URBANISM AND CULTURAL LANDSCAPES IN NORTHEASTERN SYRIA

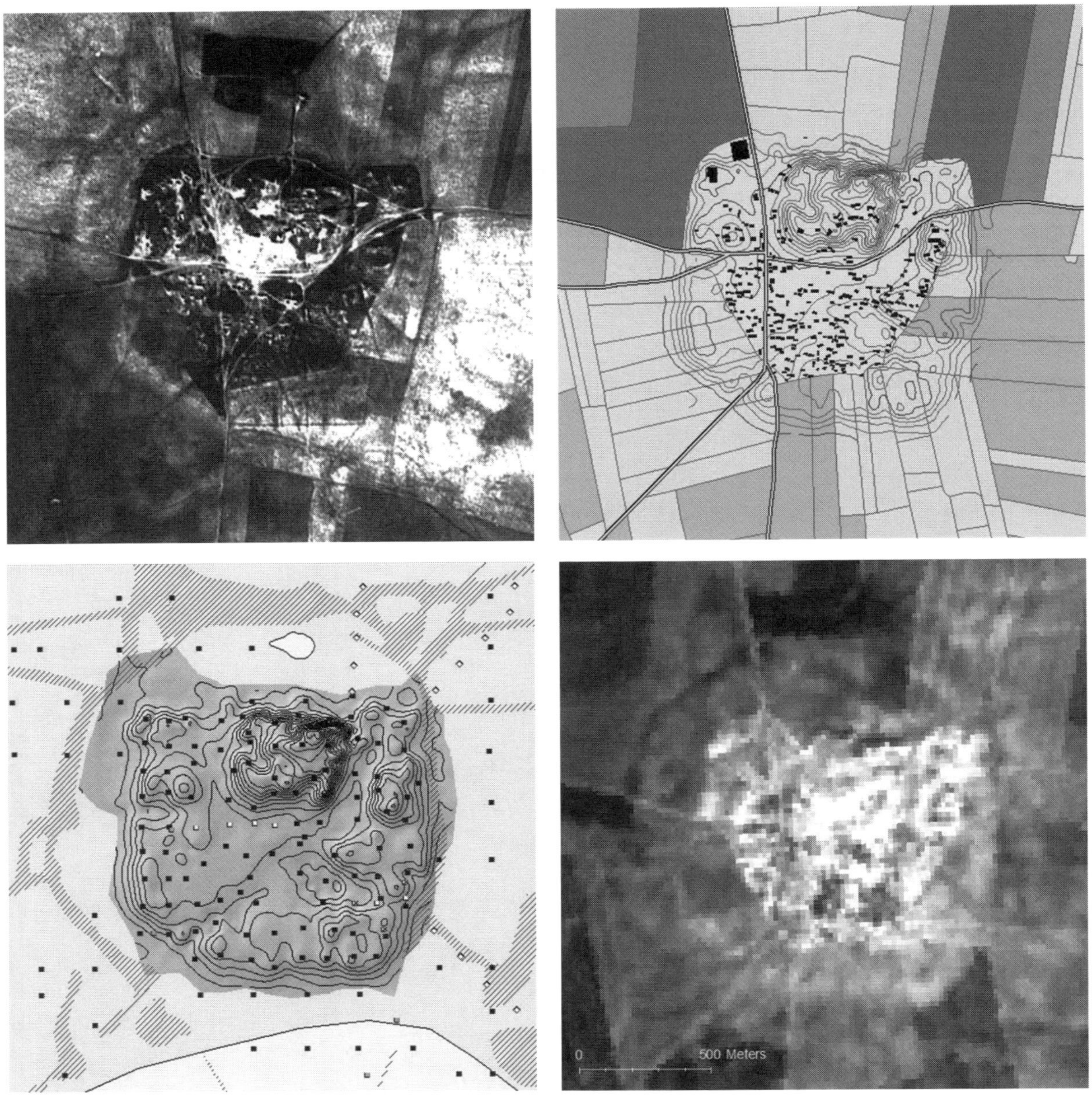

The mound of Hamoukar. Clockwise from upper left: CORONA photograph (December 1967); modern village and field system (ca. 2005); ASTER satellite image; surface collection units

TELL HAMOUKAR • VOLUME 1

URBANISM AND CULTURAL LANDSCAPES IN NORTHEASTERN SYRIA

THE TELL HAMOUKAR SURVEY, 1999–2001

by

JASON A. UR

with contribution by

McGuire Gibson, Tell Hamoukar Series Editor

ORIENTAL INSTITUTE PUBLICATIONS • VOLUME 137
THE ORIENTAL INSTITUTE OF THE UNIVERSITY OF CHICAGO

Library of Congress Control Number: 2010939630
ISBN-10: 1-885923-73-2
ISBN-13: 978-1-885923-73-8
ISSN: 0069-3367

The Oriental Institute, Chicago

ORIENTAL INSTITUTE PUBLICATIONS • VOLUME 137

Series Editors
Leslie Schramer
and
Thomas G. Urban
with the assistance of
Rebecca Cain

Series Editors' Acknowledgments
Aliya Bagewadi, Felicia Whitcomb, and Natalie Whiting assisted in the publication of this volume.

Spine Illustration

Topographic plan showing relative frequency of pottery of the Late Chalcolithic/Uruk period (4000–3000 B.C.) collected from the surface at Hamoukar in 1999

Printed by McNaughton & Gunn, Saline, Michigan

TABLE OF CONTENTS

LIST OF ABBREVIATIONS

A.D.	anno domini
ASL	above sea level
B.C.	before Christ
B.P.	before present
ca.	*circa*, approximately
cm	centimeter(s)
dm	diameter
e.g.	*exempli gratia*, for example
esp.	especially
et al.	*et alii*, and others
etc.	*et cetera*, and so forth
fig(s).	figure(s)
GIS	Geographic Information System
GPS	Global Positioning System
ha	hectare
i.e.	*id est*, that is
kg	kilogram(s)
km	kilometer(s)
m	meter(s)
mm	millimeter(s)
NJP	North Jazira Project
n(n).	footnote(s)
no(s).	number(s)
P	Period
pers. comm.	personal communication
pl(s).	plate(s)
SRTM	Shuttle Radar Topography Mission
sq.	square
THS	Tell Hamoukar Survey
UTM	Universal Transverse Mercator

LIST OF FIGURES

LIST OF MAPS

LIST OF TABLES

SERIES EDITOR'S PREFACE

McGuire Gibson

This book by Jason Ur, on the settlement history and geography of Hamoukar and its surrounding region, is the first in a series of final reports on the Oriental Institute's archaeological research program at this extraordinary site in northeastern Syria.

Hamoukar has been recognized for almost a century as a site of great importance, one that could add significantly to our knowledge of the early history not only of northeastern Syria but also of Mesopotamia in general. Since the 1930s, archaeologists visited the site and several noted the scatter of Uruk sherds on its surface, which made it a focus of attention especially after the finding of Uruk colonies on the Euphrates at Habuba Kabira Sud and Jebel Aruda. The Oriental Institute's involvement in Hamoukar began in 1998, when I made a trip to Syria at the invitation of then Director of Antiquities and Heritage, Dr. Sultan Muhesen. My primary research at Nippur, in Iraq, had been halted since 1990, due to the international embargo on Iraq. I had then shifted my fieldwork to Yemen, but I was finding that doing archaeology there, while fascinating in itself, was not a good preparation for my students, since it was too far removed geographically, artifactually, and methodologically (not enough mudbrick) from Iraq. Work in Syria would be far more relevant to the Mesopotamian sequence and to the ongoing discourse on the origins, development, collapse, and redevelopment of civilization for which Iraq and Syria had central and connected roles. In addition, the Oriental Institute had not carried out an excavation in Syria since the 1970s, and it was well past time for it to resume investigations there.

I was told that I would be shown a number of sites that were endangered by natural or man-made intrusions in eastern Syria, with the idea that I should choose one for a salvage excavation. With an official of the State Organization in Raqqa, I visited several intriguing mounds in the Balikh Valley, and along the Euphrates, including Tell Blebis, an Uruk-period site overlooking the eastern side of the river, in which there was fresh evidence of illicit digging. I also visited the impressive prehistoric site of Tell Zeidan, which Gil Stein, a decade later, has begun to excavate as a joint Syrian-American project. Going on to the Der ez-Zor area, I was taken to two other sites, both with heavy Classical overburdens, and from there I went up the Khabur Valley, which had for years been the focus of a major campaign of excavations by numerous Syrian and foreign excavators. In that area, I examined several mounds, mostly from the third and first millennia B.C. Although it was not on the list of sites that I was to be shown, I asked to visit Hamoukar, since I had heard so much about it. Arriving on the site as a storm began to gather, I had only a limited time to look over the high mound and examine some of the pottery on the surface.

On my return to Damascus, I wrote up a report, listing about ten sites in order of preference, with Blebis at the top. In fact, any of the sites would have been acceptable because there were important research questions that could be answered by excavations on any of them. But Blebis, having clearly southern Uruk sherds and being located on a high point that made it likely that it was a fortified strongpoint, much like Jebel Aruda farther north on the other side of the river, was of most immediate interest to me. I did, however, add a final paragraph saying that of all the sites I visited, Hamoukar was clearly the most threatened, since it had on it a village that was continuing to grow, and that it even had a paved road through it. Clearly the site would be lost to archaeology fairly quickly if something were not done.

I returned to Chicago with the notion that we might be working at Blebis, which was fairly small and thus relatively easy to investigate effectively in a few seasons. I was, therefore, surprised to receive a letter saying that we had been granted Hamoukar, one of the prime sites in Syria, and definitely one that would require a long-term commitment. As will be seen in this volume, the Hamoukar high mound and its immediately adjacent low mound, measuring 105 hectares, is one of the largest pre-Classical sites in Syria. The survey reported in this volume and subsequent excavations have proven that there is a southern extension of the site that brings it to four times that size. In short, Hamoukar was larger than Nippur, the city I had been excavating for years in Iraq, although not as high, nor as complex in terms of occupation history.

From the beginning, it was understood that this was to be a Syrian-American Joint Expedition. Mr. Muhammad Maktash acted as the Syrian co-director for the first season (fall 1999). Dr. Amr al-Azm was the co-director for the second and third seasons (fall 2000, 2001). Subsequent seasons have been under the co-direction of Dr. Clemens Reichel and Dr. Salam al-Quntar.

During the first season, while we were opening several excavation areas on the mound, we were given permission to do a detailed surface pick-up and analysis of the entire site of Hamoukar, as well as make walking transects and geomorphological investigations in the immediate vicinity. While Tony Wilkinson did the geomorphological investigations, especially on hollow ways and a ditch/moat adjacent to the north edge of the lower town, Jason Ur utilized a topographic map of the site created by John Sanders and Carrie Hritz to work out a systematic sampling of the surface remains. The existence of a living village on much of the southern part of the lower town, as well as a few buildings on the high mound, made his work virtually impossible to do in some squares. But, as subsequent excavations have shown, his analyses proved to be very predictive of the remains to be found on the mound. A few sherds of Halaf and Ubaid date, found in Late Chalcolithic 3 archaeological contexts at Area B but not in the surface pick-up, hint at an even earlier history of the site.

Ur's prompt working out of a basic ceramic sequence for the survey was extremely useful not just for the survey but for the entire team carrying out area excavations. Those ceramic types have held up well as diagnostic indicators, although many additions and refinements have been made to the sequence. Ur himself added many of those refinements in the second season, during the fall of 2000, when he, assisted by Lamya Khalidi and Carlo Colantoni, greatly expanded the survey. They were allowed to collect sherds from sites within a five-kilometer radius from the edges of Hamoukar and its southern extension (which he reports under the name Tell al-Fukhar). The effectiveness of a walking survey, combined with a prior analysis of satellite images to show possible locations of sites, is indicated by the fact that, within the five-kilometer area, Ur discovered sixty sites, whereas available maps showed no more than ten. The implications of this great difference in recovery of data for estimates of an area's settlements and derived population size are obvious, and we are made aware of the inadequacy of earlier survey methodology. Often, the sites show up on satellite images merely as light spots in the middle of fields, marking very small hamlets, which older survey methods would have missed.

Several larger ancient villages are, today, under modern villages. By comparing CORONA images with more recent images, it is possible to gauge the change in modern land use, detailing a great increase in settled occupation in the area since the 1960s. Hamoukar itself, for instance, had only two buildings on it in the earliest CORONA images; today, there are more than 250 structures. This process of modern re-occupation and farming of an area that was, for centuries, essentially pastoral, is only the latest evidence of a fluctuating pattern of settlement and abandonment that is evidenced at Hamoukar itself, in the vicinity of the site, and in the entire northern part of Syria. Ur's work at Hamoukar thus supplements his and Tony Wilkinson's survey results in the wider region of northern Mesopotamia, both in Syria and Iraq, which give a basis for detailed ecological and demographic analyses that were not possible before. It also allows Hamoukar to be analyzed in terms of its place on a major route that funneled people and commerce east and west, intersected by other routes that linked the mountains to the northeast with the Euphrates system.

I want to take this opportunity to lay out the general scheme of investigations and the staff for the first three seasons at Hamoukar, for which I was the director. We began the first season's work at Hamoukar on September 9 and ended on October 31, 1999. For that season, we rented a house in the nearby border town of Yarubiya, making the half-hour trip to and from the site every day.

In addition to the co-directors, Gibson and Maktash, the team consisted of Tony Wilkinson (landscape studies and survey), Judith A. Franke (site supervisor, Area B), Amr al-Azm (paleobotanist), John C. Sanders (architect), Clemens Reichel (site supervisor, Area A), Jason Ur (landscape, survey), Carrie Hritz (site supervisor, Area C), Peggy Sanders (draftsperson), and Abdulillah Salameh and Brigitte Watkins (area excavators). Mahmoud Kattab, an employee of the Directorate's Raqqa office who was seconded to the expedition, proved to be indispensable, not only in supplying material needs, but also solving a variety of problems.

This was a very productive season, with a long step trench in Area A that gave a glimpse of occupations from Late Chalcolithic 3, Late Uruk, Ninevite 5, Akkadian, and early Islamic times. Especially notable was a city wall in the Late Chalcolithic 3 level. In Area B, which was chosen because the surface was littered with southern Uruk sherds, we found that just below the surface, we were already down to Late Chalcolithic 3, with artifact-rich buildings, including a major hoard of stamp seals. The Uruk IV level, evidenced by the surface sherds and the contents of some pits, had eroded away and must be sought upslope to the north. At Area C, where we put in one small pit to gauge the importance of the occupations because we were thinking of building a dig house there, we found a small part of a building with a niched buttress, which seemed to indicate a public building. This find led us to abandon the idea of building on this part of the site. Also on C there were some modern substantial buildings belonging to two compounds that we would have liked to use as the core of a dig house, but they were involved in legal proceedings, and we were told that we would not be able to rent them. Wanting to expand the excavations in Area C, we sought permission to demolish the houses. We were given written permission to take down the houses, and we did so at the end of the season. What we did not know was that there was a missing step: the permission from the judge in the legal case to allow the demolition. In the next season, we had to pay a very large penalty to the owners of the houses.

After the season, we prepared preliminary reports for the Directorate General of Antiquities and Heritage, and others were published in *Antiquity* (2000) and *Iraq* (2002). Jason Ur published a separate article on the survey in *Iraq* (2002).

The second season was not as intensive as the first, since we were building an expedition house on the northwestern end of the site. The co-directors, Amr al-Azm and I, along with Mahmoud Kattab, arrived on August 17, 2000, to begin construction, having already arranged to have several thousand mudbricks made before we arrived. Mahmoud oversaw much of the construction of the house. During the season, the entire staff occupied a couple of houses in the village very close to the construction site. The actual research season, which lasted from September 16 to October 26, was concentrated on refining Ur's survey and conducting further excavations in Areas B and C. In Area C, Carrie Hritz, Salam al-Quntar, and later Mark Altaweel excavated several houses of Neo-Assyrian date and then, below, exposed parts of two buildings of the third millennium, including the one with the niched buttress that we had encountered in the first season. Meanwhile, Tony Wilkinson, Mark Altaweel, and Coleen Coyle cut several pits in the Southern Extension, to ascertain the nature of the occupation there. Dr. Amr al-Azm spent much of the season processing ancient botanical remains, with the help of Affamia Kattab, an archaeobotany student from the University of Damascus. Two members of the Directorate General of Antiquities and Heritage, Wurud Ibrahim and Imad Mousa, joined us to work on conservation of artifacts and mapping, respectively. Betsy Kremers, a volunteer from Chicago, photographed all the small objects from the previous season, as well as from the current campaign. A preliminary report was submitted for publication to the Directorate General of Antiquities.

In the third season, September and October 2001, we occupied the new expedition house and renewed or initiated excavation in a number of areas. Area B was a major focus of activity, as was Area C. We also opened new operations in Areas E, G, and H. These last three areas were all located in the lower reaches of the mound where surface sherds indicated that, with a minimum amount of digging, we might expose buildings of the third millennium B.C. We also ran a trench, Area F, perpendicular to our old step trench, Area A, to determine for sure that the large wall that we had found in the Late Chalcolithic 3 was, in fact, a city wall. More recent geomagnetic survey initiated by Reichel has thus far traced the wall for more than half of the circuit of the high mound.

In order to carry out the expanded program of excavation in the third season, we had a much larger staff than before, including students from the University of Damascus and several specialists from the Department of Antiquities and Museums. Dr. Amr al-Azm was again the co-director, and we had two assistant directors, Clemens Reichel and Salam al-Quntar. Clemens served as the architect for this season and Salam was in charge of Area F, assisted by George Muammar ibn Yakub. Area C was once more under the supervision of Carrie Hritz, assisted by Stephanie Reed, Saqr Muhammad, and Martin Mackinson. Area B, excavated by Lamya Khalidi, Jonathan Tenney, and Bassim Muhammad, produced hundreds of Late Chalcolithic 3 artifacts in superb context. Peggy Sanders, who was with us to draw objects for the last month of the dig, was invaluable in the documentation of the seal impressions and other finds from this area and others. Area E, very close to the expedition house on the western edge of the site, was supervised by Carlo Colantoni, Bashar al-Dakhil Jasim, and Colleen Coyle, the last of whom was also registrar. Areas G and H were located in wheat fields that had just been harvested. Within a few centimeters of the surface, Jason Ur and Tariq Ahmad, with the later addition of Carlo Colantoni and Salam al-Quntar, exposed houses of post-Akkadian date, with many artifacts left in situ (Colantoni 2005; Colantoni and Ur in press; Ur and Colantoni 2010). The great number of artifacts from all areas was a challenge to conserve and register, but this season we had the invaluable conservation skills of Ghassan Abdul Aziz, who worked on not only fragile clay sealings and bone artifacts but also many of the reconstructable pots that were numerous in both Areas C and H. Thaer Fayad carried out the flotation of soil samples to recover ancient seeds under the direction of Dr. al-Azm. Serving once again as a solver of all problems was Mahmoud Kattab. Ivan Mahar, a very good cook from Qamishli, made all our lives better. Tony Wilkinson joined us for about two weeks and carried out landscape studies.

A major summary account on the first three seasons (Gibson et al. 2002) appeared in *Akkadica*, along with detailed reports on the seals and sealings by Reichel (2002), the survey by Ur (2002b), and a landscape piece by Wilkinson (2002). A report on the third season was submitted for publication to the Directorate General of Antiquities (Gibson and al-Azm 2002–03).

In closing, I wish to acknowledge the encouragement and aid of the successive Directors General of Antiquities with whom I worked: Dr. Sultan Muhesen and Dr. Abdul Razzak Muazz. Dr. Michel Maqdisi in Damascus and Sayyid Abdul Messieh Bagdo in Hasakah must also be thanked for their advice and help.

ACKNOWLEDGMENTS

It is a pleasure to acknowledge the permission and encouragement of the Directorate General of Antiquities and Museums of the Syrian Arab Republic. In particular, I thank the current and former Directors General, Abd al-Razzak Moaz and Sultan Muhesen, the Director of Excavations, Michel al-Maqdisi, and the Director for Hassake province, Abd al-Massieh Baghdo. The directors of the Syrian-American Hamoukar Expedition, McGuire Gibson of the University of Chicago Oriental Institute and Amr al-Azm of the University of Damascus, were kind enough to entrust the survey to my direction.

By its very nature, any archaeological study is a collaborative undertaking, this one perhaps more so than most. On the 2000 Tell Hamoukar Survey, I had the good fortune to have Carlo Colantoni and Lamya Khalidi, both of the University of Cambridge, as field team members. Their good humor, professionalism, and tolerance of dozens of kilometers of field scatter transects cannot easily be repaid. For the short 2001 survey season, I had the cheerful assistance of Tarek Ahmed of the University of Damascus. The 1999 surface collection of Hamoukar made use of the topographic data collected by John Sanders and Carrie Hritz.

My greatest intellectual debts are to the University of Chicago archaeologists who served as my mentors. McGuire Gibson was the first to inspire me with ancient Mesopotamia, and I benefited greatly from his encyclopedic knowledge of its history and archaeology. The text of this volume was also substantially improved by Mac's close reading. The intellectual and methodological debt I owe to Tony Wilkinson should be obvious. I hope that I have gained some of his unique ability to read the landscape, and I am grateful for his willingness to involve me in several of his field projects. Gil Stein kept me grounded in anthropology by encouraging a broadly comparative, issue-oriented approach to the past. David Schloen challenged me to go beyond sites and landscapes to consider larger questions of society.

Other colleagues at Chicago have also been most helpful. Members of the present excavation team at Hamoukar, directed by Clemens Reichel and Salam al-Quntar, have kept me appraised of recent excavation results; information on the Hamoukar Southern Extension (THS 25) provided by Salam al-Quntar, Lamya Khalidi, and Khalid Abu Jayyab has been especially important in my interpretations of that site. Other interpretations spring from discussions with fellow members of the University of Chicago-Argonne National Labs Modeling Ancient Settlement Systems (MASS) Project. In particular, I must thank Magnus Widell for his eagerness to discuss cuneiform issues of relevance to ancient land use. Most of the THS data was digitized, processed, or analyzed using the facilities of the Center for Ancient Middle Eastern Landscapes (CAMEL) at the Oriental Institute, directed by Tony Wilkinson and later by Scott Branting. Carrie Hritz and Jesse Casana served as valuable sounding boards in developing my GIS and remote-sensing skills there. Nicholas Kouchoukos in the Department of Anthropology was a great source of expertise on GIS. John Sanders, head of the Oriental Institute Computer Lab, has given me excellent advice on myriad computer issues over the last ten years, and many thanks go to Charles Jones, Oriental Institute Research Archivist at the time of this research.

Outside of Chicago, I am grateful to Marc Lebeau, Augusta McMahon, Geoff Emberling, and Joan and David Oates for allowing my participation in excavation and survey at Tell Beydar, Chagar Bazar, and Tell Brak. Henry Wright and Eric Rupley of the Tell Brak Survey offered helpful suggestions on survey methodology and ceramic typology. My subsequent participation in excavation and survey work at Tell Brak (2002–2006) and conversations with Brak members have had a great impact on my thinking, and I thank David and Joan Oates, Geoff Emberling, Helen McDonald, Henry Wright, and the other team members.

Many other colleagues offered specific advice, skills, or data. On ceramic chronology, I benefited from the expertise of several individuals: Olivier Nieuwenhuyse provided advice and imagery for late Neolithic pottery; Stefano Valentini and Harriet Martin shared illustrations and commented on the forms of the early third millennium; Joan Oates and Augusta McMahon offered their detailed knowledge and manuscripts on later third millennium pottery in advance of publication; Jules Frane cheerfully discussed early second-millennium ceramics; and Lidewijde de Jong and Jennifer Gates-Foster offered advice and extensive references on Hellenistic and Roman pottery in the Near East. Many of the sherds and the small finds were drawn by Peggy Sanders, Carlo Colantoni, and Lamya Khalidi. Statistical tests for operator differences were undertaken by Emily Hammer. Several individuals and institutions generously provided data to the survey. Rudolph Dornemann sent slides from his 1976 visit to Hamoukar, which comprise the earliest ground photographs of the site available at present. Topographic maps were made available to me by the Cartographic Library at the Institut Français du Proche Orient in Damascus and by Lauren Ristvet. The hydrology in several figures and maps 2 and 3 were derived by Devin White from 30 m SRTM topographic data. I was especially fortunate to receive soil maps, unpublished reports, and invaluable advice from the geomorphologist and modern discoverer of hollow ways, Willem Van Liere. Martin Fowler provided the acquisition times for CORONA scenes listed in table 4.1. All of these individuals have my deepest gratitude.

Funding for the Tell Hamoukar Survey came from several sources. The Helen Rich Travel Fund of the Oriental Institute and the University of Chicago Ryerson Fund provided several seasons' worth of travel and living expenses. The American Schools of Oriental Research 2000–2001 Mesopotamian Fellowship funded the 2001 season and the excavations in Area H. The 2002 University of Chicago Walsh Award for Computing in the Humanities enabled me to acquire software and imagery. Finally, a Whiting Fellowship in 2003 allowed me to analyze and write up the late fourth- through early second-millennium data, which formed a major component of my 2004 University of Chicago dissertation.

Finally, I must thank my family for their encouragement over the last ten years: Joseph and Lynne Ur, Tara and Joseph Veneracion, and Bill and Gloria Currie. This volume is dedicated with love to my wife Heather Mell, who has shown great patience with Hamoukar over the last eight years.

BIBLIOGRAPHY

Abdi, Kamyar

2003 "The Early Development of Pastoralism in the Central Zagros Mountains." *Journal of World Prehistory* 17: 395–448.

Abu al-Soof, B.

1966 "Short Sounding at Tell Qalinj Agha (Erbil)." *Sumer* 22: 77–82.

Adams, Robert McC.

1965 *Land Behind Baghdad: A History of Settlement on the Diyala Plains*. Chicago: University of Chicago Press.

1970 "Tell Abu Sarifa: A Sassanian-Islamic Ceramic Sequence from South Central Iraq." *Ars Orientalis* 8: 87–119.

1978 "Strategies of Maximization, Stability, and Resilience in Mesopotamian Society, Settlement, and Agriculture." *Proceedings of the American Philosophical Society* 122: 329–35.

1981 *Heartland of Cities: Surveys of Ancient Settlement and Land Use on the Central Floodplain of the Euphrates*. Chicago: University of Chicago Press.

2005 "Intensified Large-scale Irrigation as an Aspect of Imperial Policy: Strategies of Statecraft on the Late Sasanian Mesopotamian Plain." In *Agricultural Strategies*, edited by J. Marcus and C. Stanish, pp. 17–37. Cotsen Advanced Seminar Series 2. Los Angeles: Cotsen Institute of Archaeology.

Adams, Robert McC., and Hans J. Nissen

1972 *The Uruk Countryside: The Natural Setting of Urban Societies*. Chicago: University of Chicago Press.

Ainsworth, William F.

1842 *Travels and Researches in Asia Minor, Mesopotamia, Chaldea, and Armenia*. London: John W. Parker.

Akkermans, P. M. M. G.

1988 "The Period V Pottery." In *Hammam et-Turkman* I: *Report on the University of Amsterdam's 1981–84 Excavations in Syria*, edited by M. N. Van Loon, pp. 287–349. Istanbul: Nederlands Historisch-Archaeologisch Instituut.

Akkermans, P. M. M. G., and Glenn Schwartz

2003 *The Archaeology of Syria: From Complex Hunter-Gatherers to Early Urban Societies (ca. 16,000–300 B.C.)*. Cambridge: Cambridge University Press.

Alcock, Susan E.

1991 "Urban Survey and the *Polis* of Phlius." *Hesperia* 60/4: 421–63.

Alcock, Susan E.; John F. Cherry; and Jack L. Davis

1994 "Intensive Survey, Agricultural Practice and the Classical Landscape of Greece." In *Classical Greece: Ancient Histories and New Archaeologies*, edited by I. Morris, pp. 137–70. New Directions in Archaeology. Cambridge: Cambridge University Press.

Alden, John R.

1988 "Ceramic Ring Scrapers: An Uruk Period Pottery Production Tool." *Paléorient* 14: 143–50.

Algaze, Guillermo

1989 "The Uruk Expansion: Cross-Cultural Exchange in Early Mesopotamian Civilization." *Current Anthropology* 30: 571–608.

1993 *The Uruk World System: The Dynamics of Expansion of Early Mesopotamian Civilization*. Chicago: University of Chicago Press.

2001 "Initial Social Complexity in Southwestern Asia: The Mesopotamian Advantage." *Current Anthropology* 42: 199–233.

Algaze, Guillermo; Ray Breuninger; Chris Lightfoot; and Michael Rosenberg

1991 "The Tigris-Euphrates Archaeological Reconnaissance Project: A Preliminary Report of the 1989–1990 Seasons." *Anatolica* 17: 175–240.

Alizadeh, Abbas

2004 "Mobile Pastoralism and Prehistoric Exchange," in *Persiens antike Pracht: Bergbau, Handwerk, Archäologie*, edited by T. Stöllner, R. Slotta, and A. Vatandoust, pp. 76–91. Bochum: Deutsches Bergbau-Museum.

Alizadeh, Abbas; Nicholas Kouchoukos; Tony J. Wilkinson; A. M. Bauer; and M. Mashkour

2004 "Human-Environment Interactions on the Upper Khuzestan Plains, Southwest Iran. Recent Investigations." *Paléorient* 30: 69–88.

Alizadeh, Karim, and Jason A. Ur
2007 "Formation and Destruction of Pastoral and Irrigation Landscapes on the Mughan Steppe, North-Western Iran." *Antiquity* 81: 148–60.

al-Quntar, Salam
2009 The Role of Craft Specialisation and Exchange in the Emergence of Early Mesopotamian Urbanism. Ph.D. dissertation, Cambridge University.

Altaweel, Mark
2005 "The Use of ASTER Satellite Imagery in Archaeological Contexts." *Archaeological Prospection* 12: 151–66.
2006 "Excavations in Iraq: The Ray Jazirah Project, First Report." *Iraq* 68: 155–81.

Ammerman, Albert J.
1981 "Surveys and Archaeological Research." *Annual Review of Anthropology* 10: 63–88.
1985 "Plow-Zone Experiments in Calabria, Italy." *Journal of Field Archaeology* 12: 33–40.

Anastasio, Stefano
1999 "Prospection archéologique du Haut-Khabur occidentale (Syrie du N.E.): Preliminary Information on the Pottery of the Iron Age." In *Iron Age Pottery in Northern Mesopotamia, Northern Syria and South-Eastern Anatolia* (Papers Presented at the Meetings of the International "table ronde" at Heidelberg [1995] and Nieborów [1997] and Other Contributions), edited by A. Hausleiter and A. Reiche, pp. 173–91. Altertumskunde des Vorderen Orients 10. Münster: Ugarit-Verlag.

Archi, Alfonso
1998 "The Regional State of Nagar According to the Texts of Ebla." In *About Subartu: Studies Devoted to Upper Mesopotamia*, edited by M. Lebeau, vol. 2, pp. 1–15. Subartu 4. Turnhout: Brepols.

Archi, Alfonso, and Maria Giovanna Biga
2003 "A Victory over Mari and the Fall of Ebla." *Journal of Cuneiform Studies* 55: 1–44.

Ault, Bradley A.
1999 "Koprones and Oil Presses at Halieis: Interactions of Town and Country and the Integration of Domestic and Regional Economies." *Hesperia* 68: 549–73.

Bachmann, F.
1998 "Das keramische Inventar eines urukzeitlichen Gabäudes in Tell Sheikh Hassan / Syrien." In *About Subartu: Studies Devoted to Upper Mesopotamia*, edited by M. Lebeau, vol. 1, pp. 89–129. Subartu 4. Turnhout: Brepols.

Bagg, Ariel M.
2000 *Assyrische Wasserbauten: Landwirtschaftliche Wasserbauten im Kernland Assyriens zwischen der 2. Hälfte des 2. und der 1. Hälfte des 1. Jahrtausends v. Chr.* Baghdader Forschungen 24. Mainz am Rhein: Philipp von Zabern.

Ball, Warwick
1997 "Tell Shelgiyya: An Early Uruk 'Sprig Ware' Manufacturing and Exporting Centre on the Tigris." *Al-Rāfidān* 17: 93–104.

Ball, Warwick; David Tucker; and Tony J. Wilkinson
1989 "The Tell al-Hawa Project: Archaeological Investigations in the North Jazira." *Iraq* 51: 1–66.

Ball, Warwick, and Tony J. Wilkinson
2003 "Ninevite 5 Town and Country in Northwestern Iraq." In *The Origins of North Mesopotamian Civilization: Ninevite 5 Chronology, Economy, Society*, edited by E. Rova and H. Weiss, pp. 335–59. Subartu 9. Turnhout: Brepols.

Banning, E. B.
2002 *Archaeological Survey*. Manuals in Archaeological Method, Theory, and Technique. New York: Kluwer Academic/Plenium Publishers.

Bartl, Karin
1994 *Frühislamische Besiedlung im Balīh-Tal/Nordsyrien*. Berliner Beiträge zum Vorderen Orient 15. Berlin: Dietrich Reimer.
1996 "Balīh Valley Survey: Settlements of the Late Roman/Early Byzantine and Islamic Period." In *Continuity and Change in Northern Mesopotamia from the Hellenistic to the Early Islamic Period* (Proceedings of a Colloquium Held at the Seminar für vorderasiatische Altertumskunde, Freie Universität Berlin, 6th–9th April 1994), edited by K. Bartl and S. R. Hauser, pp. 333–48. Berliner Beiträge zum Vorderen Orient 17. Berlin: Dietrich Reimer.

Beck, C. M.
1991 "Cross-cutting Relationships: The Relative Dating of Ancient Roads on the North Coast of Peru." In *Ancient Road Networks and Settlement Hierarchies in the New World*, edited by C. D. Trombold, pp. 66–79. New Directions in Archaeology. Cambridge: Cambridge University Press.

Bernbeck, Reinhard
1993. *Steppe als Kulturlandschaft: Das 'Agig-Gebiet Ostsyriens vom Neolithikum bis zur islamischen Zeit.* Berliner Beiträge zum Vorderen Orient, Ausgrabungen 1. Berlin: Dietrich Reimer.

Bettini, Lidia
1998 "Testimonianze sulla Ǧazīra presso i geografi arabi medievali." In *Tell Barri/Kahat* 2: *Relazione sulle campagne 1980–1993 a Tell Barri/Kahat, nel bacino del Habur (Siria)*, by P. E. Pecorella, pp. 317–34. Documenta Asiana 5. Rome: Istituto per gli studi Micenei ed Egeo-Anatolici.

Biga, Maria Giovanna
1998 "The Marriage of Eblaite Princess Tagrish-Damu with a Son of Nagar's King." In *About Subartu: Studies Devoted to Upper Mesopotamia*, edited by M. Lebeau, vol. 2, pp. 17–39. Subartu 4. Turnhout: Brepols.

Bintliff, John L.
2000 "The Concepts of 'Site' and 'Offsite' Archaeology in Surface Artefact Survey." In *Non-destructive Techniques Applied to Landscape Archaeology*, edited by M. Pasquinucci and F. Trément, pp. 200–15. Archaeology of Mediterranean Landscapes 4. Oxford: Oxbow Books.

Bintliff, John L., and A. M. Snodgrass
1985 "The Cambridge/Bradford Boeotian Expedition: The First Four Years." *Journal of Field Archaeology* 12: 123–61.
1988 "Off-Site Pottery Distributions: A Regional and Interregional Perspective." *Current Anthropology* 29: 506–13.

Blaylock, Stuart R.
1999 "Iron Age Pottery from Tille Höyük, South-Eastern Turkey." In *Iron Age Pottery in Northern Mesopotamia, Northern Syria and South-Eastern Anatolia* (Papers Presented at the Meetings of the International "table ronde" at Heidelberg [1995] and Nieborów [1997] and Other Contributions), edited by A. Hausleiter and A. Reiche, pp. 263–86. Altertumskunde des Vorderen Orients 10. Münster: Ugarit-Verlag.

Boehmer, Rainer Michael
1974 "Keramik aus der Umgebung von Batas." *Sumer* 30: 101–08.

Boese, Johannes
1995 *Ausgrabungen in Tell Sheikh Hassan* I: *Vorläufige Berichte über die Ausgrabungskampagnen 1984–1990 und 1992–1994*. Schriften zur vorderasiatischen Archäologie 5. Saarbrücken: Saarbrücker Druckerei und Verlag.

Boghossian, Roupen
1952 *La Haute-Djézireh.* Aleppo: Imprimerie Chiraz.

Braidwood, Robert J., and Linda S. Braidwood
1960 *Excavations on the Plain of Antioch*, Vol. 1: *The Earlier Assemblages, Phases A–J*. Oriental Institute Publications 61. Chicago: University of Chicago Press.

British Admiralty
1943 *Syria.* April 1943 edition. Geographical Handbook Series B.R. 513. British Admiralty, Naval Intelligence Division.

Buccellati, Giorgio, and Marilyn Kelly-Buccellati, editors
1988 *Mozan* I: *The Soundings of the First Two Seasons*. Bibliotheca Mesopotamica 20. Malibu: Undena.
1999 "Das archäologische Projekt Tall Mozan/Urkesh." *Mitteilungen der Deutschen Orient-Gesellschaft zu Berlin* 131: 7–16.
2002 "Tar'am-Agade, Daughter of Naram-Sin, at Urkesh." In *Of Pots and Plans: Papers on the Archaeology and History of Mesopotamia and Syria Presented to David Oates in Honour of his 75th Birthday*, edited by L. al-Gailani Werr, J. Curtis, H. Martin, A. McMahon, J. Oates, and J. Reade, pp. 11–31. London: Nabu.

Buckingham, James S.
1827 *Travels in Mesopotamia.* 2 volumes. London: H. Colburn.

Buringh, P.
1960 *Soils and Soil Conditions in Iraq.* Baghdad: Ministry of Agriculture.

Butzer, Karl W.
1995 "Environmental Change in the Near East and Human Impact on the Land." In *Civilizations of the Ancient Near East*, edited by J. Sasson, vol. 1, pp. 123–51. New York: Charles Scribner's Sons.

Cameron, Verney L.
1880 *Our Future Highway.* 2 volumes. London: MacMillan.

Campbell, B.
1989 "The Roman Pottery from Seh Qubba, North Iraq." In *The Eastern Frontier of the Roman Empire*, edited by D. French and C. Lightfoot, vol. 1, pp. 53–65. British Archaeological

Reports, International Series 533. Oxford: British Archaeological Reports.

Campbell, Stuart

1995 "The Halaf Pottery." In *Excavations at Kharabeh Shattani*, edited by D. Baird, S. Campbell, and T. Watkins, vol. 2, pp. 55–90. Edinburgh: University of Edinburgh Department of Archaeology.

1996 "Rescue Excavations at Ginnig and Khirbet Garour in the North Jazira." *Sumer* 48: 6–10.

2007 "Rethinking Halaf Chronologies." *Paléorient* 33: 103–36.

Castel, Corrine

2000 "La photographie aérienne au service d'une archéologie pionnière en Haute-Djéziré syrienne." In *Aux origines de l'archéologie aérienne: A. Poidebard (1878–1955)*, edited by L. Nordiguian and J.-F. Salles, pp. 93–107. Beirut: Presses de l'Université Saint-Joseph.

Charpin, Dominique

1987 "Shubat-Enlil et le pays d'Apum." *Mari: Annales de recherches interdisciplinaires* 5: 129–40.

1990 "Conclusions et perspectives: Tell Mohammed Diyab, une ville du pays d'Apum." In *Tell Mohammed Diyab: Campagnes 1987 et 1988*, edited by J.-M. Durand, pp. 117–22. Cahiers de N.A.B.U. 1. Paris: SEPOA.

1992 "De la vallée du Tigre au 'triangle du Habur': Un engrenage géopolitique?" In *Recherches en Haute Mésopotamia: Tell Mohammed Diyab, campagnes 1990 et 1991*, edited by J.-M. Durand, pp. 97–102. Mémoires de N.A.B.U. 2. Paris: SEPOA.

2004 "Histoire politique du Proche-Orient Amorrite (2002–1595)." In *Mesopotamien: Die altbabylonische Zeit*, edited by D. Charpin, D. O. Edzard, and M. Stol, pp. 23–482. Orbis Biblicus et Orientalis 160/4. Fribourg: Academic Press; Göttingen: Vandenhoeck & Ruprecht.

Cherry, John F.

1983 "Frogs Round the Pond: Perspectives on Current Archaeological Survey Projects in the Mediterranean Region." In *Archaeological Survey in the Mediterranean Area*, edited by D. R. Keller and D. W. Rupp, pp. 375–416. British Archaeological Reports, International Series 155. Oxford: Oxford University.

Chisholm, Michael

1962 *Rural Settlement and Land Use: An Essay in Location*. London: Hutchinson.

Colantoni, Carlo

2005 Traces of Tradition: Northern Mesopotamian Urbanism from the Late 3rd through Early 2nd Millennium B.C. Ph.D. dissertation, Cambridge University.

Colantoni, Carlo, and Jason A. Ur

In press "The Architecture and Pottery of a Late 3rd Millennium B.C. Residential Quarter at Tell Hamoukar, Northeastern Syria." *Iraq* 73 (2011).

Courty, Marie-Agnès

1994 "Le cadre paléographique des occupations humaines dans le bassin du Haut-Khabur (Syrie du Nord-Est). Premiers Résultats." *Paléorient* 20: 21–59.

1998 "The Soil Record of an Exceptional Event at 4000 B.P. in the Middle East." In *Natural Catastrophes during Bronze Age Civilizations*, edited by B. J. Peiser, T. Palmer, and M. E. Bailey, pp. 93–108. British Archaeological Reports, International Series 728. Oxford: Archaeopress.

1999 "The 4000 yr B.P. Impact Event: The Birth of a Scientific Hypothesis." *The Observatory, A Review of Astronomy* 119: 168–71.

2001 "Evidence at Tell Brak for the Late EDIII/Early Akkadian Air Blast Event (4 kyr B.P.)." In *Excavations at Tell Brak*, Vol. 2: *Nagar in the Third Millennium B.C.*, by D. Oates, J. Oates, and H. McDonald, pp. 367–72. Cambridge: McDonald Institute for Archaeological Research; London: British School of Archaeology in Iraq.

Crawford, Osbert Guy Stanhope

1953 *Archaeology in the Field*. London: Phoenix House.

Cribb, Roger

1991 *Nomads in Archaeology*. New Studies in Archaeology. Cambridge: Cambridge University Press.

Cruells, Walter

2006 "Chagar Bazar préhistorique: Esquisse de la séquence d'évolution et la périodisation." In *Chagar Bazar (Syrie)*, Vol. 1: *Les sondages préhistoriques (1999–2001)*, edited by Ö. Tunca and A. M. Baghdo, pp. 121–42. Louvain: Peeters.

Curtis, John

1989 *Excavations at Qasrij Cliff and Khirbet Qasrij*. London: British Museum.

Curtis, John, and Anthony Green
1997 *Excavations at Khirbet Khatuniyeh*. London: British Museum Press

Curvers, Hans H., and Glenn Schwartz
1990 "Excavations at Tell al-Raqa'i: A Small Rural Site of Early Urban Northern Mesopotamia." *American Journal of Archaeology* 94: 3–23.

Dalley, Stephanie; C. B. F. Walker; and John D. Hawkins
1976 *The Old Babylonian Tablets from Tell al Rimah*. London: British School of Archaeology in Iraq.

Danti, M.
2000 Early Bronze Age Settlement and Land Use in the Tell es-Sweyhat Region, Syria. Ph.D. dissertation, University of Pennsylvania.

Day, D. A.; J. M. Logsdon; and B. Latell, editors
1998 *Eye in the Sky: The Story of the CORONA Spy Satellites*. Smithsonian History of Aviation Series. Washington, D.C.: Smithsonian Institution Press.

de Vaumas, É.
1956 "La Djézireh." *Annales de Géographie* 65: 64–80.

Debruyne, Michel
1997 "A Corbelled Akkadian Grave (Field F)." In *Tell Beydar, Three Seasons of Excavations (1992–1994): A Preliminary Report*, edited by M. Lebeau and A. Suleiman, pp. 145–54. Subartu 3. Turnhout: Brepols.

Deckers, Kathleen, and Simone Riehl
2007 "Fluvial Environmental Contexts for Archaeological Sites in the Upper Khabur Basin (Northeastern Syria)." *Quaternary Research* 67: 337–48.

Dillemann, Louis
1962 *Haute Mésopotamie orientale et pays adjacents*. Paris: Paul Geuthner.
1979 "Les Français en Haute-Djezireh (1919–1939)." *Revue Française d'histoire d'Outre-Mer* 66: 33–58.

Dion, Paul-Eugène
1997 *Les Araméens à l'âge du fer: Histoire politique et structures sociales*. Paris: Librairie Lecoffre.

Dohmann-Pfälzner, Heike, and Peter Pfälzner
2001 "Ausgrabungen der Deutschen Orient-Gesellschaft in der zentralen Oberstadt von Tall Mozan/Urkes. Bericht über die in Kooperation mit dem IIMAS durchgeführte Kampagne 2000." *Mitteilungen der Deutschen Orient-Gesellschaft zu Berlin* 133: 97–139.

Dorna-Metzger, Francesca
1996 "Hellenistic and Parthian-Roman Pottery from the Upper Khabur Survey: A Preliminary Study." In *Continuity and Change in Northern Mesopotamia from the Hellenistic to the Early Islamic Period* (Proceedings of a Colloquium Held at the Seminar für vorderasiatische Altertumskunde, Freie Universität Berlin, 6th–9th April 1994), edited by K. Bartl and S. R. Hauser, pp. 363–75. Berliner Beiträge zum Vorderen Orient 17. Berlin: Dietrich Reimer.

Drennan, R. D.
1988 "Household Location and Compact versus Dispersed Settlement in Prehispanic Mesoamerica." In *Household and Community in the Mesoamerican Past*, edited by R. R. Wilk and W. Ashmore, pp. 273–93. Albuquerque: University of New Mexico.

Dunnell, Robert C., and William S. Dancey
1983 "The Siteless Survey: A Regional Scale Data Collection Strategy." In *Advances in Archaeological Method and Theory*, edited by M. B. Schiffer, vol. 6, pp. 267–87. New York: Academic Press.

Durand, Jean-Marie
2004 "Peuplement et sociétés à la époque amorrite: (1) Les clans bensim'alites." In *Nomades et sédentaires dans le Proche-Orient ancien*, edited by C. Nicolle, pp. 111–97. Amurru 3. Paris: Éditions Recherche sur les Civilisations.

Eidem, Jesper; Irving L. Finkel; and Marco Bonechi
2001 "The Third Millennium Inscriptions." In *Excavations at Tell Brak*, Vol. 2: *Nagar in the Third Millennium B.C.*, by D. Oates, J. Oates, and H. McDonald, pp. 99–120. Cambridge: McDonald Institute for Archaeological Research; London: British School of Archaeology in Iraq.

Eidem, Jesper, and David A. Warburton
1996 "In the Land of Nagar: A Survey around Tell Brak." *Iraq* 58: 51–64.

Emberling, Geoff; Jack Cheng; Torben E. Larsen; Holly Pittman; Tim B. B. Skuldeboel; Jill Weber; and Henry T. Wright
1999 "Excavations at Tell Brak 1998: Preliminary Report." *Iraq* 61: 1–41.

Emberling, Geoff, and Helen McDonald
2003 "Excavations at Tell Brak 2001–2002: Preliminary Report." *Iraq* 65: 1–75.

Ergenzinger, Peter, and Hartmut Kühne

1991 "Ein regionales Bewässerungssystem am Habur." In *Die rezente Umwelt von Tell Sheikh Hamad und Daten zur Umweltrekonstruktion der assyrischen Stadt Dur-Katlimmu*, edited by H. Kühne, pp. 163–90. Berlin: Dietrich Reimer.

Ergenzinger, Peter; Hartmut Kühne; and Harald Kurschner

1988 "The Reconstructions of Environment, Irrigation, and Development of Settlement on the Habur in North-East Syria." In *Conceptual Issues in Environmental Archaeology*, edited by J. Bintliff, pp. 108–28. Edinburgh: University Press.

Falconer, Steven E., and Stephen H. Savage

1995 "Heartlands and Hinterlands: Alternative Trajectories of Early Urbanism in Mesopotamia and the Southern Levant." *American Antiquity* 60: 37–58.

FAO (Food and Agriculture Organization of the United Nations)

1959 *United Arab Republic Syrian Region Country Report*. Rome: Food and Agriculture Organization of the United Nations.

1966 *Étude des ressources en eaux souterraines de la Jazireh syrienne*. Rome: Food and Agriculture Organization of the United Nations.

Farr, T. G.; P. A. Rosen; E. Caro; R. Crippen; R. Duren; S. Hensley; M. Kobrick; M. Paller; E. Rodriguez; L. Roth; D. Seal; S. Schaffer; J. Shimada; J. Umland; M. Werner; M. Oskin; D. Burbank; and D. Alsdorf

2007 "The Shuttle Radar Topography Mission." *Reviews of Geophysics* 45: RG2004.

Felli, Candida

2003 "Developing Complexity: Mid- to Late Fourth-Millennium Investigations; The Northern Middle Uruk Period." In *Excavations at Tell Brak*, Vol. 4: *Exploring an Upper Mesopotamian Regional Centre, 1994–1996*, edited by R. Matthews, pp. 53–95. Cambridge: McDonald Institute for Archaeological Research; London: British School of Archaeology in Iraq.

Fentress, Elizabeth

2000 "What Are We Counting For?" In *Extracting Meaning from Ploughsoil Assemblages*, edited by R. Francovich and H. Patterson, pp. 44–52. Archaeology of Mediterranean Landscapes 5. Oxford: Oxbow Books.

Fielden, K. J.

1981 The Chronology of Settlement in Northeast Syria During the Later Fourth and Third Millennia B.C. in the Light of Ceramic Evidence from Tell Brak. Unpublished Ph.D. dissertation, Corpus Christi College, Oxford University.

Fiey, Jean-Maurice

1964 "The Iraqi Section of the Abbasid Road Mosul-Nisibin." *Iraq* 26: 106–17.

1977 *Nisibe, métropole syriaque orientale et ses suffragants des origines à nos jours*. Louvain: Secrétariat du Corpus SCO.

Fincke, Jeanette C.

1993 *Die Orts- und Gewässernamen der Nuzi-Texte*. Répertoire Géographique des Textes Cunéiformes 10. Wiesbaden: Ludwig Reichert.

Finkbeiner, Uwe

1991 *Uruk: Kampagne 35–37, 1982–1984: Die archäologische Oberflächenuntersuchung (Survey)*. Ausgrabungen in Uruk-Warka, Endberichte 4. Mainz am Rhein: Philipp von Zabern.

Fish, Suzanne K., and Stephen A. Kowalewski, editors

1990 *The Archaeology of Regions: A Case for Full-Coverage Survey*. Smithsonian Series in Archaeological Inquiry. Washington, D.C.: Smithsonian Institution Press.

Flannery, Kent V., editor

1976 *The Early Mesoamerican Village*. Studies in Archaeology. New York: Academic Press.

Fleming, Daniel E.

2004 *Democracy's Ancient Ancestors: Mari and Early Collective Governance*. Cambridge and New York: Cambridge University Press.

Fletcher, J. P.

1850 *Notes from Nineveh, and Travels in Mesopotamia, Assyria and Syria*. Philadelphia: Lea & Blanchard.

Forbes, F.

1839 "A Visit to the Sinjár Hills in 1838, with Some Account of the Sect of Yezídís, and of Various Places in the Mesopotamian Desert, between the Rivers Tigris and Khábúr." *Journal of the Royal Geographical Society of London* 9: 409–30.

Forlanini, Massimo

2006 "Étapes et itinéraires entre Assur et l'Anatolie des marchands paléo-assyriens: Nouveaux documents et nouveaux problèmes." *Kaskal* 3: 147–75.

Forni, N.
2003 "Land Tenure and Labour Relations." In *Syrian Agriculture at the Crossroads*, edited by C. Fiorillo and J. Vercueil, pp. 309–33. FAO Agricultural Policy and Economic Development Series 8. Rome: Food and Agriculture Organization of the United Nations.

Fortin, Michel
1999 *Syria: Land of Civilizations*. Montreal: Éditions de l'Homme.

Fowler, M. J. F.
2004 "Archaeology through the Keyhole: The Serendipity Effect of Aerial Reconnaissance Revisited." *Interdisciplinary Science Reviews* 29: 118–34.

Francovich, Riccardo, and Helen Patterson, editors
2000 *Extracting Meaning from Ploughsoil Assemblages*. Archaeology of Mediterranean Landscapes 5. Oxford: Oxbow Books.

Frane, Julia E.
1996 The Tell Leilan Period I Habur Ware Assemblage. Ph.D. dissertation, University of North Carolina-Chapel Hill.

Fuller, Michael, and Neathery Fuller
1987–88 "Tell Tuneinir on the Habur: Preliminary Report on Three Seasons." *Annales archéologiques de Syrie* 37–38: 279–90.
1994 "Tuneinir." *American Journal of Archaeology* 98: 157–58.

Gaffney, C.; Vincent Gaffney; and M. Tingle
1985 "Settlement, Economy or Behaviour? Micro-Regional Land Use Models and the Interpretation of Surface Artefact Patterns." In *Archaeology from the Ploughsoil: Studies in the Collection and Interpretation of Field Survey Data*, edited by C. Haselgrove, M. Millett, and I. Smith, pp. 95–107. Sheffield: Department of Archaeology and Prehistory, University of Sheffield.

Gaffney, Vincent; John L. Bintliff; and B. Slapsak
1991 "Site Formation Processes and the Hvar Survey Project, Yugoslavia." In *Interpreting Artefact Scatters: Contributions to Ploughzone Archaeology*, edited by A. J. Schofield, pp. 59–77. Oxford: Oxbow Books.

Gallagher, William R.
1994 "Assyrian Deportation Propaganda." *State Archives of Assyrian Bulletin* 8: 57–65.

Gallant, T. W.
1986 "'Background Noise' and Site Definition: A Contribution to Survey Methodology." *Journal of Field Archaeology* 13: 404–18.

Gasche, Hermann; James A. Armstrong; S. W. Cole; and V. G. Gurzadyan
1998 *Dating the Fall of Babylon: A Reappraisal of Second-Millennium Chronology*. Mesopotamian History and Environment Series 2, Memoirs 4. Ghent: University of Ghent; Chicago: The Oriental Institute.

Gelb, Ignace J., and Burkhart Kienast
1990 *Die altakkadischen Königsinschriften des dritten Jahrtausends v. Chr.* Freiburger altorientalische Studien 7. Stuttgart: F. Steiner.

Gibert, A., and Maurice Fevret
1953 "La Djézireh syrienne et son réveil économique." *Revue de Géographie de Lyon* 28: 1–15, 83–99.

Gibson, McGuire
1972 *The City and Area of Kish*. Coconut Grove: Field Research Projects.
1974 "Violation of Fallow and Engineered Disaster in Mesopotamian Civilization." In *Irrigation's Impact on Society*, edited by T. E. Downing and McG. Gibson, pp. 7–19. Tucson: University of Arizona Press.

Gibson, McGuire, and Amr al-Azm
2002–03 "Tell Hamoukar." *Les annales archologiques arabes syriennes. Revue d'archéologie et d'histoire* 45–46: 85–97.

Gibson, McGuire; Amr al-Azm; Clemens Reichel; Salam al-Quntar; Judith A. Franke; Lamya Khalidi; Carrie Hritz; Mark Altaweel; Colleen Coyle; Carlo Colantoni; Jonathan Tenney; Ghassan Abdul Aziz; and Tobin Hartnell
2002a "Hamoukar: A Summary of Three Seasons of Excavation." *Akkadica* 123: 11–34.

Gibson, McGuire, and Muhammad Maktash
2000 "Hamoukar: Early City in Northeastern Syria." *Antiquity* 74: 477–78.

Gibson, McGuire; Muhammad Maktash; Judith A. Franke; Amr al-Azm; John C. Sanders; Tony J. Wilkinson; Clemens Reichel; Jason A. Ur; Peggy Sanders; Abdulillah Salameh; Carrie Hritz; Brigitte Watkins; and Mahmoud Kattab
2002b "First Season of Syrian-American Investigations at Hamoukar, Hasekeh Province." *Iraq* 64: 45–68.

Glubb, J. C.
1942 *Handbook of the Nomad, Semi-Nomad, Semi-Sedentary and Sedentary Tribes of Syria.* G.S.I. (T) Headquarters, Ninth Army. Great Britain, Army.

Goetze, Albrecht
1953 "An Old Babylonian Itinerary." *Journal of Cuneiform Studies* 7: 51–72.

Gonnella, Julia
1999 "Reliefkeramik." In *Ar-Raqqa* I: *Die frühislamische Keramik von Tall Aswad*, edited by P. A. Miglus, pp. 55–75. Mainz am Rhein: Philipp von Zabern.

Goodwin, Jacqui
1995 "The First Millennium B.C. Pottery." In *Excavations at Kharabeh Shattani,* Volume 2, edited by D. Baird, S. Campbell, and T. Watkins, pp. 91–141. Occasional Paper 18. Edinburgh: University of Edinburgh Department of Archaeology.

Göyünç, Nejat, and Wolf-Dieter Hütteroth
1997 *Land an der Grenze: Osmanliche Verwaltung im heutigen türkisch-syrisch-irakischen Grenzgebiet im 16. Jahrhundert.* Istanbul: EREN.

Green, Anthony
1999 "The Ninevite Countryside: Pots and Places of the Eski Mosul Region in the Neo-Assyrian and Post-Assyrian Periods." In *Iron Age Pottery in Northern Mesopotamia, Northern Syria and South-Eastern Anatolia* (Papers Presented at the Meetings of the International "table ronde" at Heidelberg [1995] and Nieborów [1997] and Other Contributions), edited by A. Hausleiter and A. Reiche, pp. 91–126. Altertumskunde des Vorderen Orients 10. Münster: Ugarit-Verlag.

Guérin, Alexandrine
1996 "L'occupation abbasside de Nasibin: Typologie et chronologie préliminaires de la céramique prospectée en surface." In *Continuity and Change in Northern Mesopotamia from the Hellenistic to the Early Islamic Period* (Proceedings of a Colloquium Held at the Seminar für vorderasiatische Altertumskunde, Freie Universität Berlin, 6th–9th April 1994), edited by K. Bartl and S. R. Hauser, pp. 377–400. Berliner Beiträge zum Vorderen Orient 17. Berlin: Dietrich Reimer.

Guest, Evan
1966 "The Vegetation of Iraq and Adjacent Regions." in *Flora of Iraq*, Vol. 1: *Introduction*, edited by E. Guest, pp. 55–108. Baghdad: Ministry of Agriculture.

Guichard, Michael
2002 "Le Šubartum occidental à l'avènement de Zimrî-Lîm." In *Florilegium marianum* 6: *Recueil d'études à la mémoire d'André Parrot*, edited by D. Charpin and J.-M. Durand, pp. 119–68. Paris: SEPOA.

Gut, Renate Vera
1995 *Das prähistorische Ninive: Zur relativen Chronologie der frühen Perioden Nordmesopotamiens.* Baghdader Forschungen 19. Mainz am Rhein: Philipp von Zabern.

Haase, Claus-Peter
1996 "Madīnat al-Fār: The Regional Late Antique Tradition of an Early Islamic Foundation." In *Continuity and Change in Northern Mesopotamia from the Hellenistic to the Early Islamic Period* (Proceedings of a Colloquium Held at the Seminar für vorderasiatische Altertumskunde, Freie Universität Berlin, 6th–9th April 1994), edited by K. Bartl and S. R. Hauser, pp. 165–71. Berliner Beiträge zum Vorderen Orient 17. Berlin: Dietrich Reimer.

Hallo, William W.
1964 "The Road to Emar." *Journal of Cuneiform Studies* 18: 57–88.

Harper, R. P.
1980 "Athis—Neocaesareia—Qasrin—Dibsi Faraj." In *Le Moyen Euphrate: Zone de contacts et d'échanges,* edited by J.-C. Margueron, pp. 327–48. Leiden: E. J. Brill.

Hauser, Stefan R.
1996 "The Production of Pottery in Arsacid Ashur." In *Continuity and Change in Northern Mesopotamia from the Hellenistic to the Early Islamic Period* (Proceedings of a Colloquium Held at the Seminar für vorderasiatische Altertumskunde, Freie Universität Berlin, 6th–9th April 1994), edited by K. Bartl and S. R. Hauser, pp. 55–85. Berliner Beiträge zum Vorderen Orient 17. Berlin: Dietrich Reimer.

Hayes, P. P.
1991 "Models for the Distribution of Pottery around Former Agricultural Settlements." In *Interpreting Artefact Scatters: Contributions to Ploughzone Archaeology*, edited by A. J. Schofield, pp. 81–92. Oxford: Oxbow Books.

Helwing, Barbara
2000 "Regional Variation in the Composition of Late Chalcolithic Pottery Assemblages." In *Chronologies des pays du Caucase et de*

l'Euphrate aux IVe–IIIe millénaires, edited by C. Marro and H. Hauptmann, pp. 145–61. Paris: Institut Français d'Études Anatoliennes d'Istanbul.

Hijara, Ismail

1973 "Excavations at Tell Qalinj Agha (Erbil) Fourth Season 1970." *Sumer* 29: 3–12 (Arabic section).

Hill, James Brett

2004 "Land Use and an Archaeological Perspective on Socio-Natural Studies in the Wadi Al-Hasa, West Central Jordan." *American Antiquity* 69: 389–412.

Hillenbrand, Carole

1990 *A Muslim Principality in Crusader Times: The Early Artuqid State*. Leiden: Nederlands Instituut voor het Nabije Oosten.

Hindle, Brian P.

1982 *Medieval Roads*. Shire Archaeology 26. Princes Risborough: Shire Publications.

1993 *Roads, Tracks and Their Interpretation*. London: Batsford.

Hole, Frank

1980 "Archaeological Survey in Southwest Asia." *Paléorient* 6: 21–44.

1997 "Evidence for Mid-Holocene Environmental Change in the Western Khabur Drainage, Northeastern Syria." In *Third Millennium B.C. Climate Change and Old World Collapse*, edited by H. N. Dalfes, G. Kukla, and H. Weiss. NATO ASI Series I, Vol. 49. Berlin and Heidelberg: Springer.

1999 "Economic Implications of Possible Storage Structures at Tell Ziyadeh, NE Syria." *Journal of Field Archaeology* 26: 267–83.

2001 "A Radiocarbon Chronology for the Middle Khabur, Syria." *Iraq* 63: 67–98.

2002–2003 "Khabur Basin Project, 1986–2001." *Les annales archéologiques de Syrie* 45–46: 11–20.

2007 "Agricultural Sustainability in the Semi-Arid Near East." *Climate of the Past* 3: 193–203.

Hole, Frank, and R. Smith

2004 "Arid Land Agriculture in Northeastern Syria: Will This Be a Tragedy of the Commons?" In *Land Change Science: Observing, Monitoring and Understanding Trajectories of Change on the Earth's Surface*, edited by G. Gutman, A. C. Janetos, C. O. Justice, E. F. Moran, J. F. Mustard, R. R. Rindfuss, D. Skole, B. L. Turner, II, and M. A. Cochrane, pp. 209–22. Dordrecht: Kluwer.

Holland, Thomas A.

2006 *Excavations at Tell es-Sweyhat, Syria*, Vol. 2: *Archaeology of the Bronze Age, Hellenistic, and Roman Remains at an Ancient Town on the Euphrates River*. Oriental Institute Publications 125. Chicago: The Oriental Institute.

Honigmann, E., and C. E. Bosworth

2006 "Nasībīn, Nasībīn." *Encyclopedia of Islam*. 2nd edition. Leiden and Boston: Brill.

Hoskins, W. G.

1988 *The Making of the English Landscape*. 2nd edition. London: Hodder & Stoughton.

Hütteroth, W.-D.

1990 "Villages and Tribes of the Ğezīra under Early Ottoman Administration (16th Century): A Preliminary Report." *Berytus* 38: 179–84.

1992 "Settlement Desertion in the Gezira between the 16th and the 18th Century." In *The Syrian Land in the 18th and 19th Century: The Common and the Specific in the Historical Experience*, edited by T. Philipp, pp. 285–94. Stuttgart: Franz Steiner.

Hyslop, J.

1991 "Observations about Research on Prehistoric Roads in South America." In *Ancient Road Networks and Settlement Hierarchies in the New World*, edited by C. D. Trombold, pp. 28–33. Cambridge: Cambridge University Press.

Ibn Hawqal, M.

2001 *La configuration de la terre = Kitab surat al-ard*. Paris: Maisonneuve et Larose.

Ibrahim, Jabir Khalil

1986 *Pre-Islamic Settlement in Jazirah*. Baghdad: Republic of Iraq, Ministry of Culture and Information, State Organization of Antiquities and Heritage.

Jackson, John

1799 *Journey from India towards England, in the year 1797, by a Route Commonly Called Overland*. London: C. Woodfall.

Jamieson, Andrew S.

1999 "Neo-Assyrian Pottery from Tell Ahmar." In *Iron Age Pottery in Northern Mesopotamia, Northern Syria and South-Eastern Anatolia* (Papers Presented at the Meetings of the International "table ronde" at Heidelberg [1995] and Nieborów [1997] and Other Contributions), edited by A. Hausleiter and A. Reiche, pp. 287–308. Altertumskunde des Vorderen Orients 10. Münster: Ugarit-Verlag.

Jans, Greta, and Joachim Bretschneider
1998 "Wagon and Chariot Representations in the Early Dynastic Glyptic." In *About Subartu: Studies Devoted to Upper Mesopotamia*, edited by M. Lebeau, vol. 2, pp. 155–94. Subartu 4. Turnhout: Brepols.

Joannès, Francis
1996 "Routes et voies de communication dans les archives de Mari." In *Amurru* 1: *Mari, Ébla et les Hourrites*, edited by J.-M. Durand, pp. 323–61. Paris: Éditions Recherche sur les Civilisations.

Kaschau, Gundela
1999 *Lidar Höyük: Die Keramik der Mittleren Bronzezeit*. Archaeologica Euphratica 3. Mainz am Rhein: Philipp von Zabern.

Kepinski, Christine
2007 "Continuity and Break at the End of the Third Millennium B.C.: The Data from Tilbeşar, Sajur Valley (South-Eastern) Turkey." In *Sociétés humaines et changement climatique à la fin du troisième millénaire: une crise a-t-elle eu lieu en haute Mésopotamie?*, edited by C. Kuzucuoğlu and C. Marro, pp. 329–40. Varia Anatolica 19. Istanbul: Institut Français d'Études Anatoliennes Georges-Dumézil.

Kepinski-Lecomte, Christine
2001 "Tell Khoshi et l'urbanisation de la Djezireh au IIIe millénaire." In *Études Mésopotamiens: Recueil de textes offert à Jean-Louis Huot*, edited by C. Breniquet and C. Kepinski, pp. 265–86. Paris: Éditions Recherche sur les Civilisations.

Kessler, K.
1996 "Nisibis." *Der Neue Pauly* 8: 962–63.

Kettenhofen, Erich
1993 *Das Sasanidenreich*. Tübinger Atlas des Vorderen Orients B VI 3. Wiesbaden: Ludwig Reichert.

Khalidi, Lamya, and Salam al-Quntar
2008 "Obsidian Production and Exchange during the Late Chalcolithic II Period at Tell Hamoukar and Tell Brak." Paper delivered at the International Congress on the Archaeology of the Ancient Near East, Rome, 2008.

Khalidi, Lamya; Bernard Gratuze; and S. Boucetta
2009 "Provenance of Obsidian Excavated from Late Chalcolithic Levels at the Sites of Tell Hamoukar and Tell Brak, Syria." *Archaeometry* 51: 879–93.

Khoury, Dina Rizk
1997 *State and Provincial Society in the Ottoman Empire: Mosul, 1540–1834*. Cambridge Studies in Islamic Civilization. Cambridge: Cambridge University Press.

Kiepert, Richard
1893 *Syrien und Mesopotamien zur Darstellung der Reise des Dr. Max Freiherrn von Oppenheim, vom Mittelmeere zum Persischen Golf, Östliches Blatt (1:850,000)*. Berlin: Dietrich Reimer.

Killion, T. W.
1992 "Residential Ethnoarchaeology and Ancient Site Structure: Contemporary Farming and Prehistoric Settlement Agriculture at Matacapan, Veracruz, Mexico." In *Gardens of Prehistory: The Archaeology of Settlement Agriculture in Greater Mesoamerica*, edited by T. W. Killion, pp. 119–49. Tuscaloosa: University of Alabama.

Kinneir, John M.
1818 *Journey through Asia Minor, Armenia, and Koordistan in the Years 1813 and 1814*. London: J. Murray.

Koizumi, Tatsundo
1993 "Ubaid Pottery from Kashkashkok II: Typology and Chronology." *Al-Rāfidān* 14: 19–67.

Koliński, Rafal
2007 "The Upper Khabur Region in the Second Part of the Third Millennium B.C." *Altorientalische Forschungen* 34: 342–69.

Kouchoukos, Nicholas
1998 Landscape and Social Change in Late Prehistoric Mesopotamia. Ph.D. dissertation, Yale University.

Kramer, Carol
1980 "Estimating Prehistoric Populations: An Ethnoarchaeological Approach." In *L'Archéologie de l'Iraq: Perspectives et limites de l'interprétation anthropologique des documents*, edited by M.-T. Barrelet, pp. 315–34. Paris: Éditions du Centre National de la Recherche Scientifique.

Kühne, Hartmut
1995 "The Assyrians on the Middle Euphrates and the Habur." In *Neo-Assyrian Geography*, edited by M. Liverani, pp. 69–87. Quaderni di Geografia Storica 5. Rome: Università di Roma "La Sapienza."

Kühne, Hartmut, editor

2005 *Magdalu/Magdala: Tall Šēh Hamad von der postassyrischen Zeit bis zur römischen Kaiserzeit.* Berichte der Ausgrabung Tall Šēh Hamad/Dūr-katlimmu 2. Berlin: Dietrich Reimer.

Kupper, Jean-Robert

1957 *Les nomades en Mésopotamie au temps des rois de Mari.* Paris: Les Belles Lettres.

Kuzucuoğlu, Catherine, and Catherine Marro, editors

2007 *Sociétés humaines et changement climatique à la fin du troisième millénaire: Une crise a-t-elle eu lieu en haute Mésopotamie?* Varia Anatolica 19. Istanbul: Institut Français d'Études Anatolienne Georges-Dumézil.

Layard, Austen Henry

1853 *Discoveries in the Ruins of Nineveh and Babylon.* London: Putnam.

Lázaro, A.

1988 "The Period X Pottery." In *Hammam et-Turkman* I: *Report on the University of Amsterdam's 1981–84 Excavations in Syria*, edited by M. N. van Loon, vol. 2, pp. 499–559. Leiden: Nederlands Historisch-Archeologisch Instituut te Istanbul.

Le Mière, Marie

2000 "L'occupation proto-Hassuna du Haut-Khabur occidental d'apres la ceramique." In *Prospection archéologique du Haut-Khabur occidental (Syrie du N.E.),* Vol. 1: *Bibliothèque archéologique et historique T. 155*, edited by B. Lyonnet, pp. 127–49. Beirut: Institut Français d'Archéologie du Proche-orient.

Le Mière, Marie, and Olivier Nieuwenhuyse

1996 "The Prehistoric Pottery." In *Tell Sabi Abyad: The Late Neolithic Settlement*, edited by P. M. M. G. Akkermans, pp. 119–284. Leiden: Nederlands Historisch-Archaeologisch Instituut te Istanbul.

Le Strange, Guy

1905 *The Lands of the Eastern Caliphate: Mesopotamia, Persia, and Central Asia from the Moslem Conquest to the Time of Timur.* Cambridge: Cambridge University Press.

Lebeau, Marc

1990 "Esquisse d'une histoire de la Haute Mésopotamie au début de l'Age du Bronze." *Zeitschrift für Assyriologie* 80: 241–96.

1993 *Tell Melebiya, cinq campagnes de recherches sur le Moyen Khabour (1984–1988).* Akkadica Supplémentum 9. Leuven: Peeters.

1997 "La situation géographique, la topographie et les périodes d'occupation de Tell Beydar." In *Tell Beydar, Three Seasons of Excavations (1992–1994): A Preliminary Report*, edited by M. Lebeau and A. Suleiman, pp. 7–19. Subartu 3. Turnhout: Brepols.

2000 "Stratified Archaeological Evidence and Compared Periodizations in the Syrian Jezirah During the Third Millennium B.C." In *Chronologies des pays du Caucase et de l'Euphrate aux IVe–IIIe millénaires*, edited by C. Marro and H. Hauptmann, pp. 167–92. Paris: Institut Français d'Études Anatoliennes d'Istanbul.

Lebeau, Marc, and Elena Rova

2003 "Périodisation de Tell Beydar." In *Tell Beydar, the 1995–1999 Seasons of Excavations. A Preliminary Report*, edited by M. Lebeau and A. Suleiman, pp. 7–14. Subartu 10. Turnhout: Brepols.

Lebeau, Marc, and Antoine Suleiman, editors

2003 *Tell Beydar, the 1995–1999 Seasons of Excavations. A Preliminary Report.* Subartu 3. Turnhout: Brepols.

Lemke, G., and M. Sturm

1997 "δ^{18}O and Trace Element Measurements as Proxy for the Reconstruction of Climate Changes at Lake Van (Turkey): Preliminary Results." In *Third Millennium B.C. Climate Change and Old World Collapse*, edited by H. N. Dalfes, G. Kukla, and H. Weiss, pp. 653–78. NATO ASI Series I, Vol. 49. Berlin and Heidelberg: Springer.

Lewis, Norman N.

1987 *Nomads and Settlers in Syria and Jordan, 1800–1980.* Cambridge: Cambridge University Press.

Lightfoot, C. S.

1988 "Facts and Fiction: The Third Siege of Nisibis (A.D. 350)." *Historia* 37: 103–25.

Lines [Oates], Joan

1954 "Late Assyrian Pottery from Nimrud." *Iraq* 16: 164–67.

Lipiński, Edward

2000a "The Linguistic Geography of Syria in Iron Age II (c. 1000–600 B.C.)." in *Essays on Syria in the Iron Age,* edited by G. Bunnens, pp. 125–42. Ancient Near Eastern Studies, Supplement 7. Leuven: Peeters.

2000b *The Arameans: Their Ancient History, Culture, Religion.* Leuven: Peeters.

Lipo, C. P., and T. L. Hunt

2005 "Mapping Prehistoric Statue Roads on Easter Island." *Antiquity* 79: 158–68.

Litak, R.; M. Barazangi; W. Beauchamp; D. Seber; G. Brew; T. Sawaf; and W. al-Youssef

1997 "Mesozoic-Cenozoic Evolution of the Intraplate Euphrates Fault System, Syria: Implications for Regional Tectonics." *Journal of the Geological Society, London* 154: 653–66.

Liverani, Mario

1994 Comments to "The Structure and Dynamics of Dry-Farming States in Upper Mesopotamia," by T. J. Wilkinson. *Current Anthropology* 35/5: 508–09.

Lloyd, Seton

1940 "Iraq Government Soundings at Sinjar." *Iraq* 7: 13–21.

1954 "Sultantepe (Part II)." *Anatolian Studies* 4: 101–10.

Lloyd, Seton, and Fuad Safar

1945 "Tell Hassuna: Excavations by the Iraq Government Directorate General of Antiquities in 1943 and 1944." *Journal of Near Eastern Studies* 4: 255–89.

Lovelock, P.

1984 "A Review of the Tectonics of the Northern Middle East Region." *Geological Magazine* 121: 577–87.

Lumsden, Stephen

1999 "Neo-Assyrian Pottery from Nineveh." In *Iron Age Pottery in Northern Mesopotamia, Northern Syria and South-Eastern Anatolia* (Papers Presented at the Meetings of the International "table ronde" at Heidelberg (1995) and Nieborów (1997) and Other Contributions), edited by A. Hausleiter and A. Reiche, pp. 3–15. Altertumskunde des Vorderen Orients Band 10. Münster: Ugarit-Verlag.

Lupton, Alan

1996 *Stability and Change: Socio-Political Development in North Mesopotamia and South-East Anatolia 4000–2700 B.C.* British Archaeological Reports, International Series 627. Oxford: British Archaeological Reports.

Lyonnet, Bertille

1990 "Prospection archéologique du site de Mohammed Diyab." In *Tell Mohammed Diyab: Campagnes 1987 et 1988*, edited by J.-M. Durand, pp. 71–115. Paris: SEPOA.

1996a "La prospection archéologique de la partie occidentale du Haut-Khabur (Syrie du nord-est): Méthodes, résultats et questions autour de l'occupation aux IIIe et IIe millénaires Av. N.È." *Amurru* 1: 363–76.

1996b "Settlement Pattern in the Upper Khabur (N.E. Syria) from the Achaemenids to the Abbasid Period: Methods and Preliminary Results from a Survey." In *Continuity and Change in Northern Mesopotamia from the Hellenistic to the Early Islamic Period (*Proceedings of a Colloquium Held at the Seminar für vorderasiatische Altertumskunde, Freie Universität Berlin, 6th–9th April 1994), edited by K. Bartl and S. R. Hauser, pp. 349–61. Berliner Beiträge zum Vorderen Orient 17. Berlin: Dietrich Reimer.

1998 "Le peuplement de la Djéziré occidentale au début du 3e millénaire, villes circulaires et pastoralisme: Questions et hypothèses." In *About Subartu: Studies Devoted to Upper Mesopotamia*, edited by M. Lebeau, vol. 1, pp. 179–93. Subartu 4. Turnhout: Brepols.

Lyonnet, Bertille, editor

2000 *Prospection archéologique du Haut-Khabur occidental (Syrie du N.E.)*, Vol. 1: *Bibliothèque archéologique et historique T. 155*. Beirut: Institut Français d'Archéologie du Proche-orient.

Mahmoud, Asad; Reinhard Bernbeck; Hartmut Kühne; Peter Pfälzner; and Wolfgang Röllig

1988 "Die Ausgrabung auf dem Tall 'Ağağa/Šadikanni 1982." *Damaszener Mitteilungen* 3: 141–84.

Mallowan, M. E. L.

1936 "The Excavations at Tall Chagar Bazar, and an Archaeological Survey of the Habur Region, 1934–5." *Iraq* 3: 1–86.

Mason, R. B.

1995 "New Looks at Old Pots: Results of Recent Multidisciplinary Studies of Ceramics from the Islamic World." *Muqarnas* 12: 1–10.

Matney, Timothy, and Guillermo Algaze

1995 "Urban Development at Mid–Late Early Bronze Age Titriş Höyük in Southeastern Anatolia." *Bulletin of the American Schools of Oriental Research* 299/300: 33–52.

Matney, Timothy; Lynn Rainville; Kemalettin Köroğlu; Azer Keskin; Tasha Vorderstrasse; Nursen Ö. Fındık; and Ann Donkin

2007 "Report on Excavation at Ziyaret Tepe, 2006 Season." *Anatolica* 33: 23–74.

Matsutani, Toshio, editor
1991 *Tell Kashkashok: The Excavations at Tell No. II*. Tokyo: Institute of Oriental Culture, University of Tokyo.

Matthews, Roger
2003a "A Chiefdom on the Northern Plains: Early Third-Millennium Investigations: The Ninevite 5 Period." In *Excavations at Tell Brak,* Vol. 4: *Exploring an Upper Mesopotamian Regional Centre, 1994–1996*, edited by R. Matthews, pp. 97–191. Cambridge: McDonald Institute for Archaeological Research; London: British School of Archaeology in Iraq.
2003b "Traces of Early Complexity: Late Fifth- to Early Fourth-Millennia Investigations." In *Excavations at Tell Brak,* Vol. 4: *Exploring an Upper Mesopotamian Regional Centre, 1994–1996*, edited by R. Matthews, pp. 25–51. Cambridge: McDonald Institute for Archaeological Research; London: British School of Archaeology in Iraq.

Matthews, Wendy
2003c "Microstratigraphic Sequences: Indications of Uses and Concepts of Space." In *Excavations at Tell Brak*, Vol. 4: *Exploring an Upper Mesopotamian Regional Centre, 1994–1996,* edited by R. Matthews, pp. 377–88. Cambridge: McDonald Institute for Archaeological Research; London: British School of Archaeology in Iraq.

Mattingly, David
2000 "Methods of Collection, Recording and Quantification." In *Extracting Meaning from Ploughsoil Assemblages*, edited by R. Francovich and H. Patterson, pp. 5–15. Archaeology of Mediterranean Landscapes 5. Oxford: Oxbow Books.

McAdam, Ellen
1995 "The Proto-Hassuna Pottery." In *Excavations at Kharabeh Shattani,* Vol. 2: *The 1983 Season of Excavation*, edited by D. Baird, S. Campbell, and T. Watkins, pp. 32–54. Edinburgh: University of Edinburgh Department of Archaeology.

McClellan, Tom L.; Rodger Grayson; and Cliff Ogleby
2000 "Bronze Age Water Harvesting in North Syria." In *La Djéziré et l'Euphrate Syriens de la protohistoire à la fin du IIe millénaire av. J.-C.: Tendances dans l'interprétation historique des donnés nouvelles*, edited by O. Rouault and M. Wäfler, pp. 137–55. Subartu 7. Turnhout: Brepols.

McClellan, Thomas L., and Anne Porter
1995 "Jawa and North Syria." *Studies in the History and Archaeology of Jordan* 5: 49–65.

McCoan, J. C.
1879 *Our New Protectorate, Asia in Turkey*. London: Chapman & Hall.

McDonald, Helen, and N. Jackson
2003 "A House on the Hill: Second-Millennium Investigations; The Middle Bronze Age." In *Excavations at Tell Brak*, Vol. 4: *Exploring an Upper Mesopotamian Regional Centre, 1994–1996*, edited by R. Matthews, pp. 271–319. Cambridge: McDonald Institute for Archaeological Research; London: British School of Archaeology in Iraq.

McDonald, Robert A., editor
1997 *Corona Between the Sun and the Earth: The First NRO Reconnaissance Eye in Space.* Bethesda: American Society for Photogrammetry and Remote Sensing.

McEwan, Calvin W.; Linda S. Braidwood; Henri Frankfort; Hans G. Güterbock; Richard C. Haines; Helene J. Kantor; and Carl H. Kraeling
1958 *Soundings at Tell Fakhariyah*. Oriental Institute Publications 79. Chicago: University of Chicago Press.

McMahon, Augusta
1998 "The Kuyunjik Gully Sounding, Nineveh, 1989 & 1990 Seasons." *Al-Rāfidān* 19: 1–32.

McMahon, Augusta, and Philippe Quenet
2007 "A Late Third Millennium B.C. Pottery Assemblage from Chagar Bazar (Area D, Phase II)." In *Chagar Bazar (Syrie)* II: *Les vestiges "post-akkadiens" du chantier D et études diverses*, edited by Ö. Tunca, A. McMahon, and A. e.-M. Baghdo, pp. 69–242. Leuven: Peeters.

Mehner, H.
1983 "Die Mechanisierung der Landwirtschaft in Irak, Iran und Syrien." *Berichte über Landwirtschaft* 61: 633–59.

Meijer, Diederik J. W.
1986 *A Survey in Northeastern Syria*. Publications de l'Institut historique-archéological Néerlandais de Stamboul 58. Istanbul: Nederlands Historisch-Archaeologisch Instituut te Istanbul.
1990 "An Archaeological Surface Survey: Some Assumptions and Ideas." In *Tall al-Hamidiya* 2 (Symposium: Recent Excavations in the Upper Khabur Region, Berne, December 9–11,

1986), edited by S. Eichler, M. Wäfler, and D. Warburton, pp. 31–45. Orbis Biblicus et Orientalis, Series Archaeologica 6. Freiburg: Universitätsverlag; Göttingen: Vandenhoeck & Ruprecht.

Menze, B. H.; Jason A. Ur; and Andrew G. Sherratt
2006 "Detection of Ancient Settlement Mounds: Archaeological Survey Based on the SRTM Terrain Model." *Photogrammetric Engineering & Remote Sensing* 72: 321–27.

Michalowski, Piotr
1986 "Mental Maps and Ideology: Reflections on Subartu." In *The Origins of Cities in Dry-Farming Syria and Mesopotamia in the Third Millennium B.C.*, edited by H. Weiss, pp. 129–56. Guilford: Four Quarters.
1999 "Sumer Dreams of Subartu: Politics and the Geographical Imagination." In *Languages and Cultures in Contact: At the Crossroads of Civilizations in the Syro-Mesopotamian Realm*, edited by K. Van Lerberghe and G. Voet, pp. 305–15. Orientalia Lovaniensia Analecta 96. Leuven: Peeters.

Miglus, Peter A.
1999 *Ar-Raqqa* I: *Die frühislamische Keramik von Tall Aswad.* Mainz am Rhein: Philipp von Zabern.

Miglus, Peter A., and F. M. Stępniowski
1999 "Formen, Verzierung und Verteilung der Keramik." In *Ar-Raqqa* I: *Die frühislamische Keramik von Tall Aswad*, edited by P. A. Miglus, pp. 19–54. Mainz am Rhein: Philipp von Zabern.

Miller, N. F.
1984 "The Use of Dung as Fuel: An Ethnographic Example and an Archaeological Application." *Paléorient* 10/2: 71–79.

Miller, N. F., and T. Smart
1984 "Intentional Burning of Dung as Fuel: A Mechanism for the Incorporation of Charred Seeds into the Archaeological Record." *Journal of Ethnobiology* 4.

Millet, M.
1991 "Pottery: Population or Supply Patterns? The Ager Tarraconensis Approach." In *Roman Landscapes: Archaeological Survey in the Mediterranean Region*, edited by G. Barker and J. Lloyd, pp. 18–26. London: British School at Rome.

Mitford, Edward Ledwich
1884 *A Land March from England to Ceylon Forty Years Ago.* 2 vols. London: W. H. Allen.

Monchambert, Jean-Yves
1984a "Le futur lac du Moyen Khabour: Rapport sur la prospection archéologique menée en 1983." *Syria* 61: 181–218.
1984b "Prospection archéologique sur l'emplacement du futur lac du Moyen Khabour." *Akkadica* 39: 1–7.

Montagne, Robert
1932 "Quelques aspects du peuplement de la Haute-Djeziré." *Bulletin d'études orientales de l'Institut français de Damas* 2: 53–66.

Moore, Andrew M. T.; Gordon C. Hillman; and Anthony J. Legge
2000 *Village on the Euphrates: From Foraging to Farming at Abu Hureyra.* Oxford: Oxford University Press.

Moore, John
1993 *Tille Höyük* 1: *The Medieval Period.* London: British Institute of Archaeology at Ankara.

Moorey, P. R. S.
2001 "Clay Models and Overland Mobility in Syria, c. 2350–1800 B.C." In *Beiträge zur vorderasiatischen Archäologie, Winfried Orthmann gewidmet*, edited by J.-W. Meyer, M. Novák, and A. Pruß, pp. 344–51. Frankfurt am Main: Johann Wolfgang Goethe-Universität.

Morandi Bonacossi, D.
2000 "The Linguistic Geography of Syria in Iron Age II (c. 1000–600 B.C.)." In *Essays on Syria in the Iron Age*, edited by G. Bunnens, pp. 349–96. Ancient Near Eastern Studies, Supplement 7. Leuven: Peeters.

Muir, Richard
2000 *The New Reading the Landscape: Fieldwork in Landscape History.* Exeter: University of Exeter Press.

Nicolle, Christophe, editor
2004 *Nomades et sédentaires dans le Proche-Orient ancien: Compte rendu de la XLVI*[e] *Rencontre assyriologique internationale.* Paris: Éditions Recherche sur les Civilisations.
2006 *Tell Mohammed Diyab* 3: *Travaux de 1992–2000 sur les buttes A et B.* Paris: Éditions Recherche sur les Civilisations.

Nieuwenhuyse, Olivier
2000 "Halaf Settlement in the Khabur Headwaters." In *Prospection archéologique du Haut-Khabur occidental (Syrie du N.E.)*, Vol. 1:

Bibliothèque archéologique et historique T. 155, edited by B. Lyonnet, pp. 151–260. Beirut: Institut Français d'Archéologie du Proche-orient.

2007 *Plain and Painted Pottery: The Rise of Late Neolithic Ceramic Styles on the Syrian and Northern Mesopotamian Plains*. Turnhout: Brepols.

Nieuwenhuyse, Olivier, and Tony J. Wilkinson

2008 "Late Neolithic Settlement in the Area of Tell Beydar (NE Syria)." In *Beydar Studies* 1, edited by M. Lebeau and A. Suleiman. Subartu 21. Turnhout: Brepols.

Nishiaki, Yoshihiro

2000 "Palaeolithic and Neolithic Stone Industries from the Khabur Basin, Northeast Syria." In *Prospection archéologique du Haut-Khabur occidental (Syrie du N.E.)*, Vol. 1: *Bibliothèque archéologique et historique T. 155*, edited by B. Lyonnet, pp. 77–124. Beirut: Institut Français d'archéologie du proche-orient.

Nishiaki, Yoshihiro, and Marie Le Mière

2005 "The Oldest Pottery Neolithic of Upper Mesopotamia: New Evidence from Tell Seker al-Aheimar, the Khabur, Northeast Syria." *Paléorient* 31: 55–68.

Nissen, Hans J.

2002 "Uruk: Key Site of the Period and Key Site of the Problem." In *Artefacts of Complexity: Tracking the Uruk in the Near East*, edited by J. N. Postgate, pp. 1–16. Iraq Archaeological Reports 5. Warminster: British School of Archaeology in Iraq.

Nokandeh, Jebrael; Eberhard W. Sauer; Hamid O. Rekavandi; Tony J. Wilkinson; Ghorban A. Abbasi; Jean-Luc Schwenninger; Majid Mahmoudi; David Parker; Morteza Fattahi; Lucian S. Usher-Wilson; Mohammad Ershadi; James Ratcliffe; and Rowena Gale

2006 "Linear Barriers of Northern Iran: The Great Wall of Gorgan and the Wall of Tammishe." *Iran* 44: 1–52.

Nordiguian, L., and J.-F. Salles, editors

2000 *Aux origines de l'archéologie aérienne: A. Poidebard (1878–1955)*. Beirut: Presses de l'Université Saint-Joseph.

Northedge, Alastair

1981 "Selected Late Roman and Islamic Coarse Wares." In *The River Qoueiq, Northern Syria, and Its Catchment: Studies Arising from the Tell Rifa'at Survey 1977–1979*, edited by J. Matthers, pp. 109–28. British Archaeological Reports, International Series 98. Oxford: British Archaeological Reports.

Northedge, Alastair, and R. Falkner

1987 "The 1986 Survey Season at Sāmarrā'." *Iraq* 49: 143–73.

Nouss, Izzat

1951 La population de la République syrienne: Étude démographique et géographique. Ph.D. dissertation, Paris.

Numoto, Hirotoshi

1988 "Excavations at Tell Fisna." *Al-Rāfidān* 9: 1–72.

Oates, David

1968 *Studies in the Ancient History of Northern Iraq*. London: British Academy.

Oates, David, and Joan Oates

1958 "Nimrud 1957: The Hellenistic Settlement." *Iraq* 20: 114–57.

1959 "Ain Sinu: A Roman Frontier Post in Northern Iraq." *Iraq* 21: 207–42.

1976 "Early Irrigation Agriculture in Mesopotamia." In *Problems in Economic and Social Archaeology*, edited by G. d. G. Sieveking, I. H. Longworth, and K. E. Wilson, pp. 109–35. London: Duckworth.

1990 "Aspects of Hellenistic and Roman Settlement in the Khabur Basin." In *Resurrecting the Past: A Joint Tribute to Adnan Bounni*, edited by P. Matthiae, M. Van Loon, and H. Weiss, pp. 227–48. Leiden: Nederlands Historisch-Archaeologisch Instituut.

1991 "Excavations at Tell Brak 1990–91." *Iraq* 53: 127–45.

1993 "Excavations at Tell Brak 1992–93." *Iraq* 55: 155–99.

2001a "The Excavations." In *Excavations at Tell Brak*, Vol. 2: *Nagar in the Third Millennium B.C.*, by D. Oates, J. Oates, and H. McDonald, pp. 15–98. Cambridge: McDonald Institute for Archaeological Research; London: British School of Archaeology in Iraq.

Oates, David; Joan Oates; and Helen McDonald

1997 *Excavations at Tell Brak*, Vol. 1: *The Mitanni and Old Babylonian Periods*. Cambridge: McDonald Institute for Archaeological Research; London: British School of Archaeology in Iraq.

2001 *Excavations at Tell Brak*, Vol. 2: *Nagar in the Third Millennium B.C.* Cambridge: McDonald Institute for Archaeological Research; London: British School of Archaeology in Iraq.

Oates, Joan

1959 "Late Assyrian Pottery from Fort Shalmaneser." *Iraq* 21: 130–46.

1987 "A Note on 'Ubaid and Mitanni Pottery from Tell Brak." *Iraq* 49: 193–98.

1997 "The Pottery." In *Excavations at Tell Brak*, Vol. 1: *The Mitanni and Old Babylonian Periods*, by D. Oates, J. Oates, and H. McDonald, pp. 61–80. Cambridge: McDonald Institute for Archaeological Research; London: British School of Archaeology in Iraq.

2001a "Equid Figurines and 'Chariot' Models." In *Excavations at Tell Brak*, Vol. 2: *Nagar in the Third Millennium B.C.*, by D. Oates, J. Oates, and H. McDonald, pp. 279–293. Cambridge: McDonald Institute for Archaeological Research; London: British School of Archaeology in Iraq.

2001b "The Third Millennium Pottery." In *Excavations at Tell Brak*, Vol. 2: *Nagar in the Third Millennium B.C.*, by D. Oates, J. Oates, and H. McDonald, pp. 151–94. Cambridge: McDonald Institute for Archaeological Research; London: British School of Archaeology in Iraq.

2002 "Tell Brak: The 4th Millennium Sequence and Its Implications." In *Artefacts of Complexity: Tracking the Uruk in the Near East*, edited by J. N. Postgate, pp. 111–22. Iraq Archaeological Reports 5. Warminster: British School of Archaeology in Iraq.

2005 "Archaeology in Mesopotamia: Digging Deeper at Tell Brak." *Proceedings of the British Academy* 131: 1–39.

Oates, Joan; Augusta McMahon; P. Karsgaard; Salam al-Quntar; and Jason A. Ur

2007 "Early Mesopotamian Urbanism: A New View from the North." *Antiquity* 81: 585–600.

Oates, Joan, and David Oates

1997 "An Open Gate: Cities of the Fourth Millennium B.C. (Tell Brak 1997)." *Cambridge Archaeological Journal* 7: 287–97.

2001b "The Late Third Millennium in the Khabur." In *Beiträge zur vorderasiatischen Archäologie Winfried Orthmann gewidmet*, edited by J.-W. Meyer, M. Novák, and A. Pruß, pp. 386–89. Frankfurt am Main: Johann Wolfgang Goethe-Universität.

2001c *Nimrud: An Assyrian Imperial City Revealed.* London: British School of Archaeology in Iraq.

2002 "The Reattribution of Middle Uruk Materials at Brak." In *Leaving No Stones Unturned: Essays on the Ancient Near East and Egypt in Honor of Donald P. Hansen*, edited by E. Ehrenberg, pp. 145–54. Winona Lake: Eisenbrauns.

Oded, Bustenay

1979 *Mass Deportations and Deportees in the Neo-Assyrian Empire*. Wiesbaden: Ludwig Reichert.

Oguchi, Hiromichi

1987 "Tell Musharifa." In *Researches on the Antiquities of Saddam Dam Basin Salvage and other Researches*, edited by M. S. Demirji, pp. 49–54. Baghdad: Ministry of Culture and Information, Republic of Iraq.

2000 "The 'Late' Khabur Ware Problem Once Again." *Al-Rāfidān* 21: 103–26.

2003 "20th Century B.C. North Mesopotamia: An Archaeological Dilemma." *Al-Rāfidān* 24: 83–100.

Oppenheim, A. Leo

1977 *Ancient Mesopotamia: Portrait of a Dead Civilization.* Revised edition. Chicago: University of Chicago Press.

Orssaud, Dominique

1991 "La céramique." In *Halabiyya-Zenobia, Place forte du limes oriental et la Haute Mésopotamie au VIe siècle*, Vol. 2: *L'architecture publique, religieuse, privée et funéraire*, edited by J. Lauffray, pp. 260–75.Bibliothèque archéologique et historique 138. Paris: P. Geuthner.

Orthmann, Winfried

1997 "Chuera, Tell." In *The Oxford Encyclopedia of Archaeology in the Ancient Near East*, edited by E. Meyers, pp. 491–92. Oxford: Oxford University Press.

2002 *Die aramäisch-assyrische Stadt Guzana: Ein Rückblick auf die Ausgrabungen Max von Oppenheims in Tell Halaf.* Saarbrücken: Saarbrücker Druckerei und Verlag.

Parker, Bradley J.

2001 *The Mechanics of Empire: The Northern Frontier of Assyria as a Case Study in Imperial Dynamics.* Helsinki: Neo-Assyrian Text Corpus Project.

2003 "Archaeological Manifestations of Empire: Assyria's Imprint on Southeastern Anatolia." *American Journal of Archaeology* 107: 525–57.

Pearce, Julie

2000 "The Late Chalcolithic Sequence at Hacinebi Tepe, Turkey." In *Chronologies des pays du Caucase et de l'Euphrate aux IVe–IIIe millénaires*, edited by C. Marro and H. Hauptmann, pp. 115–43. Paris: Institut Français d'Études Anatoliennes d'Istanbul.

Perrin de Brichambaut, G., and Carl Christian Wallén

1963 *A Study of Agroclimatology in Semi-Arid and Arid Zones of the Near East*. World Meteorological Organization Technical Note No. 56. Geneva: Secretariat of the World Meteorological Organization.

Peterson, T. C., and R. S. Vose

1997 "An Overview of the Global Historical Climatology Network Temperature Database." *Bulletin of the American Meteorological Society* 78: 2837–49.

Pfälzner, Peter

1988 "Tell Bderi 1985: Bericht über die erste Kampagne." *Damaszener Mitteilungen* 3: 223–386.

1990 "Tell Bderi, the Development of a Bronze Age Town." In *The Near East in Antiquity: German Contributions to the Archaeology of Jordan, Palestine, Syria, Lebanon, and Egypt*, edited by S. Kerner, vol. 1, pp. 63–79. Amman: Goethe-Institute and Al Kutba Publishers.

1995 *Mittanische und mittelassyrische Keramik: Eine chronologische, funktionale und produktionsökonomische Analyse*. Berichte der Ausgrabung Tall Šēh Hamad/Dūr-katlimmu 3. Berlin: Dietrich Reimer.

1997 "Wandel und Kontinuität im Urbanisierungsprocess des 3. Jtsds. in Nordmesopotamien." In *Die orientalische Stadt: Kontinuität, Wandel, Bruch: 1. Internationales Colloquium der Deutschen Orient-Gesellschaft, 9.–10. Mai 1996 in Halle/Saale*, edited by G. Wilhelm, pp. 239–65. Saarbrücken: Saarbrücker Drukkerei und Verlag.

1998 "Eine Modifikation der Periodisierung Nordmesopotamiens im 3. Jtsd. v. Chr." *Mitteilungen der Deutschen Orient-Gesellschaft zu Berlin* 130: 69–71.

Pfälzner, Peter; Anne Wissing; and Christian Hubner

2004 "Urbanismus in der Unterstadt von Urkeš: Ergebnisse einer geomagnetischen Prospektion und eines archäologischen Surveys in der südöstlichen Unterstadt von Tall Mozan im Sommer 2002." *Mitteilungen der Deutschen Orient-Gesellschaft zu Berlin* 136: 41–86.

Philip, G.; D. Dononghue; A. Beck; and N. Galiatsatos

2002 "CORONA Satellite Photography: An Archaeological Application from the Middle East." *Antiquity* 76: 109–18.

Pierobon-Benoit, R.

1998 "Tra l'Ellenismo e il Medioevo: Dati e problemi a Tell Barri." In *Tell Barri/Kahat 2: Relazione sulle campagne 1980–1993 a Tell Barri/Kahat, nel bacino del Habur (Siria)*, edited by P. E. Pecorella, pp. 199–256. Documenta Asiana 5. Rome: Istituto per gli studi Micenei ed Egeo-Anatolici.

Pigulevskaja, Nina V.

1963 *Les villes de l'état Iranien aux époques parthe et sassanide: Contribution à l'histoire sociale de la Basse Antiquité*. Paris: Mouton.

Plog, Stephen; Fred Plog; and Walter Wait

1978 "Decision Making in Modern Surveys." In *Advances in Archaeological Method and Theory*, Vol. 1, edited by M. B. Schiffer, pp. 384–421. New York: Academic Press.

Poidebard, Antoine

1934 *La trace de Rom dans le désert de Syrie*. Bibliothèque Archéologique et Historique 18. Paris: P. Geuthner.

Pollock, Susan, and C. Coursey

1995 "Ceramics from Hacinebi Tepe: Chronology and Connections." *Anatolica* 21: 101–41.

Porada, Edith; Donald P. Hansen; Sally Dunham; and S. Babcock

1992 "Mesopotamia." In *Chronologies in Old World Archaeology*, 3rd edition, edited by R. W. Ehrich, pp. 77–121. Chicago: University of Chicago Press.

Porter, Venetia

1981 *Medieval Syrian Pottery*. Oxford: Ashmolean Museum.

Postgate, Carolyn; David Oates; and Joan Oates

1997 *The Excavations at Tell al Rimah: The Pottery*. Iraq Archaeological Reports 4. Warminster: Aris & Phillips.

Postgate, J. Nicholas

1994 "How Many Sumerians per Hectare? Probing the Anatomy of an Early City." *Cambridge Archaeological Journal* 4: 47–65.

Postgate, J. Nicholas, editor

2002 *Artefacts of Complexity: Tracking the Uruk in the Near East*. Iraq Archaeological Reports 5. Warminster: British School of Archaeology in Iraq.

Rainville, Lynn

2003 "Results from Micro-archaeology in 2001 and 2002." In "Excavations at Tell Brak 2001–2002: Preliminary Report," by Geoff Emberling and Helen McDonald, pp. 63–72. *Iraq* 65: 1–75.

Reade, Julian

1968 "Tell Taya (1967): Summary Report." *Iraq* 30: 234–64.

1982 "Tell Taya." In *Fifty Years of Mesopotamian Discovery*, edited by J. Curtis, pp. 72–78. London: British School of Archaeology in Iraq.

1997 "Taya, Tell." In *The Oxford Encylopedia of Archaeology in the Ancient Near East*, edited by E. Meyers, vol. 5, pp. 158–60. Oxford: Oxford University Press.

2001 "Assyrian King-Lists, the Royal Tombs of Ur, and Indus Origins." *Journal of Near Eastern Studies* 60: 1–30.

Redford, Scott

1998 *The Archaeology of the Frontier in the Medieval Near East: Excavations at Gritille, Turkey*. Archaeological Institute of America Monographs, new series, 3. Philadelphia: University Museum Publications.

Redman, Charles L.

1982 "Archaeological Survey and the Study of Mesopotamian Urban Systems." *Journal of Field Archaeology* 9: 375–82.

Redman, Charles L., and P. J. Watson

1970 "Systematic, Intensive Surface Collection." *American Antiquity* 35: 279–91.

Reichel, Clemens

2002 "Administrative Complexity in Syria during the 4th Millennium B.C.: The Seals and Sealings from Tell Hamoukar." *Akkadica* 123: 35–56.

Reichel, Clemens, editor

In prep. *The Origins and Development of Urbanism in NE Syria: The 2001–2007 Seasons at Hamoukar*. Oriental Institute Communications. Chicago: The Oriental Institute.

Riccardi, Roberta Venco

1970–71 "Sasanian Pottery from Tell Mahuz (North Mesopotamia)." *Mesopotamia* 5/6: 427–82.

1984 "Sasanian Pottery from Choche (Artisans' Quarter) and Tell Baruda." In *Arabie orientale, Mésopotamie et Iran méridional de l'age du fer au début de la période islamique*, edited by R. Boucharlat and J.-F. Salles, pp. 49–57. Paris: Éditions Recherche sur les Civilisations.

Richelson, J.

2003 "A 'Rifle' in Space." *Air Force Magazine* June 2003: 72–75.

Rick, J. W.

1976 "Downslope Movement and Archaeological Intrasite Spatial Analysis." *American Antiquity* 41: 133–44.

Ristvet, L.

2005 Settlement, Economy, and Society in the Tell Leilan Region, Syria, 3000–1000 B.C. Ph.D. dissertation, University of Cambridge.

Roaf, Michael

1984 "Excavations at Tell Mohammed Arab in the Eski Mosul Dam Salvage Project." *Iraq* 46: 141–56.

Roaf, Michal, and R. Killick

1987 "A Mysterious Affair of Styles: The Ninevite 5 Pottery of Northern Mesopotamia." *Iraq* 49: 199–230.

Roberts, D. G., and D. Barrett

1984 "Nightsoil Disposal Practices of the 19th Century and the Origin of Artifacts in Plowzone Proveniences." *Historical Archaeology* 18: 108–15.

Römer-Strehl, Christiane

2005 "Untersuchungen zur Keramik der Seleukidischen und parthisch-römischen Zeit vom Tall Šēh Hamad." In *Magdalu/Magdala: Tall Šēh Hamad von der postassyrischen Zeit bis zur römischen Kaiserzeit*, edited by H. Kühne, pp. 197–312. Berlin: Dietrich Reimer.

Rosen, Arlene Miller

1986 *Cities of Clay: The Geoarchaeology of Tells*. Chicago: University of Chicago Press.

Rosen, S. A.

2003 "Early Multi-Resource Nomadism: Excavations at the Camel Site in the Central Negev." *Antiquity* 77: 749–60.

Rossel, S.; F. Marshall; J. Peters; T. Pilgram; M. D. Adams; and D. O'Connor

2008 "Domestication of the Donkey: Timing, Processes, and Indicators." *Proceedings of the National Academy of Sciences* 105: 3715–20.

Rossmeisl, I.

1989 "Late Bronze Age Pottery of Tell Sabi Abyad." In *Excavations at Tell Sabi Abyad*, edited by P. M. M. G. Akkermans, pp. 337–56. British Archaeological Reports, International Series 468. Oxford: British Archaeological Reports.

Rothman, Mitchell S.

2001a "The Local and the Regional: An Introduction." In *Uruk Mesopotamia and Its*

Neighbors: Cross-Cultural Interactions in the Era of State Formation, edited by M. S. Rothman, pp. 3–26. Santa Fe: School of American Research Press.

2002a "Tepe Gawra: Chronology and Socio-Economic Change in the Foothills of Northern Iraq in the Era of State Formation." In *Artefacts of Complexity: Tracking the Uruk in the Near East*, edited by J. N. Postgate, pp. 49–77. Iraq Archaeological Reports 5. Warminster: British School of Archaeology in Iraq.

2002b *Tepe Gawra: The Evolution of a Small, Prehistoric Center in Northern Iraq*. University Museum Monograph 112. Philadelphia: University of Pennsylvania Museum of Archaeology and Anthropology.

Rothman, Mitchell S., editor

2001b *Uruk Mesopotamia and Its Neighbors: Cross-Cultural Interactions in the Era of State Formation*. Santa Fe: School of American Research Press.

Rova, Elena

1988 *Distribution and Chronology of the Nineveh 5 Pottery and of its Culture*. Contributi e materiali di archeologia orientale 2. Rome: Università degli studi di Roma "La Sapienza."

1999–2000 "A Tentative Synchronisation of the Local Late Chalcolithic Ceramic Horizons of Northern Syro-Mesopotamia." *Mesopotamia* 34–35: 175–99.

2000 "Early Third Millennium B.C. Painted Pottery Traditions in the Jezirah." In *Chronologies des pays du Caucase et de l'Euphrate aux IVe–IIIe millénaires*, edited by C. Marro and H. Hauptmann, pp. 231–54. Paris: Institut Français d'Études Anatoliennes d'Istanbul.

2003 "The III Millennium Pottery Morphology: The Typology Principles, the Coding System and some Preliminary Results." In *Tell Beydar, the 1995–1999 Seasons of Excavations: A Preliminary Report*, edited by M. Lebeau and A. Suleiman, pp. 395–489. Subartu 10. Turnhout: Brepols.

Sachau, Eduard

1883 *Reise in Syrien und Mesopotamien*. Leipzig: F. A. Brockhaus.

Sallaberger, Walther

1996 "Grain Accounts: Personnel Lists and Expenditure Documents." In *Administrative Documents from Tell Beydar (Season 1993–1995)*, edited by F. Ismail, W. Sallaberger, P. Talon, and K. Van Lerberghe,pp. 89–106. Subartu 2. Turnhout: Brepols.

2004 "A Note on the Sheep and Goat Flocks: Introduction to Texts 151–167." In *Third Millennium Cuneiform Texts from Tell Beydar (Seasons 1996–2002)*, edited by L. Milano, W. Sallaberger, P. Talon, and K. Van Lerberghe, pp. 13–21. Subartu 12. Turnhout: Brepols.

2007 "From Urban Culture to Nomadism: A History of Upper Mesopotamia in the Late Third Millennium." In *Sociétés humaines et changement climatique à la fin du troisième millénaire: Une crise a-t-elle eu lieu en haute Mésopotamie?*, edited by C. Kuzucuoğlu and C. Marro, pp. 417–56. Varia Anatolica 19. Istanbul: Institut Français d'Études Anatoliennes Georges-Dumézil.

Sallaberger, Walther, and Jason A. Ur

2004 "Tell Beydar/Nabada in Its Regional Setting." In *Third Millennium Cuneiform Texts from Tell Beydar (Seasons 1996–2002)*, edited by L. Milano, W. Sallaberger, P. Talon, and K. Van Lerberghe, pp. 51–71. Subartu 12. Turnhout: Brepols.

Sanlaville, Paul

1989 "Considérations sur l'évolution de la Basse Mésopotamie au cours des derniers millénaires." *Paléorient* 15: 5–27.

Sawaf, T.; D. al-Saad; A. Gebran; M. Barazangi; J. Best; and T. Chaimov

1993 "Stratigraphy and Structure of Eastern Syria Across the Euphrates Depression." *Tectonophysics* 220: 267–81.

Schiffer, M. B.; A. P. Sullivan; and T. C. Klinger

1978 "The Design of Archaeological Surveys." *World Archaeology* 10.

Schneider, E.

1999 "Die eisenzeitliche Keramik von Tell Sheikh Hassan (Syrien)." In *Iron Age Pottery in Northern Mesopotamia, Northern Syria and South-Eastern Anatolia* (Papers Presented at the Meetings of the International "table ronde" at Heidelberg [1995] and Nieborów [1997] and Other Contributions), edited by A. Hausleiter and A. Reiche, pp. 325–46. Altertumskunde des Vorderen Orients 10. Münster: Ugarit-Verlag.

Schneider, G.

1989 "A Technological Study of North-Mespotamian Stone Ware." *World Archaeology* 21: 30–50.

Schneider, Gerwulf, and Malgorzata Daszkiewicz

2001 "Stone Ware and Ninevite 5: Notes on Composition and Technology of Pottery from Tell

Brak." In *Excavations at Tell Brak*, Vol. 2: *Nagar in the Third Millennium B.C.*, by D. Oates, J. Oates, and H. McDonald, pp. 194–216. Cambridge: McDonald Institute for Archaeological Research; London: British School of Archaeology in Iraq.

Schwartz, Glenn M.
1988a *A Ceramic Chronology from Tell Leilan, Operation 1*. Yale Tell Leilan Research 1. New Haven: Yale University Press.
1988b "Excavations at Karatut Mevkii and Perspectives on the Uruk/Jemdet Nasr Expansion." *Akkadica* 56: 1–41.
1994 "Before Ebla: Models of Pre-State Political Organization in Syria and Northern Mesopotamia." In *Chiefdoms and Early States in the Near East: The Organizational Dynamics of Complexity*, edited by G. J. Stein and M. S. Rothman, pp. 153–74. Madison: Prehistory Press.
2001 "Syria and the Uruk Expansion." In *Uruk Mesopotamia and Its Neighbors: Cross-Cultural Interactions in the Era of State Formation*, edited by M. S. Rothman, pp. 233–64. Santa Fe and Oxford: School of American Research Press.
2007 "Taking the Long View on Collapse: A Syrian Perspective." In *Sociétés humaines et changement climatique à la fin du troisième millénaire: Une crise a-t-elle eu lieu en haute Mésopotamie?*, edited by C. Kuzucuoğlu and C. Marro, pp. 45–67. Varia Anatolica 19. Istanbul: Institut Français d'Études Anatoliennes Georges-Dumézil.

Senior, Louise, and Harvey Weiss
1992 "Tell Leilan 'Sila Bowls' and the Akkadian Re-organization of Subarian Agricultural Production." *Orient-Express* 1992: 1–6.

Sheets, P., and T. L. Sever
1991 "Prehistoric Footpaths in Costa Rica: Transportation and Communication in a Tropical Rainforest." In *Ancient Road Networks and Settlement Hierarchies in the New World*, edited by C. D. Trombold, pp. 53–65. Cambridge: Cambridge University Press.

Sherratt, Andrew G.
2004 "Spotting Tells from Space." *Antiquity* 78.

Simpson, St John
1996 "From Tekrit to the Jaghjagh: Sasanian Sites, Settlement Patterns and Material Culture in Northern Mesopotamia." In *Continuity and Change in Northern Mesopotamia from the Hellenistic to the Early Islamic Period* (Proceedings of a Colloquium Held at the Seminar für vorderasiatische Altertumskunde, Freie Universität Berlin, 6th–9th April 1994), edited by K. Bartl and S. R. Hauser, pp. 87–126. Berliner Beiträge zum Vorderen Orient 17. Berlin: Dietrich Reimer.
2000 "Mesopotamia in the Sasanian Period: Settlement Patterns, Arts and Crafts." In *Mesopotamia and Iran in the Parthian and Sasanian Periods: Rejection and Revival c. 238 B.C.–A.D. 642*, edited by J. Curtis, pp. 57–80. London: British Museum.

Smith, M. E.; J. Novic; P. Kroefges; and A. Huster
2007 "A New Map of the Aztec-Period City of Calixtlahuaca in Central Mexico." *Antiquity* 81: Project Gallery.

Smyth, Michael P.
1998 "Surface Archaeology and Site Organization: New Methods for Studying Urban Maya Communities." In *Surface Archaeology*, edited by A. P. Sullivan, pp. 43–60. Albuquerque: University of New Mexico Press.

Snead, James E.
2002 "Ancestral Pueblo Trails and the Cultural Landscape of Pajarito Plateau, New Mexico." *Antiquity* 76: 756–65.

Snead, J. E.; C. Erickson; and W. A. Darling, editors
2009 *Landscapes of Movement: Paths, Trails, and Roads in Anthropological Perspective*. Philadelphia: University of Pennsylvania Museum Press.

Sodini, J.-P., and E. Villeneuve
1992 "Le passage de la céramique byzantine à la céramique omeyyade." In *La Syrie de Byzance à l'Islam, 7e–8e siècle*, edited by P. Canivet and J.-P. Rey-Coquais, pp. 194–218. Damascus: IFEAD.

Sohn, H.-G.; G.-H. Kim; and J.-H. Yom
2004 "Mathematical Modelling of Historical Reconnaissance CORONA KH-4B Imagery." *Photogrammetric Record* 10: 51–66.

Southgate, Horatio
1840 *Narrative of a Tour through Armenia, Kurdistan, Persia and Mesopotamia*. 2 vols. New York: D. Appleton.

Spaer, M.
1992 "The Islamic Glass Bracelets of Palestine: Preliminary Findings." *Journal of Glass Studies* 34: 44–62.

Stein, Gil J.
1999 *Rethinking World-Systems: Diasporas, Colonies, and Interaction in Uruk Mesopotamia.* Tucson: University of Arizona Press.
2000 "Material Culture and Social Identity: The Evidence for a 4th Millennium B.C. Mesopotamian Uruk Colony at Hacinebi, Turkey." *Paléorient* 25: 11–22.
2001 "Indigenous Social Complexity at Hacinebi." In *Uruk Mesopotamia and Its Neighbors: Cross-Cultural Interactions in the Era of State Formation*, edited by M. S. Rothman, pp. 233–64. Santa Fe: School of American Research Press.
2004 "Structural Parameters and Sociocultural Factors in the Economic Organization of North Mesopotamian Urbanism in the Third Millennium B.C." In *Archaeological Perspectives on Political Economies*, edited by G. M. Feinman and L. M. Nicholas, pp. 61–78. Salt Lake City: University of Utah Press.

Stein, Gil J., and M. J. Blackman
1993 "The Organizational Context of Specialized Craft Production in Early Mesopotamian States." *Research in Economic Anthropology* 14: 29–59.

Stein, Gil J., and Patricia A. Wattenmaker
1989 "Leilan 1987 Survey: Uruk Summary." *Paléorient* 15: 283–84.
1990 "The 1987 Tell Leilan Regional Survey: Preliminary Report." In *Economy and Settlement in the Near East: Analyses of Ancient Sites and Materials*, edited by N. Miller, pp. 8–18. MASCA Research Papers in Science and Archaeology 7 (supplement). Philadelphia: University Museum.
2003 "Settlement Trends and the Emergence of Social Complexity in the Leilan Region of the Habur Plains (Syria) from the Fourth to the Third Millennium B.C." In *The Origins of North Mesopotamian Civilization: Ninevite 5 Chronology, Economy, Society*, edited by E. Rova and H. Weiss, pp. 361–86. Subartu 9. Turnhout: Brepols.

Steinkeller, Piotr
1996 "The Organization of Crafts in Third Millennium Babylonia: The Case of Potters." *Altorientalische Forschungen* 23: 232–53.
1998 "The Historical Background of Urkesh and the Hurrian Beginnings in Northern Mesopotamia." In *Urkesh and the Hurrians: Studies in Honor of Lloyd Cotsen,* edited by G. Buccellati and M. Kelly-Buccellati, pp. 75–98. Urkesh/Mozan Studies 3. Malibu: Undena.

Sténuit, Marie-Eve, and Veronique Van der Stede
2003 "Du Palais au quartier de maisons privées (jonction entre le chantier F et le chantier B, campagnes 1997–1999)." In *Tell Beydar, the 1995–1999 Seasons of Excavations: A Preliminary Report*, edited by M. Lebeau and A. Suleiman, pp. 225–41. Subartu 3. Turnhout: Brepols.

Stewart, F. H.
2004 "Khuwwa." *Encyclopedia of Islam.* 2nd edition. 12: 535–36.

Stone, Elizabeth C., and Paul Zimansky
2004 *The Anatomy of a Mesopotamian City: Survey and Soundings at Mashkan-shapir.* Winona Lake: Eisenbrauns.

Streck, Michael P.
1999 "Nasībīna." *Reallexikon der Assyriologie und vorderasiatischen Archäologie* 9: 185–86.

Suleiman, Antoine, and Olivier Nieuwenhuyse, editors
2002 Tell Boueid 2. *A Late Neolithic Village on the Middle Khabur (Syria).* Subartu 11. Turnhout: Brepols.

Sumner, William M.
1979 "Estimating Population by Analogy: An Example." In *Ethnoarchaeology: Implications of Ethnography for Archaeology*, edited by C. Kramer, pp. 164–74. New York: Columbia University.
1989 "Population and Settlement Area: An Example from Iran." *American Anthropologist* 91: 631–41.
1990 "Full-Coverage Regional Archaeological Survey in the Near East: An Example from Iran." In *The Archaeology of Regions*, edited by S. K. Fish and S. A. Kowalewski, pp. 87–113. Washington, D.C.: Smithsonian Institution Press.

Sürenhagen, Dietrich
1978 *Keramikproduktion in Habuba Kabira-Süd.* Berlin: Bruno Hessling.
1986 "The Dry Farming Belt: The Uruk Period and Subsequent Developments." In *The Origins of Cities in Dry-Farming Syria and Mesopotamia in the Third Millennium B.C.*, edited by H. Weiss, pp. 7–43. Guilford: Four Quarters.
1987 "Hirbet Aqar Babira 1985." In *Researches on the Antiquities of Saddam Dam Basin Salvage and other Researches*, edited by M. S. Demirji, pp. 129–31. Baghdad: Ministry of Culture and Information, Republic of Iraq.

Sykes, M.

1907 "Journeys in North Mesopotamia." *Geographical Journal* 30: 237–54, 384–98.

Tachjian, Vahé

2004 *La France en Cilicie et en Haute-Mésopotamie: Aux confins de la Turquie, de la Syrie et de l'Irak, 1919–1933*. Paris: Karthala.

Tavernier, Jean-Baptiste

1677 *The Six Voyages of John Baptista Tavernier, Baron of Aubonne through Turky, into Persia and the East-Indies, for the Space of Forty Years*. London: William Godbid.

Taylor, Christopher C.

1972 "The Study of Settlement Patterns in Pre-Saxon Britain." In *Man, Settlement and Urbanism*, edited by P. J. Ucko, R. Tringham, and G. W. Dimbleby, pp. 109–13. London: Duckworth.

1979 *Roads and Tracks of Britain*. London: Dent.

Taylor, J. G.

1865 "Travels in Kurdistan, with Notices of the Sources of the Eastern and Western Tigris, and Ancient Ruins in their Neighborhood." *Journal of the Royal Geographic Society* 35: 21–58.

Thomas, D. H.

1975 "Nonsite Sampling in Archaeology: Up the Creek without a Site?" In *Sampling in Archaeology*, edited by J. Mueller, pp. 61–81. Tucson: University of Arizona Press.

Thompson-Miragliuolo, J.

1988 "The Outer City: Introduction and Surface Collection." In *Mozan* I: *The Soundings of the First Two Seasons*, edited by G. Buccellati and M. Kelly-Buccellati, pp. 49–56. Bibliotheca Mesopotamica 20. Malibu: Undena.

Tobler, Arthur J.

1950 Excavations at Tepe Gawra 2. *Levels IX–XX*. Philadelphia: University of Pennsylvania Press.

Tomita, Toru

1998a "Late Chalcolithic Chronology in Syria and Northern Mesopotamia." In *Excavations at Tell Umm Qseir in Middle Khabur Valley, North Syria: Report of the 1996 Season,* edited by A. Tsuneki and Y. Miyake, pp. 197–201. Al-Shark 1. Tsukuba: Department of Archaeology, Institute of History and Anthropology, University of Tsukuba.

1998b "Pottery." In *Excavations at Tell Umm Qseir in Middle Khabur Valley, North Syria: Report of the 1996 Season*, edited by A. Tsuneki and Y. Miyake, pp. 141–60. Al-Shark 1. Tsukuba: Department of Archaeology, Institute of History and Anthropology, University of Tsukuba.

Tonghini, Cristina

1998 *Qal'at Ja'bar Pottery: A Study of a Syrian Fortified Site of the Late 11th–14th Centuries.* British Academy Monographs in Archaeology 11. Oxford: Oxford University Press.

Trombold, Charles D., editor

1991a *Ancient Road Networks and Settlement Hierarchies in the New World.* New Directions in Archaeology. Cambridge: Cambridge University Press.

1991b "An Introduction to the Study of Ancient New World Road Networks." In *Ancient Road Networks and Settlement Hierarchies in the New World*, edited by C. D. Trombold, pp. 1–9. New Directions in Archaeology. Cambridge: Cambridge University Press.

Tsoar, H., and Y. Yekutieli

1992 "Geomorphological Identification of Ancient Roads and Paths on the Loess of the Northern Negev." *Israel Journal of Earth Sciences* 41: 209–16.

Underbjerg, Heidi M.

2003 "The Chipped Stone Assemblage from Areas TC and WP." In "Excavations at Tell Brak 2001–2002: Preliminary Report," by Geoff Emberling and Helen McDonald, pp. 60–63. *Iraq* 65: 1–75.

Ur, Jason A.

2002a "Settlement and Landscape in Northern Mesopotamia: The Tell Hamoukar Survey 2000–2001." *Akkadica* 123: 57–88.

2002b "Surface Collection and Offsite Studies at Tell Hamoukar, 1999." *Iraq* 64: 15–44.

2003 "CORONA Satellite Photography and Ancient Road Networks: A Northern Mesopotamian Case Study." *Antiquity* 77: 102–15.

2004–05 "Archaeological Survey and Landscape Studies in the Hamoukar Region, 1999–2001." *Annales archéologiques arabes syrienne* 47–48: 9–21. (Arabic section). Translated by S. al-Quntar.

2005a Review of *The Excavations at Tell al-Rimah: The Pottery*, by C. Postgate, D. Oates, and J. Oates. *Journal of Near Eastern Studies* 64/1: 65–68.

2005b "Sennacherib's Northern Assyrian Canals: New Insights from Satellite Imagery and Aerial Photography." *Iraq* 67: 317–45.

2009 "Emergent Landscapes of Movement in Early Bronze Age Northern Mesopotamia." In *Landscapes of Movement: Paths, Trails, and Roads in Anthropological Perspective*, edited by J. E. Snead, C. Erickson, and W. A. Darling. Philadelphia: University of Pennsylvania Museum Press.

2010a "Cycles of Civilization in Northern Mesopotamia, 4400–2000 B.C." *Journal of Archaeological Research* 18: 387–431.

2010b "Landscapes of Settlement and Movement in Northeastern Syria." http://hdl.handle.net/1902.1/14011

In press "Urban Form at Tell Brak Across Three Millennia." In *Preludes to Urbanism: Studies in the Late Chalcolithic of Mesopotamia in Honour of Joan Oates*, edited by H. Crawford and A. McMahon. British Archaeological Reports, International Series. Archaeopress, Oxford.

Ur, Jason A., and Carlo Colantoni

2010 "The Cycle of Production, Preparation, and Consumption in a Northern Mesopotamian City." In *Inside Ancient Kitchens: New Directions in the Study of Daily Meals and Feasts*, edited by E. Klarich, pp. 55–82. Boulder: University Press of Colorado.

Ur, Jason A., and Emily L. Hammer

2009 "Pastoral Nomads of the Second and Third Millennia A.D. on the Upper Tigris River, Turkey: Archaeological Evidence from the Hirbemerdon Tepe Survey." *Journal of Field Archaeology* 34: 37–56.

Ur, Jason A.; P. Karsgaard; and Joan Oates

2007 "Urban Development in the Ancient Near East." *Science* 317: 1188.

Ur, Jason A., and Tony J. Wilkinson

2008 "Settlement and Economic Landscapes of Tell Beydar and its Hinterland." In *Beydar Studies* 1, edited by M. Lebeau and A. Suleiman, pp. 305–27. Subartu 21. Turnhout: Brepols.

Valentini, Stefano

2005 "La ceramica protodynastica dell'Area G." In *Tell Barri/Kahat: La Campagna del 2002*, by P. E. Pecorella and R. Pierobon Benoit, pp. 181–90. Florence: Firenze University Press.

Van Berg, Paul-Louis, and Vincianne Picalause

2003 "Structures archéologiques et art rupestre à Khishâm (Hassake, Syrie): Campagne 1999." In *Tell Beydar, the 1995–1999 Seasons of Excavations: A Preliminary Report*, edited by M. Lebeau and A. Suleiman, pp. 555–68. Subartu 10. Turnhout: Brepols.

Van Berg, Paul-Louis; M. Vander Linden; S. Lemaitre; N. Cauwe; and V. Picalause

2004 "Desert-Kites of the Hemma Plateau (Hassake, Syria)." *Paléorient* 30: 89–100.

Van Lerberghe, Karel

1996 "The Livestock." In *Administrative Documents from Tell Beydar (Season 1993–1995)*, edited by F. Ismail, W. Sallaberger, P. Talon, and K. Van Lerberghe, pp. 107–17. Subartu 2. Turnhout: Brepols.

Van Liere, Willem J.

1961–62 "Notice géographique sur le site de la ville de Kahat-Tell Barri." *Les annales archéologiques de Syrie* 11–12: 163–65.

1963 "Capitals and Citadels of Bronze-Iron Age Syria and Their Relationship to Land and Water." *Les annales archéologiques de Syrie* 13: 109–22.

n.d. Survey of Soil, Present Land Use and Land Capabilities of the Jezireh.

Van Liere, Willem J., and Jean Lauffray

1954–55 "Nouvelle prospection archéologique dans la Haute Jezireh syrienne." *Les annales archéologiques de Syrie* 4–5: 129–48.

Van Loon, M. N., editor

1988 *Hammam et-Turkman* I. Istanbul: Nederlands Historisch-Archaeologisch Instituut.

Vercueil, J., and G. Cummins

2003 "The Livestock Sector and Policies in Syria." In *Syrian Agriculture at the Crossroads*, edited by C. Fiorillo and J. Vercueil, pp. 219–46. FAO Agricultural Policy and Economic Development Series 8. Rome: Food and Agriculture Organization of the United Nations.

Vezzoli, V.

2004 *L'insediamento di epoca islamica nell'area di Tell Leilan (Gazira settentrionale): Studio del materiale ceramico.* Tesi di Laurea quadriennale in "Lingue e Civiltà orientali." Venice: Università Ca' Foscari.

von Oppenheim, Max F.

1900 *Vom Mittelmeer zum Persischen Golf*. Vol. 2. Berlin: Dietrich Reimer.

Wattenbach, H.

2006 *Farming Systems of the Syrian Arab Republic*. Syrian Arab Republic, Ministry of Agriculture and Agrarian Reform.

Wattenmaker, P.

1997 "Kazane Höyük, 1995: Excavations at an Early City." In *18. Kazı Sonuçları Toplantısı*, pp. 81–91. Ankara: Republic of Turkey, Ministry of Culture, General Directorate of Monuments and Museums.

Weber, J.
2006 Economic Developments of Urban Proportions: Evolving Systems of Animal-Product Consumption and Distribution in the Early and Middle Bronze Ages in Syro-Mesopotamia. Ph.D. dissertation, University of Pennsylvania.

Weiss, Harvey
1983 "Excavations at Tell Leilan and the Origins of North Mesopotamian Cities in the Third Millennium B.C." *Paléorient* 9: 39–52.
1985 "Tell Leilan and Shubat Enlil." *Mari: Annales de recherches interdisciplinaires* 4: 269–92.
1986 "The Origins of Tell Leilan and the Conquest of Space in Third Millennium Mesopotamia." In *The Origins of Cities in Dry-Farming Syria and Mesopotamia in the Third Millennium B.C.*, edited by H. Weiss, pp. 71–108. Guilford: Four Quarters.
1992 "Habur Triangles: Third Millennium Urban Settlement in Subir." *N.A.B.U.* 1992: 91–94.
2000 "Causality and Chance: Late Third Millennium Collapse in Southwest Asia." In *La Djéziré et l'Euphrate Syriens de la protohistoire à la fin du IIe millénaire av. J.-C.: Tendances dans l'interprétation historique des donnés nouvelles*, edited by O. Rouault and M. Wäfler, pp. 207–17. Subartu 7. Turnhout: Brepols.
2003 "Ninevite 5 Periods and Processes." In *The Origins of North Mesopotamian Civilization: Ninevite 5 Chronology, Economy, Society*, edited by E. Rova and H. Weiss, pp. 593–624. Subartu 9. Turnhout: Brepols.

Weiss, Harvey, and Marie-Agnès Courty
1993 "The Genesis and Collapse of the Akkadian Empire: The Accidental Refraction of Historical Law." In *Akkad: The First World Empire*, edited by M. Liverani, pp. 131–55. History of the Ancient Near East Studies 5. Padova: Sargon.

Weiss, Harvey; Marie-Agnès Courty; Wilma Wetterstrom; F. Guichard; L. Senior; Richard Meadow; and A. Curnow
1993 "The Genesis and Collapse of Third Millennium North Mesopotamian Civilization." *Science* 261: 995–1004.

Weiss, Harvey; F. DeLillis; D. de Moulins; Jesper Eidem; T. Guilderson; Ulla Kasten; Torben E. Larsen; L. Mori; L. Ristvet; Elena Rova; and Wilma Wetterstrom
2002–03 "Revising the Contours of History at Tell Leilan." *Les annales archéologiques arabes syriennes* 45–46: 59–74.

Wenke, Robert J.
1975–76 "Imperial Investment and Agricultural Development in Parthian and Sassanian Khuzestan: 150 B.C. to A.D. 640." *Mesopotamia* 9–11: 31–221.

Whallon, Robert
1979 *An Archaeological Survey of the Keban Reservoir Area of East-Central Turkey*. Memoirs of the Museum of Anthropology, University of Michigan 11. Ann Arbor: University of Michigan.
1983 "Methods of Controlled Surface Collection in Archaeological Survey." In *Archaeological Survey in the Mediterranean Area*, edited by D. R. Keller and D. W. Rupp, pp. 73–83. British Archaeological Reports, International Series 155. Oxford. British Archaeological Reports.

Whitehouse, D.
1979 "Islamic Glazed Pottery in Iraq and the Persian Gulf: The Ninth and Tenth Centuries." *Annali Istituto Orientale di Napoli* 39: 45–61.

Widell, Magnus
2004 "Some Observations on the Administration, Agriculture and Animal Management of Tell Beydar." *Ugarit-Forschungen* 35: 717–33.

Wilhelm, Gernot
1989 *The Hurrians*. Warminster: Aris & Phillips.

Wilkinson, K. N.; A. R. Beck; and G. Philip
2006 "Satellite Imagery as a Resource in the Prospection for Archaeological Sites in Central Syria." *Geoarchaeology* 21: 735–50.

Wilkinson, Tony J.
1982 "The Definition of Ancient Manured Zones by Means of Extensive Sherd-Sampling Techniques." *Journal of Field Archaeology* 9: 323–33.
1988 "The Archaeological Component of Agricultural Soils in the Middle East: The Effects of Manuring in Antiquity." In *Man-Made Soils: Symposia in Environmental Archaeology*, edited by W. Groenman-van Waateringe and M. Robinson, pp. 93–114. British Archaeological Reports, International Series 410. Oxford: British Archaeological Reports.

1989 "Extensive Sherd Scatters and Land-Use Intensity: Some Recent Results." *Journal of Field Archaeology* 16: 31–46.

1990a "Early Channels and Landscape Development around Abu Salabikh: A Preliminary Report." *Iraq* 52: 75–83.

1990b *Town and Country in Southeastern Anatolia*, Vol. 1: *Settlement and Land Use at Kurban Höyük and other Sites in the Lower Karababa Basin*. Oriental Institute Publications 109. Chicago: The Oriental Institute.

1993 "Linear Hollows in the Jazira, Upper Mesopotamia." *Antiquity* 67: 548–62.

1994 "The Structure and Dynamics of Dry-Farming States in Upper Mesopotamia." *Current Anthropology* 35: 483–520.

1995 "Late-Assyrian Settlement Geography in Upper Mesopotamia." In *Neo-Assyrian Geography*, edited by M. Liverani, pp. 139–60. Quaderni di Geografia Storica 5. Rome: Università di Roma "La Sapienza."

1997 "Environmental Fluctuations, Agricultural Production and Collapse: A View from Bronze Age Upper Mesopotamia." In *Third Millennium B.C. Climate Change and Old World Collapse*, edited by H. N. Dalfes, G. Kukla, and H. Weiss, pp. 67–106. NATO ASI Vol. I, Series 49. Berlin and Heidelberg: Springer-Verlag.

1998 "Water and Human Settlement in the Balikh Valley, Syria: Investigations from 1992–1995." *Journal of Field Archaeology* 25: 63–87.

2000a "Archaeological Survey of the Tell Beydar Region, Syria, 1997: A Preliminary Report." In *Tell Beydar: Environmental and Technical Studies*, edited by K. Van Lerberghe and G. Voet, pp. 1–37. Subartu 6. Turnhout: Brepols.

2000b "Regional Approaches to Mesopotamian Archaeology: The Contribution of Archaeological Surveys." *Journal of Archaeological Research* 8: 219–67.

2000c "Settlement and Land Use in the Zone of Uncertainty in Upper Mesopotamia." In *Rainfall and Agriculture in Northern Mesopotamia*, edited by R. M. Jas, pp. 3–35. Istanbul: Nederlands Historisch-Archaeologisch Instituut te Istanbul.

2002a "Physical and Cultural Landscapes of the Hamoukar Area." *Akkadica* 123: 89–105.

2002b "The Settlement Transition of the Second Millennium B.C. in the Western Khabur." In *Of Pots and Plans: Papers on the Archaeology and History of Mesopotamia and Syria Presented to David Oates in Honour of his 75th Birthday*, edited by L. al-Gailani Werr, J. Curtis, H. Martin, A. McMahon, J. Oates, and J. Reade, pp. 361–72: Nabu Publications.

2003 *Archaeological Landscapes of the Near East*. Tucson: University of Arizona Press.

2004 *On the Margin of the Euphrates: Settlement and Land Use at Tell es-Sweyhat and in the Upper Lake Assad Area, Syria*. Oriental Institute Publications 124. Chicago: The Oriental Institute.

2005 "Approaches to Modelling Archaeological Site Territories in the Near East." In *Nonlinear Models for Archaeology and Anthropology*, edited by C. S. Beekman and W. W. Baden, pp. 123–38. Hampshire: Ashgate.

Wilkinson, Tony J., and Eleanor Barbanes

2000 "Settlement Patterns in the Syrian Jazira During the Iron Age." In *Essays on Syria in the Iron Age*, edited by G. Bunnens, pp. 397–422. Ancient Near Eastern Studies, Supplement 7. Leuven: Peeters.

Wilkinson, Tony J.; J. Christiansen; Jason A. Ur; Magnus Widell; and Mark Altaweel

2007a "Urbanization within a Dynamic Environment: Modelling Bronze Age Communities in Upper Mesopotamia." *American Anthropologist* 109: 52–68.

Wilkinson, Tony J.; C. A. I. French; W. Matthews; and Joan Oates

2001 "Geoarchaeology, Landscape and the Region." In *Excavations at Tell Brak*, Vol. 2: *Nagar in the Third Millennium B.C.*, by D. Oates, J. Oates, and H. McDonald, pp. 1–14. Cambridge: McDonald Institute for Archaeological Research; London: British School of Archaeology in Iraq.

Wilkinson, Tony J.; McGuire Gibson; J. Christiansen; Magnus Widell; David Schloen; Nicholas Kouchoukos; Christopher Woods; John C. Sanders; K.-L. Simunich; Mark Altaweel; Jason A. Ur; Carrie Hritz; Jake Lauinger; Tate Paulette; and Jonathan Tenney

2007b "Modeling Settlement Systems in a Dynamic Environment: Case Studies from Mesopotamia." In *The Model-Based Archaeology of Socionatural Systems*, edited by T. A. Kohler and S. van der Leeuw, pp. 175–208. Santa Fe: School of American Research.

Wilkinson, Tony J.; Belinda H. Monahan; and David J. Tucker

1996 "Khanijdal East: A Small Ubaid Site in Northern Iraq." *Iraq* 58: 17–50.

Wilkinson, Tony J., and D. J. Tucker

1995 *Settlement Development in the North Jazira, Iraq.* Warminster: Aris & Phillips.

Wilkinson, Tony J.; Jason A. Ur; and Jesse Casana

2004 "From Nucleation to Dispersal: Trends in Settlement Pattern in the Northern Fertile Crescent." In *Side-by-Side Survey: Comparative Regional Studies in the Mediterranean World*, edited by J. Cherry and S. Alcock, pp. 198–205. Oxford: Oxbow Books.

Wilkinson, Tony J.; Eleanor Barbanes Wilkinson; Jason A. Ur; and Mark Altaweel

2005 "Landscape and Settlement in the Neo-Assyrian Empire." *Bulletin of the American Schools of Oriental Research* 340: 23–56.

Williamson, T.

1998 "Questions of Preservation and Destruction." In *The Archaeology of Landscape: Studies Presented to Christopher Taylor*, edited by P. Everson and T. Williamson, pp. 1–24. Manchester: Manchester University Press.

Wilson, David R.

1982 *Air Photo Interpretation for Archaeologists.* New York: St. Martin's Press.

Wirth, E.

1964 "Die Ackerebenen Nordostsyriens." *Geographische Zeitschrift* 52: 7–42.

Woods, John E.

1999 *The Aqquyunlu: Clan, Confederation, Empire.* 2nd edition. Salt Lake City: University of Utah.

Wright, H. E.

1993 "Environmental Determinism in Near Eastern Prehistory." *Current Anthropology* 34: 458–69.

Wright, Henry T.

1981 "The Southern Margins of Sumer: Archaeological Survey of the Area of Eridu and Ur." In *Heartland of Cities: Surveys of Ancient Settlement and Land Use on the Central Floodplain of the Euphrates,* by R. McC. Adams, pp. 295–345. Chicago: University of Chicago Press.

2005 "Prepottery Neolithic Sites in Eastern Syria." *Paléorient* 31: 169–72.

Wright, Henry T., and Eric S. A. Rupley

2001 "Calibrated Radiocarbon Age Determinations of Uruk-Related Assemblages." In *Uruk Mesopotamia and Its Neighbors: Cross-Cultural Interactions in the Era of State Formation*, edited by M. S. Rothman, pp. 85–122. Santa Fe: School of American Research Press.

Wright, Henry T.; Eric S. A. Rupley; Jason A. Ur; Joan Oates; and Eyad Ganem

2006–07 "Preliminary Report on the 2002 and 2003 Seasons of the Tell Brak Sustaining Area Survey." *Les annales archéologiques arabes syriennes* 49–50: 7–21.

Zeder, Melinda A.

2003 "Food Provisioning in Urban Societies: A View from Northern Mesopotamia." In *The Social Construction of Ancient Cities*, edited by M. L. Smith, pp. 156–83. Washington, D.C.: Smithsonian Institution.

Zettler, Richard L.

1977 "The Sargonic Royal Seal: A Consideration of Sealing in Mesopotamia." In *Seals and Sealing in the Ancient Near East*, edited by McG. Gibson and R. Biggs, pp. 33–38. Bibliotheca Mesopotamica 6. Malibu: Undena.

Zimansky, Paul

1995 "The Origin of Nuzi Ware: A Contribution from Tell Hamida." In *Studies on the Civilization and Culture of the Hurrians,* Vol. 5, edited by D. Owen, pp. 75–87. Winona Lake: Eisenbrauns.

CHAPTER 1

INTRODUCTION

1.1. ORIGINS OF THE TELL HAMOUKAR SURVEY (THS) AND PROJECT GOALS

In recent decades, Near Eastern archaeology has embraced two spatial/geographic realities: no ancient settlement can be understood in isolation from its hinterland, and no site can be fully understood from a few excavation trenches. Both of these statements are especially true of the large settlements characterized as "urban." With these facts in mind, the Joint Expedition of the Syrian Directorate General of Antiquities and Monuments and the University of Chicago Oriental Institute to Hamoukar, in Hassake province of the Syrian Arab Republic (fig. 1.1), included a systematic surface collection of the site and an intensive full-coverage survey of its sustaining area as major components of its first three seasons in the field (1999–2001).

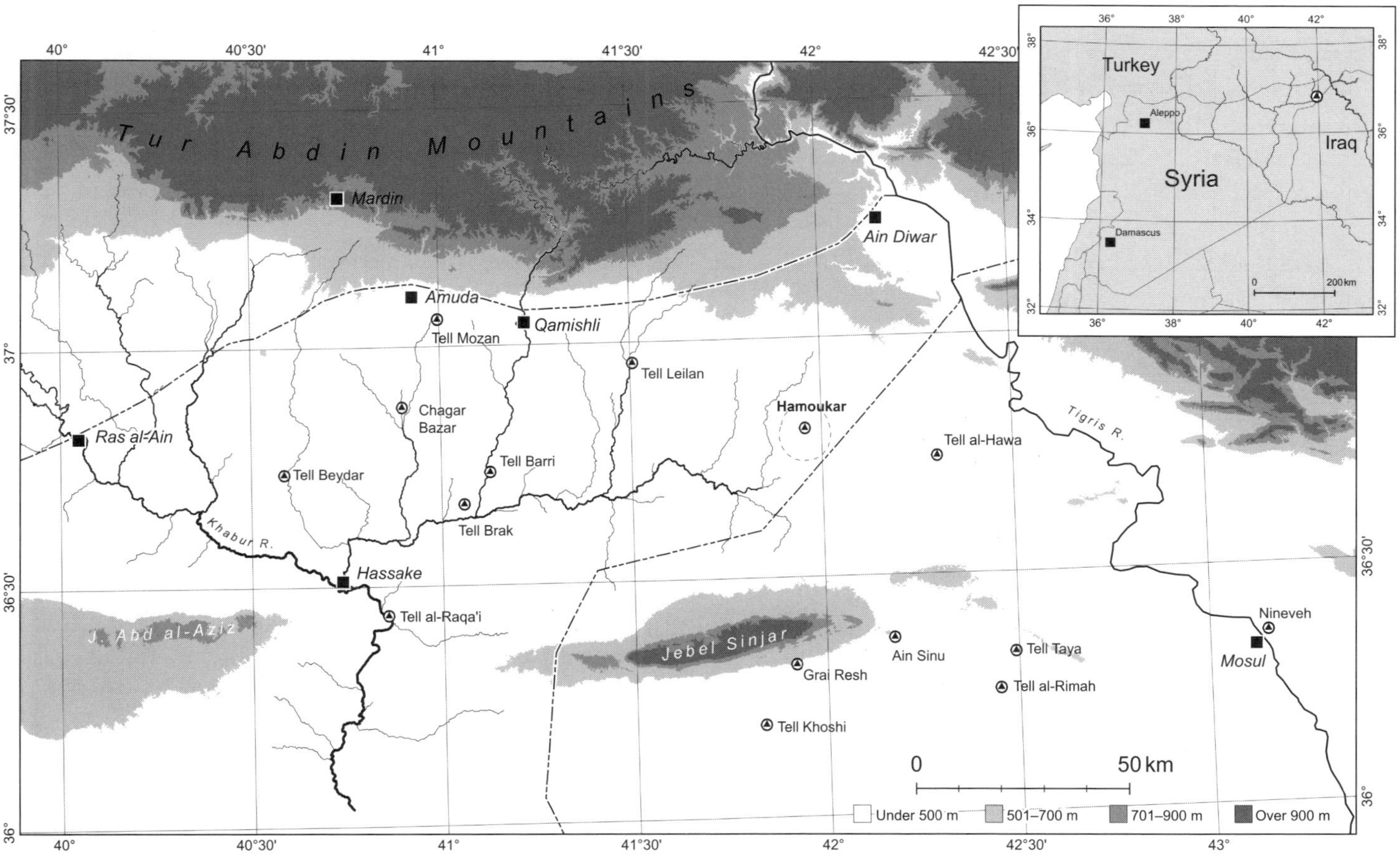

Figure 1.1. Hamoukar's location in the Upper Khabur basin, Hassake province, with other excavated sites. Inset: Hamoukar's position within the Syrian Arab Republic

Surface observation methods are increasingly a default component of any pilot or initial season of a new project. Their employment at and around Hamoukar was, however, intended to address some issues of general interest in Mesopotamian archaeology and of specific significance to Hamoukar itself. Hamoukar had been observed on the ground and in the air since the 1950s with divergent results in two particular aspects: its scale, and its role within the regional interaction sphere of the fourth millennium B.C. (the "Uruk Expansion"). With regard to the former, the initial observations of the site were done via aerial photography in the 1950s (Van Liere and Lauffray 1954–55; Van Liere 1963). In addition to the high mound and the extensive lower town, these images revealed ditches or moats (Van Liere 1963: fig. 3b) that enclosed an area of 216 ha (as estimated by Wilkinson 1994: 488). Later visitors on the ground limited their estimations to the mounded area alone (e.g., 90 ha in Weiss 1983: 44). The Hamoukar Expedition considered an empirically based estimate of Hamoukar's spatial extent to be critical for subsequent demographic interpretations.

Another site-specific research issue concerned Hamoukar's position within the Uruk Expansion in the fourth millennium. At the start of research, substantial knowledge of southern influence or colonization on the northern plains was limited to Tell Brak (Oates 2002). Hamoukar is also in this region and is even located astride one of the major routes of interregional movement proposed by Guillermo Algaze (1993: 46–48, fig. 21). Previous visitors had, however, relayed conflicting reports about its fourth-millennium surface assemblage. Some reported the full range of southern grit-tempered ceramics (e.g., Sürenhagen 1986: 14–15; Lebeau 1990: 243), while others noted only indigenous chaff-tempered wares alongside bevelled-rim bowls (e.g., Oates and Oates 1991: 140 n. 4). Should Hamoukar's fourth-millennium assemblage have a spatial distribution toward the larger of the early estimates of Hamoukar's size, it would have a major impact on our geographic models of indigenous northern Mesopotamian society or intrusive southern colonization (Stein 1999: 102). Therefore a major goal of the Hamoukar surface collection was to characterize its fourth-millennium assemblage and to map closely the relative spatial distributions of artifacts of local and southern derivation.

The site and its region also offered the opportunity to investigate larger issues of landscape and subsistence in the context of early northern Mesopotamian urbanism. Hamoukar is uniquely suited to test models developed by T. J. Wilkinson, particularly his notion of the northern Mesopotamian plains as the "Fragile Crescent" under conditions of urban growth in a dynamic landscape (2003). Using the nearby third-millennium urban center of Tell al-Hawa as a case study, Wilkinson's dynamic model of the growth and maintenance of urban settlement systems incorporates as variables demographics, agricultural yields, the spatial distribution of labor and resources, and fluctuating climate to propose a growth ceiling of approximately 100 ha in the later third millennium B.C. (1994). At a maximum extent of 66 ha (Ball, Tucker, and Wilkinson 1989), Tell al-Hawa never reached this threshold. Although its exact scale had yet to be determined, it was certain that Hamoukar was either at or above this size; it would therefore present an ideal opportunity to test this proposed threshold.

Hamoukar presented an opportunity to test Wilkinson's assumptions about dynamic relations between the settlement and its landscape that were derived from off-site archaeological features. For example, linear "hollow way" features were used to delineate sites' agricultural catchments (Wilkinson 1994), and the density of field scatters was used as a proxy indicator of the intensity of manuring (Wilkinson 1989, 1993). If these assumptions were accurate, Hamoukar's radial pattern of trackways should be even larger than that of Tell al-Hawa, and the density of field scatters should be even greater, given its hypothesized greater scale.

The Tell Hamoukar Survey (THS) was also determined to develop some methodological innovations that would make the project more than just an additional 125 sq. km of surveyed area. The Upper Khabur basin is hardly terra incognita in terms of archaeological survey: at the initiation of the Hamoukar Expedition, almost the entire basin has been subjected to reconnaissance (Mallowan 1936; Meijer 1986; Lyonnet 2000), and more intensive surveys had covered the hinterlands of Tell Brak (Eidem and Warburton 1996), Tell Beydar (Ur and Wilkinson 2008; Wilkinson 2000a), Tell Leilan (Weiss 1986; Stein and Wattenmaker 2003), and most significantly Tell al-Hawa (Wilkinson and Tucker 1995). This last survey, which is separated from the THS by only a few kilometers and the modern Syrian-Iraqi frontier, remains the largest and best-published survey project in northern Mesopotamia. Among these surveys, the THS aimed to make new methodological contributions in two areas: survey intensity and the use of previously unavailable digital technologies and remote-sensing datasets

At only 125 sq. km, the THS has the smallest geographic area of any full-coverage project yet undertaken in the Upper Khabur basin. The smaller area permitted an intensification of observation on sites and in the spaces between them. Mounded sites were spatially subdivided to a fine degree, permitting the high-resolution study of settlement expansion and contraction. The off-site landscape record could also be studied with greater intensity. Compared to the North Jazira Project, the THS was able to make almost twice as many field scatter collections within a survey universe only a quarter of its area; other surveys in the basin have omitted this research component. The Hamoukar area thus provides a small high-resolution window upon the northern Mesopotamian landscape which presents an idea of what aspects might be missed by larger and correspondingly less intensive surveys.

The THS also took advantage of new digital tools and resources. Of greatest importance was the new availability of declassified CORONA intelligence satellite photographs, taken in the 1960s. Throughout much of the Near East, previous surveys have been largely dependent on ground observation to locate sites and landscape features, although maps and aerial photographs were occasionally made available under tight control. High-resolution CORONA imagery can detect the small and unmounded sites that are often overlooked by standard survey techniques. The THS employed CORONA scenes from five missions, taken under a variety of ground conditions; together, they record a detailed picture of sites and landscapes that would be inaccessible from ground observations alone. CORONA photographs are particularly powerful for detecting the traces of premodern trackways. The THS was able to extend the hollow way patterns mapped by Wilkinson in the North Jazira (1993; Wilkinson and Tucker 1995) into the Hamoukar area and throughout the entire Upper Khabur basin.

All collections and ground observations made by the THS were recorded with handheld Global Positioning System (GPS) receivers for seamless integration into the project's Geographic Information System (GIS) spatial database. These technologies are now commonly used in archaeology, but at the time of the survey, they permitted an accuracy and ease of recording which had not been previously possible. As a result, all archaeological phenomena visited on the ground have positioning errors estimated at 5–20 m at maximum, and the maps and imagery presented in this volume have a high degree of geographic accuracy independent of their scale.

1.2. PERIODIZATION WITHIN THE TELL HAMOUKAR SURVEY

Because of the nature of the surface assemblage dataset, the subdivision of time for the purposes of archaeological survey must be done more coarsely than is generally practiced for excavated materials. It is necessary to navigate between very long periods that are too coarse to discern the major processes that are the subject of the research, and very finely subdivided periods which require an unsupportable stretching of a few chronologically sensitive types.

The survey chronology employed by the THS (table B.1) is in some ways more finely divided than those employed by previous surveys (e.g., the subdivision of the "Uruk" period into three semi-overlapping periods) and in other ways is coarser, reflecting the admission that some historically defined subdivisions simply are not visible in the record of surface artifacts. The periods and the ceramic types used to define them are discussed in detail in *Appendix B*.

1.3. THE ORGANIZATION OF THIS VOLUME

Following this introduction, *Chapter 2* presents the basin's physical environment and describes patterns of twentieth-century settlement and land use, two subjects critical for understanding past land use and transformations that are responsible for the present condition of the archaeological landscape. *Chapter 3* and *Chapter 4* detail the survey methods employed in the surface collections at Hamoukar and at the other sites in the THS, respectively, including a detailed discussion of how "sites" are defined and how the various remote-sensing datasets were employed. In *Chapter 5*, the elements of the archaeological landscape of the THS are described, including the various site morphologies and also off-site elements such as field scatters, hollow ways, and irrigation canals. In *Chapter 6* and *Chapter 7*, the spatial data for sites and landscape features are presented, with *Chapter 6* focusing on the THS region and *Chapter 7* illustrating broader patterns of settlement and landscape throughout the basin as derived from a program of CORONA imagery analysis. Finally, *Chapter 8* synthesizes the settlement and landscape data with historical studies and the results of previous surveys and excavations throughout northern Mesopotamia. A detailed catalog of the sixty sites recovered by the THS appears in *Appendix A*, and *Appendix B* presents a detailed ceramic chronology in which type frequencies are presented quantitatively and their utility as survey diagnostics are critically evaluated. *Appendix C* illustrates a selection of artifacts recovered from site surfaces.

CHAPTER 2

THE PHYSICAL ENVIRONMENT AND RECENT PROCESSES OF LANDSCAPE FORMATION

2.1. ORIGINS, HYDROLOGY, AND GEOMORPHOLOGY OF THE BASIN

Urbanism throughout northern Mesopotamia developed in an environmental context very different from that of southern Mesopotamia. The plains of the south are almost completely flat, with aggrading rivers flowing above plain level, and negligible rainfall (see especially Buringh 1960; Sanlaville 1989; Wilkinson 2003: 76–87). The northern and southern environmental contexts placed very different limits upon, and offered different opportunities for, the development of ancient urban society.

2.1.1. GEOLOGY AND GEOMORPHOLOGY

Northern Mesopotamia (figs. 2.1–2) began to take its modern form in the early Miocene Epoch (ca. 20 million years ago), when the Arabian plate separated from the African plate. By the mid-Miocene, it had collided with the Eurasian plate along the Bitlis suture in southern Turkey. The Palmyra and Sinjar troughs deformed in response to this collision, since they contained several thousand meters of under-compacted Mesozoic and Tertiary sediments. By the late Miocene–early Pliocene, the northern part of the Arabian plate was uplifted and the formation of the Taurus-Zagros orogenic zone had begun (Litak et al. 1997; Lovelock 1984; Sawaf et al. 1993).

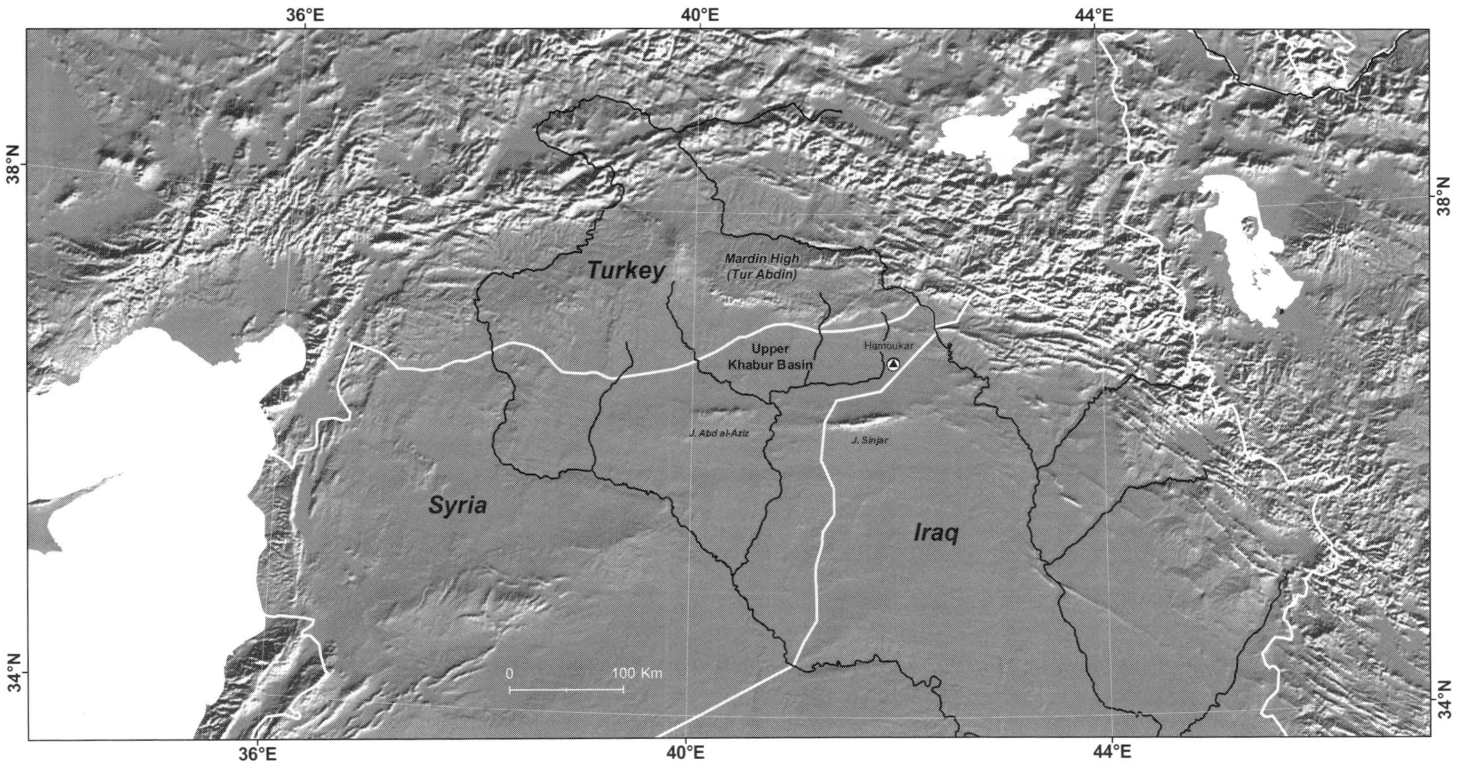

Figure 2.1 The geography of northern Mesopotamia

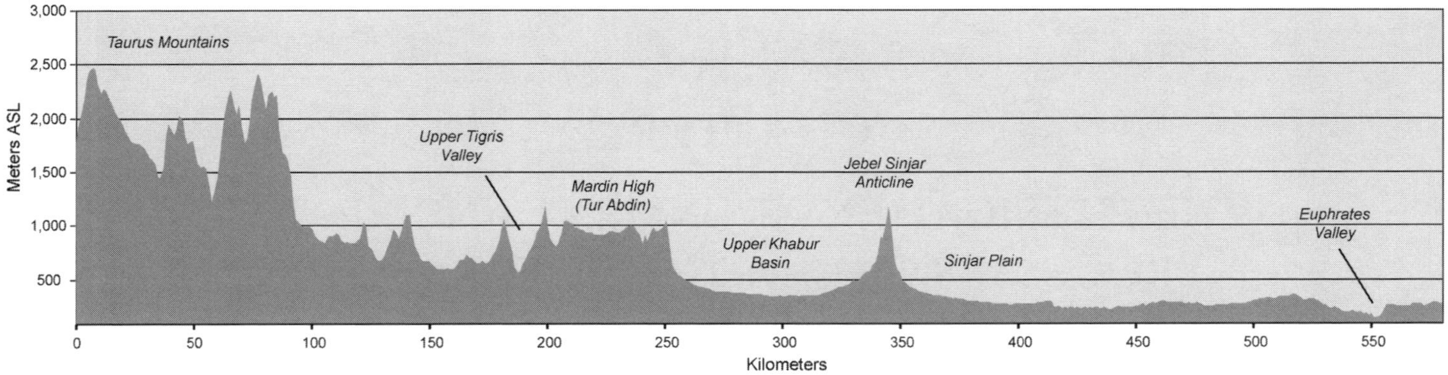

Figure 2.2. North–south section from the Taurus Mountains to the Euphrates Valley (approximately 35× vertical exaggeration)

The folding of sedimentary deposits in the Sinjar-Palmyrene trough caused the emergence of the Sinjar and Jebel Abd al-Aziz anticlines along its north edge (Sawaf et al. 1993). At the edge of the orogenic zone, the Mardin High (Tur Abdin), an ancient part of the Arabian plate that has escaped the forces that produced the Taurus Mountains to its north, was elevated. These tectonic processes reactivated structural weaknesses within the Arabian plate, causing volcanism that resulted in several basalt plateaus, including the Jebel Kaukab near Hassake and the Ardh al-Shaykh west of Tell Beydar (FAO 1966: 100–02). The uplift of the Jebel Abd al-Aziz and the Taurus range during the Mio-Pliocene and Pleistocene epochs also resulted in undulations in the Miocene substratum to the north; it is in these north–south depressions that the major wadis of the basin have formed (Courty 1994). Also at this time, a large "Paleo-Tigris" river channel drained a large catchment within the Taurus Mountains; the large water-rounded cobbles of this river have been found in deep sections at Tell Alo and near Tell Brak (Wilkinson 2002a).

Within this tectonic framework, the Upper Khabur basin has filled with rocks and sediments of Tertiary and Quaternary date (fig. 2.3), although Quaternary basalt sheets extend along the northern limits of the basin at the foot of the Turkish mountains, and Pliocene clays survive in the northeast corner and west of the Wadi Khanzir (Wilkinson 2002a). The more recent sediments have been brought into the basin by the Khabur and Jaghjagh rivers and the various seasonal wadis, which have collection basins within the Tur Abdin. The other major wadis are fed primarily by springs at the foot of the mountainous zone and the various basalt plateaus (Courty 1994). These fluvial systems flow generally north to south, and have produced a broad alluvial plain filled with eroded sediments from the Tur Abdin (fig. 2.4). At the eastern end of the basin, the Sinjar ridge has altered the flow direction to create a marshy area (*sebkha*) along the Wadi Radd.

The wadi floodplains are generally a few tens of meters wide but show considerable aggradation over the last four millennia. At the southern end of the Wadi Aweidj, a series of geomorpological trenches demonstrated variable rates of floodplain aggradation, with a particularly intense phase at the end of the third millennium B.C., where almost 3 m of sediment were rapidly deposited (Courty 1994), and similar floodplain observations have been made farther to the north near the modern Tell Tamr–Qamishli road (Wilkinson 2000a). The interfluves, on the other hand, have much shallower soils and have seen much less aggradation. These soils are at most 2 m deep on a hard quaternary substratum (Courty 1994: 32).

Throughout the Upper Khabur (fig. 2.4) and the adjacent plains of the Iraqi North Jazira, the dominant soil type is Calcic xerosol, which is very fertile (Wilkinson and Tucker 1995: 5–6; Wilkinson 1997: 70–72). These soils are classified as brown or reddish brown soils by Buringh (1960: 78) and grumusols by Van Liere (n.d.).

Soils and drainage in the eastern part of the Upper Khabur basin around Hamoukar have not received such intensive geomorphological investigation but can be described on a basic level (fig. 2.5). Hamoukar itself sits 9.5 km west of the watershed between the Tigris basin and the Upper Khabur basin (and, by extension, the Euphrates basin). To the east, surface runoff is channeled into the Wadi al-Murr, which flows into the Tigris at Eski Mosul. The Wadi Rumaylan originates within the Tur Abdin, cuts its way through the Quaternary basalts near the modern political border, and flows south into the marshes of the Radd. Drainage within the THS all originates as surface runoff from the low-relief plains to Hamoukar's northeast and flows into the Wadi Rumaylan at or below Tell al-Tash.

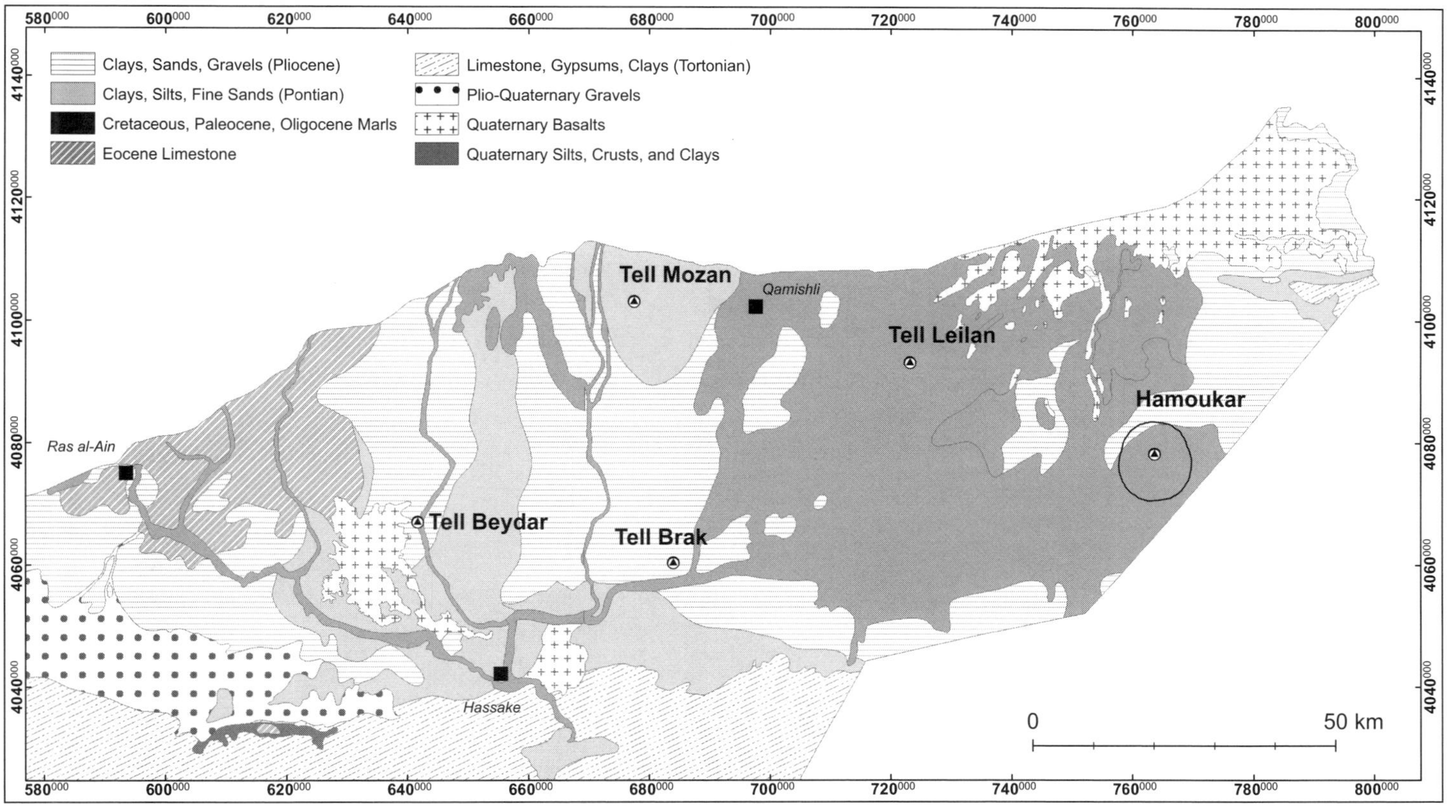

Figure 2.3. Geology of the Upper Khabur basin (based on FAO 1966: map 2)

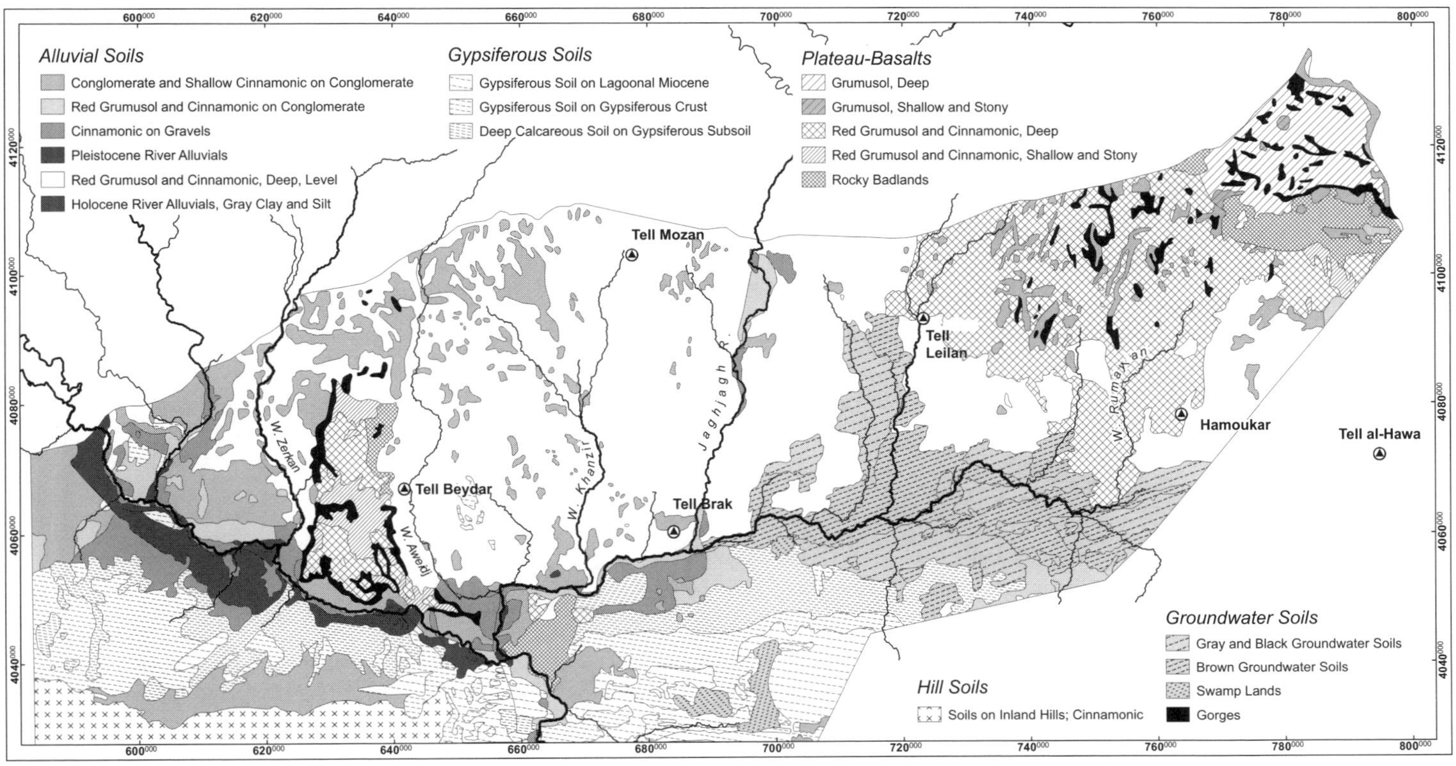

Figure 2.4. Soils and hydrology of the Upper Khabur basin

The eastern end of the basin has been divided into five zones by Wilkinson (2002a) (fig. 2.5). To the northeast of the THS region are Tertiary uplands on Pliocene sediments, now eroded but perhaps originally a continuous sheet (Zone 1). The THS region itself falls within the low-relief silt plains of Zone 2. Presently, the wadis flowing from the Zone 1 uplands into this area are mostly infilled by silt clay plow wash from millennia of agriculture and are mostly visible as dark areas on satellite imagery. Wilkinson's Zone 3 consists of low basalt plateaus of Quaternary date to the northwest of the THS region, across the Wadi Rumaylan. These basalt sheets are the southernmost extension of a broad basaltic area that stretches along the northeastern edge of the basin (see FAO 1966: fig. IV–7). Although basalt outcrops are found throughout this area, which must have been a major source of material for grindstones, it generally possesses a thick soil layer that is well suited for cultivation.

Wilkinson's Zones 4 and 5 are in areas of very low relief in the southeastern part of the basin. Zone 4 is at the lower reaches of the Wadi Rumaylan, where it exhibits branching and meandering traces and even levee formation

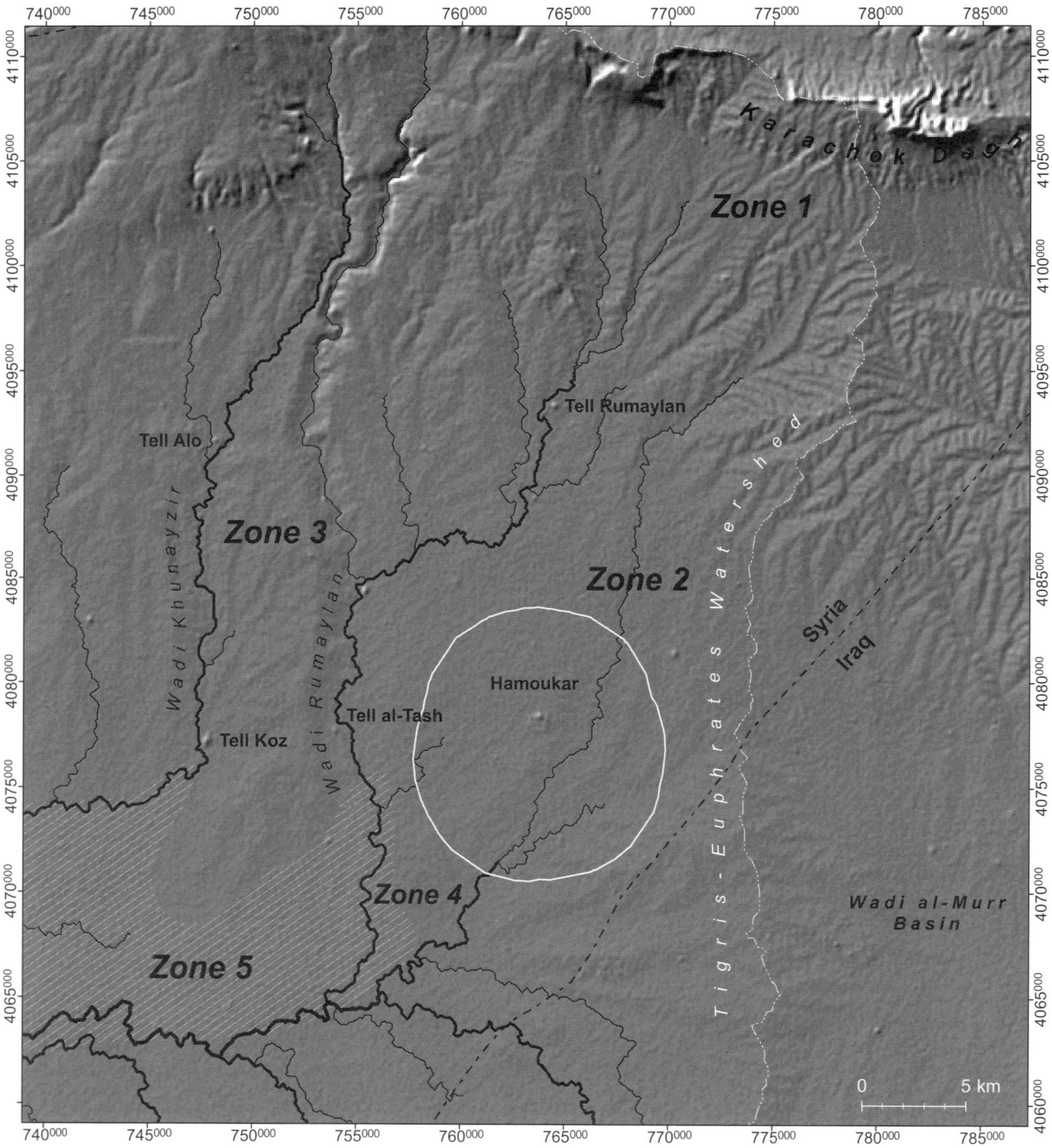

Figure 2.5. The eastern Upper Khabur basin, with geomorphological zones from Wilkinson 2002a

suggestive of irrigation channels. These cannot be dated directly at present, but the nearby large sites at Tell Koz and Tell al-Tash suggest a possible Bronze Age date (Wilkinson 2002a: 91). Finally, the wadis Rumaylan and Khunayzir flow into a broad and poorly drained salt marsh (Zone 5, the Wadi Radd).

2.1.2. CLIMATE, RAINFALL, AND VEGETATION

Today, the Upper Khabur region features a strongly seasonal Mediterranean climate, with the vast majority of rainfall occurring during the winter months. Summers are very dry (fig. 2.6A and FAO 1966: 52–57); this regime results from the southward shift of moist westerly winds in the winter and the northward expansion of the subtropical high-pressure belt in the summer (Wright 1993). Northern Iraq and northeastern Syria benefit from additional moisture in the spring that is derived from stationary low-pressure cells that advect moisture from the Persian Gulf and is precipitated orographically by the southern Taurus Mountains. The increased solar radiation and temperature of spring lead to water stress, but this late boost in rainfall can prolong the agricultural growing season and increase crop yields (Kouchoukos 1998: 321–23).

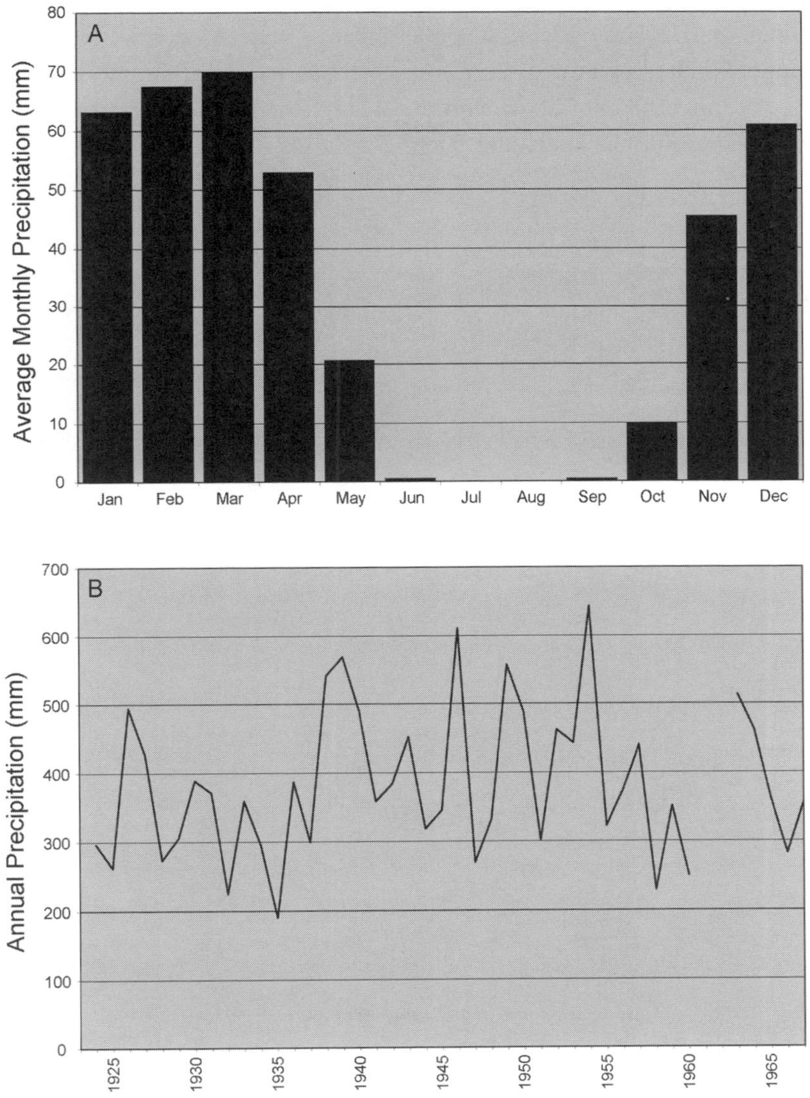

Figure 2.6. Rainfall at Mosul, Iraq.
(*A*) Average monthly precipitation between 1923 and 1967; (*B*) Annual precipitation (August–July) between 1923 and 1967. Data from the Global Historical Climatology Network database (Peterson and Vose 1997)

The distribution of rainfall in the basin varies in relationship to proximity to the Tur Abdin mountains (FAO 1966: 52–54; Perrin de Brichambaut and Wallén 1963: 7–19). The northern basin averages 400–450 mm of rain annually. This figure declines as one moves southward, such that Hassake averages just over 250 mm annually (fig. 2.7; FAO 1966: table III–2). Throughout the basin, almost all this precipitation falls between January and March. These annual averages hide a substantial degree of interannual variability, which can be as high as 20–30 percent (fig. 2.6B; see also Perrin de Brichambaut and Wallén 1963: fig. 2; FAO 1966: 55). Thus, land generally considered to be above the threshold for productive dry farming on average (the threshold is generally placed at 250 mm per year) could have crop failures in any given year.

The degree to which these modern conditions pertain to the past is currently a matter of debate between investigators using different data sources. It is generally agreed that during the last glacial maximum (late Pleistocene, 18,000 years B.P.), conditions in the Middle East were cooler and dryer. Pollen cores from lake sediments throughout the region indicate a drastic reduction in tree pollen at this time (Butzer 1995; Wright 1993). The colder temperatures resulted in reduced evaporation and therefore reduced precipitation, which caused the contraction of forests. The reduced evaporation also resulted in the raising of lake levels throughout the region, which can be documented by increases in the O^{18} isotope (Lemke and Sturm 1997). From a variety of proxy data, it has been proposed that the fourth and early third millennia B.C. were wetter than at present (Hole 1997; Deckers and Riehl 2007; Courty 1994: 45–47). The second half of the third millennium probably witnessed a drying phase, but the timing and impact of this phase are debated (Weiss et al. 1993; Courty 2001; Wilkinson 1997).

The vegetation of northern Mesopotamia has also evolved dramatically since the last glacial maximum. At the start of the Holocene Epoch, park woodland and woodland steppe vegetation characterized the plains (Moore et al. 2000: fig. 3.7). In the Upper Khabur basin, a gallery forest with an extended swamp belt existed along the Jaghjagh River in the fourth and early third millennia B.C., and the steady flow of the river at that time suggests greater vegetation cover in the basin in general (Deckers and Riehl 2007: 345–46). Aggradation of sediments in the second

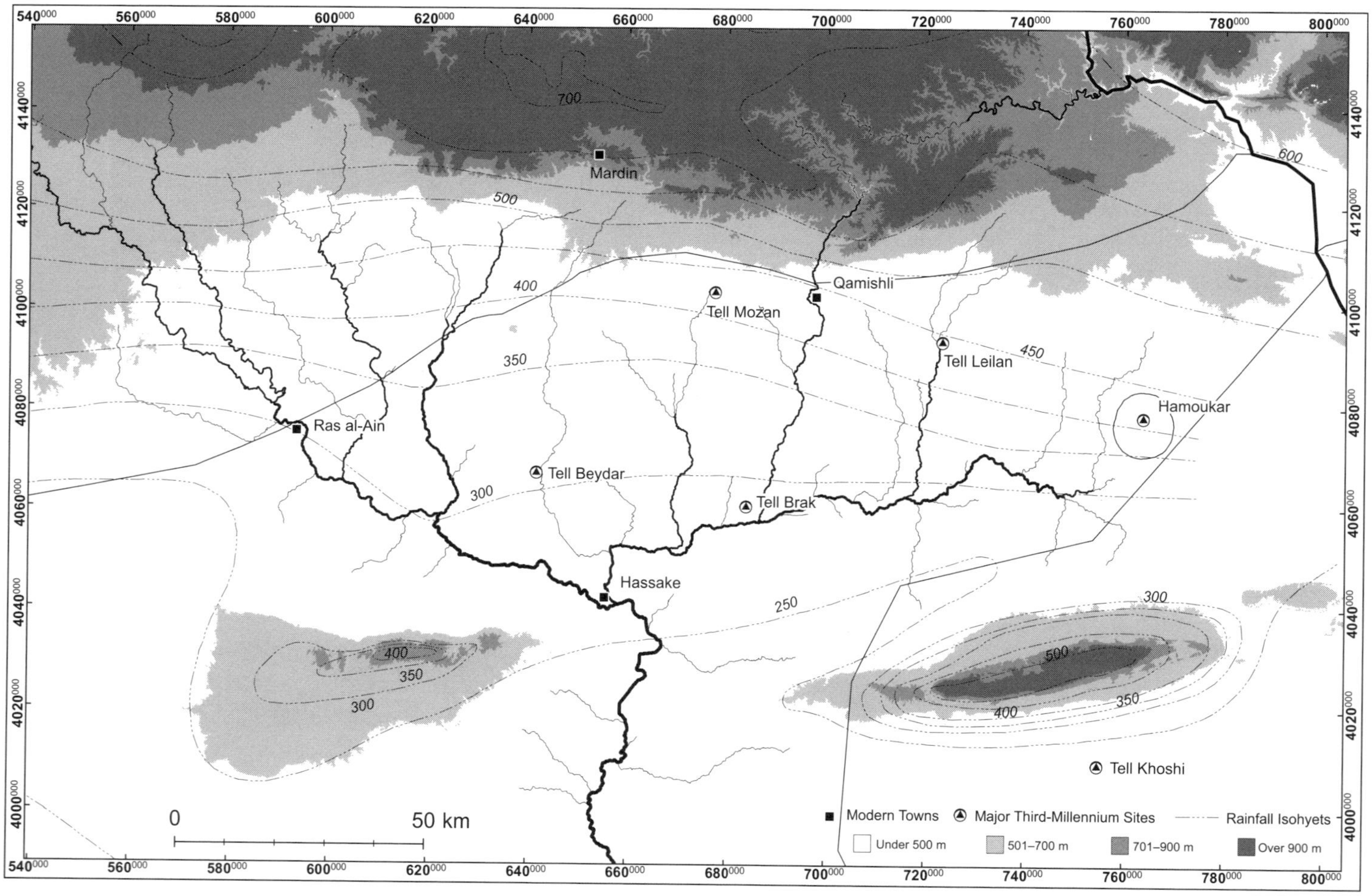

Figure 2.7. Rainfall in the Upper Khabur basin. Isohyets derived from FAO 1966: map 1

half of the third millennium B.C. has been attributed to changing vegetation patterns due to climatic drying, but was probably exacerbated by intensified human land use (Courty 1994: 48–50). Today the basin is completely deforested and badly overgrazed (Hole 2007; Hole and Smith 2004).

The climate and soils of the Upper Khabur basin are very productive for dry-farming agriculture, particularly in the northern half, where annual rainfall is more reliably above the minimum necessary for a successful crop. The superior productivity and reduced risk of irrigation agriculture compared to dry farming is well documented; under pre-industrial agricultural conditions, an irrigated field will be 50 to 100 percent more productive than a rainfed field of the same size (Weiss 1986). However, the geomorphology of the southern Mesopotamian plains restricts cultivation to the sloping sides of river levees; the soils of the basins beyond are fine-textured, poorly drained, and saline, although these factors varied through time and with changes in land use (Wilkinson 2003: 77–78). Although there are also differences in productivity between floodplain and interfluve, the soils of the Upper Khabur basin are more homogenous. Thus, on the northern plains, cultivation would not have been as geographically restricted as in the south, and much more cultivable land would have been available, although still strongly influenced by the availability of rainfall (Weiss 1986; Wilkinson 1997, 2000c). Weiss has concluded that "the dry-farming plains of northern Mesopotamia could have generated aggregate yields considerably greater than those of southern Mesopotamia" (Weiss 1986: 74), perhaps two to three times as much as in the irrigated south (Weiss 1983). The critical issue then becomes the transport of harvested cereals: bulk grains could be moved efficiently by boat on the canals of the southern plains, but the friction of overland transportation on the northern plains is prohibitively expensive beyond a certain distance (Wilkinson 1994: 503). This environmentally defined difference in transportation efficiency is a major point of divergence between the Bronze Age economies of northern and southern Mesopotamia (Algaze 2001: 76–77; Stein 2004).

2.2. RECENT SETTLEMENT AND LAND USE IN THE UPPER KHABUR BASIN

As part of the historical perspective adopted by this study, the recent history of human occupation in the Upper Khabur basin is significant not only as the most recent stage in a long sequence of settlement, but also as a critical factor in the survival of past landscapes to the present. Many parts of the Near East cycled between pastoral nomadic and sedentary agricultural economies over the last millennium, but the Upper Khabur basin appears to be unique in its combination of high agricultural potential and the long duration of nomadic control. Despite its obvious richness and potential, the basin remained a pastoral zone long after similar areas had been brought under cultivation.

The start of the most recent phase of pastoral dominance is not certain (Hütteroth 1992: 285–86). Some argue that the district of Nisibin, the most important city in the basin from the late first millennium B.C. until the founding of Hassake and Qamishli, was abandoned in the face of Abbasid overtaxation (Gibert and Fevret 1953: 8); others assume it was completely deserted as a result of the Mongol conquests of the mid-thirteenth century (e.g., British Admiralty 1943: 36; Wirth 1964: 8). Certainly in the sixteenth century, Nisibin and its immediately surrounding regions were settled, agriculturally productive, and taxed accordingly by the Ottoman government (Hütteroth 1990; Göyünç and Hütteroth 1997). Unfortunately, Ottoman tax records did not include the THS region. Control of the far eastern basin alternated between Mosul and an independent *livā* (administrative district) Akčakal'a, neither of which were included in Göyünç and Hütteroth's study. The sixteenth century was the highpoint of the Ottoman state and correspondingly a time of reduction in nomads' strength (Göyünç and Hütteroth 1997: 14–15), so it is unlikely that this political-economic snapshot is valid for earlier and later times. The last decade of the sixteenth century, however, marked the start of a long phase of pastoral domination of the Mosul countryside, as the Ottoman army simultaneously took away administrative powers from tribal groups but demanded more mutton and camels to provision their armies against the Safavids; pastoralism became more profitable than agriculture (Khoury 1997: 39–42).

At this time, the basin was dominated by Tay Arab tribes. By the mid-seventeenth century, they appear to have driven out most sedentary occupation. In 1644, Tavernier noted the "Country between [Nisibin and Mosul] being altogether desert and uninhabited. There is no Water to be found but in two places, and that not very good neither; near to which you shall see some few Herdsmen grazing their Cattel" (1677: 71).

Travelers in the basin in the eighteenth century were shocked at the decay of the once great city of Nisibin (summarized in Fiey 1977: 114–26) and found it surrounded by a largely depopulated and uncultivated plain. Norman Lewis summarizes several early accounts:

> Peasants fled rather than "entertain" soldiers on the march or Ottoman grandees on a journey. Villages were sacked in the course of local strife, ravaged by soldiers or by ex-soldiers turned bandit, raided by Kurds or beduin. The state of public security in the countryside was abysmally low; peasants received virtually no protection from beduin raiders or other disturbers of the peace. Natural disasters like drought, plague or locus infestations left empty villages in their wake. Peasants, driven to despair by the demands of rapacious "appropriators of the surplus," particularly tax-farmers and usurers, abandoned their villages in hopes of finding a living in the cities or elsewhere (Lewis 1987: 12–13).

The middle of the eighteenth century saw the arrival of the Shammar tribes, camel nomads who had been forced out of Arabia by rival tribes (Glubb 1942: 22–25; Gibert and Fevret 1953: 9; Dillemann 1979: 39). These northern Shammar proceeded to dominate the existing Tay tribes and imposed upon them and semi-sedentary Kurdish groups the *khuwa* (brotherhood tax; see Stewart 2004).

Western observers in the nineteenth and early twentieth centuries were traveling between Mosul and Nisibin (fig. 2.8); their trajectories vary but their accounts of the landscapes of the eastern part of the basin all share three main points. All were faced with crossing a dangerous and unpoliced area. Those who took the direct route, which passed just north of the THS region through Tell Rumaylan and Tell al-Hawa, exposed themselves to the greatest risk of banditry. Jackson (1799) and Buckingham (1827) traveled mostly at night and with large contingents of heavily armed persons. McCoan managed to ally himself with the Shammar to insure safe passage (McCoan 1879:

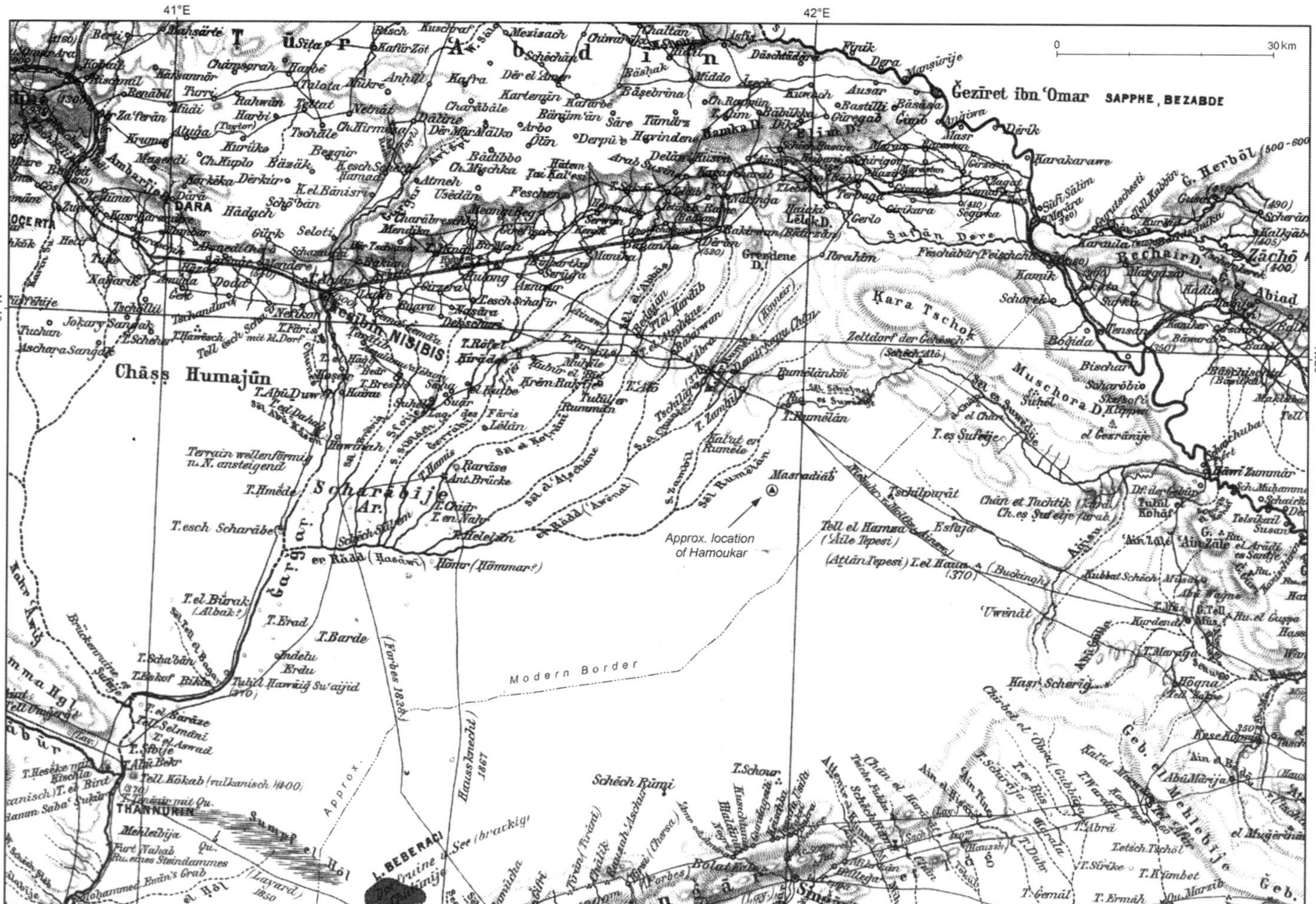

Figure 2.8. The eastern Upper Khabur basin and Iraqi North Jazira as depicted in the map of Richard Kiepert (1893)

79–84). More commonly, travelers followed closely along the southern edge of the Tur Abdin, where Kurdish settlements afforded some protection (Kinneir 1818; Fletcher 1850; Sachau 1883; von Oppenheim 1900), or along the flanks of the Jebel Sinjar among the Yezidi villages (Forbes 1839; Layard 1853). Even villages along the edge of the Tur Abdin were reportedly recently abandoned (Sachau 1883: 388), although it remains a distinct possibility that Sachau and others were observing the seasonally vacant villages of semi-nomadic Kurds (see below).

Also prominent in these nineteenth-century narratives are the presence of large camps of nomads on the plain and the absence of sedentary settlement and cultivation. The twelve miles beyond Nisibin were in "a tolerable state of cultivation" in 1813 (Kinneir 1818: 444), but the central part of the plain southeast of Aznavur was "desolate" in the 1840s (Ainsworth 1842: 120). Several travelers reported Kurdish villages in the neighborhood of Tell Leilan, southeast of Nisibin (esp. von Oppenheim 1900: 139), but these did not extend more than a 30 minutes' ride away from Nisibin itself. McCoan (1879: 80) saw no fixed settlements between Tel'afar and the immediate hinterland of Nisibin. Traveling in the spring of 1879, Cameron (1880: 220–28) reports that Kurds grazed large flocks at Tell Rumaylan because there were no water sources on the road beyond to Mosul for ten to twelve hours. He noted no cultivation whatsoever between Chilagha and Tell Hugna. Several other travelers noted that Chilagha was the interface between settlement and cultivation to the northwest and vast grassy steppe to the south and southeast (Mitford 1884: 1:265; Southgate 1840: 2:269).

Some villages that appeared "abandoned" were in fact seasonal habitations. For example, the village at Tell 'Abra was empty because its Kurdish inhabitants spent part of the year in their summer pastures out on the plain (von Oppenheim 1900: 142). The dynamism of the southeastern edge of settlement is revealed in the place names around Tell Leilan (Dillemann 1962: 68–71). North of Leilan and west of the Wadi Abbas are many abandoned places with Kurdish and Turkish names, which suggests to Dilleman that they were abandoned in recent times, probably due to beduin raids; alternately, south of Leilan and east of the Wadi Abbas most place names are Arabic and refer to tribal leaders within living memory (1962: 70).

The third recurrent observation of these early travelers was of the startling unexploited agricultural potential of these grazing lands, especially in the eastern part of the basin. Buckingham noted that east of the Wadi Khunayzir, "the rest of our way was over desert ground, though the whole tract was capable of being rendered highly fertile, being covered with a good soil, and intersected by several small rivulets of water" (Buckingham 1827: 2:2). Ainsworth (1842: 120) described the area around Tell Rumaylan as a "greensward" only in need of the application of water. The western half of the basin was similarly fertile and similarly abandoned by cultivation (Sykes 1907: 242).

These three conditions (lack of security, domination by pastoral nomads, and untapped agricultural potential) were of course closely related. The perspective of the sedentary farmer was succinctly stated by Taylor, who, speaking of the Shammar beduin, notes:

> It is hardly necessary to say that they pay no tribute whatsoever to the Turkish Government; on the contrary, their head-men receive a monthly salary from the Turks, and levy, in addition, black mail from every traveller and caravan passing through their territory, and also from all the villages and towns in the plains subjected to them. They are the curse of the country, and have totally put a stop to everything like cultivation and improvement in the splendid tracts they call their own. Under a strong and liberal government, and with the water system, climate, and soil of that part of Northern Mesopotamia terminated by the Jaghjagha and Khaboor, several thousand bales of cotton alone, of a very fair quality, might be raised annually. ... Now, however, the country is literally a desert — a vast uninhabited plain, though studded profusely with old tumuli and heaps of rubbish, the former abodes of an exuberant, peaceful, and industrious population (Taylor 1865: 54).

This settlement situation continued into the twentieth century, unaffected by either the collapse of the Ottoman empire or the initial establishment of the French mandate. It was only in 1926 that the mandate government effectively "pacified" the Upper Khabur basin, in the face of violent opposition from Kurdish tribes and the Arab Shammar (Dillemann 1979; Tachjian 2004). At this time, the near-total sedentary abandonment of the region is first documented photographically by the pioneering aerial archaeologist Antoine Poidebard (1934). In his photographs of the basin, the landscape is almost entirely devoid of settlements or agricultural field boundaries, and the only visible roads or tracks are the small braided paths of sheep and goat herds.

The human geography of the basin in the years following the imposition of French control (fig. 2.9) is vividly described by Robert Montagne (1932) and in the British Admiralty *Handbook of the Nomad* (Glubb 1942). The sedentary villages along the railway between Ras al-Ain and Nisibin were expanding due to the influx of Armenian, Kurdish, Chechen, and Assyrian refugees from Turkey and Iraq, as was the recently founded town of Qamishli, just

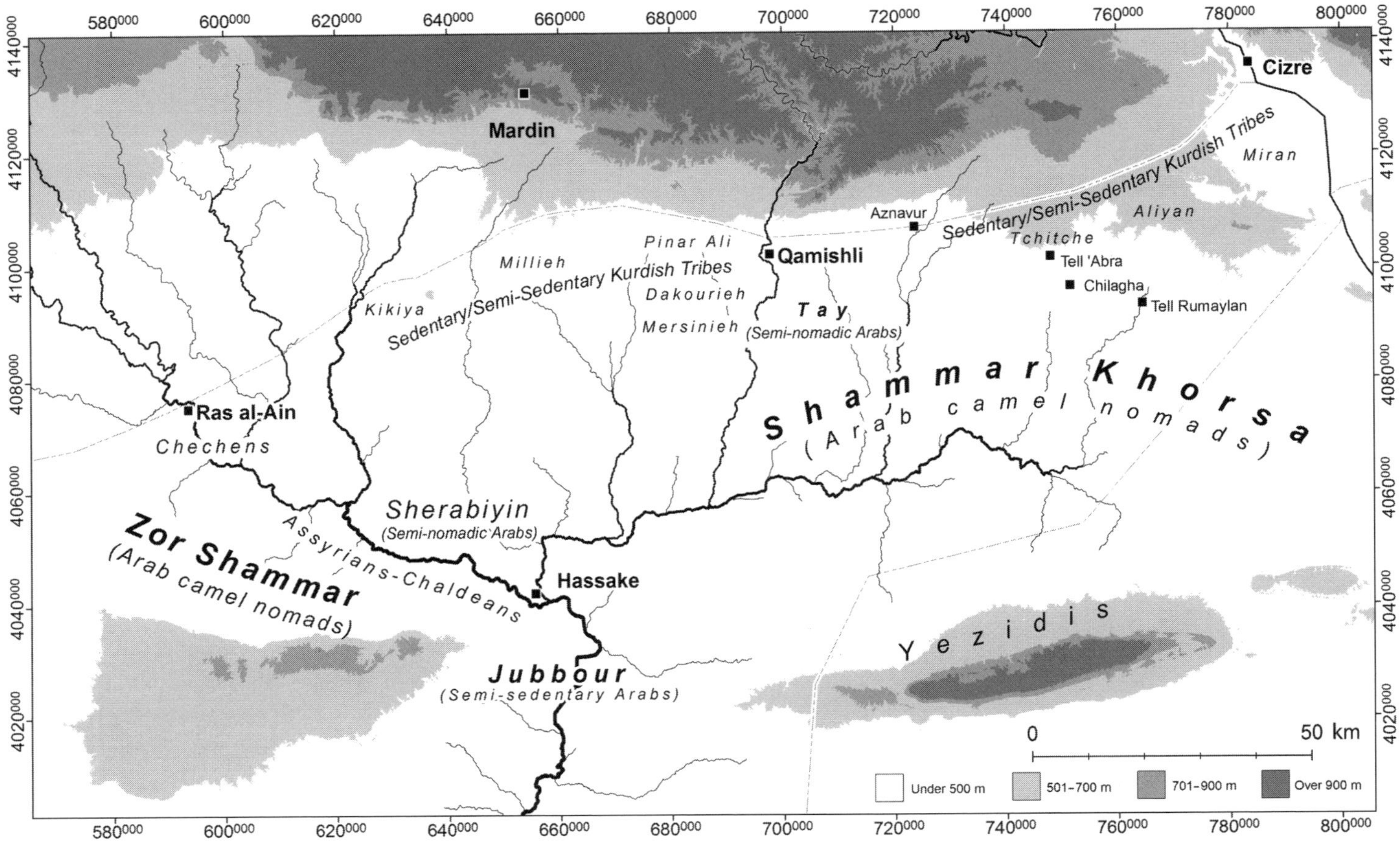

Figure 2.9. Sedentary, semi-sedentary, and nomadic groups in the pre-Mandate twentieth century. Shammar areas are winter pasture. Compiled from Montagne 1932, Gibert and Fevret 1953, Wirth 1964, and Glubb 1942

opposite Nisibin on the Syrian side of the border. The northern part of the western basin continued to be populated by the semi-nomadic Milli Kurds, while the eastern basin hosted the mostly sedentary Kikiya, Millieh, Dakourieh, Mersinieh, Pinar Ali, Aliyan, and Miran Kurdish tribes.

The small remainder of the semi-nomadic Tay Arabs summered south and southeast of Qamishli and moved their sheep flocks to the area between their cultivated land near Qamishli and the Jebel Sinjar. Several semi-sedentary groups also occupied parts of the basin at various intervals: the Baggara brought their flocks up from the Euphrates to the Jebel Abd al-Aziz in the winter; the Jubbour moved their animals onto the steppes surrounding their villages along the Jaghjagh and the Khabur; and the Sherabiyin migrated to the Jebel Sinjar from the area around Tell Safra (Glubb 1942: 77–94).

The dominant non-sedentary force continued to be the fully nomadic tribes of the Shammar beduin. Unlike the various Kurdish tribes who mostly raised sheep, these were camel breeders and therefore capable of great annual migrations. The Shammar arrived from Nejd in the mid-eighteenth century and gradually spread throughout Mesopotamia as far east as Baghdad; in the process, they seized control of the pastures of the Jubbour, Baggara, and Wulda, all formerly fully nomadic tribes who became semi-sedentary in the Jazira when faced with these losses (Glubb 1942: 24–25; Taylor 1865: 54–55). In 1875 the Shammar split. West of the Khabur River, the Shammar of Zor moved between the steppe south of the Jebel Abd al-Aziz and the Euphrates as far downstream as Ana. At the time of the British occupation, the Iraqi half split further into the Iraqi Shammar, who occupied the banks of the Tigris south of Mosul, and the Shammar Khorsa (or Syrian Shammar), who summer around Demir Kapou (now Rumaylan), Qubur el-Bid, Tell 'Abra, and along the Wadi Khunayzir and migrate to winter pastures in the salt marshes of Buwara and as far south as Ana (Glubb 1942: 22).

This phase of low settlement density (and thus low impact on the archaeological landscape) rapidly began to be reversed in the years prior to the Second World War, as formerly semi-nomadic Kurdish tribes and fully nomadic camel beduin began to settle and adopt agriculture under French encouragement (fig. 2.10). The French government also encouraged the immigration of Christian groups from Turkey and northern Iraq into the basin. Grain produc-

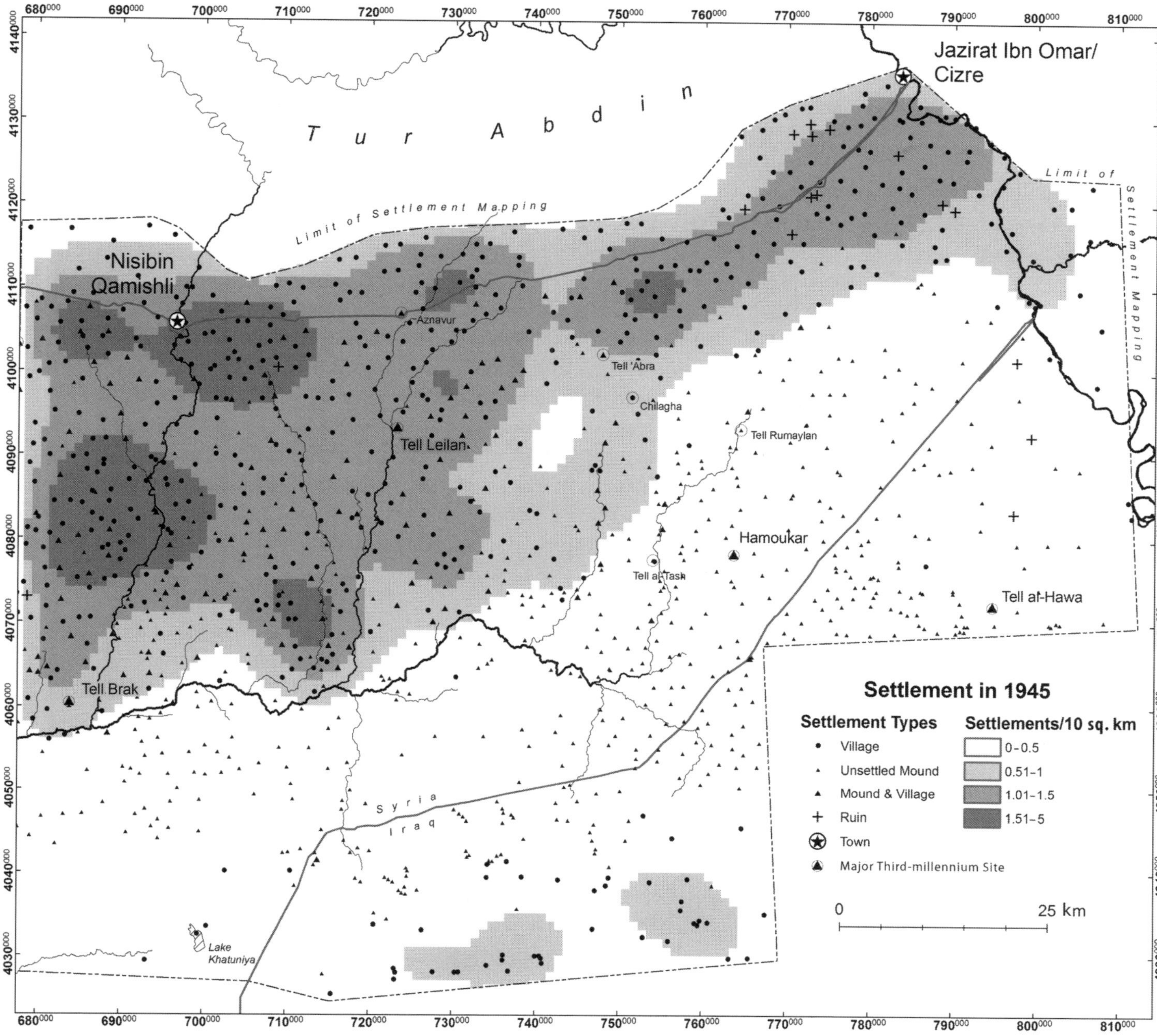

Figure 2.10. Density of settlement in the Upper Khabur basin circa 1933–1945. Settlements from French 1:200,000 Levant map series, Qamichlîyé-Sinjar (1945) and Karatchok-Dagh (1933) sheets. Compare the known settlement pattern of fifty years earlier in figure 2.8

tion more than tripled from 199,100 ha in 1937 to 643,000 ha in 1954 (de Vaumas 1956: 75; Wilkinson and Tucker 1995: 13). Cotton was first grown in the region in 1948 and had expanded from 140 to 3,300 ha by 1950, when the Korean War pulled some American producers from the market (Gibert and Fevret 1953: 86–88). By 1954, the population had ballooned from an estimated 40,000 persons in 1929 to almost 240,000 persons (Nouss 1951, cited in de Vaumas 1956: 73). A parallel and contemporaneous southward expansion of settlement and the limits of agriculture has been documented for the Iraqi North Jazira and the Sinjar Plain (Wilkinson and Tucker 1995: 12–14).

This process came latest to the southeastern part of the basin, however. In 1945, settlement and cultivation extended no farther than Tell al-Tash on the Wadi Rumaylan (Dillemann 1962: 70). As it extended south, sedentary reoccupation was focused on the low wadi floodplains, leaving the higher interfluvial areas to be recolonized later (Gibert and Fevret 1953: 10). The last part of the basin to be cultivated was the region around Tell Kotchek/Yarubiya, where the Shammar Khorsa were induced to settle by the Agrarian Reform (FAO 1966: 37; Gibert and Fevret

1953: 15). The first appearance of the modern village at Hamoukar, now called al-Hurriya, is to be placed in this context.

By 1954, the entire basin had been brought under agriculture (de Vaumas 1956: 73). Over one million hectares were cultivated, half by machine and half by animal traction. All first- and second-class cereal lands were under cultivation, which extended into even marginal zones and areas considered not suitable for cultivation. Writing around 1955, Van Liere noted that "the Jezireh developed so rapidly during the last 15 years that there is hardly a parallel in the whole of the Middle East" (Van Liere n.d.: 27). Most of this unprecedented growth was due to the rapid introduction of, and heavy reliance upon, mechanization, especially in the marginal areas (Wirth 1964; Mehner 1983).

The context of mechanization was the expansion of capitalist investment in agriculture. With the start of World War II, capitalists based in Aleppo began to contract for agricultural rights with the Kurdish aghas or Arab shaykhs who controlled the land; very few landowners cultivated their land themselves (Boghossian 1952: 134–40; Wirth 1964; de Vaumas 1956: 75–76; Gibert and Fevret 1953: 94–98). In the Jazira, land rents accounted for 10–15 percent of the crop, but the percentage extracted by the owners of agricultural machinery could be as high as 45–60 percent of the crop (FAO 1959: III–4). On account of the inequality of land ownership and continued poverty of most village-based sharecroppers, the government passed the Agrarian Reform Law in September 1958. The law fixed ceilings on land ownership in rainfed areas at 300 ha plus 169 ha for dependents; the expropriated lands were to be redistributed to landless or poor farmers at the rate of 30 ha per family (FAO 1959: III–5–9; Forni 2003). These lands continue to be owned by the state and are rented to the farmers. The 1958 land reform is responsible for the current arrangement of fields in the eastern basin, and its effects are important to recognize if one is to peel back the latest layers on the landscape palimpsest as captured by CORONA (see Section 4.3).

The farmlands of the Upper Khabur basin are highly productive (Weiss 1986: 71–80). The adjacent plains of the Iraqi North Jazira produce mean yields of 700 kg of wheat and 900 kg of barley per hectare (Wilkinson and Tucker 1995: 7). These figures mask great variation, mostly tied to the amount and timing of rainfall. Two years can serve as examples (Van Liere n.d.: 27). Between August 1953 and July 1954, 656 mm of rain fell at Qamishli and 643 mm fell at Mosul. In the following year, 371 mm fell at Qamishli and 322 at Mosul. In the wet year 1954, the harvest in the basin averaged 1,200 kg of wheat on the best land, 1,000 kg on good land, 800 kg on marginal land, and 500 kg on land best suited for grazing. The following year, these averages declined to 1,000 kg, 600 kg, and 500 kg for the best, good, and marginal lands, respectively, with no yields on grazing land. All crops but the best land were considered to be failures.

In general, the lower the interannual variability, the lower the average annual rainfall threshold for continuous successful dry farming (Perrin de Brichambaut and Wallén 1963: 9–10). Therefore, short-term runs of high annual rainfall might inspire the expansion of agriculture into marginal areas, as occurred in the Syrian and Iraqi Jazira and the Sinjar Plain during the postwar years (Van Liere n.d.; Wilkinson and Tucker 1995: 13), but settlements in these areas may prove not to be viable in the long run.

2.3. HISTORY, CONTINGENCY, AND THE CREATION OF THE PRESENT ARCHAEOLOGICAL LANDSCAPE

The Upper Khabur basin has thus witnessed a dramatic shift from one end of the land-use intensity spectrum (seasonal grazing by low-density nomadic groups) to the other (intensified and mechanized agriculture by sedentary communities). In the span of only twenty to thirty years, the plain went from near-abandonment to complete agricultural and sedentary colonization. The historical patterns of settlement and land use reviewed in this section are particularly vivid due to the written accounts, which certainly fill in a major gap in archaeological research (i.e., the post-Mongol Islamic period). This recent history of settlement in the basin is critical for understanding the formation of the present landscape and its unparalleled degree of preservation of ancient features. Furthermore, although they are historically contingent, these settlement processes might be cautiously used to understand similar transitions in the past which are only hinted at by shifts in numbers and sizes of sites.

As discussed in detail below, the basin has until recently preserved a quantity and variety of landscape features seen rarely, if at all, elsewhere in comparable alluvial areas of the Near East. Archaeological landscapes can be placed on a continuum between landscapes of destruction and landscapes of survival, based on a combination of natural taphonomic processes and contingent settlement histories (Taylor 1972; Williamson 1998; Wilkinson 2003). Simply put, some landscapes are more likely to suffer greater attrition through time than others. Desert and mountain areas tend to feature landscapes of survival, because once human activities have left traces, environmental conditions are unlikely to encourage destructive human resettlement. For example, the harsh conditions of the central Negev allow the preservation of pastoral nomad sites from the early third millennium B.C. (Rosen 2003). Alternately, areas with moderate climates, sufficient rainfall, and fertile soils will attract settlement and encourage its continuation or resettlement. Continuous settlement in such a region will lead to progressive attrition of earlier landscape features through time.

The Upper Khabur basin therefore appears to be a classic landscape of destruction. As reviewed above, geologically and geomorphologically, the basin is well suited for extensive agriculture. Continental-scale tectonics have produced an enclosed basin; the hills to the north inspire orogenic rainfall that runs off across it, and they contain springs along its south edge, both of which provide moisture for the basin. The alluvial sediments have formed fertile soils. Even when the basin was almost completely given over to pasture in the last centuries, the density of tells suggest to visitors the underlying potential for agriculture. Because of this agricultural potential, in the past, and especially in the last half century, archaeologists have assumed that the basis for local political power and the inspiration for foreign conquest was control over agricultural surpluses (Weiss 1986; Weiss et al. 1993). Within the Taylor-Williamson framework, we should expect that relatively few early landscape features would survive, having been effaced by subsequent agricultural settlement.

The landscape situation is a bit more complicated. If one looks at the average annual rainfall isohyets (fig. 2.7), almost the entire basin is above the 250 mm/year threshold for successful dry farming. As discussed above, however, these averages mask substantial interannual variability in rainfall. On a wet year, the 250 mm isohyet might shift southward, but more importantly, it could shift to the north on a dry year, leaving sedentary communities in the southern part of the basin without sufficient rainfall for their crops. The latter was the situation of the 1954/1955 growing season, when most crops in the basin failed. Crop failure was not spatially uniform, however; agriculture in the far northeast of the "bec du canard," near the Tigris, continued to return high yields. This area has the highest average annual rainfall in the Syrian Jazira.

In sum, the Upper Khabur basin is not uniform in its long-term agricultural potential; interannual variation in rainfall means that cultivation is increasingly risky as one moves south. In Wilkinson's taphonomic classification, the basin falls into Zone 3, a marginal rainfed steppe where relative preservation is expected to be high (2003: 41–43). This classification certainly describes the southern part of the basin around Tell Brak and especially the steppe beyond it toward the Jebel Abd al-Aziz and the Jebel Sinjar; the northern part is expected to be far less marginal, barring any dramatic shifts in climate such as those proposed for the later third millennium B.C. (Weiss et al. 1993).

Thus far, landscape preservation and destruction have been described solely in environmental terms: climate, geology, and soils determining the possibilities for initial sedentary occupation and the likelihood of subsequent reoccupation. The record of the last several centuries, however, demonstrates that nonpredictable sociopolitical factors play a strong role in landscape preservation. Lack of sedentary occupation was related not to climatic marginality, but to a lack of security in the face of extortionate beduin, Kurdish, and Yezidi tribes and an Ottoman government presence extractive in its own right.

Here we see the role of historical contingency in landscape preservation. It was the imposition of centralized control over the basin by Ottoman and French mandatory governments, rather than a climatic amelioration, that led to the expansion of settlement in the sixteenth century and since 1926 (Göyünç and Hütteroth 1997; de Vaumas 1956). The landscape impacts of the twentieth-century sedentary expansion can be documented by comparing historical aerial and satellite photographs from the 1950s and '60s to recent high-resolution commercial satellite imagery, with ground confirmation via field survey. The sixteenth-century expansion is presently only known through a textual study of Ottoman tax records (Göyünç and Hütteroth 1997), but a case can be made that it is connected to a pronounced void in the basinwide distribution of ancient trackways (see Section 7.3.2).

The high degree of landscape preservation in the basin up until recent decades thus results from a unique combination of patterned landscape creation and transformation starting in at least the third millennium B.C. and environmental conditions that were dynamic but remained generally suitable for both intensive agriculture and extensive pasture. The creation of much of what survives of the premodern landscape features, especially hollow ways and field scatters, can be attributed to the phase of urbanism of the later third millennium B.C. (Period 7), with other durable elements being added in the late Sasanian to Early Islamic periods (Periods 16–17). This urbanization was not limited to the Upper Khabur basin and adjacent alluvial plains, and it is likely that its landscape impact was also to be found elsewhere in northern Mesopotamia. However, these other areas, for example the Harran Plain around Kazane Höyük and the Idlib region around Ebla, had their own subsequent settlement histories that did not include the lengthy pastoral interlude of the Upper Khabur basin.

The above review of recent settlement history provides more than just an explanation for the current patterns and condition of the archaeological landscape; it also provides a model for the patterns of pastoral nomadic-agriculturalist interaction and processes of nomadization and sedentarization in the deeper past. At present, the understanding behind archaeological processes of abandonment and resettlement is dominated by monocausal explanations involving normative response to postulated climate change: sedentary agricultural communities abandoned their settlements when the climate dried, only to return upon amelioration. The environment of the Upper Khabur basin was undeniably dynamic, and even short-term reductions in rainfall could have a substantial impact on the viability of settlement systems expanded beyond the point of resilience (Wilkinson 1994, 1997). The situation of the last centuries complicates climatically driven interpretations of past settlement shifts by demonstrating the possibility that they were the result of sociopolitical, rather than climatic, instabilities.

CHAPTER 3

THS FIELD METHODOLOGY 1: THE HAMOUKAR SURFACE COLLECTION

3.1. PREVIOUS ARCHAEOLOGICAL OBSERVATIONS

At the time that excavations commenced, in autumn 1999, Hamoukar had never been excavated but had been the subject of repeated visits and speculation regarding its size and settlement history. These speculations were often based on analysis of aerial photographs without ground control, or on brief site visits. The 1999 surface collection of the mound at Hamoukar was intended to reconcile these often conflicting observations, in addition to the broader research goals outlined in *Chapter 1*.

The earliest archaeologists to visit the Upper Khabur basin avoided the Hamoukar area, preferring to move between the Yezidi villages on the fringes of the Jebel Sinjar (Layard 1853) or along the southern edge of the Tur Abdin (von Oppenheim 1900). The southeastern portion of the basin was the domain of the Shammar, and both Layard and von Oppenheim traveled under heavy guard.

The earliest observations of Hamoukar were made from the air. Although Poidebard (1934) never ventured so far east, Hamoukar came to the attention of Willem Van Liere and Jean Lauffray in the course of an aerial survey undertaken for the Syrian Ministry of Agriculture. From aerial photographs, they recognized the site as "un des plus vastes de toute la haute Jezireh — 1 kilomètre carré," and associated it with a series of ancient trackways (Van Liere and Lauffray 1954–55: 137). Subsequently, Van Liere (1963: fig. 3b) published a scaled photo interpretation which showed Hamoukar's main features: the high mound, the lower town, the outer depression, and associated hollow ways. On this site plan, the mounded area of the site measured 116 ha but the circular depression encompassed 216 ha (calculated in Wilkinson 1994: 488). Primarily on the basis of its large size, he proposed to identify Hamoukar with the Mitanni capital Waššukanni (Van Liere 1963: 120).

Since Van Liere's discussion, Hamoukar has been visited repeatedly. Diederik Meijer included it as part of his survey of the eastern basin; he reported Uruk/Amuq F sherds, metallic ware, and Khabur ware (Meijer 1986: 19). Subsequent informal visits provided evidence to place Hamoukar within the framework of the Uruk Expansion (Sürenhagen 1986: 14–15; Schwartz 1988b; Lebeau 1990: 243; Weiss 1983: 44). Others, however, report only local chaff-tempered ceramics in the fourth millennium (Oates and Oates 1991: n. 4; Schwartz 1994: 164 n. 19).

Almost fifty years after Van Liere's observations, the scale of the site remained unclear, with estimates ranging from 90 to 216 ha, and the question of whether it grew to that size in the fourth millennium or as part of the urban expansion of the later third millennium remained unanswered. The systematic surface collection of the mound, undertaken in the first season of the project, was designed to clarify these issues. A preliminary report appeared in the journal *Iraq* (Ur 2002b), but is now superseded by the results presented in *Chapter 6*.

3.2. MORPHOLOGY, SETTLEMENT, AND SURFACE CONDITIONS

The interpretation of surface collection data is based on the assumption that, all other things being equal, the location of material on the surface is directly related to the location of ancient settlement below the surface (e.g., Redman and Watson 1970: 279–80). Interpretation, however, is rarely so straightforward. A range of post-abandonment processes, both natural and cultural, can alter the composition of the surface assemblage. To account for these processes at Hamoukar, it is necessary to review the mound's morphology, its most recent settlement history, and the conditions of the surface at the time of the surface collection.

3.2.1. MORPHOLOGY OF THE MOUND

Hamoukar's present form is the result of over 2,000 years of settlement and can be classed with a handful of other mounds in the basin with similar settlement histories. The most apparent feature is its 15 ha high mound, which at its peak rises 18 m above the plain, measured at the north (figs. 3.1–2).[1] At its base, it approximates a 500 × 400 m rectangle. Its slopes conform generally to common patterns of mound erosion in northern Mesopotamia (Rosen 1986: 31–33). The northern slopes face the direction of the prevailing wind. This situation encourages parallel slope retreat, wherein the relatively sharp angle of the slope at the time of abandonment is maintained while the position of the slope itself gradually moves backward. The south-facing slopes, however, are struck obliquely by wind and rain, which encourages slope decline. This process removes materials from the top and redeposits them at the base, creating a longer and more gentle slope. The two processes operate at different rates: the north-facing slopes support greater vegetation, which acts to retain the soil, while the low-vegetation southern slopes offer less resistance to erosional forces. The resulting asymmetrical profile (see fig. 3.4 Section A–A′) is almost universal among simple conical mounds on the plain (see, e.g., the topographical maps in Stein and Wattenmaker 2003), but also characterizes other large mounds such as Tell Brak.

The high mound exhibits internal characteristics that distinguish it from high mounds of comparable size elsewhere in the basin. Rather than having a plateau shape, it rises to a high point at its northeastern corner. This arrangement almost certainly resulted from its settlement history after the fourth millennium B.C. In Ninevite 5 times and later, it appears that only parts of the high mound were occupied (see *Chapter 6*). The mound is drained by three primary gullies. The largest is a broad feature that completely dominates its western half. Smaller gullies cut into the mound near its southeastern corner and its northern edge. Each of the three has produced a colluvial fan of eroded material at its base, the size of which appears proportional to its gully's runoff collection area. Two gullies also drain

Figure 3.1. The high mound at Hamoukar, with the step trench in Area A, viewed from the north

[1] The topographic survey of Hamoukar was carried out by John C. Sanders and Carrie Hritz. The resulting coordinates were input into the ArcGIS Spatial Analyst's spline tool to produce an interpolated surface of the surveyed areas. The 1 m contour dataset was derived from the interpolated surface.

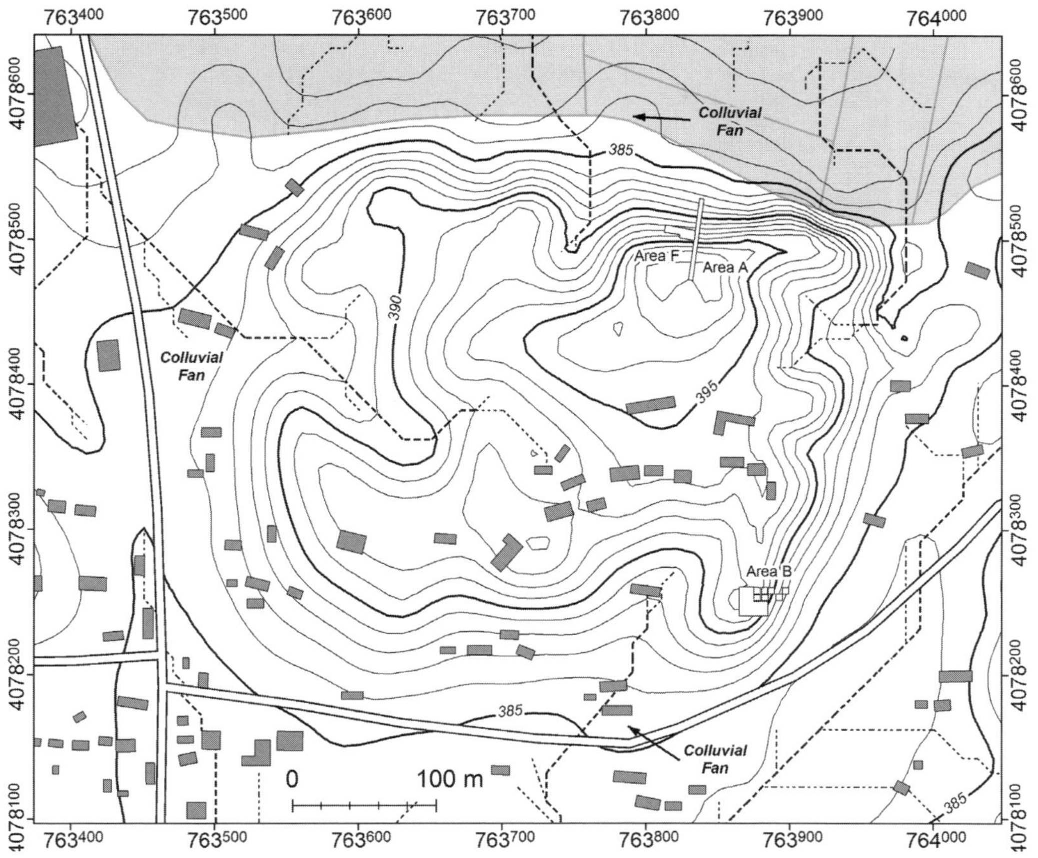

Figure 3.2. Topography, hydrology, and features of the high mound at Hamoukar. Surface drainage is indicated by dashed lines; gray rectangles are modern houses and outbuildings. Oriented with north at top

the eastern edge, including a substantial one at the northeastern corner, whose corresponding colluvial fan has been largely taken away for brick and roofing materials by the villagers of Hamoukar/al-Hurriya.

The high mound is located at the northern edge of an extensive lower town (fig. 3.3). The area of the lower town and high mound together encompasses 105 ha, making Hamoukar one of the largest Bronze Age urban centers in northern Mesopotamia, surpassed only by Tell Mozan and possibly by Tell Taya. The lower town averages a 3–4 m elevation above the surrounding plain although with considerable internal variation. The largest elevated area on the lower town stretches from its northeastern corner south along its eastern edge. This ridge is actually three discrete mounded areas, resulting from three chronologically distinct post-third-millennium reoccupations (from north to south, Iron Age, Hellenistic, and first millennium A.D., respectively; see *Chapter 6*). The middle of these three is a considerable mound in its own right which rises 6 m over the level of the lower town. Two other elevated areas, at the southeastern corner and at the western edge, do not appear to be related to pre- or post-third-millennium settlement.[2] Instead, these elevations may be due to monumental structures that are more resistant to erosion.

Depressed areas on the lower town can be related to patterns of natural drainage and to elements of ancient topography, and it is likely that a recursive relationship existed between the two. The largest feature is a shallow depression that curves around the eastern, southern, and southwestern sides of the high mound, with a broad extension running to the southwestern edge of the lower town. This feature probably originated as an area of mudbrick extraction during the initial occupation of the high mound and prior to the settlement of the lower town; it would have also accumulated runoff from the high mound, discouraging settlement while the lower town grew up around it. At present it serves to drain the southern half of the high mound and all but the northwestern corner of the lower town.

---

[2] Interestingly, the French military cartographers included this western mound on the 1:200,000 map of the region, along with the high mound; they did not, however, indicate the full lower town (see fig. 4.5).

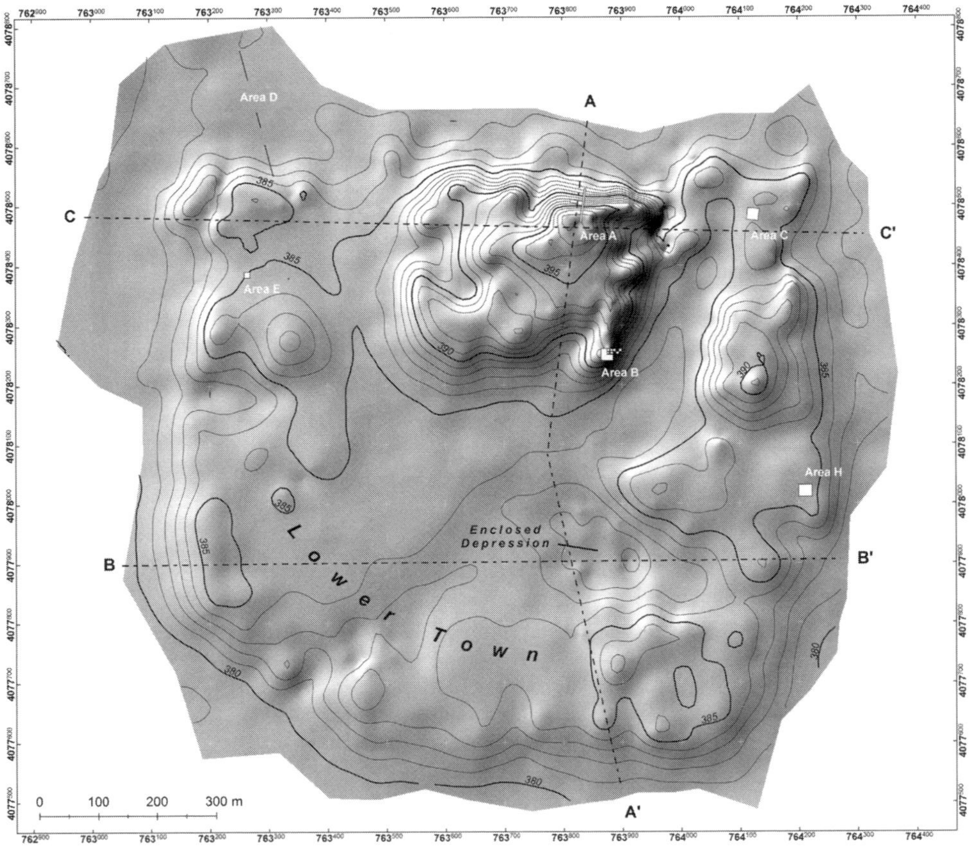

Figure 3.3. Topography and morphological features of the lower town (see fig. 3.4 for profiles)

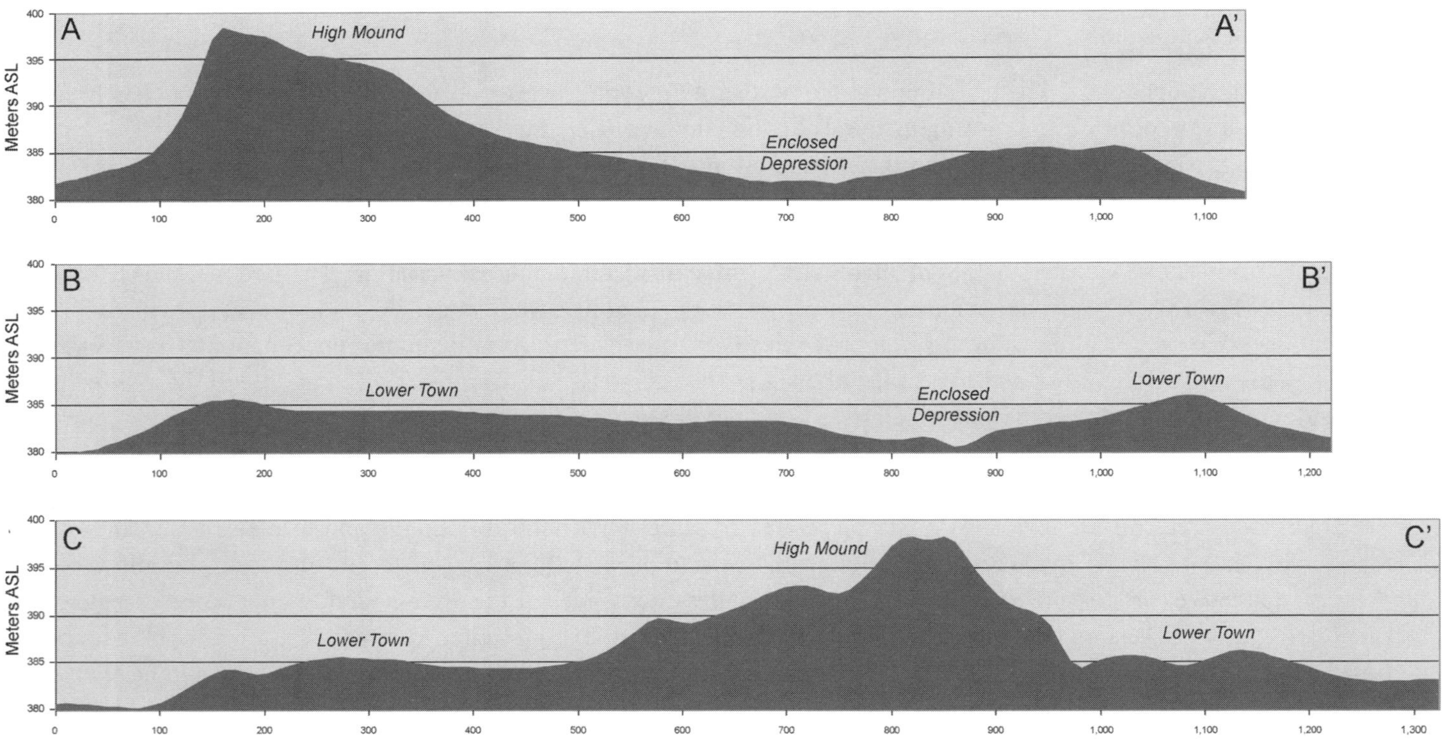

Figure 3.4. Vertically exaggerated topographic profiles across Hamoukar (see fig. 3.3 for profile locations). (*A–A′*) North–south profile across the high mound summit, lower town, and its enclosed depression; (*B–B′*) East–west profile across the southern lower town; (*C–C′*) East–west profile across the high mound and northern lower town

Part of this large depressed area is an internal drainage basin, near the center of the lower town. Such enclosed depressions are commonly found in association with sites of the last two millennia and are best interpreted as the remains of mudbrick extraction pits that have not had time to become infilled with plow wash or aeolian sediments (see Section 5.1.2 and Wilkinson and Tucker 1995: 32–35). They are rarely associated with sites as early as the third millennium B.C., so it is tempting to associate this feature with the poorly understood first-millennium A.D. settlement 100 m to its northeast. However, it may have largely attained its present form in the last fifty years; in the earliest CORONA images, this area shows neither elevated vegetation growth nor moisture retention.

Finally, the edges of the lower town are notched in several places by re-entrant contours. The most prominent, at the southwestern corner, has been deepened by its position at the outflow point for lower-town surface runoff, but was probably a preexisting feature. Others, most notably at the center of the western edge and at the east edge, appear unrelated to surface runoff. The most likely interpretation for all these features is that they mark the position of former gates into the lower town. It may be preferable to consider them as major access points, since the topography of the lower town gives no indication that it was walled. This interpretation is strongly supported by off-site evidence from the surrounding landscape. All the major re-entrants are directly associated with hollow ways (see below).

Beyond the mounded site there are several subtle landscape features that attracted attention long before the start of the Chicago Hamoukar Expedition. Van Liere noted a "double circular ditch" around the mound, which he mapped from aerial photographs but did not otherwise describe (fig. 3.5). On his scaled plan, Van Liere's inner

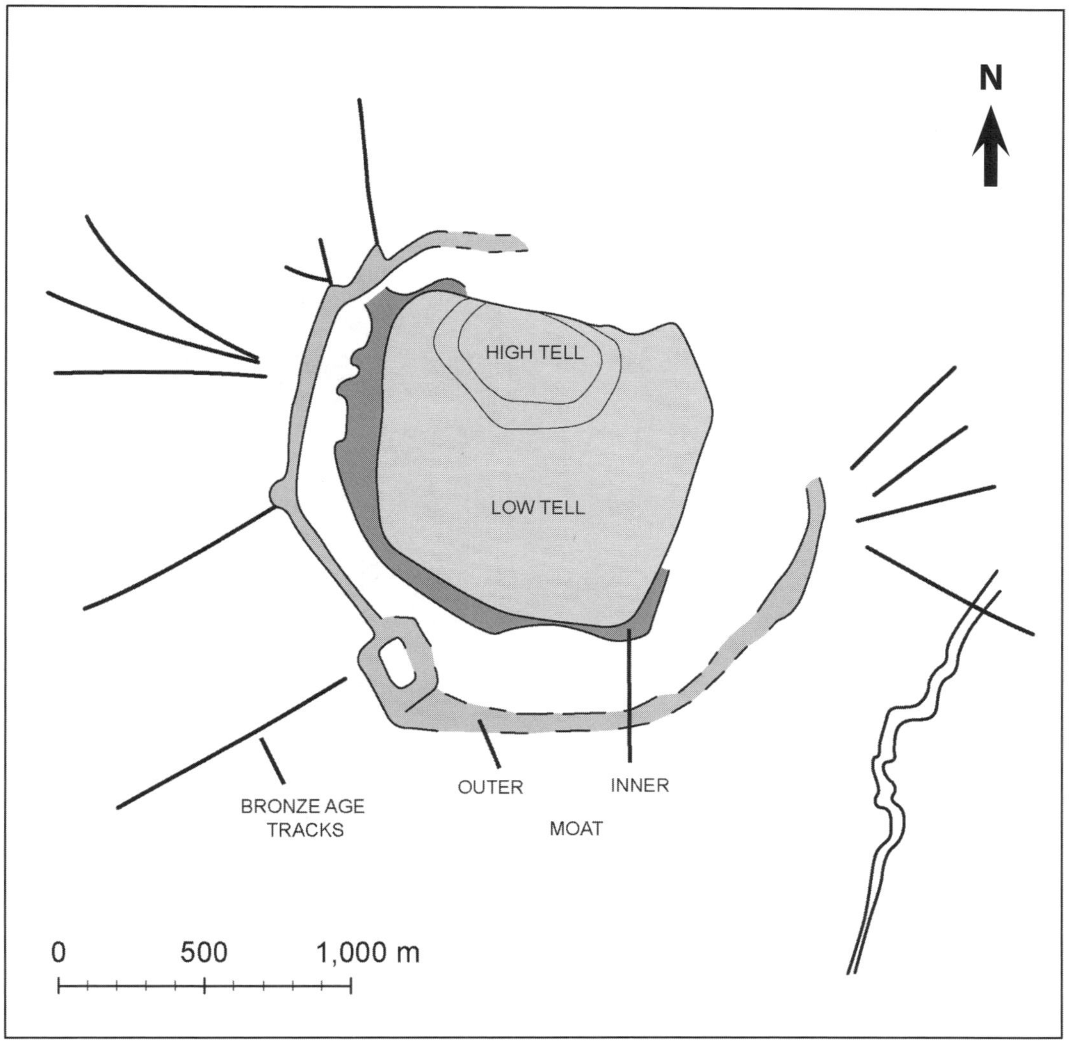

Figure 3.5. Van Liere's plan of Hamoukar with linear features and ditches (based on Van Liere 1963: fig. 3b)

ditch ranges between 110 m wide at the western lower town, to 70 m wide at the southeast. The outer ditch varies between 40 and 60 m in width and includes several rectilinear features along its southwestern extent. The north and east sides of the outer ditch are either poorly understood (indicated by dashes) or unreconstructed by Van Liere. Beyond the outer ditch, Van Liere identified twelve linear features as "Bronze Age tracks": four converging on a single point on the eastern outer ditch, and the others connecting with the outer ditch at various points along its western half. Van Liere's plan includes the ephemeral wadi that flows to the east of Hamoukar, but does not indicate other landscape aspects such as modern structures, tracks, or fields.

With the exception of the northwestern part of the outer ditch and the two southwestern tracks, none of these features can be seen on the ground today, and the aerial photographs employed by Van Liere are not accessible at present. These features can, however, be reconstructed from the five CORONA missions that covered the THS region, especially Mission 1117 from May 1972 (fig. 3.6). The outer ditch in the field northwest of Hamoukar is particularly clear, and closely corresponds in dimensions to Van Liere's plan. The inner ditch in this area, however, appears to be less of a linear feature than a generally disturbed area, perhaps an area of extensive brick pits. The southwestern outer ditch also appears to be a line of large depressions.

The ditches on Hamoukar's other sides are more difficult to interpret from CORONA. The fields north of Hamoukar were already transformed by small-scale irrigation by 1965 and do not show a continuation of the ditch. Van Liere's reconstruction of the southern and eastern outer ditch finds no support from CORONA either. Like the southwestern section, the eastern extent appears to be a somewhat linear arrangement of depressions. Van Liere's hypothetical southern extent would have crossed over the northern part of the Southern Extension (THS 25, Khirbat al-Fakhar; see Section 4.5).

Figure 3.6. Hamoukar's circular depression and associated hollow ways (CORONA 1117, 25 May 1972)

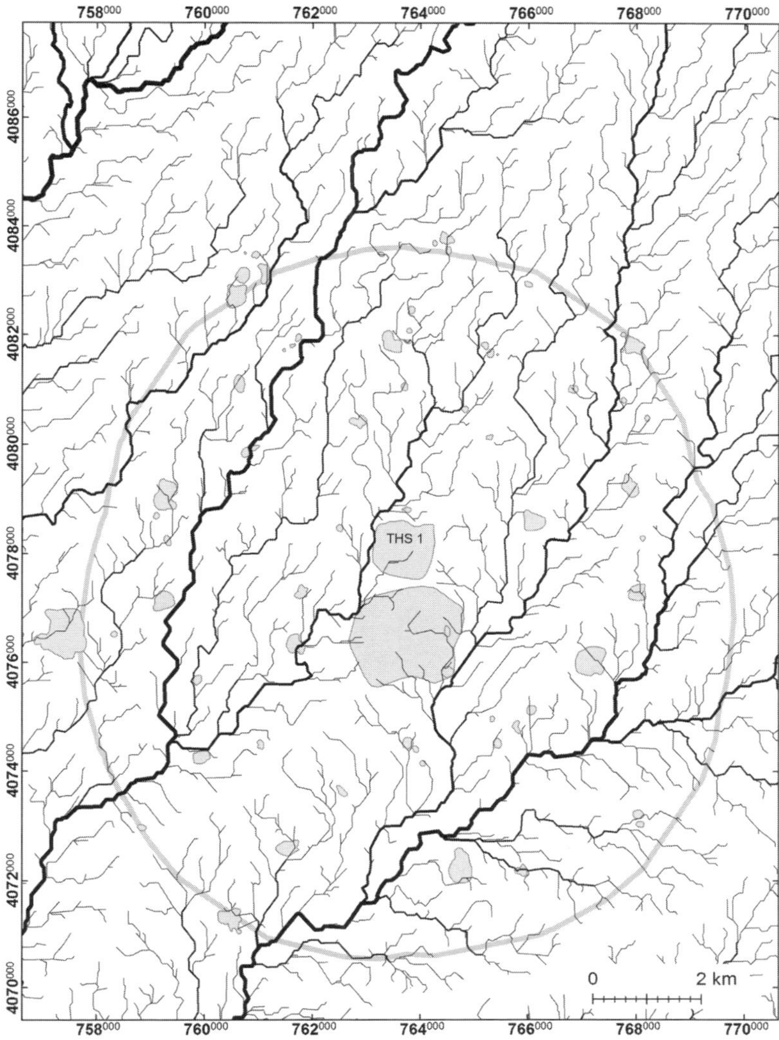

Figure 3.7. Surface drainage in the THS area. Modeled from the 30 m SRTM digital elevation dataset

These depressed features do not appear to be regular enough to be interpreted as a defensive moat, following Van Liere. They are more likely to have resulted from a recursive process of surface runoff and excavation for building materials. The drainage pattern visible on the surface today is the result of natural patterns and human intervention (Section 5.4), but the hydrology as modeled from Shuttle Radar Topography Mission (SRTM) digital terrain data indicates that a broad area of the plain to the north-northeast would have drained along Hamoukar's western edge (fig. 3.7). This interpretation is supported by the Area D geomorphological trench near the northwestern corner of the lower town (Wilkinson 2002a: 95–99). The trench through the outer ditch contained poorly sorted calcium carbonate accretions, along with some potsherds of later third-millennium fabric. Wilkinson interprets this deposit as originating from locally eroded soils and probably representing local drainage formed under the influence of human modifications. Specifically, it may represent the capture of natural drainage by a hollow way to the north, which redirected runoff into the borrow-pitting area near Hamoukar (Wilkinson 2002a: 97–98). Further runoff would have continued out of this area toward the southwest via the hollow way near Hamoukar's western edge, which would explain its continued deep profile (see figs. 5.20 and 5.25 Profile P). Similar hollow way-directed surface runoff has been documented at Tell Brak and elsewhere (Wilkinson et al. 2001: 6–7; shown schematically in Wilkinson 1993: fig. 8).

Van Liere's radial network of hollow ways can be confirmed and extended via CORONA imagery (fig. 3.8). All the features he noted on Hamoukar's west side appear on multiple CORONA images, and most can be followed for several kilometers farther south and west. On the other hand, the four features he identified on Hamoukar's eastern

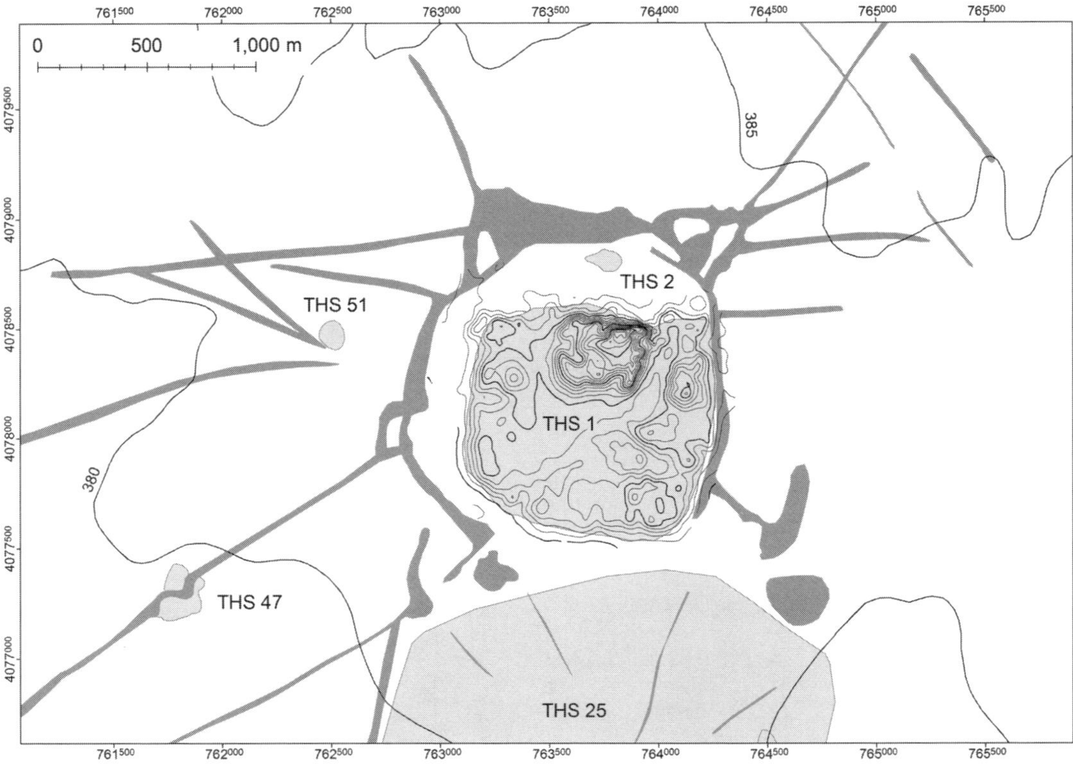

Figure 3.8. Topography and depressed features in the Hamoukar area, derived from CORONA photographs (Missions 1102, 1108, and 1117)

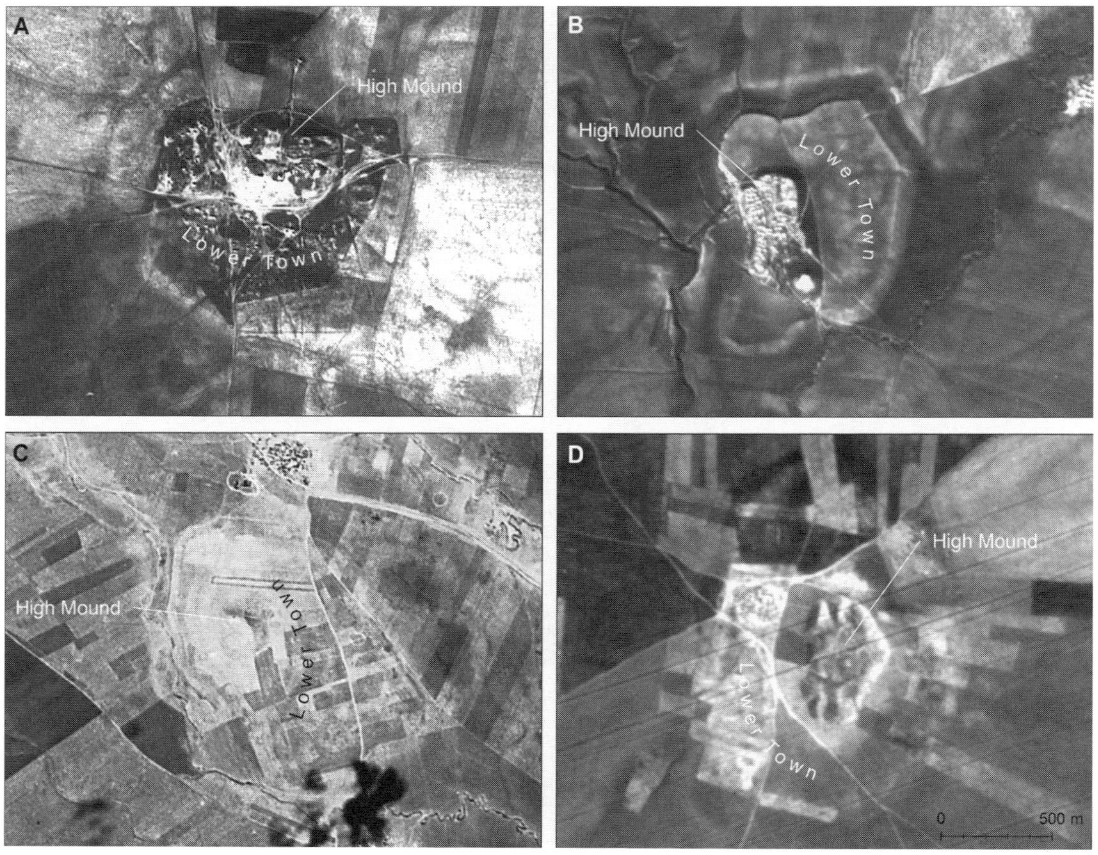

Figure 3.9. Site morphologies of mid- to late third-millennium B.C. urban centers in northern Mesopotamia. (*A*) Hamoukar, 105 ha (CORONA 1102-1025DF007); (*B*) Tell Leilan, 90 ha (CORONA 1108-1025DA004); (*C*) Kazane Höyük, 90 ha (CORONA 1104-1009DA005); (*D*) Tell Mozan, 120 ha (CORONA 1021-2120DF007). All to the same scale

side cannot be identified on CORONA, and three features converging on Hamoukar's northeastern corner are apparent on several CORONA photographs but do not appear on his plan.

Hamoukar's system of hollow ways is discussed in greater detail below (Section 5.3), but in the present context, they provide further support for the interpretation of the areas of re-entrant topographic contour lines on the edges of the lower town as gates or points of controlled access. For example, the point on the western lower town edge is the likely terminus of at least four hollow ways, and a fifth lines up closely with the re-entrant at the southwestern corner (fig. 3.8). Hollow ways line up with probable ancient gates at Tell Beydar and Tell Leilan as well (Ur and Wilkinson 2008).

Although it has some unique characteristics, Hamoukar is thus morphologically similar to several other large northern Mesopotamian sites, especially those that were also part of the flourishing urbanism of the later third millennium B.C. (fig. 3.9). The closest parallels appear to be with Tell Mozan (Buccellati and Kelly-Buccellati 1999) and Kazane Höyük (Wattenmaker 1997), where later third-millennium lower towns grew up around older high mounds. Hamoukar is also broadly similar to Tell Leilan (Weiss 1983), Tell al-Hawa (Ball, Tucker, and Wilkinson 1989), and Tell Khoshi (Kepinski-Lecomte 2001), although their morphologies differ due to circumvallation and partial resettlement in the early second millennium B.C., features that are not present at Hamoukar.

3.2.2. MODERN SETTLEMENT ON HAMOUKAR

The village at Hamoukar (now called al-Hurriya) must be discussed not only because it is the largest settlement of the present settlement pattern of the region (see Section 6.11), but also because it presented a major challenge to the collection of the surface units and their interpretation. It consists of some 800 persons living in low-density house compounds over an approximate area of 40 ha. It is difficult to determine when this settlement originated. At the turn of the nineteenth century, the area between Nisibin/Qamishli and Tell Leilan was lightly settled by Kurdish tribal groups (von Oppenheim 1900: 139–44; see also Section 2.2 above); Hamoukar's Kurdish name suggests it was at least known to these groups.[3] However, these Kurdish villages were in the midst of the summer pasturelands of the Arab Shammar tribal confederacy, to whom they paid a protection tax (*khuwa*) (Montagne 1932: 61). Today, the villagers of al-Hurriya are almost all Shammar Arabs and former dependents, so the village must have appeared sometime after the establishment of French control over the basin in 1926 (Montagne 1932: 55; Tachjian 2004: 322–25), and probably only shortly before the time of full agricultural colonization around 1954. The French 1:200,000 series Qamichlîyé-Sinjār map sheet (surveyed in 1936) labels Hamoukar as a mound but does not indicate contemporary settlement or tracks (see fig. 4.5). Van Liere's plan, based on mid-1950s aerial photographs, does not indicate any modern settlement (fig. 3.5; Van Liere 1963: fig. 3b).

By the time of the earliest CORONA mission, in May 1965, the site could be reached via modern tracks and the high mound and lower town appear to be settled in some form. In the photographs from this and most other CORONA missions, resolution and focus are not sufficient to identify individual structures, with the exception of Mission 1105 from 14 November 1968. In this scene, a handful of permanent structures can be recognized in a very dispersed pattern (fig. 3.10A; see also fig. 5.20). A pair of isolated structures existed on the high mound and low-density houses stretched across the western lower town and directly south of the high mound. By 2005, occupational density had increased in the central part of the lower town and new structures had appeared along the northeastern and eastern edges of the lower town (fig. 3.10B). The land on the lower town given over to agriculture remained unchanged between 1968 and 2005. When faced with population growth, the villagers responded by increasing density, rather than by expanding the size of the settlement.

[3] In Kurdish, Hamoukar means "mound of Hamo." It is thus redundant to include the Arabic "Tell" before the name since it already includes the Kurdish element *kar*/*gir*. The full name Tell Hamoukar is retained here on occasion because of previous usage, and because it reflects well the multiethnic character of the settlement and the Upper Khabur region in general.

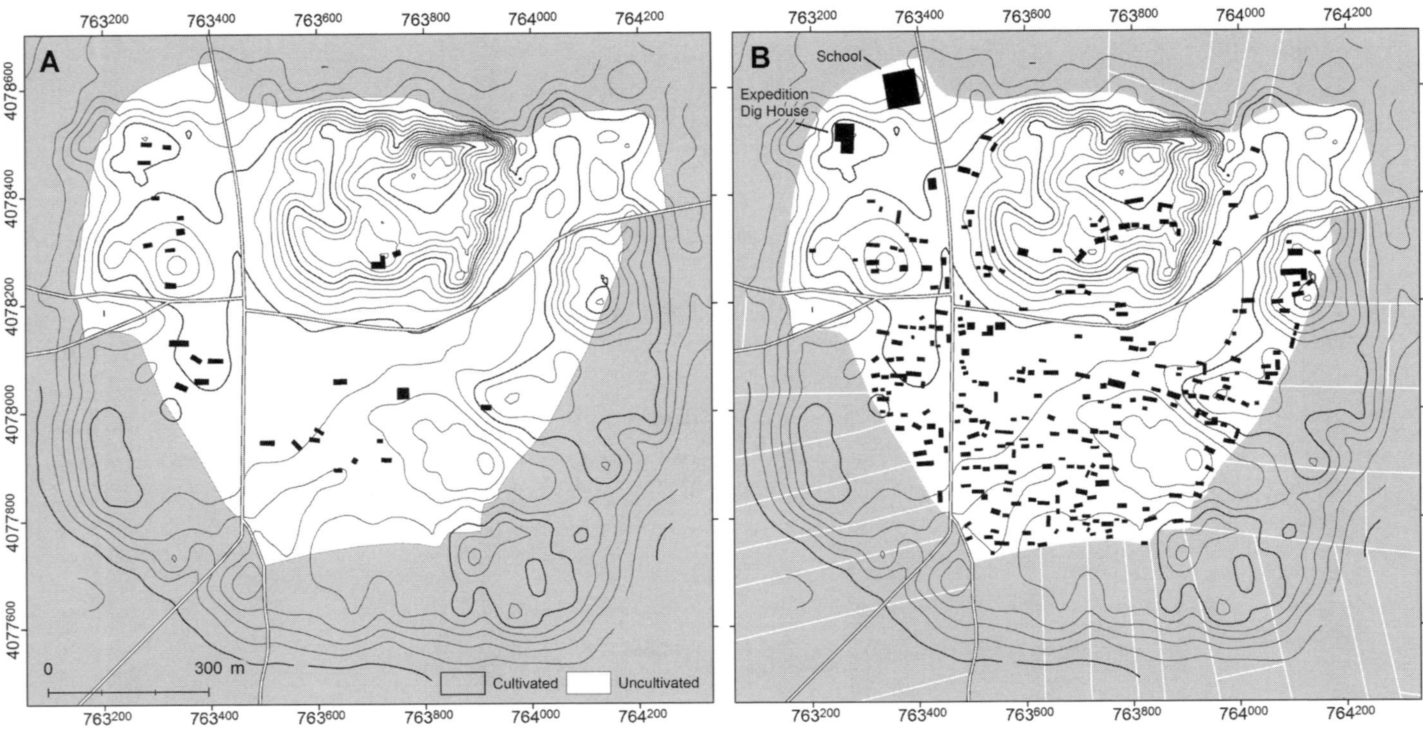

Figure 3.10. Growth of al-Hurriya village at Hamoukar in the later twentieth century. (*A*) Permanent structures in 1968 (from CORONA 1105); (*B*) Permanent structures circa 2005 (from SPOT)

3.2.3. CURRENT LAND USE AND SURFACE CONDITIONS

At Hamoukar and throughout the Upper Khabur basin, modern settlement and land use has impacted the archaeological record. Modern villages cling to the southern slopes of tell sites and cover over low-mounded sites, making collection difficult or impossible. The mechanized disc plowing of grain fields has the ability to shift settlement debris across the surface of a site and can obscure field scatters. As Hassake province has become more integrated into the global economy, former wheat fields have been converted into irrigated cotton fields, which sometimes necessitates the dramatic alteration of the slope of a field in order to facilitate proper gravity flow. Irrigation often renders field scatters inaccessible and in some cases has resulted in the obliteration of hollow ways and even entire sites. Construction of roads and railways in the area has also resulted in the leveling of sites. Built roads of gravel and asphalt are particularly destructive to hollow ways. Because modern villages tend to be on or adjacent to tells, the modern roads connecting these villages obscure the ancient tracks connecting the tells. These issues are by no means unique to the Upper Khabur basin, and indeed large-scale modification of the landscape as part of state-sponsored agricultural products has been going on for several millennia (Hole 1980: 22–23). The ways in which modern settlement impacts the surviving remains of ancient settlement must be borne in mind when interpreting survey data.

All these transformative processes have been active at Hamoukar since its resettlement around the middle of the twentieth century. The surface collection recognized three general classes of land use on the mound at Hamoukar:

- Bare tell surface. These areas of the site are essentially unused space and remain relatively undisturbed. They are, however, kept devegetated by village herd grazing and occasional irregular trampling via animal, foot, and wheeled traffic. In general, they tend to have very high visibility of surface artifacts and a relatively high proportion of small sherds, often smaller than the THS's collection threshold, although in areas of greater slope they are subjected to sheet erosion, which reveals larger sherds. Bare tell surfaces characterize much of the high mound and the fringes of the lower town along its northern and northwestern edges.

- Disturbed surface. These areas are found in close proximity to the houses of the modern village and are highly variable in surface condition and artifact density. In some areas, small-scale excavation by villagers has produced undulating surfaces characterized by loose soil, various forms of modern debris (organic household waste, glass and metal debris, and construction materials), and occasionally assemblages of large sherds with fresh breaks. In other areas, village women have swept surfaces and tamped them down with water, resulting in a compact surface devoid of any cultural material, ancient or modern. Disturbed surfaces cluster around village houses on the southern edge of the high mound and across the lower town, particularly in the areas west and northeast of the enclosed depression. Areas with routine and systematic trampling (i.e., tracks) were also classified as disturbed surfaces. When possible, these areas were avoided for collection unit placement.

- Cultivated fields. Large tracts of Hamoukar's lower town are presently under cultivation. These fields extend across the southwestern, southern, and southeastern areas. At the time of collection (autumn 1999) none were under crops. The nature of their surface assemblages varied depending on their position in the agricultural rotation and could be subdivided into:
    - Fallow land. These fields had lain undisturbed for at least the past agricultural season (1998–1999). Fallow fields on the lower town presented the most ideal collecting conditions: village herds had removed almost all vegetation and pulverized clumps of earth into a smooth surface, leaving large and small sherds highly visible.
    - Plowed land. These fields had been given a plowing in advance of seeding, to occur later in the fall. Plowing occasionally brings to the surface larger and generally more diagnostic sherds, but tends to obscure smaller or finer forms.

The different visibility conditions and sherd assemblages characteristic of these surface classes must be borne in mind when interpreting the distribution of surface materials. The very small sherds characteristic of bare tell surfaces were the least likely to be diagnostic; therefore, low numbers of diagnostic sherds for any given period from such a surface may indicate only a chronologically unhelpful collection, rather than a lack of past occupation of that space. Collections from disturbed areas are often similarly small and nondiagnostic, but are occasionally very abundant, especially when they represent the sweepings from a village house courtyard. These latter collections are the most likely to be removed from their original place of deposition, however, and therefore collections from disturbed areas are considered to have the highest potential spatial error. Collections from cultivated surfaces have also been subjected to lateral movements, in this case via repeated plowing. However, several controlled archaeological experiments have demonstrated that such movement is relatively modest (e.g., Ammerman 1985; Rick 1976). Indeed, collections from agricultural fields, both plowed and fallow, are the most likely to be spatially connected to their point of initial deposition.

3.3. SURFACE COLLECTION AT HAMOUKAR

Given the size and topography of Hamoukar itself, examining every square meter of its surface would have been prohibitively time consuming in both collection and ceramic processing, so it was decided to sample the site according to a non-probabilistic systematic scheme. When faced with similar sites of similar scale, archaeologists have applied similar strategies to other large urban centers such as the Mesoamerican cities of Sayil (Smyth 1998) and Calixtlahuaca (Smith et al. 2007), and the Greek *polis* of Phlius (Alcock 1991).

3.3.1. THE SYSTEMATIC SAMPLING STRATEGY

Probabilistic sampling at the level of the site has been attempted in Near Eastern archaeology, most notably in the Keban Reservoir Survey (Whallon 1979, 1983) and elsewhere in southeastern Turkey (Redman and Watson 1970), and within the Upper Khabur basin at Tell Mozan (Thompson-Miragliuolo 1988). The strength of a random probabilistic approach is that it enables a statistically valid estimation of the total population; its primary drawback is that it may result in uneven coverage. Neither Whallon nor Thompson-Miragliuolo ultimately used their probabilistic samples to estimate the full sherd population of their sites. Whallon concluded that a simple non-probabilistic systematic sampling method would be ideal, since archaeologists are more interested in mapping the spatial distribution of sherds than in estimating their total numbers on the surface (1979: 291).

Following Whallon's conclusions, the surface collection at Hamoukar aimed for spatially even coverage via a non-probabilistic systematic approach. A 100 m grid was imposed on the 105 ha mounded area of the site, and one 100 sq. m sample unit was collected from as close to the center of each as was possible under local access and visibility conditions (fig. 3.11). The 110 units thus represent just over a 1 percent sample of the total mounded area. At the time this strategy was devised, it was thought that even the smallest identifiable occupations would be contiguous and about 1 ha in size; subsequently, based on observations in the broader survey of the Hamoukar region and at the early urban center at Tell Brak (Ur, Karsgaard, and Oates 2007), it has become clear that settlement areas can be dispersed, of variable density, or both. The relatively low-intensity collection at Hamoukar was well suited to identifying areas of continuous high-density settlement, but it is possible that this strategy would have missed small or patchy areas of settlement.

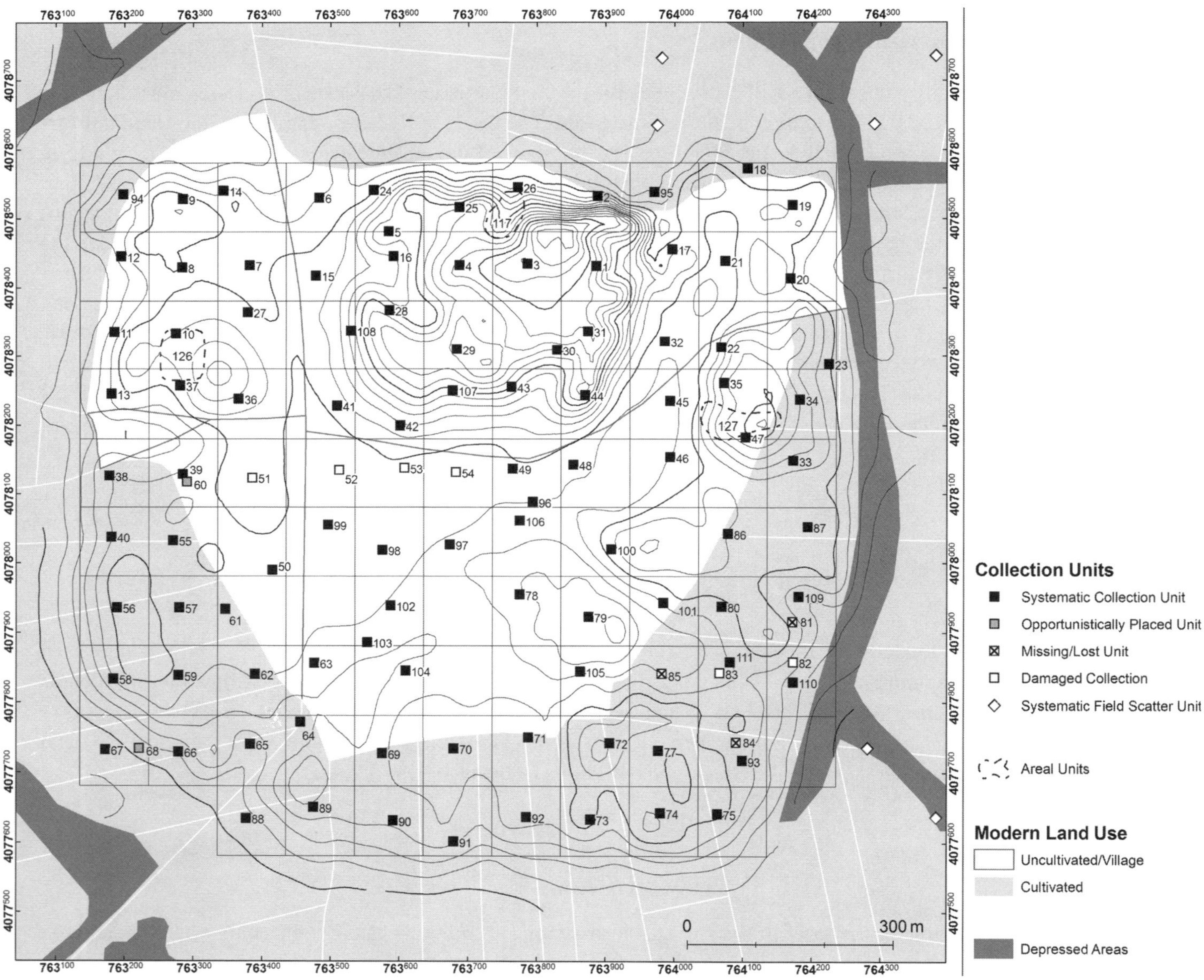

Figure 3.11. Systematic, opportunistic, and areal collection units at Hamoukar

As a check on this sampling strategy, supplementary areal collections were subsequently made in three places. Collection units 117, 126, and 127, each between 0.3 and 0.5 ha, were placed to confirm unexpected results from systematic sampling.

3.3.2. PLACEMENT OF COLLECTION UNITS

Although the excavation's topographic survey created an arbitrary metric site grid for positioning excavation trenches, the surface collection used the Universal Transverse Mercator (UTM) projection grid (Zone 37 north) to locate each sample unit by means of handheld GPS receivers. The UTM grid has several benefits over an arbitrary grid or the Geographic Coordinate System (latitude and longitude). It is almost infinitely extensible without the need to resort to negative coordinates. Those coordinates are given in meters north and east, rather than degrees, minutes, and seconds, which makes them more intuitive for measuring distance and area. Finally, a GPS receiver can be used to navigate to a position very easily with a single operator. Positioning via tape and compass is not feasible on a site as large as Hamoukar. Theodolite positioning is time consuming and difficult, given the presence of village houses that block lines of sight and require multiple survey stations.

A GPS receiver is, however, inherently less accurate. At the time of the Hamoukar surface collection (September/October 1999), the U.S. Department of Defense systematically degraded the accuracy of the GPS satellite network for all non-military applications. In order to minimize the deliberate distortion, all positions were calculated by taking continuous readings over a period of time and then averaging the northing and easting coordinates. The error was thus reduced, but still was approximately 20–30 m, based on comparing these positions with ortho-rectified SPOT images. After this policy, called "Selective Availability," was removed on 1 May 2000, the positioning error in the basin was reduced to 5–10 m. Given the spatially inexact nature of surface assemblages, both pre- and post-Selective Availability positioning errors were considered to be acceptable.

A preliminary map of intended collection unit locations was created by placing a 100 m grid over the site in alignment with the edges of the lower town. This operation was simplified by the fact that Hamoukar is almost a perfect kilometer square with sides aligned with the cardinal directions. The centerpoint of the grid square at the top of the high mound was calculated (763885 m E, 4078431 m N, the position of Collection Unit 1) and the locations of the rest of the collection units were determined by intervals of 100 m on the X and Y axes from this point; the unit to its north was to be located 763885 m E, 4078531 m N, and so forth. A Garmin GPS 48 model handheld GPS receiver was used to navigate to these positions.

In many cases, collection at the intended position was not possible because of recent surface disturbance. On several occasions, the center of a grid square fell within an animal pen or a house courtyard; collection in such household contexts was determined to be unnecessarily intrusive. In any case, walled courtyards and outdoor activity areas associated with household compounds are carefully maintained, to the great detriment of the surface assemblage. Most surfaces are regularly swept clean of all debris, modern and ancient. As a result, several hectares of the site in the densest part of the modern village could not be collected. In other instances, sample units fell on paved or gravel tracks. On a few occasions, intended sample units fell on an area of heavily trampled tell surface on which the surface sherds had been ground into small and undiagnostic fragments. In these circumstances, the position of the unit was adjusted to the closest location with a reasonable assemblage. In addition, three opportunistic collections were made (Units 50, 60, and 68) at positions where recent digging or plowing had turned up chronologically significant assemblages outside of the systematic grid. This method could therefore be accused of lacking methodological rigor, but it was decided that a set of somewhat opportunistically located, yet productive, sample units would be of greater utility in documenting the occupational history of the site than a rigidly systematic set of samples, some of which may contain too few sherds to be of analytical use (see also Gallant 1986: 406).

Once the intended location (or a suitable nearby alternative) was located, its coordinates were recorded and then fixed as the northwestern corner of the collection unit. The 10 × 10 m unit was laid out via metric tape and walked in five passes, under the assumption that sherds would be visible at 1 m on each side of the line of the pass. Identical methods were used for off-site field scatter collection (see Section 5.2.1 and fig. 5.9). Artifacts collected were not limited to the standard diagnostic forms (rims, bases, handles, decorated sherds, etc.); all body sherds larger than 1 cm were collected, as well as lithics, kiln slag and ceramic wasters, and basalt fragments.

Three supplementary opportunistic collections were made in areas where the systematic sampling strategy had produced ambiguous or unexpected results (see fig. 3.11). These units were areal and intended to produce a large number of diagnostics; since collection was opportunistic, they are not used in analyses of surface density. Unit 117 was placed in a gully roughly 50 m west of the step trench in Area A, with the goal of testing for several periods found in the excavations but not in the systematic surface collections nearby. Unit 126 was placed on a relatively undisturbed area amid village houses near the western edge of the lower town, on the northwestern slope of a localized elevation. It was intended to confirm the results of the systematic collection, which found no evidence for additional periods of occupation that might explain the localized mounding. Finally, Unit 127 was placed on the western slope of the prominent mound on the eastern edge of the lower town. Systematic collection in this area had revealed body sherds and small diagnostic fragments of Seleucid pottery; Unit 127 was intended to collect larger diagnostics for publication purposes.

3.4. ANALYSIS

On the mound at Hamoukar, the THS collected 15,901 artifacts from 110 collection units. Several collections were discarded after being tampered with (either by dogs or small children) and had to be re-collected; the original units have not been used in determining sherd densities, although their diagnostics generally provided confirmation to the results of the systematic units. The total area of all samples was 11,000 sq. m, slightly more than 1 percent of the site. Of the 15,169 potsherds, 1,883 (12.4%) were diagnostic; of these, 1,191 were typeable with reference to the survey typology (see *Appendix B*). Thus 7.9 percent of all sherds, and 63.3 percent of all diagnostic sherds, ultimately proved to be chronologically useful.

3.4.1. DISTRIBUTION AND RELIABILITY OF THE SURFACE ASSEMBLAGE

From the surface of Hamoukar proper, the collection units had a mean average of 151 sherds per 100 sq. m, from a low of 21 sherds per 100 sq. m up to 436 sherds per 100 sq. m (fig. 3.12). Areas of low sherd density (<100 sherds/100 sq. m) occur south of the high mound on disturbed surfaces within the modern village, where courtyards and other exterior spaces were heavily trampled and swept clean of all debris, including ancient pottery. In other areas, intermediate sherd density (101–150 sherds/100 sq. m) could be attributed to extreme trampling that broke up surface sherds into fragments smaller than the collection minimum; this was particularly true for a large and flat area at the northwestern corner of the lower town.

Areas of high sherd density (>150 sherds/100 sq. m) include the high mound, the northeastern corner of the lower town, and points along the western edge of the lower town. In the case of the high mound, the high sherd density found along its southern slopes (especially Units 30, 44, 49, 107, and 108) can be explained with reference to the general principles of tell erosion in the Near East (see Section 3.2.1). Along the western edge of the lower town, and to a lesser extent elsewhere along the site edge, elevated sherd densities are probably due to a combination of erosion and modern plowing; the large amount of sherds with fresh breaks lends support to the latter cause. The high density of the northeastern lower town also can be related to its recent history: this area featured a recently abandoned segment of the modern village that was no longer maintaining the exterior spaces as was the rest of the village.

3.4.2. DISTRIBUTION OF FABRIC TYPES

Given the disagreement among previous visitors with regard to the date of Hamoukar's urban expansion (fourth millennium or later third millennium B.C.) and the unresolved nature of its fourth-millennium settlement (purely indigenous, exclusively southern Uruk, or both), the surface collection was especially concerned to differentiate between fourth- and third-millennium assemblages and also to distinguish between local and intrusive components of the fourth-millennium assemblage. An initial concern was that diagnostics of the local Late Chalcolithic assemblage (Period 5b) would be systematically underrepresented. Non-finewares of this time are heavily chaff tempered and

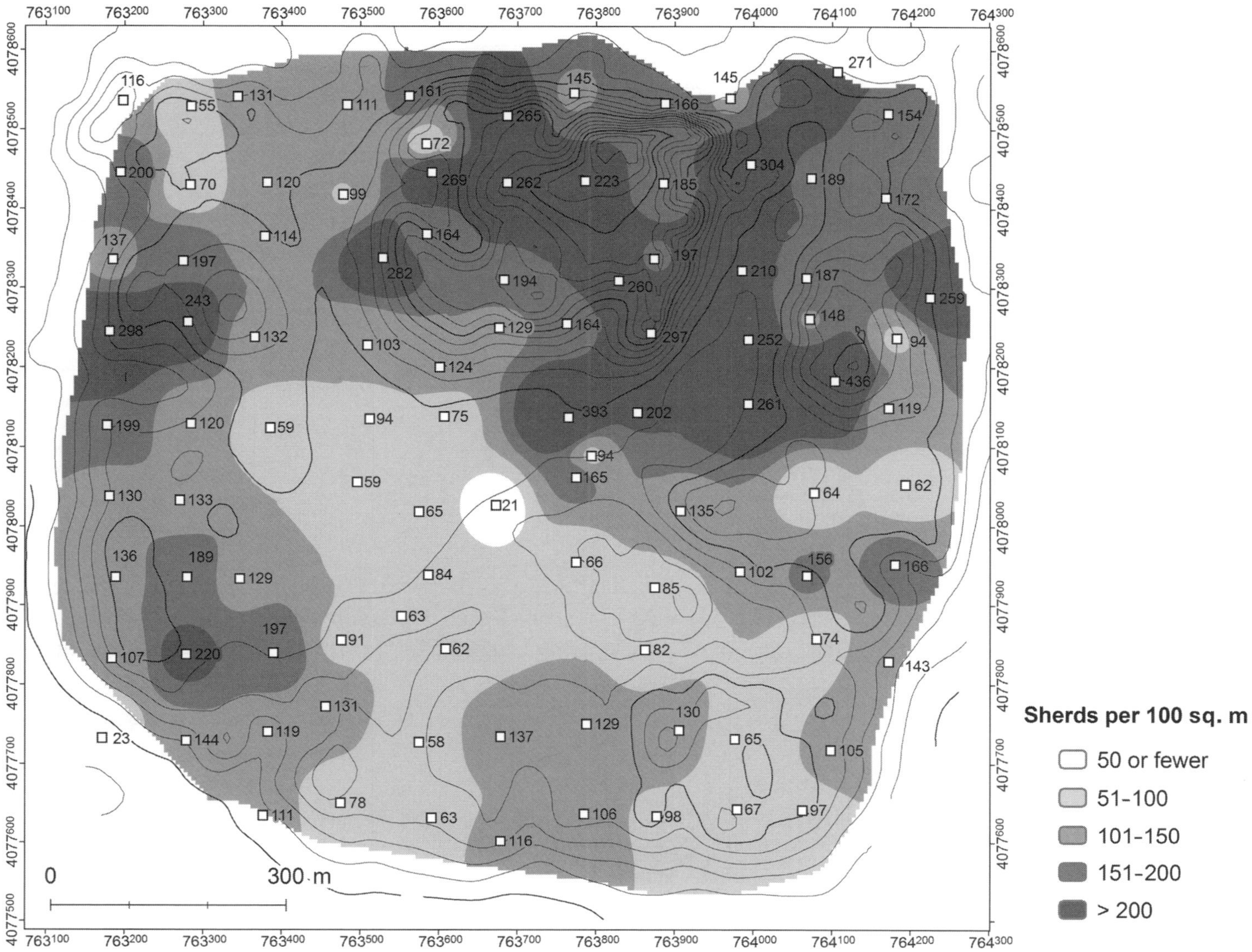

Figure 3.12. Density of surface ceramics at Hamoukar. Point values are the total number of collected sherds from 100 sq. m collection units

poorly fired (see Section B.2.5) and are therefore more likely to erode into non-diagnostic lumps when left exposed or repeatedly plowed over on the surface. If this proved to be the case, a diagnostics-only collection would systematically underrepresent fourth-millennium ceramic densities and thus underestimate the scale of fourth-millennium Hamoukar.

Ultimately, Period 5b diagnostics proved to be robust enough to be recognizable in surface assemblages, at Hamoukar and within the broader THS region. Nonetheless, the distribution and density of body sherds provides a useful confirmation of the validity of densities of diagnostic types from the collection units. Toward this end, all systematically collected sherds from Hamoukar's surface were classified into one of nine general fabric groups (table 3.1). These groups are admittedly coarse, designed to be useful under macroscopic visual inspection and without the need to make fresh breaks. This system concentrates on surface color and characteristics and the most visible aspects of temper and firing.

The assemblage most easily distinguished is that of the fourth millennium (Period 5b), because the morphological and technological characteristics of the non-finewares are not to be found in any other period of occupation at Hamoukar. These red-brown surface, reduced core, coarse chaff-tempered sherds (Fabric F5) are easily distinguished from the evenly fired buff to green sherds of the third millennium B.C. (Fabric F3), the other major settlement period (fig. 3.13). The system works imperfectly for other periods. For example, fourth-millennium finewares

Table 3.1. Fabric classification used in the systematic surface collection of Hamoukar

Type	*Fabric Description*	*Possible Date(s)*
F1	Small, worn, and unclassifiable	—
F2	Green to greenish yellow fineware with wheel striations	Periods 6–7
F3	Green to greenish yellow common ware with fine chaff and sand temper	Periods 6–7
F4	Red to brown, black core cooking ware with abundant grit temper	—
F5	Orange to red surfaces with thick reduced core and frequent coarse chaff temper	Period 5b
F6	Orange to yellow well-fired fabric with abundant sand temper	Period 5a, 13
F7	Yellow to buff with pink core, chaff temper	Periods 5b, 11
F8	Yellow to orange fineware, often slipped	Period 5b
F9	Red to orange, heavily grit-tempered fabric	Period 13

(Fabric F8) can only be distinguished from third-millennium finewares (Fabric F2) by their general lack of wheel striations, and both the southern Uruk (Period 5a) and Hellenistic (Period 13) assemblages are heavily sand and grit tempered (Fabric F6). It is also likely that late Sasanian–Early Islamic body sherds were classified in the third-millennium fabric classification.

3.4.3. DISTRIBUTION OF PRODUCTION ACTIVITIES

One of the most attractive aspects of a holistic approach is the possibility of demarcating the internal spatial organization of activities within the city; indeed, in collections of single-period sites, it may be the primary research objective (see especially Stone and Zimansky 2004). There are several reasons why the Hamoukar surface collection could only make this attempt in a very general sense. Hamoukar has not been subjected to the intensive wind deflation that has left activity-related artifacts densely concentrated on the surface; it is argued above that the lateral movement from plowing is limited, but it is still substantial enough to disperse artifacts to the extent that they do not concentrate enough for ancient activities to be apparent. Even if the surface assemblage was well suited for identifying activities, the necessary intensity of collection was unfeasible due to the limited time and labor resources of the Hamoukar surface collection. It is possible to plot the distribution of a few production-related artifact types across the surface of the site, but only at a very coarse level that might be able to identify the relative frequency of certain activities within broad zones of the site, but cannot resolve individual workshops or *suq*-like concentrations, as was possible at Abu Duwari (Stone and Zimansky 2004: 340–72).

The distribution of lithics (fig. 3.14) appears to be unrelated to either ancient patterns of behavior or subsequent transformations. A slightly elevated density was found on parts of the high mound but also on slight prominences on the eastern and western lower towns. This is particularly odd, since the former is an area of Hellenistic settlement (Period 13). The wide but low-density distribution of lithics (almost all production debris) is not surprising, given that lithic technology remained in use up to the end of the third millennium (see, e.g., Underbjerg 2003; Rainville 2003) and perhaps even later. There also appear to be no significant differences in the patterning of obsidian versus chert or flint.

The distribution of ceramic processing debris (kiln slag and wasters) occurs across the entire site, again at a low density (fig. 3.15). Slag was much more common than overfired sherds. The wasters recovered in systematic collection could never be identified by type. A few localized areas of dense kiln slag were found on the high mound and on the interior parts of the lower town, but substantial concentrations clustered along the eastern and western edges of the site. This is unsurprising, given that pottery firing is a fuel-intensive craft that produces ash and smoke. Although not detected by the systematic collection, informal observations in the area immediately southeast of the high mound found many fragments of stacked kiln wasters. This prominence probably supported specialized mass production of small bowls at the end of the third millennium, as is known from contemporary neighbors such as Tell Leilan (Senior and Weiss 1992; Stein and Blackman 1993).

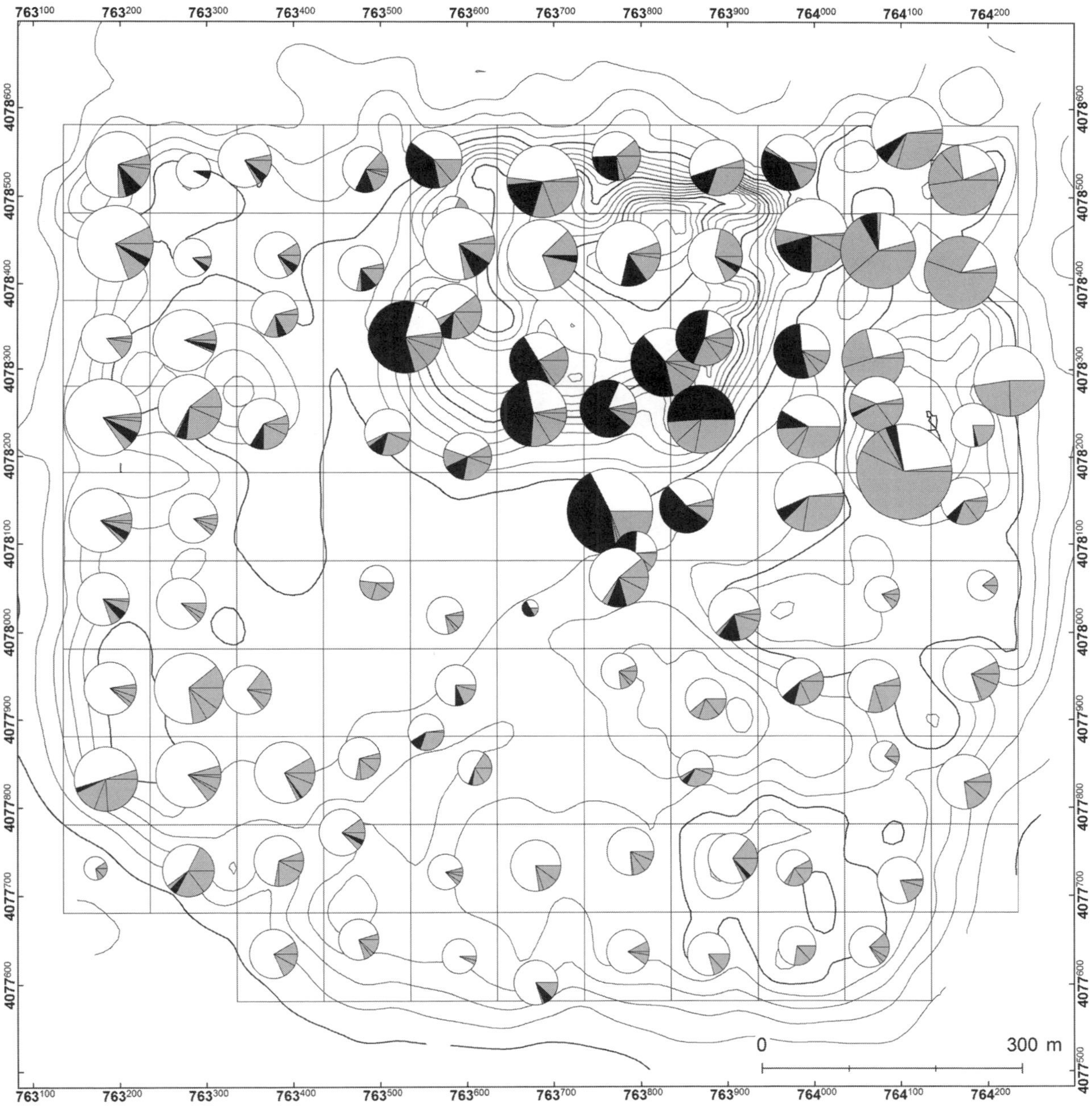

Figure 3.13. Distribution of ceramic fabric classes at Hamoukar. Period 5b coarse ware (F5) in black; Period 7 common ware (F3) in white; all other fabric classes in gray. For total numbers of sherds, see figure 3.12

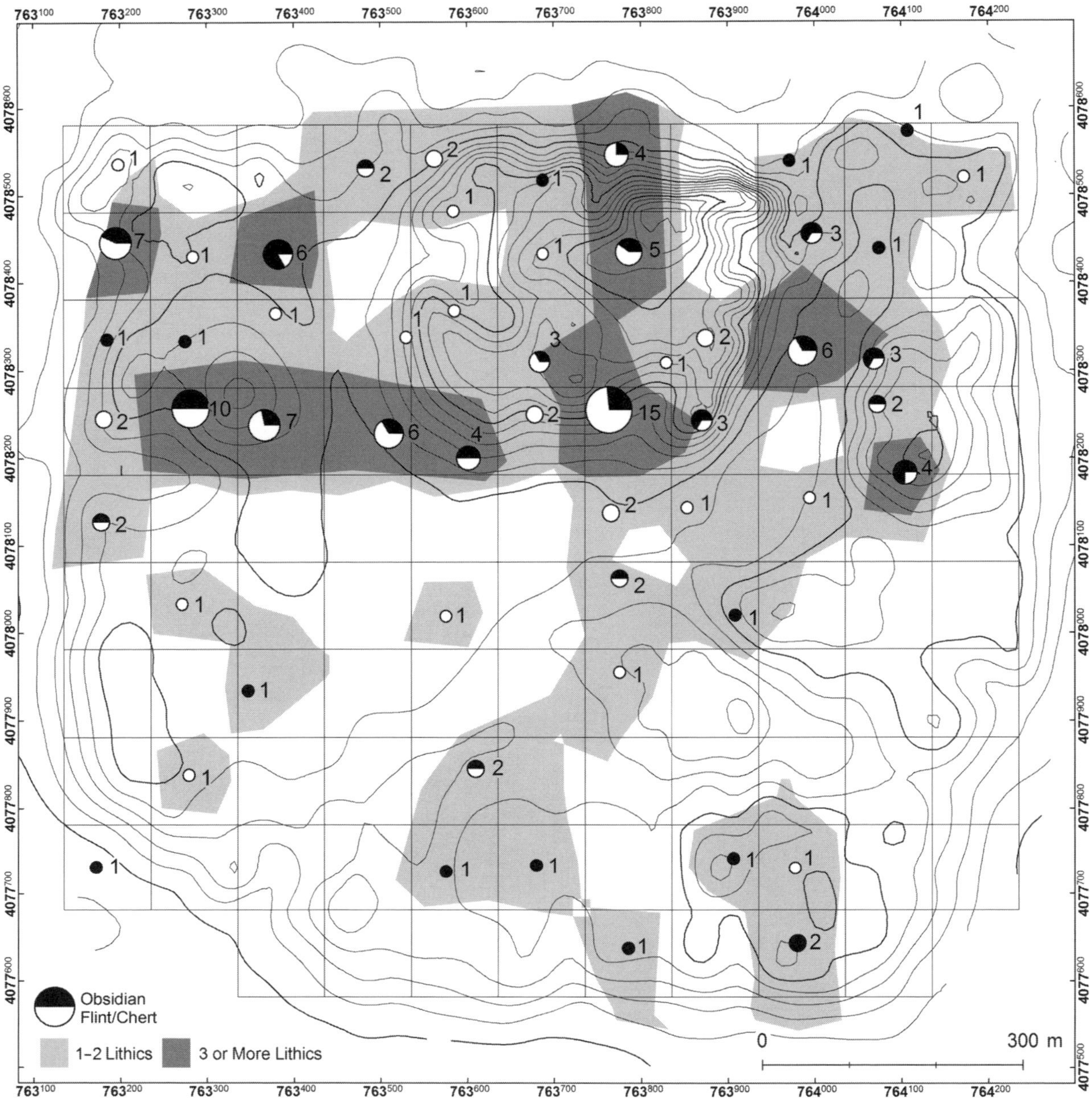

Figure 3.14. Distribution of lithic artifacts at Hamoukar. Point values are the total number of lithics from 100 sq. m collection units

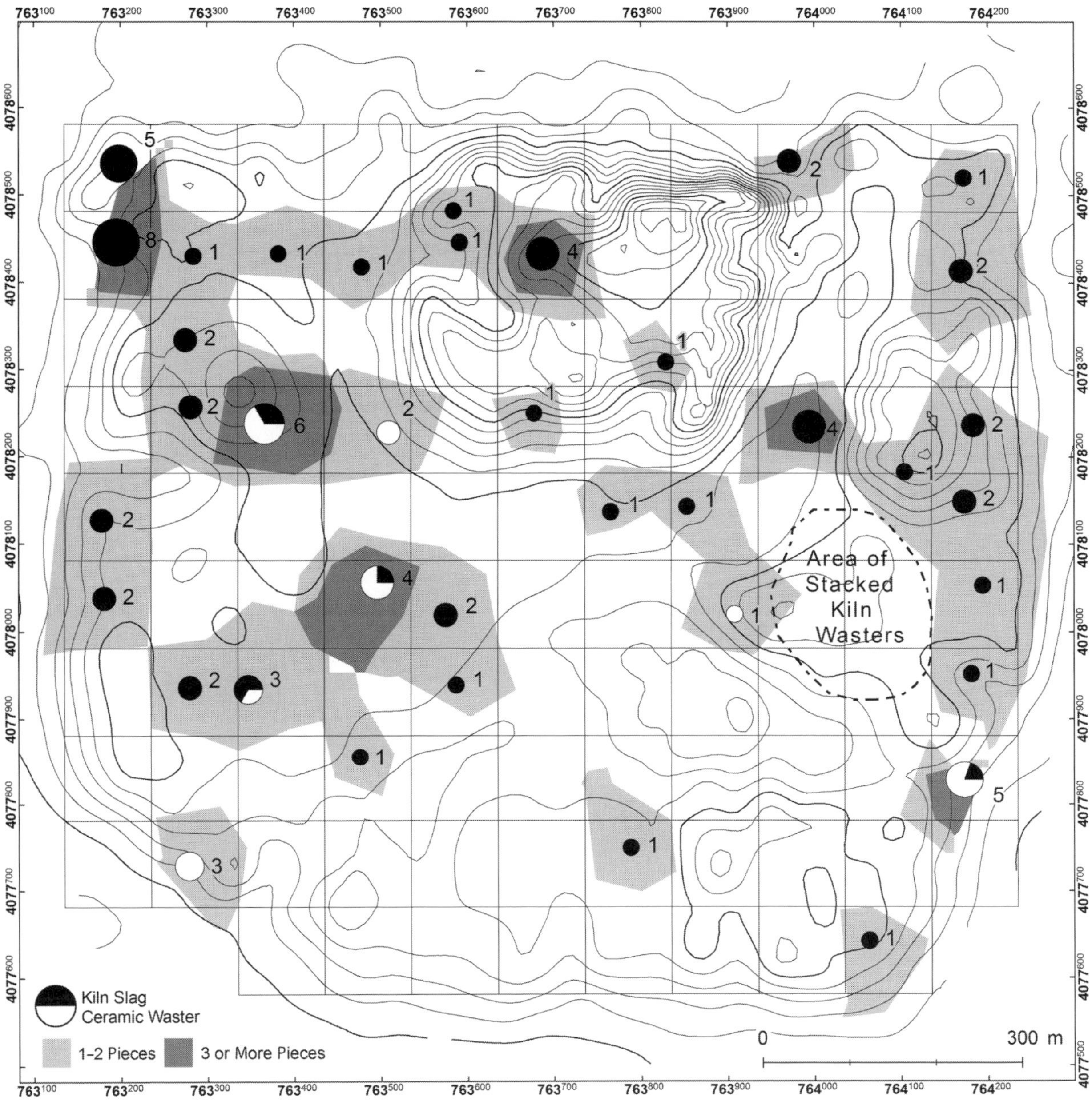

Figure 3.15. Distribution of ceramic manufacturing debris at Hamoukar. Point values are the total number of artifacts from 100 sq. m collection units

CHAPTER 4

THS FIELD METHODOLOGY 2: THE TELL HAMOUKAR SURVEY

4.1. INTRODUCTION

As part of the Hamoukar Expedition's holistic approach, the results of excavation and surface collection on Hamoukar itself were integrated with a still larger regional scale. Toward this end, the Expedition included a field survey component as part of its initial research design. In designing our methodology, we attempted to place the THS within the full-coverage tradition of Near Eastern survey while including intensity and sampling methods more typical of Mediterranean and New World survey. The properties or variables of the survey strongly affect the nature of the results and the interpretations that can be made of them (Banning 2002; Plog, Plog, and Wait 1978; Schiffer, Sullivan, and Klinger 1978). After contextualizing the THS within the history of archaeological survey in the Upper Khabur basin, these variables will be reviewed and placed within the methodological framework of the THS.

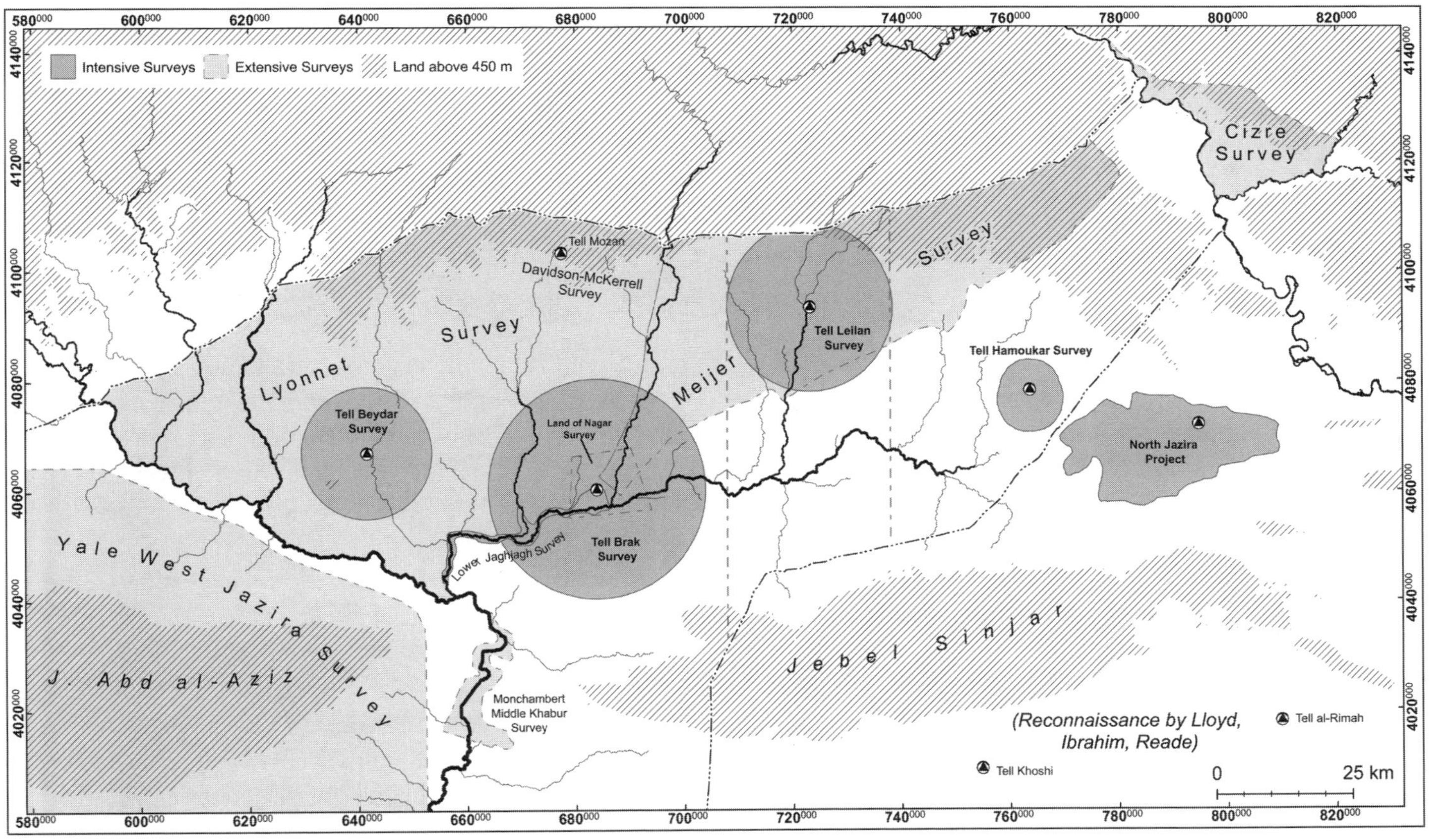

Figure 4.1. Intensive and extensive surveys in the Upper Khabur basin and adjacent areas

4.1.1. PREVIOUS SURVEY IN NORTHERN MESOPOTAMIA

The evolution of landscape studies in northern Mesopotamia has proceeded in a very different manner than in southern Mesopotamia (reviewed in Wilkinson 2000b). In the south, Adams' extensive initial projects (1965, 1981; Adams and Nissen 1972) were followed by more geographically focused surveys (Gibson 1972; Wright 1981) and only recently by intensive projects at the microregional (Wilkinson 1990a) or site (Stone and Zimansky 2004) level. Adams' grand syntheses, based on low-intensity observation of a broad geographic region, could then be tested against more intensive observations in smaller areas.

Surveys in northern Mesopotamia (fig. 4.1) have proceeded in a far less coordinated manner. Aside from anecdotal observations by early visitors such as von Oppenheim and Mallowan, initial survey in the region was primarily aerial: Poidebard's survey of the Roman eastern frontier in the late 1920s (Poidebard 1934; Castel 2000), and Van Liere's more systematic observations of sites and road networks (1961–62, 1963; Van Liere and Lauffray 1954–55). These investigations included only opportunistic ground visits. Modern survey in the region began with Fielden's Lower Jaghjagh Survey (1981) and Meijer's survey of the basin east of the Jaghjagh (1986), which included a visit to Hamoukar. In adjacent areas in northern Iraq and southeastern Turkey, extensive surveys were undertaken by Reade (1968: 235–37), Ibrahim (1986), and Algaze and colleagues (Algaze et al. 1991; Parker 2001).

Subsequent survey in the basin has been mostly intensive and focused on the hinterlands of excavated sites: the surveys around Tell Leilan (Weiss 1986; Stein and Wattenmaker 2003; Ristvet 2005), Tell Beydar (Wilkinson 2000a, 2002b; Ur and Wilkinson 2008), Hamoukar (Ur 2002a, 2002b, 2003, 2004–05), Tell Brak (Eidem and Warburton 1996; Oates 2005; Ur, Karsgaard, and Oates 2007; Wright et al. 2006–07), and Tell al-Hawa (Wilkinson and Tucker 1995). At the same time, extensive survey has continued in the western part of the basin (Lyonnet 1996a, 2000) and the Jebel Abd al-Aziz region (Hole 2002–03; Kouchoukos 1998).

Thus the development of settlement and landscape studies in northern Mesopotamia, and the Upper Khabur basin in particular, has proceeded in the opposite manner as in southern Iraq: a series of mostly site-centric small surveys, undertaken independently with different levels of intensity and often employing divergent methodologies and ceramic indicators.

4.1.2. INTENSITY OF SURVEY

The THS differs from previous surveys in northern Mesopotamia most strongly in its intensity. Survey intensity can be understood as the relative amount of effort expended on a unit of space (Sumner 1990: 93; Plog, Plog, and Wait 1978) and is generally inversely proportional to the size of the survey area. The earliest surveys in the Near East covered vast areas very rapidly, with a heavy reliance on aerial photography (see Sumner 1990: 87–91 for an overview). Such low-intensity methodologies allow a large area to be surveyed because less energy is expended on each square unit. The larger component (sites of greater size) of entire settlement systems can be recovered relatively quickly; however, the disadvantage to a low-intensity approach is that the surveyor is much more likely to miss sites, particularly smaller ones (Redman 1982: 377–78).

Low-intensity survey will probably locate the larger political and economic centers, but the poorer recovery rates for small sites skews our understanding of settlement hierarchies in periods of social complexity and can dramatically impact reconstructions of prehistoric periods, when most or all sites were very small. For these reasons, the level of intensity in Near Eastern survey has increased in recent decades, although vehicle-based survey is still the norm. Walking transects are almost universally employed in New World, European, and Mediterranean surveys, where low landscape visibility, low site obtrusiveness, and high landscape attrition through continuous settlement make them a necessity. Perhaps because low visibility and obtrusiveness have been considered to be less of a factor in the Near East, few surveys have adopted pedestrian transects.

Ultimately, the degree of intensity must be dictated by the research goals of the survey itself as well as factors such as visibility and obtrusiveness. The THS intended to recover settlement patterns that would document the formation and decline of urbanism; therefore, the rural settlement component was significant, and a high degree of intensity was necessary. Because of the extremely favorable properties of visibility and obtrusiveness that characterize the basin (see Section 2.3), it was decided that an acceptable level of intensity to recover these smaller sites could be achieved *without* the use of systematic pedestrian transects. In the Hamoukar area in particular, initial reconnaissance aimed at testing the utility of CORONA satellite photographs demonstrated that few if any sites were invisible from the air, under certain ground conditions (see Section 4.3 below). It can therefore be said that all parts of the survey area were fully and intensely studied using remote-sensing data. Using imagery from various CORONA missions, every square kilometer of the THS area was intensively investigated for sites and landscape features prior to fieldwork. During the survey itself, areas with potential sites were more intensively observed than areas which appeared to be devoid of settlement on the images.

Justification for this approach, and further evidence that it was not causing sites to be missed, came from a limited set of walking transects. These were conducted not for the purposes of identifying sites, but for the documentation of off-site "field scatters" of pottery and other artifacts at 200 m intervals (see Section 5.2). Nonetheless, fieldwalkers were instructed to scan the ground on either side of them while moving from one field scatter sample unit to the next, specifically looking for site-level sherd scatters, gray anthropogenic soils, and mounding. The 200 m interval between these transects would be considered very large by the standards of North American and Mediterranean survey (e.g., Mattingly 2000). Given the local conditions of visibility and obtrusiveness discussed above, and the fact that these transects were limited to high visibility fallow fields, it is estimated that fieldwalkers could discern mounding at 100 m to either side, anthropogenic soils at 50 m, and site-level sherd scatters at 5 m. Since almost all sites in the THS exhibited some mounding, it is unlikely that many sites were missed during fieldwalking. Although not intended to recover sites, the field scatter transects served as a useful check on the CORONA-based preliminary site identifications: all sites noted in almost 80 km of transects had already been identified from the satellite photographs.

If one uses recovered sites per square kilometer as an indicator of intensity, the THS appears to be one of the most intensive surveys undertaken in the Mesopotamian world (fig. 4.2; see also Wilkinson, Ur, and Casana 2004). A clear correlation exists between small survey regions and higher sites per square kilometer ratios. In northern Mesopotamia, only the Lower Jaghjagh Survey (Fielden 1981) recovered more sites per square kilometer. However, this survey, and the survey of the Middle Khabur region (Monchambert 1984b, 1984a), were limited to river floodplains and lower terraces.

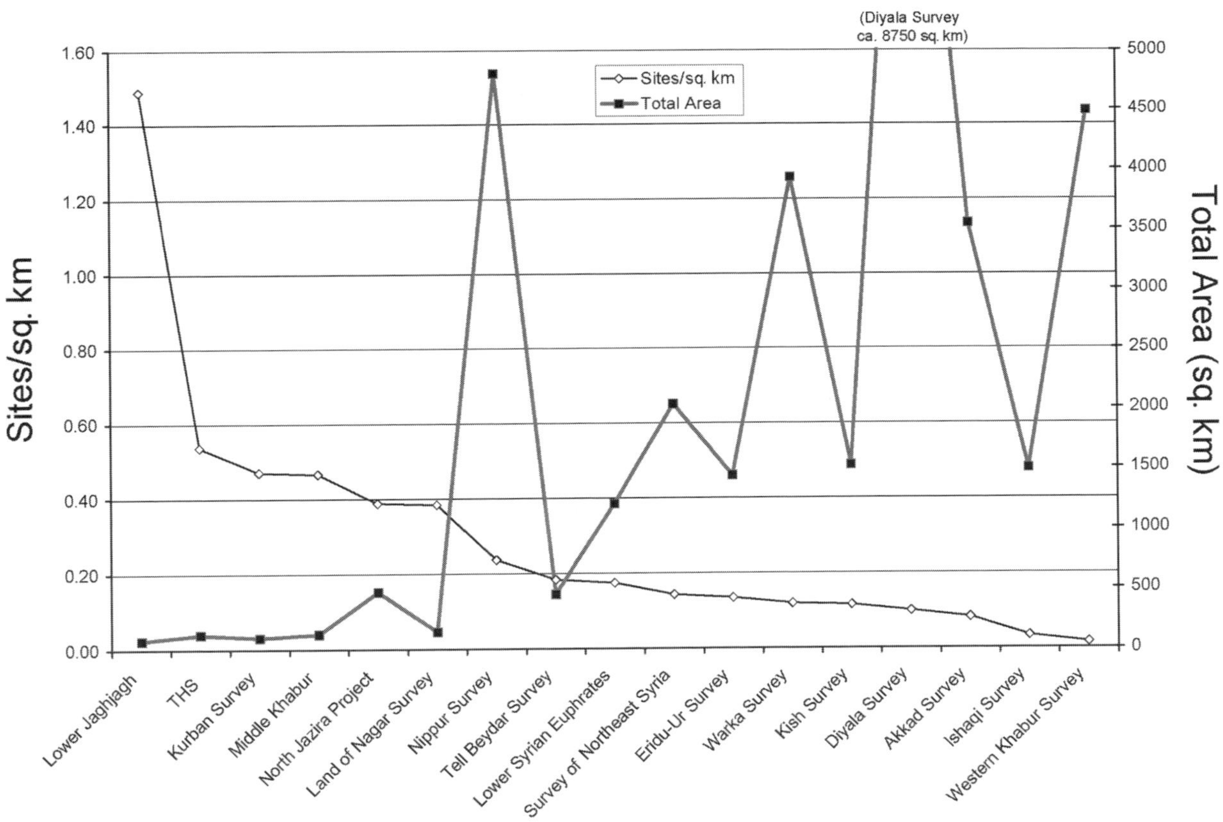

Figure 4.2. Recovery rates for Mesopotamian surveys since the 1950s

The high recovery rate of the THS was enabled by its small survey universe relative to other Mesopotamian surveys, particularly compared to the enormous areas of Adams' surveys in southern Iraq. However, site density is much lower than in most Mediterranean surveys (Cherry 1983: fig. 1; Wilkinson, Ur, and Casana 2004: fig. 14.1). It is unlikely that an increase in intensity — for example, by adopting exclusively field transects at close interval — would have increased the number of sites recovered. The lower site density found in alluvial Mesopotamian regions is a reflection of real differences in settlement continuity and nucleation between Mesopotamia and the Mediterranean world (Wilkinson, Ur, and Casana 2004: 195–96).

4.2. THE HAMOUKAR SURVEY REGION

4.2.1. DEFINITION OF THE SURVEY UNIVERSE

Ideally, the limits of the area to be surveyed will be co-terminous with a geographic, cultural, or political entity. Some processual archaeologists have even suggested that an arbitrarily defined universe is not worth studying (Plog, Plog, and Wait 1978: 384). Such programmatic statements are not helpful in the Middle East, where the definition of survey boundaries can be a sensitive political issue, defined by local and national antiquities officials rather than by foreign research strategies. In any case, it would be nearly impossible to survey properly a unitary cultural or political entity, because these evolve through time: a territory that was an entire kingdom or ethnic zone at one time may be only a small part of a much larger entity at another time. To complicate matters further, such a scale change could occur within a single ceramic period.

As part of the Hamoukar Expedition's agreement with the Directorate General of Antiquities and Monuments in Damascus, the Tell Hamoukar Survey was arbitrarily defined by a 5 km distance from the edge of the excavation concession. Because the concession included the immense "Southern Extension" (THS 25, Khirbat al-Fakhar), the area is egg shaped, totaling 125 sq. km. The survey universe is geographically homogeneous (Wilkinson 2002a) and at no time corresponded to a political or cultural entity in its entirety.

4.2.2. AGRICULTURE AND ARCHAEOLOGICAL DESTRUCTION

At present, the THS region is an entirely agricultural landscape. With the exception of village land, tracks, roads, and adjacent land, every square meter of land is used for agricultural purposes. In any given year some proportion may be held fallow or used for pasture, but this is a temporary situation. The precise time of origin for these circumstances can be fixed to between the French "pacification" of 1926 and the time of the first CORONA missions in the area in May 1965, and probably the decade following the end of the Second World War. Prior to this agricultural colonization, the THS region, and indeed the majority of the Upper Khabur basin, was pastureland dominated by Arab tribes of the Shammar confederation (see Section 2.2).

This extension of agriculture and especially its postwar mechanization has had a substantial impact on the preservation of landscape features. With the exception of the highest mounds, the slopes of which are too steep, almost all sites are presently under agricultural fields. Most sites have probably been reduced in height, since agriculture has removed the steppe vegetation that anchors the soil; sites are now much more susceptible to aeolian deflation and erosion via surface runoff. In only a few cases have entire sites been leveled altogether; these were almost certainly very low and spatially small, if we can extrapolate from CORONA imagery.

Whether via plow or erosion, therefore, the surface assemblages of many sites have been diffused to some extent across the landscape. Based on experimental studies of plowzone movement of artifacts elsewhere (Ammerman 1985; Rick 1976), it is unlikely that such movement has dramatically altered the spatial extent of surface assemblages, but it is important to recognize that these processes have been in effect. What we are mapping is therefore the surface assemblage following some fifty years of intensive mechanized agriculture, in addition to undocumented but similar agricultural processes likely extending back seven or eight millennia.

The transformation by agriculture of the off-site record is far more dramatic, although in different ways for different features. The stripping of natural vegetation and constant tilling of the landscape, and the movement of sediments that results from these activities, have obscured many landscape features with subtle topographic expression. Hollow ways and canals have especially suffered, and now must be mapped primarily from historic CORONA photographs. This churning of the upper soil horizons has, however, maintained the visibility of field scatters by keeping them close to the surface.

4.2.3. PASTORALISM AND LANDSCAPE VISIBILITY

The pastoral component of the modern economy of the area greatly enhances landscape visibility. At present, small herds are maintained by village households year round, and larger herds are trucked into the basin from elsewhere in Syria on a seasonal basis. In both cases, grazing rights are based on contracts with local landowners (Vercueil and Cummins 2003).

Grazing herds benefit landscape visibility in two ways. After the harvest, they remove the remains of cereal crops to reveal the earth beneath. A well-grazed field in the basin will exhibit only stray bits of chaff and a telltale scatter of sheep and goat dung. Just as important, their hooves break up clods of soil which cast shadows and otherwise obscure visibility. In the extreme brightness of summer and autumn daylight in the basin, the high contrast between reflective surface and shadow can impact field scatter recovery, especially in low-density areas.

4.3. APPLICATIONS OF REMOTE-SENSING DATASETS

The full-coverage methodology of the THS relied heavily on remote-sensing datasets to identify and locate potential sites and landscape features.

4.3.1. CORONA SATELLITE PHOTOGRAPHY AND ITS INTERPRETATION

With the declassification of the imagery from the CORONA program (Day, Logsdon, and Latell 1998; McDonald 1997), scholars in dozens of fields gained a valuable research tool. CORONA was the United States' first intelligence satellite program, originally designed to give American military planners an estimate of Soviet nuclear missile capabilities. In thirteen years of operation (1959–1972), it produced over 800,000 images that covered 557 million square miles, the equivalent of the entire land surface of the earth almost ten times over (Day, Logsdon, and Latell 1998: 6). During its existence, the program used an evolving set of cameras. The last two cameras, used on KH-4A and KH-4B programs, had a highest resolution of 9 feet and 6 feet, respectively. Because the CORONA satellites carried film cameras, rather than digital sensors, the film had to be physically returned to earth via parachute, where it was collected in midair by military planes. The photographs from the CORONA program were declassified by executive order on 22 February 1995.

Subsequently, imagery from the higher-resolution KH-7 has also been declassified. This "spotter" satellite provided highly detailed imagery of features of interest first identified by CORONA (Richelson 2003). For the Upper Khabur basin, KH-7 coverage is limited to the area immediately surrounding Qamishli. Photographs from both CORONA and KH-7 programs can now be previewed and ordered via the United States Geological Survey (USGS) Web site.[4] CORONA imagery is particularly valuable for Near Eastern archaeology, and studies utilizing these images are beginning to appear in print (Fowler 2004).

[4] http://EarthExplorer.usgs.gov.

One aspect of CORONA imagery that is frequently mentioned as one if its greatest benefits to archaeology is its age (Philip et al. 2002: 110; Ur 2003). The CORONA program documented the landscape of the late 1960s and early 1970s. In the intervening three decades, human activity has done much to alter this landscape. Towns and villages have expanded, covering over ancient sites; roads have been built; and new crops and plowing methods have damaged sites and landscape features. The CORONA images have preserved many features that have been radically transformed or removed altogether. In the THS area, cultivation in general and the expansion of irrigated cotton fields in particular have resulted in the destruction of the microtopography of many hollow ways and has even obliterated several sites. However, the CORONA images were produced before the expansion of cotton agriculture, so these features and sites can still be mapped. For example, THS 8, a Halaf site, appears in the CORONA images as a very small light spot. When it was visited by the survey team in autumn 2000, it lay in the middle of a large fallow cotton field, which had eradicated its edges. Because the process of making the irrigation furrows had destroyed the mounding of the site, masked the lighter color of the anthropogenic soils, and reduced sherd visibility, it is possible that even intensive fieldwalking might have overlooked this site.

Unlike modern digital systems like Landsat and ASTER, CORONA photographs were acquired on film. They must be scanned and geometrically corrected, which is a difficult process given the peculiarites of the CORONA cameras (Sohn, Kim, and Yom 2004). All scenes were geocorrected with reference to 10 m resolution orthorectified panchromatic SPOT imagery available from the U.S. National Geospatial-Intelligence Agency's Raster Roam interface.[5] Additional ground-control points were collected in the field using handheld GPS receivers. Throughout the basin, local tracks and field systems have remained remarkably stable between the time of CORONA acquisition and the time of the SPOT image acquisition (most acquired in the early 1990s). The most accurate ground-control points were therefore intersections of local tracks and field boundaries (fig. 4.3). Also useful was the track of the Qamishli–Mosul railway; in several cases the points where tracks crossed wadis also were useful. Several prominent features proved to be difficult to use for ground control, especially tells and other archaeological sites, the center-points and boundaries of which are too imprecise. Paved inter-village roads also proved difficult to use because their locations in SPOT almost never coincide spatially with their unpaved antecedents visible in CORONA imagery.

Image georeferencing was undertaken within the ERDAS Imagine program using a second-order polynomial warp and cubic convolution interpolation. The scenes were projected into the UTM projection and coordinate system for Zone 37 using the WGS 1984 datum. All georeferenced images were output to a resolution of 2 m. The positioning error fluctuates across any given scene but rarely exceeds 15 m. These images are now available online for free download (Ur 2010b).

In an environment such as the Upper Khabur basin, CORONA images can be used to great effect in identifying sites, mapping off-site archaeological features, and reconstructing ancient environments. The THS relied primarily on five missions, each with distinct properties and strengths (table 4.1). Preliminary site and feature identifications from CORONA imagery were tested in the field during reconnaissance in the 1999 season in order to gain ground control for further image interpretation (Ur 2002b). Because of the demonstrated utility of the CORONA images, it was decided that a high level of site recovery could be maintained without fieldwalking. Therefore sites were visited directly by vehicle, without making systematic ground transects for the purposes of locating sites. However, systematic transects were made during field scatter collection, and these served to confirm this decision. No additional sites were identified during field scatter collection that had not already been identified through CORONA image interpretation.

[5] http://geoengine.nga.mil/geospatial/SW_TOOLS/NIMAMUSE/webinter/rast_roam.html.

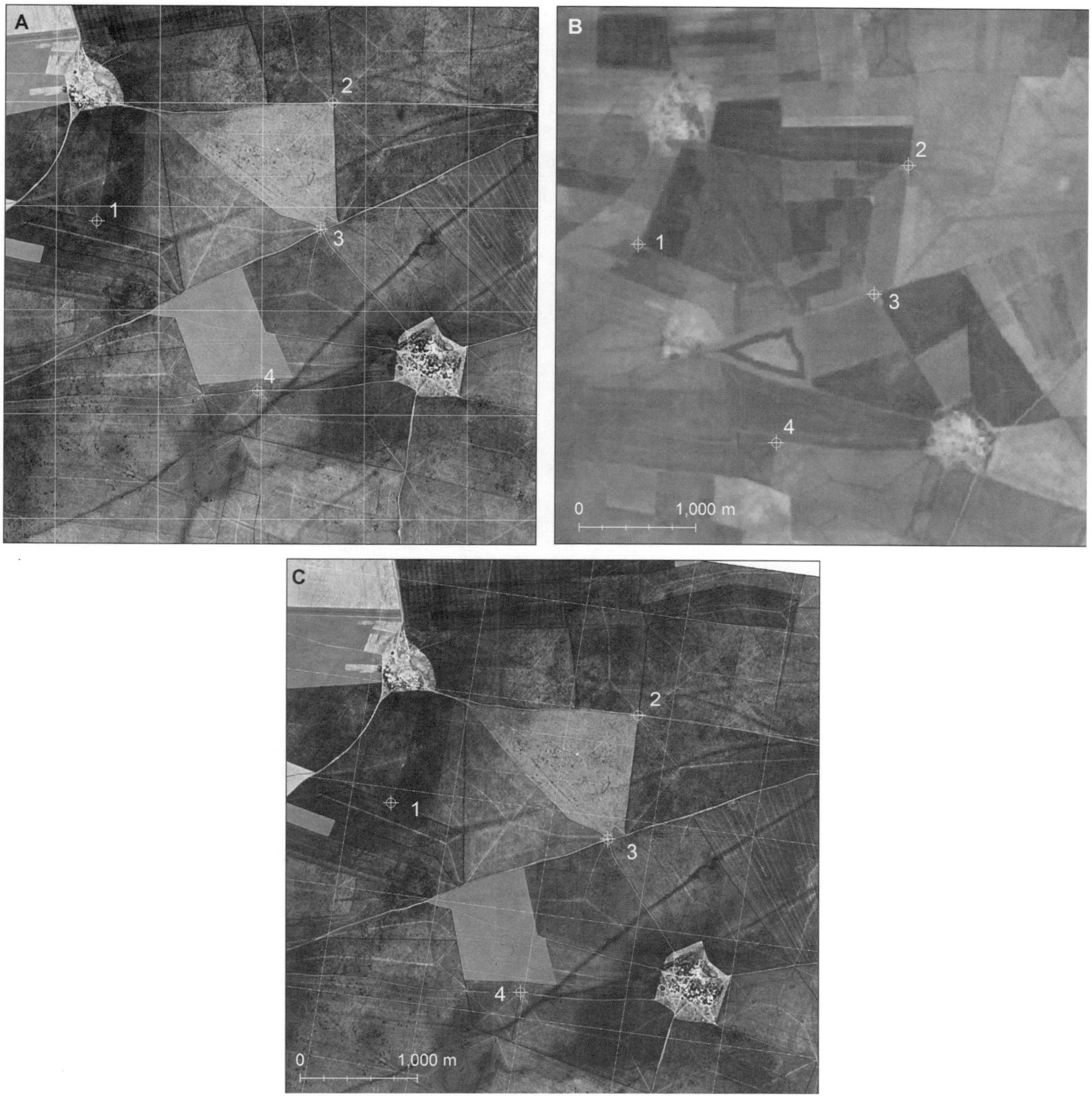

Figure 4.3. Georeferencing of CORONA photographs to SPOT imagery. (*A*) Unreferenced CORONA scene with four suitable georeferencing points and arbitrary grid (1117-1025DF147, 25 May 1972); (*B*) Georeferenced 10 m SPOT image with the same four points (8 March 1990); (*C*) Georeferenced CORONA scene. Note the warping in the grid between the unreferenced and georeferenced CORONA scenes

Table 4.1. CORONA missions used in the THS and their characteristics

Mission and Rotation	*Frames*	*Date and Time*	*Strengths*	*Weaknesses*	*General Notes*
1021-2120D	F007, F008, F009, F010	26 May 1965, 7:40 A.M.	Moist and vegetated ground at time of acquisition; good for hollow ways and other depressed features	Lower resolution than other missions used	The only mission with a KH-4A camera used by the THS; coverage between the Balikh and the western basin
1102-1025D	F006, F007, F008, F009	11 December 1967, 1:23 P.M.	Sites and hollow ways	—	THS region is close to nadir, therefore optimal resolution and least geometric distortion
1105-1025D	F056, F057, F058, F059, F060	5 November 1968, 12:37 P.M.	Tracks, field boundaries, and built structures	Acquired prior to start of winter rains; ground is too dry for hollow way visibility	Mission camera with the sharpest focus. Western basin at nadir; does not extend into eastern basin
1105-2170D	F049, F050, F051	14 November 1968, 11:14 P.M.	Tracks, field boundaries, and built structures	Acquired prior to start of winter rains; ground is too dry for hollow way visibility; some cloud cover in eastern basin	Mission camera with the sharpest focus
1108-1025D	A004, A005, A006, A007, A008	6 December 1969, 12:36 P.M.	Sites and surrounding alluvial sediments have maximally discrete signatures	—	Nadir at THS/ North Jazira Project area; extends from Jaghjagh to trans-Tigridian zone
1117-1025D	F145, F146, F147, F148, F149, F150	25 May 1972	Hollow ways, wadis, natural drainage	Site sediments are apparently saturated and are often indistinguishable from surrounding fields	Soft focus; negatives have sharp latitudinal striations

4.3.2. DIGITAL ELEVATION MODELS

Although the basin might appear to be flat, its slight topography defines patterns of drainage and therefore has been an important variable for settlement and land use for millennia. Furthermore, its microtopography, in the form of mounded sites and depressed linear features, represents most of the archaeological features of interest. At the time of survey, the only topographic data available was the 1:50,000 scale Arabic series (discussed below). Subsequently, a 90 m resolution global dataset from the SRTM has become available (Farr et al. 2007).[6] Each pixel is slightly less than one hectare, so the resolution is too coarse to detect many sites in the THS area. However, it does resolve the largest and highest mounds in the basin very well (Sherratt 2004) and can be used for computer automated detection of mounds across the Fertile Crescent (Menze, Ur, and Sherratt 2006).

The 90 m version of the SRTM dataset resolves the morphology of Hamoukar's high mound and lower town, as well as the high mounds within the THS (fig. 4.4). Its primary utility for the THS, however, is that it reveals the subtle mounding of THS 25 (Khirbat al-Fakhar) and also allows a general characterization of the slope and the primary north-northeast to south-southwest drainages in the area, none of which are apparent from the ground. The

[6] http://www2.jpl.nasa.gov/srtm/.

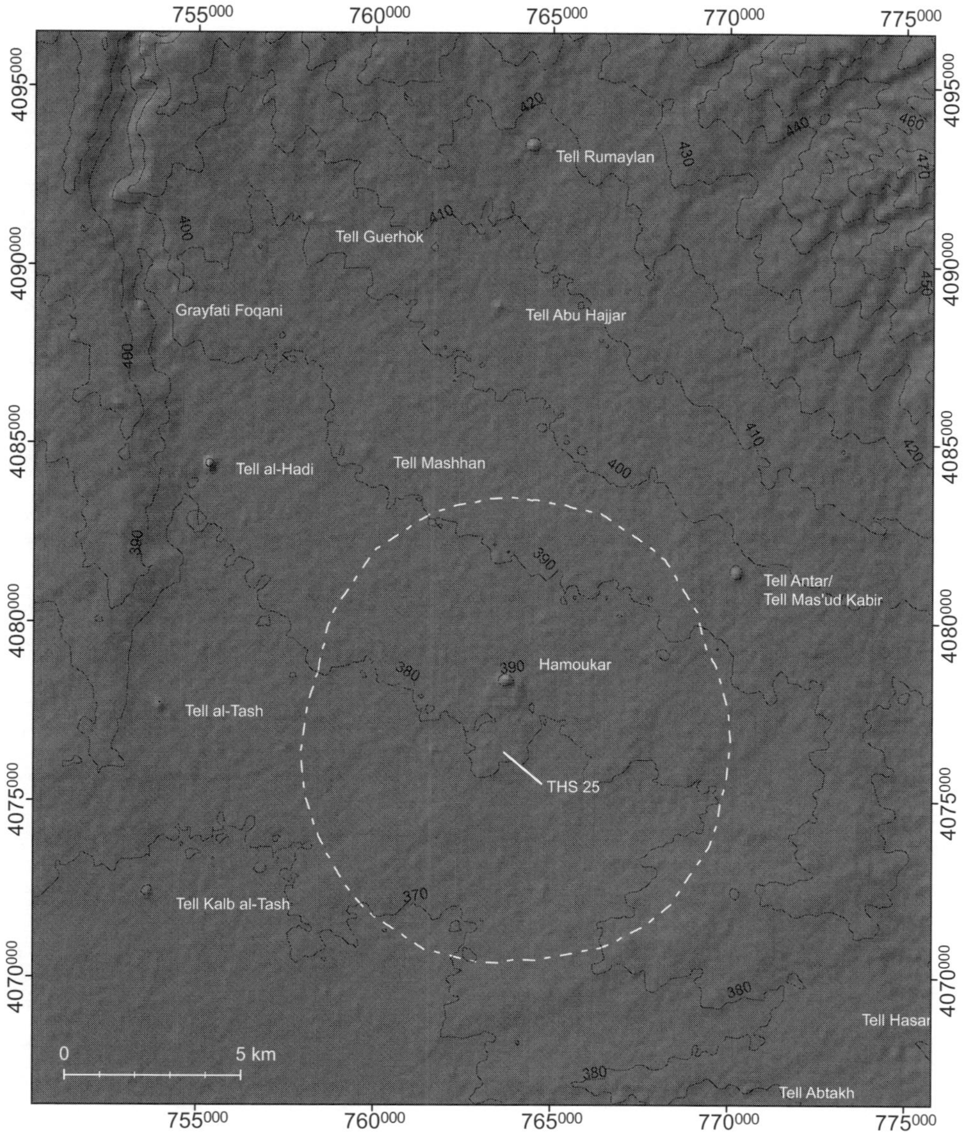

Figure 4.4. Hillshaded topography of the THS area derived from 90 m SRTM terrain data. Contours at 10 m intervals

30 m version of the SRTM dataset is not publicly available; however, a vector surface drainage model was derived from these data by Devin White and made available to the THS (see fig. 3.7 and hydrology in maps 2–3).

4.3.3. TOPOGRAPHIC AND HISTORICAL MAPS

Place names on maps with distinctive elements such as *khirba* and *tell* ("ruin" and "mound" in Arabic), or *gir* ("mound" in Kurdish) can be useful indicators of where sites might be found beneath modern villages. Two map series were incorporated into the THS spatial database. The first was the French 1:200,000 Levant series produced by the Service Géographique des forces Françaises du Levant. The sheets relevant to the THS were Qamichlîyé-Sinjār (1945 provisional edition) and Karatchok-Dagh (1933 and 1950 editions). All editions were based on surveys conducted in 1936 or earlier. The 50 m contour interval gives only a general indication of regional terrain, but contains iconic indications of mounded places, which are often named. Within the THS region, fourteen mounded sites are indicated, including all six of the high mounds and most of the complex mounded sites (fig. 4.5).

Of much greater utility were the topographic maps produced by the Syrian Military Surveying Administration. The THS area was covered by the Bab al-Hadid and the Janub Bab al-Hadid sheets from the 1:50,000 series, and the Yarubiya (Tell Kotchek) 1 sheet from the 1:25,000 series. These series' contour intervals (5 m and 2.5 m, respectively) often indicated mounded sites and occasionally internal topographic detail as well. Their mid-1960s publication date makes them nearly contemporary with the CORONA photographs used in this study and were therefore useful aides in image interpretation.

Using these remote-sensing and map datasets, it was possible to identify potential sites prior to the start of fieldwork. These preliminary identifications guided site visits.

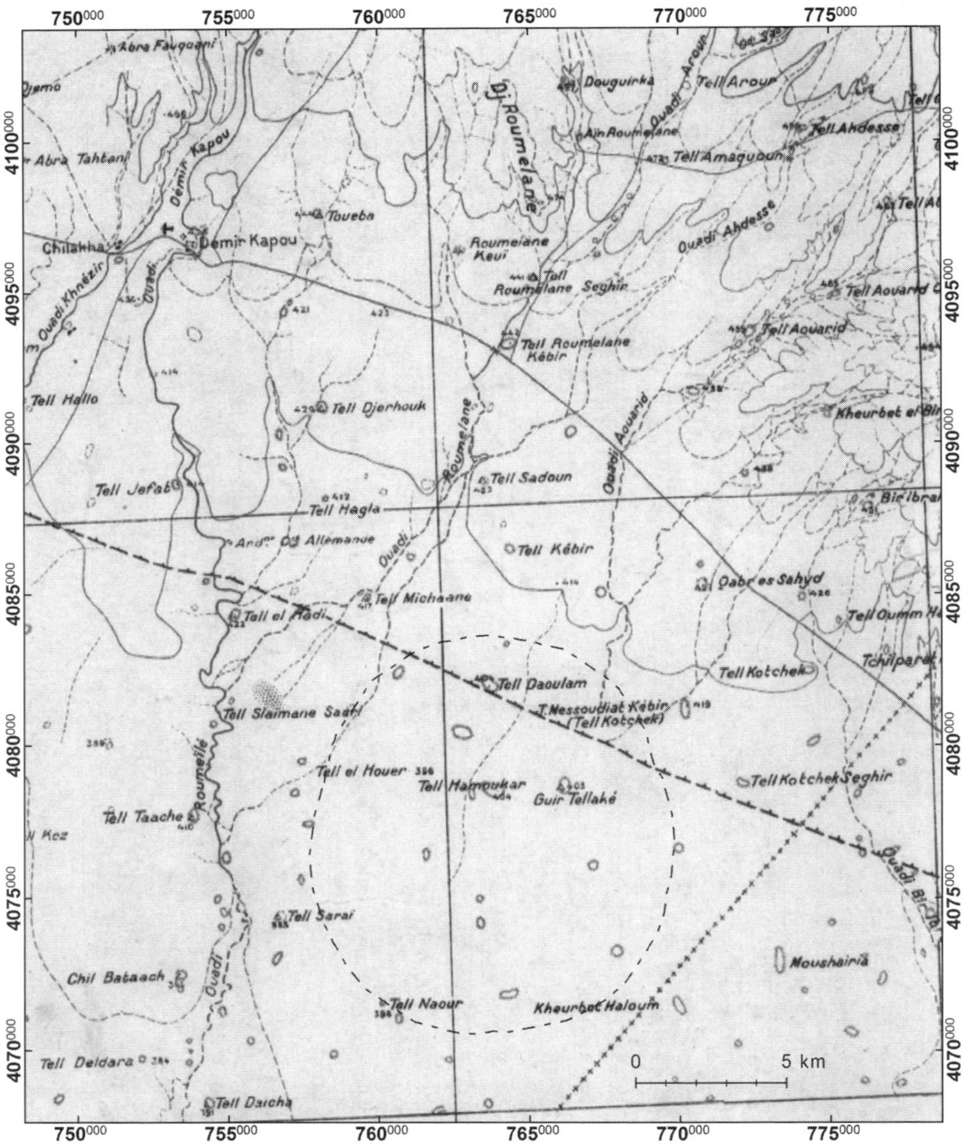

Figure 4.5. Karatchok-Dagh 1:200,000 scale map of the THS area (surveyed in 1932, printed in December 1933)

4.4. FIELD MAPPING AND ARTIFACT COLLECTION

4.4.1. SAMPLING VERSUS FULL COVERAGE

Sampling methods are common in European archaeology and almost universal in North American survey, where they are considered to be necessary for practical reasons. In these often temperate climates, both visibility and site obtrusiveness are quite low, so a sampling approach allows smaller areas to be investigated at a high intensity, with the results being extrapolated to the survey universe as a whole. In the Near East, the arid or semi-arid climate coupled with millennia of timber clearance, agriculture, and overgrazing have produced conditions of high visibility and sites of high obtrusiveness (see Section 2.3), so that sampling is often considered unnecessary.

The main advantage of a full-coverage approach over a sampling strategy is that it allows for the recovery of the full hierarchical size-range settlement patterns (Sumner 1990). Sampling strategies provide an accurate view of the distribution of settlements when they are homogeneous, numerous, and uniformly distributed across the landscape. However, when settlement is nucleated, the likelihood of not recovering a center is increased (see Bintliff 2000: 201 for Greek examples); this is called the Teotihuacan Effect when rare or unique phenomena are missed (Flannery 1976: 131–36). Furthermore, Near Eastern archaeologists have traditionally been less concerned with estimations of total population than with hierarchical settlement patterns, an issue that can only be approached via a full-coverage strategy (see papers in Fish and Kowalewski 1990).

The THS adopted a varied collection methodology, employing systematic sampling strategies for surface collections at Hamoukar (see Section 3.3) and Khirbat al-Fakhar (THS 25, see Section 4.5), within a full-coverage framework for the entire THS region. At the level of the survey universe, full coverage was necessitated by the goals of recovering complete settlement patterns. In the past, full-coverage surveys have been most successful in areas of high visibility with low topography and highly obtrusive sites (Ammerman 1981: 64–65), such as the Upper Khabur basin. The use of CORONA satellite photographs allowed the surveys to take advantage of soil color and texture, obtrusive properties of sites that are apparent from a vertical perspective (see above).

4.4.2. FIELD IDENTIFICATION OF SITES AND BOUNDARY DETERMINATION

Sites were identified and their boundaries determined by three primary variables: high density of surface artifacts, the presence of mounding, and the presence of lighter sediments of anthropogenic origin. In most cases, these three indicators covaried closely.

Artifact density, primarily potsherds, was assessed qualitatively. The THS opted against applying thresholds of artifact density to define the area of sites, for two reasons. Logistically, systematic density measurement across and beyond the limits of all sites in the region would have made surface collection prohibitively intensive, and was deemed unnecessary in light of the utility of the other two indicators, mounding and soil color. Only in the case of THS 25 (Khirbat al-Fakhar), when those other indicators were absent or could not be determined, did the survey attempt to define site boundaries via fluctuations in density of surface sherds.

Furthermore, patterns of ceramic production and consumption can change through time, especially with relation to production technologies, distribution patterns (Millet 1991), and density of settlement. For these reasons it was decided that relative fluctuations, as opposed to a universal threshold of artifact density, would more accurately define site areas. For example, on the later third-millennium B.C. lower town of Hamoukar, density rarely dropped below 100 sherds per 100 sq. m (see Section 3.4). On small prehistoric sites (Period 4 and earlier), artifact density was much lower, almost certainly because ceramic production was less specialized and residential density was lower. Finally, differences in surface visibility related to ground conditions also would have an impact on absolute quantities of sherds recovered, but would presumably not impact shifts in relative density.

It must be emphasized that, in northern Mesopotamia, it is relative density of artifacts, not merely presence of them, that indicates habitation sites, as a result of the ancient practice of distributing settlement-derived debris onto the fields as a crop amendment. These manuring scatters can be distinguished from direct settlement debris by density and sherd morphology (see discussion in Section 5.2). If presence of artifactual material alone were used as a site indicator, nearly the entire THS region would be considered a site.

Site *mounding* is the hallmark of Near Eastern archaeological sites and characterizes almost every site in the THS area, to varying degrees. Above a certain height threshold, mounded sites have attracted cemeteries of sedentary and nomadic communities and have remained uncultivated. These sites are relatively well preserved and are slowly eroding according to a well-documented pattern (see Section 3.2.1 and Rosen 1986). Lower sites, however, are less likely to be granted the cultural protection that a cemetery provides, and those that do not host modern villages are almost all presently under cultivation. These sites are eroding much faster than the high mounds, but only a few sites have had their mounding completely erased by agriculture. For logistical reasons, the spatial limits of mounded areas were assessed qualitatively in the field.

Soil color is a highly distinctive property of sites of long duration, presumably resulting from human activities and related natural processes such as mudbrick manufacture and decay, burning of organic materials, the concentration of settlement debris and human and animal wastes, and the breakdown of the upper soil horizons through continuous and concentrated disturbance. After site abandonment, the resulting soils are lighter in color and finer in texture than the reddish brown soils that characterize this part of the Upper Khabur basin (see Section 2.1). This property of archaeological sites produces a distinctive signature on CORONA satellite photographs and other remote-sensing datasets (fig. 4.6), but sites' lighter soils are also clearly visible from the ground, and from distances of up to several hundred meters under certain sunlight conditions (fig. 4.7). During site visits, changes in soil color were assessed qualitatively, but could be later confirmed against georeferenced CORONA imagery.

In an ideal situation, a site's boundary would be definable by a simultaneous shift in all three variables. When moving from the site to the unoccupied terrain beyond, relative sherd density would drop abruptly, soil color would change from gray to reddish brown, and there would be either a marked drop in elevation or the slope would decrease to zero (fig. 4.8). When all three variables could be tracked, it was clear that they were often linked in precisely this manner. In practice, the THS relied mostly on a combination of changes in soil color (as defined by a site's signature on a CORONA photograph) and mounding (as defined by ground observation). In several instances where low sites had been deep-plowed or bulldozed for irrigated cotton fields (e.g., THS 57, 58, 59), their boundaries were defined entirely by their signature on CORONA photographs.

4.4.3. FIELD COLLECTION OF SITES

Potential sites identified from maps, CORONA photographs, and other imagery sources were visited and confirmed by the three main site criteria discussed in the previous section.

The majority of sites were collected by full areal coverage, generally following the methodology used in the collections of Tell al-Hawa (Ball, Tucker, and Wilkinson 1989) and Tell Mohammed Diyab (Lyonnet 1990) and in the surveys of the Iraqi North Jazira and the Tell Beydar region (Wilkinson and Tucker 1995; Wilkinson 2000a). Sites were spatially subdivided into collection areas, usually on the basis of topography (fig. 4.9). Discrete mounded areas, spurs defined by eroding gullies, and central high points were all candidates for separate collection. In general, gullies were used as boundaries for sub-areas; collections within them were avoided because sherds from such active areas will have traveled farther from their point of original deposition than sherds found on a more stable surface. However, because they are erosionally active, gullies attract a higher density of larger (and thus more diagnostic) sherds, and they were deliberately targeted on sites where sherd density was otherwise too low to provide a reliable ceramic dating.

Ideally, collection areas were kept to around 1–2 ha, and flat or otherwise topographically homogenous areas of a site were often arbitrarily divided if they exceeded that size. High mounds or other areas suspected of containing deeply buried occupations were often subdivided into smaller units. Collection area corners and significant points along area boundaries were marked with highly visible nylon flags and their positions recorded via GPS. These points were used to construct collection area polygons in an ArcGIS spatial database to allow their accurate measurement.

Within collection areas, collections were made by walking slow transects at varying intervals. For highly mounded small collection areas, transects tended to be tightly spaced; in larger areas of less mounding, transects were widely spaced to evenly cover the area. Unlike the strategy adopted for the collection of Hamoukar itself, only diagnostic sherds (rims, bases, handles, and decorated pieces) and artifacts were kept, with no attempt at "vacuuming" the surface. Sherd collections were intended to be representative but not unmanageably large. Therefore, some

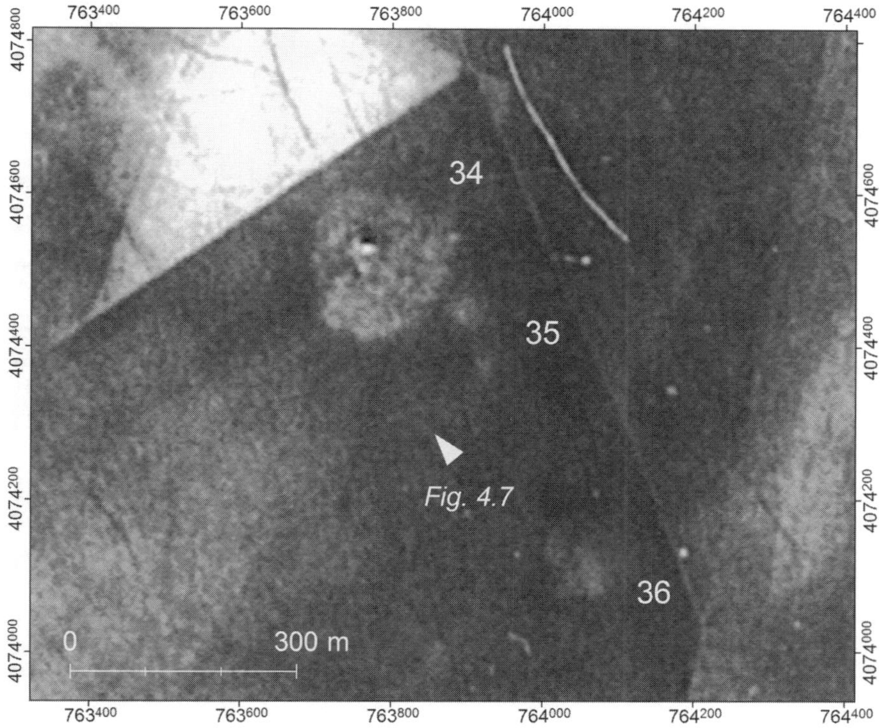

Figure 4.6. Anthropogenic soil color in a CORONA photograph (1102-1025DF007, 11 December 1967)

Figure 4.7. Anthropogenic soil color and site mounding at THS 34. The view is to the northwest, across the southwestern slope of the mound. For the position of this view see figure 4.6

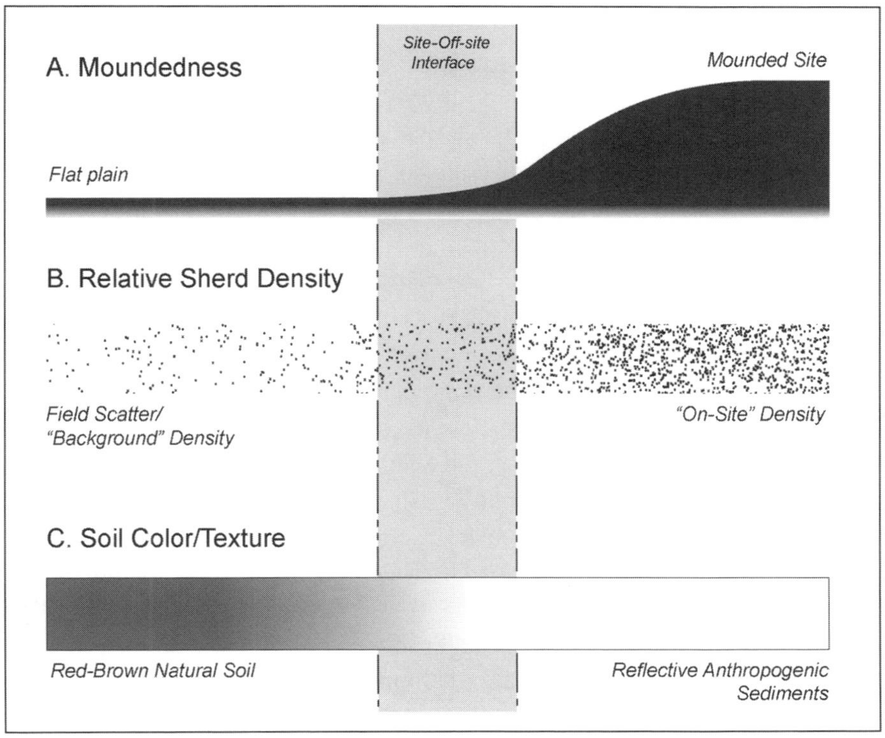

Figure 4.8. Idealized cross section showing the relationship between (*A*) mounding, (*B*) sherd density, and (*C*) soil color at a hypothetical low-mounded site

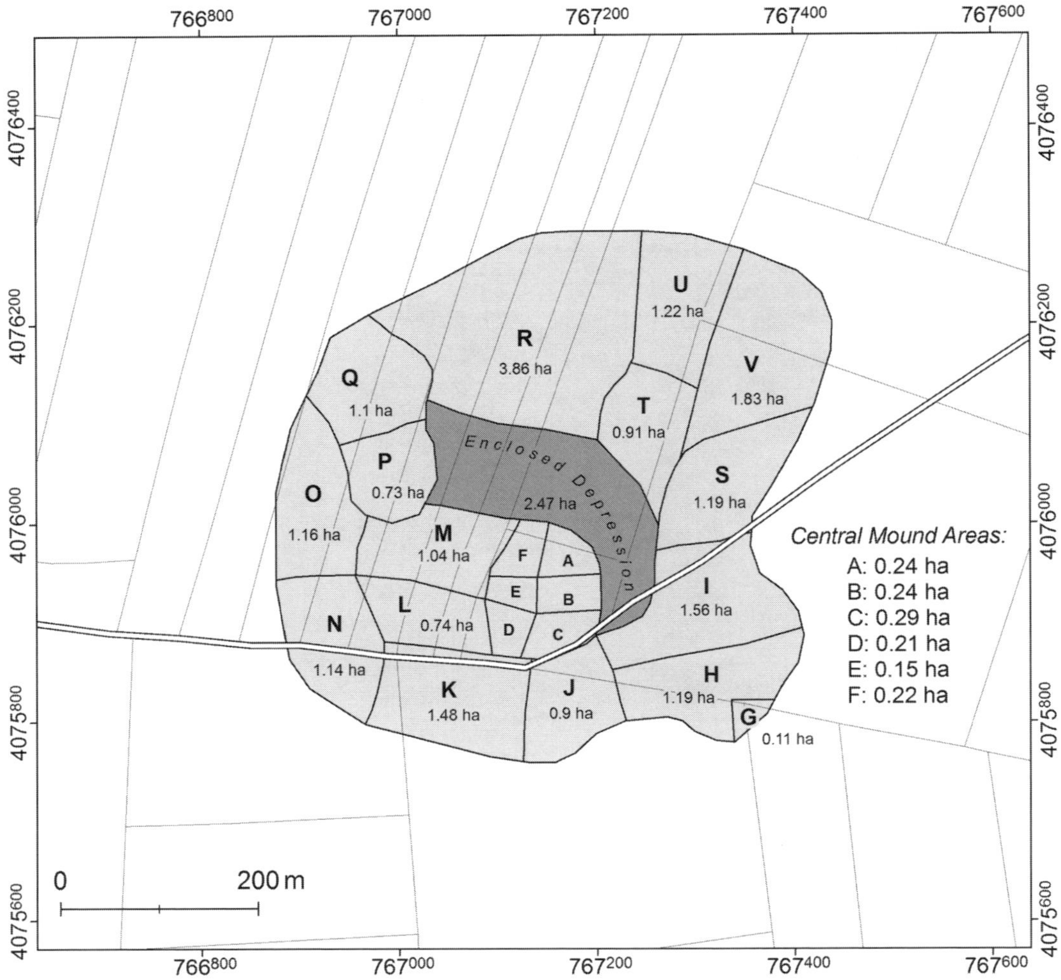

Figure 4.9. Example of site subdivision at a large and topographically complex site: THS 24

areas were collected fully but at low intensity (see below), and it is possible that small or deeply buried occupations were not detected.

The survey was intended to be intensive and full coverage, for the reasons outlined above. In recording sites, the aims of the team were to make discrete collections of surface artifacts within well-defined units that could be related to each other and to the morphology of the site as a whole (see above). This approach was intended to allow the accurate diachronic mapping of settlement within the site, as well as to document natural and cultural processes that may have had an effect on the surface distribution of material culture.

Field recording made heavy use of GPS receivers. The THS conducted field seasons both prior to and after the discontinuation of the U.S. Department of Defense's "Selective Availability" accuracy degradation in 2000. However, all sites mapped prior to the removal of Selective Availability were remapped in the 2000 season of the THS, when the positioning error was as low as 4–5 m. The exception was Hamoukar itself (see Section 3.3). In general, GPS receivers are very accurate in the Khabur basin because the landscape has low relief, it is almost completely deforested, and the horizon is normally visible in all directions. The signals of four or more satellites are required for a three-dimensional position, but positions based on strong signals from nine to ten satellites were not uncommon.

Site maps were produced using GPS positions. Initially, the perimeter of the site was mapped by taking positions at 50–100 m intervals. The site boundary was defined by a subjective combination of mounding edge, sherd scatter density, and distribution of lighter anthropogenic soil (see Section 4.4.2). These positions were simultaneously plotted in the field notebook at a scale appropriate to the size of the site (e.g., 1:5,000 for a large tell with an extensive lower town, or 1:1,000 for a low prehistoric mound). Next the internal details of the site were positioned and drawn on the plan. Mapped features might include the center or top of the site, existing survey benchmarks, erosional gullies, modern villages and roads, and any other notable modern or ancient features. From this plan, relative contour lines were approximated to indicate the general steepness of the mound slopes.

The THS did not limit its field observations and mapping to habitation sites, however. More than half of its field time was spent investigating off-site archaeological features, especially field scatters and hollow ways. These features and the field methods used to record them are described in detail in *Chapter 5* and synthesized with the settlement record in *Chapter 6*.

4.5. HYBRID COLLECTION METHODOLOGY AT THS 25 (KHIRBAT AL-FAKHAR)

The survey methodology for the THS region beyond the central site of Hamoukar was based on assumptions about the properties of the sites that were likely to be found: their size range, the nature of site boundaries, and the character of their surface assemblages. One site proved to be so dramatically at odds with the "target parameter" assumptions that the site identification, mapping, and collection methodology described in Section 4.4 could not be applied without modification.

The broad expanse of THS 25 (Khirbat al-Fakhar) lies directly south of Hamoukar itself; its northern edge comes within 200 m of the southern edge of Hamoukar's middle to late third-millennium (Period 7) lower town. Although the complex of low mounds at its core has been previously noted by visiting archaeologists, its full extent, 300 ha, was only appreciated when CORONA satellite photographs became available (fig. 4.10A). At present, its enormous size, unique morphology, and early date (predominantly Period 4, Late Chalcolithic 1–2) leave it unparalleled in Mesopotamian archaeology, with the possible exception of early urban Tell Brak (Ur, Karsgaard, and Oates 2007). The central complex posed no particular challenge to the survey methodology, but the enormous scale of the entire site precluded the full-coverage method employed elsewhere in the THS. Ultimately it was decided to employ a hybrid method, combining a full-coverage approach applied to the central mounded complex with a systematic sampling strategy derived from the THS field scatter program.

4.5.1. THS 25 SITE MORPHOLOGY

THS 25 (Khirbat al-Fakhar) consists of a central complex of low mounds surrounded by a broad flat expanse that appears unmounded at present but is covered with a variable scatter of sherds and lithics (fig. 4.10B). The central mounded complex is large (31.3 ha) but not otherwise atypical for first- and second-millennium A.D. sites in the Upper Khabur basin and adjacent areas of the Iraqi North Jazira. Most of this area is contiguous, along an east–west axis, the exception being a 3.5 ha low mound to the south. At present, most of this area is under rainfed cultivation, with the exception of a small discrete mound (Area B) at the west end of the complex.

Surrounding this mounded complex on all sides is a broad expanse of fields that today do not appear to be mounded or to have unusually light soil color (fig. 4.11). A closer inspection reveals a scatter of handmade ceramics and mostly obsidian lithic material covering over 275 ha. The surface assemblage in this area is variable. Some areas have a light but site-level scatter, whereas others appear to be of midden density. Throughout, however, sherd densities are too high to be interpreted as field scatter, and the sherds themselves have the size and edge morphology of recently plowed settlement debris. This outer area is presently intensively cultivated, with pump irrigation of cotton fields especially dense in its northwestern quadrant and along its northern edge. Given its proximity to the later third-millennium city of Hamoukar, it is likely that it has seen intensive agriculture in the past as well. These ancient and recent agricultural practices appear to have obliterated any internal topography that may have existed in the site.

There are two areas within the outer expanse that appear to have avoided these processes. At the eastern and southeastern edges of the complex are two low mounds, both of which are under cultivation but still retain their topography. Both were given separate site designations (THS 26 and THS 27, respectively) and have other periods of occupation, but both should be considered as part of THS 25 during the early Late Chalcolithic period (Period 4).

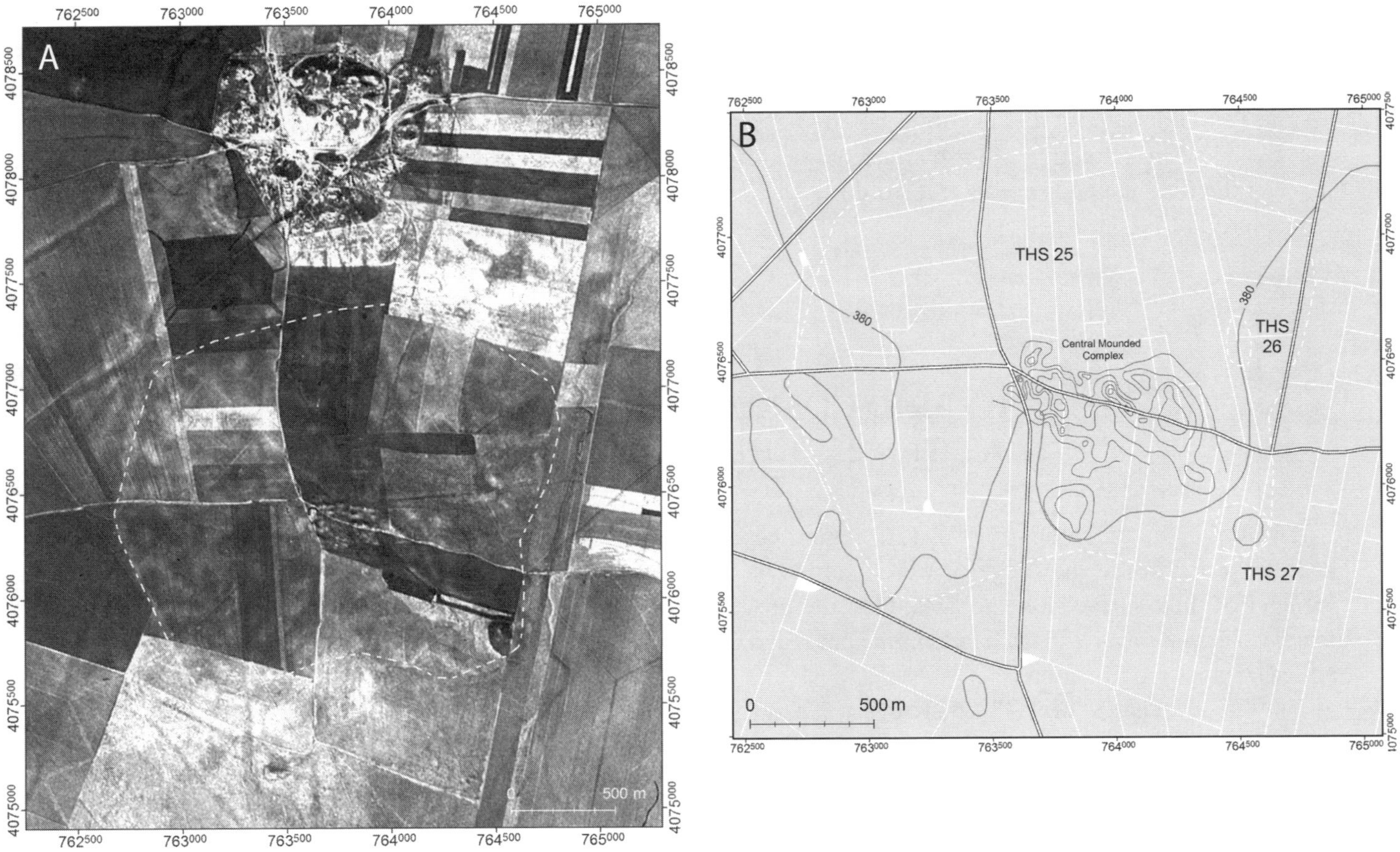

Figure 4.10. (*A*) CORONA photograph of THS 25 (1108-1025DF007, 6 December 1969). (*B*) Topography and modern features at THS 25. The 380 m contour is derived from Syrian 1:50,000 topographic maps; the contours of central mounded complex are derived from the field sketch plan and are not tied to absolute elevation

Figure 4.11. THS 25. In the distance is the central mounded complex; in the foreground is the unmounded area of the site. Note the lack of soil discoloration in the latter

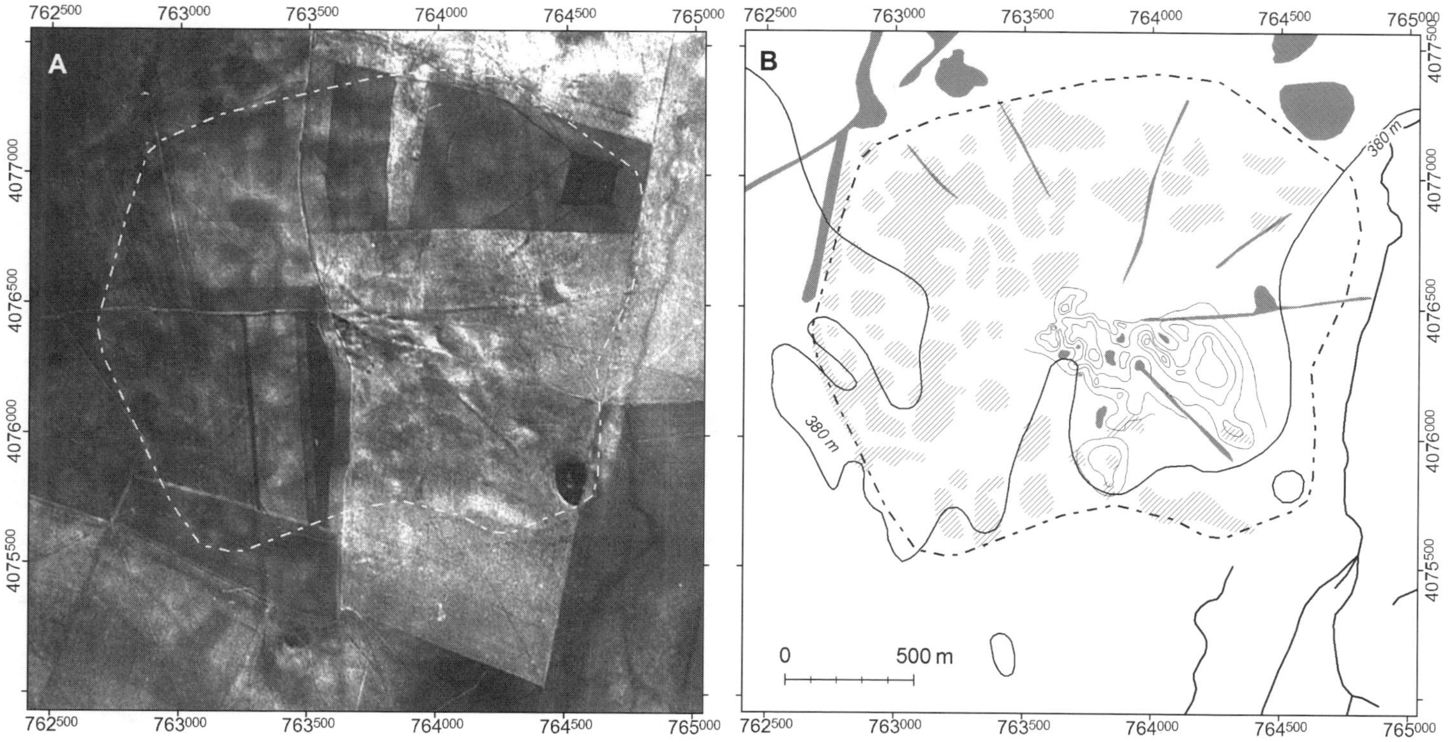

Figure 4.12. (*A*) CORONA photograph of mottled outer area of THS 25 (1102-1025DF007, 11 December 1967); (*B*) Interpreted depressed areas (gray) and areas of anthropogenic soils (hatched) with topography from Syrian 1:50,000 maps (380 m contour) and field sketch of central mounded area

Some clues to internal variability in the outer areas of THS 25 come from CORONA Missions 1102 and 1108. Some fields have a distinctly mottled character; lighter reflective areas alternate with darker areas (fig. 4.12A). These light areas have the same signature as low mounds elsewhere in the THS. Thus it appears likely that the THS 25 outer areas were once characterized by dispersed low mounds with intervening unsettled areas. Intensive mechanized agriculture since the time of CORONA acquisition in the 1960s appears to have removed their topography and to have homogenized any discrete pockets of lighter soils or sherd scatters.

While all internal mounding now appears to be gone, the entire complex may still retain some slight elevation above the surrounding plain (fig. 4.12B). The 1:50,000 Syrian topographic maps show a slight elevation where the 380 m contour extends around it to the south. Furthermore, the 90 m resolution SRTM Digital Elevation Data also characterizes the THS 25 area as a local plateau over the drainages on either side.

4.5.2. AREAL COLLECTION AT THE CENTRAL MOUNDED COMPLEX

The combination of discrete areas of low mounds and intervening depressed areas (probably borrow pits for mudbrick materials) made this central area well suited for the standard THS areal collection methodology. The complex was subdivided into seventeen areas (Areas A–Q) and collected (fig. 4.13). It quickly became clear that Late Chalcolithic 1–2 (Period 4) diagnostic types were extremely abundant. To avoid overburdening the sherd processing system, these were processed by type and count in the field; only diagnostics of other periods were kept for processing at the dig house.

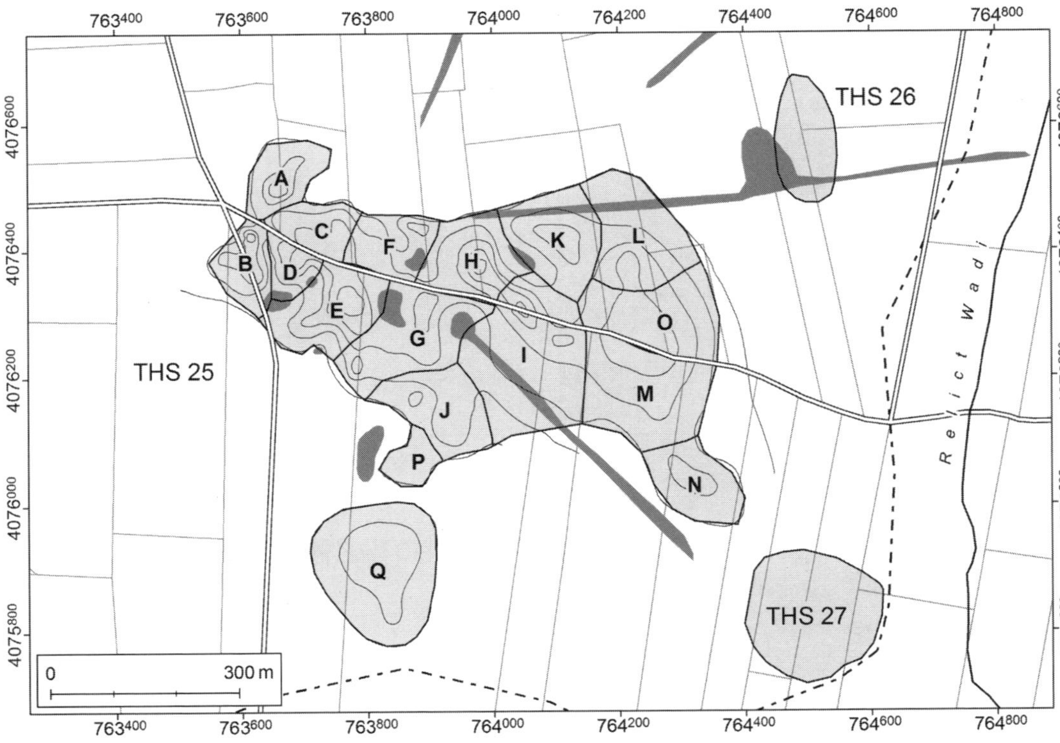

Figure 4.13. Central mounded area at THS 25 with collection areas

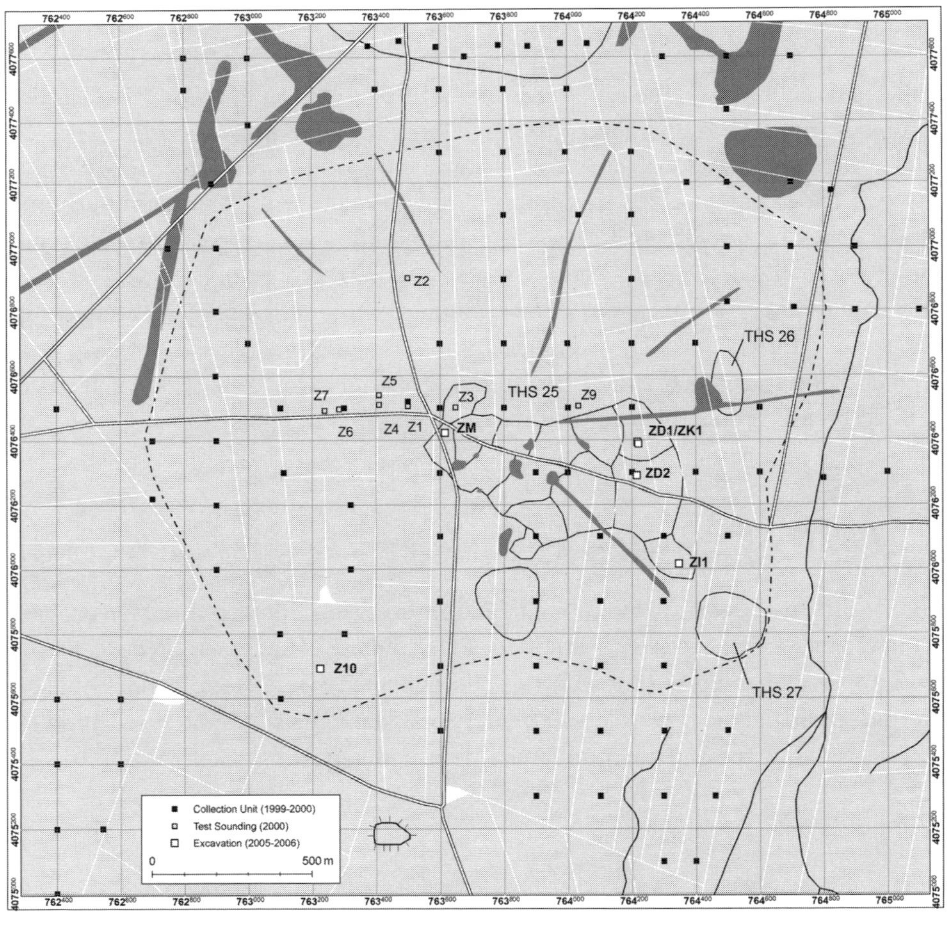

Figure 4.14. Position of collection units on THS 25 with systematic collection units, soundings, and excavation trenches

4.5.3. SYSTEMATIC SAMPLING IN THE OUTER AREAS

The large size of the outer area rendered impractical the areal collections undertaken on the central mounded area; a sampling strategy had to be adopted. A weeklong non-systematic reconnaissance over the site in 1999 revealed its approximate scale and demonstrated the chronological homogeneity of its surface assemblage; furthermore, it suggested that it might be possible to demarcate the edges of THS 25 (Khirbat al-Fakhar) from its mottled signature on CORONA satellite imagery. For these reasons, the goals in collecting the outer areas of the site differed from the goals in collecting other sites in the THS: rather than identifying changes in settlement area through time, the THS was primarily concerned with establishing the density of the surface assemblage and using variations in density to indicate its boundaries. Because of its unprecedented size, a well-documented empirical basis for the estimation of its size was deemed to be critical. The collection of representative diagnostic types was less important than quantitative information on surface artifact density.

Using surface artifact density to define the boundaries of THS 25 is complicated by the close proximity of Hamoukar to the north. The fields surrounding the later third-millennium (Period 7) site are covered with field scatter of especially high density, since these areas were the most easily manured with Hamoukar-derived settlement debris (see Section 5.2). Therefore it was anticipated that the fields beyond the boundaries of THS 25 would still have a substantial sherd assemblage.

The transition from site-level to field scatter density would be an important one, so the THS opted simply to extend its field scatter sampling program across THS 25. As with field scatter collection, a 200 m interval was maintained between units. Some alternations of the standard field scatter collection methodology were necessary for on-site collection, however. With regard to placement, units were placed on a broader range of surface visibilities, since densities were often so high that even low-visibility land surfaces produced site-level collections. In areas of very high density, where full collection of 100 sq. m would have produced thousands of sherds, a smaller area was collected, often only 4 sq. m (a 2 × 2 m unit).

In practice, it was not possible to sample large areas of the site, particularly at the northwest, because of the presence of standing cotton fields. Furthermore, field conditions prevented comparable collections in several areas beyond the site's edge. It was possible, however, to demonstrate dramatic reductions in artifact density south, east, and northwest of the outer area. Where it could be demonstrated, the limits of the Late Chalcolithic 1–2 (Period 4) sherd scatter corresponded to the extent of surface mottling on CORONA imagery. The total extent of THS 25 is thus estimated to be 300 ha. Within this area, sixty units were collected, with an average sherd density of 1,540 sherds per 100 sq. m.[7] The pattern of settlement at THS 25 and its significant implications for our understanding of late fifth-millennium society is discussed in *Chapters 6* and *8*, respectively.

[7] The average sherd densities per 100 sq. meters at Hamoukar and THS 25 cannot be compared directly because they were collected using different methodologies. Collection at Hamoukar excluded very small sherds, whereas THS 25 was collected using the field scatter collection methodology (see Section 5.2).

CHAPTER 5

ELEMENTS OF THE ARCHAEOLOGICAL LANDSCAPE

The most obtrusive signature of past human activity is the habitation site, but the site is only one element in the complex archaeological palimpsest of the Mesopotamian landscape. The THS attempted to record systematically not only habitation sites but also off-site elements such as tracks, canals, and field scatters.

5.1. SITES AND SETTLEMENTS

5.1.1. SITES AND THEIR DEFINITION

It has been noted that "the decision whether or not a specific cluster [of artifacts] is a site has frequently been based on the researcher's implicit assumptions about what the surface manifestations of a site should be. If the number of decision-makers in a survey is small, then the results should at least be consistent for that survey, but they will not be readily comparable to the results from other surveys" (Gallant 1986: 417). The definition of a "site" is an etic one, based on the archaeologist's assessment of site boundaries rather than on any inherent quality of the archaeological remains themselves. Functionally, sites are not limited to places of habitation. They can be temporary activity areas, industrial areas such as mines, or cemeteries. Some archaeologists have advocated moving the level of analysis from the arbitrarily defined "site" down to the level of the surface artifacts of which it is composed (Dunnell and Dancey 1983); others have gone further to suggest that the "site" be done away with altogether, for analytical purposes (Thomas 1975). The most agreeable definition comes from Gallant (1986: 416): "Sites are those areas with discrete accumulations of artifacts demonstrating higher levels of density and continuity in relation to the overall regional pattern of artifact distribution when visibility is not a distorting factor." Whereas other "formalized" definitions might prescribe a minimum sherd density, this definition has the benefit of flexibility in the face of variable visibility conditions (see also Plog, Plog, and Wait 1978: 389).

Traditionally, most surveys have treated site definitions with what might be called "benign neglect" (Gallant 1986: 408): a site is assumed to be too obvious to require explicit definition. Such is often the case for Near Eastern survey, where sites are generally equated with tells. However, intensive survey has found that the classic Near Eastern tell is only one of several site morphologies, and not even the most common (see below and Wilkinson 2003: table 4.1).

The terms "site" and "settlement" are not used synonymously in this volume. Sites are the traces of former loci of human activity that have survived to the present, after their transformation by a range of natural and cultural processes. These processes include mudbrick collapse, water erosion, wind deflation, soil formation, plowing, earth leveling, or reoccupation. Most sites have resulted from a combination of several or all of the preceding. On the other hand, settlements are living places where human communities concentrate their activities on a permanent basis. The former are directly accessible to archaeologists via surface collection and excavation, and indirectly through remote-sensing datasets; the latter are no longer accessible but can only be reconstructed from etic interpretations of the surviving remains (i.e., the site). Throughout this volume, "site" is used to refer to the place as it exists at present, and "settlement" refers to the place as a living social and economic entity in the past.

5.1.2. GENERAL CLASSIFICATION OF SEDENTARY SITES

The archaeological criteria for identifying sites and delineating their boundaries are reviewed in Section 4.4.2. Among the sedentary sites, it is possible to discern several general categories, based on clustering variables for site properties, especially height, microtopography, sediment texture, associated landscape features, and period of occupation.

Low mounds are generally less than 5 m high and tend toward a simple round or oval shape without internal topographic features (fig. 5.1). They average around 1 ha and rarely exceed 3 ha. Low mounds are most often the remains of prehistoric settlements that have had sufficient time to erode into their present shape, but can also have Late Bronze Age (Period 10) or Iron Age (Period 11) occupation. They rarely have any associated landscape features. Their low height offers little impediment to cultivation, and almost all are presently under agricultural fields.

High mounds are greater than 5 m high and can be as tall as 20 m in the THS area (fig. 5.2). They are the product of continuous settlement at a single significant place, often over millennia. The most typical chronological pattern at high-mounded sites is an initial prehistoric core topped by a third-millennium B.C. (Periods 6–7) reoccupation and with terminal Khabur (Period 8) settlement. These sites are most likely to be christened *tells* in their modern Arabic names. Throughout the Upper Khabur basin and adjacent areas, high mounds are disproportionately associated with broad hollow way features (Ur and Wilkinson 2008) and dense field scatters (Wilkinson 1989). Their steep sides discourage cultivation, so most have compact and stable surfaces with relatively low sherd density.

It is not uncommon for settlement of the Late Bronze Age and later to have returned to high mounds, but generally at a reduced scale and accompanied by more extensive *lower town* settlement (Wilkinson 2002b). Lower towns are rarely more than 3 m high and develop adjacent to an older settlement on one or more sides (e.g., THS 16, 37, 41, 54). Lower towns are not chronologically limited to any particular periods. However, the most extensive lower towns are those of the Late Bronze and Iron Ages (especially in the central basin; see Wilkinson 2002b); later lower town occupations tend to be smaller. Elsewhere in the basin, lower towns formed in earlier periods while the high mound was still substantially occupied, especially on the major later third-millennium urban centers such as Tell Mozan, Tell Leilan, and Tell Brak. In the THS region, early lower town formation was limited to Hamoukar itself (see Section A–A′ in fig. 3.3).

Lower towns often include depressed or excavated areas ("enclosed depressions") at their center or around their edges (fig. 5.3). These features came into being as mudbrick extraction pits, and they often continue to be used for such purposes since their depressed morphology captures moisture. The sharpness of their edges is inversely proportional to their age. Low- and high-mounded sites were at one time associated with enclosed depressions but their greater age has allowed them to be infilled by plow wash and aeolian sediments or obscured by later settlement.

Complex mounded sites might be thought of as lower towns without associated high mounds. These sites are composed of multiple topographically discrete low mounds, often arranged around a central enclosed depression (e.g., THS 10, 18, 25, 45). Complex mounded sites might incorporate an earlier prehistoric mound, but tend to spread outward rather than upward; occupation is generally Iron Age or later but complex mounded sites are especially typical of the Islamic periods. Being later in time, they are strongly associated with narrow hollow way features and occasionally with possible canals. Many appear to have only recently come under cultivation, and their soils are often finer and ashier than on older sites.

Finally, several *unmounded* sites were recovered in the THS area. Several probably retained some topographic expression until recently being plowed out (e.g., THS 21, 57, 58, 59) or leveled for irrigated cotton (e.g., THS 35). In all these examples, the sites' original dimensions could be reconstructed from CORONA photographs, in which their signatures appeared identical to those of low-mounded sites elsewhere in the survey region. Three sites, however, were flat or nearly flat but without any indication of recent deep plowing or leveling (THS 22, 30, 31). All had permanent Late Chalcolithic occupation (either Period 4 or 5b), and all appear to have had a transient middle to late third-millennium (Period 7) presence. All unmounded sites, whether recently leveled or not, could be identified by their signature on CORONA photographs.

5.1.3. THE SIGNATURE OF ARCHAEOLOGICAL SITES ON CORONA IMAGERY

These general classes of archaeological sites have different properties of obtrusiveness that render them more or less recoverable by archaeological survey. These properties result in distinctive signatures on CORONA satellite

Figure 5.1. A site with low-mound morphology: THS 39

Figure 5.2. A site with high-mound morphology: THS 41, facing southwest

Figure 5.3. The enclosed depression at THS 43 between the multiperiod western low mound (Areas A–F) and the Period 14 lower mound to the east (Area G), facing south

photographs. To match the properties with their CORONA signature, the THS included ground-control acquisition as a component of its 1999 pilot season. Anomalies identified on CORONA images were visited in the field and their spatial and spectral patterning were matched to the archaeological phenomena on the ground. In this manner, it was possible to develop a set of signature keys for interpreting the various CORONA scenes in different seasons and under different moisture and vegetation conditions (on the place of CORONA in THS methodology, see Section 4.3.1).

High mounds are the most easily identified by ground survey because their topographic prominence stands out strongly on an otherwise low-relief plain. Traditional low-intensity survey in the Near East is well suited to recovering sites of this class. High mounds are easily identified on CORONA imagery by the shadows they cast. These shadows appear on the northwestern side of high mounds for scenes acquired in the morning, and on the northeastern side for afternoon acquisitions; at the same time, the corresponding southern side is highly illuminated (fig. 5.4). Late fall or winter scenes (e.g., Missions 1102 and 1108) are preferable to summer scenes for detecting moundedness, since the lower altitude of the sun in the winter causes shadows to be lengthened.

The other morphological site classes are also recognizable on CORONA images. Under certain moisture and land-use conditions, sites can appear as lighter spots on a background of darker soils. This lighter signature is a product of the anthropogenic nature of the soils of sites, which lack the developed soil structure of the surrounding fields (see Section 4.4.2 and fig. 4.6). Reflectivity coincides with finer sediment size, a result of the breakdown of mudbrick architecture (Wilkinson, Beck, and Philip 2006). There are several exceptions, however. The signature appears to be inverted under very wet conditions, when known archaeological sites appear darker than the surrounding terrain. This is the case for sites in the Mission 1117 imagery, taken at the very end of May 1972, which was an

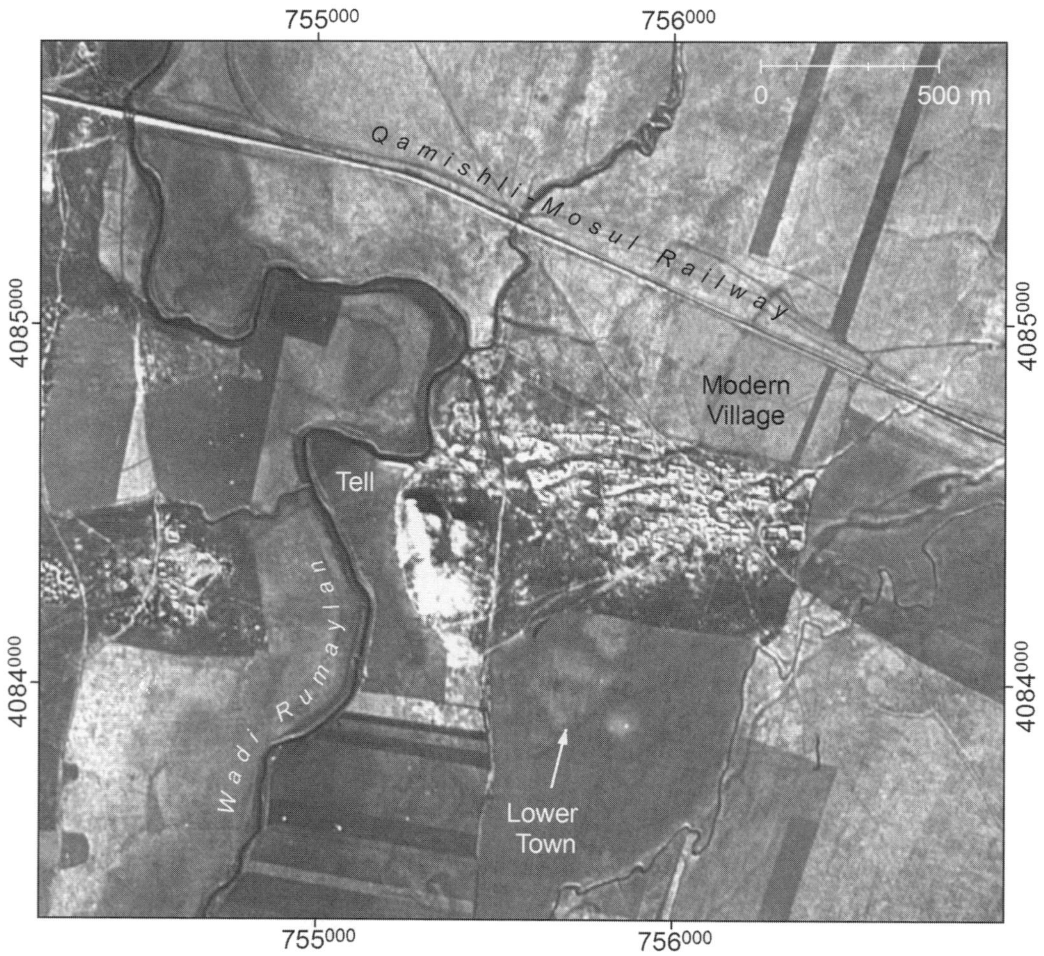

Figure 5.4. The high mound (40 m) at Tell Hadi, on the Wadi Rumaylan. The southern and western slopes of the mound are illuminated, while the northern slopes are in shadow (CORONA 1108-1025DA004, 6 December 1969)

extremely wet month at the end of a wetter-than-average rainy season (fig. 5.5A).[8] Under such conditions, anthropogenic soils may become saturated and therefore highly absorptive of light. Likewise, under conditions of extreme dryness at the height of summer, or following the harvest when sites and off-site areas are equally covered by dry chaff, differences in soil texture between sites and the surrounding terrain may not be visible (fig. 5.5B).

Complex mounded sites have a very distinctive pattern of alternating areas of light and dark on most CORONA scenes. As with low or unmounded sites, the areas of enhanced reflectivity are due to the finer sediments resulting from the erosion of mudbrick and a general lack of soil structure. The intervening dark areas mark streets and other open spaces between structures, and especially enclosed depressions, the areas excavated to make mudbricks (fig. 5.6). These depressions collect runoff moisture from the surrounding mounded areas, which in turn promotes vegetation growth. These two interrelated variables, higher moisture and vegetation, are responsible for the darker signature.

For complex mounded sites, the contrast between reflective mounded areas and absorptive depressions can be an effective relative indicator of age. For recently abandoned sites, the contrast is sharp; in some cases, it is still possible to make out internal features like streets and even individual structures, as at Tell Umm Hidur (fig. 5.6). With time, streets, courtyards, and enclosed depressions accumulate eroded sediments redeposited by wind and surface runoff, and formerly undulating surfaces become smooth. If the site surface remains stable, it will become further homogenized by the physical, chemical, and biological processes of soil formation. Although conditions vary locally, often only the largest enclosed depressions retain expression on CORONA images from Late Bronze Age (Period 10) and Iron Age (Period 11) sites; earlier settlements have been transformed into low mounds that appear internally homogeneous on CORONA.

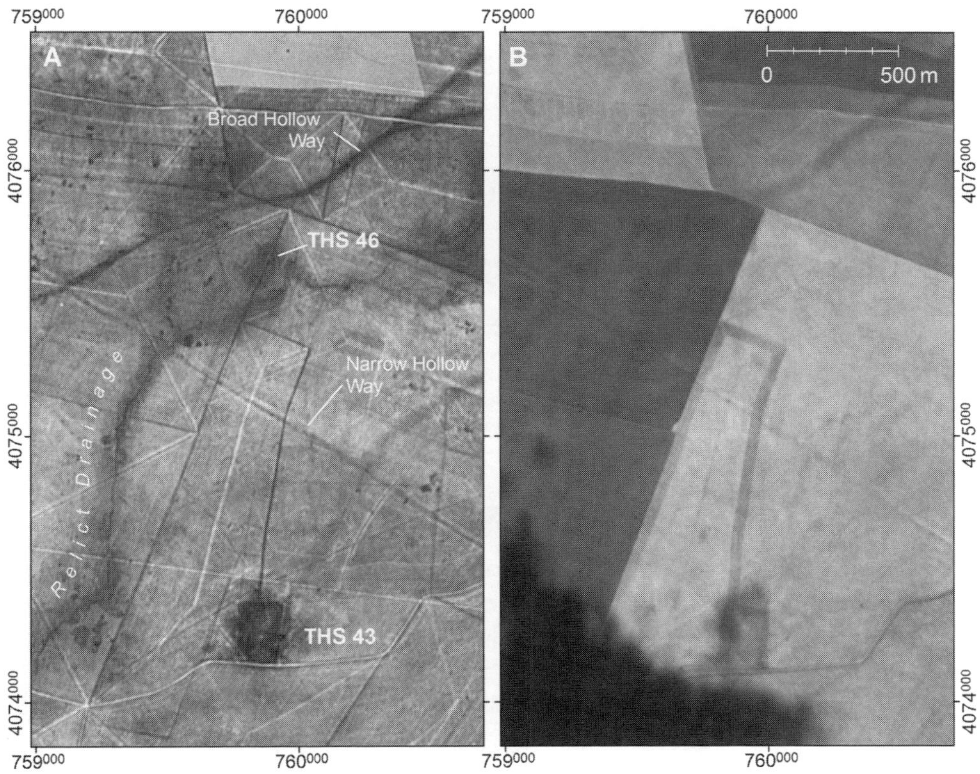

Figure 5.5. The effects of ground moisture on feature visibility in CORONA. (*A*) Saturated soils of sites and landscape features in the spring (CORONA 1117-1025DF147, 25 May 1972); (*B*) The same area before the start of the rainy season (CORONA 1105-2170DF051, 14 November 1968)

[8] In the 1971/1972 precipitation year, 587 mm fell on Qamishli. Between 1952 and 1990, rainfall in May at Qamishli averaged 30.4 mm, but in May 1972 the town received 117 mm, making it one of the wettest recorded [Global Historical Climatology Network (GHCN) Version 2 Precipitation].

Figure 5.6. Tell Umm Hidur, a complex mounded site southeast of the THS region with visible mudbrick architecture and abundant associated hollow way features (CORONA 1108-1025DA006, 6 December 1969)

The signature of areas of former settlement on CORONA photographs is thus dependent on several variables, especially ground moisture, ground cover, and land use. It is therefore critical to employ multiple missions that acquired imagery from different seasons, stages of the agricultural calendar, and positions in fields' crop rotations. In the missions exploited by the THS (see Section 4.3.1 and table 4.1), high mounds were visible in all, but low mounds and complex mounded sites often only appeared in one or two, due to particularly favorable local ground conditions.

5.1.4. NOMADIC OR NON-PERMANENT OCCUPATIONS

In alluvial areas of Mesopotamia, the presence of non-sedentary groups within past landscapes is difficult to document in a non-ambiguous way, or simply cannot be recovered at all. In the Upper Khabur basin, very light scatters of material are sometimes interpreted as the traces of seasonally present pastoral nomads (Lyonnet 1996a: 371–72), or it is assumed that they would have been found in the open steppe between the intensely used infields of sedentary settlements (Wilkinson 2000c). Their presence has also been inferred from disparities between high population size and low agricultural resources (Kouchoukos 1998: 391–93), or overabundance of cereal storage alongside low populations (Hole 1999). Pastoral nomads are not always archaeologically invisible, however. Seasonal campsites of pastoralists are in some cases rather substantial and may involve durable substructures upon which tents were erected each year (Cribb 1991; Alizadeh 2004; Ur and Hammer 2009), but such circumstances are far less common on broad steppe or alluvial areas.

Written sources, however, are non-ambiguous, beginning at least in the early second millennium B.C., when groups moved between the Euphrates at Mari and the Upper Khabur and Sinjar plains (Kupper 1957; Fleming 2004; Nicolle 2004). Northern Mesopotamia was the realm of the Aramean tribes in the late second and early first millennia B.C. (Lipiński 2000; Dion 1997), and various urban-based sources mention troublesome tribal groups in the basin in close vicinity thereafter (e.g., in the late tenth century, Ibn Hawqal 2001: 204). With the exception of the sixteenth century, the plains of northern Mesopotamia have been almost entirely given over to pastoral nomads for at least the last half millennium (see Section 2.2). Although the basin is almost entirely under cultivation at present, it is not uncommon for households from elsewhere in Syria to move their animals by truck onto rented harvested fields in the basin during the summer months (Vercueil and Cummins 2003).

Matters are further complicated by the range of variation within a pastoral economic mode and their different potential archaeological signatures. Over the last several centuries, the basin has hosted fully nomadic camel beduin but also a range of Arab and Kurdish semi-nomads and semi-sedentary communities (Glubb 1942: 1). These latter often left villages of permanent mudbrick structures to lead their animals out into the steppe, especially during the winter absence of the Shammar (von Oppenheim 1900: 142–43). These seasonally occupied villages would of course erode into mounds just as permanently settled ones would. Furthermore, groups could and did move along the continuum from sedentary agriculturalists to fully nomadic pastoralists throughout Mesopotamian history (Adams 1978). The Tay Arabs had once been fully nomadic like the Shammar, but adopted a semi-nomadic economy once the Shammar seized their pastures in the eighteenth century, and the semi-sedentary Kurdish tribes became full-time agriculturalists with the firm establishment of the Turkish-Syrian frontier in the 1930s.

Thus there is no doubt that the sequence of sedentary settlement patterns produced by archaeological survey in the basin is failing to represent an economically and politically significant component of human society and land use. The THS methodology was designed to document sedentary occupations without overwhelming the collections processing; therefore seasonal or impermanent occupations are unlikely to have been identified. More intensive surface collection methodologies, such as those made by Lyonnet's survey of the western basin (2000), are better suited to recover ephemeral occupations. The tradeoff is of course that fewer sites can be collected and more time must be devoted to the processing of very large collections.

Nonetheless, the THS did document several small collections of ceramics of the later third millennium B.C. (Period 7) that are interpreted, following Lyonnet (1996a), as the traces of non-permanent settlements. Nine small and low-mounded sites had such collections amid more abundant assemblages of other, generally earlier, periods (see the discussion in Section 6.4.2). It cannot be determined if these occupations were of pastoral nomads or of seasonal agricultural laborers from nearby towns and cities. Although the latter has been very common in the context of the modern cotton industry (Forni 2003: 331–32; Wattenbach 2006: 40–41), they may not have been a component of the premodern economy.

Complicating our interpretation of low-density assemblages is the presence of field scatters throughout the basin, deriving not from settlement but from manuring practices (see Section 5.2). The THS distinguished the two based on sherd morphology: field scatters are small and highly abraded, whereas sherds possibly deriving from non-permanent occupations are larger and show less wear. It must be admitted that the vast spread of artifactual material covering all parts of the basin where systematic observations have been made surely do contain some artifacts from campsites; however, the latter simply cannot account for the enormous volume of surface material.

Aside from the later third millennium, it seems likely that similar patterns existed in other periods and particularly between the major phases of nucleated settlement. Thus we resist referring to times of low sedentary occupation as periods of "abandonment" in favor of a general understanding that sedentary agriculture is but one economic adaptation found in the history of the Upper Khabur basin, albeit the one with the most robust landscape signature.

5.2. TRACES OF INTENSIFICATION: FIELD SCATTERS

As survey archaeologists have moved to study the landscape with increasing intensity, they have noticed that artifactual material is not restricted to obvious archaeological sites, but can be found in the fields beyond at lower density (Wilkinson 1982). This material is mostly comprised of sherds but also includes roof tiles, kiln slag, and lithics. In any given regional context, the density of these "field scatters" appears to be conditioned by several factors, most generally proximity to archaeological sites. Variation in density between regions is correlated with environment (Bintliff and Snodgrass 1988): wind erosion in semi-arid regions can remove soils but leave sherds behind, resulting in very high density; in temperate areas, higher rainfall can result in the burial of surface artifacts. As a result, the "halo" around a Roman site in England (average rainfall 750 mm/year) might be less than one sherd per 100 sq. m, but over 2,000 sherds per 100 sq. m in Oman (80 mm/year) (Bintliff and Snodgrass 1988: fig. 2; Wilkinson 1982).

Field scatters were first recognized in western Europe where, ironically, they are the least visible archaeologically (Wilkinson 1989: 31–32; Gaffney, Gaffney, and Tingle 1985). They have been most systematically studied in association with medieval Islamic sites in coastal Iran and Oman (Wilkinson 1982, 1988), Roman-Byzantine southeastern Anatolia (Wilkinson 1990b), and Bronze Age northern Mesopotamia (Wilkinson and Tucker 1995; Ur 2002a). In the 1970s and '80s, survey methods became increasingly intensive in the Mediterranean, to the point where all modern survey projects not only record off-site scatters but also use the same intensive methods for the collection of traditional sites (Alcock, Cherry, and Davis 1994; Bintliff and Snodgrass 1985; papers in Francovich and Patterson 2000).

In the Near East, field scatters are interpreted by Wilkinson as the remains of ancient manuring, a practice that features prominently in his model of the relationship between third-millennium urbanization and intensive agriculture (1994, 1997). The THS region provided an opportunity to test this model, which was based largely on Wilkinson's observations of field scatters in the North Jazira Project survey area (Wilkinson and Tucker 1995). Given the proximity of the THS and the North Jazira Project areas (Tell al-Hawa is only 31 km from Hamoukar, and the survey boundaries are at one point only 2.3 km apart), it seemed likely that similar manuring techniques would have been practiced at Hamoukar and its contemporary satellites. Furthermore, at 98 ha in settled area, Hamoukar's middle to late third-millennium (Period 7) population would have been even more subject to the necessity of agricultural intensification than its neighbors at 66 ha Tell al-Hawa. On these bases, a broad program of field scatter sampling was considered critical to the reconstruction of past landscapes in the THS region.

5.2.1. THS FIELD SCATTER COLLECTION METHODOLOGY

The THS field scatter collection program methods followed previous Near Eastern surveys but with previously unavailable positioning technologies. Collections have mostly employed a systematic sampling methodology, and have been undertaken exclusively by Wilkinson (1982, 1989) with some variation in intervals and placement strategies. Around Tell Sweyhat, sherds were collected from 100 sq. m surface units at 500 m or 100 m intervals, whereas in the Iraqi North Jazira, intervals varied between 300 m and 50 m; in both cases these observations were supplemented by walking tallys (Wilkinson 1989: 36; 2004: 59–65). Around Sweyhat and in the North Jazira Project area, transects radiated outward from the major sites, but were placed on a grid in the area around Kurban Höyük (Wilkinson 1990b: 68–69). These methods are far less intense than standard Mediterranean survey (e.g., Bintliff 2000; Mattingly 2000), but they allow a much broader area to be covered. Wilkinson sampled some 117 sq. km around Tell al-Hawa (Wilkinson and Tucker 1995), whereas in the first three seasons of the highly intensive Boeotian Expedition survey, only 13.7 sq. km were explored (Bintliff and Snodgrass 1985: 135).

When faced with the necessity of documenting field scatters over a 125 sq. km survey area with only three team members, the THS adopted a systematic sampling method similar to Wilkinson's. A pilot program of three radial transects in the 1999 season demostrated the presence of significant scatters and the feasibility of systematic collection (Ur 2002b: 27–28). For the 2000 season, units were collected in transects separated by 200 m, and placed at 200 m intervals (fig. 5.7). These transects were oriented either north–south or east–west and followed whenever possible the grid of the UTM coordinate system, as indicated by handheld GPS receivers.

Although the primary goal in walking these transects was not site recognition, the terrain to either side of the transects was scanned while walking between collection units. These transects offer a degree of confirmation that sites were not being missed by the remote sensing-intensive site recognition methodology: in over 77 km of transects, no site was identified that had not already been spotted on CORONA imagery.

Because variation in sherd density can result from differences in ground visibility, some archaeologists have coded the visibility of each collection unit and used this score to "correct" the raw artifact counts (e.g., Bintliff 2000; Gallant 1986; Gaffney, Bintliff, and Slapsak 1991), although others have expressed skepticism in this method (Mattingly 2000). The THS attempted to circumvent this issue by limiting transects and collection units to fields of comparable visibility (either fallow in the previous winter or harvested, heavily grazed, and not yet plowed) while skipping over low-visibility fields (especially recently plowed fields, ungrazed fields with dense chaff cover, and those with standing summer cotton crops). Variation in visibility was thus reduced, although not eliminated (see

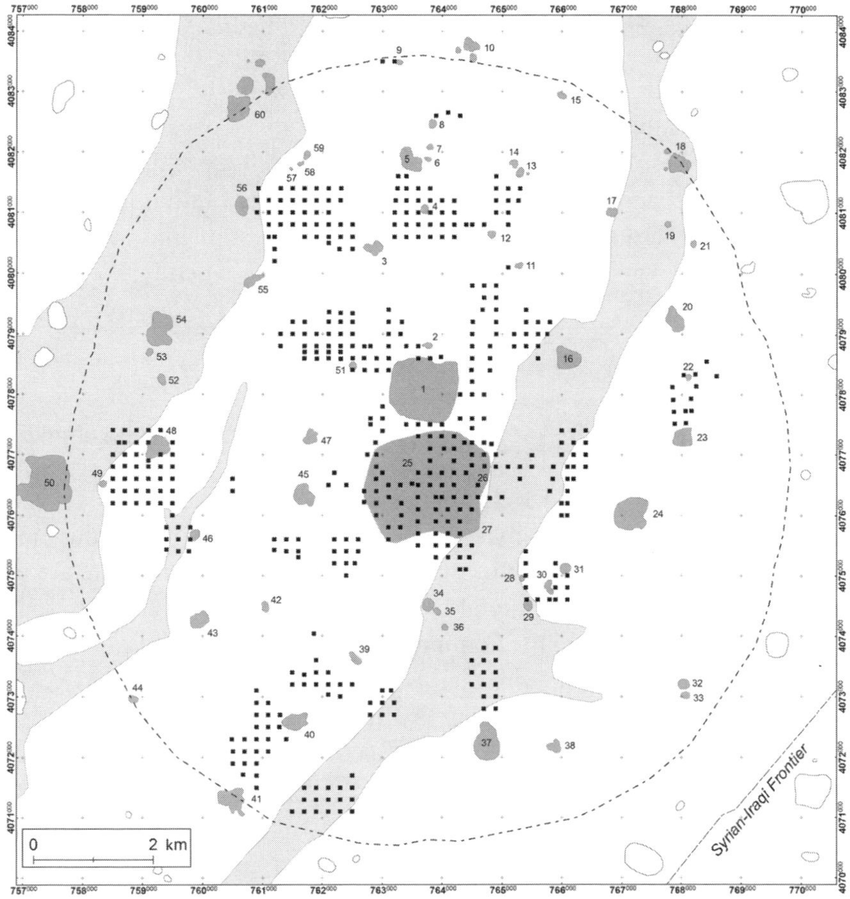

Figure 5.7. Distribution of systematic field scatter units in the THS region, with floodplain areas and surveyed sites indicated

Figure 5.8. Field scatter collection on a high-visibility fallow field, with simulated unit boundaries

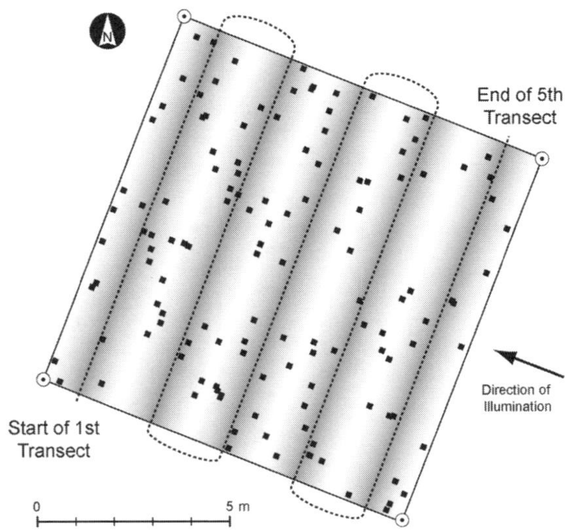

Figure 5.9. Schematic illustration of a field scatter collection unit

also Wilkinson and Tucker 1995: 20–21). In some cases, transects and collection units deviated slightly from the UTM grid to avoid low-visibility positions, but these deviations did not exceed 20 m.

Once a collection unit had been positioned, a 10 × 10 m square was laid out (fig. 5.8). The orientation of the square varied depending on the position of the sun: the first side of the square was paced out by walking directly toward the collector's shadow. The resulting orientation insured that the back-and-forth transects through the square could be made with the collector's shadow directly to one side, rather than falling in the transect path and creating sharp lighting contrasts that lower sherd recovery (fig. 5.9). Collection of a single unit took generally 12–15 minutes and collectors attempted to spend approximately this amount of time on collections so that collection intensity would not be a significant variable.

5.2.2. DENSITY AND DISTRIBUTION OF FIELD SCATTERS

In the 2000 season, the THS collected 474 field scatter units. Sixty of these units were within the bounds of THS 25 (Khirbat al-Fakhar), the 300 ha low-density settlement of the late fifth millennium (Period 4; see fig. 4.14). These units and several others that fell within 50 m of the edge of an archaeological site are excluded from the analyses that follow, leaving 393 off-site units with a total of 14,981 sherds collected. Overall sherd density was high, averaging over 38 sherds per 100 sq. m. No collection unit failed to produce at least a single sherd, and units with five or fewer sherds were rarer than units with more than fifty sherds in the THS area (fig. 5.10). The placement of field scatter collection units was dictated to a large extent by the desire to maintain comparable visibility conditions; as a result, the distribution of units (fig. 5.7) leaves many areas uninvestigated. Ultimately, over 77 km of transects were walked.

Before discussing the density and spatial distribution of field scatters, it is important to rule out observation differences between collectors as a potential source of variation. Elsewhere in the eastern Mediterranean, field projects have avoided this potential problem by having a single individual make all off-site collections (e.g., Gallant 1986;

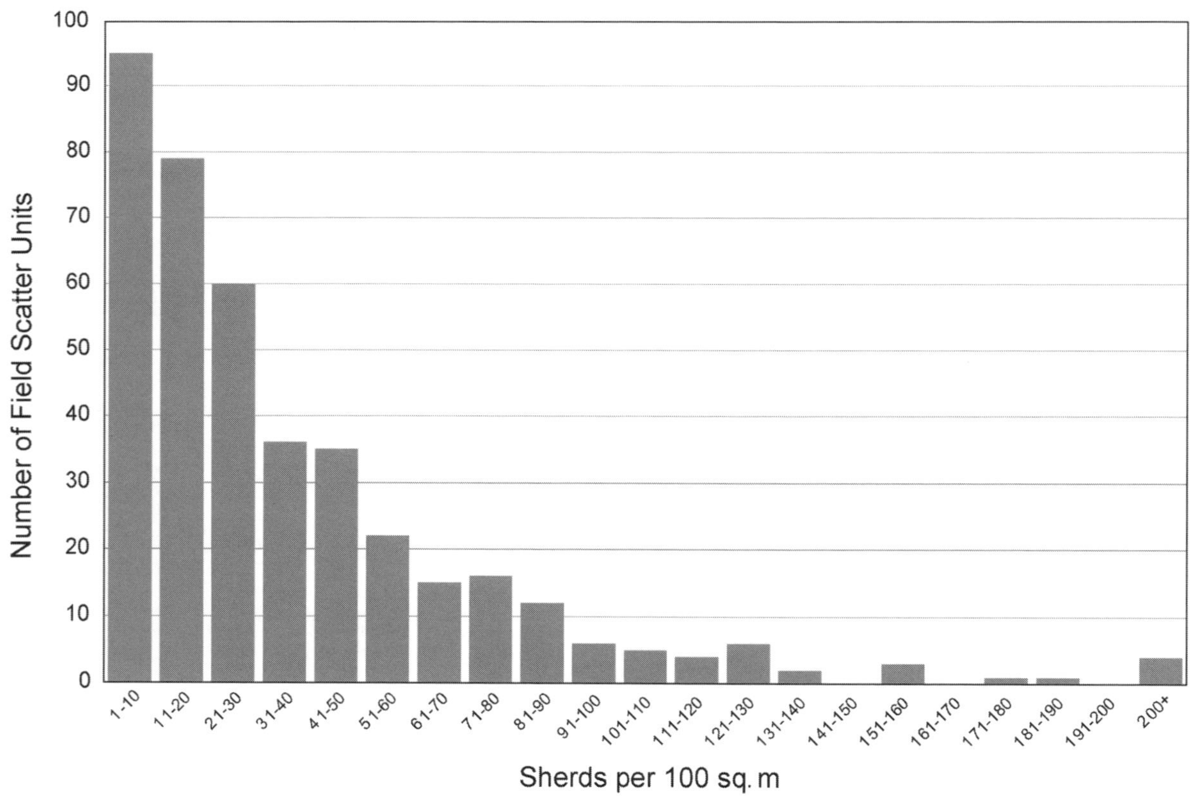

Figure 5.10. Histogram of collection units and field scatter density. No units produced zero sherds

Wilkinson and Tucker 1995: 20). In order to cover more area, the THS used three collectors (fig. 5.11). To test for operator biases, an initial set of transects was run as a training exercise, with no apparent differences between the collectors. After all units were collected, a statistical test was run on the data. The transects were assigned to the three collectors randomly throughout the survey and the distribution of the three resulting sets of sherd counts are approximately normal when log-transformed, so a one-way analysis of variance (ANOVA) was performed. The calculated F ratio (1.175) is less than the F critical value ($F_{(.001,2,380)} = 7.035$), so the differences between the counts for the three operators are statistically insignificant at the 0.1% level. On this basis, we believe that variation in field scatter density is related to a combination of ancient agricultural practices (see below) and subsequent natural and cultural transformations, and that differences in collection rates between individual collectors did not contribute significantly to variation in scatter density.

The Wilkinson model predicts that field scatters will be densest in proximity to large settlements, and indeed the densest field scatters occur within 3 km of Hamoukar (fig. 5.12). Of the eighty units of 60 or more sherds per 100 sq. m, seventy-two fall in this zone. However, within that 3 km area, there is a substantial range of variation (mean of 50 sherds/100 sq. m with a standard deviation of 45.6).

Sherd density per 100 sq. m was plotted by distance from Hamoukar, both on a unit-by-unit basis (fig. 5.12) and by average within concentric rings of 500 m intervals (fig. 5.13). Within 2 km, sherd density averages over 80 sherds per 100 sq. m but exhibits great variability. After a spike at 1,500–2,000 m, average density declines steadily and after another small spike at 3,500–4,000 m, plateaus around 20 sherds per 100 sq. m.

Hamoukar was the largest, but not the only, Period 7 (middle to late third-millennium) settlement in the THS; therefore density was also plotted by distance from the permanently occupied Period 7 settlements (THS 1, 16, 37, 41, 54; see figs. 5.14 and 5.15). Densities beyond 3,500 m in these figures should be viewed with caution; given the distribution of Period 7 settlements, almost all areas of the THS region are within 3,500 m of a site of that period (note the number of collection units in fig. 5.15). For example, the tremendous spike in the average at 3,500–4,000 m is derived from a single collection unit less than 100 m from an almost completely leveled Halaf site (THS 8). Furthermore, study area edge effects are probably significant: the few units that are beyond 3,500 m may be located closer to an unsurveyed site beyond the THS limits. Bearing these caveats in mind, density still averages 80 sherds per 100 sq. m within 500 m of Period 7 sites and declines gradually to 29 sherds per 100 sq. m at 3,000–3,500 m, beyond which density figures are not reliable.

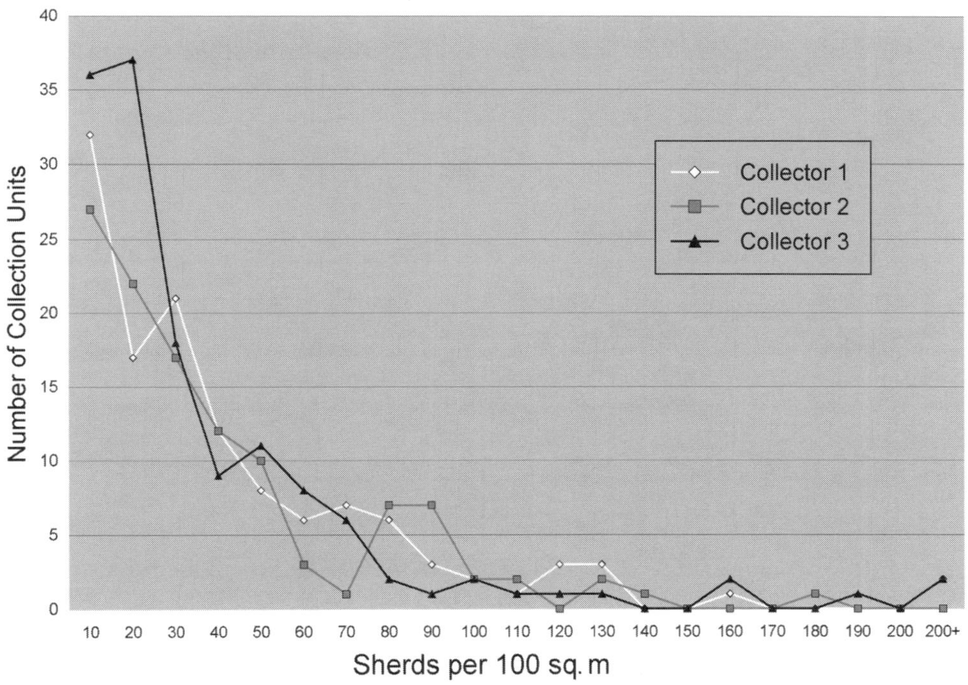

Figure 5.11. Histogram of collection units and field scatter density, by collector

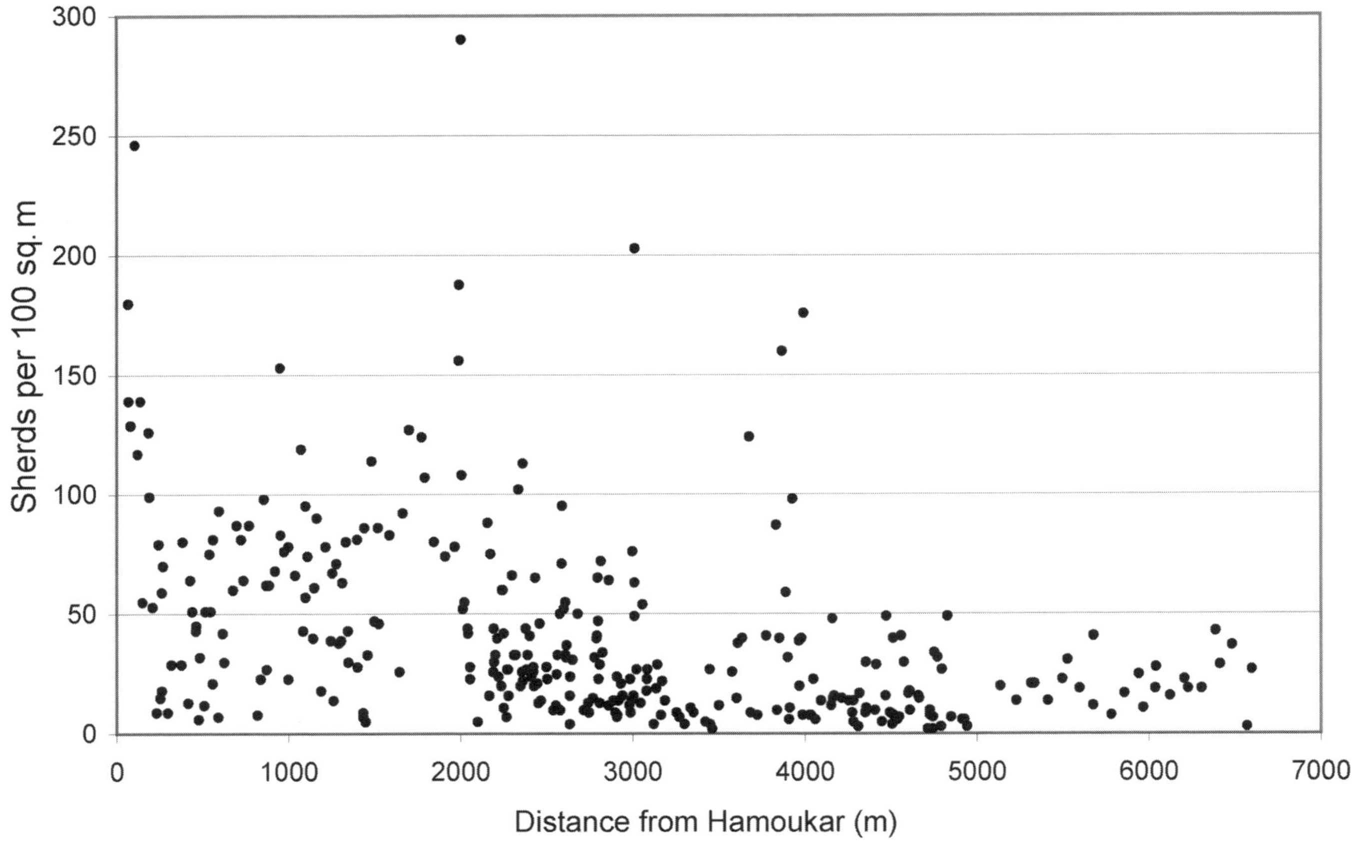

Figure 5.12. Field scatter density in relation to distance from Hamoukar

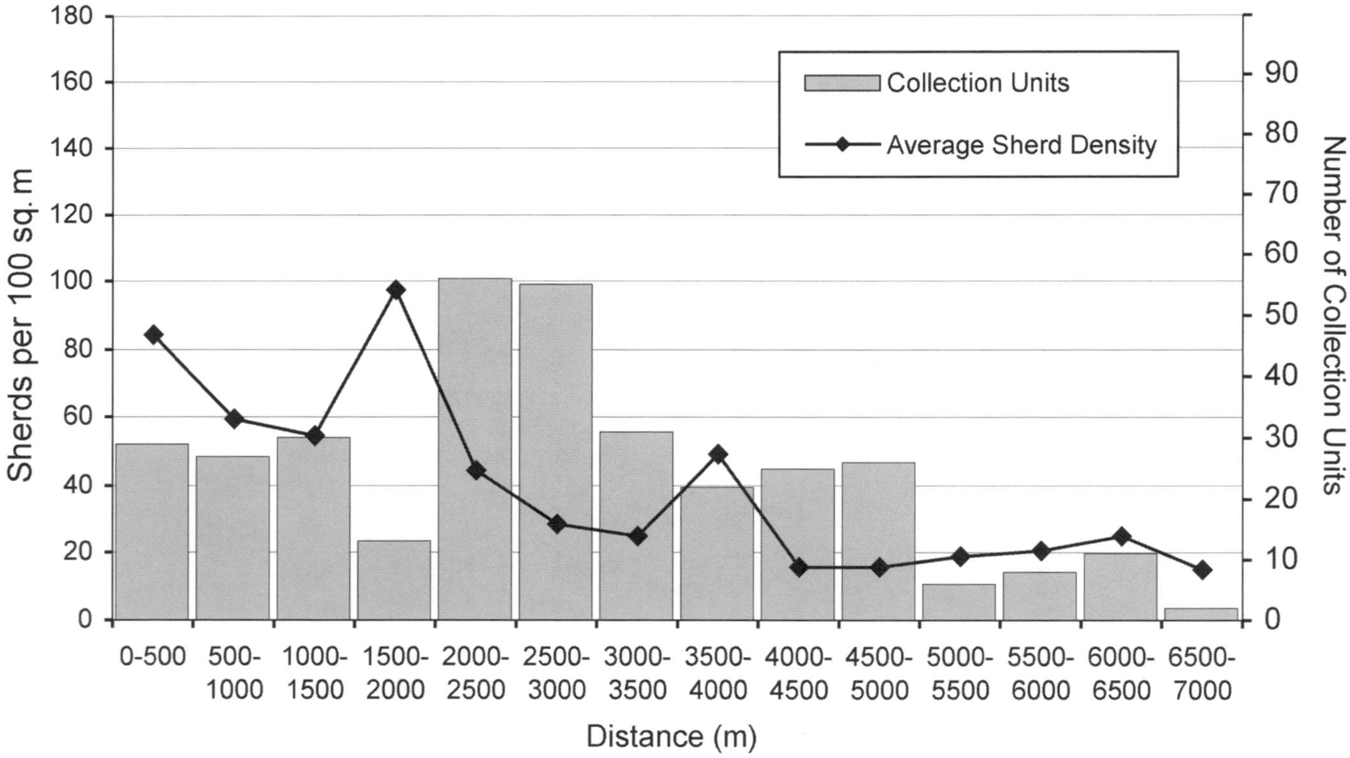

Figure 5.13. Average field scatter density (black lines) and number of collection units (gray bars) with distance from Hamoukar

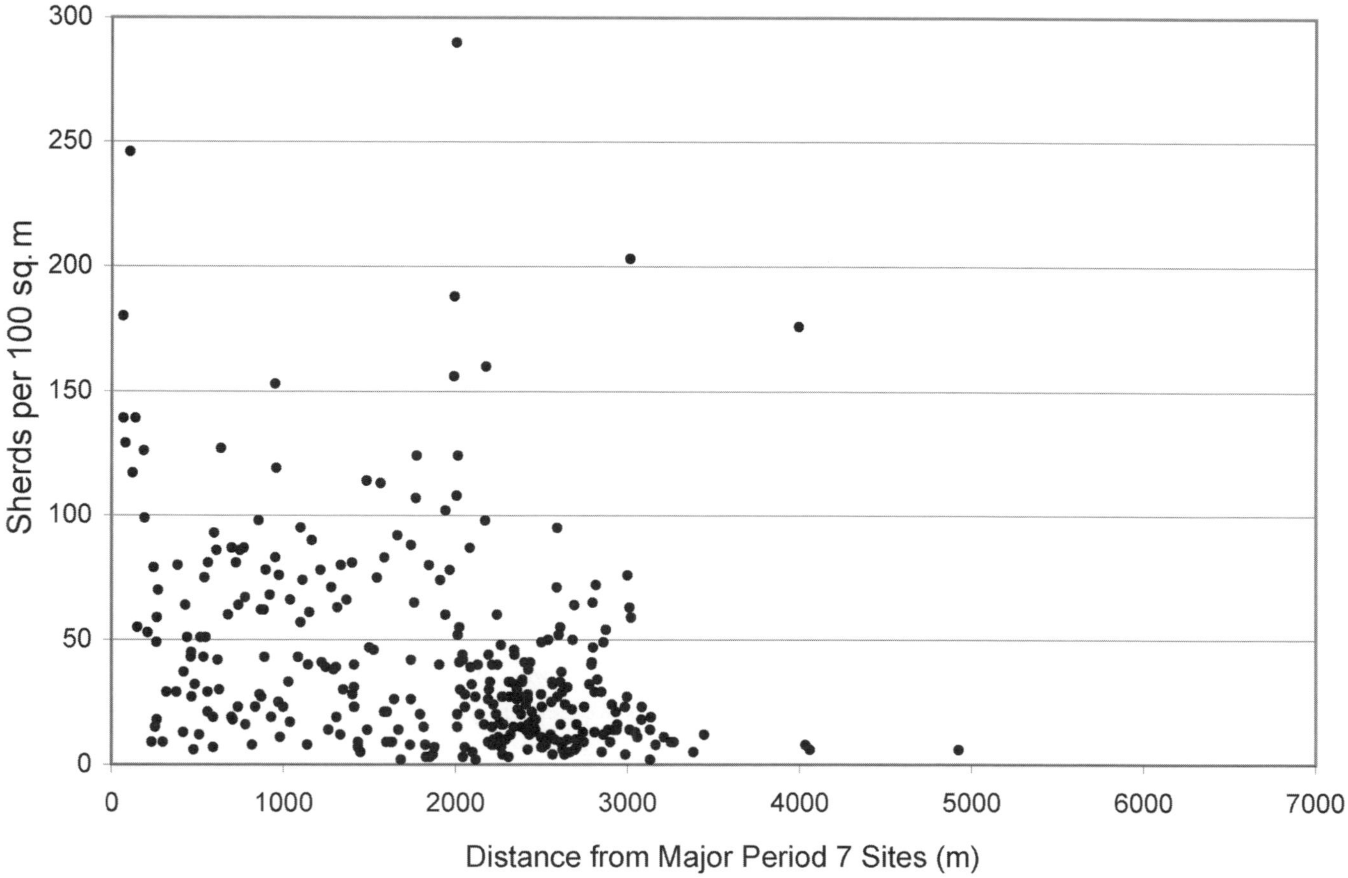

Figure 5.14. Field scatter density in relation to distance from major Period 7 sites

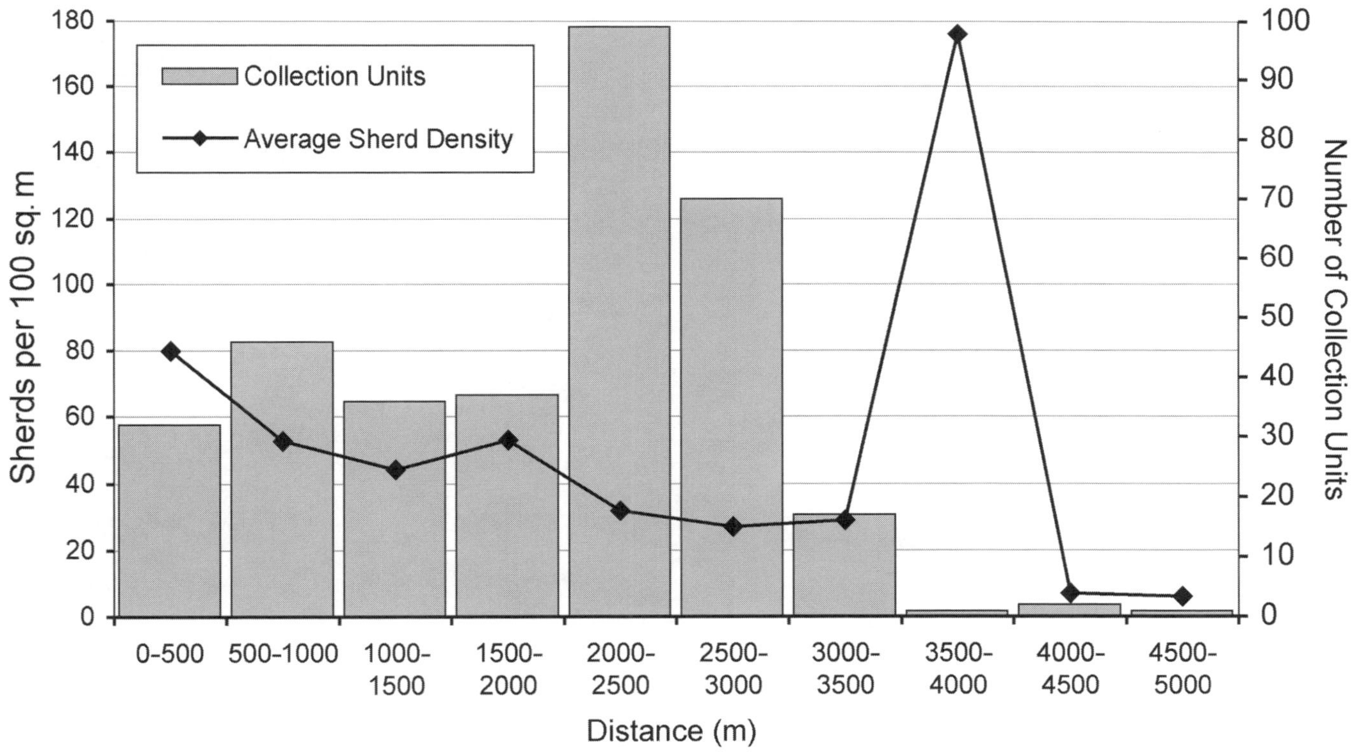

Figure 5.15. Average field scatter density (black lines) and number of collection units (gray bars) with distance from major Period 7 sites

Overall, field scatters in the THS area are more variable than those in the nearby North Jazira Project area (Wilkinson and Tucker 1995: 21–23, figs. 14–18). Around Hamoukar itself, field scatters are generally dense; this is particularly true of the fields to the northwest, northeast, and far north (south of THS 5), where average density often exceeds 60 sherds/100 sq. m. However, isolated areas of low density exist within these areas of high density, despite identical visibility conditions.

The situation is more complicated around Hamoukar's Period 7 satellites. The fields around THS 16 exhibit similar densities to Hamoukar itself, but their proximity to Hamoukar might mean that these scatters are related to Hamoukar rather than THS 16. No units were collected within 2 km of THS 54, and the units collected north of THS 37 were almost all within a zone of aggradation in the eastern drainage (see Section 5.2.3). Thirty-nine units were collected on the plain north of THS 41; their average density (23.5 sherds/100 sq. m) is in excess of the "background" scatter around sites such as THS 48 and 50, but much lower than the scatters in the vicinity of Hamoukar itself. This pattern appears to match that of the adjacent North Jazira area, where Tell al-Hawa's satellites exhibited field scatter halos only to around 1 km from the site edge (Wilkinson and Tucker 1995: 22, fig. 60).

5.2.3. PRESERVATION AND TRANSFORMATION OF FIELD SCATTER SURFACE ASSEMBLAGES

Absolute counts of sherds in the field cannot be taken at face value because various patterned processes have transformed the landscape. Areas of low field scatter density are generally distant from Hamoukar. In two places, these low densities seemed anomalous, given their proximity to sites of middle to late third-millennium (Period 7) date and despite high visibility. When plotted on CORONA imagery, two such areas in the southern THS region

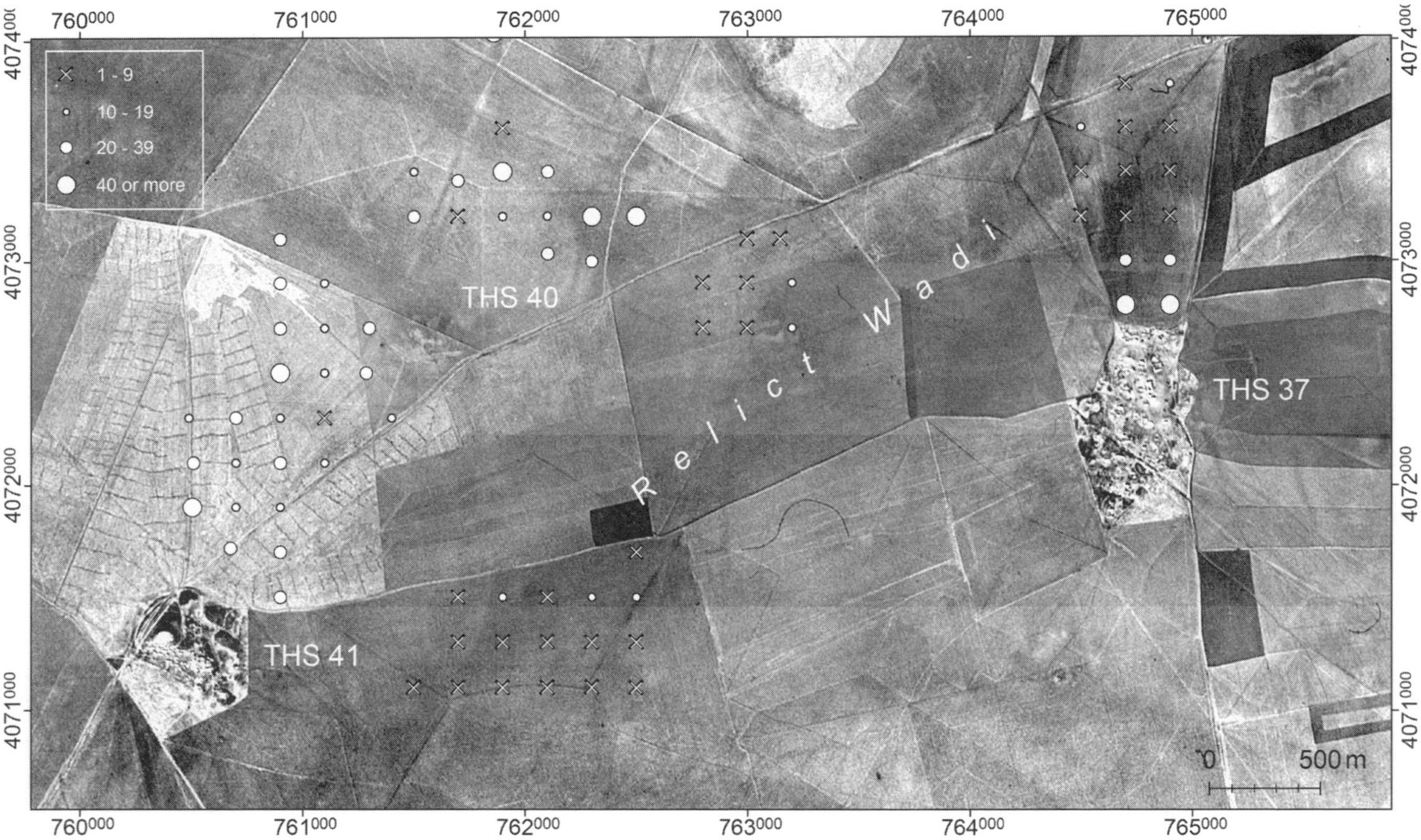

Figure 5.16. The effects of wadi infilling via plow wash on field scatter density in the area of THS 37 and 41 (CORONA 1108-1025DA006, 6 December 1969). Quantities are in sherds per 100 sq. m

(east of THS 41 and north of THS 37) fell within the valley fill of the easternmost drainage (fig. 5.16). Although hydrological modeling indicates that runoff should concentrate into surface drainage in these areas (Section 2.1), they are at present entirely flat; the former wadi has been completely filled in with plow washed sediments and is invisible on the ground (although it is visible farther to the north near Hamoukar). In these cases, it is highly likely that field scatters have been obscured by in-washed sediments.

Although more speculative, irrigation may also have impacted the field scatter record. There are traces of small-scale irrigation systems north and west of the THS region (see Section 5.4). No traces survive of small distributary canals, but the few large channels that can be identified leave the possibility that the northwestern quadrant of the THS may have been irrigated at some point. If irrigation did occur in this area, it may be responsible for the low (but not absent) scatters there (discussed in the next section).

5.2.4. DIRECT AND ASSOCIATIONAL DATING OF FIELD SCATTERS

When diagnostic types can be recognized in sherd scatter collections, they are predominantly of Period 7 (middle to late third millennium) (see also Wilkinson and Tucker 1995: 22–23); however, the great majority of the collected sherds are battered and abraded beyond recognition.

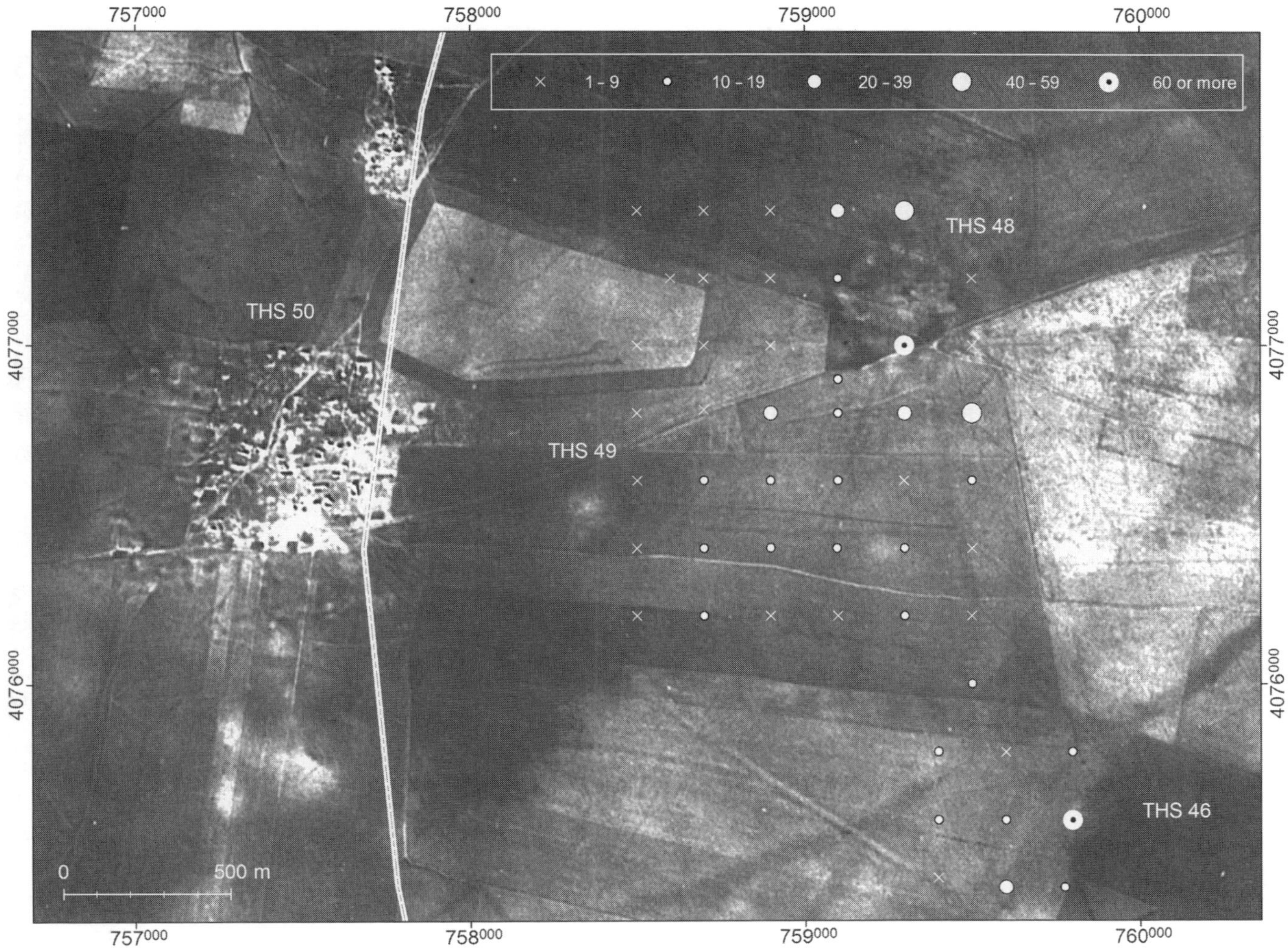

Figure 5.17. Low-density field scatters between the large Period 11 site at THS 48 and the large Periods 16–17 site at THS 50 (CORONA 1102-1025DF006, 11 December 1967)

An alternative method for dating field scatters comes from spatial association with sites of known occupation dates. The close association of dense field scatters with the large mid- to late third-millennium center at Hamoukar agrees well with Wilkinson's (2003: 117–18) findings around other contemporary medium to large centers in northern Mesopotamia such as Kurban Höyük, Titriş Höyük, Tell Sweyhat, and Tell al-Hawa. Major sites of other times of settlement expansion, Period 11 (Iron Age/Neo-Assyrian) and Periods 16–17 (Sasanian–Early Islamic), are not associated with field scatters in the THS region.

For example, an extensive area of high visibility was sampled between the 7.6 ha Iron Age settlement at THS 48 and the 60 ha Sasanian–Early Islamic town at THS 50 (fig. 5.17). Also in this area are small sites of Period 1 (Proto-Hassuna) and Period 4 (Late Chalcolithic 1–2) (THS 49 and 46, respectively). Fifty units were collected, averaging 15.5 sherds per 100 sq. m. If we disregard the four units within 50 m of the edges of THS 46 and 48, that average falls to 11.6 sherds per 100 sq. m. This average density is probably lowered by the inclusion of ten units that fall in areas identified as aggraded areas of former watercourses, northwest of THS 48 and west of THS 46. The low densities in these areas may be analogous to the low densities around THS 37 and 41 discussed in the previous section. These thirty-six units average 12.6 sherds per 100 m, which is likely to be the general "background" level of field scatter for non-aggrading surfaces in the THS region (compare with Wilkinson and Tucker 1995: 21). It remains a possibility, however, that this area may have been irrigated, and therefore these densities may have been lowered via sediment aggradation (see above and Section 5.4).

5.2.5. INTERPRETATION OF FIELD SCATTERS

Prior to intensive and systematic investigation of off-site areas, the presence of cultural material beyond site limits was generally explained as the result of chance events, such as "the mythical donkey off whose back pots are supposed to have fallen, leaving trails of sherds in otherwise unimportant zones of the landscape" (Bintliff and Snodgrass 1988: 507). Such an explanation cannot account for the near-continuous distribution of field scatters. Others interpret scatters as evidence of low-intensity activities that were undertaken outside of the settlement (Gaffney, Gaffney, and Tingle 1985), and still others emphasize the ability of natural erosion and plowing to relocate artifacts from settlements into the surrounding fields (reviewed in Bintliff and Snodgrass 1988: 507–08; Alcock, Cherry, and Davis 1994). Yet another interpretation might see field scatters as the low-density debris from the campsites of pastoral nomads, which do not leave mounding or durable soil discoloration. All these processes contributed to some extent to the off-site record in the THS region, but even taken together, they cannot account for the continuous nature of the phenomenon.

The most plausible explanation, which takes into consideration the ubiquity of the scatters as well as their spatial patterning, is that field scatters derive from ancient manuring practices (Wilkinson 1982; Bintliff and Snodgrass 1988). Cultivation removes nutrients such as nitrogen and phosphorus from the soil, which decreases yields; manuring can reintroduce nutrients to maintain or elevate agricultural productivity. Manuring can be done directly by pasturing animals on the fields to be manured, but this method is of little value in semi-arid regions, where dung dries out quickly. In order to be effective, manure should be composted; therefore, manure and other organic material was first collected at a settlement and then taken out to be distributed on the fields.

Settlement-based composting of animal, human, and other types of organic wastes and their use as fertilizer are well documented by historical and ethnographic data from the Near East and China (reviewed in Wilkinson 1982: 324–25; 1989: 40–41), in the Classical World (Alcock, Cherry, and Davis 1994: 145–57), and even in New World contexts (Killion 1992). The mechanism for the incorporation of sherds and other artifacts is described by Wilkinson: "... byres were emptied, cess pits cleaned, and streets were systematically scoured. These 'night soils,' or composts of them, were then hauled from the settlements and spread in a zone adjacent to the city. Such enterprises inevitably incorporated a miscellany of artifacts into the manure and all but the largest of these artifacts would eventually be spread on the fields as part of the manure" (1982: 324). At several classical towns in Greece, excavated household byres have been found full of sherds and roof tiles; soil analysis shows extremely high levels of phosphorous, as would be expected if organic wastes had been composted in them (Ault 1999). A nineteenth-century byre in Philadelphia was also packed with non-organic household debris that was deliberately introduced so that liquid wastes would leach slowly (Roberts and Barrett 1984).

It is possible that in the hinterlands of the larger settlements, it was not composted manure that was being deposited but rather the ashes from burnt dung that had been used for fuel. In Wilkinson's "agro-ecological" model of dung use, when wood fuel is readily available, dung will be used for manure; when wood fuel is unavailable, dung will have to be burnt and thus will be unavailable for manure (Miller 1984; Miller and Smart 1984). Dung ash is still valuable for crop nutrition, however, and would still be deposited on fields. Because this ash derives from a settlement context, it is more likely to be deposited in conjunction with other inorganic settlement debris, and this latter component survives in the topsoil. Therefore, high field scatter densities reflect not only manuring but also hint indirectly at the more intensive use of dung as fuel in a wood-poor environment.

In the Near East and Mediterranean, the "manuring hypothesis" has been met with both enthusiastic acceptance and considerable skepticism. The reaction has tended toward the latter in the Near East (see, e.g., comments by Oates and Schwartz to Wilkinson 1994: 510–11). For the Mediterranean area, Alcock and colleagues note that "in the traditional model of Greek agriculture, manuring was down-played, but the danger now lies in the opposite direction … the 'manuring hypothesis' is inadequate as the *only* explanation for off-site pottery distributions; whether it was nonetheless the *chief* factor … is still *sub judice*, and in any case probably varied substantially with time and place, in ways that would repay exploration" (1994: 157; see also Gaffney, Gaffney, and Tingle 1985; Fentress 2000).

Despite these criticisms, manuring remains the most convincing general explanation for the distribution and volume of off-site surface artifacts in the THS area. We reconstruct a cyclical movement of nutrients between the settlement and the fields in its hinterland. Nutrients came into the settlement as cereal and animal products; there they were prepared, consumed, and discarded, either as food remains or as burnt or composted dung, ultimately to be taken back out to the fields as manure (Ur and Colantoni 2010). Beyond a certain point, manure ceases to be economically feasible to transport: "Midden and manure-stack material is usually in short supply and heavy to transport. Its use will, therefore, tend to be limited to the more intensive arable land, as close as practicable to its source"

Figure 5.18. Field scatter evidence for intensive cultivation in the immediate hinterland of Hamoukar, with sites and modern field boundaries. Point and interpolated surface values are in sherds per 100 sq. m

(Hayes 1991: 82). Therefore, if manuring produced the sherd distributions found in the fields, one would expect densities to be higher closest to the presumed center of collection and distribution (Wilkinson 1982).

The fields to the west, north, and east of Hamoukar were probably heavily manured during Hamoukar's major phase of expansion in Period 7 (fig. 5.18). This zone of intensive cultivation extended between 2 and 3 km from the site itself and possibly farther. If this intensive zone also included the fields to the south, the abandoned surface of THS 25 would have also come under cultivation. Unfortunately, the THS had not developed a methodology for distinguishing third-millennium field scatter from late fifth-millennium settlement debris during the 2000 field season. Farmers at Hamoukar's major Period 7 neighbors also engaged in manuring their fields. Spatially limited manuring at a lesser intensity occurred around THS 41 and 37 but cannot be confirmed around the others.

Elsewhere in the THS, anomalous patches of high-density scatters were found in areas of otherwise low sherd density. Frequently, these patches can be explained as the products of erosion or recent smearing by plowing from nearby habitation sites. However, it is equally possible that they represent manuring strategies more spatially and chronologically limited than those employed by later third-millennium farmers at Hamoukar. For example, the one or two high-density collection units found immediately offsite near the Period 11 (Iron Age/Neo-Assyrian) sites at THS 48 (fig. 5.17) and THS 23 (see fig. 5.7) might be interpreted as small-scale manuring of vegetable gardens. The 200 m interval sampling strategy employed by the THS was designed to document extensively patterned manuring as already known from other third-millennium towns and cities in northern Mesopotamia; a proper investigation of the variable scatters around these Period 11 sites and the Period 7 satellites of Hamoukar would require a higher-resolution collection methodology.

Field scatters can suggest the area of *intensive* cultivation, but not the total arable land, which could have extended much farther beyond it. This broader area of lower-intensity cultivation can be approximated via a second off-site archaeological phenomenon, the hollow way.

5.3. ANCIENT MOVEMENT: HOLLOW WAYS

The linear features that cross the plains of the Upper Khabur basin and elsewhere in northern Mesopotamia have been documented and correctly identified as transport routes since the late 1920s. Elsewhere, the traces of ancient movement survive only in fragmentary form (Trombold 1991a; Snead, Erickson, and Darling 2009), but the unique circumstances of preservation in the basin discussed in *Chapter 2* have allowed nearly complete networks to be recovered. The THS documented dozens of hollow way features on the ground, and subsequent imagery analysis has permitted the mapping of over 6,000 km of tracks in the Khabur basin alone.

An important terminological distinction between the two main types of routes must be made at the start. Within archaeological literature, a dichotomy has been drawn between *roads*, which are formal, intentionally constructed features, and *tracks* or *paths*, which are the informal, non-constructed results of human or animal movement (Crawford 1953: 60–62; Trombold 1991b: 3; Hyslop 1991: 29). Formal features tend to be very straight and of a defined width and are likely to disregard topographic relief along their course. Tracks, on the other hand, are the result of intentional individual decisions, but their formation as landscape features is the unintended consequence of the whole of these decisions rather than the product of a single action or decision. They tend to take the path of least resistance, which generally involves the avoidance of steep slopes or uneven ground.

In the Upper Khabur basin, almost all known ancient paths of movement, and the majority of present ones as well, were informal and non-constructed. The building materials for formal roads were unavailable locally and would have been prohibitively expensive to import. It is therefore inappropriate to use the term "road" with reference to the linear features in the Upper Khabur basin. Identically formed features in Costa Rica are referred to as "paths" (Sheets and Sever 1991), but this term carries connotations about size, function, and means of transportation that are inappropriate for the case at hand. As demonstrated below, networks of movement in the Upper Khabur basin carried a range of traffic (pedestrians, animals, wheeled vehicles) for a range of purposes. Furthermore, the landscape features now visible via remote sensing and occasionally on the ground are not the ancient features themselves but rather their remains transformed by cultural and natural processes. Here we refer to the archaeological features as hollow ways, the ancient features as tracks, and the general corridors of movement (without reference to any specific hollow way or track) as routes.

5.3.1. RECONSTRUCTING ANCIENT MOVEMENT IN NORTHERN MESOPOTAMIA

Hollow ways, also called linear hollows (Wilkinson 1993) or routes rayonnantes (Van Liere and Lauffray 1954–55), are linear depressions that represent the surviving traces of ancient tracks (fig. 5.19). As archaeological phenomena, they can be found in diverse geographical contexts all over the world, but are best known in Britain (Crawford 1953; Hoskins 1988; Taylor 1979; Hindle 1993). British hollow ways can be as deep as 20 feet when aided by water erosion (Hindle 1982: 11), but often survive only as crop or soil marks (Wilson 1982: 137–38). Pre-Columbian sunken footpaths in the Costa Rican rainforest are only 30–70 cm wide and are also marked by vegetation differences (Sheets and Sever 1991). Elsewhere in the Middle East, analogous ancient tracks formed on the loess of the northern Negev (Tsoar and Yekutieli 1992).

In northern Mesopotamia, the depth of hollow ways ranges from as little as 50 cm to almost 2 m (Wilkinson 1993; Wilkinson and Tucker 1995). Widths may vary from 30 to 100 m, but can be as large as 200 m; however, their edges fade subtly into the surrounding landscape, making exact measurements somewhat subjective. Their patterning is most frequently in the form of radial systems extending outward from sites in a spoke-like pattern, which is closely associated with the central site (Van Liere and Lauffray 1954–55: 136, 145). However, longer interregional hollow ways that run through the areas of two or more sites also exist (Wilkinson and Tucker 1995: 26, table 4).

Hollow ways form through a combination of compaction and erosion that results from the continuous passage of human and animal traffic across fine-textured soils. Tsoar and Yekutieli (1992: 211–12) have identified two formation mechanisms. During wet months, soil consistency (its natural resistance to pressure) is lowered by high moisture content, so that movement compacts the surface of the track. In the dry season, aeolian movement predominates. Human and animal traffic lifts silt and clay particles, which the winds are not strong enough to erode on their own; once lifted, the winds can then transport them. The end result is that the "reiteration of such erosion action on

Figure 5.19. Oblique view across a broad hollow way near Profile D, facing south (see fig. 5.23 for location and fig. 5.25 for profile cross section). The eastern end of the Jebel Sinjar is visible in the background

paths and roads reduces them to a lower level than the surrounding plain and gives the roads the appearance of a gutter" (Tsoar and Yekutieli 1992: 212). Once formed, hollow ways can channel surface runoff and may even redirect the flow of nearby wadis (Wilkinson and Tucker 1995: fig. 25).

The movement of farmers to and from their fields led to hollow way formation, but the daily movement of animals to pasture would have accounted for twelve times as much compaction/disturbance (Wilkinson 1993: 559; see also Taylor 1979: 163–68). Herd traffic may explain in part why northern Mesopotamian hollow ways can be very broad. More difficult to quantify is the impact of wheeled traffic on hollow way formation processes. Vehicles themselves do not survive, but clay models of carts and chariots have been found in third-millennium B.C. levels throughout Mesopotamia (Oates 2001a; Moorey 2001) and they are a frequent motif on the cylinder seals from Tell Beydar (Jans and Bretschneider 1998). The frequent mention of the cartwright (nagar ^{giš}gigir$_2$) in the Beydar texts (Sallaberger 1996: 95) may indicate that wheeled transport was employed not only for the textually documented visits of the ruler of Nagar with large teams of draft animals, but also for more mundane activities, such as the hauling of settlement-derived manure out to the fields (see Section 5.2 above) and the movement of cereal harvests into the settlements.

Of great importance in the formation of hollow ways is the presence of constraints on human and animal movement by cultivated fields. In Britain, Richard Muir has observed that, "where tightly confined by dwellings and private property defined by hedgerows the track was far more likely to develop a linear, deeply incised and rutted form than it was when traversing open, upland commons, where travelers were free to select whichever of several branches offered the easiest 'going,' while stock being driven could spread unconfined across the drift or drove" (Muir 2000: 113; see also Hindle 1982: 21). Animals and people could not walk freely through fields under cultivation, but once they were beyond such fields, their movement, and therefore the accompanying processes of compaction and erosion, was not limited to a linear path. In theory, therefore, the terminal ends of radial hollow ways can serve as a proxy indicator of the limits of cultivation for that site (Ur and Wilkinson 2008; Wilkinson 2005; Wilkinson et al. 2007a). This method of delimiting the agricultural hinterland of a settlement is discussed below.

Although captured opportunistically in the photographs of Poidebard (1934; Nordiguian and Salles 2000) in the late 1920s and early 1930s, hollow ways in the Khabur basin were first systematically studied by Van Liere and Lauffray using thousands of aerial photographs (1954–55; Van Liere 1963; see fig. 3.5). Hollow ways became a focus of research again in a series of surveys and landscape projects undertaken by T. J. Wilkinson in several regions of northern Mesopotamia (Wilkinson 1990a, 1993; Wilkinson and Tucker 1995: 24–28). These studies involved interpretation of aerial photographs but included detailed ground measurement of hollow ways and studies of the effects of subsequent natural and cultural processes on their preservation. More recently, McClellan and colleagues have proposed that hollow ways are not the traces of tracks but rather a deliberately excavated system of channels designed to redirect surface runoff toward settlements for irrigation and consumption (McClellan, Grayson, and Ogleby 2000; McClellan and Porter 1995). This hypothesis recognizes the impacts of hollow ways on the basin's hydrology, but is problematic in several ways, particularly in that hollow ways run over watersheds and other topographic features in ways that would impede water flow (see discussion in Ur and Wilkinson 2008).

A broader component of the THS included a basinwide reassessment of the initial map of Van Liere and Lauffray (see *Chapter 7*). The original 1:10,000 scale aerial photographs are not accessible, so the reassessment made use of declassified CORONA satellite photographs and other remote-sensing datasets, and included field observations within the THS area.

5.3.2. HOLLOW WAYS IN REMOTE-SENSING SOURCES

Hollow ways in the THS area were initially identified by their distinctive signatures on CORONA satellite photography (Ur 2003). Their depressed troughs collect moisture and therefore appear as dark lines on the images (fig. 5.20). Depending on the season and position in the agricultural calendar, these marks are either soil marks resulting from wetter soils, or crop marks from enhanced vegetation growth (cereals in the winter, weeds in the summer) in the troughs. During the growing season, cereals grow more lushly; in the summer, vegetation is limited to weeds, particularly *Prosopis farcta*, a spiky perennial (Guest 1966: 92–93; see also fig. 5.24 below).

Some hollow ways appear with lighter margins on either side of the trough. The sloping sides encourage drainage, and therefore the margins tend to be drier with less vegetation than either the hollow way trough or the surrounding terrain. Occasionally, this margin occurs on the northern side only, because this side is generally uphill throughout the basin but also because in the Northern Hemisphere it is better angled to reflect sunlight. Frequently, hollow ways lack these lighter margins; ground visits have established that these features are no longer "hollow," although they still tend to support denser vegetation. Erosion of the surrounding fields have infilled these marginless hollow ways; presumably their dark signature can be explained by greater moisture retention in the now-buried ancient surface. When these two signatures are related to their surrounding topography, the reasons become clear. Hollow ways with light margins tend to run parallel to the natural slope of the landscape, channeling runoff and maintaining their depressed morphology or even increasing it via runoff erosion. Hollow ways without margins often run perpendicular to the slope, causing them to act as catchment for eroding sediments; the trough of the hollow way becomes filled, although the buried track surface still retains moisture.

Hollow ways can be distinguished from modern tracks, roads, and wadis in CORONA photographs. Informal dirt tracks, generally no wider than 3–4 m, predominated at the time when CORONA imagery was acquired. Although often depressed as much as 50 cm below the surrounding fields, they are much shallower than hollow ways. Their relative narrowness and shallowness result in a small runoff catchment, so these modern tracks hold much less moisture than ancient hollow ways. Because they are in use, their surfaces are disturbed and vegetation-free, and therefore highly reflective. The distinctive signature of modern tracks, a thin white line, is easily distinguished from hollow ways.

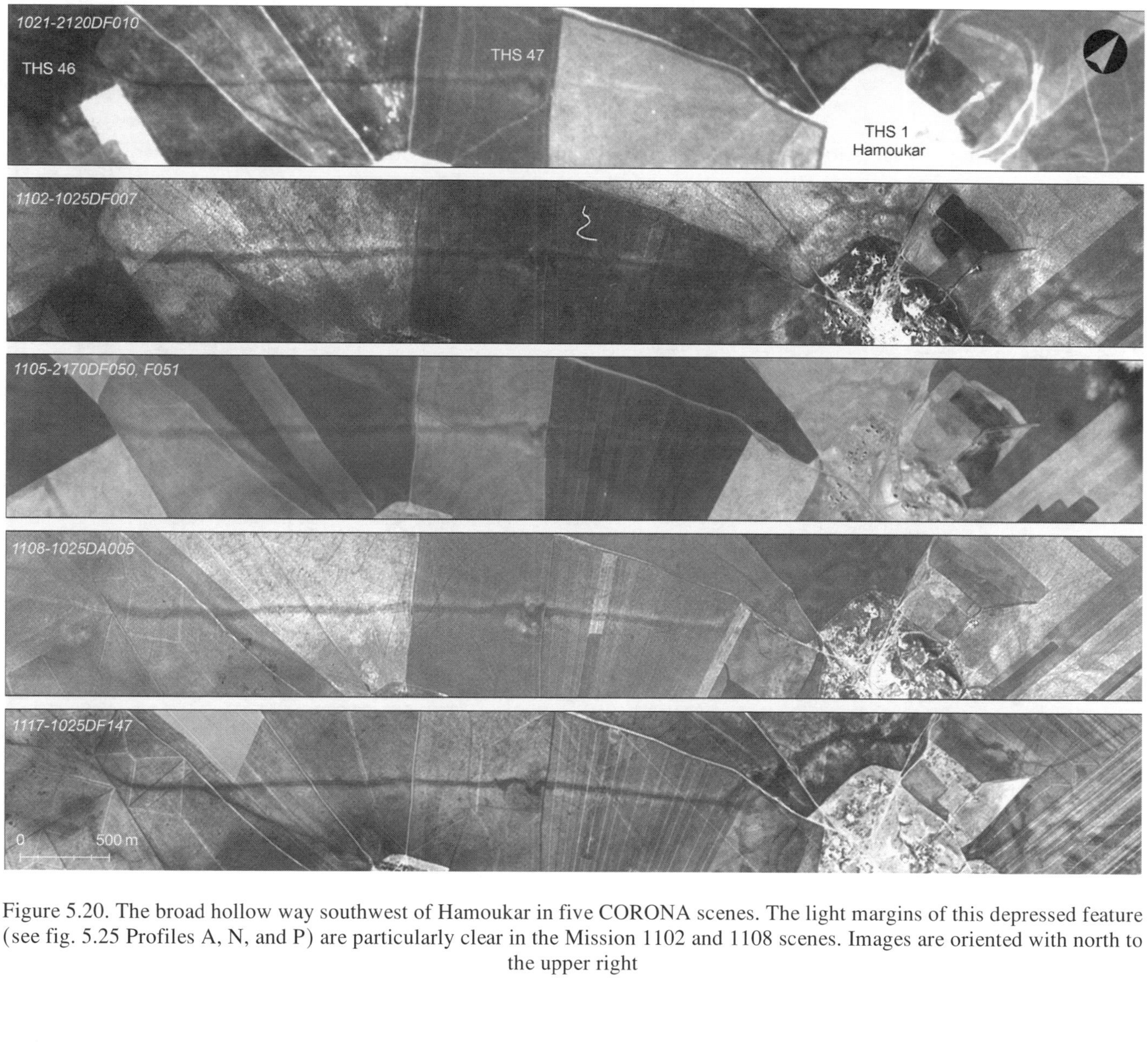

Figure 5.20. The broad hollow way southwest of Hamoukar in five CORONA scenes. The light margins of this depressed feature (see fig. 5.25 Profiles A, N, and P) are particularly clear in the Mission 1102 and 1108 scenes. Images are oriented with north to the upper right

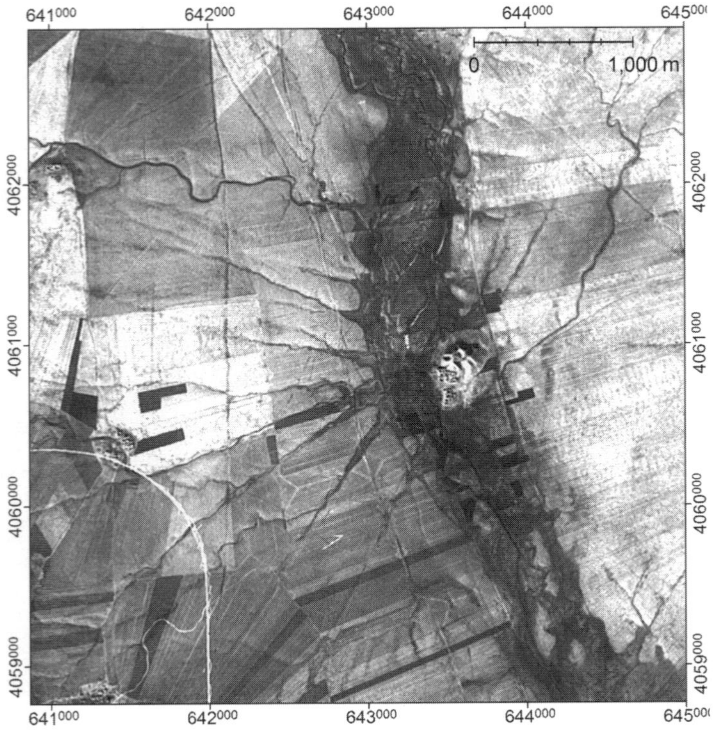

Figure 5.21. Radiating hollow way features near Tell Jamilo (TBS 59, Lyonnet no. 14). Surface runoff from the west has produced meandering within their depressions (CORONA 1102-1025DF006, 11 December 1967)

Wadis and hollow ways have a similar (although unintentional) hydrological function in that they both channel runoff rainfall. The main wadis in the basin were in existence prior to the Holocene (Courty 1994: 35) and through time they have assumed the sinuous shape typical of watercourses in a low-gradient alluvial environment. Hollow ways, on the other hand, remain highly linear, especially when running perpendicular to the slope of the terrain. Their depressed morphology means that they become hydrological features, and in the millennia since their formation, hollow ways can develop secondary meandering features, under certain topographically and hydrologically ideal conditions (fig. 5.21). These conditions are rare, and in most cases linear hollow ways are easily distinguished from sinuous wadis.

Other imagery sources are less useful for mapping hollow ways. The spring 1955 aerial photograph series used by Wilkinson to map sites and features in the North Jazira (Wilkinson and Tucker 1995; also used to trace Neo-Assyrian canals in Ur 2005b) unfortunately does not extend far beyond the present Syrian-Iraqi frontier, although it could be used to map features east and northeast of the THS. More recent digital sources proved problematic for a variety of reasons. Landsat and ASTER scenes are particularly sensitive to differences in moisture and vegetation (Altaweel 2005), but have a coarser resolution (30 m and 15 m, respectively), and often fail to detect smaller hollow ways (fig. 5.22). More recent high-resolution commercial systems such as

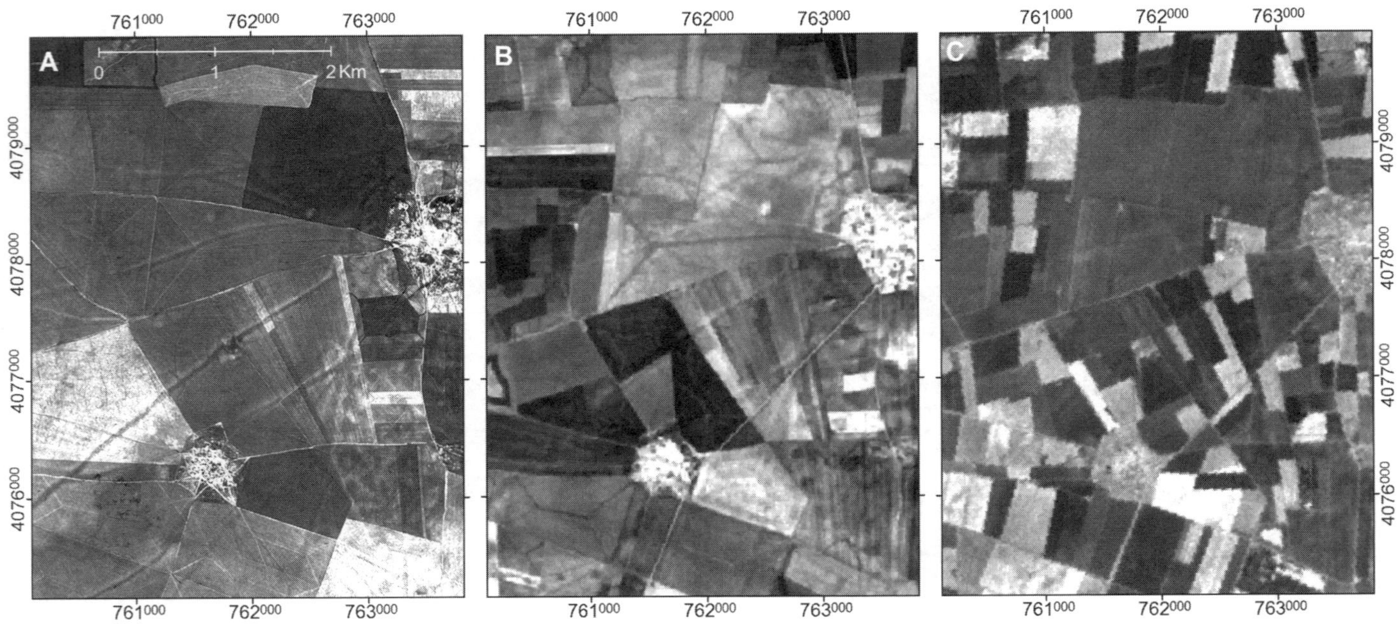

Figure 5.22. Comparison of remote-sensing datasets for hollow way feature visibility. (*A*) CORONA 2 m panchromatic (1102-1025DA005, 11 December 1967), (*B*) SPOT 10 m panchromatic (8 March 1990); (*C*) ASTER 15 m near-infrared band 3 (18 October 2004). The major southwestern hollow way from Hamoukar's western edge is at least partially visible in all three, but most features are visible solely in the CORONA scene

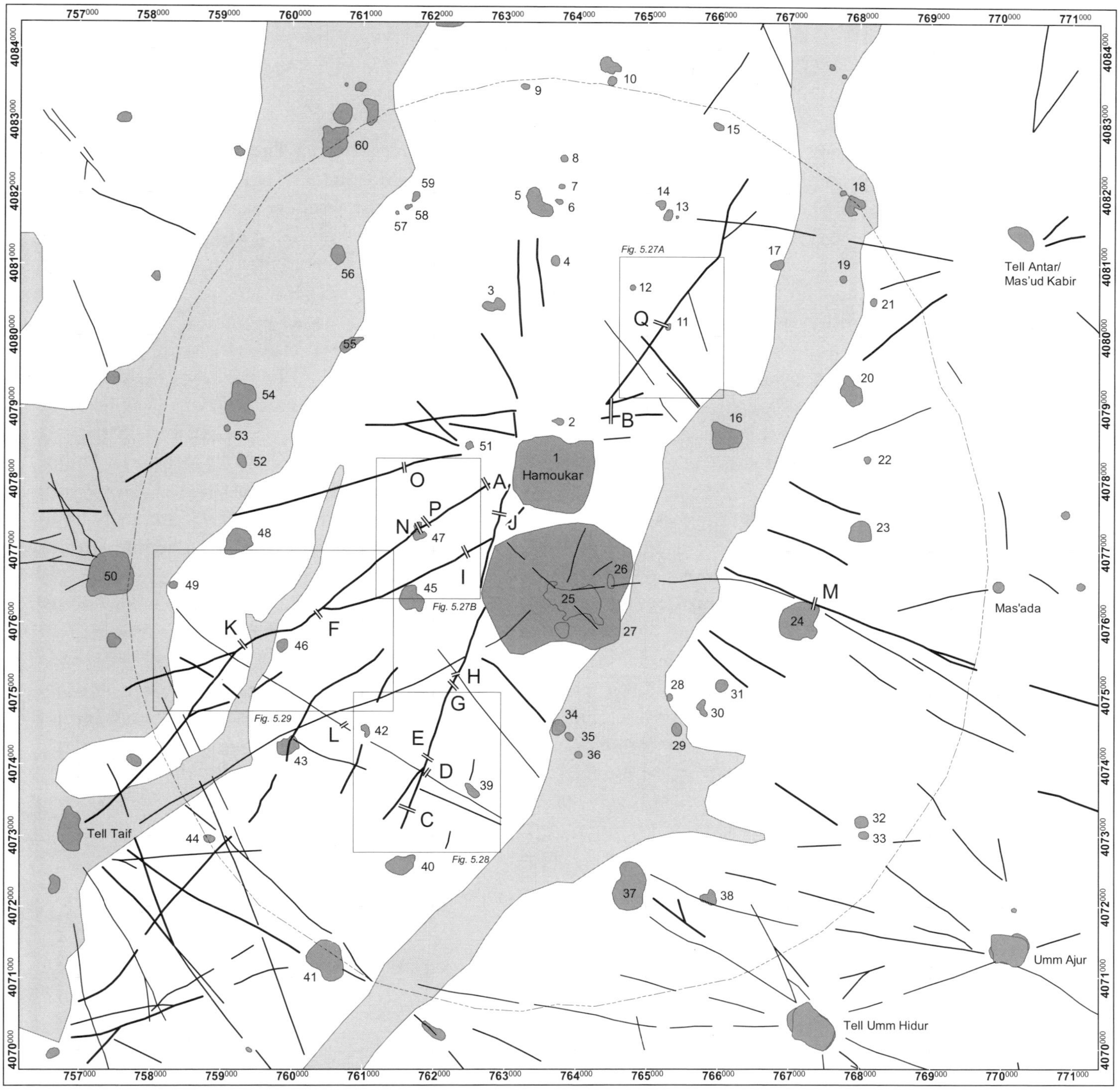

Figure 5.23. Broad and narrow hollow ways, sites, and measured profiles in the THS region

QuickBird (0.6 m), Ikonos (1 m) and SPOT (2.5 m pan-sharpened) most commonly acquire imagery during times of lowest cloud cover, which tend to be the times of poorest visibility of hollow ways. These systems also capture the present landscape, in which many hollow ways visible in 1960s CORONA have been effaced via plow wash or even deliberate leveling.

Within the bounds of the THS region, 106.6 km of hollow ways could be recognized and seventeen profiles were measured (fig. 5.23). The broader basinwide pattern of features is described in *Chapter 7*.

5.3.3. GROUND OBSERVATIONS OF HOLLOW WAYS IN THE THS REGION

The survey intended to test on the ground Van Liere and Lauffray's (1954–55) classification of hollow ways into narrow and broad types, and their observation that the broad hollow ways appeared to be associated with Bronze Age tell sites, whereas the narrower routes were found in association with small "farms" of the first millennium A.D. The THS measured seventeen profiles of hollow ways as part of its off-site program. The profiling methodology was kept technologically simple, employing only an optical level, a stadia rod, and a laser rangefinder (fig. 5.24). The level was set up on the plain on a line perpendicular to the hollow way. The height of the instrument was measured, and then elevations were measured off the stadia rod at roughly 10 m intervals along this perpendicular line. Horizontal distance was measured with the rangefinder, which was found to be accurate to ±1 m at distances up to 400 m. The positions of these profiles, labeled A through O, are indicated in figure 5.23.

Of the seventeen profiles (fig. 5.25), two (N at THS 47 and Q at THS 11) ran across hollow ways in places where later settlement had artificially deepened them (discussed below). Two other profiles (F and K) ran across a single hollow way in two places where it no longer had any topographic expression. Although it was visible as soil or crop marks in CORONA photographs, by the 2000 field season (and probably millennia before), it had been entirely filled with sediment, probably at the same time that the adjacent small drainage became infilled.

In the remaining thirteen profiles, it was possible to measure widths and depths (fig. 5.26). The broader hollow ways, as determined from imagery analysis, do appear to be wider than those that had been classified as narrow prior to fieldwork. They average 97 m wide, whereas the narrow class averages 45 m wide. Based on an admittedly limited sample of profiles, narrow hollow ways tend to be shallower than the average broad hollow way, but their depths fall within the range of variation of the broad class. It does appear that the narrow hollow ways are proportionally deeper; this situation almost certainly stems from their relative chronology, discussed below. It must be emphasized that these measurements were taken across hollow ways at the modern ground surface, which is not equivalent to the ancient surface of the track, which could be buried beneath eroded sediments or even washed away. In the former case, the hollow way trough is likely to be shallower than the ancient track, and in the latter, the trough is probably deeper (Wilkinson 2003: 111–12). Furthermore, determination of widths and depths depends on somewhat subjective assessments of the point at which the sloping sides plane out and the elevation of the original ground surface. Hollow ways in the THS region do appear to be roughly classifiable as broad or narrow, as initially suggested by Van Liere and Lauffray (1954–55); however, it is apparent that they display considerable variation in form which is related to location and preservation in addition to chronology.

Figure 5.24. Profile measurement across a broad hollow way (Profile C in fig. 5.25), facing east. Note the enhanced growth of *Prosopis* at the bottom of the feature's trough at the position of the stadia rod

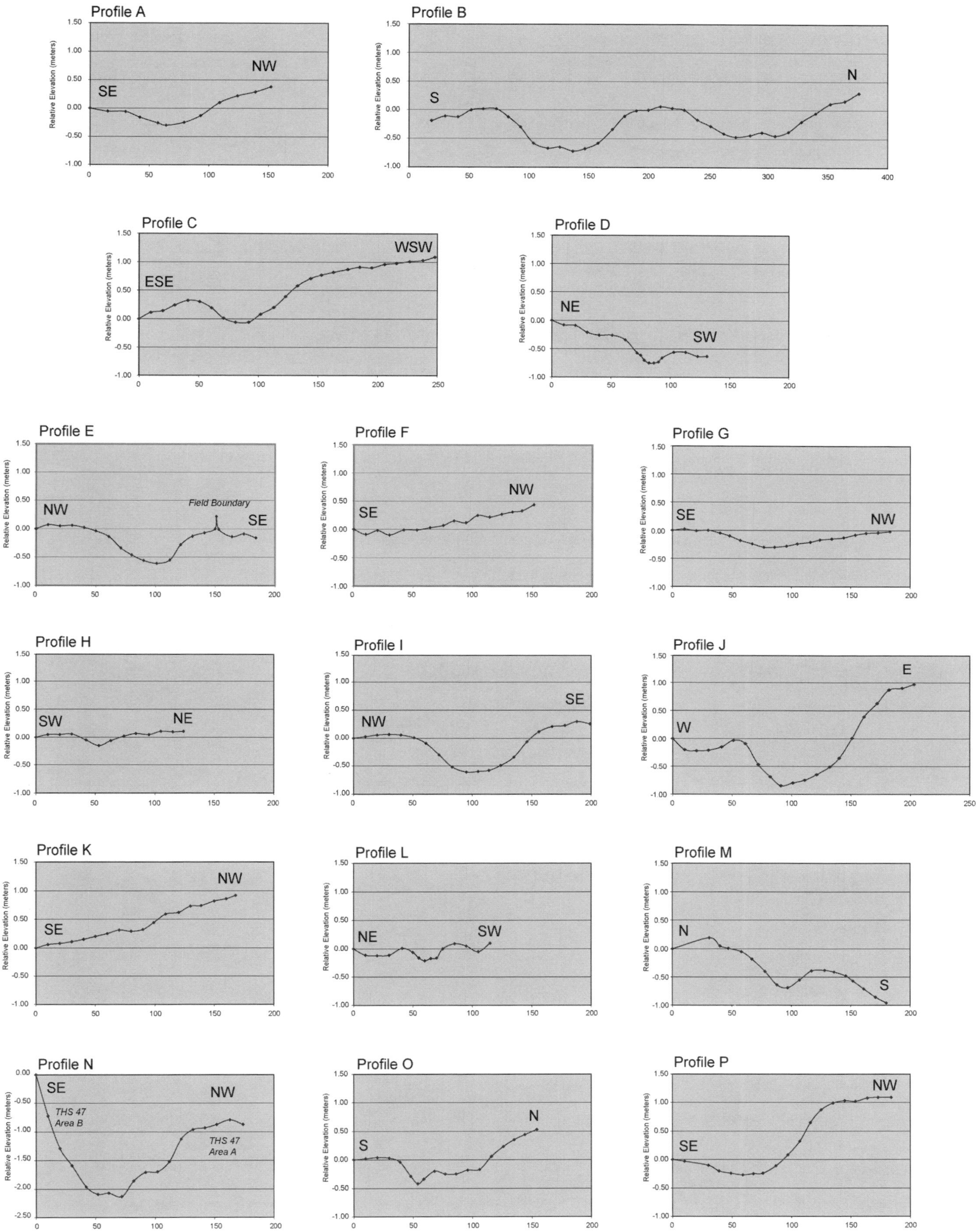

Figure 5.25. Profiles of hollow ways in the THS region. For profile locations, see figure 5.23. Vertical exaggeration approximately 47×

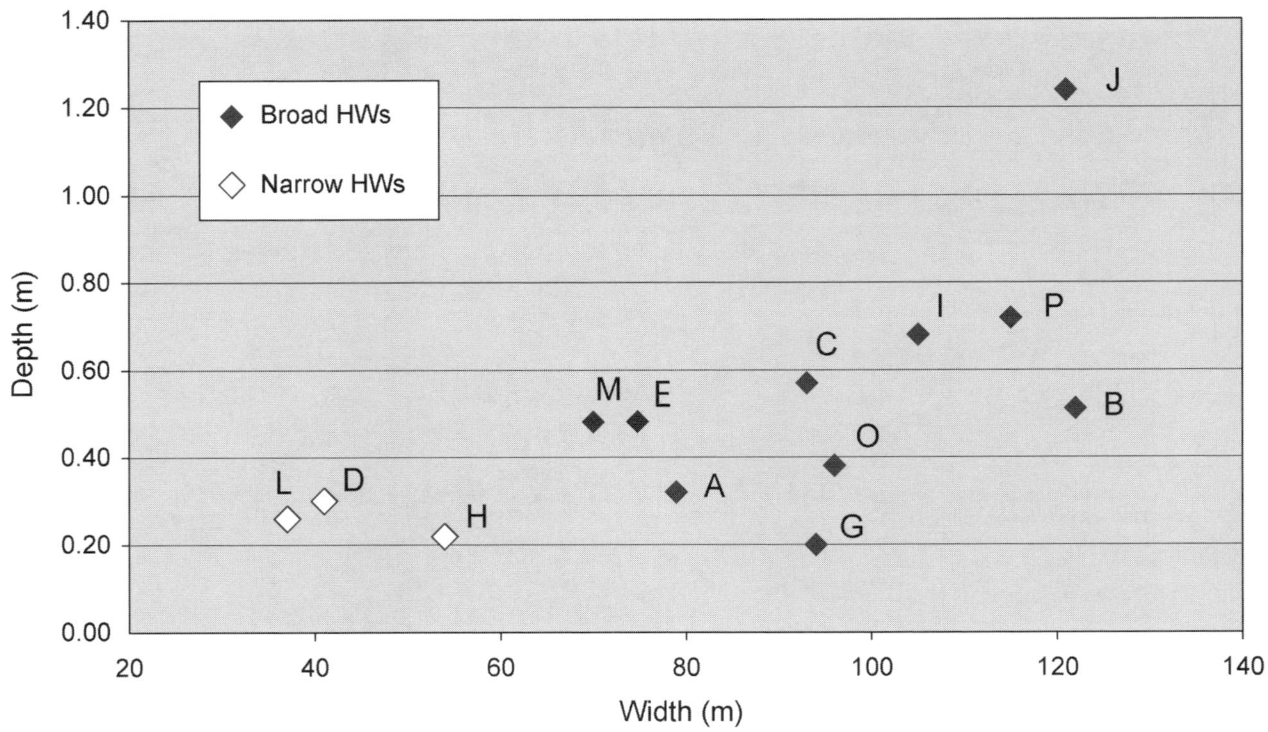

Figure 5.26. Depths and widths of thirteen hollow ways (HW) in the THS region

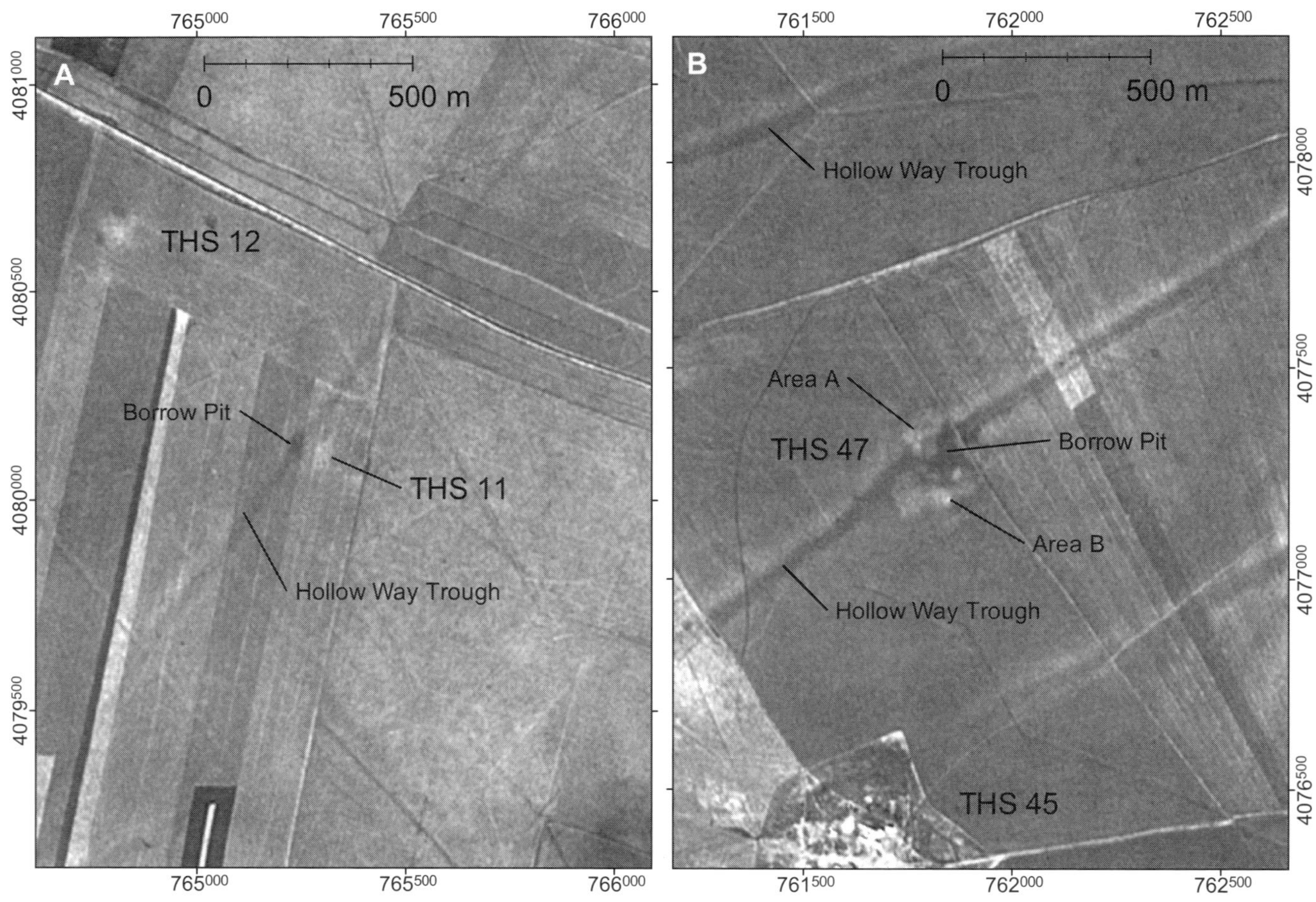

Figure 5.27. The reuse of hollow ways as borrow pits (CORONA 1108-1025DA005, 6 December 1969). (*A*) Period 10 reuse at THS 11; (*B*) Reuse in Periods 10 and 14 at THS 47

5.3.4. DATING OF HOLLOW WAYS

Ascribing a time of use to a non-constructed landscape feature can be exceedingly difficult. Without milestones or some other type of historical record, there is little intrinsically datable about a road or track. Roads can have lives that extend far beyond the time of their construction; often it is a simple matter to maintain them, or they can continue as tracks. Direct dating of non-constructed informal routes is possible only in extraordinary cases, for example Costa Rican footpaths sealed by tephra layers (Sheets and Sever 1991). Relative dating is possible when stratigraphic relationships between landscape features exist (e.g., Beck 1991). Such relative dating is possible in only a few cases in the Upper Khabur basin.

Dating hollow ways by their association with sites has been the method used by researchers in the Upper Khabur basin since at least the 1950s, when close associations of hollow ways with sites of the Bronze Age and Byzantine/Sasanian era were proposed by Van Liere and Lauffray (1954–55; Van Liere 1963). Although these early researchers were working before the establishment of proper ceramic chronologies, recent systematic and intensive archaeological survey has generally confirmed these associational datings, and further specified a phase of intense hollow way formation in the third millennium B.C. (Wilkinson 1993; Ur 2003; discussed in detail in Ur and Wilkinson 2008).

Hollow way associations are strongest with third-millennium mounds, but these are always multiperiod sites, so use in other periods cannot be excluded. The massive size of fourth-millennium Tell Brak and its elaborate radial system of hollow ways is particularly suggestive of an early date (Wilkinson et al. 2001; Ur 2003: fig. 8; Ur, Karsgaard, and Oates 2007). The THS area shows much less chronological range in hollow way associations. Large Late Chalcolithic (Periods 5a–b) sites such as THS 40 are not unequivocally associated with hollow ways, nor is THS 24, the large second-millennium town (Periods 8–10).

Associational dating must be done cautiously because some hollow ways had afterlives as features unrelated to movement. Hollow ways themselves were attractors for subsequent settlement because of their unintended impact on local hydrology. Their depressed morphology collected surface runoff during their use and long afterward. In the THS area, several settlements grew up along hollow ways long after they had ceased to function as transportation corridors. At THS 11, to the northeast of Hamoukar, a small Late Bronze Age (Period 10) village formed on a broad hollow way that extended from Hamoukar's northeastern corner (fig. 5.27A). A second hollow way from Hamoukar's western lower town (fig. 5.27B) was first dug out for brick material by the residents of another Period 10 village (THS 47 Area B); excavation was resumed over a thousand years later by the residents of a Parthian–Roman (Period 14) settlement (THS 47 Area A). In both cases, profiles across the borrow pits were much deeper than elsewhere along the same hollow ways (see fig. 5.25 Profile N). It is surely not coincidental that both of these hollow ways were especially hydrologically active, being precisely parallel to the slope of the plain. The hollow way at THS 11 drained the plain northeast of Hamoukar, and the feature at THS 47 was its continuation. Certainly these sites are "associated" with these hollow ways, but these associations have nothing to do with their initial formation and communication use.

5.3.5. HOLLOW WAY PATTERNING IN THE THS REGION

Building on the foundational work of Van Liere and Lauffray (1954–55) and Wilkinson (1993; Wilkinson and Tucker 1995), large areas of the Upper Khabur basin have been remapped via georeferenced CORONA satellite photographs. Spatial patterning across the basin and in adjacent parts of the North Jazira in Iraq is presented and discussed in *Chapter 7*.

The Hamoukar region itself is crossed by dozens of routes, used at different times and for different purposes (fig. 5.23). The majority are to be found in the southwestern quadrant of the survey region, between Hamoukar and the poorly drained Radd marsh area at the bottom of the Wadi Rumaylan. These features generally run down the slope of the terrain, which drops 1.9 m per km on a north-northeast–south-southwest line. It is therefore tempting to attribute this remarkable preservation to their unintended hydraulic effects. On the other hand, a second lower concentration of linear features occurs to the east of Hamoukar and these features are almost precisely perpendicular to the slope of the terrain.

The majority of hollow ways of the broad class are associated with Hamoukar itself, which covered 98 ha in Period 7 (see Section 6.4.2). Hamoukar is of course a multiperiod site, so any hollow way aligned with the high mound could have already been in use in the fourth millennium B.C.; this may be true of the linear features to the northeast of the site. However, the elaborate network of routes to the southwest of Hamoukar appear to be focused on a specific point at the western edge of the lower town, where a gully probably marks the location of an ancient gate or point of access (see fig. 3.8). Fewer hollow ways are aligned with similar gullies at the southwestern and southeastern edges of the lower town. The 1999 surface collection has demonstrated that these parts of the lower town were only occupied in late Period 6 and throughout Period 7 (i.e., mid- to late third millennium; see Section 6.4.2), suggesting that this was the time that the associated hollow ways were carrying traffic.

Hamoukar's Period 7 satellites have less unequivocal spatial relationships with hollow ways. One feature west of Hamoukar appears to align with THS 54 but fades out over 2 km distant from the latter site. Likewise, a major north–south route from Hamoukar's putative western gate aligns directly with THS 41, but fades out even farther away. Several routes align with THS 37, but may be more related to its Sasanian–Early Islamic (Periods 16–17) settlement (see below). THS 16 has several routes associated with it, but none conclusively link to another Period 7 site.

If the frame is expanded to include unsurveyed sites just beyond the bounds of the THS, intersite connections are far more apparent (see map 2). One branch of the major southwest route from Hamoukar's western edge leads to Tell Taif, which also is directly connected to THS 41. Tell Antar is surrounded by a radial pattern of hollow ways, one of which extends toward THS 16. The routes that run east-southeast from Hamoukar past THS 24 run toward Tell al-Samir, a major Period 7 town in the North Jazira Project survey area.

The preceding discussion is limited to the broad class of hollow ways; the narrower routes have an entirely different set of associations. In the THS area, the closest association is with the large town of al-Botha (THS 50), which has an elaborate set of radiating routes to its northwest and two long and straight routes running to the southeast; one of the latter two routes articulates with the lower town of THS 37. THS 37 is in turn connected via a narrow hollow way with THS 45 and a pair of unsurveyed sites to its southeast (Tell Umm Hidur and Umm Ajur). All the surveyed settlements in this network show major signs of occupation during Periods 16–17. The limited set of

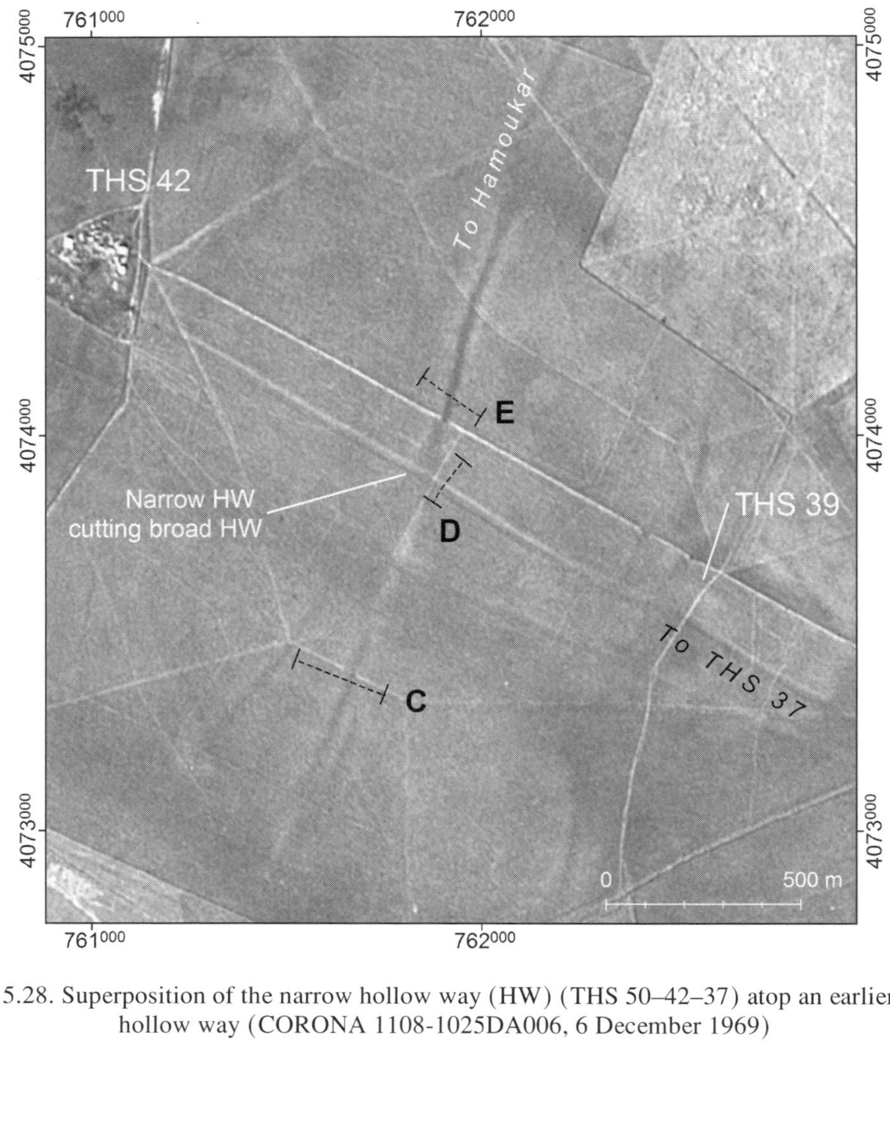

Figure 5.28. Superposition of the narrow hollow way (HW) (THS 50–42–37) atop an earlier broad hollow way (CORONA 1108-1025DA006, 6 December 1969)

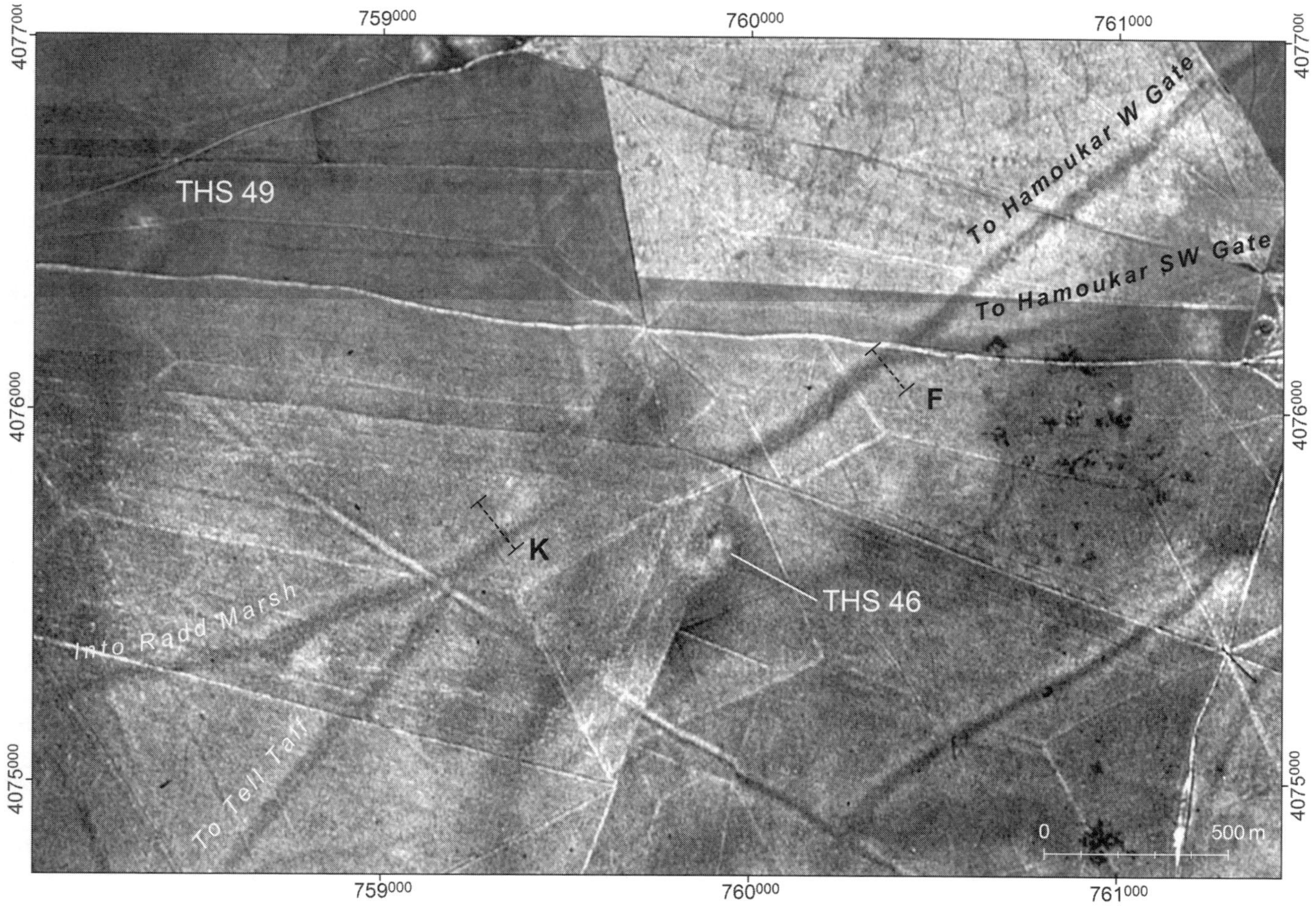

Figure 5.29. Convergence of hollow ways at a wadi crossing (CORONA 1108-1025DA005, 6 December 1969)

well-dated narrow linear features in the THS region thus appears to confirm the proposed dating of Van Liere and Lauffray (1954–55). The relative dating of the two classes is also apparent from CORONA image analysis of the area north THS 40, where a narrow hollow way can be seen to cut through a broad hollow (fig. 5.28). In general, the narrow hollow ways are proportionally deeper than those of the broad class, probably because erosion has had less time to fill them with sediment.

In rare cases, hollow way features allow other elements of the ancient landscape to be dated. For example, the major route running southwest from Hamoukar is joined by a second route to its south (fig. 5.29); the combined route then crosses over the small drainage immediately northwest of THS 46. At the opposite side, the route splits into a southern branch leading to Tell Taif and a northern branch that disappears into the floodplain of the Wadi Rumaylan. At present, this drainage has no topographic expression and is recognizable only from CORONA photographs. The proximity of the Period 4–early Period 5b site at THS 46 suggests that this drainage was flowing at least seasonally at the end of the fifth or beginning of the fourth millennium. Its continued flow into the late third millennium is implied by the hollow way pattern, which is suggestive of a river or wadi crossing. Its demise as a hydrological feature may be related to the possible irrigation traces north of the THS area, where the flow of this drainage appears to have been tapped in order to irrigate the area around Tell Mashhan (see below and fig. 5.30).

Viewed together, the off-site data from field scatters and hollow ways present strong evidence for intensive exploitation and manipulation of the landscape surrounding early urban Hamoukar, paralleling the situation at contemporary Tell al-Hawa, Tell Brak, and Tell Sweyhat. The implications for the subsistence economy are explored in *Chapter 8*.

5.4. CANAL IRRIGATION

At present, discussions of the subsistence economy of the basin prior to the Iron Age disregard the possibility of irrigation agriculture. Irrigation on the southern Mesopotamian plains is certainly of great antiquity (reviewed in Wilkinson 2003: 87–91), and can be demonstrated empirically on the Zagros flanks as early as the sixth millennium B.C. (Oates and Oates 1976). Irrigation was present by the Iron Age along the middle and lower stretches of the Khabur River (Ergenzinger and Kühne 1991) and certainly the Assyrian empire had adapted irrigation technology for the rainfed Assyrian plains (see recent syntheses in Bagg 2000; Ur 2005b). Within the basin, evidence appears to be limited to historical sources for Jaghjagh irrigation around Nisibin, starting in the Sasanian period but only defined spatially and quantitatively for the sixteenth century A.D. (discussed in Section 7.3.2).

Small-scale irrigation systems are common in the THS region today, but all are fed by diesel pumps that tap the receding ground water; such sources would have been unavailable in the pre-industrial past. Nonetheless, on

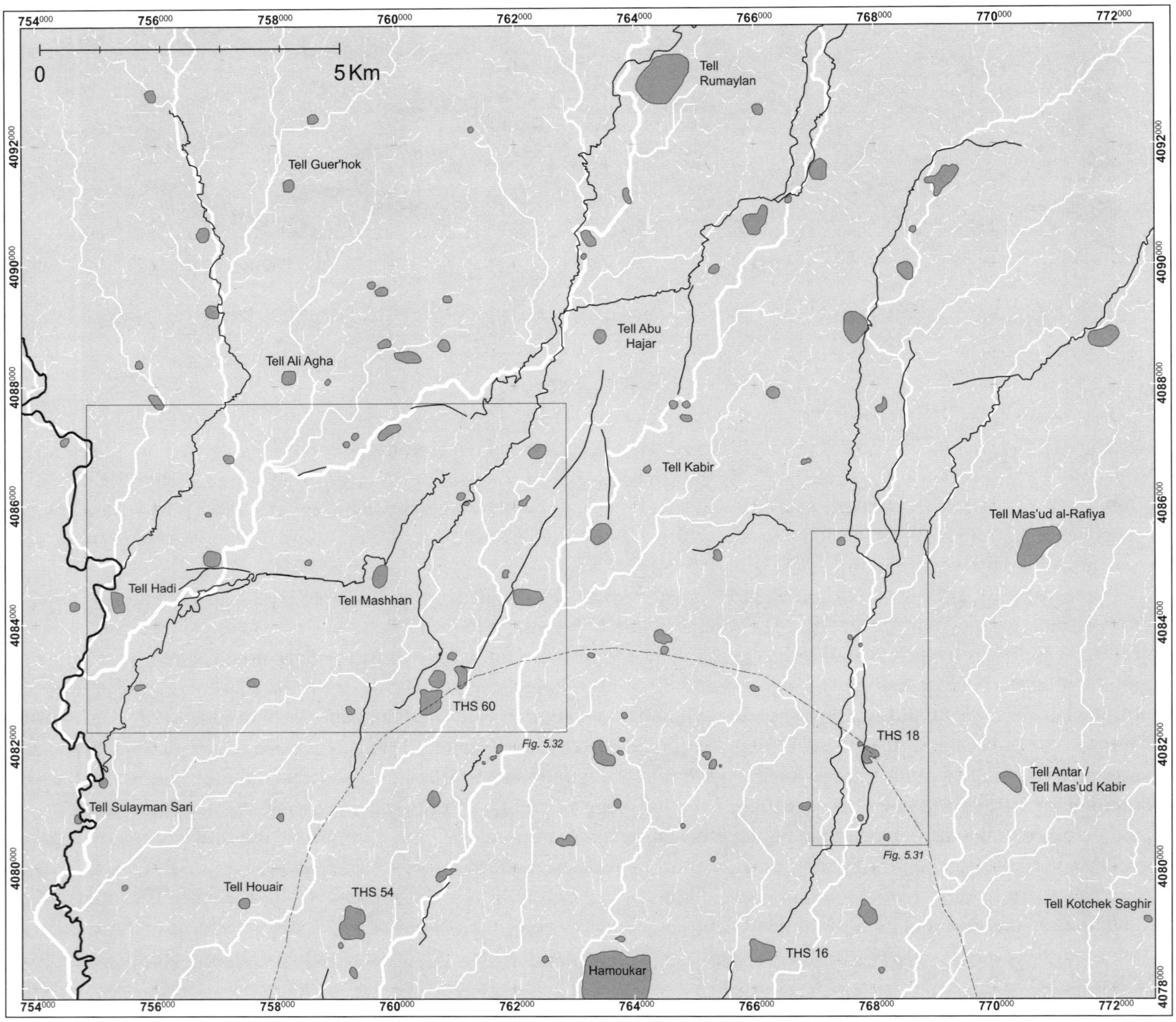

Figure 5.30. Modeled drainage (white) and wadis and possible canal features (black) visible in CORONA imagery

CORONA photographs there are traces of features that might be interpreted as artificial watercourses, particularly on the northeastern and western limits of the THS area (fig. 5.30). Two areas stand out. At or above Ramadaniya, an offtake leaves the eastern drainage and runs to its west toward THS 18, where it weaves through the occupation mounding and continues to the south (fig. 5.31). The straightness of this feature leaves no doubt that it is not a natural watercourse, and its behavior within the archaeological site at THS 18 is more suggestive of a canal than a track. Settlement at THS 18 began in the Halaf (Period 2) period but reached its greatest extent in Khabur (Period 8), Sasanian–Early Islamic (Period 16), and later times. The sharp preservation of the canal feature argues for a later dating.

A second canal system existed near Tell Mashhan, a small conical mound now covered by a substantial modern village (fig. 5.32). On CORONA imagery, Mashhan appears to be on the course of a tributary drainage of the Wadi Rumaylan, but hydrological modeling suggests that this feature is artificial, and natural drainage would have flowed through a relict feature to the northwest (see fig. 2.5, and compare fig. 5.32 with fig. 5.30). At some point, probably now covered by modern settlement, a canal head distributed the water of this drainage into several offtakes, the largest of which runs west to Tell Hadi. A canal to the east ran into the THS area's western drainage, which raises the possibility that this drainage may be partly or wholly a cultural feature. It certainly explains why the extent of the dark soils in this area is so broad.

Proposing a date for this irrigation network is difficult. Tell Mashhan falls beyond the THS limits and was not visited or collected, and the brief inspection of the mound complex at the northwestern survey limits (THS 60) revealed Parthian–Roman (Period 14) ceramics but other periods of settlement cannot be excluded. THS 50 and 54 both lay within the drainage/irrigation zone of these canals, and, like THS 18, both have major Sasanian and Islamic components (60 ha and 14.7 ha, respectively). Other canals like the ones around Tell Mashhan can be found near Tell Rumaylan on CORONA photographs. It is not possible to assign dates of use to these features, but it seems most likely that they are late first to early second millennium A.D., based on their proximity to sites of known occupation periods.

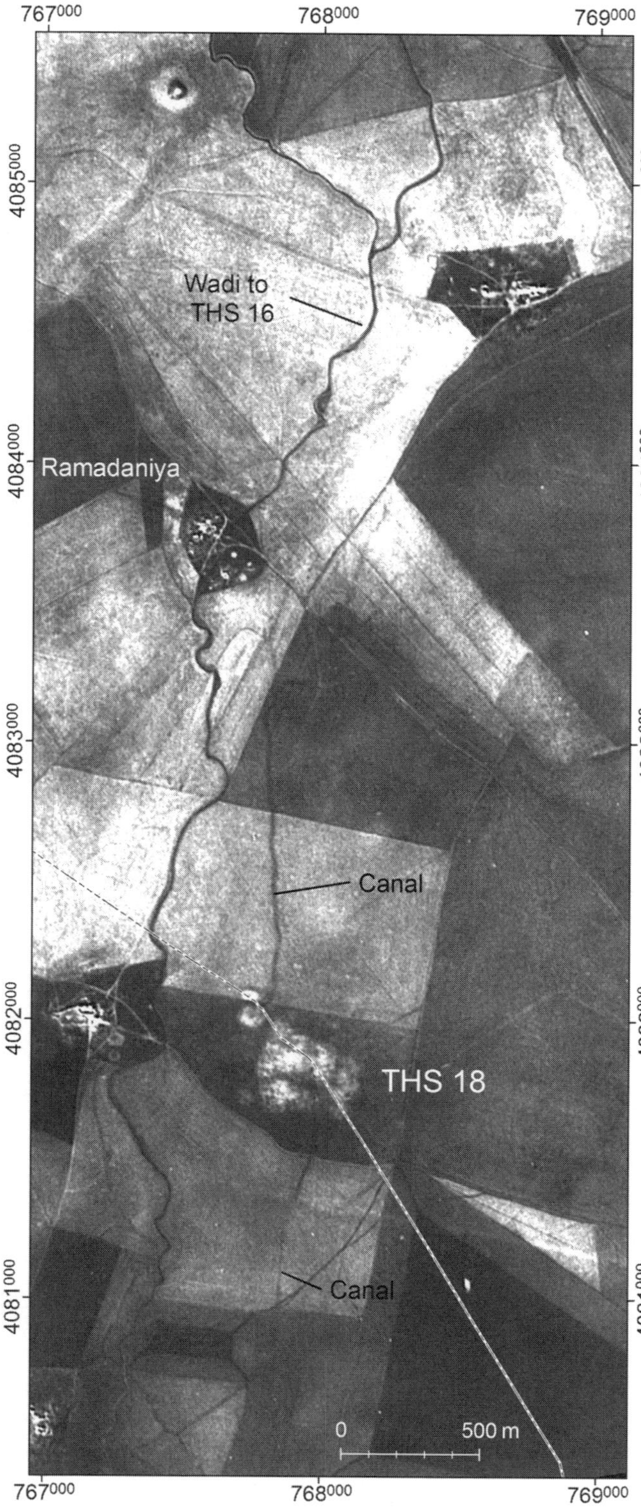

Figure 5.31. Canal feature between Ramadaniya and THS 18 (CORONA 1102-1025DF006, 11 December 1967)

Closer to Hamoukar, multiple dark meandering lines appear in the THS eastern drainage, some of which are suggestive of small-scale intra-floodplain irrigation. In particular, there are several features in the drainage southeast of THS 27. These features could be be non-contemporary wadi courses within a dynamic natural regime; however, the reconstructed patterning suggests a former weir. Firm conclusions cannot be drawn from remote-sensing data alone.

On present evidence, irrigation appears not to have played an important economic role in the THS region until the last fifty years. In the adjacent plains north and west, however, it had a more considerable but still undefined role. There is little more to be said about irrigation in these areas in the absence of geomorphological investigations and surface collections of associated sites. We can make some general statements about irrigation's impact on the preservation of earlier landscape elements, however. The apparent lacuna in hollow ways between Hamoukar and Tell Rumaylan, a large third-millennium town, is surprising given their large size, proximity, and general patterns of feature association in the THS area and elsewhere in northern Mesopotamia. This lacuna is almost certainly the result of small-scale local irrigation systems having obscured them. An identical process around Nisibin, but on a much larger scale, has altered the Bronze Age landscape record to the west of Tell Leilan and is discussed in *Chapter 7*.

Figure 5.32. Drainage and canal features around Tell Mashhan (CORONA 1108-1025DA005, 6 December 1969)

CHAPTER 6

SETTLEMENT PATTERNS IN THE HAMOUKAR REGION

The THS recovered sixty sites, which together represent eight millennia of settlement history (map 1). The focus of this chapter is on the presentation of the shifting patterns of settlement; they are interpreted more generally, compared with patterns elsewhere in northern Mesopotamia and the Near East, and placed into larger historical contexts in *Chapter 8*.

In the standard manner for the presentation of archaeological settlement patterns, they are presented here by chronological period. In assessing them, it is important to refer to the caveats presented in *Appendix B*, especially with regard to site contemporaneity. These problems are greater in the pre-Ubaid and post-Bronze Age periods, when other evidence suggests a lack of continuity in ancient settlement.

A recurrent aspect of Mesopotamian settlement must be borne in mind when assessing these patterns. In all periods there was a strong tendency to return to places formerly settled, rather than to begin a new settlement on virgin ground. This tendency expressed itself in several forms. Most obvious is the high-mounded tell, which is the physical manifestation of the long-term importance of a single place. Settlement on tells may or may not have been continuous. Continuity is suggested by surface collections with sherds from chronologically adjacent periods, but the pervasive importance of place in the past means that these places could have been sequentially reoccupied in a manner that would be invisible in the surface archaeology (i.e., abandonment and reoccupation could have occurred within a single ceramically defined period).

In other cases, settlement returned to sites but not in the precise positions of earlier settlement. These reoccupations often took the form of lower-town settlements which were discrete from, but spatially contiguous with, abandoned tells. In these cases, it is clear that there has been a cultural break of some sort within the sequence of settlement (i.e., a lack of settlement continuity at the site), but that the place itself retained some significance that drew settlers back to it.

Resettlement was not limited to high mounds and adjacent areas. Small and low mounds also exhibit multiple periods of settlement. Indeed, 75 percent of all sites in the THS area had more than one period of occupation (fig. 6.1). This percentage is probably an underestimation. At thirteen sites, only a single period was recognized by the THS. However, five of these were heavily damaged with poor surface visibility, and two received only brief visits without formal collection. Under better visibility conditions, or if full collections had been made, it is likely that most if not all these sites would have revealed multiple periods of occupation.

This durable pattern of settlement continuity and reoccupation has an impact on our ability to recognize early phases of settlement on multiperiod sites. Simply put, the greater the number and duration of reoccupations, the more likely that the earliest phases will be obscured and will fail to be recovered by survey. Therefore, it is highly likely that some prehistoric sites lay unrecognized under later high mounds. Most Period 1–3 (Proto-Hassuna–northern Ubaid) sites are in the range of 1–2 ha. Such a site could easily hide in the core of the 15 ha Hamoukar high mound, invisible to surface collection and superficial step trenches alike. For the same reason, when these early buried occupations are detectable, it is inherently the result of post-occupational transformation (e.g., well digging or terracing by later inhabitants, or tell slope erosion). We have attempted to take these processes into consideration in the size estimations for deeply buried occupations presented below, but it is important to remember that they are more tenuous than estimations of, for example, a plowed-out Islamic site.

We will assess site numbers and aggregate settled area through time, but we have elected not to employ many of the quantitative spatial analyses commonly applied in recent Near Eastern survey publications, such as rank-size and nearest-neighbor analyses (e.g., Falconer and Savage 1995; Lupton 1996). These methods can be used as a heuristic device to characterize overall patterns of distribution and scale (Wilkinson and Tucker 1995: 79–81). However, their standard interpretation involves assumptions that may not be appropriate for premodern societies. For example, the rank-size index is used to characterize the level of "integration" of settlement systems, based on settlement patterns in industrial, capitalist Western Europe. We should not expect Near Eastern communities to have made similar decisions about how they distributed themselves spatially. Furthermore, these methods tend to be highly synchronic,

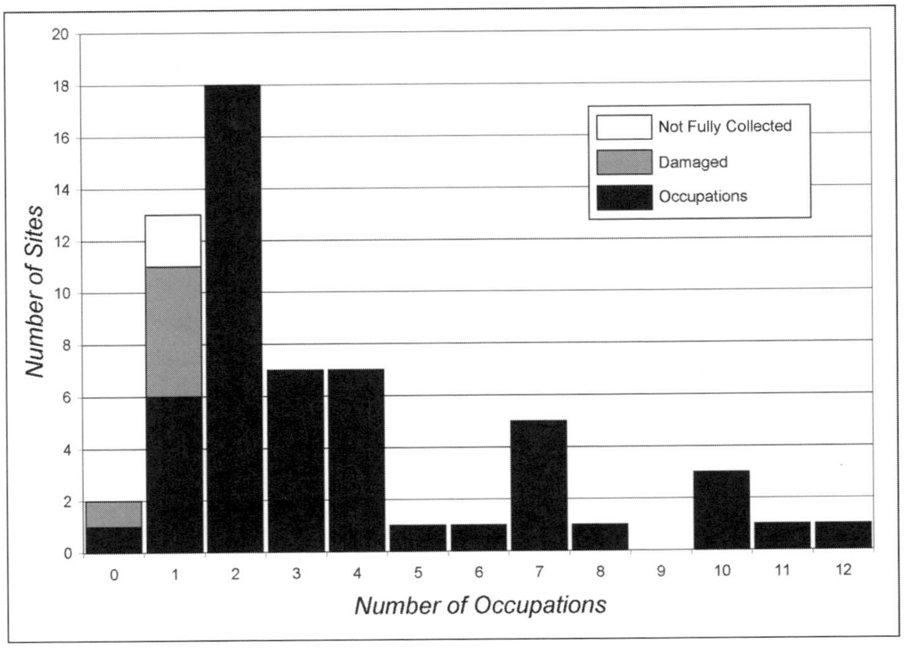

Figure 6.1. Histogram of occupations per site. For sites with zero occupations, surface collections did not recover sufficiently datable assemblages. Number of occupations are probably underestimated at damaged sites or sites that were not fully collected

and assume that settlement in each period resumed on a sort of landscape blank slate. In the analysis that follows, it is assumed that antecedent settlement and land use were variables that later settlers were aware of and considered when making decisions about settlement and land use. As discussed above, tells became meaningful places that were preferentially resettled. The landscape impact of middle to late third-millennium (Period 7) urbanism was particularly important: substantial tell formation at this time attracted lower-town resettlement in later periods, the depressed tracks were later used as brick pits (see Section 5.3.4) and the exhausted agricultural soils surrounding Hamoukar may have discouraged resettlement for several centuries. Previous landscapes of settlement were visible to later settlers in the form of mounds, and it is assumed that they continued to be meaningful. Abandoned mounds were always a part of the landscape, so on the distribution maps for each period, all previously settled mounds are indicated. Even if they were no longer settled, these features served variously as cemeteries, landmarks, campsites, and places whose symbolic importance would have conditioned the way people interacted with them and the landscape around them.

In most cases, demography has been approached very cautiously. There is a large body of literature in Near Eastern archaeology that explores the possibility of converting settled area into population estimates (Kramer 1980; Sumner 1979, 1989; Postgate 1994). Based on these ethnographic and archaeological studies, populations in northern Mesopotamia have been approximated using a ratio of 100–200 persons per settled hectare (Stein and Wattenmaker 1990; Wilkinson 1994; Wilkinson et al. 2007a). It is almost certainly incorrect to assume that there existed a single cultural norm regarding the proper settlement density throughout the eight thousand years of settlement studied here. We should expect that in the late Neolithic, when many activities took place outside the house walls, there would be greater intra-village, inter-household space and a correspondingly lower density of persons per hectare. Application of the Bronze Age ratio would therefore overestimate prehistoric populations. Within chronological periods, settlement density might vary by economic factors, such as the prevalence of village-based flocks, or according to the size of the settlement. The former might result in lower density; the latter might do the same, if the settlement hosted "public" (i.e., non-residential) structures. Conversely, cities could also have higher overall density, if their walls limited spatial growth. The institutional heterogeneity of urban places introduces a further complication, in that density certainly fluctuated *within* settlements, especially large ones. In that case, a single person-to-area ratio cannot be applied to the entire settlement. For these reasons, the temptation to convert settled area into population is resisted, with the exception of an analysis of Period 7 settlement and land use (see Section 8.3.3).

6.1. INITIAL VILLAGE SETTLEMENT

Paleolithic and early Neolithic settlement can now be recognized in the Upper Khabur basin, but sites of such early date are exceedingly uncommon and tend to be found along the two perennial rivers of the basin (Nishiaki 2000; Nishiaki and Le Mière 2005; Wright 2005). None were recovered in the THS area or by intensive survey in areas of similarly deep alluvial soils. The exception is the 0.4 ha site of Ginnig in the Iraqi North Jazira (Campbell 1996). The absence of recovered sites should, however, not be equated with a lack of human occupation; the ephemeral remains of early non-sedentary sites are easily effaced by later settlement and agriculture.

6.1.1. PERIOD 1: PROTO-HASSUNA

The earliest recovered sites in the THS region are of the Proto-Hassuna (Le Mière 2000; Nieuwenhuyse 2007) or Pre-Halaf (Akkermans and Schwartz 2003: fig. 4.2) phase of the Late Neolithic period (ca. 6500–5900 B.C.). The six sites cumulatively cover 12.54 ha and range from 5.17 ha (THS 56) to 1.01 ha (THS 49). With the exception of THS 56, all sites are between 1.01 and 2.28 ha (table 6.1). All Period 1 sites are low mounds which were either under cultivation at the time of collection or had been cultivated in recent years. It is probable that since their abandonment all came under cultivation on occasion, so it can be assumed that their sediments and surface artifacts have been subjected to lateral movement over the millennia. Therefore, the estimations of site size reflect the habitation area and an unquantifiable area of post-occupational horizontal smearing. This is true for sites of all periods, but the greater age of Period 1 sites means that these forces have been in operation for a longer time and therefore may have had a greater impact than on more recent sites.

It is striking that none of the recovered Period 1 sites ultimately grew into high mounds. All were reoccupied at least once before the present with the possible exception of THS 49, which did not receive a formal collection, but none were basal layers of high multiperiod mounds. This pattern is in contrast to the results of surveys in the

Table 6.1. Period 1 sites and areas

Site	*Area (ha)*
56	5.17
39	2.28
4	1.47
44	1.46
12	1.15
49	1.01
6	12.54

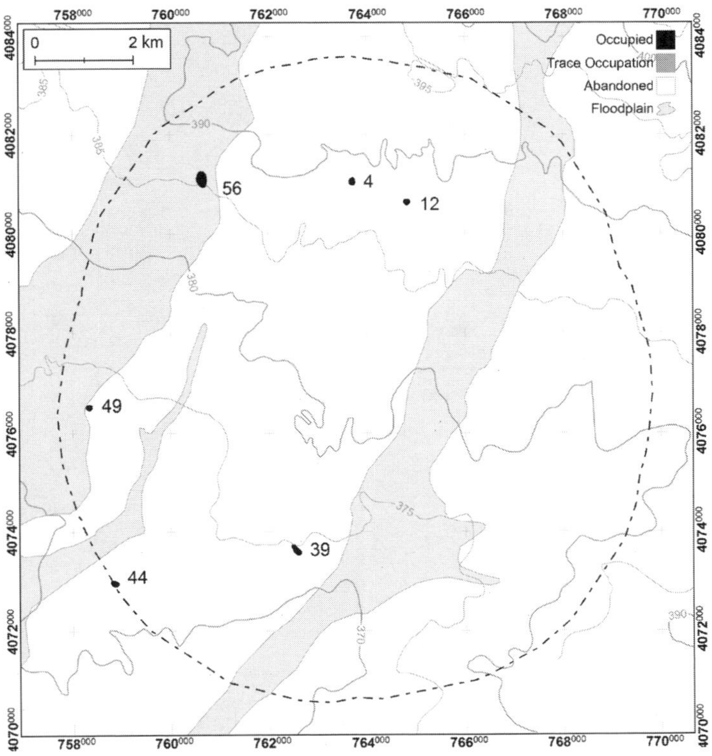

Figure 6.2. Period 1 sites in the THS region

western basin, where late Neolithic sherds were found on high mounds, albeit at very low densities (Le Mière 2000; Nieuwenhuyse 2000, 2007). It is therefore possible that the lower-intensity collection methodology employed by the THS overlooked deeply buried Period 1 occupations at multiperiod sites; the recovered settlement pattern is probably an underrepresentation of settlement during this phase. Nonetheless, the density of Period 1 sites in the THS region (20.8 sq. km/site) is roughly comparable to the 17.6 sq. km per site of the Iraqi North Jazira (Wilkinson and Tucker 1995: 45), which used a collection methodology similar to the THS.

The recovered Period 1 sites are evenly distributed throughout the survey region (fig. 6.2). Of the six, three are close to the edges of the major northeast–southwest drainages, including THS 56, the largest site; the other three are on the watershed between them. No Period 1 settlements were found east of the eastern drainage, toward the Tigris-Euphrates watershed.

6.1.2. PERIOD 2: HALAF

Recovered sites more than doubled to thirteen in Period 2. Two (THS 16 and 24) had only minor sherd assemblages, but these low sherd numbers can be attributed to subsequent settlement overburden. Average site size grew from Period 1, although the sites remained small. Occupations averaged 2.43 ha and ranged from 0.77 ha at THS 9 to traces of a 6.25 ha settlement beneath the central mound at THS 24. Total settled area almost tripled to 31.6 ha (table 6.2).

The distribution of recovered Period 2 sites is even throughout the THS (fig. 6.3). As in Period 1, there appears to be no systematic association with the major surface drainages; as many sites were located on the watershed between them as were located adjacent to their floodplains. Settlements appear to the southeast of the eastern drainage for the first time at THS 32.

Unlike the pattern in the previous period, Period 2 sites were found at basal levels of multiperiod sites (e.g., THS 18 and 24) and even high mounds (THS 16 and 41). We are therefore more confident in the ability of the collection methodology to recognize Period 2 sites. In addition to demographic expansion, the higher recovery rate

Table 6.2. Period 2 sites and areas

Site	*Area (ha)*	
	Settled	*Trace*
20	4.70	—
56	3.65	—
32	2.61	—
41	2.40	—
18	1.95	—
52	1.78	—
8	1.39	—
15	1.20	—
51	1.18	—
43	0.79	2.12
9	0.77	—
24	—	6.25
16	—	0.81
13	22.42	9.18
	31.60	

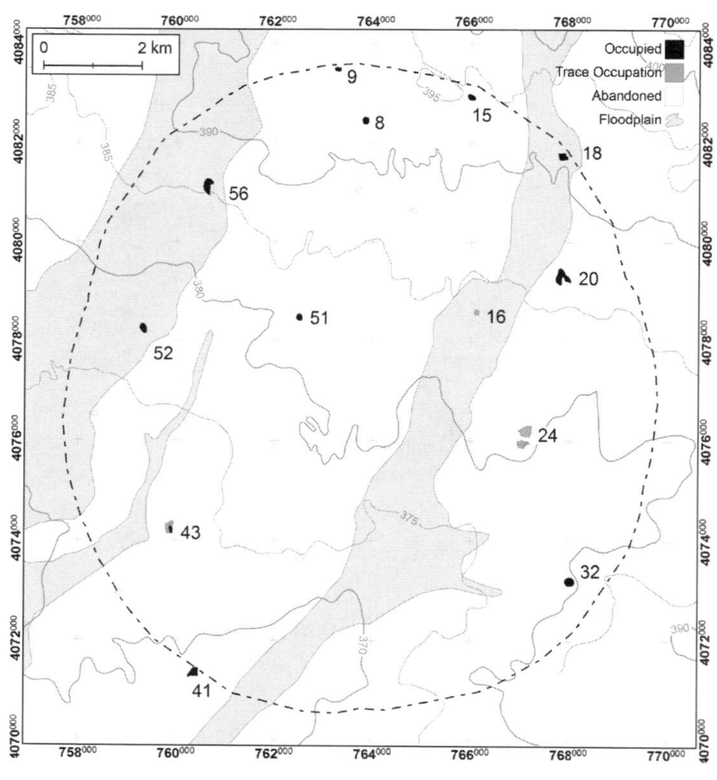

Figure 6.3. Period 2 sites in the THS region

may be related to non-demographic factors, such as longer duration of settlement within ceramic phases, increased production and consumption of pottery, and perhaps higher visibility and survival of painted potsherds. However, it remains a possibility that Period 2 settlement was overlooked at multiperiod sites.

Only a single Period 1 site, THS 56, continued to be settled in Period 2, and at a reduced scale. Even this low percentage (17% of Period 1 sites occupied again in Period 2) may be misleading. Throughout the Near East prior to the Ubaid period, settlements rarely survived for more than a few generations (Akkermans and Schwartz 2003: 151–53). The necessarily coarse chronological periods employed by archaeological surveys can provide little evidence to contradict this excavation-based conclusion. Indeed, the single-period Halaf sites (THS 8 and 52) and the others with only one or two other periods of occupation are all low mounds, which suggests that settlements were too short-lived to build up much settlement debris. For both Periods 1 and 2, it can be assumed that the settlement distribution maps represent, to some degree, a picture of non-contemporaneous settlements within a single ceramic phase.

6.1.3. PERIOD 3: NORTHERN UBAID

Following Period 2, settlement in the THS area underwent a substantial contraction. Only two Period 3 sites were recovered, for a total settled area of 3.59 ha (table 6.3). The sites are small low mounds of 1.57 and 2.02 ha, in line with the scale of previous settlement in the region. However, the density of settlement (1 site/62.5 sq. km) represents a considerable abandonment of the region by sedentary populations and is much lower than the 11.05 sq. km per site in the Iraqi North Jazira (43 Ubaid sites in 475 sq. km; Wilkinson and Tucker 1995: 40). Given the continuing density of settlement only some dozen kilometers to the east, it appears unlikely that any climatic or environmental factor could explain the low settlement in the THS region. Both sites are immediately adjacent to the eastern drainage (fig. 6.4), leaving the watersheds abandoned, but it is unwise to generalize from such a small number of sites.

Table 6.3. Period 3 sites and areas

Site	*Area (ha)*
29	2.02
26	1.57
2	3.59

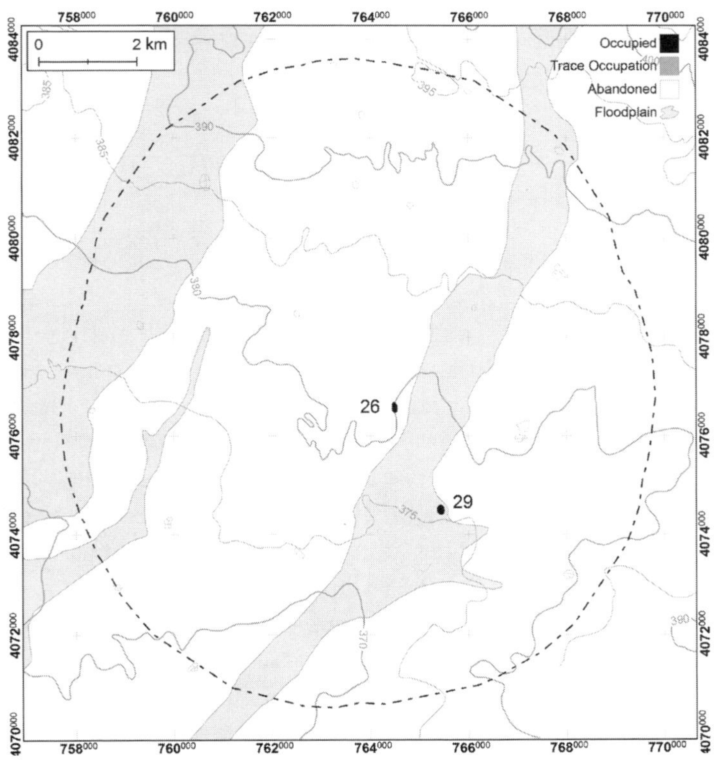

Figure 6.4. Period 3 sites in the THS region

The two small Period 3 mounds appear to be new settlements on previously unoccupied land. The smaller site, THS 26, rises only 2 m above the plain but was also settled in the Late Chalcolithic 1–2 period (Period 4). THS 29, in contrast, is 4 m high, but otherwise was only settled ephemerally in the Abbasid period (Period 17); the majority of its bulk probably derives from its Period 3 occupation. The apparent reduction in settlement from Period 2 to Period 3 may therefore be an artifact of the decrease in settlement mobility described by Akkermans (Akkermans and Schwartz 2003: 159–61). Instead of shifting settlement location every few generations, as may have happened in Period 2, the Period 3 population in the THS appears to have remained at THS 29 throughout most, if not all, of the time of the northern Ubaid ceramic tradition.

In light of the possible shift in settlement continuity, it is difficult to draw any demographic conclusions about changes in site numbers and densities between Periods 2 and 3. Long-term continuous settlement of a place will often lead to increased intrasite population density. Can the thirteen potentially short-lived and non-contemporaneous settlements of Period 2 be equated with the single long-settled and potentially higher-density settlement of Period 3? The apparent duration of Period 3 settlement at THS 29 suggests that a site-to-site correlation between Halaf- and Ubaid-period settlement is inappropriate. However, given that the neighboring North Jazira plain did not undergo a similar reduction in site numbers (Wilkinson and Tucker 1995: 40–41), it is difficult to argue against a substantial reduction in sedentary occupation of the THS region.

Settlement in the late Neolithic and early Chalcolithic periods (Periods 1–3) must be considered in light of considerable issues of contemporaneity, occupation duration, site visibility, and archaeological recovery rates. Even with these caveats, the patterns in the THS area agree with patterns found elsewhere in northern Mesopotamia: small villages of short duration and even distribution.

6.2. PERIOD 4: LATE CHALCOLITHIC 1–2

The late fifth millennium saw the appearance of a type of settlement which, on present evidence, is unique in the Near East. The sherd scatter at THS 25, also called the Hamoukar Southern Extension and known locally as Khirbat al-Fakhar, covered 300 ha (see the detailed discussion in Section 4.5.1). The scale of this site is unprecedented and was not equalled until the rise of the Early Dynastic cities of southern Mesopotamia in the early third millennium B.C. (Adams 1981: 81–94).

6.2.1. THE THS 25 SETTLEMENT COMPLEX

The hybrid areal-systematic sampling method employed at THS 25 revealed a remarkable distribution of surface artifacts. All sub-areas of the 31.3 ha central mounded complex had particularly rich surface assemblages of Period 4 diagnostic types, as did the smaller mounds at THS 26 and THS 27. It is difficult to determine the degree to which the mounding of these areas was a result of Period 4 settlement and not later reoccupation in the first millennia B.C. and A.D. Excavation at the western end of the complex has revealed only Islamic occupation, whereas several soundings at the eastern end have produced only evidence for Period 4 settlement (al-Quntar 2009).

Beyond the central mounded complex, the sampled sherd scatter was of variable but generally high density (fig. 6.5). The lowest-density collection units were in the southwestern quadrant of the outer site, with densities of 52 and 84 sherds per 100 sq. m, but the field from which they came had low visibility. Elsewhere, density was often greater than 1,000 sherds per 100 sq. m. In the outer areas, type numbers were not recorded, but collectors noted no types other than those from Period 4. Collection coverage was uneven, particularly in the northwestern and southwestern quadrants of the outer site, due to the presence of cotton crops and other visibility-reducing ground conditions. The samples collected, however, did allow a connection between high sherd density and mottled coloration on CORONA satellite photographs. Systematic collections beyond areas of mottling, especially to the south and east, had remarkably lower density. On this basis, the reconstructed extent of the site's sherd scatter is 300 ha.

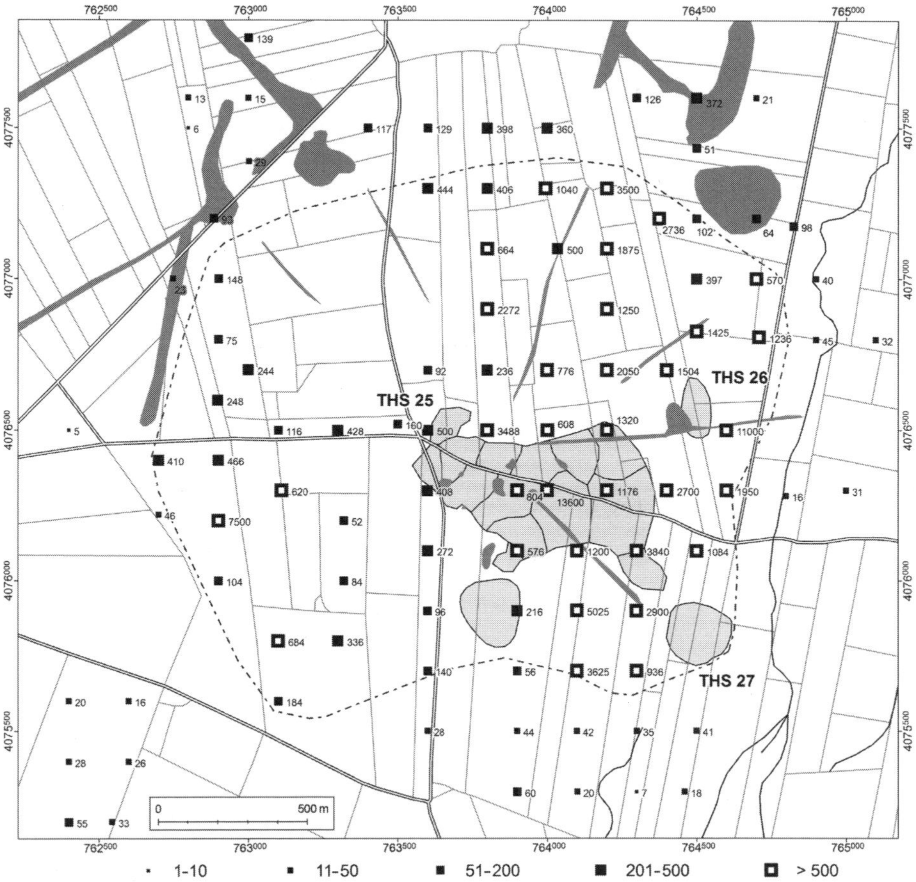

Figure 6.5. Density of surface sherds at THS 25

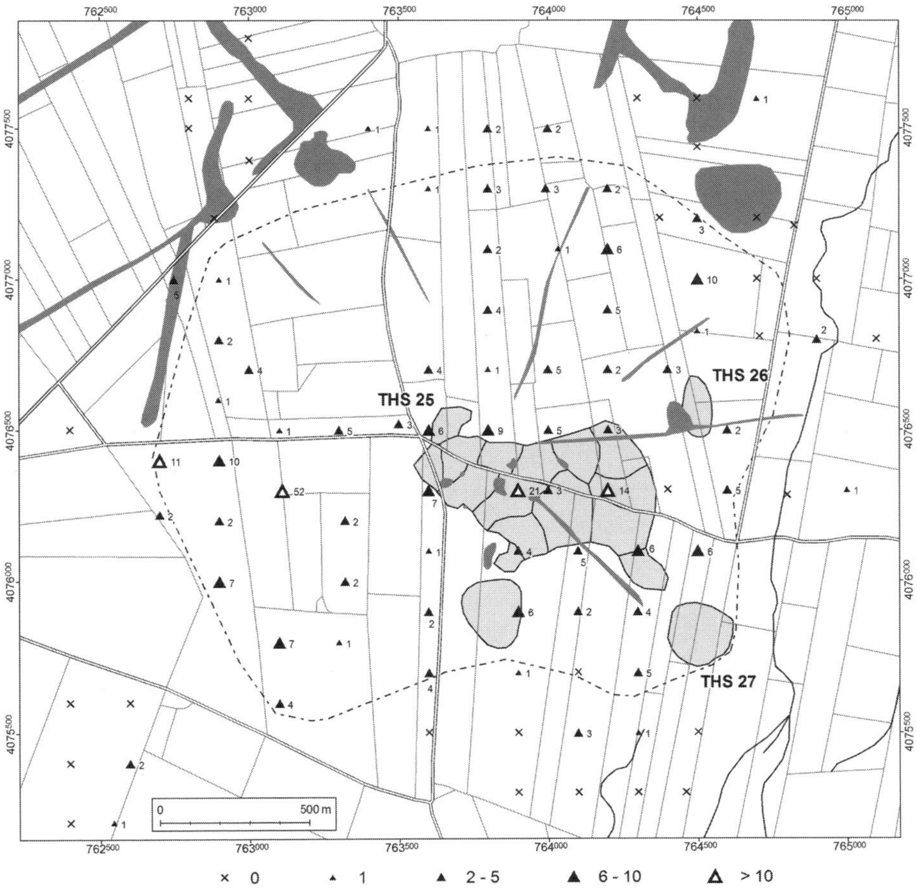

Figure 6.6. Distribution of obsidian at THS 25

The distribution of obsidian also marks THS 25 as a unique place (fig. 6.6). All collection units produced not only flakes from tool manufacture but also the tools themselves, most frequently in the form of long blades. Prismatic obsidian cores were also noted across the site outside of systematic collections.

In its scale, morphology, ceramic and lithic surface assemblage, and early date, THS 25 is a unique site. It is certainly inappropriate to interpret it in the same manner as one might the other large sites in the basin, such as Hamoukar. For example, application of commonly employed ratios of persons per hectare would yield population estimates between 30,000 and 60,000 persons in the settlement. The apparent high degree of ceramic consumption, and the frequent occurrence of large storage vessels, argues for at least semi-sedentary if not fully sedentary occupation of all parts of the complex. However, the intermittent and non-contiguous distribution of anthropogenic soils visible in CORONA (see fig. 4.12) suggests the possibility of low-density dispersed settlement patterns within the outer parts of the site.

6.2.2. PERIOD 4 SETTLEMENT IN THE THS REGION

If one were to disregard THS 25, Period 4 would otherwise appear to be a return to the settlement patterning of Period 2, with an identical number of sites (13; 12 major occupations and 1 trace occupation). Excluding THS 25, site area averages 1.88 ha, slightly smaller than the 2.43 ha of Period 2; total settled area was 25.32 ha, compared to 31.6 ha in Period 2 (table 6.4).

Spatially, however, Period 4 patterning shifted away from the even distribution of Period 1–2 sites, and might signify the first appearance of routes of communication that would become significant in the third millennium and later (fig. 6.7). The watershed between the major drainages had, with the exception of the general abandonment of Period 3, been settled since the earliest documented appearance of sedentary groups on the plain; in Period 4, villages clustered especially around the eastern drainage, but two sites were found along the small drainage at the southwestern part of the survey area. Only two sites (THS 10 and 32), representing about 11 percent of the non-THS 25 settled area, were unequivocally located on higher ground between drainages. It appears that proximity to surface drainage had become a more important factor in making decisions about settlement placement than in previous

Table 6.4. Period 4 sites and areas

Site	Area (ha)	
	Settled	*Trace*
7	31.26	275.35*
18	—	3.00
27	3.48	—
31	2.39	—
46	2.22	—
17	2.09	—
30	2.06	—
32	1.60	—
26	1.57	—
10	1.24	—
15	1.20	—
44	0.85	—
21	0.82	—
13	50.78	278.35

* 275.35 ha of settlement at THS 25 is extensive or dispersed, rather than trace settlement

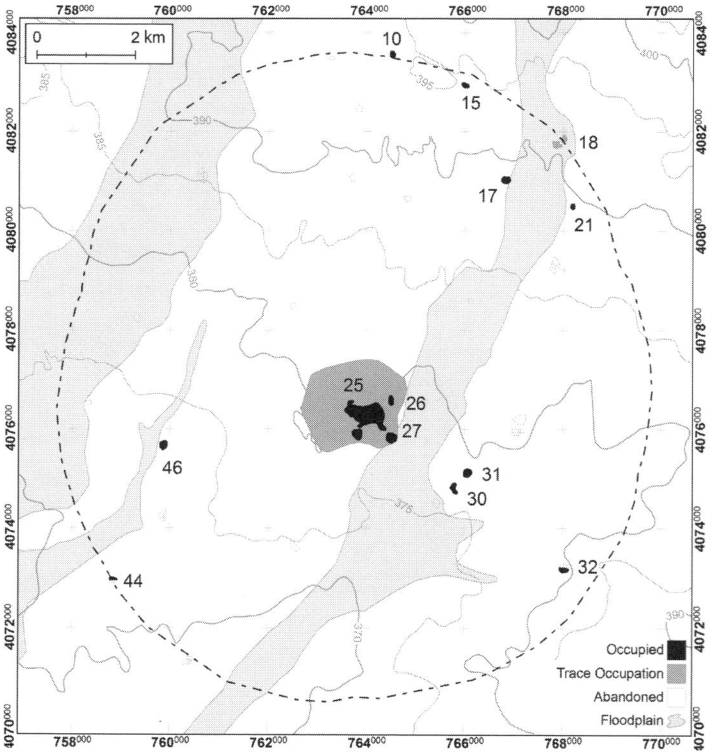

Figure 6.7. Period 4 sites in the THS region

times; whether this shift was a response to a dynamic climate, a function of endogenous socioeconomic change (e.g., a shift to perennial site occupation or changes in the agro-pastoral economy), or both, remains to be determined.

In Period 4, a clear linearity of patterning is apparent for the first time. The clearest alignment runs southeast to northwest from THS 32, through the paired sites THS 30 and 31, and then crosses the eastern drainage at the THS 25–26–27 settlement complex, which appears to have been its terminus. A second alignment runs along the northeastern edge of the survey area, also aligned southeast to northwest; it begins at THS 21, crosses the eastern drainage to THS 17, and then continues north-northwest to THS 15 and THS 10. The position of this group at the survey boundary makes it difficult to interpret; its linearity could be a function of the arbitrary end of archaeological observations. If this string of sites does indeed mark a route of communication, the THS could only document a short segment without obvious termini at either end.

This general southeast–northwest alignment through the eastern basin is an archaeologically and historically important one that became particularly durable and ultimately incised into the landscape. This route between the Tigris at the area of Mosul and the southern edge of the Tur Abdin at the emergence of the Jaghjagh River has been considered significant in the Uruk Expansion (Algaze 1993), the later third-millennium B.C. urban phase (Ur 2003; Wilkinson 1993), the Old Assyrian trading network (Charpin 1992), caravan trade between Mediterranean powers and the east clear up to the early twentieth century A.D. (see Section 2.2; Oates 1968; Fiey 1964). Although the Period 4 pattern appears to follow this alignment, it cannot be associated with any specific trackway features, as is possible for the later third millennium and the first millennium A.D. (see Section 5.3 and *Chapter 7*). The most obvious rationale for such movement in Period 4 is economic: the great abundance of non-local obsidian cores, debitage, and tools on its surface identify THS 25 as a major locus of obsidian trade at the end of the fifth millennium B.C. (Khalidi, Gratuze, and Boucetta 2009).

The two outlying sites in the southwestern part of the THS region may also mark routes of movement, although the evidence is far more ambiguous. THS 46 sits on the eastern side of a small drainage, precisely at the point of an archaeologically documented crossing point (see fig. 5.29). To its south, THS 44 sits astride another major route in later times (see map 2). Both of these later routes led from Hamoukar into the Radd marsh and presumably down the Wadi Radd to Tell Brak and the southern basin. The Period 4 occupations at THS 44 and 46 cannot be unequivocally associated with the nearby hollow ways, which appear to be Period 7 in date.

A second long-term pattern, the general tendency to reoccupy previously settled places, also appears to have its beginnings in Period 4. Although only one of the two Period 3 settlements was also occupied in Period 4, four others were founded on abandoned Period 1 and 2 sites. Overall, these five were almost 40 percent of Period 4 sites. The paired sites THS 30 and 31 were founded in close proximity to the former Period 3 settlement at THS 29 (THS 30 is only 330 m northeast of THS 29). Although continuity at individual archaeological sites is low, this general area, which was at the confluence of the major eastern drainage with two more ephemeral ones from the Tigris-Euphrates watershed, had long-term significance. Settlement shifted among these three sites in a northwestern direction such that at least one was occupied in Periods 3, 4, and 5, and two were resettled on a non-permanent basis in Period 7.

6.3. PERIOD 5: INDIGENOUS AND INTRUSIVE COMMUNITIES IN THE FOURTH MILLENNIUM

With the abandonment of THS 25 around the start of the fourth millennium B.C., settlement returned to a pattern of small villages, although at this time with multiple nucleated towns. Because of the presence of culturally independent and chronologically non-coterminous ceramic traditions (discussed in Section B.2), contemporaneity is particularly difficult to establish. Because the chaff-tempered indigenous ceramic tradition (Period 5b) predates the appearance of ceramics of the southern Mesopotamian Uruk tradition (Period 5a), the former is presented independently from the latter. This section concludes with a discussion of the feasibility of the temporal integration of the Period 5b and 5a settlement patterns.

6.3.1. PERIOD 5B: FOURTH-MILLENNIUM SITES WITH "INDIGENOUS" CERAMIC TYPES

The eighteen sites and 49.9 ha of settled area in Period 5b represent a slight increase in site numbers, but a slight decline in total settled area (excluding the unmounded areas of THS 25), from Period 4 (fig. 6.8, table 6.5). Most sites continued to be small villages, but average size grew to 2.77 ha due to the appearance of substantial towns at THS 1 (Hamoukar, 15.31 ha) and THS 40 (Khirbat Melhem, 8.57 ha). Most sites concentrated along the eastern drainage and adjacent parts of the watersheds; in particular, the eastern part of the THS now hosted many sites. The left bank of the small southwestern drainage supported two sites (THS 43 and 46).

The earliest unambiguous supra-village site appeared at Hamoukar and grew to over 15 ha (fig. 6.9). Period 5b sherds occur across the entire the high mound, although at variable density, which is to be explained by factors other than spatial patterning of ancient settlement. The high density of sherds along the southern flanks and the low density to the north is the direct result of differential erosion of slopes of different aspect. The low Period 5b sherd density on the central high mound must be related to substantial overburden of Periods 6 and 7 in addition to the overall small size of sherds on its heavily trodden surface (see Section 3.4).

The interpolated distribution of Period 5b sherds shows 11.8 ha of dense scatter (3 or more typed diagnostics/100 sq. m) and an additional 19.1 ha of low-density scatter (1–2 sherds/100 sq. m), covering roughly 31 ha. However, after considering post-occupational natural and cultural transformative processes, it is likely that actual settlement was restricted to the 15 ha area of the high mound itself. It is not certain that fourth-millennium settlement at Hamoukar was continuous, but the entire sequence of Late Chalcolithic 3–4 ceramics appear in the Area A step trench (Gibson et al. 2002a, 2002b). The Area B excavations emphasized horizontal exposure but have nonetheless revealed several meters of Late Chalcolithic 4 levels at the southeastern corner of the high mound (Gibson et al. 2002a; Reichel 2002). From the surface collection and excavation data, it appears that the entire 15.31 ha of the high mound was settled in Period 5b, although whether it attained this size already in the Late Chalcolithic 3 is uncertain.

Table 6.5. Period 5 sites and areas

Site	*Area (ha)*	
	Period 5b	*Period 5a*
1	15.31	15.31
40	8.57	7.50
3	—	3.79
20	3.53	—
38	3.22	—
32	2.61	—
31	2.39	—
46	2.22	—
18	1.95	—
41	1.54	—
33	1.33	—
15	1.20	—
2	1.08	1.08
24	0.90	—
44	0.85	—
36	0.84	—
16	0.81	—
43	0.79	0.46
22	0.76	—
19	49.90	28.14

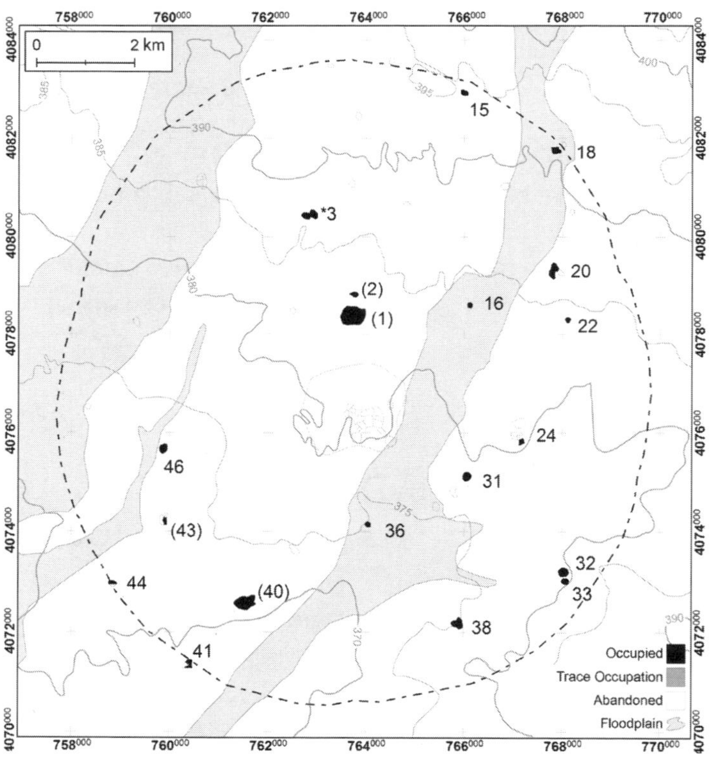

Figure 6.8. Period 5a and 5b sites in the THS region. Period 5a sites labeled with an asterisk; sites with Period 5a and 5b sherds labeled in parentheses; all other sites Period 5b

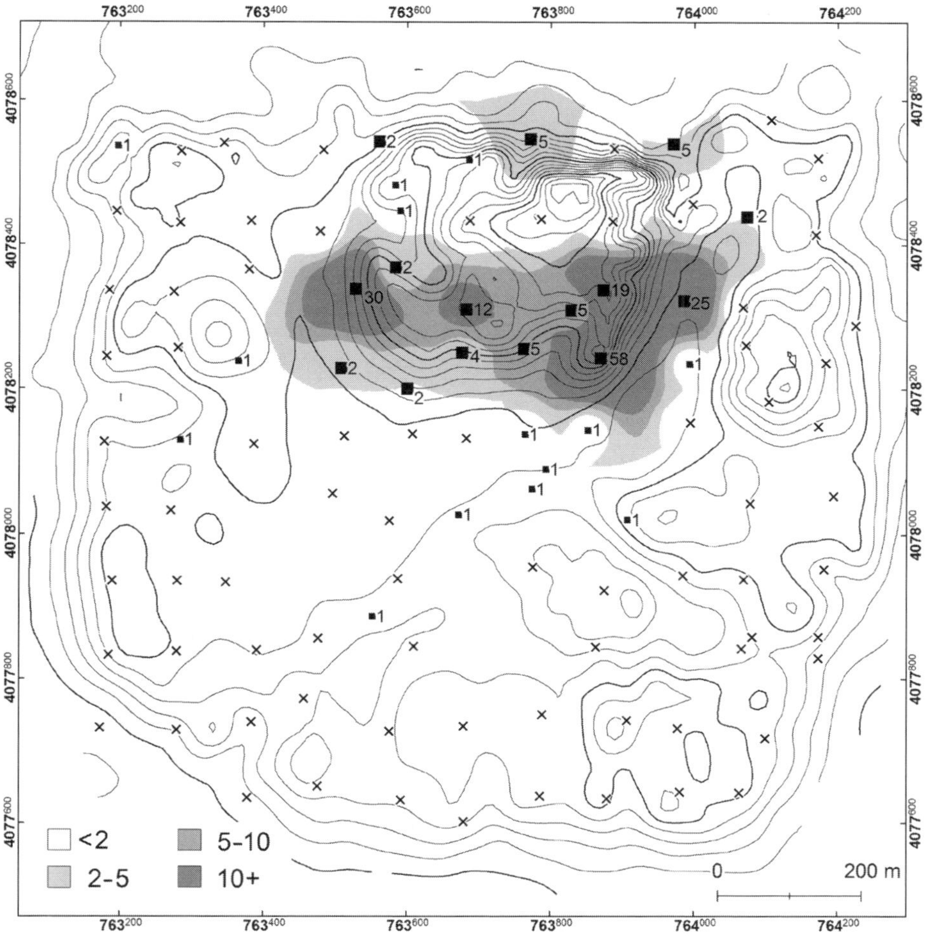

Figure 6.9. Distribution of Period 5b sherds at Hamoukar

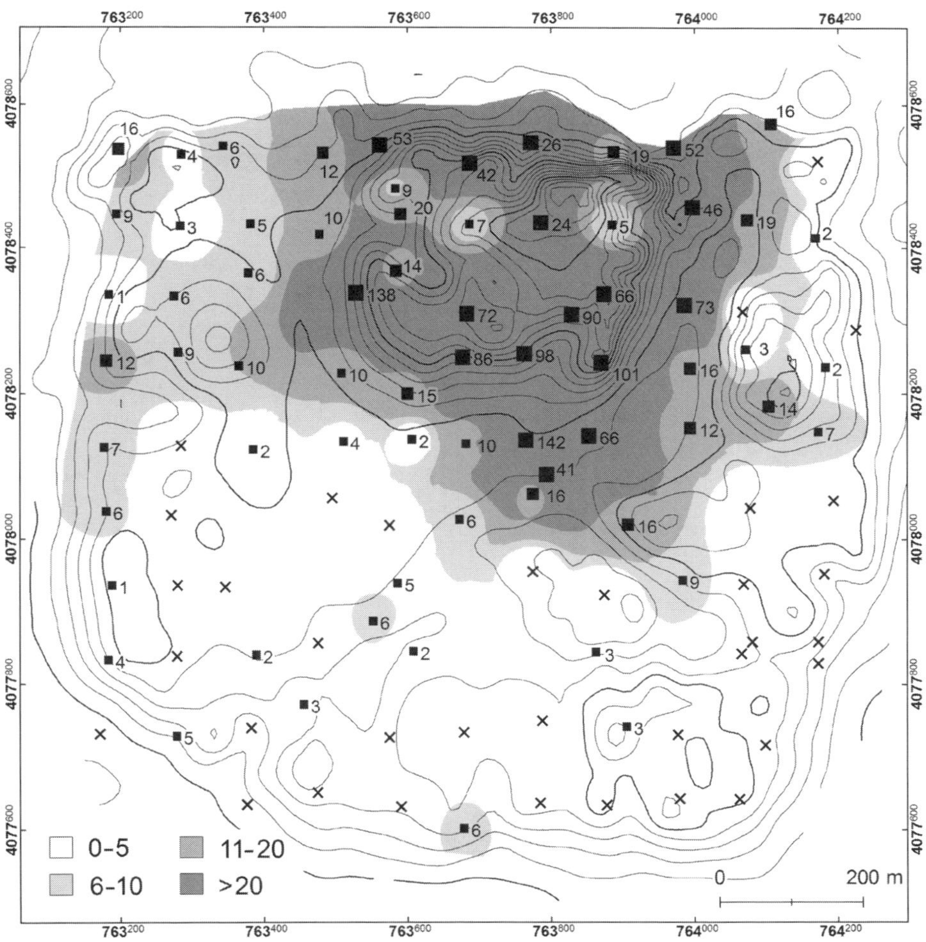

Figure 6.10. Distribution of reduced-core coarse chaff-tempered sherds (F5) at Hamoukar

The THS also quantified body sherds of the standard Period 5b fabric (Type F5; see table 3.1) and plotted their distribution (fig. 6.10). The spatial distribution appears identical to the distribution of typed diagnostics (fig. 6.9), which suggests that the pattern of ceramic consumption (and by extension, former settlement) derived from the latter is not skewed by taphonomic transformations of Period 5b sherds on the surface.

The increased settlement of the eastern portion of the THS region was matched by the apparent complete abandonment of the plain north and west of Hamoukar itself. Indeed, the only sites on the watershed between the two major drainages were Hamoukar and its closely related satellite THS 2.

6.3.2. PERIOD 5A: FOURTH-MILLENNIUM SITES WITH NON-LOCAL CERAMIC TYPES

The fourth-millennium settlement pattern is complicated by the presence of sherds of the southern Uruk ceramic tradition (designated here as Period 5a). On the surface of Hamoukar, the distribution of Period 5a ceramic types is identical to the distribution of the approximately contemporary local sherds (fig. 6.11). The recovered sherds were almost exclusively from bevelled-rim bowls (T5a/1; see fig. B.14B). Previous visitors to Hamoukar had reported abundant southern types and the Area A step trench produced the full grit-tempered southern assemblage (Gibson et al. 2002b: fig. 21), so their paucity was unexpected. It is possible that the THS sampling methodology simply missed areas with southern ceramics. To check this possibility, a non-systematic areal collection unit (117) was placed in a gully in the northern slope of the high mound (see fig. 3.11); it produced bevelled-rim bowls but also many southern

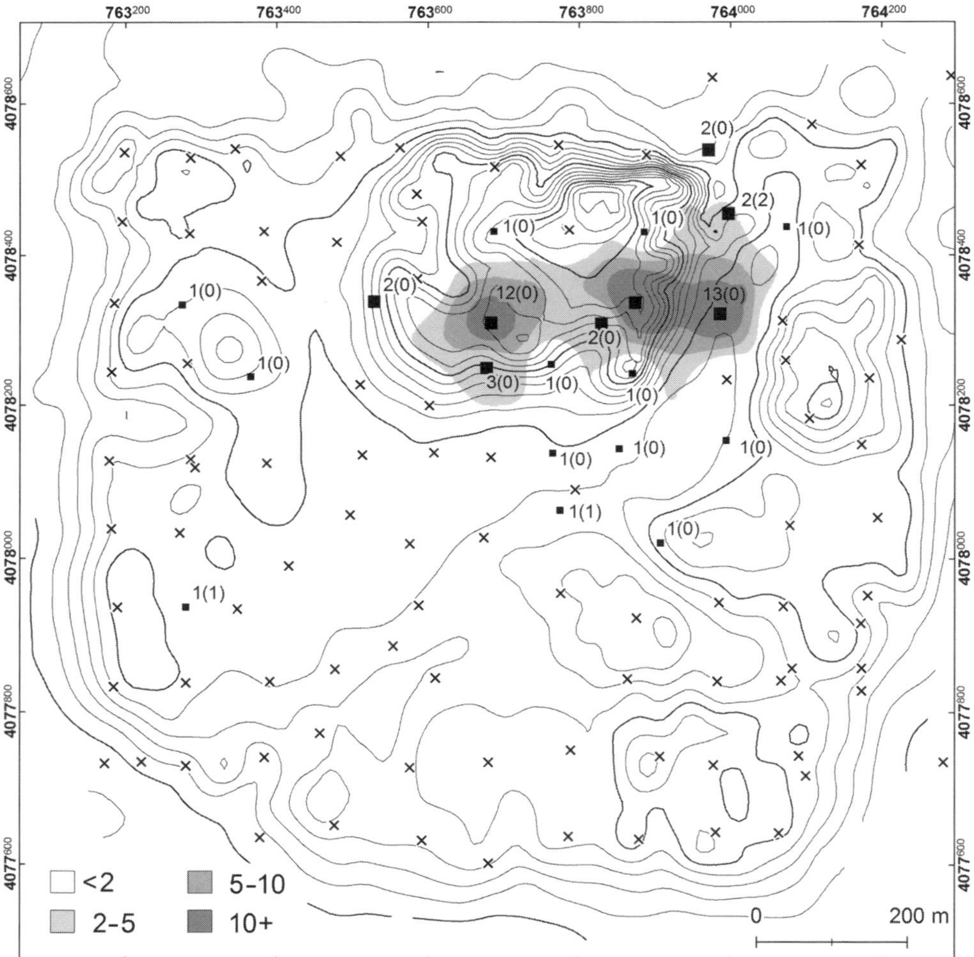

Figure 6.11. Distribution of Period 5a sherds at Hamoukar.
Number of grit-tempered (non-bevelled-rim bowl) sherds in parentheses

Uruk oblique-rimmed bowls (T5a/5). However, visiting archaeological teams have made informal pickups and even systematic collections at Hamoukar for a number of years prior to 1999, and these appear to have targeted the southern Uruk sherds on the high mound (Ur 2002b: 15, 19–20). Cumulatively, these collections may have had an impact on the surface assemblage.

At present, it appears that southern Uruk settlement covered the same 15.31 ha area of the high mound as the indigenous settlement. A possible exception may be the southeastern spur of the high mound, where excavations in Area B have produced purely local material culture, excepting a few cylinder seal impressions (Reichel 2002). Hamoukar was certainly a regional center in Period 5, but its scale was an order of magnitude smaller than some of the pre-1999 size estimations (Ur 2002b: 15).

Including Hamoukar, southern Mesopotamia-derived types occurred on four of the sixteen Period 5b sites (fig. 6.8, table 6.5). There are differences in relative densities among the sites. THS 1 was predominantly local in nature but with a substantial bevelled-rim bowl surface collection. THS 40 was predominantly southern but with local ceramics in all collection areas. The surface assemblage of THS 2 was overwhelmingly southern in character but still contained local types (fig. 6.12). THS 43 was a small local settlement with a handful of southern sherds. A fifth site (THS 3) produced exclusively southern sherds, but the collection was far too meager to draw any conclusions (5 sherds total).

The Uruk Expansion was of greater duration than previously appreciated, and ceramic indicators for the Middle (Late Chalcolithic 4) and Late Uruk (Late Chalcolithic 5) have been proposed (see Section B.2.6 and Schwartz 2001). Although conical cups (T5a/7) were abundant, none collected by the THS had the pinched lip characteristic of Late Chalcolithic 4. On the other hand, drooping spouts (T5a/3), the primary Late Chalcolithic 5 indicator, were recovered at THS 2, 40, and 43, and in the excavations at Hamoukar Area A. These two ceramic types are too few and too infrequent to exclude the possibility of Late Chalcolithic 4/Middle Uruk settlement, but it does seem likely that the southern Mesopotamian colonization or contact was more intensive later in the fourth millennium.

Figure 6.12. THS 2. The lighter soil of the low mound is visible between the two pairs of figures. The eastern half of the site (at right) has been bulldozed for cotton fields. View facing north, from the high mound of Hamoukar

6.3.3. CONTEMPORANEITY OF PERIOD 5A AND 5B SETTLEMENT

The partial temporal overlap of the ceramic traditions used here to define Period 5a and 5b settlement presents a great methodological challenge to presenting a single map of contemporaneous settlement. For analytical purposes, the THS was unable to distinguish systematically between Late Chalcolithic 3 and *indigenous* Late Chalcolithic 4 surface assemblages within Period 5b, nor could it separate Middle (*intrusive* Late Chalcolithic 4) and Late Uruk (*intrusive* Late Chalcolithic 5) assemblages within Period 5a. Furthermore, the duration of the indigenous Late Chalcolithic 4 ceramic tradition is in question: does it continue to the end of the fourth millennium (i.e., contemporary with intrusive Late Chalcolithic 5 ceramics)? These issues cannot be solved via surface observations alone.

6.4. THE GROWTH AND COLLAPSE OF URBAN SETTLEMENT IN THE THS REGION IN THE THIRD MILLENNIUM

The end of the fourth millennium witnessed a dramatic reorganization of settlement in the THS region. Four Period 6 sites were recognized by the THS. Only three of the seventeen Period 5 sites (THS 1, 16, and 41) were also occupied in Period 6, but actual continuity of settlement is uncertain; only the assemblage from THS 41 included post-Uruk painted vessels (T5b/10; see Roaf 1984; Rova 1999–2000, 2000) and painted Ninevite 5 ceramics (T6/1).

6.4.1. PERIOD 6: NINEVITE 5

Three of the four Period 6 sites were 1.18 ha or less (THS 16, 41, and 51). The fourth, Hamoukar itself, grew substantially in the later phases of Period 6, but is difficult to assess (table 6.6). A confident description of Period 6 settlement at Hamoukar is prevented by the difficulties of the ceramic assemblage. Of the eighty-six Period 6 sherds recovered at Hamoukar, only seventeen (20%) were decorated; the majority were of the various non-decorated and long-lasting ceramic types that are less useful for chronology. They occurred across the entire mounded site in low density and in discontinuous patches (fig. 6.13). The distribution on the high mound appears to be limited to its uppermost part, above the 394 m contour line; the southwestern spur may have been unoccupied at this time. On the

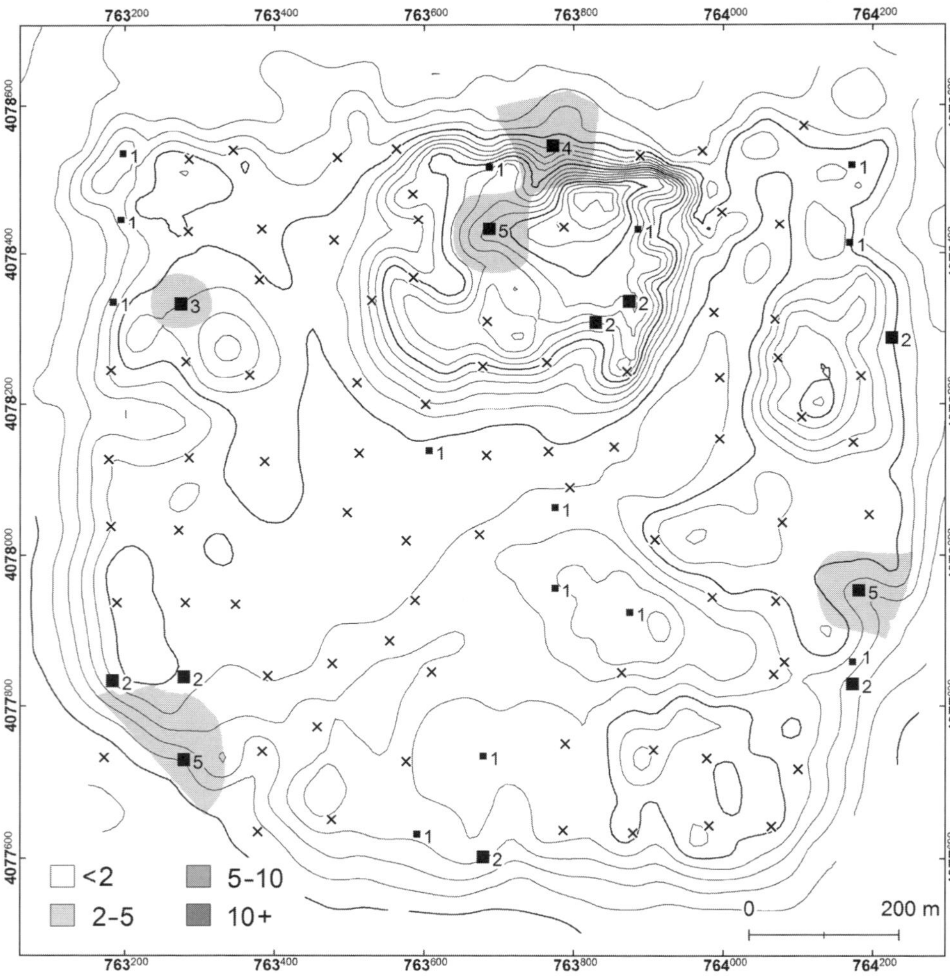

Figure 6.13. Distribution of Period 6 sherds at Hamoukar

lower town, Period 6 sherds were abundant at the plowed-out edges of the site, particularly the southwestern and southeastern corners. At the southwestern corner, a non-systematic point collection (Unit 68; see fig. 3.11) was placed to collect an anomalous assemblage of some thirty large fragments of pointed-base cups (T6/7), which may represent one or more disturbed burials. Finally, the low-density scatter in the center of the lower town coincides with a 2–3 ha topographically low area. If this enclosed depression represents an area of brick pits dug for the construction of later settlement in this area, it may be a window into earlier Ninevite 5 layers.

From the interpolated surface densities shown in figure 6.13, only 3.9 ha featured a dense distribution of Period 6 sherds, with an additional area of 24.8 ha of low-density scatter. This discontinuous low-density pattern does not directly reflect the distribution of Period 6 settlement, however. The possibility of extensive low-density settlement can no longer be dismissed outright; although uncommon, such sites exist at THS 25 in Period 4 (see Section 6.2) and at Tell Brak in Periods 4–5 (Ur, Karsgaard, and Oates 2007). At these sites, interpretation of surface artifact distributions is simplified by a relative lack of later reoccupation. Such is not the case at Hamoukar, where subsequent settlement in Period 7 has impared the visibility of Period 6 levels, especially away from the eroding edges of the lower town (see fig. 6.15). In all likelihood, the distribution of Period 6 sherds represents the places where Ninevite 5 levels are currently archaeologically visible. Furthermore, because of the nature of the Ninevite 5 ceramic assemblage (see Section B.2.7), areas of low-density scatters must carry more significance than a scatter of comparable density from a period with more robust diagnostic types. It is probable that settlement at this time covered the entire lower town. On the high mound, settlement shrank to the area enclosed by the 394 m contour (roughly 8 ha), leaving the southwestern spur and the small Area B spur vacant. In total, settlement covered 98 ha.

When it is possible to be chronologically specific, the ceramics recovered were mostly late in the Ninevite 5 sequence. Of the decorated types, no painted sherds were found during systematic collection. When decorated types were found, the majority were of the somewhat carelessly done late excised tradition typical of the terminal Ninevite 5 period at Tell Leilan (Weiss 2003). Thus the Period 6 figure of 98 ha for Hamoukar describes the site in the terminal phase of the Ninevite 5 period. At present, it is impossible to estimate the size of earlier third-millennium settlement at Hamoukar, although it was almost certainly limited to the high mound; if we exclude areas where the

Table 6.6. Period 6 sites and areas

Site	*Area (ha)*
1	98.00
16	0.81
41	0.67
51	1.18
4	100.66

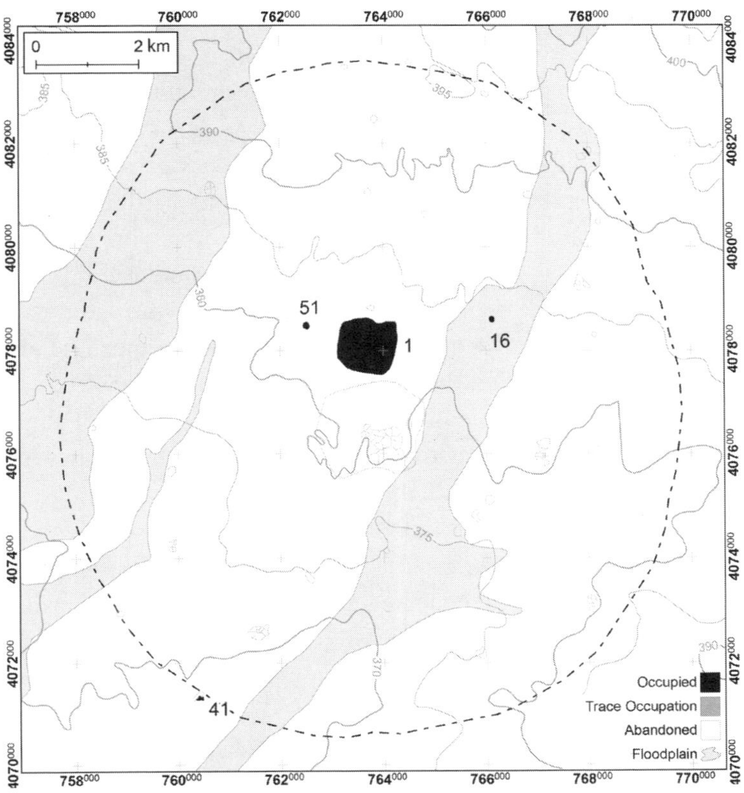

Figure 6.14. Period 6 sites in the THS region

uppermost levels are Period 5 (e.g., the southeastern spur around Area B), it may have been as small as 8 ha. The massive expansion of settlement, which formed the lower town, appears to be contemporary with and parallel to the sudden urbanization at Tell Leilan, which grew from 15 ha to 90 ha in Leilan period IIId (ca. 2600–2500 B.C.; Weiss and Courty 1993: 35–36), and Tell al-Hawa, where the expansion of settlement onto a lower town also occurred at this time (Ball and Wilkinson 2003: 340–41).

The difficulties in identifying non-decorated Ninevite 5 sherds in surface assemblages apply equally to the regional collection (fig. 6.14, table 6.6). The small quantity of Ninevite 5 sherds recovered by the survey consist mostly of chronologically insensitive bases and beaded rims. None of the rather crudely excised decorated types of this time were found on the other three sites, so there is no evidence that Hamoukar had any neighbors within the survey region at the end of Period 6.

The sparseness of settlement in the Hamoukar area can be connected to the near total abandonment of the region southwest of Tell al-Hawa (Wilkinson and Tucker 1995: 49 and fig. 37). There appear to be no environmental reasons for such an abandonment at this time; to the contrary, the early third millennium B.C. was a time of elevated rainfall (Hole 1997). The abrupt linear dropoff in settlement in the North Jazira Project area suggests a social or political reason, which cannot be detailed on the basis of settlement pattern data alone.

6.4.2. PERIOD 7: MID- TO LATE THIRD MILLENNIUM B.C.

At Hamoukar, Period 7 diagnostic sherds are distributed evenly and densely across the entire lower town and high mound (fig. 6.15). Areas of low sherd density are limited to the southern and western slopes of the high mound, the northeastern corner of the lower town, and the area of the enclosed depression. The low-density areas of the high mound may have been unsettled at this time, but other explanations can be offered for the latter two areas. At the northeastern corner of the lower town, the mid- to late third-millennium layers were sealed by Period 11 (Iron Age/ Neo-Assyrian) settlement, as suggested by the surface collection (see Section 6.6) and confirmed by the excavation in Area C (Gibson et al. 2002a: 20). The enclosed depression may have originated as an area of brick pits dug either during the construction of the Period 7 lower town settlement or by later inhabitants of a settlement that may exist beneath the modern village.

As was done with the chaff-tempered body sherds of Period 5b, the distribution of third-millennium B.C. common ware body sherds was also plotted (Type F3, fig. 6.16) for comparison with the distribution of diagnostics. Fabrics throughout the third millennium are generally buff, yellow, or a pale greenish color, fairly evenly fired and tempered with fine chaff and/or small amounts of sand. In general, fabric alone cannot be used to indicate settlement, but at Hamoukar this fabric type is distinct enough from the heavily chaff-tempered reduced-core fourth-millennium fabric (F5) and the heavily dark grit- and sand-tempered Seleucid–Hellenistic fabrics (F6 and F9) to be useful at a very general level. Overall, the distribution of Period 7 common ware body sherds mirrors the distribution of Period 7 diagnostics. Density was low within the modern village, as was overall sherd density (see fig. 3.12), and also on the southern slopes of the high mound and on the northeastern corner of the lower town.

Unlike the preceding period, ceramic types from this time are robust and distinctive (see Section B.2.8). In particular, because of its fabric, T7/5 stoneware can be identified easily even from body sherds. The distribution of this type leaves no doubt that Hamoukar was a massive urban settlement (fig. 6.17). All of the lower town and high mound was occupied, with the possible exception of the southern and western slopes of the high mound. Excavation thus far has confirmed this assessment: all trenches in the lower town (Areas C, E, G, and H) have encountered remains of this period. On the northern high mound, the Area A step trench recovered late Period 6 through Period 7 levels, but the excavations at Area B, at the southeastern corner of the high mound, found Period 5 levels directly beneath the surface. Aside from the western and southern slopes of the high mound, where low sherd density appears to correspond to unoccupied areas, comparable low density in the lower town probably represents the effects of later occupation or brick-pit excavation. The entire lower town was densely settled, whereas only 8 ha of the 15 ha high mound appear to have been occupied. The total settled area of Period 7 Hamoukar was approximately 98 ha.

Including Hamoukar, the THS region hosted seven sites with substantial Period 7 surface assemblages (table 6.7, fig. 6.18). The three other Period 6 sites remained settled, and new small settlements appeared at THS 37 and THS 54. Sherds were abundant on the surfaces of these six sites for an aggregate area of 114.85 ha. With the exception of THS 51, all are high-mounded tell sites, which is the classic site morphology for third-millennium B.C. northern Mesopotamia (Wilkinson 2003: 100–11; Wilkinson, Ur, and Casana 2004). Three of these tell sites (THS

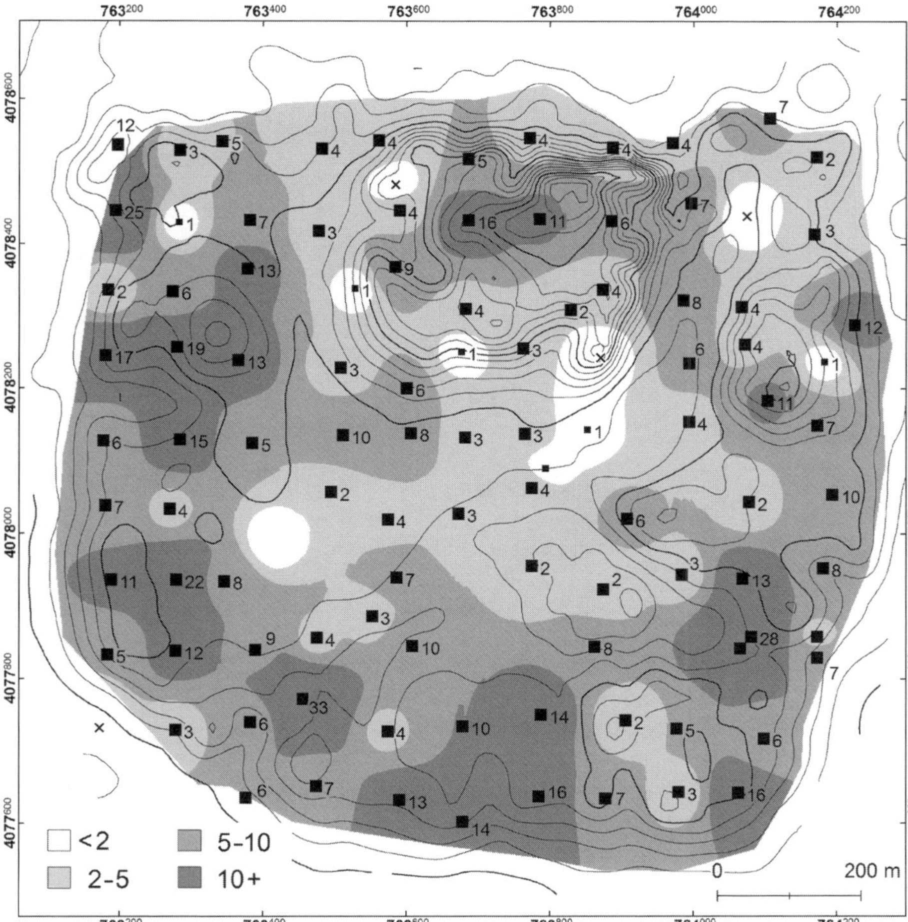

Figure 6.15. Distribution of Period 7 sherds at Hamoukar

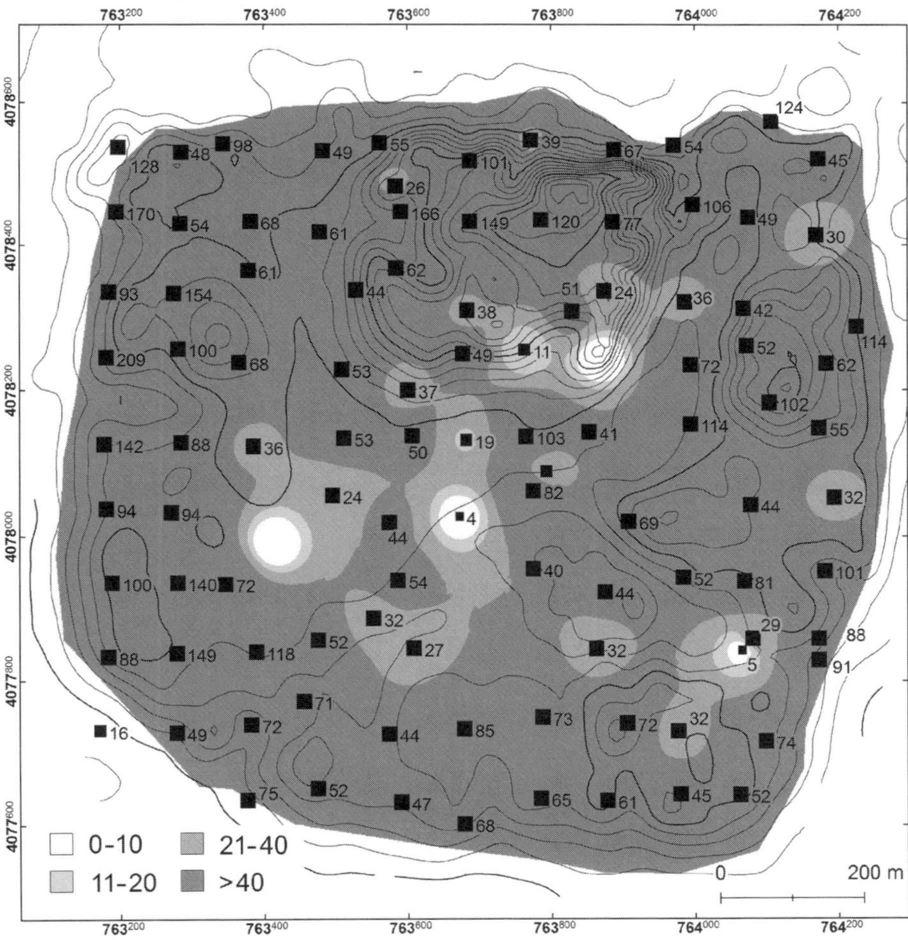

Figure 6.16. Distribution of yellow-green fine chaff- and sand-tempered sherds (F3) at Hamoukar

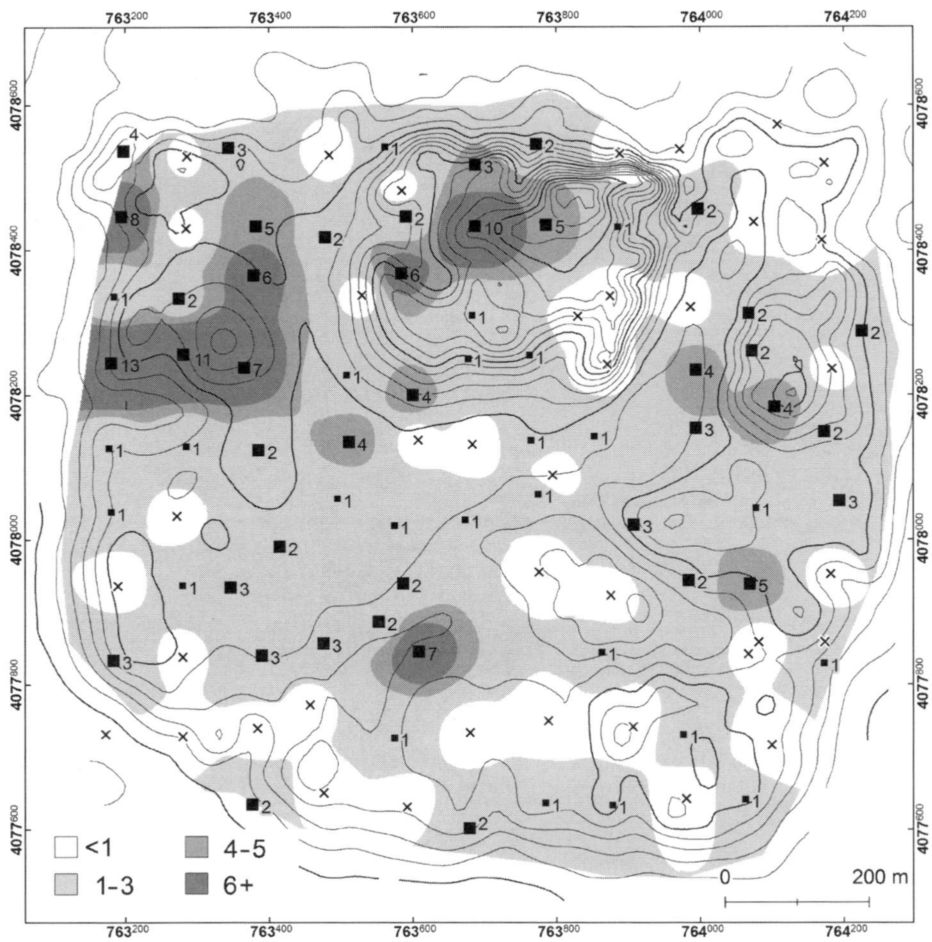

Figure 6.17. Distribution of T7/5 stoneware at Hamoukar

Table 6.7. Period 7 sites and areas

Site	Area (ha)	
	Settled	Trace
1	98.00	—
54	5.71	—
45	—	3.05
31	—	2.39
37	2.33	—
30	—	2.06
41	1.64	—
51	1.18	—
20	—	1.15
12	—	1.15
47	—	1.06
16	0.81	—
22	—	0.76
11	—	0.62
32	0.56	—
15	110.23	12.24
	122.47	

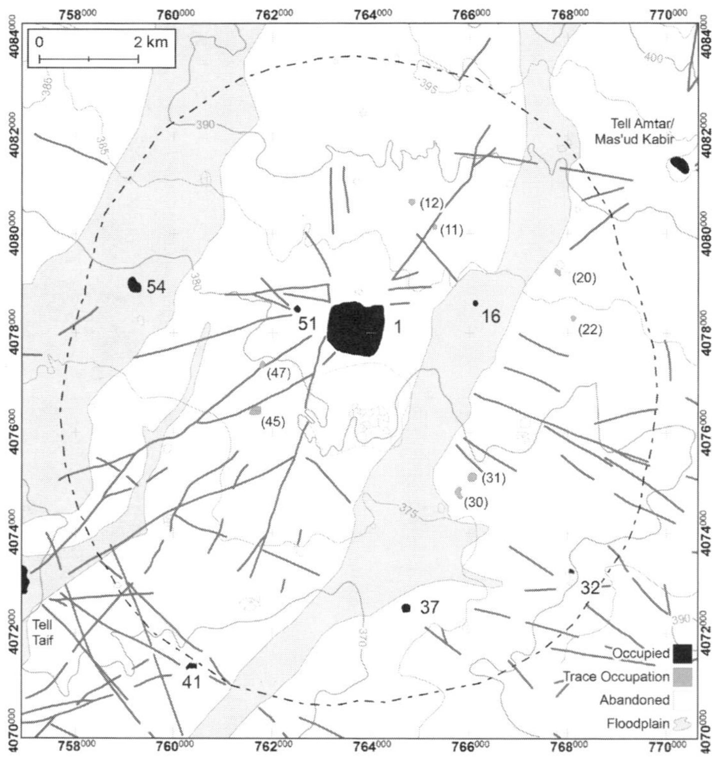

Figure 6.18. Period 7 sites in the THS region. Sites labeled in parentheses are non-permanent

16, 37, and 41) are arrayed along the eastern drainage. Settlement along wadis is the predominant pattern of third-millennium sites elsewhere in the basin.

These settlements were most likely generalized habitation sites, with the possible exception of THS 51, a 1.18 ha low mound only 600 m west of the edge of Hamoukar's lower town. It is positioned at the convergence of three hollow ways and is aligned with Hamoukar's probable western gate (see fig. 3.8). Its size and location might suggest a specialized function. If tied to interregional trade with places to the west, it may have served a caravanserai-like role. If it is to be connected to the local economy, it may have been a place for animal or cereal processing or trade, as these commodities made their way from the western fields and pastures in toward the city. Unfortunately, the surface assemblage offers no further functional clues.

Period 7 sherds were found far more widely distributed than just these seven main sites: in all, thirty-one of the sixty sites had at least one diagnostic sherd. This distribution of sherds cannot be taken at face value to represent nucleated ancient settlement. Many of these diagnostics arrived via ancient manuring, when the surfaces of abandoned sites were put under cultivation in the mid-third millennium B.C. (see Section 5.2). The basis for this assessment is not only their infrequency but also their battered condition. On these criteria, Period 7 surface collections from sixteen of these thirty-one sites are interpreted as field scatter.

Of the other fifteen sites, seven are the prominent mounded sites described above. The remaining eight sites (THS 11, 12, 20, 22, 30, 31, 45, and 47) had small assemblages, but in a less abraded condition than would be expected from field scatter. All were small (average size 1.53 ha) and most were very low. The simultaneous appearance of small low- or non-mounded hamlets and a major urban center appears to be unique to the THS region. Urban expansion at Tell al-Hawa (Wilkinson and Tucker 1995: fig. 37) resulted in the extinction of small satellites, rather than their formation. The Tell Leilan Survey showed that Leilan's expansion was accompanied by a corresponding expansion of nearby Tell Mohammed Diyab, but no new settlements were founded anywhere within the survey region (Stein and Wattenmaker 2003: 365).

6.4.3. THE POST-AKKADIAN PERIOD AND THE QUESTION OF URBAN COLLAPSE

The determination of post-Akkadian (Early Jazira V) settlement on Hamoukar hinges on the spatial distribution of T7/4 comb-incised decoration (see discussion in Section B.2.8). Comb-incised sherds were very common in the final-phase strata of the lower town excavations in Areas C, E, and H (Gibson et al. 2002a: fig. 18). At Hamoukar, the uneven distribution of T7/4 sherds (fig. 6.19) is reminiscent of the Period 6 pattern; however, as the last phase of occupation for much of the lower town, it cannot result from the obscuring effects of later settlement. Taken at face value, the post-Akkadian pattern appears to be one of scattered pockets of low-density settlement across 38.7 ha of the high mound and lower town. Because there exists only a single post-Akkadian diagnostic type, however, each of its occurrences must carry proportionally more weight than would a single occurrence of a type for a period characterized by a more robust assemblage of survey types. It seems reasonable to assume, given the data at hand, that post-Akkadian settlement at Hamoukar remained at roughly the same size or was somewhat reduced. The nature of that settlement cannot be determined from surface remains, although excavations into late Akkadian or early post-Akkadian levels on the Hamoukar lower town (Colantoni 2005; Colantoni and Ur in press; Ur and Colantoni 2010) do not suggest impoverishment.

Following the post-Akkadian period, Hamoukar was completely abandoned for at least one thousand years. Earlier visitors have reported early second-millennium pottery (Van Liere 1963; Meijer 1986: 19; 1990: 34–35). However, no sherds of the distinctive and highly visible red painted Khabur ware (T8/1) were found in any of the systematic or non-systematic collection units in 1999. A possible explanation for this divergence of observations may lie in the Period 13 (Hellenistic) sherds that cover a small prominence on the eastern edge of the lower town (see Section 6.8). These sherds frequently have red painted rims, which can appear superficially similar to Khabur ware if their abundant dark grit temper and divergent rim morphologies are not taken into consideration.

Within the THS region, comb-incised sherds were not limited to Hamoukar. They occurred in quantities of three or more at all of the other major Period 7 occupations (THS 16, 37, 41, and 54). The non-permanent settlements may have ceased to be used by this time; only THS 22 produced a single sherd. Alternately, the settlement system had certainly collapsed by about 2000–1900 B.C., since no sherds were found of what is known as the Middle Bronze I period in southeastern Anatolia (see, e.g., Kaschau 1999). A distinct set of these types, which have now been identified in the Upper Khabur basin at Chagar Bazar Area D (McMahon and Quenet 2007), were explicitly

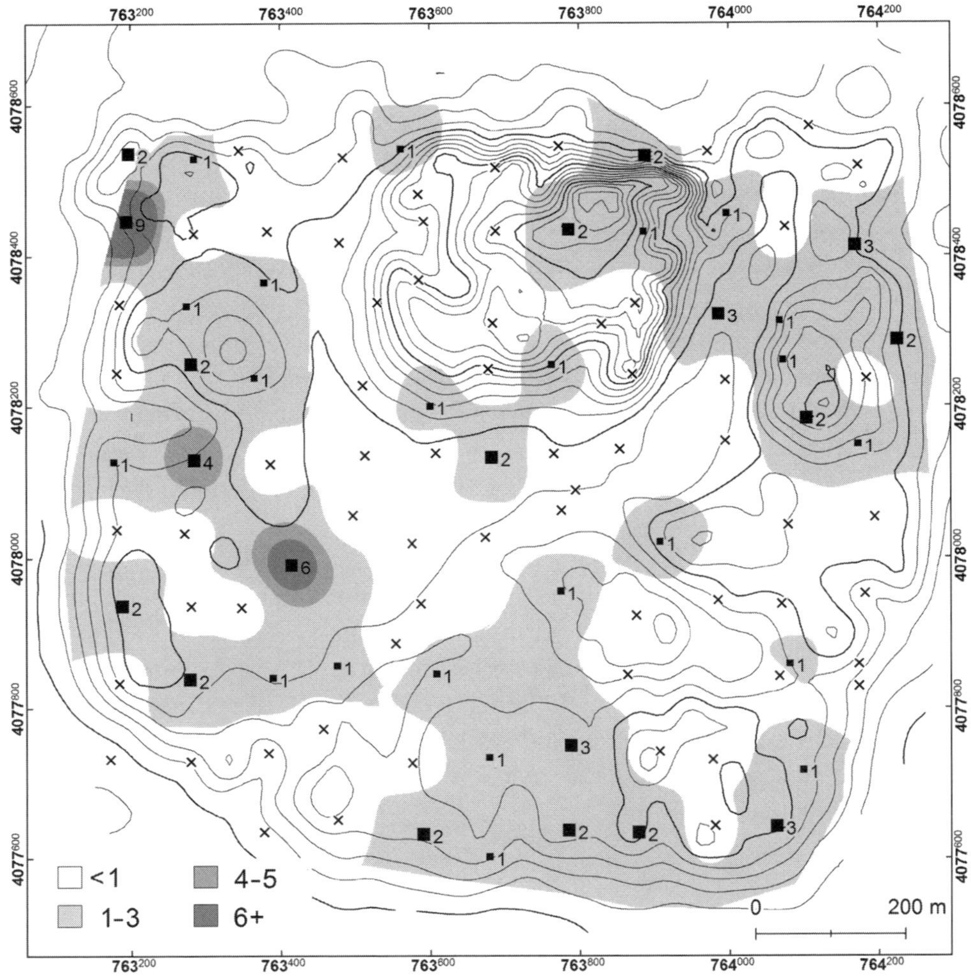

Figure 6.19. Distribution of T7/4 comb-incised sherds at Hamoukar

searched for in an attempt to trace settlement continuity, but none were recovered from Hamoukar or any other site in the THS region.

6.5. VILLAGES AND TOWNS IN THE SECOND MILLENNIUM B.C.

The height of urban nucleation in Period 7 in the THS region was never to be repeated. Although political units with their centers outside the THS area, and possibly including the region within them, continued to grow in scale in the second millennium, settlement within the THS was characterized by towns and villages.

6.5.1. PERIOD 8: EARLY SECOND MILLENNIUM B.C.

When settlement resumed in the Hamoukar area, it returned to five of the seven sites that had been occupied on a permanent basis at the end of the third millennium, with the exception of Hamoukar itself (THS 16, 32, 37, 41, and 54; fig. 6.20). At the same time, settlers returned to several sites that had not been settled since the fourth millennium or earlier (THS 10, 18, and 24). In a single case (THS 58), a wholly new settlement was founded. The focus of

Table 6.8. Period 8 sites and areas

Site	*Area (ha)*
24	10.41
18	5.80
54	5.71
32	2.61
41	2.40
37	2.33
10	1.24
16	0.81
58	0.54
9	31.85

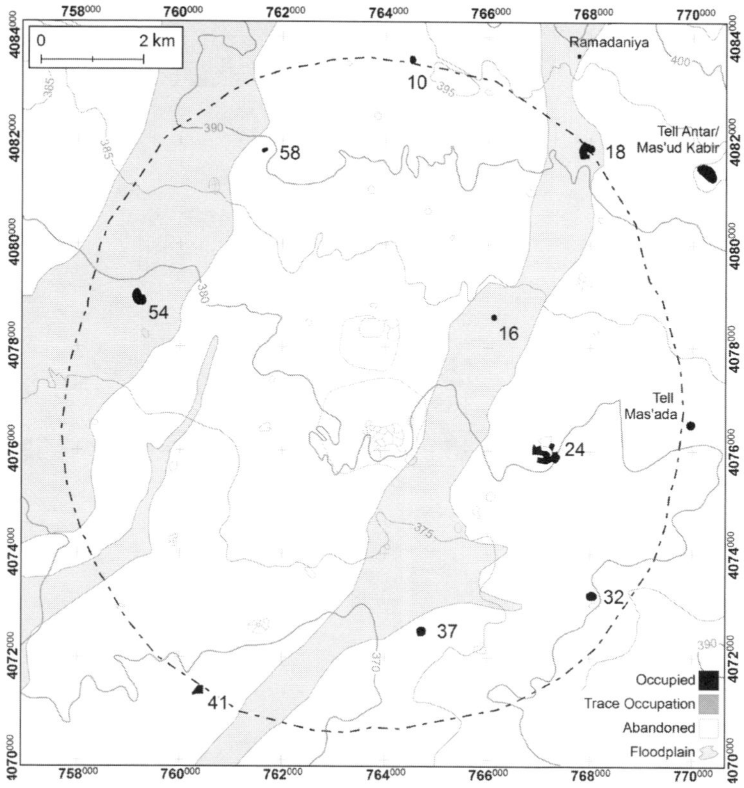

Figure 6.20. Period 8 sites in the THS region

settlement shifted to the 10.41 ha Khirbat al-ʻAbd (THS 24), which would remain an important settlement into the Islamic period. In total, the survey documented nine sites covering a total of 31.85 ha (table 6.8).

Several Period 8 towns lay immediately outside the survey area and were therefore not systematically collected. These include Tell Antar (now known as Tell Mas'ud Kabir) to the northeast, Mas'ada to the east, and Tell Hadi on the Wadi Rumaylan to the west. The former site produced a single Old Babylonian tablet surface find (Meijer 1986: 19, 44–45).

The linear patterning of sites and association with hollow ways apparent to Wilkinson (Wilkinson and Tucker 1995: 55) in the adjacent North Jazira is not as clear in the THS region. The northern alignments of sites and features, through Tell al-Hawa and Tell al-Samir respectively, continue north of the THS region, in the directions of Tell Rumaylan and Tell Mas'ud Kabir. The southern alignment, through North Jazirah Project sites 123, 96, and 140, is aligned with the southern part of the THS, but the patterning of sites and hollow ways farther west does not present a logical continuation. Movement along this axis is documented in the early second millennium by cuneiform itineraries that describe direct movement between the towns of Apqum (Tell Abu Marya) and Šubat-Enlil (Tell Leilan), with three stops between them (Goetze 1953; Hallo 1964). If this route were a straight transect, it would have skirted the southern edges of the THS and North Jazira survey regions. However, the presence of a route does not necessarily imply a corresponding track. It is argued in Section 5.3 that hollow ways form not only as a result of high populations but also a highly intensive agricultural and pastoral economy which channeled human and animal traffic onto tracks. This intensity of production occurred in Period 7 but not Period 8. Early second-millennium caravan traffic may therefore have moved through this corridor without adhering to a single physical track. The historical framework of settlement and communication in Period 8 is discussed further in *Chapter 8*.

6.5.2. PERIOD 10: LATE BRONZE AGE

During the second half of the second millennium B.C., settlement more than doubled to twenty-one sites, and occupied area almost doubled to 58.8 ha (fig. 6.21, table 6.9). At this time, the THS entered into a phase of extensive

Table 6.9. Period 10 sites and areas

Site	*Area (ha)*
24	16.06
23	7.54
54	7.26
37	4.85
45	3.05
47	2.61
48	2.02
18	1.95
13	1.67
4	1.47
42	1.36
14	1.31
20	1.17
12	1.15
16	1.12
35	1.06
53	1.02
41	0.76
11	0.62
58	0.54
57	0.19
21	58.78

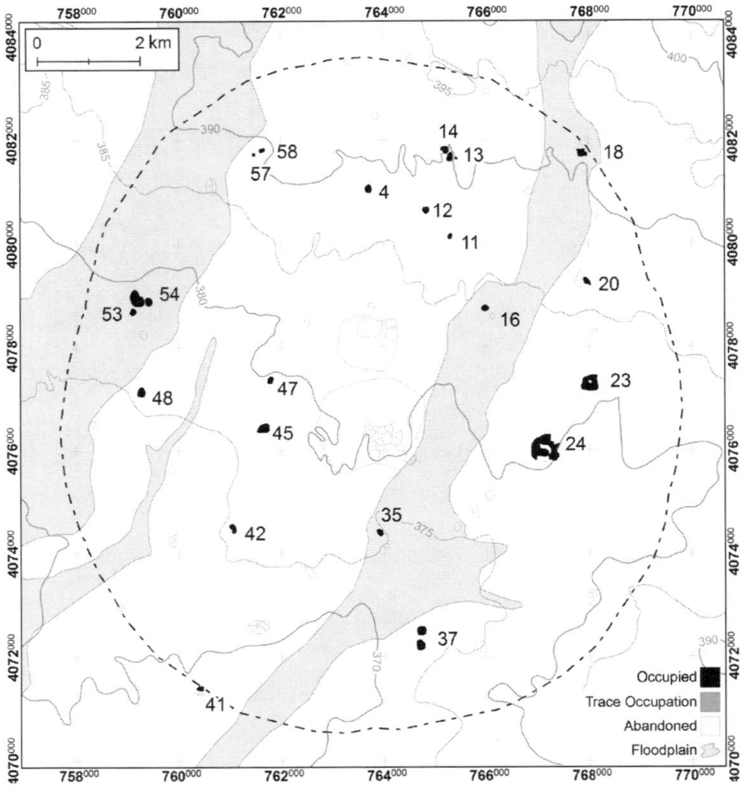

Figure 6.21. Period 10 sites in the THS region

non-nucleated settlement which continued well into the first millennium B.C. Continuity from the previous period is remarkable: seven of the nine Period 8 sites (78%) were also occupied in Period 10. Six of the new settlements were placed on the ruins of former mounds, and eight were wholly new.

The largest settlement continued to be Khirbat al-ʻAbd (THS 24), which grew to 16.06 ha. Large villages existed at nearby at THS 23 (7.54 ha), and on the western drainage at THS 54 (7.26 ha; if THS 53 is considered to be part of THS 54, the complex is 8.28 ha). The other eighteen sites were all villages averaging 1.55 ha.

Within this settlement array, clusters can be perceived. In the northern survey area, five sites totalling 6.22 ha cluster in a circle of 2 km diameter. Two of the largest sites, THS 23 and THS 24, are just over a kilometer apart. Smaller pairs are to be found at THS 57 and THS 58 (200 m) and THS 45 and THS 47 (800 m). Overall, no linearity is apparent, and there does not appear to be any relationship between site size and proximity to water. On the contrary, many Period 10 sites are on the watershed between the two major drainages. To some extent, the abandoned landscape of the later third millennium was a factor in their positioning; at least two sites (THS 11 and THS 47) fell astride major northeast–southwest hollow ways, which were used as borrow pits for mudbrick (see Section 5.3.4).

6.6. PERIOD 11: DISPERSAL IN THE IRON AGE

Despite dramatic political and social changes at the end of the second millennium, continuity characterized the general nature of Period 11 settlement. Site numbers grew by one to twenty-two, while total settled area expanded by 10 ha to 70.61 ha (table 6.10, fig. 6.22). Twelve Period 10 sites (57%) were also occupied in Period 11. These settlements were not unchanged, however; they saw a net loss of 7.47 ha (17%) over their size in Period 10. The most dramatically reduced site was THS 24, which shrank from 16.06 ha to 1.76 ha, an 89 percent reduction. Nearby THS 23 also was reduced, by 48 percent. The centers, small though they were, shifted to the western THS region at THS 54 (7.26 ha) and THS 48 (7.56 ha). Seven of the new Period 11 sites were founded atop the ruins of long-abandoned settlements, one of which was Hamoukar. Three sites (THS 34, 55, and 59) were entirely new foundations.

After at least a millennium, settlement returned to Hamoukar. Period 11 sherds were common in four collection units at the northeastern corner of the lower town, covering an estimated 3.06 ha (fig. 6.23). The surface assessment was confirmed by the excavations in Area C, which revealed 0.6 m of Period 11 deposits built on top of the long-abandoned Period 7 lower-town surface (Gibson et al. 2002a, 2002b). The shallowness of the Period 11 deposits suggests a brief occupation. The site appears to have been more than just a self-sufficient agricultural village; excavations have produced signs of wealth in the form of baked-brick pavements, palace ware, metal objects in burials, and a cylinder seal (Gibson et al. 2002a).

Despite aspects of continuity, Period 11 settlement differs from the previous pattern in two potentially meaningful ways. Although the two major Period 10 towns, THS 24 and 23, shrank in size, average site size rose from 2.80 ha in Period 10 to 3.21 ha in Period 11. If we exclude the upper-tier settlements (arbitrarily defined as greater than 7 ha), villages grew on average from 1.87 ha to 2.79 ha. Furthermore, the spatial distribution in Period 11 exhibits less clustering than in Period 10. With the exception of THS 34 and 35, which probably represent a single settlement, sites occur at 1.5 to 3.0 km intervals throughout the survey region, with the exception of the southeast, where settlement appears to have been sparse.

Table 6.10. Period 11 sites and areas

Site	*Area (ha)*
48	7.56
54	7.26
10	5.54
23	4.70
55	3.92
3	3.79
27	3.48
40	3.36
34	3.21
41	3.18
1	3.06
45	3.05
18	3.00
43	2.91
32	2.61
20	1.84
24	1.76
13	1.67
42	1.36
59	1.15
16	1.12
35	1.06
22	70.59

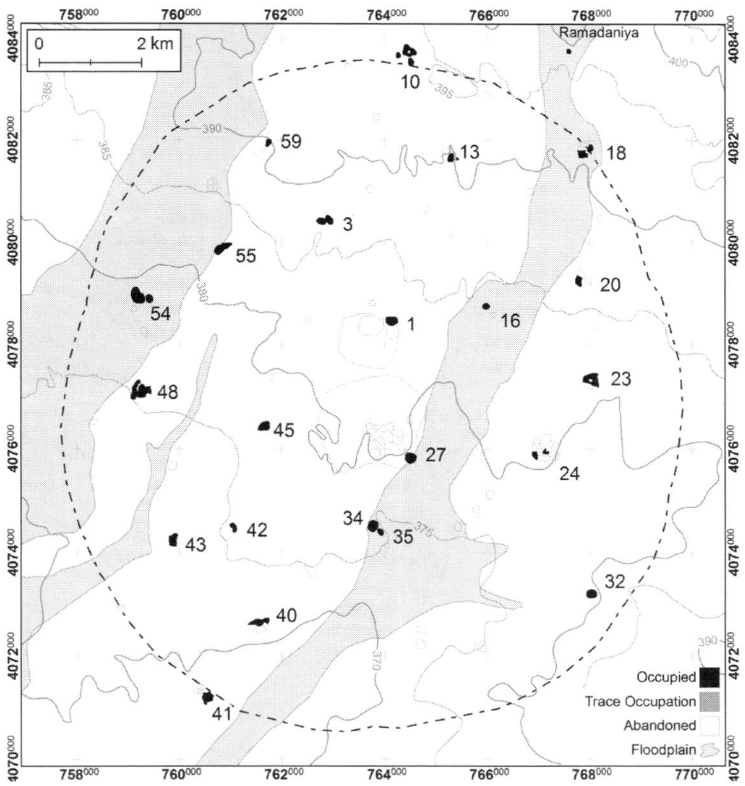

Figure 6.22. Period 11 sites in the THS region

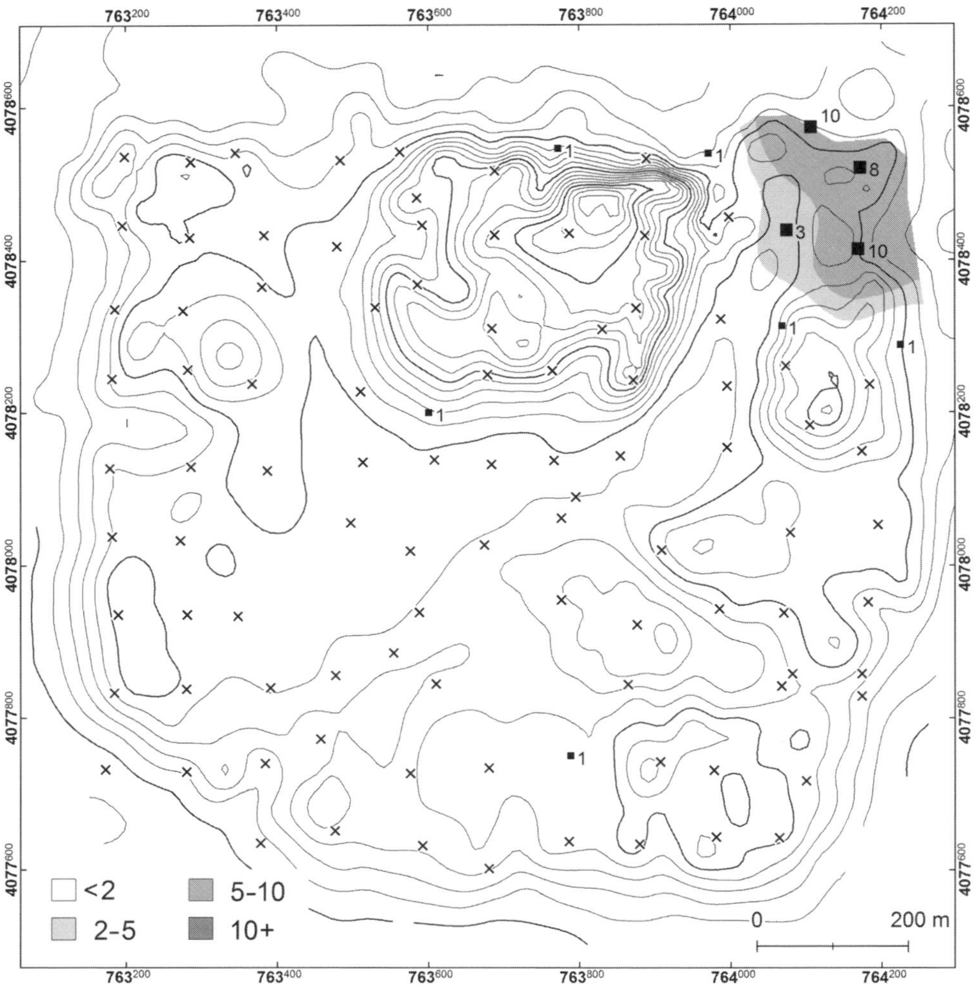

Figure 6.23. Distribution of Period 11 sherds at Hamoukar

In terms of numbers of sites, Period 11 was the time of maximum settlement expansion in the THS region. The large number of sites and their even distribution appears to be a broad regional pattern, mirrored in the adjacent North Jazira (Wilkinson and Tucker 1995: 60–62; Wilkinson, Ur, and Casana 2004) and the nearby Cizre Plain (Parker 2003). What differs between the regions is the patterning before and after the Period 11 expansion. In the THS region, the general characteristics of the expansion already existed in Period 10, which was a time of settlement contraction in the North Jazira. Conversely, the Period 11 expansion in the North Jazira continued into Period 13 with a net decline of only a single site, whereas the THS region lost over a third of its sites. In the Cizre Plain, both Periods 10 and 13 were characterized by relatively sparse settlement, compared to the expansion in numbers in Period 11 (Parker 2003: 60–78).

The dramatic expansion of site numbers in Period 11 was not matched by an equivalent expansion of total settled area. The landscape was filled with apparently homogenous small villages. Its 70.61 ha of settlement is one of the high points in THS settlement history, but this area was only a fraction of that settled earlier in Period 7 (127.09 ha) or later in Periods 16–17 (112.16 ha).

6.7. PERIOD 12: "POST-ASSYRIAN"

In absolute terms, Period 11 covers a long time span, from the start of the first millennium B.C. to the Seleucid period, roughly 1000 to 320 B.C. In an attempt to isolate the end of this span, Wilkinson (Wilkinson and Tucker 1995: 101–02) identified a series of "post-Assyrian" types, most of which appear to be hybrids of Period 11 and Period 13 types. These preliminary types were applied in the THS as Period 12 (see discussion in Section B.2.11).

Because of the tenuous chronological placement of these types, we offer here only a preliminary assessment of Period 12 settlement. One or more sherds were recovered from twenty-two sites (table 6.11). Of these, seventeen (77.3%) were also occupied in Period 11, thirteen (59.1%) were also occupied in Period 13, and eleven (50%) were occupied in both periods. Only two sites with Period 12 sherds (9.1%) were not occupied in either Period 11 or Period 13. Only six (27.3%) Period 11 sites and two (14.3%) Period 13 sites had no Period 12 sherds in their surface assemblages. Although the counts are low, these figures suggest a close relationship between the distribution of Period 12 sherds and settlements of the preceding and succeeding periods. We hesitate to draw any further conclusions before stratigraphic evidence for the placement of these types is available.

Table 6.11. Sites with Period 12 sherds, with areas of Period 11 and Period 13 settlement for comparison. Sherd counts include all site sub-areas

Site	*Period 12 (sherds)*	*Period 11 (area in ha)*	*Period 13 (area in ha)*
1	2	3.06	5.06
3	5	3.79	3.79
5	—	—	2.00
10	3	5.54	4.85
13	1	1.67	—
16	2	1.12	0.81
18	—	3.00	—
20	3	1.84	—
23	3	4.70	4.39
24	14	1.76	4.02
25	2	—	7.94
26	3	—	—
27	17	3.48	—
32	10	2.61	—
34	6	3.21	—
35	—	1.06	—
37	4	—	—
40	6	3.36	—
41	4	3.18	5.66
42	2	1.36	—
43	16	2.91	1.86
45	2	3.05	1.38
48	15	7.56	1.21
51	3	—	1.18
54	4	7.26	6.26
55	—	3.92	—
59	—	1.15	—
Number of Sites	22		

Table 6.12. Period 13 sites and areas

Site	*Area (ha)*
25	7.94
54	6.26
41	5.66
1	5.06
10	4.85
23	4.39
24	4.02
3	3.79
5	2.00
43	1.86
45	1.38
48	1.21
51	1.18
16	0.81
14	50.41

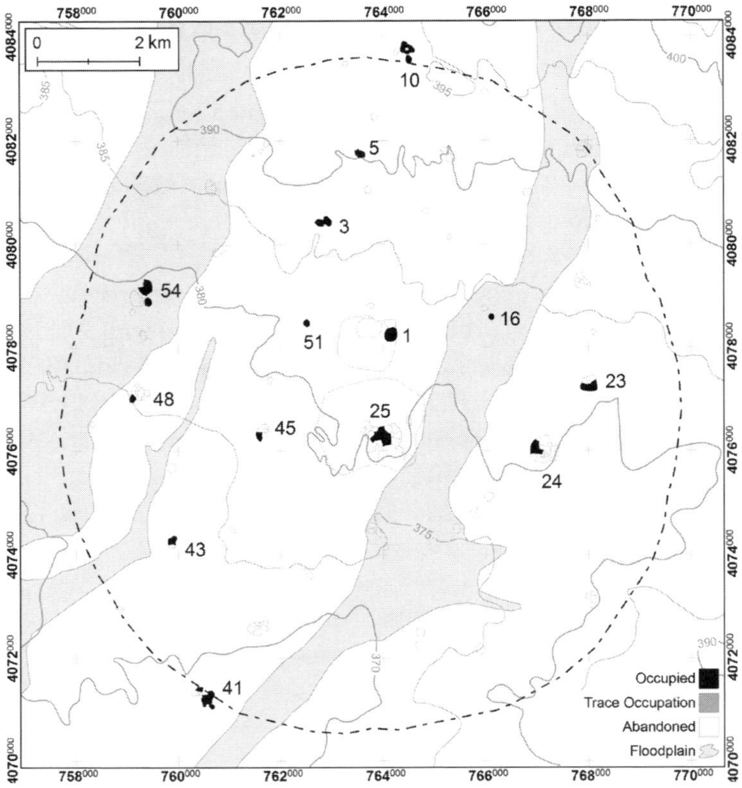

Figure 6.24. Period 13 sites in the THS region

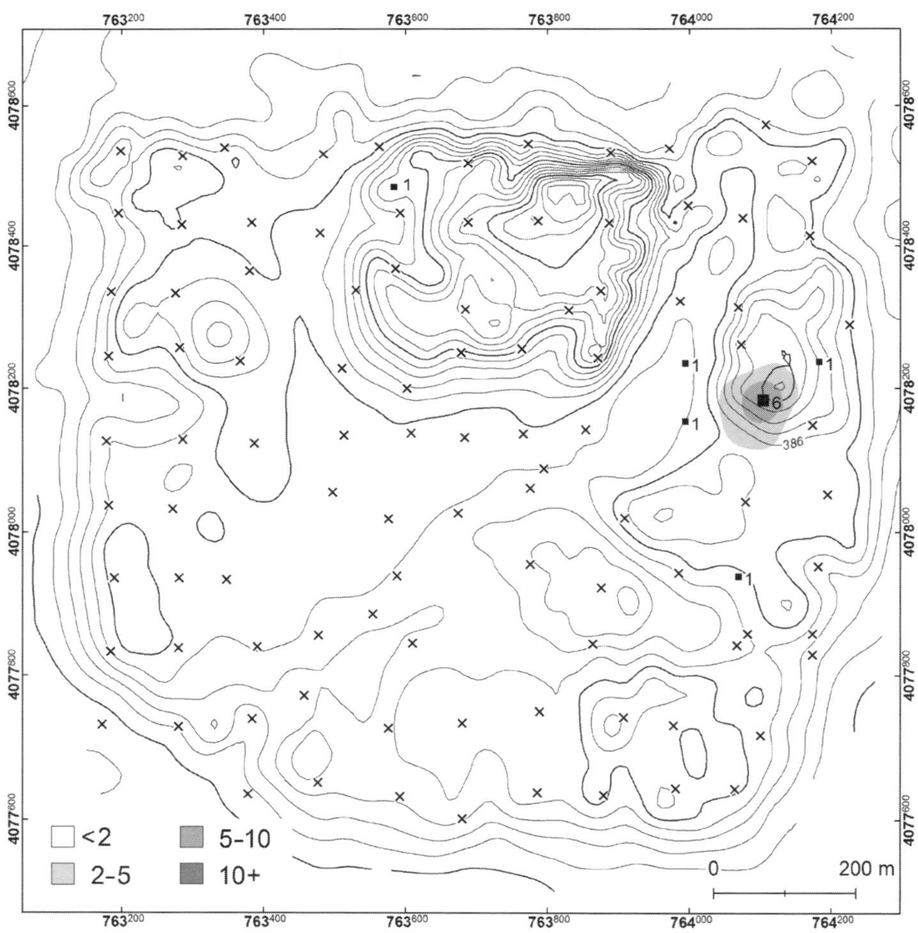

Figure 6.25. Distribution of Period 13 sherds at Hamoukar

6.8. PERIOD 13: HELLENISTIC

From Period 11 to Period 13, the THS saw a decline in numbers and settled area. Fourteen Period 13 sites, covering 50.41 ha, were occupied (table 6.12, fig. 6.24). Eleven of these sites (79% of all Period 13 sites) had also been settled in Period 11; thus continuity from Period 11 to Period 13 appears high (50%). These eleven sites had a net loss of 4.66 ha, however. THS 48, the largest Period 11 site, lost 85 percent of its settled area to become one of the smallest Period 13 villages. Two other sites appeared on abandoned mounds. One site (THS 5) appears to be an entirely new foundation, but this is likely the result of the incomplete collection from the site (see *Appendix A*).

As in the case of other periods as well, the question of whether sites with sherds of two consecutive periods were occupied continuously remains a valid one. For the transition between Periods 11 and 13, Hamoukar is a typical case. Its Period 11 occupation was a 3.06 ha village on the northeastern corner of the lower town (see previous section), an area with no obvious mounding above the general level of the rest of the lower town. The distinctive dark grit-tempered sherds of Period 13 covered an estimated 5.06 ha area on the eastern edge of the lower town, immediately south of the former Period 11 site, but spatially discrete; it is roughly defined by the 386 m contour line (fig. 6.25; note that the northern part of this mound could not be collected due to modern village houses). Unlike the Period 11 site, this area is substantially mounded above the lower town, perhaps as much as 5 m (see fig. 3.3). The height of the Period 13 mound could indicate a longer phase of occupation within the ceramically defined period. In any case, despite the close proximity of the Period 11 and Period 13 villages at Hamoukar, there is no evidence for direct continuity between the two settlements; the same could be said for several of the other "continuously occupied" Period 11–13 sites.

The THS region continued to be a landscape of villages. Period 13 sites averaged 3.60 ha. After a millennium of shifting between the eastern and western THS region, the focus of settlement was now in its center: a 7.94 ha large village at the center of THS 25, which had not been substantially occupied since the early fourth millennium B.C. The central mounded complex at THS 25 would host shifting settlement for the following two millennia.

Spatial patterning of sites does not appear to be related to the natural drainages, but does show linearity. A sequence of six sites ran south from the northern edge of the survey region (from north to south: THS 10, 5 , 3, 51, 45, and 43). These six sites represent 30 percent of the total Period 13 settled area. The spacing between them is remarkably even and their positioning is almost precisely along the crest of the watershed between the two main drainages (fig. 6.26). Furthermore, their alignment is exactly parallel to the natural slope of the terrain. No hollow ways appear to run between these sites, despite the fact that these high watershed areas have the highest hollow way preservation throughout the basin, and tracks running parallel to the slope are disproportionately preserved. The arrangement of

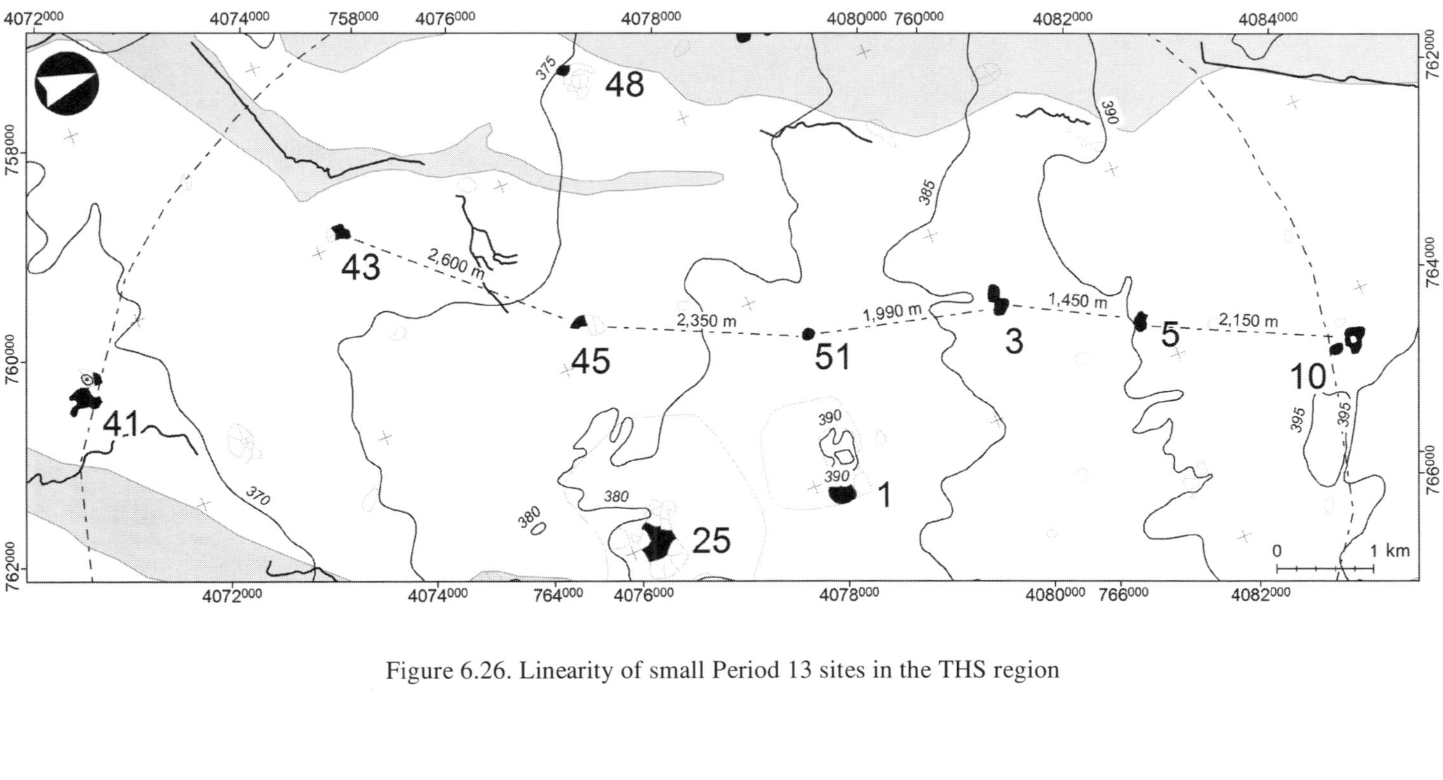

Figure 6.26. Linearity of small Period 13 sites in the THS region

these sites in relation to the land and to each other suggests that their principle of spatial organization might have been canal irrigation. Geomorphological evidence does exist for Hellenistic irrigation in the Balikh Valley to the west (Wilkinson 1998), and on CORONA scenes close to wadis in the Upper Khabur basin (see Section 5.4). However, there does not appear to be any trace of such canals between these sites on CORONA or other remote-sensing sources. The line of Period 13 sites along the watershed might represent the colonization of less desirable inter-wadi lands, and the evenness of settlement spacing hints at a centralized direction of site placement.

6.9. PERIOD 14: PARTHIAN–ROMAN

In aggregate terms, settlement remained almost constant in Period 14, with an increase of one site to a total of fifteen, covering a statistically identical area of 49.8 ha (table 6.13, fig. 6.27). Nine of these sites (57%) were also occupied in the previous period. These nine sites lost over 26 percent (9.97 ha) of their former Period 13 area, however. Six others were placed on abandoned mounds. One site, THS 60, may have been an entirely new foundation, but it received only a cursory visit and the possibility of earlier settlement cannot be excluded.

Sites were again small, on average 3.32 ha. The survey tentatively assigns a Period 14 area of 13 ha to Site 60, a complex mounded site at the northwestern edge of the survey region. Only the southern mound was visited and it did not receive a formal collection. If the other smaller mounds to its north were also fully settled in Period 14, the site would be 25.78 ha. The largest well-documented site continued to be on the central mounded complex at THS 25, which had grown by 35 percent to 10.74 ha.

The Period 14 surface assemblage at Hamoukar is difficult to interpret (fig. 6.28). Only six sherds were recovered in systematic units, and these show only slight clustering around the lower town enclosed depression. Because

Table 6.13. Period 14 sites and areas

Site	*Area (ha)*	
	Settled	*Trace*
60	13.06	—
25	10.74	—
43	4.43	—
55	3.92	—
24	3.64	—
20	2.70	—
45	2.15	—
41	1.67	—
23	1.55	—
48	1.36	—
14	1.31	—
54	1.26	—
47	1.06	—
32	0.95	—
11	0.62	—
1	—	1.00
16	50.42	1.00

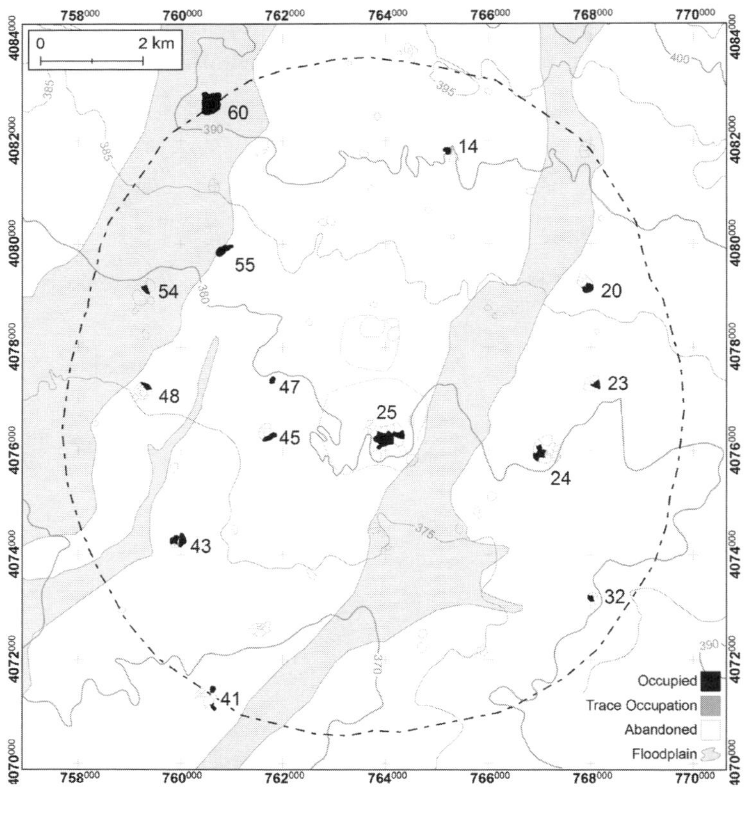

Figure 6.27. Period 14 sites in the THS region

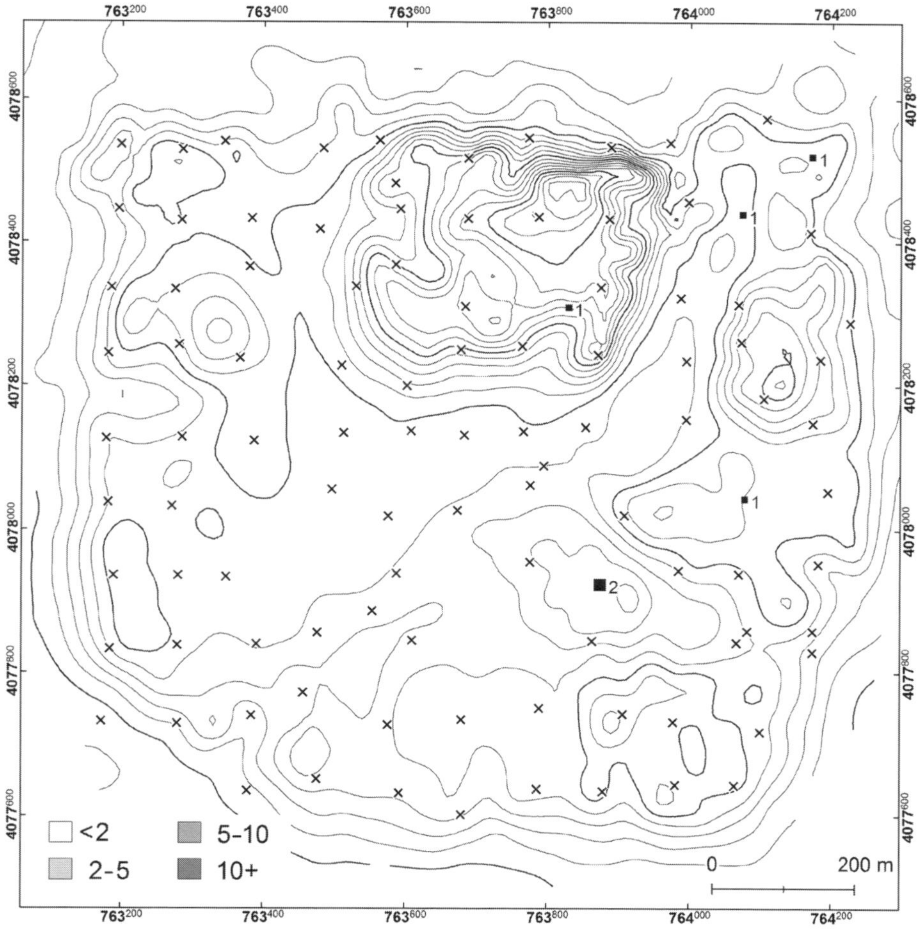

Figure 6.28. Distribution of Period 14 sherds at Hamoukar

this area produced a high percentage of untyped sherds in systematic collections, Period 14 occupation was assigned an arbitrary 1 ha area.

No obvious spatial patterning exists in the THS region. Several sites may have been positioned to take advantage of the remains of third-millennium tracks as borrow pits. Two sites on the watershed between the major drainages are adjacent to hollow ways whose troughs are noticeably deepened and even widened (THS 43 and 47; see fig. 5.25 Profile N and fig. 5.27). Hollow way reuse for brick material extraction may have been period-specific; the other concentration occurred in Period 10.

The multiple channels around THS 60 also hint at the possibility of irrigation in Period 14. Artificially straightened channels are visible in CORONA photographs farther west (fig. 5.32) and also to the northeast, but cannot be dated by association since they were beyond the THS limits. Period 14 irrigation is highly speculative at present.

6.10. SASANIAN–LATE ISLAMIC SETTLEMENT

After Period 14, the ceramic chronology of the THS becomes much less reliable. The last 1,500 years of settlement history in northern Mesopotamia are particularly frustrating to landscape archaeologists, who are presented with a wealth of off-site features on a scale not seen since the late third millennium B.C. alongside vivid textual descriptions from Arab geographers and Western travelers. Yet archaeological sequences are non-existent, imprecise, or too distant from northern Mesopotamia to aid in interpretation. When faced with this situation in southern Iraq,

Robert McC. Adams (1970) targeted a sounding at a stratified Sasanian–Islamic site, but up to the present no such corrective has been possible in the north.

Sasanian and Islamic pottery assemblages are increasingly the focus of study (see Sections B.2.15–17), but there remains an emphasis on glazes, which occur infrequently on the surface. The THS adopted the types used by Wilkinson and Tucker (1995: 105–08) with little modification. Many of these types were based on their presence on apparently single-period sites within the North Jazira survey area, rather than on stratified assemblages. Site distributions for Periods 15–20 must be considered with caution in light of the tenuousness of the typological groupings. At present, the periods overlap and therefore should not be considered as sequential.

6.10.1. PERIOD 15: SASANIAN

The THS identified only four Period 15 sites (table 6.14, fig. 6.29). They appear to demonstrate nucleation of settlement under reduced demographic conditions; total site area was 23.48 ha but average site size grew from Period 14 to 5.87 ha. THS 54 grew to over 9 ha, and a similarly large village appeared at THS 24. All four sites had been settled in the previous period, but spatial continuity *within* sites was low. Despite their relatively large areas, Period 15 settlement at THS 24, 41, and 54 did not overlap with any areas of Period 14 settlement; indeed, at THS 24 and 41, Period 15 occupation shifted to the opposite sides of the site.

Period 15 settlement patterns therefore show not settlement continuity, but rather a recurring pattern of decision-making about settlement placement. Since Period 11, settlers had preferentially sought out previously occupied places to build their communities (see Section 6.11). The THS recognized five ceramically defined periods covering a range of approximately 1,800 years, with a total of forty-nine occupations between them, but only three of these occupations were placed on previously unsettled ground. It is impossible to say what brought people back to these

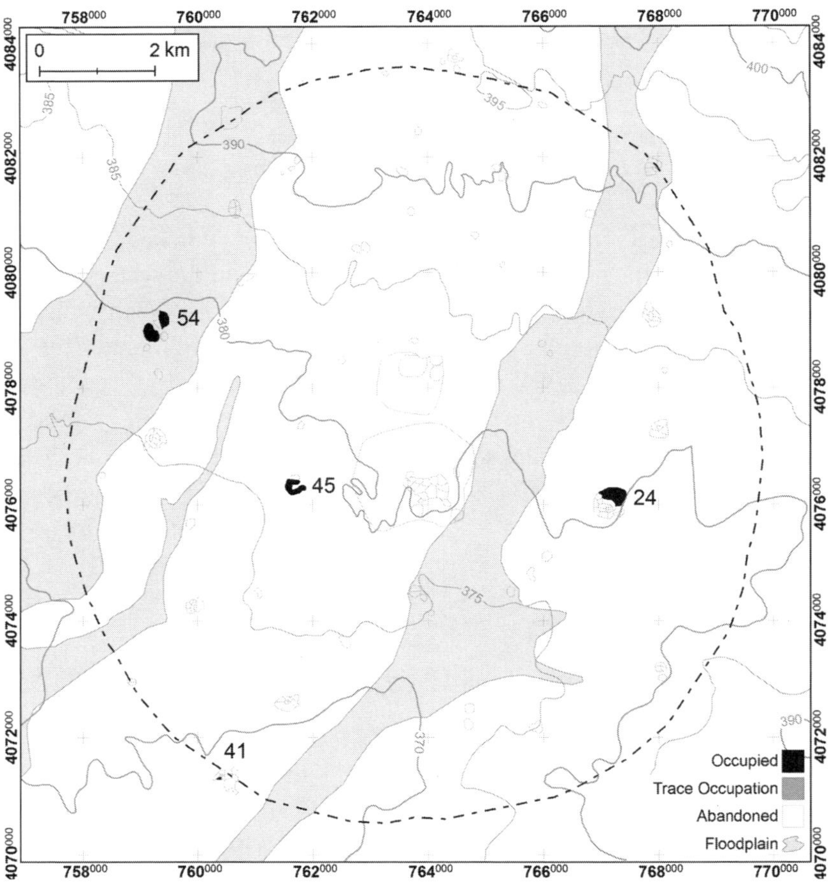

Figure 6.29. Period 15 sites in the THS region

places (or what kept them there over long spans), but it is certain that the mounds of former settlements had become meaningful and therefore preferentially resettled. The THS region includes 125 sq. km upon which to plant a new community, but sedentary groups repeatedly limited themselves to the few hundreds of hectares of pre-existing mounds.

Table 6.14. Periods 15–20 sites and areas.
Note that sites with both "settled" and "trace" areas are only counted with the "settled" sites

Site	*Area (ha)*								
	Period 15	*Period 16*		*Period 17*		*Period 19*		*Period 20*	
	Settled	*Settled*	*Trace*	*Settled*	*Trace*	*Settled*	*Trace*	*Settled*	*Trace*
3	—	—	—	—	3.79	—	—	—	—
5	—	—	—	2.00	—	2.00	—	—	—
6	—	0.60	—	—	—	—	—	—	—
7	—	0.62	—	0.62	—	—	—	—	—
9	—	—	—	0.77	—	—	—	—	—
16	—	0.81	—	0.81	—	—	—	—	—
18	—	2.44	—	6.44	—	6.44	—	1.04	—
20	—	—	1.78	—	—	—	—	—	—
23	—	—	—	—	—	—	—	—	2.84
24	9.01	9.49	—	5.21	—	—	—	0.53	—
25	—	3.53	—	7.12	—	5.22	—	0.95	—
29	—	2.02	—	—	—	—	—	—	—
32	—	0.65	—	—	—	—	—	—	—
37	—	2.52	—	—	—	—	—	—	—
38	—	—	—	—	—	3.22	—	—	—
39	—	—	—	—	—	2.28	—	—	—
40	—	—	—	1.35	—	—	—	—	—
41	0.17	0.72	3.18	—	—	—	—	—	—
42	—	—	—	—	—	1.36	—	—	—
44	—	—	—	—	—	—	0.85	—	0.85
45	5.13	6.59	—	—	—	—	—	—	—
48	—	1.66	0.93	2.76	—	1.10	—	—	—
50	—	60.00	—	60.00	—	—	—	—	—
54	9.16	14.70	—	7.44	—	2.73	—	—	—
55	—	3.92	—	3.92	—	—	—	—	—
56	—	—	—	1.52	—	—	—	—	—
Total Sites	4	15	3	13	1	8	1	3	2
Total Area	23.47	110.27	5.89	99.96	3.79	24.35	0.85	2.52	3.69

6.10.2. PERIOD 16: LATE SASANIAN–EARLY ISLAMIC

The late Sasanian through Abbasid span (Periods 16–17) was the third and final major time of settlement expansion in the THS region. The THS assigned sixteen sites to Period 16, including all four Period 15 sites (table 6.14, fig. 6.30). At two sites (THS 41 and 48), part of the settled area was minor or low-density occupation; the entire THS 20 was considered a minor occupation.

The estimation of total settled area for Period 16 is complicated by the site of al-Botha (THS 50). Because the site is only partially within the survey region and is covered by a modern village, the THS made only two small areal sample collections near its eastern edge. The full extent of the site covers 60 ha and is associated with an array of narrow hollow ways. In the 1960s, some mounds were still preserved well enough to suggest individual structures at a low density (see fig. 5.17). The small collections produced diagnostics of Periods 16 and 17, but the rest of the site was not formally collected. The analysis presented here credits the site with 60 ha in both periods, but its nearly flat nature seems to indicate a short occupation. Aside from THS 50, the region had a town at THS 54 (14.70 ha) and THS 24 continued to be a large village on the eastern side of the survey region (9.49 ha). THS 45 reached its maximum size at this time (6.59 ha). Other sites were in the range of a few hectares, and a few very small sites might be the traces of isolated hamlets or farmsteads.

6.10.3. PERIOD 17: ABBASID

Period 17 witnessed fourteen sites (13 major occupations, 1 minor occupation) over 103.75 ha (table 6.14, fig. 6.30). This figure assumes full occupation of THS 50. Nine of these sites had already been settled in Period 16, and the other five were placed on previously settled mounds. Although site numbers and settled area changed little or

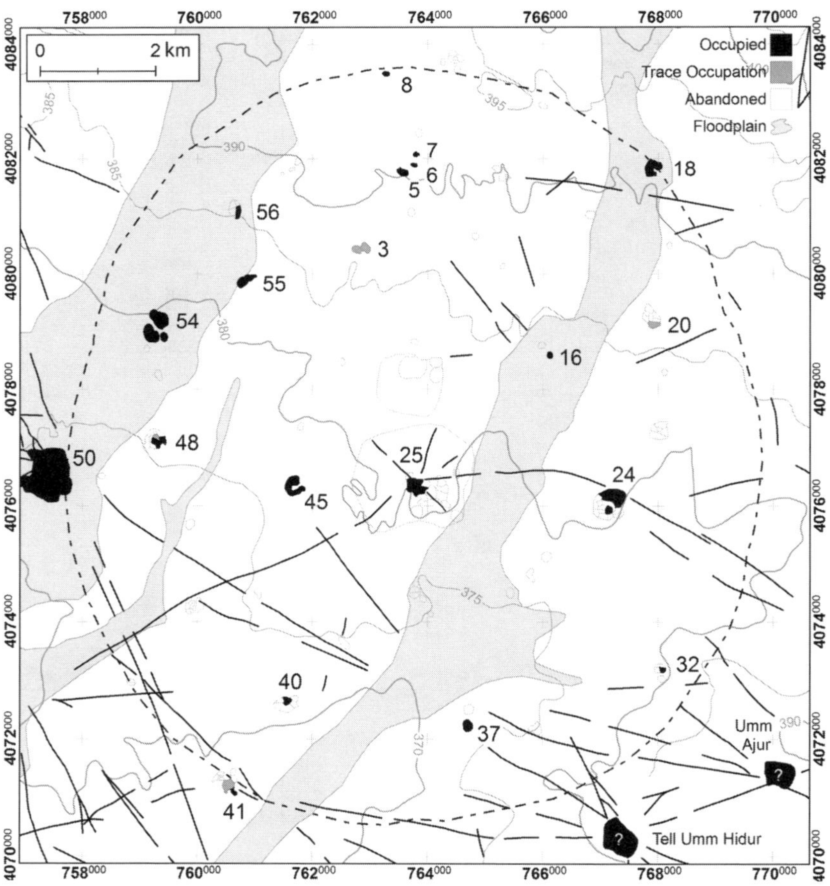

Figure 6.30. Period 16–17 sites in the THS region. Settlement at Tell Umm Hidur and Umm Ajur has not been confirmed by ground observations

not at all, several continuously occupied sites saw major changes. Settled area at THS 54 was halved to 7.44 ha and large parts of the lower town of THS 24 were abandoned, while growth occurred at THS 18 and THS 25.

6.10.4. SETTLEMENT AND LAND USE IN PERIODS 16–17

Including THS 50, Periods 16 and 17 witnessed a geographic expansion that rivals the height of urbanism in the later third millennium B.C. However, a direct demographic comparison is probably inappropriate. Period 7 urban centers and small villages across the basin have been subjected to excavation, which has revealed uniformly dense urban fabrics. We do not have comparable horizontal exposures of Period 16–17 levels, but the spatial signature of THS 50 on CORONA photographs appears to be of low-density dispersed structures within the boundaries of the site. In demographic terms, the total area of Period 16 settlement is likely to represent only a fraction of the Period 7 population.

Periods 16–17 also appear to parallel Period 7 in terms of landscape impact. Sites are again associated with hollow ways, often in radial patterns. These later hollow ways can often be distinguished morphologically by their narrowness and ratio of width to depth (see Section 5.3). Within the survey area, particularly well-preserved radial hollow ways are preserved around THS 25 and THS 50. These features articulate with morphologically identical radial systems around Umm Ajur and Tell Umm Hidur, two unsurveyed sites to the southeast of the THS region. As with the third-millennium hollow ways, constraint by surrounding agricultural fields must have been a factor in keeping human and animal traffic on these tracks, but field scatter evidence for high-intensity cultivation is lacking. It seems probable that the Period 16–17 network of tracks formed under typical conditions of agricultural production; the pattern of tracks from other earlier periods probably looked no different. Unlike the Period 7 hollow ways, which survive because they were deeply incised under conditions of intense disturbance, the Period 16–17 tracks survive simply because little time has passed. Furthermore, the intervening years have witnessed some of the lowest sedentary occupation of the basin since the late Neolithic period.

Another aspect of landscape modification may be unique to Periods 16–17. Traces of irrigation canals can be identified on CORONA photographs on the plain north and west of the THS region, but only convincingly at a few places within the THS. One such place is at the northeastern edge, at THS 18 (see fig. 5.31). The narrow channel runs southward from a wadi offtake outside the survey area and continues along the eastern edge of the drainage; it skirts the western edge of THS 18 before fading out just over a kilometer to the south. THS 18 reached its maximum size in Periods 17 and 19, which, along with the ephemerality of the signature, is the reason for attributing the channel an Islamic date. Dating landscape features is always difficult, and THS 18 was also occupied in earlier times, including a substantial Period 8 settlement. Without proper geomorphological investigations, dating of canals in the THS region must be considered highly provisional.

6.10.5. PERIODS 18–19: MIDDLE TO LATE ISLAMIC

The ceramic types used by Wilkinson and Tucker (1995: 107) to define occupation of the Middle Islamic period (here Period 18, ca. A.D. 1000–1300) were very uncommon. Only five sherds of T18/1 sgraffito ware were recovered, three sherds from THS 18 and one each from THS 6 and THS 16. Given the tenuousness of the survey typology for this period, this pattern must be interpreted with caution.

The strong reduction in site numbers and area in Period 19 does, however, appear to reflect a real collapse of sedentary occupation of the THS region. Eight sites had major occupation and one only minor or trace occupation, totalling 25.20 ha, or only 24 percent of Period 17 settled area (table 6.14). These sites were mostly small, with the exception of more substantial villages at THS 18 (6.44 ha) and THS 25 (5.22 ha). In the latter case, this area represents a considerable reduction from its Period 17 extent.

The nine sites are evenly dispersed throughout the THS area (fig. 6.31). Although the THS did not recognize Period 19 settlement at THS 50, several sites along its southeastern track remained occupied (THS 38, 39, and 42). The small-scale irrigation system at THS 18 may also have been in use.

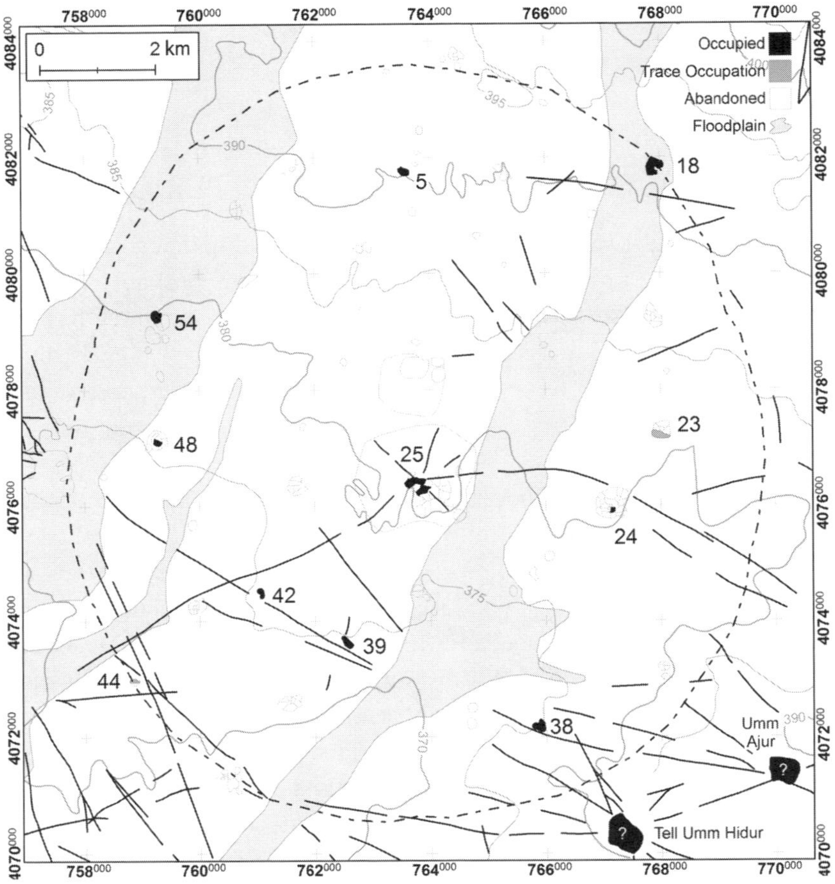

Figure 6.31. Period 19–20 sites in the THS region. Settlement at Tell Umm Hidur and Umm Ajur has not been confirmed by ground observations

6.10.6. PERIOD 20: LATE ISLAMIC

With only five sites covering 6.21 ha, Period 20 was the nadir of sedentary occupation in the THS (table 6.14, fig. 6.31). Ceramic types are admittedly insecure, being based entirely upon surface associations. Nonetheless, the low density of occupation is precisely what would be expected, given the vivid descriptions of the plain by eighteenth- and nineteenth-century travelers (see Section 2.2). The first characterization as abandoned "desert" comes from 1644 (Tavernier 1677: 71), and similar descriptions continue up until the years following the establishment of French mandatory control in 1926. The plain was by no means devoid of human occupation during this time; it simply did not take the form of sedentary agricultural villages. The THS region held the summer pastures of Tay and later Shammar camel nomads; during the absence of these tribes in the winter, Kurdish semi-nomads brought their sheep and goats into the area. It is possible, therefore, that some of these few Period 19–20 sites might have been seasonal campsites rather than perennially occupied villages.

Based on the pattern of Periods 19–20, the THS does not appear to have participated in the textually-documented resurgence of settlement and agriculture under Ottoman rule in the sixteenth century (Hütteroth 1990; Göyünç and Hütteroth 1997).

6.11. MODERN SETTLEMENT IN THE THS REGION

The "final" pattern of settlement is of course the current one (fig. 6.32). Within the 125 sq. km of the THS region, 106 sites comprising 441 ha could be identified as places of substantial human activity. All consist of at least a single structure, and most also includ various animal outbuildings and other structures, borrow pits, and other non-cultivated activity areas. They were determined by a combination of ground observation and remote-sensing imagery interpretation. The boundaries of "sites" in figure 6.32 represent both houses and the non-cultivated areas adjacent to them; no attempt has been made to distinguish areas of dense housing from other parts of the site. Based on non-systematic observations, all surfaces featured various bits of obviously modern artifacts (glass, cloth, wood fragments, metal, plastic, cement and other building debris, and un-decomposed organic refuse) which would qualify these areas as "site" according to the criteria applied to mounds. Thus, the 69.2 ha village at Hamoukar includes the approximately 40 ha of densely packed village houses south and southwest of the high mound on the lower town, but also the uncultivated and lightly occupied parts of the high mound and lower town to its east and west (see fig. 3.10).

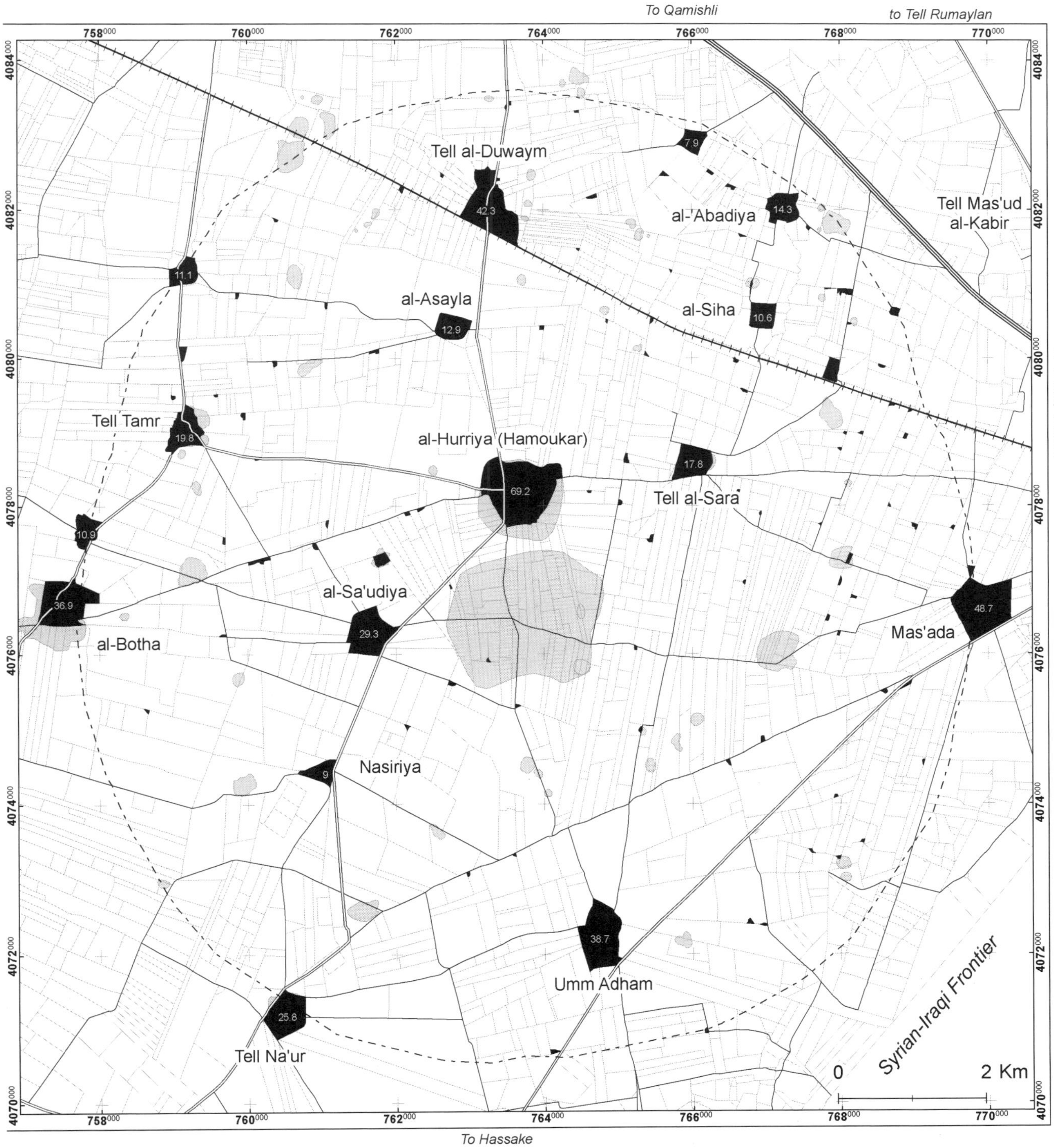

Figure 6.32. Modern settlement in the THS region, with area in hectares

Modern settlements can be divided into two groups: villages and isolated farmsteads. The largest is the 69.2 ha village at Hamoukar (now officially called al-Hurriya). Other large villages include Tell al-Duwaym (42.3 ha), Mas'ada (48.7 ha), al-Botha (36.9 ha), Umm Adham (38.7 ha), and Tell Na'ur (25.8 ha). On the French 1:200,000 maps based on surveys of the 1930s, none of these places appear, but by the late 1960s when CORONA photographs were taken, they are all present. The British series of 1955 aerial photographs used by Wilkinson is mostly restricted to the Iraqi side of the border, but a few scenes capture a picture of settlement on the Syrian side, which appears identical to the pattern of the late 1960s. Thus it seems that the pattern of villages in the THS region emerged in the 1940s or early 1950s. The eighteen large and small villages comprise over 93 percent of the settled area (413 ha).

Among the fields surrounding these villages are dozens of isolated farmsteads, generally consisting of only a single residential structure. They are most frequently placed in the corner of an agricultural field where it is adjacent to a track. Their areal extents are rarely as large as 2 ha but most are much smaller; seventy-eight farmsteads are under 0.5 ha. These eighty-eight farmsteads account for 83 percent of settled places, but only 6 percent of the total settled area.

Unlike all previous periods, the modern settlement pattern formed under conditions for which there exist detailed written accounts and even historical maps and satellite imagery. The major villages formed when Shammar groups were forced to settle on their former summer pastures. As had been the case for several millennia, they chose to settle on or adjacent to the mounded areas of ancient settlements. Nucleation was almost certainly encouraged by the fact that the land itself had quickly become consolidated under the control of agricultural capitalists in Qamishli or Aleppo. The local villagers were mostly tenant farmers who lacked the rights to move out onto the surrounding land.

The appearance of isolated farmsteads is a recent departure from this pattern. Close observation of CORONA photographs occasionally reveals isolated features in the fields. However, they occur in the middle of fields rather than at their corners, lack associated tracks, and are not brightly illuminated on their southern faces. Furthermore, they are much more common in late summer and early fall CORONA scenes than in spring scenes. For these reasons, the few isolated structures in 1960s CORONA photographs are more likely to be tents of remnant pastoralists or seasonal laborers.

Isolated farmsteads were occasionally found on or near small mounds in the survey; for example, THS 23, THS 32, and THS 47 each had a single structure at one edge or immediately adjacent. A comparison of field notes from 1999–2001 with SPOT satellite imagery taken within the last several years reveals that they have become more common, but farmsteads from the late 1990s have not grown into small villages.

6.12. GENERAL TRENDS IN SETTLEMENT IN THE THS REGION

Overall site numbers and settled area are displayed as a histogram in figure 6.33. Settlements in the THS area have been generally in the form of small villages and relatively low density, with three major exceptions. The first is a phase of urban nucleation in Period 7, when permanently settled sites were few but settled area was high. This situation was of course the result of Hamoukar's urban growth, which placed almost 90 percent of the settled area within its boundaries. The second was the great dispersal of small villages in Periods 10 and 11 (Late Bronze Age and Iron Age/Neo-Assyrian). Unlike other periods with small average site size, these periods were characterized by high site density and an even distribution of sites throughout the surveyed region. Finally, Periods 16 and 17 (Sasanian and Early Islamic) witnessed both growth in site numbers and a great expansion of settled area, although the interpretation of this growth depends on the density of population within these places, and the extent of THS 50 at this time.

When the entire sequence of settlement since the seventh millennium B.C. is considered, the degree to which settlement remained in place or returned to previously settled places is striking (fig. 6.34). The percentages of *de novo* settlement in a given period has not exceeded 50 percent since before Period 5b (Late Chalcolithic), and has remained at 20 percent or less since Period 10 (Late Bronze Age). The survey did not recover a single settlement founded on virgin terrain in the last 1,400 years. This pattern cannot be explained by invoking a steadily shrinking supply of unsettled land; even at present, the total area of former or current settlement is a small fraction of the available space within the survey region (see map 1). In cases where continuity of settlement across ceramic periods can

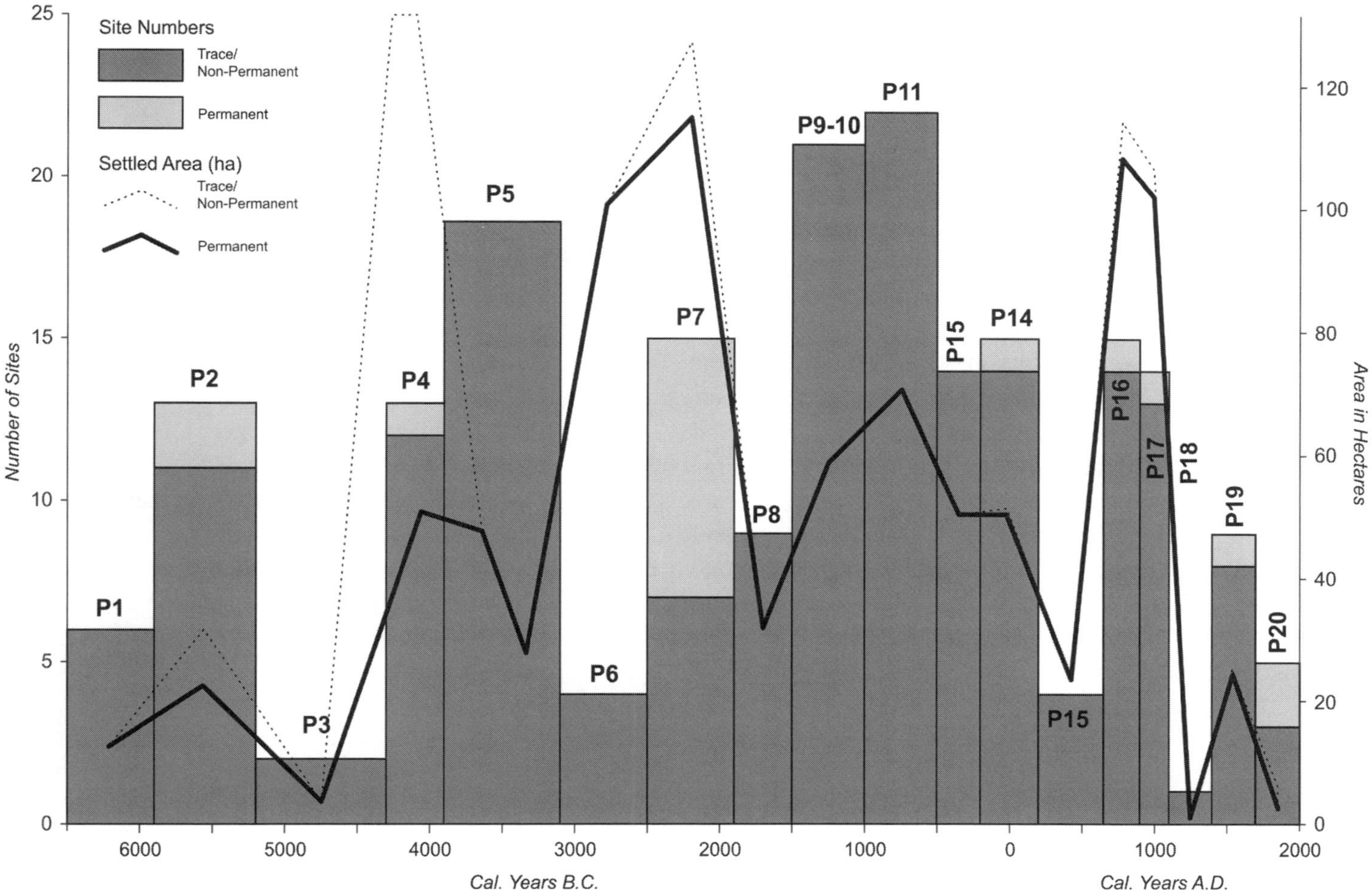

Figure 6.33. Number of sites (bars) and total settled area in hectares (lines). Width of bars approximates the length of the ceramically defined survey period

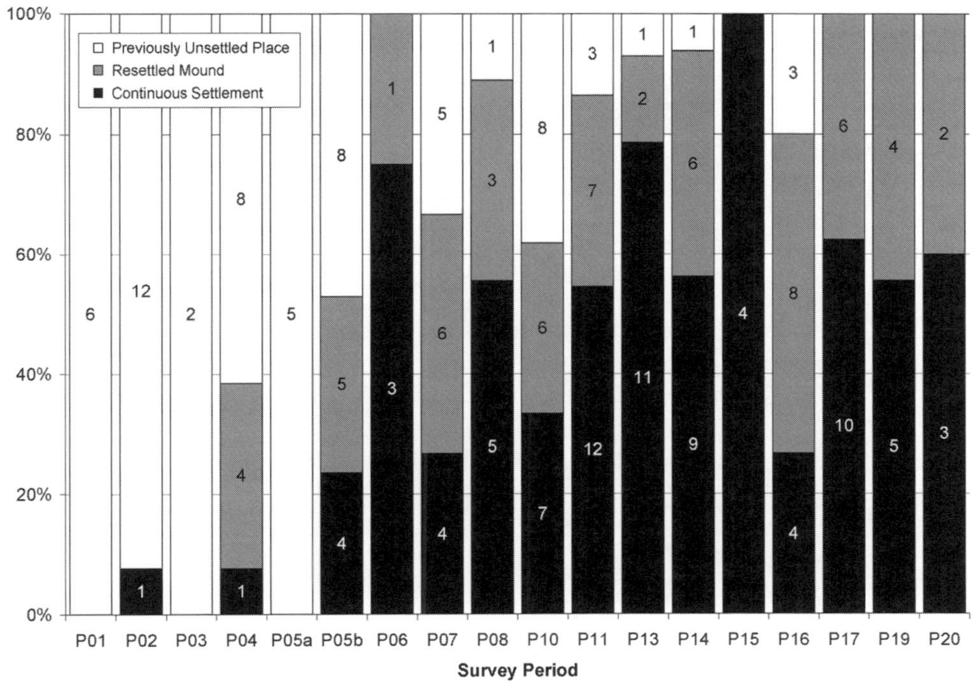

Figure 6.34. Settlement continuity, resettlement of previously settled places, and foundation of new settlements

be hypothesized, settlement stability likely resulted from long-term patterns of land tenure and other strong associations among communities and particular agricultural and pastoral landscapes. In the cases where settlement returned to a place that had been abandoned for centuries or millennia, it seems certain that places retained some meaning that compelled settlers to return there. The significance of such places may have been specific to a particular place for a particular group, as in the case of a pastoral nomadic community which opts to settle on a mound within its ancestral pasture grounds. Mounds might have a more generalized meaning, as in the case of settlers who have a general understanding of mounds as the appropriate place for human communities to reside. The meanings with which people regarded these places are lost to us now, but whether places had specific or general meanings to settlers can probably be related to the duration of their abandonment; the longer a place remained abandoned, the less likely that a pastoral or any other group might retain specific memories of that place, its history, and its former inhabitants.

Modern settlement in the THS region may depart rather dramatically from the pattern of the last centuries, but present communication routes have a deep ancestry. When the eastern Upper Khabur basin was the pasturelands of the Shammar, the "desert route" between Nisibin and Mosul left Tell Rumaylan and ran toward Tell al-Hawa. The stretch of this route between Rumaylan and Yarubiya (formerly called Tell Kotchek) was paved by the French mandatory government (visible in the far northeastern corner of fig. 6.32), although in 2000 it was in such poor condition that wheeled traffic drove in the fields alongside it. As the southern part of the basin became less dangerous, the new German-built railway ran to the south, crossing the THS at Tell al-Duwaym. In the 1980s, a new paved road was installed from Qamishli to Yarubiya, running between the French road and the railway. The physical trackways do not overlap precisely, but the general trend of interregional movement from the Tigris at Nineveh/Mosul to Nisibin/Qamishli has remained unchanged since at least the Middle Bronze Age and probably much earlier.

CHAPTER 7

LANDSCAPES OF MOVEMENT IN NORTHERN MESOPOTAMIA

The environmental and historical conditions of the Upper Khabur basin over the last several centuries have resulted in unparallelled preservation of landscape features up to the present, if we define "present" as the time of CORONA imagery acquisition in the late 1960s and early 1970s. Premodern tracks and roads survive in many places, for example, the American Southwest (Snead 2002), Costa Rica (Sheets and Sever 1991), and Easter Island (Lipo and Hunt 2005). In each of these landscapes, features amounting to tens of kilometers can still be recognized. By comparison, imagery analysis in the Upper Khabur basin and adjacent areas has recovered over six thousand kilometers of premodern trackways. In the density, aggregate length, and early date of the surviving features, the basin is one of the best-preserved landscapes of movement, not just in the Near East, but worldwide.

This high degree of survival permits a new empirically based approach to past patterns of communication. Research on routes and general lines of movement has proceeded on the basis of point patterns of archaeological sites (e.g., for the Upper Khabur, Lebeau 1997: fig. 2) or the backward projection of historically known routes (Algaze 1993). Frequently these studies rely heavily on cuneiform sources, especially itineraries (Hallo 1964; Charpin 1992; Joannès 1996). The physical manifestations of these movements are assumed to be no longer accessible.

In fact, remote-sensing sources show that ancient tracks do survive and sometimes demonstrate patterning that contradicts the assumptions upon which previous reconstructions have been based. This chapter presents the results of a program of hollow way mapping which was designed to confirm and expand the results of the pioneering efforts of Van Liere and Lauffray (1954–55) in the Upper Khabur basin and Wilkinson (1993; Wilkinson and Tucker 1995) in the adjacent Iraqi North Jazira. The aerial photographs used by Van Liere and Lauffray were not available, so this program relied primarily on declassified CORONA and KH-7 satellite photographs (see Section 5.3.2 and Ur 2003), augmented by SPOT and QuickBird imagery when available. The project's aim was to produce a geographically accurate database of hollow way features and associated sites in a GIS framework. The patterning of tracks across the entire basin is presented on maps 2 and 3. The methods and sources for the construction of the spatial database are discussed, and specific landscape characteristics of the basin's subregions are described briefly.

7.1. METHODOLOGY

The approximate positioning of many features was known prior to the start of fieldwork in the Hamoukar region. The new program of mapping began by comparing the identified hollow ways of Van Liere and Lauffray (1954–55) and Wilkinson (1993; Wilkinson and Tucker 1995) with their corresponding signatures on CORONA photographs (see Section 5.3.2). With a solid understanding of these signatures, it was then possible to remap large areas and to expand mapping coverage. In total, 17,140 sq. km were systematically investigated (fig. 7.1). At the same time, hollow ways identified from CORONA were visited on the ground, opportunistically in the areas around Chagar Bazar (spring 1999) and Tell Beydar (autumn 2000) and systematically in the THS region (autumn 1999 and 2000).

Unlike the THS area, which was covered in its entirely by five different CORONA missions, the basinwide mapping program often had to rely on only one or two missions for broad areas. The best coverage was to be found in the central and eastern basin, between Tell Beydar and the THS region; often three or more missions could be analyzed. For the western basin, the flanks of the Jebel Abd al-Aziz, and the Middle Khabur region, analysis was often limited to Mission 1021, which employed a low-resolution KH-4A camera, and Mission 1105, which was notable for the sharpness of its focus, but which was unfortunately flown under dry ground conditions, when the soil moisture and vegetation differences by which hollow ways are identified were at a minimum (see table 4.1). It is

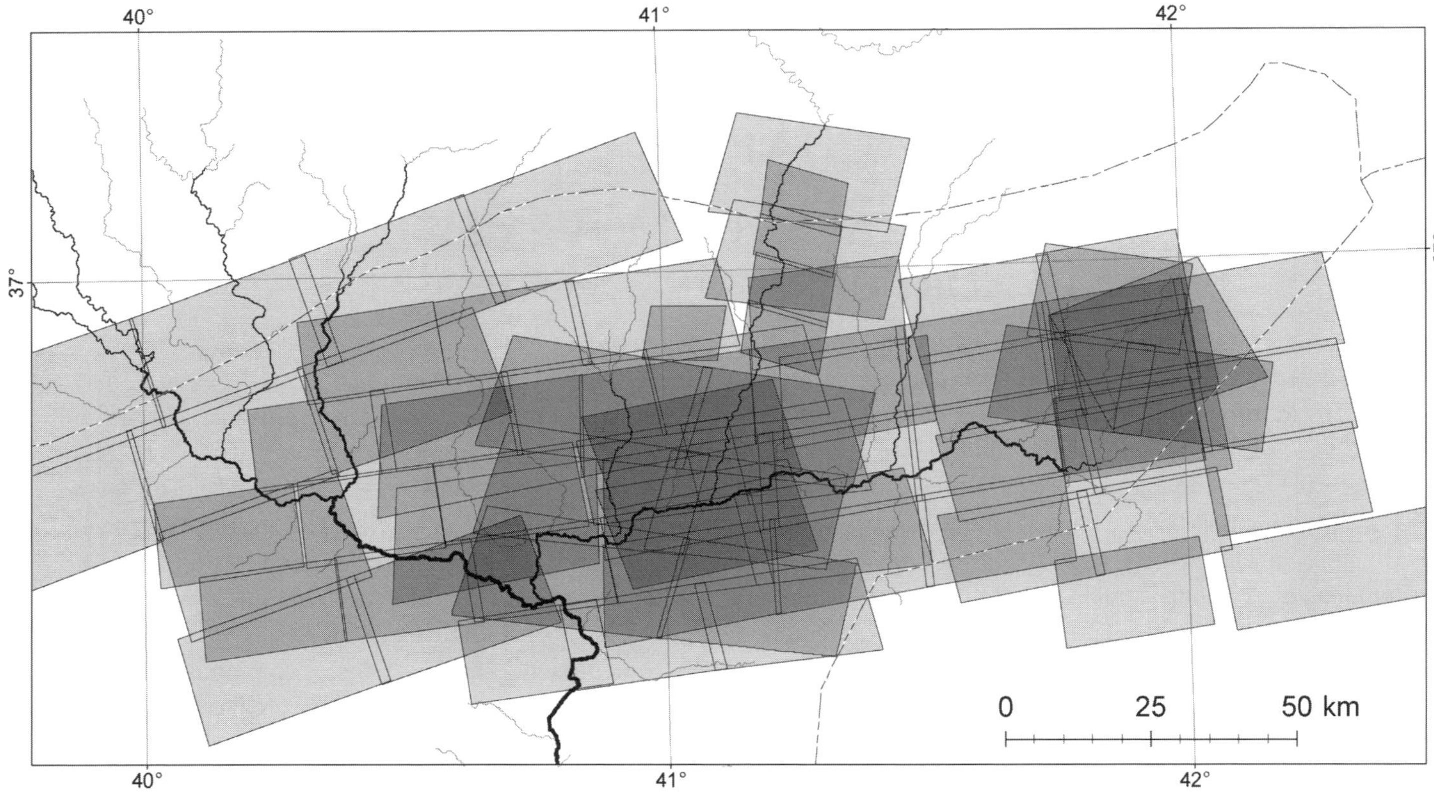

Figure 7.1. The distribution of CORONA scenes used for the program of hollow way mapping in the Upper Khabur basin. For descriptions of the missions, see table 4.1

likely, therefore, that the pattern of hollow ways for these regions are an underrepresentation of features surviving into the 1960s.

The construction of the spatial database handled the results of Van Liere and Lauffray and Wilkinson differently. Wilkinson had access to both aerial photographs and accurate topographic maps and his resulting hollow way maps (Wilkinson and Tucker 1995: figs. 6 and 24) are spatially accurate. These maps could be georeferenced and their features vectorized with relatively little geocorrection necessary. The features were then reconciled with features visible in SPOT and CORONA Mission 1102 imagery. The Iraqi North Jazira in map 2 includes some features not in the published North Jazira Project maps (the Mission 1102 imagery was acquired under more favorable ground conditions than Wilkinson's 1955 aerial photographs), but the general patterning of radial and long-distance features does not differ significantly.

The map of Van Liere and Lauffray, on the other hand, could be used as a general guide to the distribution and density of features, but its geographic inaccuracy was too great for its features to be vectorized directly. Even were this possible, it would not be desirable, since the features on the foldout map included with the 1954–55 article had been simplified in the transition from large-scale aerial photographs to the small-scale basinwide map, a fact already noted by McClellan and colleagues (2000: 137–38). This situation can be confirmed by comparing the few aerial photo examples (e.g., Tell Aswad Foqani, Van Liere and Lauffray 1954–55: pl. 3) and large-scale site plans in Van Liere's later publication on Bronze Age cities (1963) with their hollow ways on the 1954–55 map (see Section 3.2 for the example of Hamoukar).

Image analysis proceeded according to the methods described in Section 5.3.2. Because ground confirmation was impossible for areas outside of survey permit boundaries, decisions about what features were the remains of ancient tracks were as conservative as possible. The CORONA signature of a hollow way has already been described, but it is worth noting two situations when the basinwide mapping program did not include features matching that signature: when such features could be attributed to post-World War II agricultural practices and when they had potentially resulted from natural drainage processes.

Agricultural re-colonization began almost immediately after the French mandatory government established firm control of the basin from the various Arab and Kurdish nomadic groups (see Section 2.2), but mechanized agricultural methods did not become widespread until the years following World War II (Mehner 1983; Wirth 1964). By the time of the CORONA missions, common practice was to plow fields starting from the outer edges and spiralling inward in increasingly smaller circuits. This plowing pattern produces a distinctive signature that appears envelope-shaped from a vertical perspective (fig. 7.2). Often this plow envelope will appear light colored, but in many cases it can have the darker linear appearance of a hollow way. For this reason, dark linear features that articulate directly with the corner of a modern agricultural field on CORONA imagery must be considered as potentially recent features. In practice, almost all such features were disregarded.

The second situation in which a feature with the signature of a hollow way would not be mapped as such was when it might have resulted from natural surface runoff. In general, wadis and gullies in the basin have a meandering morphology that is easily distinguished from straight hollow ways. In some cases, however, it can be difficult to establish with certainty that a feature is anthropogenic, particularly when the depressed feature is only a couple hundred meters or less long. Thus, linear features whose direction coincided with the natural slope of the surrounding terrain were evaluated carefully. In general, the only time that features which clearly were serving a hydraulic function at present were designated as hollow ways was when two such features flowed into a wadi directly across from each other (fig. 7.3). Such an arrangement is unlikely under natural conditions and was used as a criterion for evaluating features in the Negev (Tsoar and Yekutieli 1992). Complicating the decision about whether such a feature was a former track is the situation in which a hollow way has captured runoff and is now in the direction of surface flow (fig. 7.4).

Notes on the Maps. The accompanying maps 2 (eastern basin) and 3 (western basin) present 6,531 hollow way segments stretching in aggregate over 6,025 km. In many cases it has been possible to assign features to broad and

Figure 7.2. The archaeological palimpsest of recent plow envelopes and ancient features.
(*A*) CORONA photograph (1108-1025DA005, 6 December 1969); (*B*) Interpretation (hollow ways in solid black, modern tracks and field boundaries in solid white, plow envelopes in dashed white)

Figure 7.3. Hollow way features southwest of Kaka Sa'id, near Tell Brak (CORONA 1102-1025DF007, 11 December 1967)

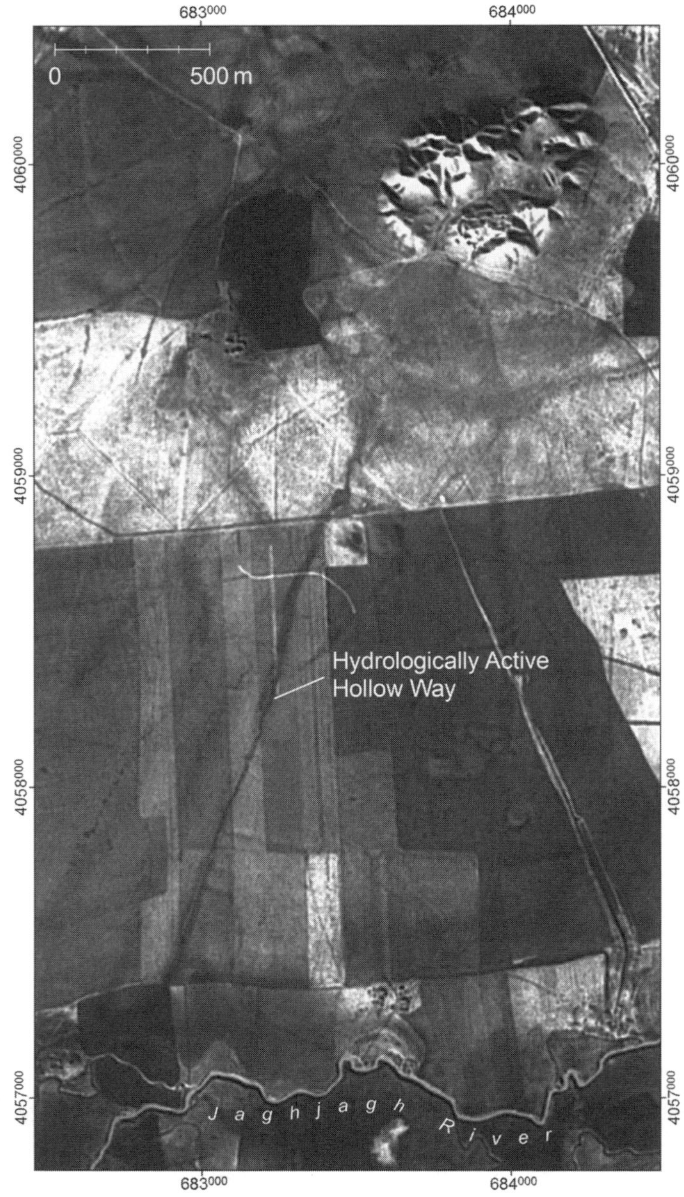

Figure 7.4. Hydrologically active hollow way draining the Tell Brak settlement complex into the Jaghjagh River (CORONA 1102-1025DF007, 11 December 1967)

narrow classes, the former being predominantly later third millennium B.C. and the latter generally dating to the later first millennium A.D. Without ground control, and under varying ground visibility conditions, it was not always possible to make this assignment, and many features remain unclassified. The sites were derived from published archaeological surveys (Eidem and Warburton 1996; Fielden 1981; Kouchoukos 1998; Lyonnet 2000; Meijer 1986; Monchambert 1984b; Ristvet 2005; Stein and Wattenmaker 2003; Weiss 1986; Weiss et al. 2002–03; Wilkinson 2000a; Wilkinson and Tucker 1995) and supplemented by analysis of CORONA imagery and topographic data from Arabic 1:50,000 scale maps and the SRTM digital elevation dataset. No attempt has been made to adhere to a common standard of transliteration for Arabic, Kurdish, and Turkish place names, and they derive from various French, Arabic, English, and Russian maps as well as from common archaeological usage. Sites have been assigned to one of five classes based on their morphology as described by excavators and surveyors or from their CORONA signature: Tell/High Mound (greater than 7 m high), Low Mound (less than 7 m high), Complex Mounded, Complex with a High Mound, and Unclassified (for a description of these types, see Section 5.1.2 and Wilkinson and Tucker 1995: 15–16). Although all recognizable hollow ways have been included on the maps, for sites, this map should be considered comprehensive only within the Hamoukar, Tell Beydar, and North Jazira Project survey areas. Premodern irrigation has been included only in places where it may have affected hollow way preservation or where discussed in the text. The positions of all sites and landscape features have been corrected using orthorectified SPOT imagery and are correct to within 20 m.

Contour lines are derived from low pass-filtered 90 m SRTM digital terrain data as processed by the Consultative Group on International Agricultural Research Consortium for Spatial Information (CGIAR-CSI). The surface drainage data was processed by Devin White from filtered 30 m SRTM digital terrain data. In many places, the surface hydrology in maps 2 and 3 differs substantially from the drainage in the French 1:200,000 and Syrian Arabic 1:50,000 topographic maps of the basin. The former derives from digital terrain data (acquired January 2000), whereas the latter was drawn from aerial photographs. The hydrology of these topographic maps conflates natural drainage with deliberately dug canals and even hollow ways that have captured surface runoff. Because of the coarse resolution of the digital terrain data (30 m), the position of the modeled drainage can be up to 100 m off, but in general it coincides very well with patterns visible in CORONA. Where the divergences between modeled and visible drainage patterns are great, deliberate human modification of the hydrology for irrigation is frequently responsible, especially in the areas of Nisibin/Qamishli and Tell Qarasa (see figs. 7.5 and 7.6 below), and between Hamoukar and the Wadi Rumaylan (see fig. 5.30).

7.2. GENERAL PATTERNS OF HOLLOW WAYS THROUGHOUT THE BASIN

7.2.1. RADIAL PATTERNING

The most common pattern in the Upper Khabur basin is one in which the hollow ways radiate out from a central site. Sometimes features articulate directly with another site; in other cases, the tracks simply fade out. It is assumed that the former conveyed human and animal traffic between settlements for a variety of economic and social purposes, whereas the latter results from movement of farmers, herders, and their animals to and from fields and pasture (Wilkinson 1993; Ur 2009). Given the overwhelmingly agricultural nature of society in the basin from the Neolithic period up to the present, it is unsurprising that fading hollow ways make up a large majority of all features.

Radial patterning occurs not only around sites in the most opportune areas for agriculture, but also in some marginal areas, both in terms of soils and rainfall. For example, most of the major *Kranzhügeln* of the later third millennium B.C. (Period 7) along the northern flanks of the Jebel Abd al-Aziz (Hole 2002–03; Kouchoukos 1998) feature well-developed radial systems.

Radial patterning is not limited to Period 7 sites, however. In the THS region, strong radial systems formed around THS 50 and the Islamic component of THS 25; other noteworthy examples are discussed below. In general, it is assumed that all past permanent agricultural settlements developed radial patterns, which are widely known cross-culturally and emerge from principles of agricultural movement that may be universal in dry-farming economies (Chisholm 1962). The third-millennium systems in the basin survive because they were so deeply etched; the late Sasanian and Islamic (Periods 16–17) systems survive because little time has passed, and the region became used for pasture after the collapse of settlement. At the time of CORONA photograph acquisition, it was the most recent layer of the landscape palimpsest. In all likelihood, the latter system would have also characterized earlier periods for which no tracks survive.

7.2.2. INTER-SITE PATTERNING

As mentioned above, many radial elements do not simply fade out but connect directly with other sites. The sites in the interconnected network of broad radial systems in the basin are, when they have been dated, mid- to late third millennium B.C. in date. The conclusion that must be drawn from this pattern is that most movement during this major phase of early urbanism was highly local. For example, we can assume that there was much movement between Nagar (Tell Brak), the major political capital, and Nabada (Tell Beydar), an important regional center. There were multiple possible routes a traveler could take, each involving a series of segments between intermediate sites such as Tell Bati, Tell Mansur, and Tell Aswad Foqani, to name a few. Despite the political and economic importance of these two places, it does not appear that a direct route between them existed (Sallaberger and Ur 2004). Inter-site patterning for later periods is similar but there tend to be greater distances between interconnected settlements.

7.2.3. LONG-DISTANCE ROUTES

Northern Mesopotamia first came to the attention of Western visitors because it was an east–west transportation corridor that avoided the environmental and nomadic difficulties of the desert route to the south and the logistical problems of the mountain route to the north. In particular, the stretch between Mosul and Nisibin, which runs through or just north of the THS region (see Section 2.2), was an important one at least as far back as the time of the Old Assyrian caravan trade and almost certainly much earlier. Wilkinson's analysis of aerial photographs of the Iraqi North Jazira demonstrated three trajectories of hollow ways leading from Eski Mosul on the Tigris northwest and into Syria. Analysis of CORONA imagery shows that these three routes continued farther toward the northwest (discussed below).

Elsewhere in the basin, it is more difficult to discern interregional paths of movement on the ground. As mentioned above, the dense network of interconnected radial routes in the central and western basin certainly enabled interregional movement, but the surviving traces do not privilege one or even a few routes. It is occasionally possible to recognize segments aligned with major Islamic places (e.g., Ras al-Ain and Tell Majdal), but none can be traced as extensively as can the Nisibin–Mosul route. The major exception comes from Tell Tuneinir in the Middle Khabur region, where a well-preserved trackway leads east of the Jebel Kaukab toward Tell Brak and Nisibin.

7.3. HOLLOW WAY PATTERNING BY BASIN SUBREGION

The following sections give brief descriptions of hollow way patterning within several subregions of the basin. The primary intention is simply to present the surviving evidence for past movement; description and analysis are kept brief.

7.3.1. THE EASTERN UPPER KHABUR BASIN

In terms of its hollow way landscape, the eastern part of the Upper Khabur basin (generally defined here as the region between the Tigris-Euphrates watershed east of Hamoukar and the Jaghjagh River) is an extension of the adjacent Iraqi North Jazira, the landscape of which has been studied in detail (Wilkinson 1993; Wilkinson and Tucker 1995). Within the Syrian frontier, however, the continuous stretch of undulating plains between Yarubiya and Qamishli is bounded by two areas of poor preservation that appear to have constrained the surviving hollow way traces into a band between Hamoukar and Tell Leilan (see map 2).

To the south, the relief of the plain is almost completely negligible and in the past, the waters of the Wadis Rumaylan, Khunayzir, and Jarrah have backed up to create marshy ground in the winter and spring. Although sites appear to be abundant in areas of high ground within the Radd marsh, almost no traces of former tracks can be identified. Sediment aggradation conditions were exacerbated at some indeterminate time by irrigation along the lower reaches of the Rumaylan and Khunayzir (Wilkinson 2002a: 90–91). Another example can be seen on the Wadi Jarrah just below Tell Qarasa (fig. 7.5). The Wadi Braybich was diverted just north of Tell al-ʿAmri into a channel that ran south for 2 km to a second weir, from which its waters were sent in several directions. Some channels flowed back into the Braybich while others drained into the Jarrah. It is not possible to propose a date for these canals, but morphologically they are likely to be recent, perhaps as part of the expansions of settlement in the basin during the Abbasid or early Ottoman periods. Tracks that might have existed in the Radd marsh and along its northern edges have been wiped clear by this combination of natural and cultural landscape transformations.

Figure 7.5. Irrigation channels off of the Wadi Braybich in the area of Tell Qarasa (CORONA 1102-1025DF006, 11 December 1967)

The absence of hollow ways to the north of the Hamoukar–Leilan corridor can be also be explained by natural and cultural processes. This area recieves more rainfall (see fig. 2.7), which renders agriculture a less risky undertaking. It is therefore likely that this area has hosted more continuous sedentary occupation, which would have resulted in higher attrition of landscape features, although the intensive surveys that might support this hypothesis have yet to be carried out. Environmental and historical processes may have operated hand in hand. When pastoral nomadic groups gained political ascendancy in this region following the sixteenth century A.D., sedentary groups retreated northward to the Tur Abdin foothills for security reasons (see Section 2.2 and fig. 2.10). The combination of higher rainfall, more continuous agricultural occupation, and more pronounced local topographic relief would have removed hollow ways either through plowing, local soil movement, or both.

Finally, localized loss of hollow way features appears to have occurred within the narrow floodplains of the major wadis. Certainly this is due to local aggradation of sediments within the floodplains, but, again, small-scale irrigation cannot be ruled out. For example, the component of the third-millennium track between Hamoukar and Tell Leilan was erased by subsequent irrigation below Tell Mashhan (see Section 5.4 and fig. 5.32).

The zones of hollow way survival are thus the high areas between the major drainages. This pattern is especially striking at Hamoukar itself, where hollow ways survive abundantly on a broad spur that extends about 10 km southwest of Hamoukar before fading into the Radd marsh.

At the same time, this corridor of survival was certainly a major route of interregional movement for millennia and continuing up to the present, when automotive and rail traffic between Qamishli and Mosul passes through this area. In the Iraqi North Jazira, Wilkinson identified three major interregional hollow way routes running northwest from Eski Mosul on the Tigris: two on the north side of the Jebel al-Qusayr (running through Tell al-Hawa and Tell al-Samir, respectively, and both passing through Tell Uwaynat) and one on the south side. All three routes continue into the eastern Upper Khabur basin. The northernmost continued from Tell al-Hawa to Tell Hayal, Chilparat, al-Jahishiya, and as far as Tell Mas'ud al-Rafiya, beyond which it appears to have been effaced by the irrigated zone north of the THS region. Beyond this area, a few hollow ways appear to align on the area of Tell Alo, but do not articulate well with any identified sites.

The interregional route through Tell al-Samir does not survive immediately to its west, but can be found again at the modern border, where it continues directly toward Hamoukar. It disappears into the irrigated zone on the left side of the Wadi Rumaylan, but reemerges to run from Tell Sulayman Sari through Tell Jaddawi, Tell Haddad, Tell Abu Far'a, Tell Mohammed Diyab, and up to Tell Leilan. Probably because of the large irrigation system southeast of Nisibin, this route cannot be followed any farther beyond Leilan to the northwest.

The southernmost route through Tell Qirdishan, Yasah, and Kharaba al-Kabir is more difficult to follow beyond the Iraqi North Jazira area. It might have continued on another route on the same northwestern alignment which originated at Rajim Hassan and continued to Umm Ajur, Umm Adham, and finally al-Botha near the edge of the Wadi Rumaylan floodplain.

Another major route runs into the basin from the gap between the eastern end of the Jebel Sinjar and the western end of the Jebel Ishkaft. There are several sites here, but features appear to articulate with a complex mounded site called Tell Shura. One route leads north to Tell Udhan and into the North Jazira survey area. Another stretches almost 18 km to an unnamed complex mounded site, where the track splits: one track goes to another unnamed complex mounded site and on to Tell Umm Hidur; the other goes to Tell al-Jahash and probably connected thereafter with the southernmost northeastern route through the North Jazira area.

These routes are difficult to date and, indeed, were probably used in multiple periods. However, the major sites along the north–south route from Tell Shura are all site complexes that have not had time to erode into featureless mounds; these particular features are probably Islamic, although the route itself was certainly used earlier. The major series of hollow ways between Tell al-Samir and Tell Leilan all articulate with high-mounded sites of the later third millennium B.C. The upper route through Tell al-Hawa articulates with important third-millennium and late sites and probably was used at both times, and likely others as well.

Radial systems around sites are not as common in the eastern basin as they are in the central plain, but several stand out. Perhaps the best preserved is around Tell Rumaylan, which perseveres in an area of otherwise poor hollow way survival. Other well-preserved radial systems surround Tell Koz, Tell Haddad, Tell Abu Qadayr, Tell Abu Far'a, and Tell Mohammed Diyab. Radial systems around Tell Leilan, Tell Qarassa, and Tell Khamis appear to be truncated by later landscape transformation via irrigation, especially on the west side of the Wadi Jarrah. Other linear features in the area between the Wadi Jarrah, the Radd marsh, and the Jaghjagh River are disjointed segments on high ground which survived the impact of the Nisibin irrigation system (see Section 7.3.2 below). The exception is Tell Farfara, an enormous site with radiating features on all sides.

Many of these sites are multiperiod, but all were widely occupied during the later third millennium B.C. (Meijer 1986; Weiss 1986; Stein and Wattenmaker 2003). Radiating patterns were not limited to the third millennium, however. The best example is the site of Chilparat Tay, a low 44 ha walled settlement (see fig. 7.2) that is often assumed to have been Roman Thebeta (see Poidebard 1934: pl. 160), although the relative lack of mound erosion suggests that it is more recent. Southeast of the THS region, the sites at Umm Ajur, Tell Umm Hidur (see fig. 5.6), Tell al-Jahash, and Khirbat Touayrash all have the complex morphology of late settlements and are interconnected by radial networks of narrow hollow ways.

The hollow ways identified via CORONA photographs for this region are far more numerous than those appearing on the basinwide map of Van Liere and Lauffray (1954–55). A perfect spatial correspondence is not to be expected, given that the map was produced prior to digital cartography and digitally georeferenced imagery. Van Liere and Lauffray recognized the major radial systems, but their map does not reflect the high degree of interconnection along the route between Hamoukar and Tell Leilan. Their map also appears only to indicate the broad class of hollow ways; the elaborate network of narrow tracks around Chilparat Tay, for example, is not indicated. The reasons for these discrepancies are not clear, but may be related to the nature of their aerial photographs (e.g., they might have been taken under dry conditions). It is also possible that they chose to exclude small features from their small-scale, large-format map, since they were able to identify narrow features on the few photographs published with the map (Van Liere and Lauffray 1954–55).

7.3.2. THE UPPER JAGHJAGH REGION

The northern central plain around Qamishli, where the Jaghjagh River emerges from the Tur Abdin, has been mentioned already as a zone of destruction of ancient trackways; therefore little can be said about communication and movement based on archaeological evidence. However, this region is worth a brief examination because it contains the largest landscape feature in the basin, outside of the network of hollow ways: a system of irrigation canals covering at least 350 sq. km, which has gone almost entirely unrecognized by archaeologists and historians, with the exception of Louis Dillemann (1962: 51–54, fig. 5; see also Göyünç and Hütteroth 1997: 60–64).

The system has been partially reconstructed using a declassified KH-7 satellite photograph taken 1 October 1965 (fig. 7.6). Offtakes from the Jaghjagh took off at and below the modern Turkish village of Baverni and flowed around and through Nisibin, which today is partly in Syria and partly under the Turkish town of Nusaybin. The main feeder canal appears to have run along the top of the watershed between the Jaghjagh and the Wadi Braybich to the east. Traces of offtakes from this main system can be recognized as far south as Tell Hamidi; below this point, canals appear to irrigate more restricted areas along the left bank of the Jaghjagh and the floodplains of wadis to the east (e.g., west of Tell Farfara). Smaller more localized systems tapped wadis to the west of Nisibin; some of these features can be traced almost as far south as Tell Brak (see map 3 and Section 7.3.3).

At present it is difficult to date this system using archaeological evidence. The main feeder runs through the area surveyed by Meijer, but this research was carried out before local ceramic sequences were well understood, and he also did not consistently note the presence of Islamic material (Meijer 1986: 33 n. 15). Lyonnet's survey was restricted to the west of the Jaghjagh, with the exception of Nisibin itself (Lyonnet 2000: no. 70; see also Lyonnet 1996b; Guérin 1996). From texts, however, it is possible to propose the times in which this system might have been in use. Nasibina was an important provincial capital of the Neo-Assyrian empire (Streck 1999), and since major irrigation systems had been installed in the imperial heartland (Ur 2005b) and around other provincial capitals (e.g., Tell Sheikh Hamad/Dur-Katlimmu; Ergenzinger and Kühne 1991), it is possible that the system was founded at that time. Nisibin continued to be an important political, economic, and especially religious center into the first millennium A.D. (Pigulevskaja 1963; Kessler 1996), and the Jaghjagh River played an important role in the failed seige of Nisibin in 350 by Shapur II (Lightfoot 1988). Medieval geographers made note of the pleasant gardens in the town (Honigmann and Bosworth 2006: 94; Ibn Hawqal 2001: 204; Le Strange 1905). In the sixteenth century, Ottoman tax records indicate many irrigated crops coming from the Nisibin sanjak (Göyünç and Hütteroth 1997: 62–64, 113–15). By the time Western travelers began to make observations, the system had certainly fallen out of use (see Section 2.2), and today all irrigation along the upper Jaghjagh is done by local small-scale diesel pumps rather than surface channels. The remains of the system which survive, visible in figure 7.6, are preserved because they are used as field boundaries for dry-farmed or pump-irrigated fields.

7.3.3. THE CENTRAL BASIN

Hollow ways in the central part of the basin, defined here as the region between the Jaghjagh River and the Wadi Aweidj (map 3), were well preserved up to the 1960s and have received much archaeological attention since Van Liere and Lauffray's initial publication (1954–55), particularly around Tell Brak (McClellan, Grayson, and Ogleby 2000; McClellan and Porter 1995; Wilkinson et al. 2001; Ur 2003, 2009) and the Tell Beydar Survey region (Wilkinson 2000a; Sallaberger and Ur 2004; Ur and Wilkinson 2008).

As in the eastern basin, the pattern of trackways appears to be limited to the north by higher rainfall, more intensive agriculture, and long-term continuous settlement, all of which have had a destructive impact on hollow ways. For example, Tell Mozan, which falls in this northern zone, appears to be the only major later third-millennium urban center in the basin without an elaborate network of associated features. Toward Qamishli, irrigation has contributed to this destruction. The area between the Jaghjagh at Qamishli and the wadi that passes through Tell Abu Rassain is as heavily irrigated as the land southeast of Qamishli. This same wadi was the source of a long feeder canal that originated near Naqara and can be traced for over 17 km to the area of Gir Zil Kabir. Another system starts near Guir Messine and can be traced almost as far as Tell Brak; this system is probably responsible for the curious void in hollow ways around Tell Zabib and Tell al-Faris. The strong divergence between the surface hydrology visible on CORONA photographs and the network derived from digital terrain data suggests that the degree to which the natural drainage has been transformed by human action is still underappreciated for this region.

Figure 7.6. Irrigation channels below Nisibin/Qamishli (KH-7 402200009H027, 1 October 1965).
See maps 2 and 3 for an interpretation

Two basaltic areas in the central basin also show little evidence for tracks. Most obvious is the Jebel Kaukab, an extinct volcano east of Hassake that covers 73 sq. km. Tracks did not form on its thin soils, with the exception of one hollow way at its southern end. It seems most likely that traffic went around it; for example, several deeply incised hollow ways from Tell al-Aswad skirt the basalt along its eastern edge (Oates and Oates 1990: 240, pl. 66a–b). The other basaltic area falls between the Wadis Zerkan and Aweidj and the Khabur River and is known variously as the Ardh al-Shaykh and the Hemma Plateau. The main basaltic area covers 250 sq. km, with other smaller outcrops to the north. The plateau's edges are a zone of survival, particularly for rock art and desert kites (Van Berg and Picalause 2003; Van Berg et al. 2004), but track features are very uncommon. They are not, however, entirely absent. A set of features articulates with TBS 23, a small Iron Age mound (Wilkinson et al. 2005: 41), and a long sequence stretches 10 km across its southwestern quadrant. The infrequency of hollow ways on these thin soils probably corresponds to long-term patterns of low-intensity unconstrained traffic. If we can assume that these were pastoral zones, there would not have been agricultural fields to constrain movement, and therefore hollow ways would not have formed except under unusual conditions (see Section 5.3.1).

The third zone of the central basin with a low occurrence of hollow ways falls around the modern provincial capital at Hassake (fig. 7.7). Starting in the 1920s, the town grew rapidly under French protection (de Vaumas 1956). By the time of the CORONA photographs in the 1960s, the area was densely populated and had a developed irrigation infrastructure which drew off the Khabur waters and even moved them up the lower Jaghjagh even beyond the confluence with the Wadi Aweidj. The lack of hollow ways in the Hassake region can be attributed to these recent cultural transformations.

With the exception of these zones of landscape destruction, CORONA photographs record thousands of kilometers of hollow ways inscribed into the terrain of the central basin. Unlike the eastern basin, there is no dominant route of movement. Interregional travel appears to have proceeded from settlement node to settlement node, generally without long intersite segments. Within the interconnected radial systems, it is possible to discern several east–west routes, for example:

- Tell Jamilo — Tell Aswad Foqani — Tell Mouerik Jowani — Tell Chemma — Tell Nourek (25 km)
- Tell Beydar — Tell Kaferu — Tell Bati — Tell Chemma — Tell Mansur — Tell Alo — Guir Bejinnk Jowani (31 km)
- Tell al-Shur Gharbi — Tell Shur — Tell Habbu — Tell Warchek — Tell Hanou — Tell Douzek — Tell Cholma Foqani — Tell Salandar — Germayr — Tell Chagar Bazar (41 km)

The most commonly occurring hollow way pattern in the central basin is a radiating set of features around high multiperiod mounds containing a substantial later third-millennium B.C. component. Hollow ways average 3–4 km in length, and most fade out without articulating with another site. The most spectacular radial

Figure 7.7. The provincial capital at Hassake, at the confluence of the lower Jaghjagh and Khabur rivers (CORONA 1105-1025DF059, 5 November 1968)

system occurs around Tell Brak (Ur 2003: fig. 8; Wilkinson et al. 2001) and may have originated in the fourth millennium, given Brak's early urban growth (Ur, Karsgaard, and Oates 2007). Radial systems occur around several sites with excavated later third-millennium remains, for example, Chagar Bazar, Tell Arbid, and Tell Beydar. On the Jaghjagh, Tell Hamidi and Tell Barri both have partial systems that have probably been damaged by subsequent irrigation (for the latter, see Van Liere 1961–62). The most spectacularly preserved radial networks occur around sites along the minor wadis in the center of this region, especially at Tell Cholma Foqani (fig. 7.8), Tell Salandar, Tell Effendi, Tell Mansur, Tell Bati, and Tell Aswad Foqani. Period 7 sites along the Wadi Aweidj also preserve strong radial systems, for example, Tell Jamilo (see fig. 5.21).

Features also radiate out from the point where the Jaghjagh River bends south to flow toward Hassake, just above its confluence with the Wadi Aweidj. Several high mounds cluster at this point (Tell Berzane, Safaya, and especially Tell Bazari), and early observers noted the remains of a stone bridge near Safaya (von Oppenheim 1900: 27; for a photograph, see Poidebard 1934: pl. 118).

Most of the features in the central basin discussed above have been of the broad variety, probably datable to the later third millennium B.C., but narrow features also survive. In particular, traffic on narrow hollow ways went up the right bank of the lower Wadi Aweidj and radiated out from the bridge at Safaya in two directions: toward Nisibin to the northeast, and across the interfluvial areas to the north-northwest (presumably toward Mardin). The Sasanian–Islamic town around the Castellum at Tell Brak is also associated with a series of narrow features, in addition to traces of local irrigation from the Jaghjagh. Elsewhere, isolated narrow hollow ways articulate with low complex mounded sites.

Again, the map of Van Liere and Lauffray (1954–55) agrees with the relatively high density of hollow ways in the central basin, but the details of specific radial networks appear to be simplified for publication at small scale, and the degree of interconnection is underrepresented.

Figure 7.8. Radial hollow way patterning around Tell Cholma Foqani (CORONA 1105-1025DF056, 5 November 1968). For an interpretation, see map 3

7.3.4. THE WESTERN BASIN

The density of preserved hollow ways is low in the western basin, defined as the area between Ras al-Ain and the Ardh al-Shaykh plateau and encompassing the Wadis Jirjib and Zerkan. This situation cannot be blamed on soils or rainfall, which do not differ appreciably from those of the central basin (see figs. 2.4 and 2.7). On the other hand, Chechen refugees began to resettle the area around Ras al-Ain already in the 1860s (Lewis 1987: 96–103), and an irrigation system was installed along the Khabur River. It is possible that earlier Iron Age (Orthmann 2002) or Hellenistic (McEwan et al. 1958) settlement may have also removed traces of earlier landscapes in this region. Finally, the hollow way mapping program used only Missions 1021 and 1105 for the western basin. The former mission used the lower-resolution KH-4A camera, and imagery from the latter mission was acquired prior to the start of the rainy season and could identify hollow ways only under certain field conditions. It is possible that with additional remote-sensing sources, more hollow ways might be identified; however, the earlier mapping effort by Van Liere and Lauffray (1954–55) describes a similarly low density of features.

The surviving features tend to be isolated track segments and non-interconnected small radial systems around high mounds. The best-preserved systems are along the Wadi Zerkan at Tell Harmal, Tell Abu Rassine, and Tell al-Ward (Van Liere and Lauffray recognized no features around the latter site). Along the Wadi Jirjib and the region farther west, hollow ways are infrequent. A few radial systems can be identified, however. Two large sites on the Turkish side of the frontier, Tell Chanafes and Büyükboğaziye, both had developed systems. On the Khabur River, a series of features ran west from Tell Jenediya, and a widely spaced set of hollow ways appears to radiate out from Tell Fakhariya. The major Iron Age/Neo-Assyrian city at Tell Halaf (ancient Guzana) does not appear to have generated a track network.

Interregional routes have not been recognized in the western basin. The sole exception is a fragmentary alignment on the southern uplands between the Wadi Jirjib and the Wadi Zerkan, which appears to align with Tell Fakhariya/Ras al-Ain to the northwest and with Tell Tamr to the southeast. This alignment suggests that traffic did not always adhere to the valley of the Khabur River.

Van Liere and Lauffray recognized elaborate radial systems around the *Kranzhügeln* of the Wadi Hammar basin. The CORONA-based hollow way mapping program only investigated the eastern part of this region and at low intensity. Non-systematic observations of imagery from the 1021 and 1105 missions confirm that hollow ways are associated with many of these sites, but cannot verify that their patterning corresponds to the mapping of Van Liere and Lauffray.

7.3.5. NORTHERN FLANKS OF THE JEBEL ABD AL-AZIZ AND THE UPPER KHABUR RIVER

The plain between the Jebel Abd al-Aziz and the Khabur River is well outside the region of reliable annual rainfall (see fig. 2.7), but nonetheless has seen several phases of substantial sedentary occupation. The survey component of the Yale West Jazira Project (Hole 2002–03; Kouchoukos 1998) revealed large settlements of the third millennium B.C. and smaller reoccupations during the Iron Age, Byzantine, and Islamic periods. In recent centuries, this zone has been the summer domain of the Shammar al-Zor camel nomads (Glubb 1942: 26–28). The area thus appears to be generally one of good landscape preservation. On the other hand, the Khabur River between Ras al-Ain and Hassake was one of the first parts of the basin to be recolonized by agriculturalists, even before the end of Ottoman control (see above), and Van Liere and Lauffray (1954–55: 146–48) detected earlier irrigation canals along its terraces. The combination of past irrigation and early resettlement suggests that the terraces along the river are less likely to preserve landscape features predating the irrigation canals.

As would therefore be expected, sites along the northern flanks of the Jebel Abd al-Aziz have well-preserved radial systems of hollow ways, especially Tell Mabtuh al-Gharbi, Tell al-Maghr, and Tell Mabtuh al-Sharqi (for the last, see also the aerial photograph in Van Liere and Lauffray 1954–55: pl. 2). These sites are major settlements of the later third millennium (Kouchoukos 1998: 368–70). Tracks radiate in the direction of the Khabur River rather than the Jebel Abd al-Aziz. The CORONA-based mapping program confirmed the general orientation and expanded the radial systems mapped by Van Liere and Lauffray around these sites. The only substantially different pattern is at Tell Mabtuh al-Sharqi. Their six features radiate to the southwest and east, whereas the majority of features visible in CORONA photographs lead to the north.

Feature preservation along the Khabur River is variable; tracks into the steppe to the south often survive for kilometers, but few survive on the lower terraces close to the river. In this riverine zone, two sites are worthy of mention. Tell Majdal is a 4.5 ha high mound with a 60 ha lower town on the right bank of the Khabur (fig. 7.9). It is associated with an extensive radiating group of hollow ways on the upper terraces and stretching 5 km out into the Abd al-Aziz steppe. One track to the south-southeast appears to mark the route toward the middle Khabur region (see map 3). Surface collection indicates dense third-millennium and medieval Islamic occupation (Lyonnet 2000: 20, 34, site no. 8). Tell Majdal is often identified with classical Magdalathum (e.g., Poidebard 1934; Dillemann 1962).

The second significant site from a landscape perspective is a complex of mounds 9 km upstream from Tell Majdal (fig. 7.10). On the left bank is a 20 ha semicircular walled site now called Tell ʻArbush. Poidebard identified it as classical Thallaba and also recognized a paved roadway and a pair of camps at Tell Barij and to its south on the river's edge (see map in Poidebard 1934: pl. 137). On the right bank and slightly downstream is a 4.5 ha high mound called Tell Harmaz. The landscape around this complex of mounds is particularly abundant with landscape features. A few fragmentary hollow way segments lead northeast from Tell ʻArbush toward the Ardh al-Shaykh plateau. Poidebard (1934: 150) proposed that a route ran between Thallaba and the fortification at Tell Bati, and these few segments do indeed line up with a better-preserved set of narrow features which cross the Wadi Aweidj at Tell Kashkashok and lead directly to Bati. To the northwest, the complex appears to be the destination of a long track across the southwestern Ardh al-Shaykh plateau. Poidebard also identified a segment of paved road south of the site, also visible on CORONA. Another set of broad tracks radiate south from Tell Harmaz across the Khabur's upper terraces toward the Jebel Abd al-Aziz. Some segments are still preserved on the lower terraces as well. On the floodplain, on the river's right bank, are traces of at least two large canals. The head of one of the canals originated directly opposite Poidebard's proposed camp at Tell Barij; the second began about 1.5 km farther upstream (see map

Figure 7.9. Tell Majdal and associated hollow way features (CORONA 1105-1025DF59, 5 November 1968)

Figure 7.10. Sites and features in the Thallaba area (CORONA 1105-1025DF059, 5 November 1968). For interpretation, see map 3 and Poidebard 1934: plate 137

3). Both appear to have been dug through a spur in the terrace to arrive in the area around Tell Majdal. The survival of landscape features on the lower terraces around 'Arbush-Harmaz is particularly surprising, given the well-documented pattern of recent intensive irrigation.

7.3.6. THE MIDDLE KHABUR REGION

We are particularly well informed about settlement below Hassake due to survey (Monchambert 1984a–b) and salvage excavations in advance of the construction of a barrage across the Khabur River. Prior to its construction, the riverine terraces had been settled and cultivated by small-scale irrigation since the 1920s (see photographs in Poidebard 1934), although it had been almost entirely given over to pasture when visited by Layard (1853: 268–73), who claimed that, "from its mouth to its source, from [Circesium] to Ras-al-Ain, there is now no single permanent human habitation on the Khabour. Its rich meadows and its deserted ruins are alike become the encamping places of the wandering Arab" (Layard 1853: 284). Layard noticed abandoned canals, which have now been studied using aerial photographs and geomorphological investigations (Ergenzinger and Kühne 1991; Ergenzinger, Kühne, and Kurschner 1988).

The hollow way mapping program analyzed only the northern part of the salvage project area, and did not attempt to include the many visible remains of irrigation canals. Furthermore, the radial systems mapped by Van Liere and Lauffray on the south side of the Jebel Abd al-Aziz (e.g., around Tell Muazar; Poidebard 1934: pl. 133) were not investigated. Only Mission 1105 was employed, and hollow ways may therefore be underrepresented. In this and other steppic regions on the edges of the Upper Khabur basin, image analysis is made difficult by a lack of ground control and land-use conditions that differ dramatically from the more familiar areas of the central basin.

Within the floodplain, few if any unambiguous traces of former trackways can be discerned; most Bronze Age features were probably erased by irrigation systems of at least Iron Age date and later. Radial systems are absent, with the possible exception of the area west of Tell Melebiya, where several features can be traced as far as 5 km out into the steppe (fig. 7.11). At 2.5 ha, Melebiya is large by the standards of the Middle Khabur region. Major occupation was in the later third millennium B.C., with a smaller Islamic component (Lebeau 1993). Few hollow ways could be associated with its third-millennium contemporaries. The 4 ha Tell Bderi (Pfälzner 1988, 1990) might be connected to a pair of features on the steppe to the southeast. Isolated tracks appear to run toward Brak from Tell Rad Shaqrah and the two Kerma mounds.

Most preserved tracks marked longer-distance routes along the river and across the steppe toward other areas of settlement. West of the Melebiya–Bderi stretch of the Khabur River is a cluster of features generally oriented northwest to southeast; the northwestern terminus appears to have been the large site at Tell Majdal, but the destination along the Khabur River is not clear. On the left bank of the river, most features are associated with the site of Tell Tuneinir, and more specifically with its large medieval Islamic settlement (Fuller and Fuller 1987–88, 1994). Above and below the site, two parallel tracks mark shortcuts across the steppe around bends in the river. Tracks radiate into the eastern steppe in three directions. The shortest of the three can be traced for 4.5 km to the southeast, after which the terrain becomes undulating and ill-suited for feature preservation. It is tempting to connect this track with the route along the south side of the Jebel Jembe identified by Poidebard (1934: pl. 140), which led to the fortified site at al-Khan and then onto the Sinjar Plain.

The eastern track skirts the northern edge of the al-Hol marsh before arriving at the vicinity of Lake Khatuniya. This track was first noticed by Poidebard (1934: pl. 149) passing less than 100 m north of the small fortified site at Tulul Mughayr. The track's light signature differs from that of a typical hollow way and more closely resembles recent tracks. Nonetheless, its presence on Poidebard's photograph suggests some antiquity. Its light signature may have resulted from the clearance of stones from the path, a simple construction technique noted by Poidebard elsewhere in eastern Syria. The age of this feature is difficult to determine without ground control, but it is likely to have

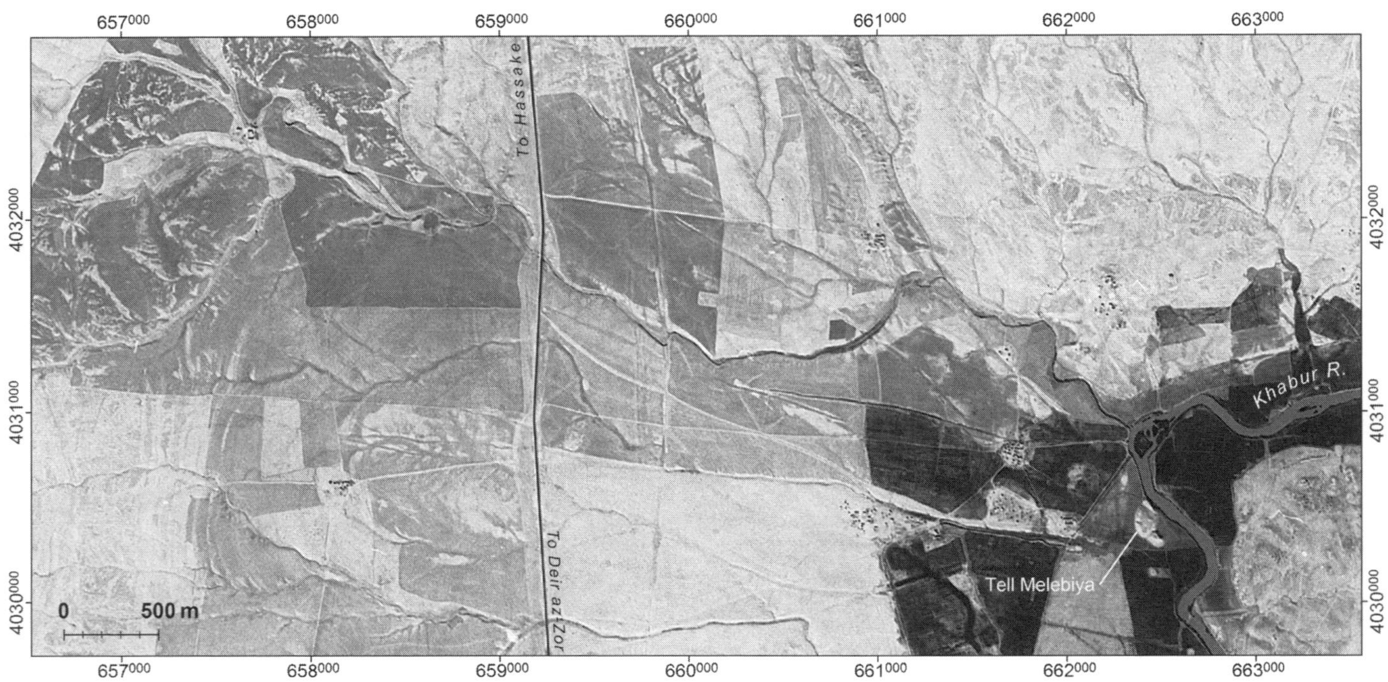

Figure 7.11. Hollow ways in the steppe west of Tell Melebiya in the Middle Khabur area (1105-1025DF060, 5 November 1968)

been used in many periods, including the twentieth century: it appears on the French 1:200,000 maps of 1945 as a "piste de 2ème classe." The present paved road between Khatuniya and Hassake runs only a few dozen meters to the south of this track for much of its preserved length.

The northeastern track runs directly across the steppe southeast of the Jebel Kaukab, in the direction of Tell Brak and presumably Nisibin beyond it. This track has a similar signature to the Khatuniya track, but survives in a far more fragmentary state. A probable fourth track ran to its west along the eastern edge of the Jebel Kaukab toward Tell Aswad (discussed in Section 7.3.3). This northern route has been a long-traveled one, and the ancient track is often difficult to discern from a series of spatially corresponding recent tracks.

7.3.7. THE PLAIN NORTH OF THE JEBEL SINJAR

The broad plain between the Radd marsh and the Jebel Sinjar is the least investigated archaeological region in the basin. Around al-Hol and Lake Khatuniya, Poidebard's aerial observations revealed complex palimpsests of open settlements, fortified structures, tracks and roads, irrigation canals, walls, and desert kites (see especially 1934: 152–54 and pl. 140). None of these sites and features have been subjected to intensive archaeological investigation in the modern era, although CORONA and QuickBird satellite coverage of the area suggests that it would be very fruitful to do so. On the Sinjar side of the modern border, Iraqi government excavations have been published only in a preliminary fashion (Altaweel 2006); on the Syrian side, little is known aside from the aerial observations of Van Liere and Lauffray (1954–55), although surveys around Brak (Wright et al. 2006–07) and Tell Leilan (Ristvet 2005; Weiss et al. 2002–03) soon will provide greater detail. The southeastern basin was one of the last areas to be recolonized by sedentary agriculturalists, and site and feature preservation appears to be very high.

The limits of hollow way preservation (and probably also formation) apparent in Van Liere and Lauffray's map could be generally confirmed, although the specific patterning derived from CORONA analysis had many differences. The east–west line of radial systems, including Tell Mosti and Tell Abu Khadhraf (fig. 7.12), are some of the clearest mapped by Van Liere and Lauffray and have been used in constructing models of third-millennium B.C. agricultural catchments (Wilkinson 1994: 493, fig. 8). The CORONA-based reassessment does not invalidate this model, but it does show a much greater complexity in the palimpsest of ancient trackways.

The area southeast of Tell Brak and south of the Wadi Radd preserves a dense concentration of hollow way features. The major radial systems around Tell Hanta, Tell Abu Jerada, and Tell Merchoudi were also recognized by Van Liere and Lauffray, but their degree of interconnection was underappreciated. Furthermore, there also exist several long alignments of tracks. One pair is aligned on Lake Khatuniya and originates from the Jaghjagh River at Kaka and Chouker. A second pair aims toward the corridor between the east end of the low Jebel Jeribe and the west end of the Jebel Sinjar, a major communication corridor in historical times (Oates and Oates 1990). Most of these features have the narrow morphology generally associated with the first millennium A.D. or later. Farther to the east are disconnected feature traces on north–south alignments, but many without obvious destinations on or beyond the Jebel, with the exception of the routes focused on its eastern end (see Section 7.3.1).

Figure 7.12. Radial hollow ways around Tell Abu Khadhraf and Tell Mosti (CORONA 1102-1025DF008-4, 11 December 1967). Note the precise gridding of the plain (squares 2,250 m per side, 506.25 ha) imposed at the time the southeastern basin was resettled by agriculturalists

CHAPTER 8

LANDSCAPES OF THE HAMOUKAR REGION THROUGH TIME

The preceding chapters describe the Hamoukar region, the methods employed by the THS in studying it, and the recovered sites and features in their spatial contexts. The survey region provides a focused window into northern Mesopotamian settlement history, but it must be remembered that it is a small and not always representative sample area within much broader interaction spheres. This final chapter contextualizes the results of the THS within larger historical and economic processes. The THS results make greater contributions for some periods than for others, and it is on these periods that the analysis below concentrates.

8.1. THE EXTENSIVE SETTLEMENT AT THS 25 AND THE LATE FIFTH MILLENNIUM IN THE THS REGION

In its initial millennia of settlement, the THS region hosted landscapes of small village settlements, patterns that agree with previous results from the North Jazira and the western Upper Khabur basin (Nieuwenhuyse 2000; Nieuwenhuyse and Wilkinson 2008; Wilkinson and Tucker 1995). The exception is the paucity of Period 3 (northern Ubaid) settlement, which remains difficult to explain.

The first radical divergence from previously documented patterns of settlement came in Period 4. In terms of the spatial distribution of surface materials (300 ha) and the very early date (Period 4; Late Chalcolithic 1–2, ca. 4400–3800 B.C.), THS 25 is at present a unique settlement in the prehistoric Near East. Uruk would not reach this size until the end of the fourth millennium (Finkbeiner 1991). Its contemporaries, such as Tepe Gawra and Tell Shelgiyya (Rothman 2002b; Ball 1997), hardly exceed 4 ha. The other sites in the THS and Iraqi North Jazira are most typical, overwhelmingly between 1 and 3 ha (see table 6.4; Lupton 1996: table C.4).

Comparisons based on scale alone are almost certainly inappropriate, however. CORONA imagery analysis, surface observations, and small soundings in its low outer areas (Wilkinson 2002a: 99–101; al-Quntar 2009) suggest that the site may have had a variable internal settlement density. The central mound appears to have been characterized by closely spaced mudbrick structures known from Gawra level XII (Rothman 2002b: fig. 3.6), which led to the mounding that characterizes it at present. The outer areas, however, lack such mounding and appear to have clusters of grayish anthropogenic soils separated by open and possibly unsettled areas (see fig. 4.12). This pattern may not be entirely unique; a similar pattern at a smaller spatial scale developed in the Late Chalcolithic 2 period at Tell Brak (Ur, Karsgaard, and Oates 2007) and might have existed at Tell al-Hawa as well (estimated at 33 ha in Lupton 1996: 127).

Interpretation of the survey and sounding data for THS 25 thus presents considerable challenges. Given the indirect but strong evidence for variable settlement density across the site, it would be inappropriate to apply the standard ratios of persons per hectare employed in the Near East to estimate its population. Two possible alternative interpretations are shifting non-permanent settlement (previously advocated by Gibson and colleagues [2002a: 12] and Wilkinson [2002a: 101]) or permanent but discontinuous settlement (Ur 2002b: 18–19). The two models are not mutually exclusive and convincing hybrid interpretations are possible.

Interpreted within the first model, THS 25 consisted of a substantial permanent settlement of approximately 30 ha (the central mounded area). Surrounding it was a vast area which was seasonally occupied by nomadic pastoralist groups. These groups may have arrived from the southern steppes for the summer months, or descended from the mountains to the north for the winter months. This model supposes shifting settlement through time; during the course of Period 4 settlement, returning groups would have occupied different parts of the outer area. Thus, the settlement signature on the ground (the extensive distribution of surface materials) and from a remote-sensing perspective (the pattern of soil discoloration visible in CORONA photographs) is a palimpsest resulting from several centuries or more of seasonal settlement in the same general area. The geographic position of the site on the Tigris-Euphrates watershed between large "conventional" settlements at Tell Brak and Tell al-Hawa may explain THS 25 as an intermediate meeting ground for mobile groups, perhaps for exchange or for religious or social gatherings (Wilkinson 2002a: 101).

Alternatively, the second model supposes permanent or at least semi-sedentary occupation of the central mounded complex and the outer zone. The central complex hosted the sort of dense and contiguous domestic and supra-domestic mudbrick architecture known from Tepe Gawra, among other places. The extensive outer area was also characterized by permanent settlement but of lower density. The patterns of soil discoloration imply spatially dispersed clusters of settlement; these might be interpreted as socially autonomous households or extended lineage groups who settled at the site for some combination of economic, political, or religious reasons, but who maintained some form of social or political independence through spatial separation. This intervening space was probably not vacant but rather held penned animals or garden crops. This latter pattern was common in Mesoamerica, where it was related to the intensity of agriculture (Drennan 1988). The dispersed Late Chalcolithic 2 settlement at Tell Brak has been interpreted in a similar fashion (Ur, Karsgaard, and Oates 2007).

It is not possible to evaluate these models fully from surface observations alone; therefore, the tentative interpretation presented here will certainly be revised by the results of the recently begun excavations on the site. There are, however, grounds for favoring a sedentary model of settlement over one that supposes shifting and seasonal reoccupation based on the evidence at hand. The discoloration seen in CORONA photographs is the result of several types of human activities, but the most significant factor is the presence of mudbrick architecture. Controlled comparison of CORONA reflectivity with that of multispectral sensors and geoarchaeological study of site sediments has demonstrated that decomposed mudbrick material makes the largest contribution to the lighter signature on panchromatic CORONA images; sites with other forms of architecture have a different signature (Wilkinson, Beck, and Philip 2006). The failure of the soundings excavated in 2000 to identify architecture is not surprising; more recent sites in the nearby Iraqi North Jazira were dramatically altered by soil formation processes (Wilkinson and Tucker 1995: 5–6, fig. 3). Furthermore, the density and form of surface ceramics does not suggest a low-density mobile population. Surface density is consistently very high (fig. 6.5), although it is possible that prior to the twentieth-century mechanization of agriculture, it had a spatial variability similar to the soil discoloration (fig. 4.12). This rate of ceramic consumption seems to be greatly in excess of that of ethnographically known non-sedentary groups. The vessel forms found in the surface assemblage included significant quantities of large storage jars, for example the T4/4 double-rimmed jar, the T4/5 flaring jar rim, the T4/8 deep straight-sided urn, and the T4/9 internally hollowed rim. The double-rimmed jar and straight-sided urn in particular are far too large for seasonal movement (see the whole examples from Tepe Gawra in Tobler 1950) and, in general, this assemblage seems to be more characteristic of sedentary agriculturalists who stored resources rather than following them according to seasonal availability. Finally, the initial appearance of Near Eastern transhumance is still a matter of debate (Cribb 1991; Alizadeh 2004; Abdi 2003). It remains to be established that such a model is not anachronistic for the late fifth millennium B.C., a time prior to the domestication of the donkey (Rossel et al. 2008) and millennia before camels enabled the long-distance migrations typical of beduin.

Based on the evidence available at present, THS 25 is best interpreted as a primarily sedentary settlement consisting of a central core zone of dense mudbrick architecture surrounded by an extensive area of low-density clusters of households. Semi-sedentary occupation of the outer areas remains a possibility, but since settlement was characterized by mudbrick architecture, storage of cereals, and intensive lithic production (Khalidi, Gratuze, and Boucetta 2009), a shifting pattern of reoccupation seems unlikely. The unique settlement at THS 25 emerged immediately prior to the appearance of the first unequivocal urban center in northern Mesopotamia at Tell Brak (Ur, Karsgaard, and Oates 2007; Oates et al. 2007), which, during its initial growth, had a dispersed spatial pattern similar to that of THS 25. At these sites, we may be seeing an initial impetus toward population agglomeration in which groups are motivated to aggregate, but prior to the emergence of the social structures that enabled the dense nucleation of the cities of the third millennium B.C. and later. It appears that the inhabitants of Brak were ultimately able to resolve these conflicting fission and fusion tendencies in the early to mid-fourth millennium (Late Chalcolithic 3–4). For unknown reasons, the earlier experiment at THS 25 was not successful; the outer areas (and possibly the central mounded complex as well) were abandoned during or at the end of the Late Chalcolithic 2 period. Sedentary occupation, now in a spatially smaller and presumably nucleated form, shifted north to Hamoukar.

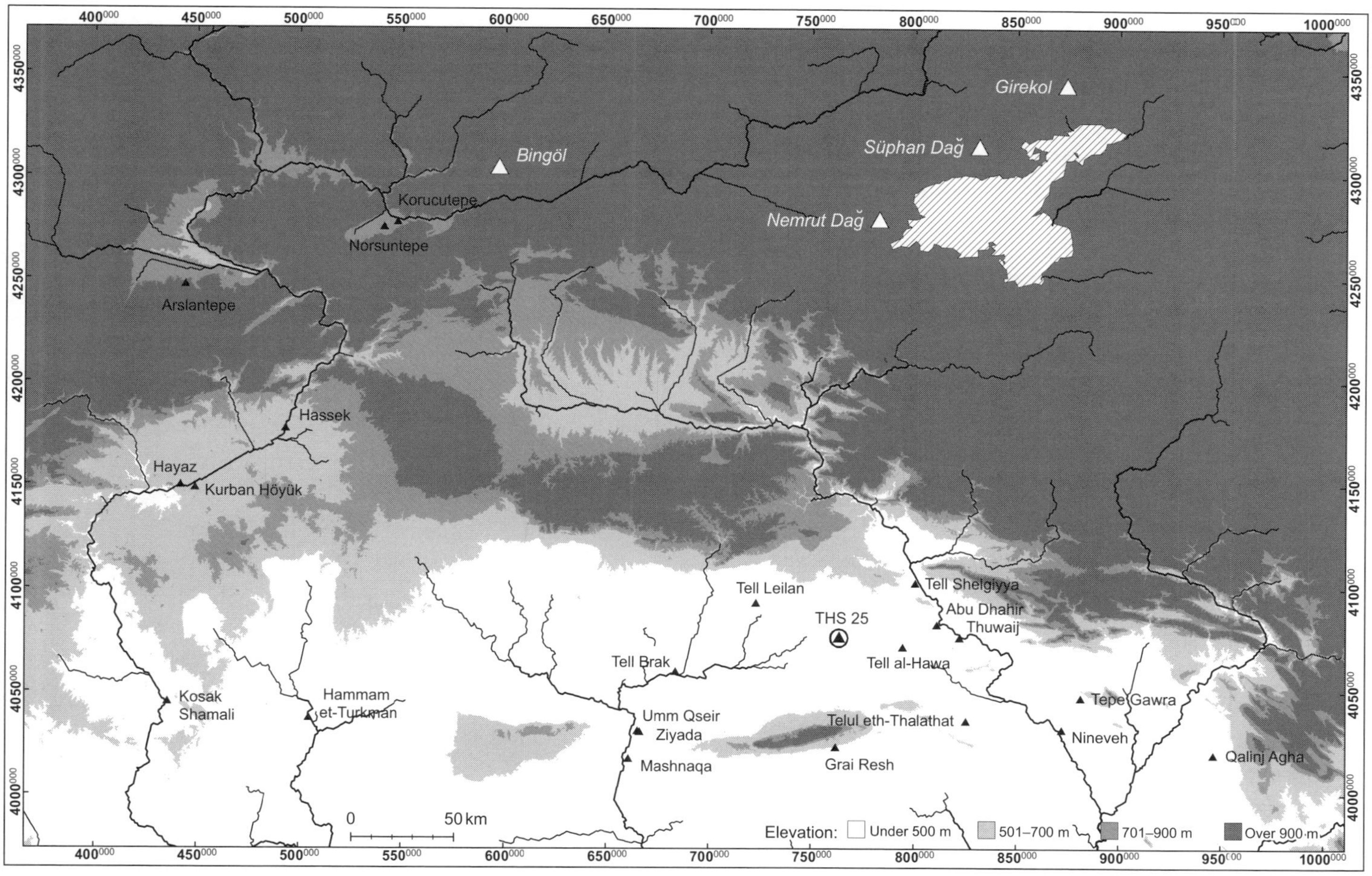

Figure 8.1. Period 4 sites in northern Mesopotamia

The forces that motivated the movement of groups into the THS 25 area can only be hypothesized, but it is likely that economic forces were significant. The surface of the site is covered by dense obsidian cores, manufacturing debris, and tools. The nearest obsidian sources are over 150 km distant at Bingöl and Nemrut Dağ (fig. 8.1). Given the broad distribution of material across the outer areas, the organization of obsidian trade and tool manufacture was not likely to have been highly centralized. Preliminary observation of use wear suggests that some tools were used locally for harvesting, but the sheer quantity of cores, blades, and debris rules out the use of obsidian merely for local consumption (Khalidi and al-Quntar 2008; Khalidi, Gratuze, and Boucetta 2009). Existing models of obsidian trade favor a "trickle trade" model, but the evidence from THS 25 indicates at least one center of manufacturing and redistribution located a great distance from the nearest source area.

8.2. HAMOUKAR'S PLACE IN THE URUK EXPANSION

An important issue, and one that cannot be solved through study of surface assemblages, concerns interpretation of sites as southern Uruk colonial enclaves or outposts, loci of exchange, or places where indigenous persons were emulating southern material culture (Stein 2000). The surface sherds come from ceramics of southern Mesopotamian type; however, their place of origin (manufactured in the south, or locally produced) cannot be determined macroscopically, nor can the ethnicity or place of origin of their consumers be identified. The pots may have arrived in these villages from afar as trade goods or their containers, to be consumed by the indigenous populations, or they might have been used by southern colonists who preferred to maintain a household inventory in the styles of their geographic homeland. To complicate matters further, there is no reason why the origins of the ceramics, and of the population consuming them, had to be identical at each site. For example, one might hypothesize that an ethnically southern community at Hamoukar traded vessels with the local northern Mesopotamians living at THS 40 (Khirbat Melhem). The resulting surface assemblage might differ only in the abundance of southern versus local ceramic types. If local potters were emulating the southern Mesopotamian styles, even this variable would be meaningless. These issues require high-resolution excavation data for a range of social and economic activities (e.g., Stein 2000).

We can, however, propose questions based on survey data. The relationship between Hamoukar (THS 1) and THS 2 is of particular interest. THS 2 is a small low mound only 200 m north of Hamoukar's high mound (fig. 6.12). The intervening space was unoccupied. Thus the large and preexisting settlement at Hamoukar developed a close but spatially discrete satellite, a pattern found elsewhere in the Upper Khabur basin in the fourth millennium at Tell Brak (Ur, Karsgaard, and Oates 2007). Spatial segregation at THS 2 raises questions about the presence and integration of a non-indigenous community. For example, did a small group of southerners establish a *kārum*-like settlement close to, but separate from, a large indigenous town? In this scenario, the southern Uruk ceramics on Hamoukar's high mound would signify trade or emulation, rather than the presence of southerners.

THS 40 was the second supra-village site with both Period 5a and 5b assemblages, but whose morphology suggests a divergent settlement history from Hamoukar within the fourth millennium. At 8.57 ha, THS 40 was just over half the size of Hamoukar (15.31 ha), but more than twice the size of any of the other Period 5a–5b settlements in the THS region. Unlike Hamoukar, the bulk of whose 18 m tell derives from the fourth millennium, THS 40 is a mostly flat site; the mounded area (Areas A–D) can probably be attributed to the later Iron Age (Period 11) village and Abbasid (Period 17) farmstead. THS 40 was thus an extensive but short-lived settlement founded on previously unoccupied land. If the drooping spouts (T5a/3) can be used as a chronological indicator, the site originated late in the fourth millennium, when Hamoukar had already grown to a substantial town 6 km to the northeast. Based on its apparently short duration, high density of southern pottery types, and foundation on *terra nova,* it is tempting to interpret it as a intrusive colony; indeed, THS 40, along with the oddly segregated satellite at THS 2, may have been the settlements of non-indigenous communities. The surface assemblage inspires compelling hypotheses, but these require excavation before conclusions can be drawn.

In the first synthesis of the Uruk Expansion by Guillermo Algaze (1989, 1993), a southern presence could only be recognized in isolation at Tell Brak and Nineveh; now it can be demostrated that the eastern Upper Khabur basin supported one of the highest densities of settlements with non-local Uruk ceramics recognized at present. Although more sites can be characterized as purely local than have evidence of an Uruk colonial presence (12 of 17 sites of Period 5), Uruk ceramics covered the two largest sites and a greater total area (28.1 out of 47.8 ha; see table 6.5). In the Iraqi North Jazira, seven sites with major southern Uruk occupation totalled 49.7 ha (Wilkinson and Tucker 1995: 43–45, fig. 35). Taken together, the THS and North Jazira Project areas include 77.8 ha of Period 5a settlement in 600 sq. km. By comparison, the Middle Euphrates, the best-studied locus of southern colonization, hosted an estimated 36.5 ha of intrusive settlement in an area of approximately 115 sq. km (about 15 km north to south in a 5–10 km wide floodplain; Lupton 1996: 54–56). An additional seven sites ranging between 1.4 and 4.4 ha fall within the limits of the 1987 Tell Leilan Survey (Stein and Wattenmaker 1989). The eastern Upper Khabur basin thus contains more than double the settled area of the Middle Euphrates cluster, although at a lower density. Whether this surface assemblage represents colonization, exchange, or emulation remains to be determined, but at minimum it can be said that northeastern Syria was heavily involved in the supra-regional interactions of the mid- to late fourth millennium.

8.3. HAMOUKAR AND ITS REGION IN THE MID- TO LATE THIRD MILLENNIUM

8.3.1. HAMOUKAR'S PLACE IN THE NORTHERN MESOPOTAMIAN URBAN SYSTEM

The results of the systematic surface collection demonstrate that Hamoukar was the largest city in the eastern Upper Khabur basin in the mid- to late third millennium (Period 7), and one of the largest centers in the dry-farming zone of northern Mesopotamia (fig. 8.2, table 8.1). Of its 105 ha mounded area, 98 ha appear to have been densely settled; the surface of 7 ha of the high mound had no Period 7 ceramic material. This area may have been kept deliberately vacant of structures, perhaps because it was reserved for large institutional households such as those known from Tell Beydar (Lebeau and Suleiman 2003) and Tell Brak Areas FS and SS (Oates, Oates, and McDonald 2001).

In comparing the sizes of the major urban centers, one notable point is that the major known political capitals were by no means the largest sites. The emerging pre-Akkadian geopolitical picture makes it clear that the three major kingdoms were centered on Ebla (Tell Mardikh), Nagar (Tell Brak), and Mari (Tell Hariri); wars were fought, luxury goods exchanged, and diplomatic marriages arranged between elites based in these capitals (Archi and Biga 2003; Archi 1998; Biga 1998; Sallaberger 2007). Yet spatially, Mardikh and Brak fall in the second tier of Period 7 urban centers. Any reconstruction of later third-millennium political entities that equates site size with position within a political hierarchy would place Tell Mozan, Tell Taya, and Hamoukar at the pinnacle of power.

It must be remembered, however, that the Mari-Ebla-Nagar tripartite political division is known from texts that only cover a span of a few generations prior to the Akkadian military campaigns in the area. The Period 7 phase of urbanism in northern Mesopotamia extends over half a millennium, so this political arrangement may not have described earlier or later phases of the later third millennium. Tell Mozan (ancient Urkesh), for example, probably attained its power in Akkadian and post-Akkadian times (Buccellati and Kelly-Buccellati 2002; Steinkeller 1998), and future discoveries may prove these other places to have assumed political centrality at times. At present, however, these spatial data suggest caution when equating site size and political hierarchy.

8.3.2. THE SUBSISTENCE ECONOMY OF HAMOUKAR

Mid- to late third-millennium Hamoukar was associated with a particularly rich array of off-site features. Taken together, they represent a well-preserved archaeological landscape; indeed, the Period 7 landscape of the Upper Khabur basin and adjacent North Jazira may be the best-preserved Bronze Age landscape in the Near East, outside of the arid desert zones (see *Chapter 7*). These features allow reconstructions of the staple economy that could not be attempted for other periods of settlement.

Hamoukar's size placed it at the limits of settlement sustainability under the conditions of dry-farming agriculture (Wilkinson 1994). An important variable in establishing these limits has to do with the distribution of agricultural labor, and it is in this regard that the eight trace or non-permanent Period 7 sites may have been significant. They can be interpreted in several ways. In general, low sherd density suggests an ephemeral occupation in which relatively few ceramics were consumed. Similarly structured surface assemblages of the early second millennium were found on small sites along the Khabur River, where they were interpreted as the traces of occupation by non-sedentary nomads (Lyonnet 1996a: 371–72). Alternatively, these places may have been seasonal encampments of agricultural laborers. These people could be envisioned as hired wage laborers (almost certainly an anachronistic term at this point in history) or entire families who lived in temporary structures or tents during certain labor-intensive points in the agricultural calendar (i.e., field preparation and harvesting).

Either interpretation describes a spatial distribution of persons that would have ameliorated labor stress on the subsistence economy at the height of Hamoukar's urban growth. Wilkinson's model of urban staple economy (1994, based on Chisholm 1962) assumes that farmers will not travel beyond five kilometers from their homes to their fields; therefore if all were based within the city itself, Hamoukar's maximum territory would require 2,620 persons to be fully cultivated. If half of Hamoukar's population were able-bodied laborers, it would have had an under-utilized agricultural labor force of at least 2,380 persons.[9] Temporary camps for Hamoukar-based agricultural workers would have expanded the agricultural territory of the city by locating some of its labor more efficiently on a seasonal basis. Of course other nucleated satellites certainly existed beyond Hamoukar's theoretical 5 km territorial maximum (probably at Tell Antar and Tell Taif), but these smaller sites (with correspondingly smaller populations) may have been experiencing labor shortages (Wilkinson 1994: 502–03). The temporary emplacement of Hamoukar-

[9] Assuming a population of at least 10,000. Able-bodied agricultural laborers would number 5,000, of which 2,620 would be required within the territory of 5 km. Thus at least 2,380 persons were "surplus labor." If Liverani (1994) is correct that a much higher percentage of the population was engaged in agriculture, then this surplus figure would need to be increased proportionally. Note that studies of urban-based agriculture on the irrigated southern plains assume much smaller proportions of agricultural labor.

Table 8.1. Comparative sizes of Period 7 urban sites in northern Mesopotamia

Period 7 Site	*Area (ha)*	*Area Source*
Tell Mozan (Urkesh)	120	Buccellati and Kelly-Buccellati (1999: 15, figs. 3, 5)
Tell Taya	95–155	Reade (1997); area of anthropogenic discoloration on QuickBird imagery is approximately 95 ha
Hamoukar	98	1999 Field Survey (see fig. 6.15)
Kazane Höyük	90	Wattenmaker (1997: 82); measured from CORONA and QuickBird imagery
Tell Leilan (Šehna)	90	Weiss (1986: 95)
Tell Hadhail	90	Weiss (1983: fig. 11)
Tell Khoshi	78	Kepinski-Lecomte (2001); measurement of mounded area on Landsat imagery
Tell Brak (Nagar)	70	Preliminary estimate from field survey 2003–2006 (Ur in press)
Tell al-Hawa	66	Ball, Tucker, and Wilkinson (1989: 34, fig. 9)
Tell Mardikh (Ebla)	65	Measurement of mounded area on QuickBird imagery
Tell Chuera	65	Orthmann (1997)
Tilbeşar	56	Kepinski (Kepinski 2007), measurement of mounded area on QuickBird imagery
Tell Mohammed Diyab	50	Lyonnet (1990: 74) and Nicolle (2006: 8, figs. 1–9)
Titriş Höyük	43	Matney and Algaze (1995: 33)
Tell Farfara	40	Ristvet (2005: 60–61)

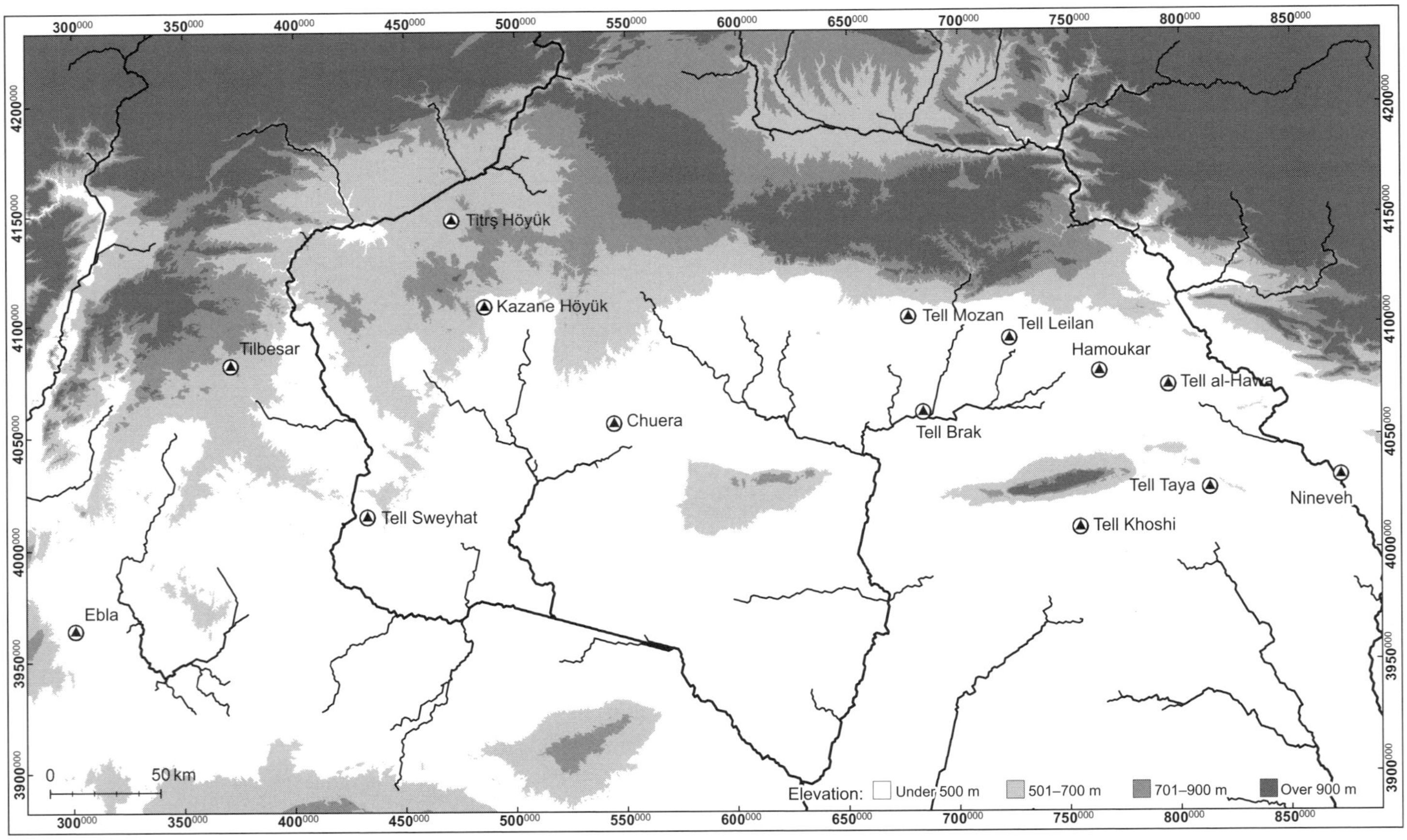

Figure 8.2. Period 7 urban places in northern Mesopotamia

based surplus labor within or at the edge of their own agricultural territories would have allowed these neighboring settlements to cultivate more land and also may have provided in-field locations for processing and transportation of their surplus cereals back to Hamoukar.

Seasonally present nomadic groups would have had a different set of relationships to the sedentary populations, but could have also solved problems of agricultural labor. Indeed, the presence of pastoral nomads might have been welcomed not only because of the opportunities for exchange in animal and other products, but also because of the nomads' potential as temporary agricultural workers. These small settlements might represent both seasonally present pastoralists and temporary laborer camps. In an urban hinterland such as Hamoukar's, the latter would represent a more efficient use of locally available labor; however, we have no way of knowing if "full employment" was a valued economic condition in the third millennium B.C.

It might be suggested that evidence for an even wider distribution of population exists in the form of field scatters. If these ephemeral sherd scatters are interpreted as settlement, even on a temporary basis, it could be possible that other areas of low-density sherds, which have been interpreted as the traces of manuring, also might have derived from similar settlement (see especially comments to Wilkinson 1994). This scenario is unlikely, because the definition of a site involves more variables than sherd density alone (reviewed in Section 4.4.2). Low-density scatters of small, highly abraded sherds recovered from unmounded areas of reddish brown soils were interpreted as field scatter. Scatters of larger sherds exhibiting similar low density but also fresh breaks almost always occurred in association with areas of mounding and grayish anthropogenic soils. Despite the low sherd density, the other two variables still suggest ancient settlement. Even the emerging dispersed pattern of in-field houses visible in the THS region today (see Section 6.11) would produce a clustered distribution of surface artifacts which would stand in stark contrast to the gradual shifts in density of the near-continuous carpet of surface artifacts (see Section 5.2).

8.3.3. LAND TENURE AND AGRICULTURAL INTENSIFICATION

As the largest urban center in the eastern basin, Hamoukar's large and nucleated population would have placed a heavy demand on its subsistence economy. The physical manifestations of these demands survive as hollow ways and field scatters. The radial patterns of hollow ways found around Period 7 (mid- to late third-millennium B.C.) settlements in the THS area and throughout the basin are primarily the products of their agricultural and pastoral economies. A large percentage simply fades out, generally between 3 and 5 km from the site; these roads that "go nowhere" conveyed farmers and plow animals out to their fields, and brought its yields back into the settlement. Sheep and goats were at least as important, if not more so, for the formation of hollow ways. As they were led through the cultivated zone to the pastures beyond, their feet were responsible for most of the surface disturbance that lowered the track. These farmers and their animals did not choose to traverse these sunken paths for reasons of efficiency; in the wet season, they were muddy and difficult. Rather, they used these paths because their movements were constrained by the presence of agricultural fields to either side (Ur 2009). Thus, in general, radial hollow ways can serve as proxy indicators for the zone of ancient cultivation and long-term patterns of land tenure; the terminal ends or fade-out points mark the interface between the arable zone and the pasture beyond (Wilkinson 1994: 492–93). A study of hollow way-defined catchments around Tell Beydar (Ur and Wilkinson 2008) demonstrated a small self-sufficient regional agricultural system: most Period 7 sites were cultivating more area than was necessary to sustain their populations, with the exception of the largest center, Tell Beydar, which would have need to import some of the surplus products of its hinterland.

An attempt to define a hollow way catchment for Hamoukar using these principles produces a 5,202 ha territory (fig. 8.3). This territory extends almost a full 5 km to the southwest, 3–4 km to the east and north, and a mere 1.4 km to the northwest.[10] Because later irrigation systems may have impacted hollow way survival (see Section 5.4), the territory may have extended farther to the northeast and particularly to the northwest.

This empirically based estimate of Hamoukar's agricultural catchment can be compared to a theoretical sustaining area derived from population estimation. Ninety-eight of Hamoukar's 105 ha were settled in Period 7, so its population may have ranged between 9,800 (assuming 100 persons/ha) and 19,600 (assuming 200 persons/ha). If

[10] Note that this territory includes the 300 ha of Khirbat al-Fakhar (THS 25). The proximity of this extensive low-mounded site makes it certain that it was subjected to cultivation along with the rest of Hamoukar's hinterland.

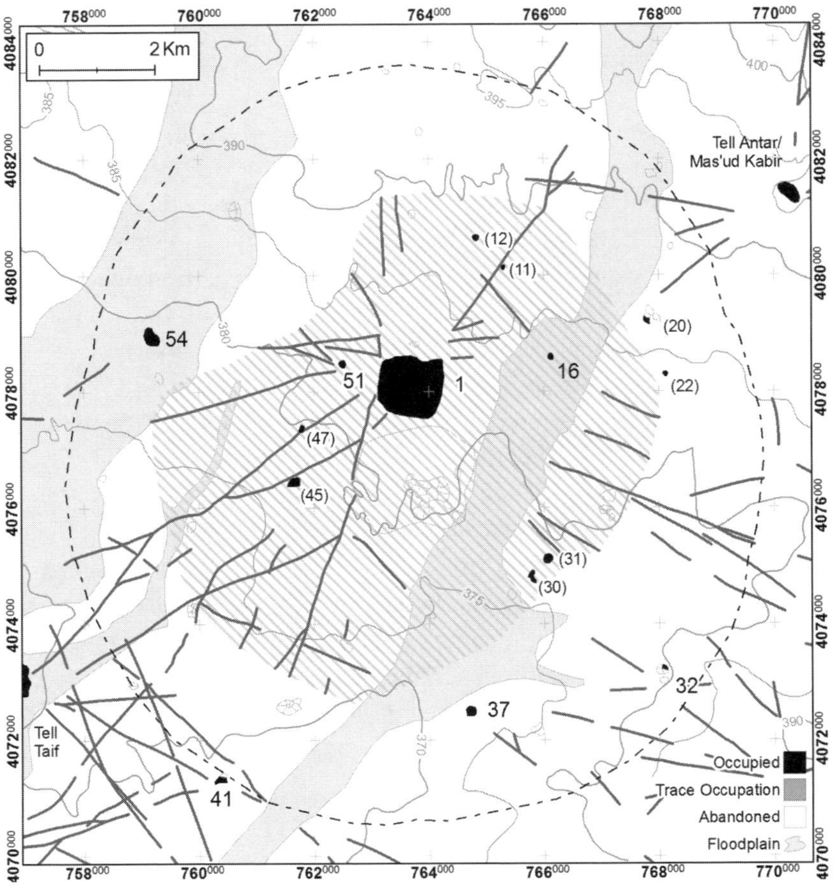

Figure 8.3. Hamoukar's Period 7 agricultural catchment as derived from fading hollow ways

each consumed 250 kg of cereals annually, a hectare yielded 500 kg, and fields were fallowed biennially, Hamoukar's farmers would have had to cultivate between 9,800 and 19,600 ha each year. Using the lower (and more probable) figure based on a density of 100 persons per ha, Hamoukar's agricultural territory as defined by hollow ways only accounts for 53 percent of that area. If fallow were violated, the inhabitants would have required cultivation of only 4,900 ha, which is 302 ha less than Hamoukar's hollow way catchment. For comparative purposes, the entire 125 sq. km area of the THS region is 12,509 ha, so if all land was fully utilized, Hamoukar would be able to sustain its population. The labor for full cultivation was available locally at Hamoukar, but was inefficiently concentrated at that site. In this light it is interesting that four of the proposed temporary agricultural settlements (THS 20, 22, 31, and 30) sit on the eastern edge of the hollow way-derived catchment (see fig. 8.3).

Wilkinson's model (1994, 1997) predicts that deficits in the center would be compensated for by surpluses at nearby satellites. Unfortunately, the THS permit only allowed the immediate hinterland of Hamoukar to be collected. Therefore, Hamoukar's major satellite settlements remain unknown. It might be proposed, based on the presence of hollow ways, that sites like Tell Antar, Tell Taif, or even Tell Rumaylan may have been such satellites (see fig. 6.18). Future fieldwork might reveal a similar settlement system along the Wadi Rumaylan, the surplus production of which might have sustained Hamoukar.

Cultivators at Hamoukar may have been tempted to forgo the fallow year in pursuit of short-term gains in production. Some evidence for violation of fallow can be found in the presence of hollow ways. The constraints of agricultural fields were crucial to their formation. Agriculture has been economically important since the earliest-known settlement in the basin, but the majority of broad features appear to have formed during a window of 1,500 years between the late fourth millennium and the early second millennium. During this time, hollow way formation was not limited to major urban centers; sites as small as 1 ha have elaborate radial patterns associated with them. Why, then, do tracks from other times not survive? Obviously, many factors go into the formation of hollow ways, but the intensity of cultivation is what set this time period apart (Ur 2009; Ur and Colantoni 2010; Ur and Wilkinson 2008). Under low-intensity cultivation, with half the fields lying fallow, there would have been many opportunities for humans and animals to move about without damaging crops; however, if cultivation was intensive, with few fallow fields, more traffic would have been constrained to the spaces between them, and the processes of disturbance and compaction would have been similarly intensified. Although other factors must be accounted for, such as duration of use and the quantity and intensity of traffic, the quantity of hollow ways dated to a given period might be an indicator of violation of fallow on a scale not seen before or since.

Full cultivation without fallow will result in a short-term increase in yields, but it is not a sustainable strategy (Gibson 1974). If all fields were cultivated, the agricultural territory in figure 8.3 would have sustained Hamoukar's population for a time, until the depletion of nutrients began to take a toll on yields. One method for ameliorating this nutrient loss would have been through manuring, which was practiced intensively around Hamoukar (see Section 5.2). At Hamoukar, as at Tell al-Hawa, manuring was one component of a strategy of agricultural intensification which ultimately enabled large nucleated populations to be sustained, for a time at least.

Even with manuring to return nutrients to the soil, annual cropping still produces declining yields through time, due to the depletion of soil moisture reserves. A recent settlement study in the Wadi al-Hasa of Jordan concluded that the abandonment and failure to resettle an area can be best explained by human-caused soil degradation (Hill 2004). The core of the THS region remained abandoned by sedentary agriculturalists long after other areas had been resettled (see Section 8.4.1 below).

These figures are based on an annual yield of 500 kg/ha, with the intention of showing the economic functioning under assumed typical conditions. However, yield is heavily dependent on the timing and quantity of rainfall each season, and a more dynamic model would have to take into account the high interannual variability in rainfall in northern Mesopotamia (for the initial results of such dynamic agent-based models for northern Mesopotamia, see Wilkinson et al. 2007a, 2007b). Five hundred kilograms was chosen here as an average value; wet seasons would certainly produce higher yields and drier seasons would produce less if not fail altogether. Catastrophic events (Weiss and Courty 1993; Weiss et al. 1993) or a run of dry years (Wilkinson 1994, 1997) might result in low yields or widespread crop failure. Hamoukar was either heavily reliant on surpluses from satellites beyond the THS region or was using short-term production strategies, which result in a fragile system that is poorly equipped to handle such fluctuations.

The previous discussion has focused almost exclusively on agriculture, which is particularly amenable to modeling; however, the economic importance of sheep and goats in the mid- to late third millennium is well documented through zooarchaeology (Zeder 2003) and ancient texts (Sallaberger 2004; Van Lerberghe 1996; Widell 2004). A particular onager-donkey hybrid (kúnga in Sumerian) was especially important for trade in the region (Archi 1998; Weber 2006). It could be suggested that livestock are the key to understanding the apparent huge agricultural surpluses in the western Khabur basin: rather than feeding people, these surpluses (see table 5.1) may have been intended, at least in part, as fodder for settlement-based herds (Danti 2000). Some clues are beginning to emerge for the presence of animals within settlements; for example, an open space near the palace at Tell Beydar was covered with the footprints of sheep (Sténuit and Van der Stede 2003: 226–27). This proposition must be further tested with new excavation methods designed to detect the presence of animals within settlements (for example, soil micromorphology and the study of micro-debitage; W. Matthews 2003; Rainville 2003).

8.3.4. AKKADIAN IMPERIAL CONTROL

In some reconstructions of late third-millennium society, the military intervention of the southern Mesopotamian-based Akkadian empire plays an important role, not only in catalyzing political and economic changes (Weiss and Courty 1993), but even in the top-down rearrangement of settlement demographics under the Akkadian ruler (Weiss 1992). Despite the frequency with which the Akkadian conquest is invoked as the cause of major transitions in the archaeological literature, it is not assigned that position in the analysis of THS area settlement and society. There are two reasons for this omission.

Site surface assemblages, which are the primary datasets employed here, are simply incapable of resolving short-lived politically defined time periods, let alone the vestiges of that political control. Potters are rarely if ever attached directly to ruling households, so there is no reason to expect ceramic styles to change with the rise and fall of political dynasties. The only type proposed to be an imperial bureaucratic tool, the "sila bowl" (Senior and Weiss 1992), occurs in levels earlier than the Naram-Sin building at Tell Brak and therefore cannot be exclusive to Akkadian rule (Oates 2001b: 182–83, 193). In the THS area, the processes of urban growth and land-use intensification appear to have begun before and continued after the phase of Akkadian political and military intervention.

More generally, there is good reason to look more closely at the evidence for the nature and duration of Akkadian "imperialization." At present, evidence for durable control over northern Mesopotamia is surprisingly slight, given its prominent position in archaeological narratives. The royal inscriptions, mostly second-millennium copies, describe conquest, destruction, and plunder; political incorporation and administration are rare or omitted. Archaeologically, there is the monumental structure with bricks stamped with the name of Naram-Sin at Tell Brak, which contained a handful of administrative tablets, but no identified living floors (Oates and Oates 2001a). However, it is important to recognize that political entities need not endure as long as their monuments. For example, the cities of eastern Europe are filled with large Soviet-built administrative buildings that are still in use and will be for generations to come. Naram-Sin controlled Nagar at some point, but without further evidence we cannot be sure if it was for a generation, a decade, or a year. Other evidence, such as inscribed votive objects and even the presence of royal daughters, speaks to interregional exchange and diplomacy, but in themselves are not evidence of control. Finally, the term "Akkadian" is often applied haphazardly to objects and sites that are thought to be contemporary with this proposed political control, but are not themselves ethnically, geographically, or politically Akkadian. A detailed review of the archaeological and epigraphic evidence for an Akkadian imperial presence in northern Mesopotamia would find that it rests at present on rather flimsy archaeological grounds and places too much faith in straightforward readings of propagandistic royal inscriptions.

8.3.5. HAMOUKAR'S ANCIENT NAME

It seems inconceivable that a city of Hamoukar's size would have remained unmentioned in contemporary written sources from Ebla or the cities of southern Mesopotamia. Based on scale alone, Van Liere (1963: 120) proposed an identification with Waššukanni, the Mitanni capital, but the absence of any surface evidence for Late Bronze Age occupation at the site renders this suggestion untenable. In the preliminary publication of the Hamoukar survey, an identification with Azuhinum was proposed (Ur 2002a: 71). The conquest of this place, and the defeat of its Hurrian-named ruler Tahiš-atal, was an event considered momentous enough by Naram-Sin to be commemorated in a year name: "The year (when) Naram-Sin won a battle against Subartu in Azuhinum (and) captured Tahiš-atal" (Gelb and Kienast 1990: 51–52; translation after Steinkeller 1998: n. 54). In Steinkeller's reconstruction of the route of Naram-Sin's army, this battle took place somewhere between Urkesh (Tell Mozan) and the Tigris River. The identification of Azuhinum with Hamoukar was based on the assumption that the Middle Bronze Age town of of the same name was a separate place near Nuzi (see references in Fincke 1993). However, a Middle Bronze Age town called Azuhinum existed close enough to Tell al-Rimah that cereals could be transported via donkey between the two places (Dalley, Walker, and Hawkins 1976: no. 145). Indeed, it was a major town in the kingdom of Shubartum, a polity north of the Jebel Iskhaft and between the Tigris and the Wadi Radd (Charpin 1992: 101). Without any trace of Khabur/Old Babylonian (Period 8) occupation, Hamoukar cannot be Azuhinum, which is more likely to be found at Tell al-Hawa, a city of 66 ha at this time (Ur 2002a: 71; Forlanini 2006: 153). Hamoukar's ancient identity remains unclear.

8.3.6. THE END OF URBAN SETTLEMENT AT HAMOUKAR AND CIVILIZATIONAL "COLLAPSE"

The Period 7 cities of northern Mesopotamia all underwent dramatic changes around the end of the third millennium B.C. (reviewed in Ur 2010a). One hypothesized explanation for this transition is the effects of an abrupt and extreme climatic event, variously described as volcanic in origin (Weiss et al. 1993; Weiss and Courty 1993) or the result of an extraterrestrial impact event (Courty 1998, 1999, 2001). This event, whatever its nature may have been, supposedly precipitated the collapse of Akkadian imperial control of northern Mesopotamia and resulted in the complete sedentary abandonment of the Upper Khabur basin. Most recently, its effects are supposed to have caused the synchronous collapse of neighboring civilizations in the Aegean, Egypt, Iran, and the Indus as well (Weiss 2000).

The evidence from Hamoukar and its region complicates this picture of climatically driven simultaneous deurbanization. Excavations in the final occupation phase of the Period 7 lower town in Areas C and H at Hamoukar show signs of violence and looting, with deliberately smashed vessels and partially articulated human remains lying on floors (Gibson et al. 2002a: 23; Ur and Colantoni 2010; Colantoni and Ur in press). The abandonment or reduction of Hamoukar should be placed within the pattern of interpolity conflict *within* greater northern Mesopotamia, which is being revealed by closer scrutiny of textual records (Sallaberger 2007; Archi and Biga 2003).

Hamoukar's abandonment also appears to occur after the abandonment of Tell Leilan. Improvements in the ceramic chronology of the later third millennium permit the identification of several distinct post-Akkadian ceramic forms, one of which (T7/4 comb-incised decoration) has proven to be useful as a survey diagnostic (see Section B.2.8). The distribution of this type across the surface of Hamoukar's lower town strongly suggests that the city persevered longer than Leilan, a city only 43 km distant from Hamoukar, but where no post-Akkadian ceramics are to be found (Weiss et al. 2002–03: 68). Furthermore, Hamoukar's permanent satellites also appear to have survived; surface collections from all of them included T7/4 comb-incised sherds.

On present chronological evidence, Hamoukar remained settled and urbanized into the post-Akkadian period, as did its hinterland. The variability in the timing of urban collapse in the Upper Khabur basin thus matches the nonsynchronous abandonments of sites along the Euphrates to the west (Kuzucuoğlu and Marro 2007). Indeed, recent reviews of the evidence (Schwartz 2007; Koliński 2007) demonstrate substantial variability in the timing of settlement abandonment in all regions of northern Mesopotamia and western Syria.

Nonetheless, none of the Period 7 cities of northern Mesopotamia emerged into the Middle Bronze Age unchanged. The variability in timing of site abandonments argues against a single precipitating climatic event, but climatic conditions still may have played a role. The intensity of the agricultural economy rendered it highly susceptible to even short-term climatic changes such as the multi-year droughts known in the last century (see, e.g., the variability in fig. 2.6). In such a case, responsibility for a collapse would be shared by the climatic shifts and the human societies that overextended their economies. Some Period 7 urban places may have had more overextended agricultural systems than others, which would be one possible explanation for variable timing of collapse in the face of a region-wide run of dry years. Drought and violence could be closely linked: dangerously low stores in one city could inspire attempts to seize the harvests of another. However, this scenario is still ultimately driven by climate, and it should be remembered that human communities routinely turn to violence for entirely political or ideological reasons.

Whatever drove this dramatic settlement reorganization, it could not have resulted in a complete year-round abandonment of the basin. Landscape memory is demonstrated by continuity of place names across this boundary. The Akkadian-period personnel list from Tell Brak (Eidem, Finkel, and Bonechi 2001: 106–07 no. 12) lists a number of presumably dependent towns in the region. After the resettlement, only one of these places is not mentioned in the tablets of the Middle Bronze Age (Charpin 1987: 132; Koliński 2007: 354). For these places to retain their names, some settlement must have survived the "collapse," or at a minimum, the basin must have been the domain of pastoral nomads who were likely descendants of the former agriculturalists. With the reappearance of written records in the early second millennium, such groups became the politically and economically dominant force (Durand 2004, Fleming 2004).

8.4. MIDDLE BRONZE AGE ECONOMY AND SOCIETY

The transition between the urbanism of the later third millennium and the wholly new pattern of small sites and mostly vacant Middle Bronze Age capitals now appears to have been highly variable in time and space. This transition has been characterized as the abandonment of the entire plain accompanied by a massive migration to the irrigated zone of southern Mesopotamia, and the return of sedentary occupation has been correlated with climatic amelioration (Weiss et al. 1993). However, it is clear that the basin was never abandoned by pastoral nomadic groups, who retained their political dominance in the small kingdoms and territorial polities that reappeared in the first centuries of the second millennium (Charpin 2004; Fleming 2004; Ristvet 2005). The situation of the last centuries of Ottoman rule in the basin provides a useful analogy. An unfavorable climate did not prevent the recolonization of the plains by sedentary agriculturalists; the observations of multiple Western travelers over several centuries describe the agricultural potential of the plain in those centuries in rich detail (see Section 2.2). Rather, resettlement was actively opposed by Tay and Shammar camel nomads and semi-nomadic Kurdish sheep pastoralists, whose political and economic organization had proven to be an effective adaptation to their physical and political environments (Glubb 1942). Pastoralism was a resilient and successful economic strategy, and mobility enabled a high degree of autonomy from the Ottoman regime. In the Late Ottoman case, the recolonization by sedentary agriculturalists required external military intervention; the Middle Bronze Age resettlement appears to have been a nonviolent endogenous process.

8.4.1. SEDENTARY AVOIDANCE OF THE HAMOUKAR AREA IN PERIOD 8

It is notable that, with the exception of THS 16, all Period 8 sites lay within 2 km of the survey limits, leaving a large vacant zone around the abandoned mound at Hamoukar (fig. 8.4). Not only did the settlements avoid Hamoukar, their modeled sustaining areas fall outside the former area of intensive cultivation, as derived from hollow ways and field scatters (see Section 8.3.3). This region went from intensive utilization at the end of the third millennium to abandonment or more likely pasturage.

The reasons for the apparent avoidance of the immediate area around Hamoukar are not certain, but two non-exclusive hypotheses can be proposed. After several centuries as the sustaining area for largest urban center in the eastern basin, the soils may have been depleted and were considered sufficient only for pasture. The coincidence between the intensity of cultivation in the late third millennium and the under-utilization of that same space in the early second millennium suggests that agricultural degradation may have discouraged the reoccupation of the central

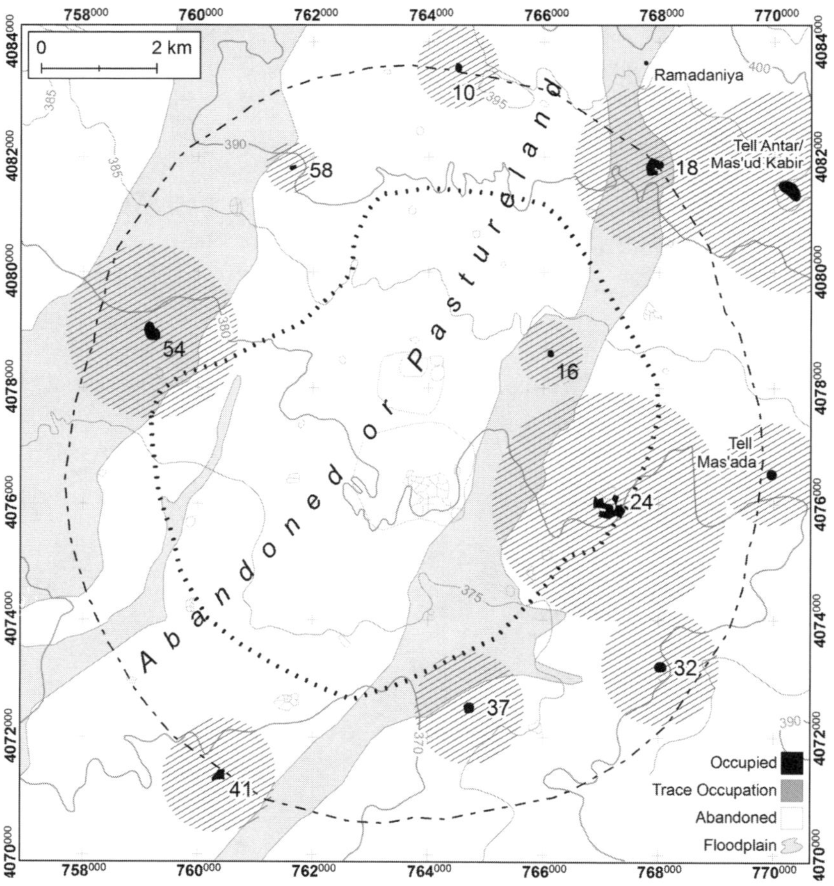

Figure 8.4. Period 8 sites and sustaining areas with Period 7 zone of intensive cultivation indicated. Sustaining areas based on 100 persons/ha, biennial fallow, and 500 kg/ha yields

THS region. It is not possible, however, to rule out social or political prohibitions against the resettlement of this territory. It is likely that some or all of Hamoukar's former inhabitants transitioned into a pastoral nomadic way of life. In such a situation, they may have retained rights to their former fields, which were now used for seasonal pasture. In either case, the resumption of sedentary agriculture in the area immediately around Hamoukar appears to have been discouraged or prevented.

8.4.2. SETTLEMENT VARIABILITY IN THE MIDDLE BRONZE AGE POLITIES OF NORTHERN MESOPOTAMIA

Within the small area of the THS, Period 8 (Khabur/Old Babylonian) settlement was dramatically reduced from its pinnacle in the later third millennium. The 31.85 ha of Period 8 settled area represented only a quarter of the total Period 7 area (see tables 6.7 and 6.8). In contrast, in the North Jazira, the 79.8 ha of Period 7 settlement doubled to 153.7 ha in Period 8.

In some areas of the basin, the early second millennium was a time of heightened settlement numbers and density. Within intensive survey areas, density across the basin is highly variable (fig. 8.5, table 8.2). The highest densities (0.095 sites/sq. km) occur around Tell Leilan (Ristvet 2005). The pattern around Leilan confirms impressionistic results of Meijer's reconnaissance in the eastern half of the basin, which noted a great abundance of painted Khabur ware sherds on 166 sites in total (Meijer 1986: fig. 34; 1990). Densities in the Iraqi North Jazira are only slightly lower (0.088 sites/sq. km). Between these two, the Hamoukar region has the lowest density in the eastern basin (0.072 sites/sq. km), despite the fact that it was the most intensively surveyed (see fig. 4.2).

The eastern basin hosted variable densities of settlement in the early second millennium, but the most dramatic variation emerges between the eastern and western basins. Seven Period 8 sites were recovered in the Tell Beydar Survey region, a density of only 0.015 sites/sq. km (Wilkinson 2002b; Ur and Wilkinson 2008: fig. 4). The assemblages of six of these sites were of such low density that they are best interpreted as the traces of non-permanent settlement by mobile pastoralists (following Lyonnet 1996a). In an inverted parallel to the eastern basin, the results from the intensive Beydar survey lend support to the more impressionistic interpretation from a reconnaissance of a broader area that most early second-millennium settlements were small and ephemeral (Lyonnet 2000).

The rich textual record, which has emerged from cuneiform finds at Chagar Bazar, Tell Leilan, Tell al-Rimah, and, above all, Mari, offers the possibility of mapping these variable survey results onto the constellation of northern Mesopotamian polities. The dense concentration around Leilan can probably be related to its preeminent political position as capital of Samsi-Addu's large territorial kingdom (under the name Šubat-Enlil), and later as the main town of the kingdom of Apum (having reverted to its earlier name Šehna; Weiss 1985; Charpin 1987). A second major town existed at Tell Mohammed Diyab, perhaps ancient Azamhul (Charpin 1990; Nicolle 2006). The long-term political significance of this region may have been accompanied by a level of security that encouraged dispersed small-scale settlement.

The similarly dense pattern found in the North Jazira Project area may correspond to Šubartum, another textually documented kingdom. The designation Subir/Šubartum and its geographic reality is a difficult issue, especially in the later third millennium (Steinkeller 1998; Michalowski 1986, 1999). Even into the early second millennium, some regard Šubartum as a term for a cultural area rather than a polity, and its location depends on the point of view of the observer (Guichard 2002; Michalowski 1999). For at least a time, however, Šubartum was a geographic entity with several associated towns including Azuhinum (see Section 8.3.5). It was located north of the Jebel Ishkaft and between the Tigris River and the Wadi Radd (Charpin 1992: 101).

The Hamoukar area appears to fall between these kingdoms. According to the tablets from Tell Leilan, Apum extended as far as the town of Šurnat, which Eidem locates at Tell Hadi on the Wadi Rumaylan (cited in Ristvet 2005: 146). Pastoralism remained important to the economy of Apum, and numerous references are made in the Leilan tablets to flocks sent to pasture in the areas to the south and southeast toward the Jebel Sinjar (Ristvet 2005: 130–33). Even more pastoralism oriented were the small kingdoms that made up the Ida-Maras confederacy in the western part of the basin. This area was the traditional summer pasture of the Binu Sim'al pastoral nomads, who attained political dominance with the dynasty of Zimri-Lim and his predecessors (Fleming 2004; Durand 2004). The meager record of sedentary occupation from the Tell Beydar and Lyonnet surveys appears to confirm this textual impression.

Table 8.2. Comparative densities of Period 8 sites in intensive survey areas (Ur and Wilkinson 2008; Wilkinson and Tucker 1995; Wilkinson 2002b; Ristvet 2005: appendix 3)

		Sites		
Survey	*Area (sq. km)*	*Sedentary*	*Trace / Non-Sedentary*	*Sites/Sq. Km*
Tell Leilan Survey	1,650	136	21	0.095
North Jazira Project	475	39	3	0.088
Tell Hamoukar Survey	125	9	—	0.072
Tell Beydar Survey	453	1	6	0.015

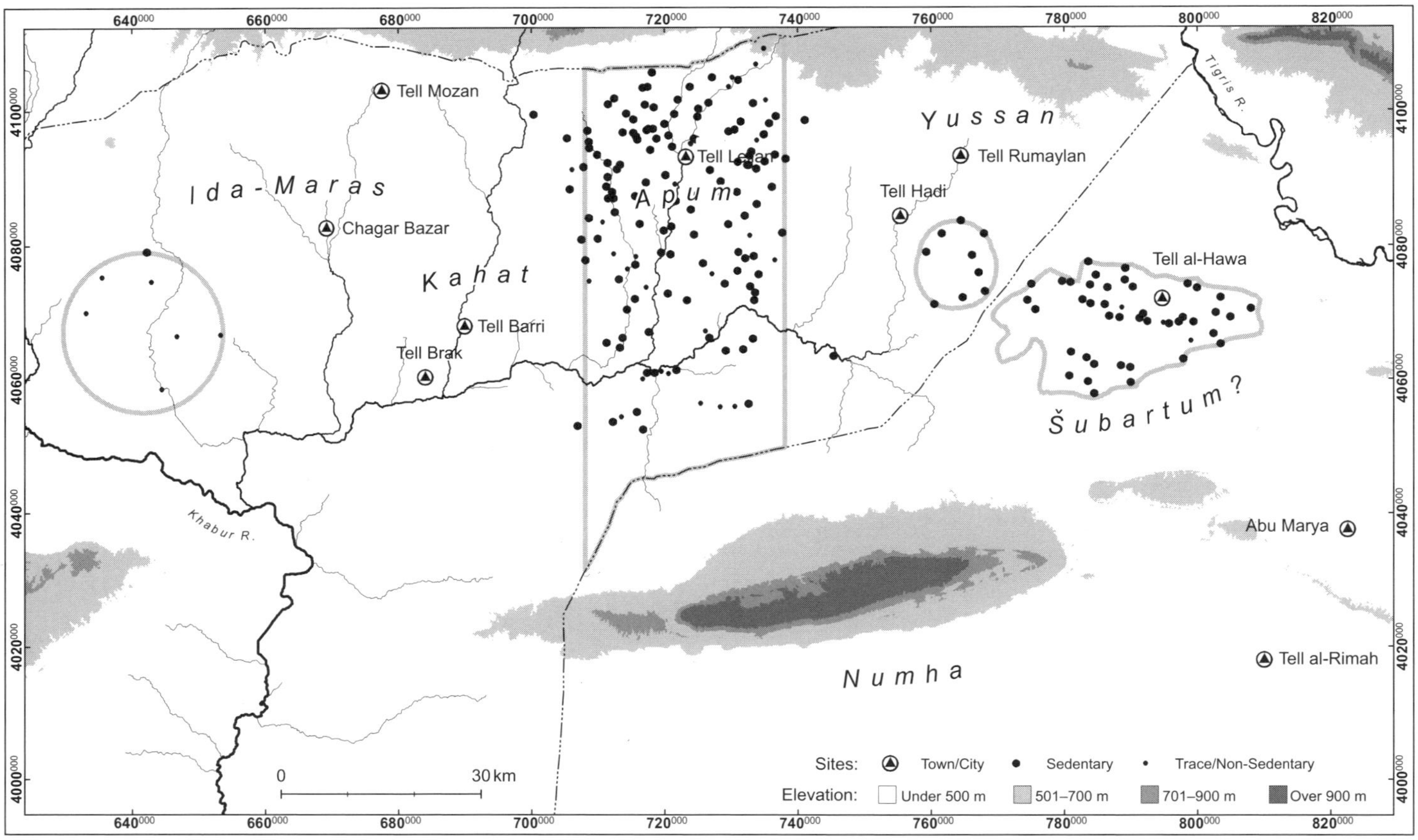

Figure 8.5. Period 8 site densities in selected survey regions (Ur and Wilkinson 2008: fig. 4; Ristvet 2005; Wilkinson and Tucker 1995: fig. 37)

8.4.3. THE THS AND THE "ROAD TO EMAR"

The THS region sits astride an overland route between the Tigris River and the resource-rich areas of Anatolia. Kings from Naram-Sin of Akkad to Samsu-iluna of Babylon have attempted to control this route (Charpin 1992: 102; Joannès 1996: 343–44). Several routes are possible and often fluctuated based on political factors. The itinerary from the era of Samsi-Addu (Hallo 1964) runs between Apqum (Tell Abu Marya) and Šubat-Enlil (Tell Leilan); this route, if direct, would have skirted the southern edge of the THS region. Another contemporary route ran from Ekallatum on the Tigris directly to Qattara (to be located at Tell al-Rimah or in its vicinity) and then on to Šubat-Enlil (Joannès 1996: 339–40). At other times, the route to Anatolia avoided the Khabur basin altogether by going up the Tigris and crossing the Tur Abdin (Forlanini 2006).

It is unlikely that the surviving landscape features (see Section 5.3 and map 2) can be connected directly with any of these routes. Within the Hamoukar area, for example, the intensity of settlement and cultivation was probably not sufficient to constrain the movement of herders and caravans onto linear tracks; indeed, it is likely that much of this area was primarily pastureland. The textual record on communication routes demonstrates that, even in times like the early second millennium, when movement was not intensive or constrained enough to inscribe durable linear tracks, some long-term corridors of human movement, such as the southeast–northwest Tigris–Nisibin route, were still in use.

8.5. THE EXTENSION OF SETTLEMENT IN THE LATE BRONZE AND IRON AGES

Following the retreat of settlement numbers and settled area in the Middle Bronze Age, the end of the second millennium saw the flourishing of a dispersed rural pattern that continued well into the first millennium (fig. 6.33). The number of sites reached its height within the THS region. From a long-term perspective, however, settled area did not increase at the same rate; thus, these settlements were numerous but small. During the Late Bronze and Iron Ages (Periods 10–11) the THS region was subsumed into large territorial empires, first the Mitanni and subsequently the Assyrian states. In the case of the latter, a rich textual record provides a historical and socioeconomic framework within which the settlement pattern of the THS can be interpreted.

8.5.1. THE INITIAL EXPANSION OF SETTLEMENT IN THE LATE BRONZE AGE (PERIOD 10)

The Upper Khabur basin was the center of power for the Mitanni kingdom, and archaeological evidence for elite occupation comes from Tell Hamidi and especially Tell Brak, where a richly appointed palace and temple complex has been excavated (Oates, Oates, and McDonald 1997). After several campaigns, the final conquest of the basin was completed by the Middle Assyrian king Adad-nerari I in the early thirteenth century B.C. (Wilhelm 1989: 38–40). By the mid-thirteenth century, Shalmaneser I established a provincial capital at Dur-Katlimmu (Kühne 1995) and the limits of Assyrian control extended to the Balikh River (Akkermans and Schwartz 2003: 348–50).

The Late Bronze Age (Period 10) settlement pattern shows a dramatic expansion of the number of settlements compared to the previous period. However, it is unclear whether this pattern is to be connected to an expansion of settlement in the Mitanni core, or colonization of conquered lands under Assyrian administration. The strong continuity in common wares between the periods of Mitanni and Middle Assyrian political control of the eastern basin render their distinction from surface materials problematic, despite recent advances in ceramic chronology (see Section B.2.10).

8.5.2. THE REAPPEARANCE OF SEDENTARY OCCUPATION AND ASSYRIAN CONTROL (PERIOD 11)

Following the territorial collapse of the Middle Assyrian state, northern Mesopotamia and western Syria fell under the control of Aramean polities that were at least in part oriented toward pastoral nomadism. One polity, Bit Bahiani, was centered at Tell Halaf (ancient Guzana) in the western Upper Khabur basin (Orthmann 2002; Dion 1997: 38–49). By the end of the ninth century, after a time when these polities were tributaries, Guzana had been incorporated into the expanding Neo-Assyrian state. With Nineveh 125 km to the southeast and the provincial capital at Nasibina 70 km to the northwest, the THS region was a rural hinterland for most of this period.

Despite the continuing high numbers of settlements, the overall population appears to have been low enough, and evenly distributed enough, to have not encouraged the adoption of intensive agricultural methods which were employed in the urban expansion of Period 7. One of the most extensive areas of field scatter sampling was the 1.5 sq. km south and west of THS 48, the largest Period 11 site in the survey region (see fig. 5.17). Density was overwhelmingly in the range of 1–20 sherds per 100 sq. m, except for within 100 m of the site boundary, where it was elevated. Thus it is possible that some small-scale manuring was practiced, perhaps related to gardens, but intensive practices over broad stretches of sustaining areas were lacking.

The expansion of settlement seen in the THS and adjacent Iraqi North Jazira regions is matched by the results of other surveys in the Upper Khabur basin (Wilkinson 1995; Wilkinson et al. 2005), the lower Khabur River and adjacent areas (Kühne 1995; Bernbeck 1993), the Upper Tigris (Parker 2003, 2001), and the Sinjar Plain (Ibrahim 1986).

The most intuitive interpretation of this settlement landscape would be that it represents small agricultural villages that were primarily concerned with their own subsistence (Wilkinson et al. 2005: 39–40; Morandi Bonacossi 2000: 365–66). Excavations of several small sites in the area have complicated this interpretation by revealing signs of wealth and status above what might be expected from self-sufficient agricultural hamlets. The 3 ha village at the northeastern corner of Hamoukar's lower town included baked brick pavements, palace ware vessels, a pottery kiln, and a cylinder seal. Similar trappings of wealth come from the nearby North Jazira Project area (Wilkinson and Tucker 1995: 61), including administrative and manufacturing functions at 2 ha Mithlai (NJP 101).

The Iron Age (Period 11) landscape of the eastern basin, as revealed by the THS and the North Jazira Project, was extensively and evenly settled (fig. 8.6). Compared to the equally rural Late Bronze Age (Period 10) pattern (see fig. 6.21), its settlements are far less clustered; the pattern has been described as one of infilling (Wilkinson et al. 2005: 40–41). Three processes can be hypothesized, and it is possible that all contributed in varying degrees to the archaeologically visible pattern.

The first possibility is that formerly mobile Aramean groups began to settle on and cultivate their former pasturelands in the basin. This process could have been entirely endogenous and independent of the policies or desires of the Neo-Assyrian state; indeed, it could have preceded the return of Assyrian influence. An analogy for this process is the reappearance of Period 8 settlement in the eastern basin following the collapse of later third-millennium urbanism (see Section 8.4.2). On the other hand, sedentarization may have been enforced by the Assyrian state, in which case the situation of the French mandatory policy of the 1930s through 1940s would be a better analogy. Cer-

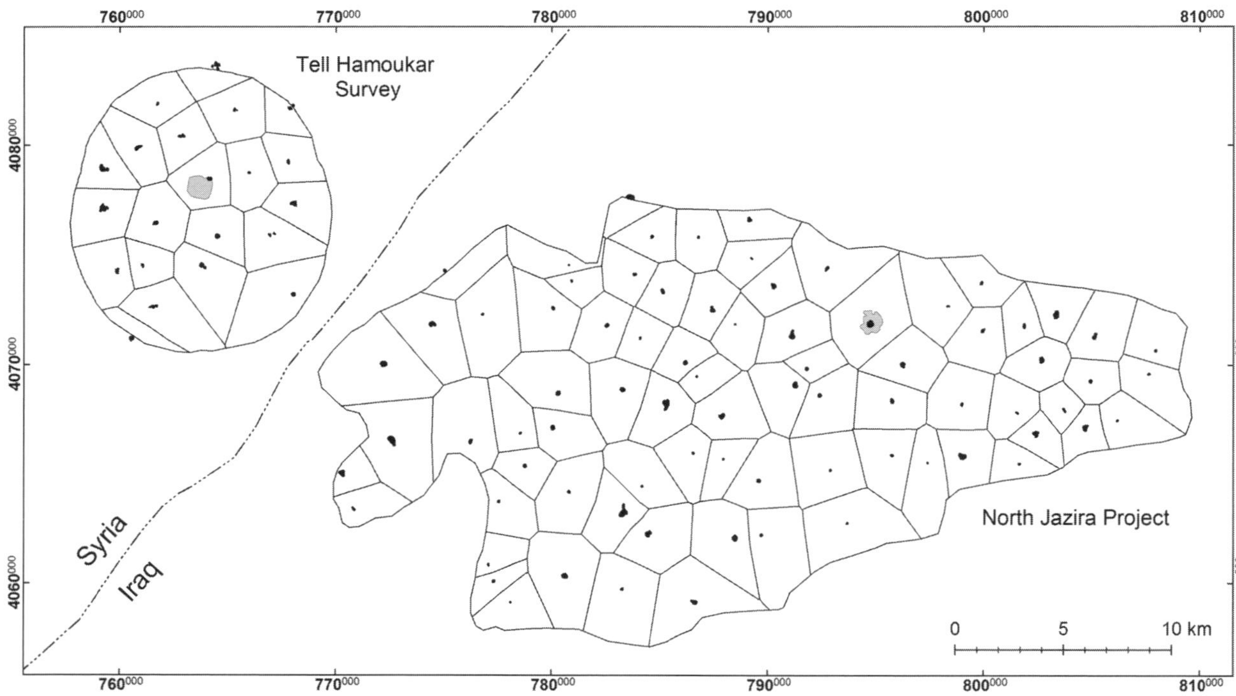

Figure 8.6. Period 11 site distributions in the THS and North Jazira Project regions. North Jazira Project data from Wilkinson and Tucker (1995: fig. 41). For comparison, the Period 7 areas of Hamoukar and Tell al-Hawa are shown in gray

tainly, the area around the Tur Abdin remained predominantly Aramaic throughout the Neo-Assyrian period (Lipinski 2000: 136).

The wealth and specialization in manufacturing at the few excavated sites in the eastern basin raises a second possibility: rural agricultural estates granted to officials by the Assyrian king. Newly conquered land would have been a redistributable resource, especially if it were previously pasture. If such land were to be granted systematically, it might explain the apparent regularity of spacing and catchment seen in the settlement pattern and Thiessen polygon-derived hypothetical catchments in figure 8.6.

A final possibility, which fits within the framework of the empire's expansion, is that these settlements resulted from the forced resettlement of conquered peoples (Oded 1979; Gallagher 1994). As a matter of policy, the Assyrian kings moved populations about within their territories for a variety of purposes including pacification, planned urbanization of new capital cities, and agricultural expansion. Sennacherib alone claimed to have relocated almost half a million persons (Oded 1979: 20–21, 28). Assyrian policy was to maintain the deportees within their household and village structures so that they would continue to be economically productive in their new settlements. The regularity of spacing in the Period 11 settlements in the eastern basin suggests a degree of planning that could be related to the even dispersal of agriculturally productive communities by imperial decision makers (Wilkinson and Barbanes 2000; Ur 2005b: 343; Wilkinson, Ur, and Casana 2004; see also Parker 2001: 82–83 for similar conclusions for the Cizre Plain).

This broadly visible pattern of Period 11 settlement throughout northern Mesopotamia has emerged as one of the greatest settlement reorganizations in the Holocene Epoch. Ultimately, problems of ceramic chronology and the lack of problem-oriented excavation on Period 11 sites render the evaluation of these possible interpretations difficult at present.

8.6. LATE SASANIAN–EARLY ISLAMIC PERIODS

The third major expansion of settlement in the THS region was in the broad ceramic period which encompasses the end of the Sasanian period and the first centuries of the Islamic period (Periods 16–17). Even more so than in previous periods, our ability to integrate this archaeological pattern with historical events and processes is hampered by chronological difficulties.

The later kings of the Sasanian empire transformed their lands through the expansion of settlements and the creation of engineered landscapes to support them. This process was most visible in the imperial core of southern Iraq. In the Diyala region, Adams (1965) estimates that the entire flow of the Diyala River was redirected into canals. The plain below Baghdad was similarly restructured into an elaborate network of settlements and canals that greatly exceeded anything before it and was not to be surpassed until the twentieth century (Adams 2005). The plains of Khuzistan underwent a similar hydraulic and settlement transformation (Wenke 1975–76; Alizadeh et al. 2004). Similar processes were occurring at the empire's northwestern and northeastern frontiers (Nokandeh et al. 2006; Alizadeh and Ur 2007). In the latter half of the Sasanian period, the frontier ran along the Jaghjagh River (Kettenhofen 1993); Nisibin was an important frontier town. Thus the THS region was at the fringes of Sasanian-held territory.

To the west of the Upper Khabur basin, a similar flourishing characterized the Early Islamic period. Simultaneously with the rise in importance of Raqqa, large settlements were founded in the Balikh, particularly Madinat al-Far (Haase 1996; Bartl 1994), and the valley showed a great density of rural settlement in the eighth and ninth centuries, as well (Bartl 1994, 1996). Both the Sasanian and Early Islamic patterns stand in stark contrast to the distribution of sites in the Iraqi North Jazira, which entered an extended phase of settlement decline in the Sasanian period (Wilkinson and Tucker 1995: 69–74).

In the case of the Jazira region between Mosul and Nisibin, the writings of medieval Islamic geographers contribute to this reconstruction of settlement and overland movement (Le Strange 1905; Bettini 1998). In the ninth century, Nisibin and its region were highly praised. The town fell into decline by the fourteenth century (Ibn Hawqal 2001: 204; Le Strange 1905: 94–95). The important route between Balad (Eski Mosul) and Nisibin described by several of these geographers has been plausibly reconstructed by several modern scholars (Le Strange 1905: 99–100; Fiey 1964; Wilkinson and Tucker 1995: 72–73). The route (fig. 8.7) left Balad and proceeded to

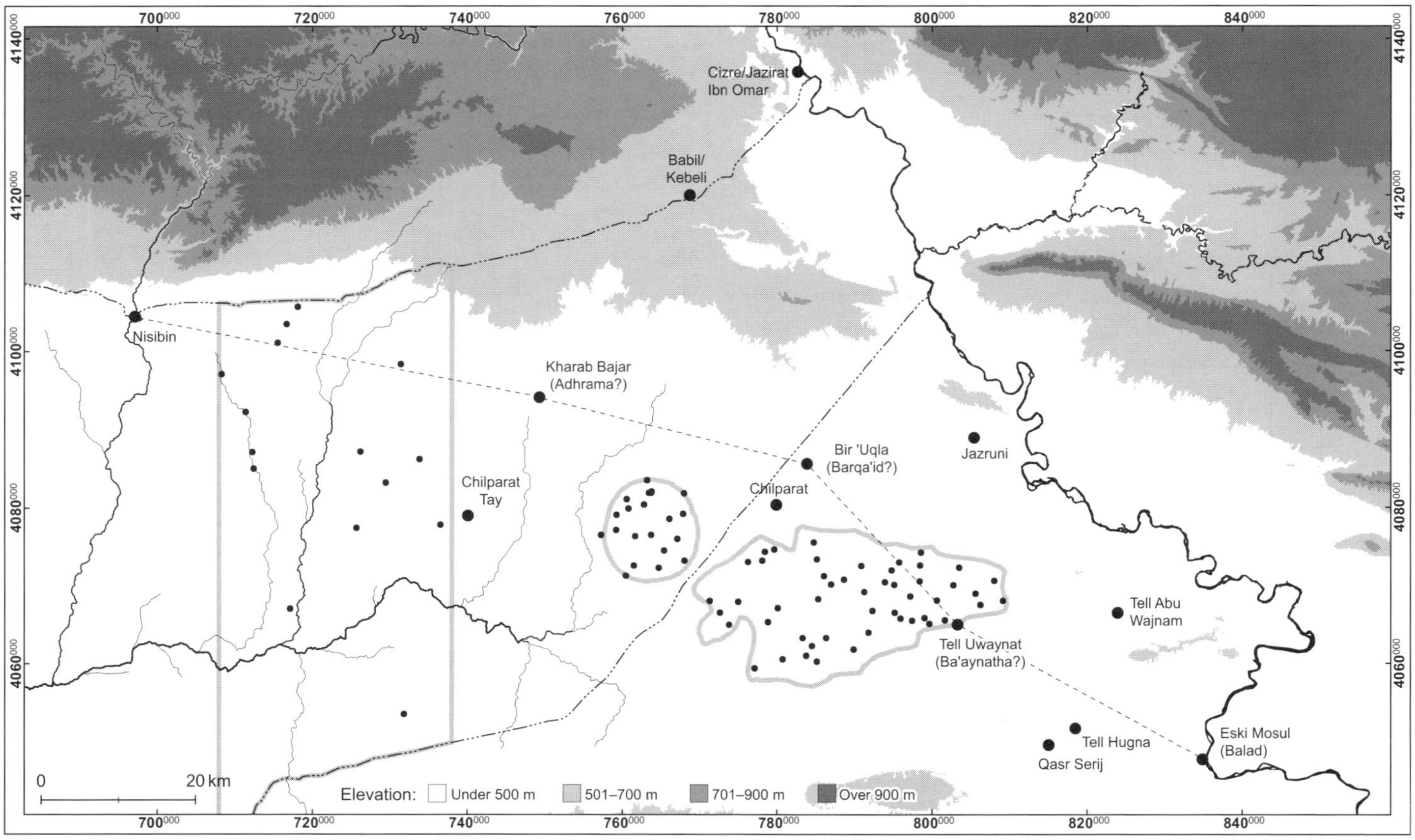

Figure 8.7. The Abbasid route between Balad and Nisibin and some major sites of the Early Islamic period (survey data from Vezzoli 2004; Wilkinson and Tucker 1995)

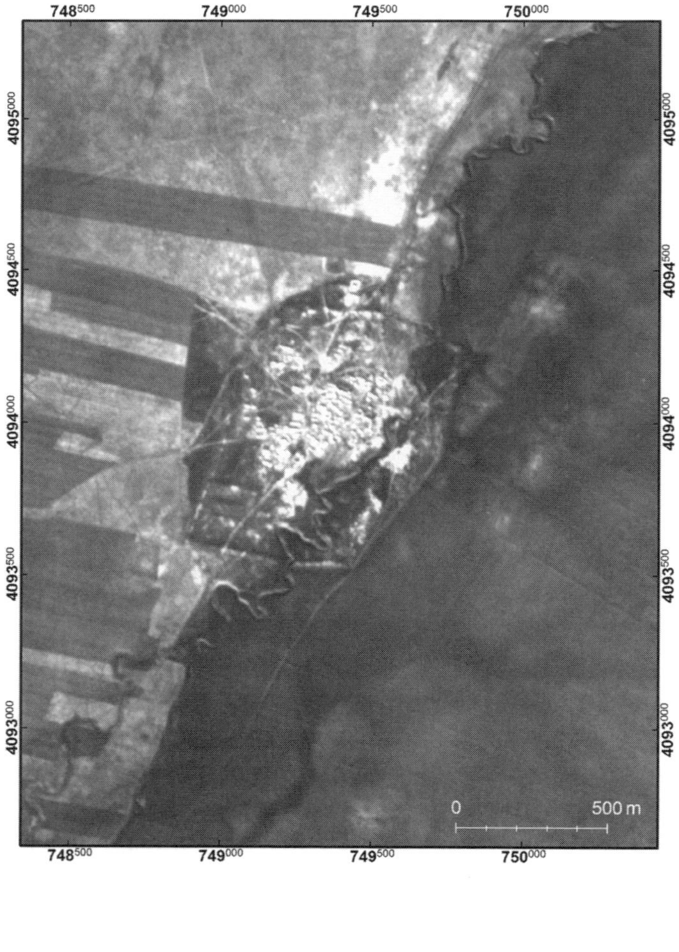

Figure 8.8. The walled town at Kharab Bajar (possibly ancient Adhrama) (CORONA 1108-1025DA004, 6 December 1969)

Ba'aynatha, a town in a particularly fertile region which Fiey (1964) places at Tell Uwaynat. The route continued to Barqa'id, which might be located at either Bir Uqla or Chilparat, two large walled sites roughly 11–13 parasangs (63–75 km) from Eski Mosul (Wilkinson and Tucker 1995: 72). The final station between Barqa'id and Nisibin was Adhrama, a town similar in size to Barqa'id. In the ninth century, the town possessed a stone palace, a double wall with a moat, and a stone bridge across the stream that ran though the town; its district was called Bayn-an-Nahrayn, or Between the Rivers (Le Strange 1905: 100). A possible (although unsurveyed) candidate for this place is a 52 ha walled site visible in CORONA (fig. 8.8) called Kharab Bajar on the French 1:200,000 maps. It falls almost directly on a line between Bir Uqla and Nisibin and closely matches the descriptions of the medieval geographers. At present, it is associated with few hollow way features (see map 2), although it lies close to the northern edge of hollow way preservation in the eastern basin.

The THS landscape record and the descriptions of the medieval geographers appear to be slightly contradictory. Although the texts describe flourishing towns and fertile agricultural districts along this route, they also mention the threat of nomadic raids, which probably inspired the construction of the town walls. The Period 16–17 sites in the THS tend to be larger than villages, but none have any obvious fortifications. If we place emphasis on these textual sources, it may be that the settlement pattern relates to either late Sasanian or earlier Abbasid (eighth- to ninth-century) settlement. At present, the ceramic chronologies for the last 1,500 years are insufficiently fine to reconcile the divergent archaeological and historical data.

8.7. MIDDLE ISLAMIC PERIOD TO PRESENT

What little is known of the history of the eastern Upper Khabur basin in the last millennium must be pieced together from indigenous histories and Western travelers' accounts. The histories (e.g., Hillenbrand 1990; Woods 1999) are largely concerned with political events, but some indications of settlement and land use can be discerned. For example, the nomadic groups within Aqquyunlu confederacy spent summers in pastures in the Taurus Mountains of eastern Anatolia and moved south to the lower plains of northern Mesopotamia for the winter. This winter region included the Upper Khabur basin, then part of the broader area known as Diyar Rabi'ah (Woods 1999: 28–31).

The low density of settlement in the THS area appears to correspond to the general lack of sedentary occupation that followed the decline of Abbasid power and the arrival of Oghuz Turkmen nomadic groups in the twelfth century. The nearby Iraqi North Jazira was already largely pasture before the arrival of the Mongols (Wilkinson and Tucker 1995: 73). Although the ceramic indicators are weak for Periods 18–19 (Middle–Late Islamic), the settlement pattern in the THS region appears to be one of a few small and ephemeral villages (see Section 6.10.5).

A change in this situation appears to have resulted from the imposition of Ottoman political control throughout much of the sixteenth century. Aspects of settlement and economy are preserved in official tax records (*mufassal defterler*) from this period, which have been studied and translated (Hütteroth 1990; Göyünç and Hütteroth 1997). The most productive and densely populated district was Mardin, in the hills above the northwestern corner of the plain (fig. 8.9). Nisibin was settled at a reduced scale from Abbasid times, but oversaw a productive irrigation economy that generated taxable quantities of rice and cotton, among other non-irrigated crops (Göyünç and Hütteroth 1997: map 3a). The fossil irrigation system (see Section 7.3.2 and fig. 7.6) was certainly in existence at that time, although it may have been created earlier.

The THS region probably fell into the liva (administrative district) of Cizre, and thus outside of the districts studied by Göyünç and Hütteroth (1997), but some clues to its status can be gleaned from its neighbor to the west. The liva Akčakal'a (Göyünç and Hütteroth 1997: 65, 234–38) extended from the Tur Abdin above Nisibin down the Wadi Jarrah and into the Radd marsh. It included a village of twenty households called Leylān, which is probably the same place as the modern Tell Leilan. Tax receipts were low compared to Nisibin or Mardin, which suggests production and population was also low; if the spatial reconstruction of Göyünç and Hütteroth (1997: map 3a) is correct, the liva was also populated at a low density. Furthermore, a large number of the liva's villages were affiliated with the Shah Nasibi tribe. In general, Akčakal'a liva appears to have been a low-density, agriculturally unproductive district on the margins of the main region of settlement between Mardin and Nisibin. The THS area east of

Akčakal'a was likely to have been similar, or perhaps even less settled as is suggested by the lack of archaeological remains.

This phase of sedentary stability under Ottoman control lasted roughly one century. Subsequently, Nisibin underwent a sharp decline (Fiey 1977: 114–28) and the basin fell under the control of pastoral nomadic groups, who appear to have prevented agricultural utilization of their pasturelands. At this point, the THS region — and the whole of this area of northeastern Syria — entered into the long phase of pastoral land use outside of the control of state governments which was much commented upon by Western travelers (see Section 2.2).

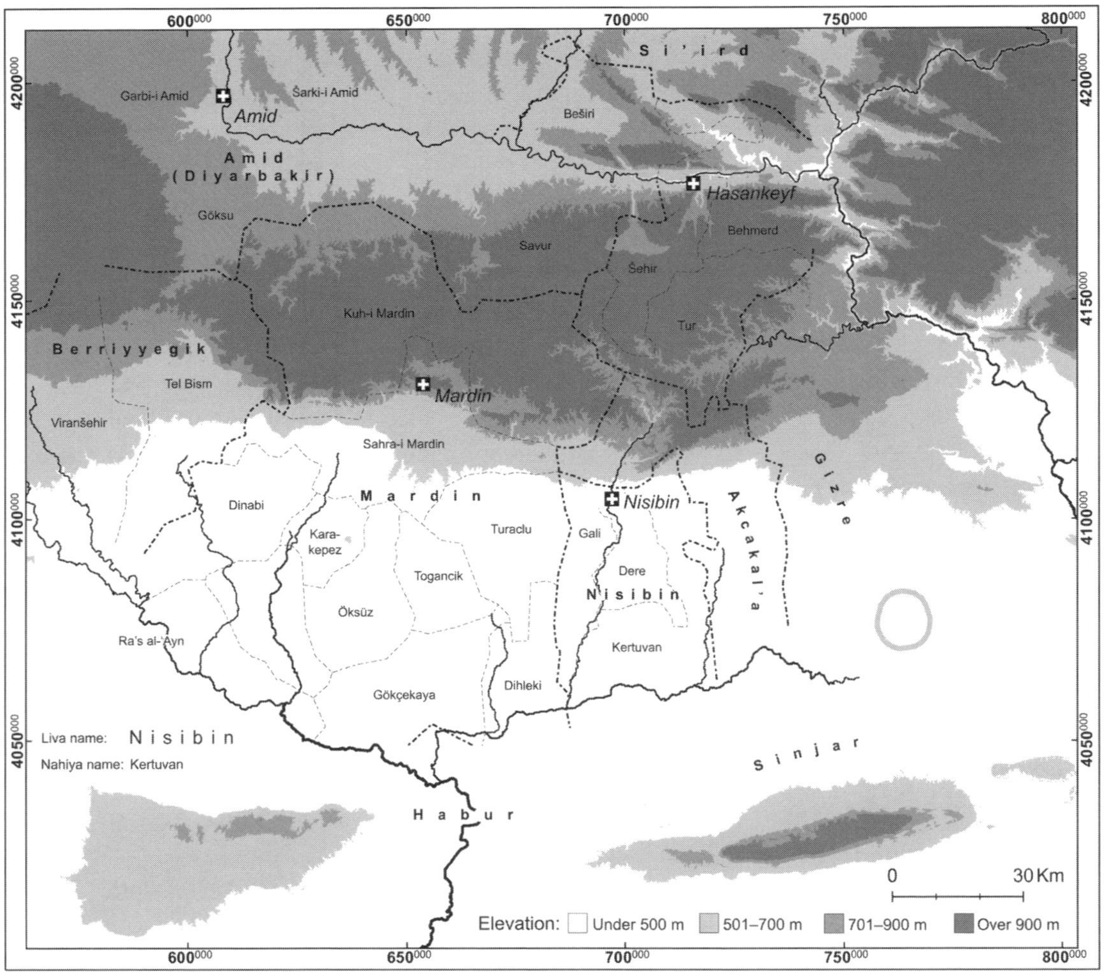

Figure 8.9. Early Ottoman administrative districts in sixteenth-century northern Mesopotamia with the THS region indicated (names and boundaries from Göyünç and Hütteroth 1997)

APPENDIX A

TELL HAMOUKAR SURVEY SITE CATALOG

During the Tell Hamoukar Survey, sites were assigned field numbers sequentially in the order of their collection. These field site numbers were used in the survey's preliminary report (Ur 2002a). For this final report, sites have been renumbered in a clockwise order and radiating outward from Hamoukar. Modern place names were derived from local informants and several recent and historical map sources, among which there are frequent disagreements.

Site positions are given in meters east and north according to the UTM projection and using the World Geodetic System (WGS) 1984 datum. For consistency, all coordinates are given in terms of the UTM Zone 37 north, although all sites in the THS east of the 42° east longitude are technically in Zone 38 north.

Site and area measurements have been rounded to the nearest tenth of a hectare. For the spatial arrangement of all features ancient (sites, areas, hollow ways, canals, and field scatters) and modern (villages, field boundaries, roads, and tracks), see map 1. In addition to site and collection area labels, *Appendix A* CORONA figures include the positions of 100 sq. m field scatter collections, labeled with the number of sherds recovered. All CORONA figures in the Appendix are at 1:20,000 scale.

For each site, a "battleship curve"-style settlement graph depicts the evolution of site size. The width of the bars is proportional to the size of the site with a ratio of 2 mm = 1 ha; the exception is THS 1 (Hamoukar), where 1 mm = 1 ha. Solid bars indicate major and trace settlement. White bars indicate possible temporary or non-permanent occupation in Period 7 (mid- to late third millennium). Gray bars indicate largely assumed settlement. Justifications for such assumptions, along with more precise details on sizes, are included in the text description for each site.

THS 1 (FIELD SITE NO. 1)

SITE NAME:

Hamoukar (Arabic 1:50,000: حموكر ; French 1:200,000: Tell Hamoûka); modern village name is al-Hurriya

SITE POSITION:

763740 E, 4078380 N (center of high mound)

SITE MEASUREMENTS AND MORPHOLOGY:

104.8 ha; a 15 m high mound with broad lower town to its east, south, and west, which averages 4–5 m above the surrounding plain. A smaller prominence (6 m above the lower town) sits at its eastern edge. See Section 3.2 for a detailed description.

SITE SUB-AREAS AND PERIODS OF OCCUPATION:

Collected as systematic sampling units at 100 m intervals, supplemented by areal collections in several areas (see Section 3.3 and table C.1).

SETTLEMENT HISTORY:

(fig. A.1) Although one or two out-of-context Halaf and Ubaid sherds have been reported by excavation team members, the earliest occupation documented by the excavations and surface collection comes from Period 5b, when the 15.3 ha high mound was occupied. Excavations in Area A suggest that settlement started in the Late Chalcolithic 3 phase. This same 15.3 ha area featured southern Uruk ceramics, mostly in the form of T5a/1 bevelled-rim bowls; drooping spouts from Area A may indicate a Late Uruk (Late Chalcolithic 5) occupation. By the end of the Ninevite 5 period (P6, equivalent to Leilan IIId), settlement had expanded to 98 ha on the high mound and lower town. The earlier Ninevite 5 extent cannot be firmly established, but probably did not expand beyond the high mound. This scale of occupation continued into the mid- to late third millennium (P7). After abandonment throughout the second millennium B.C., Hamoukar's northeast lower town was resettled in the Iron Age (P11; 3.1 ha), possibly extending into the post-Assyrian period (P12). Settlement shifted to another area of the eastern lower town in the Hellenistic period (P13; 5.1 ha). A trace settlement of the Parthian period (P14; estimated at 1 ha) probably existed to the north of the lower town enclosed depression. A small (less than 1 ha) settlement of probable Middle Islamic (P18) date was founded at the top of the high mound in Area A. Into these levels were dug Islamic burials, probably by Tay or Shammar nomadic pastoralists in the last five centuries.

SMALL FIND:

A bronze coin of Roman date (2 HM 12) was found within the village by an excavation team member (fig. A.21 no. 1).

EXCAVATIONS:

Hamoukar has been excavated since 1999 by the Syrian-American Hamoukar Expedition (Syrian Directorate General of Antiquities and Museums, and the Oriental Institute of the University of Chicago). Preliminary reports have appeared in the journals *Iraq* (Gibson et al. 2002b), *Akkadica* (Gibson et al. 2002a, Reichel 2002), and a forthcoming volume in the Oriental Institute Communications series (Reichel in prep.).

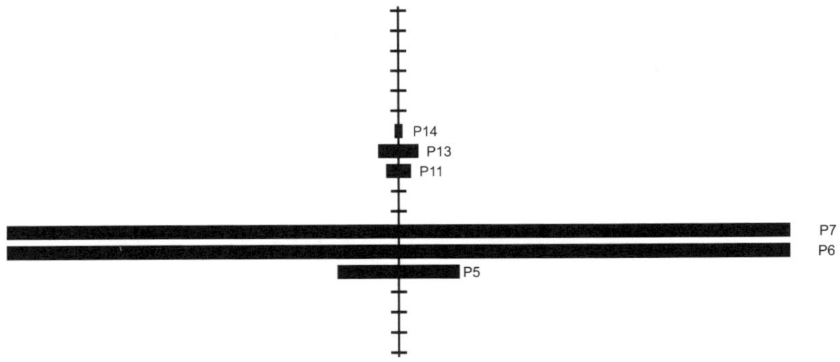

Figure A.1. Settlement graph for THS 1. 1 ha = 0.1 cm

THS 2 (FIELD SITE NO. 35)

SITE NAME:

—

SITE POSITION:

763759 E, 4078809 N (approximate center of mound)

SITE AREA AND MORPHOLOGY:

(fig. A.2) Originally an east–west-oriented oval-shaped low mound of 1 m height, 170 m east–west × 100 m north–south. The eastern half of the site has been leveled to expand a cotton field to the west; bulldozed archaeological materials from this operation are now heaped in a 1.5 m high linear dump running along the western edge of the field (see fig. 6.12), through what was probably the center of the site. From 1968 to 1972, a single structure sat at the western end of the cotton field; some concrete debris is visible, presumably from this structure. The original extent of the site has been estimated from CORONA imagery. Estimated area 1.1 ha.

SITE SUB-AREAS AND PERIODS OF OCCUPATION:

Collected as a single area; P5a, P5b (table C.2, fig. C.1)

SETTLEMENT HISTORY:

A small satellite of Hamoukar occupied exclusively in the mid- to late fourth millennium (P5). Its Late Chalcolithic 3–4 component is probably to be placed late (Late Chalcolithic 4) and likely contemporary with its southern Mesopotamian Uruk component (Late Chalcolithic 4–5).

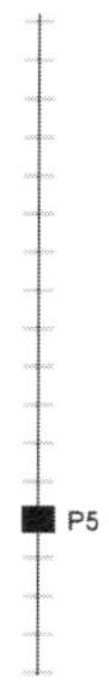

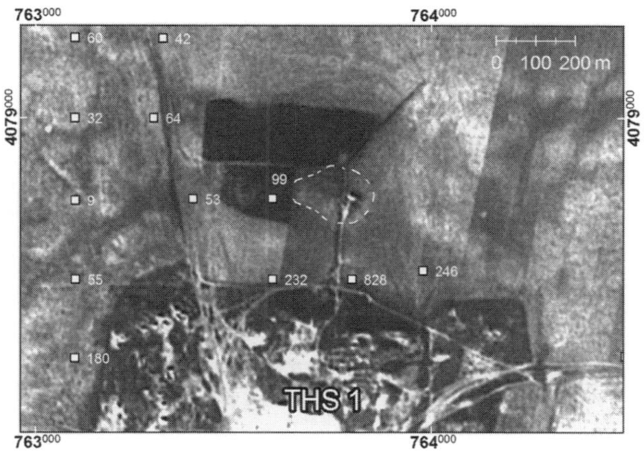

Figure A.2. THS 2 (CORONA 1102-1025DF007, 11 December 1967)

THS 3 (FIELD SITE NO. 21)

SITE NAME:

al-'Asayla (Arabic 1:50,000: الاصيلع)

SITE POSITION:

762950 E, 4080429 N (top of eastern mound, Area A)

SITE AREA AND MORPHOLOGY:

(fig. A.3) Small complex of two mounds and a 0.8 ha *Prosopis*-filled enclosed depression to the south. At east is a 2 m high elongated north–south mound (A); at west is a higher (5 m) mound (B). The two mounds cover 320 m on the long east–west axis × 140 m on the north–south axis. The summit of Area A now is covered with several large houses and associated animal outbuildings. Both areas are heavily trampled and uncultivated. Total site area covers 4.6 ha.

SITE SUB-AREAS AND PERIODS OF OCCUPATION:

(table C.3)

Area A: 2.1 ha; P5a, P11, P13, P17 (trace)

Area B: 1.7 ha; P5a, P11, P13, P17 (trace)

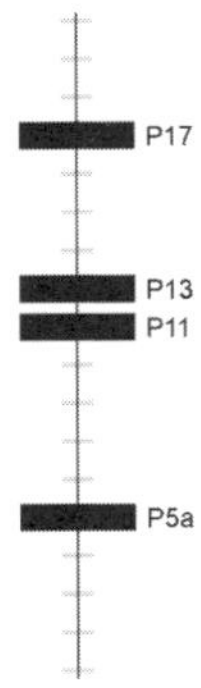

SETTLEMENT HISTORY:

The earliest settlement dates to the later fourth millennium (P5a) and appears to have been southern Uruk on both mounds (3.8 ha). Most occupation was of the first millennium B.C., when both mounds were occupied in the Iron Age and Hellenistic (P11, P13) periods (3.8 ha). Traces of settlement of the Abbasid period (P17) were also recovered on both mounds (3.8 ha).

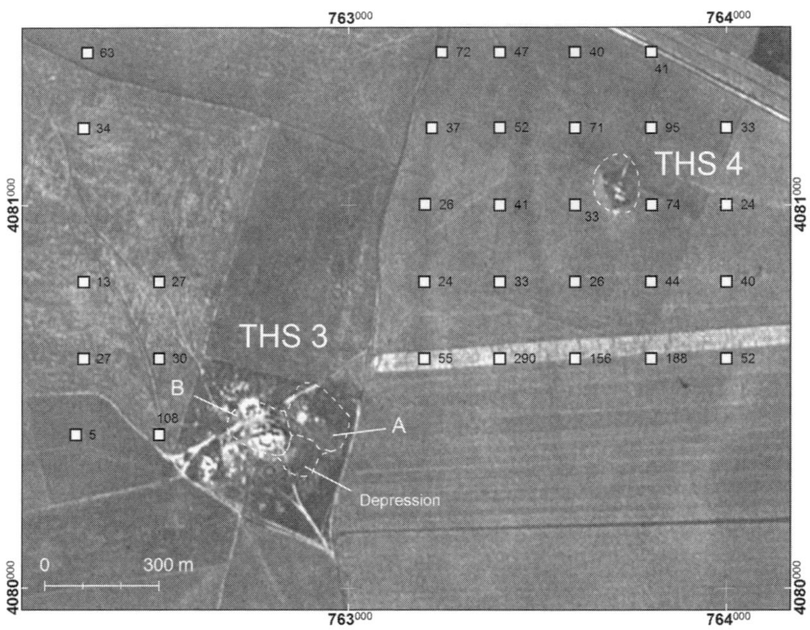

Figure A.3. THS 3 and 4
(CORONA 1108-1025DA005, 6 December 1969)

THS 4 (FIELD SITE NO. 6)

SITE NAME:

—

SITE POSITION:

763708 E, 4081053 N (center and top of mound)

SITE AREA AND MORPHOLOGY:

(fig. A.3) Small mound approximately 0.5 m high and covering 1.5 ha. Cement and rebar remains of a now-abandoned well at the site's center. Sherds frequently occurring, but all very small; some basalt fragments.

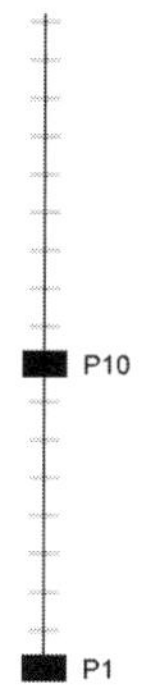

SITE SUB-AREAS AND PERIODS OF OCCUPATION:

Collected as a single area. P1, P10 (many untyped sherds of distinctive Late Bronze Age common ware fabric) (table C.4, fig. C.2)

SETTLEMENT HISTORY:

A small Proto-Hassuna (P1) settlement was later reoccupied by an equally small Late Bronze Age (P10) settlement.

THS 5 (FIELD SITE NO. 22)

SITE NAME:

Tell al-Duwaym (source: village signpost; French 1:200,000: Tell Daoulam)

SITE POSITION:

763466 E, 4081850 N (iron survey benchmark at top of Area A mound)

SITE AREA AND MORPHOLOGY:

(fig. A.4) A site complex composed of an approximately 5 m high main mound (A) with a lower (ca. 2 m) lobe stretching to the southeast (B) and 1.4 ha enclosed depression to the northeast. A large village completely covers Area A and all but the flanks of Area B; the extent of the site north and west of the Area A mound beneath the village is difficult to determine, but could be as much as 5.0 ha. Local villagers had dug out the summit of Area A to a depth of 1.5 m, leaving the iron benchmark pedestalled. Total area of the complex is 9.8 ha.

SITE SUB-AREAS AND PERIODS OF OCCUPATION:

(table C.5)

Area A: 1.4 ha; not collected

Area B: 2.0 ha; P13, P17, P19 (only southern slopes collected)

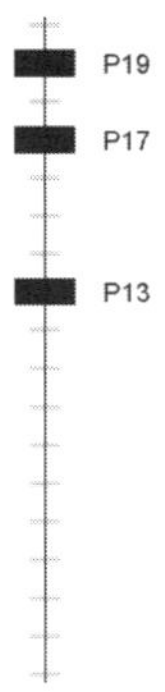

SETTLEMENT HISTORY:

It is impossible to give a complete description of the settlement history of the site because an uncharacteristically hostile reaction to the presence of the survey team prevented the collection of Area A or the 5.0 ha of the mound beneath the modern village. Its height suggests the possibility of some prehistoric occupation, and its association with hollow ways and dense field scatters may indicate settlement in the later third millennium, but no artifactual evidence exists for these proposals. Only Area B was fully collected. It was occupied in the Hellenistic period (P13; 2.0 ha) and then again in the Abbasid and Middle to Late Islamic periods (P17, P19; 2.0).

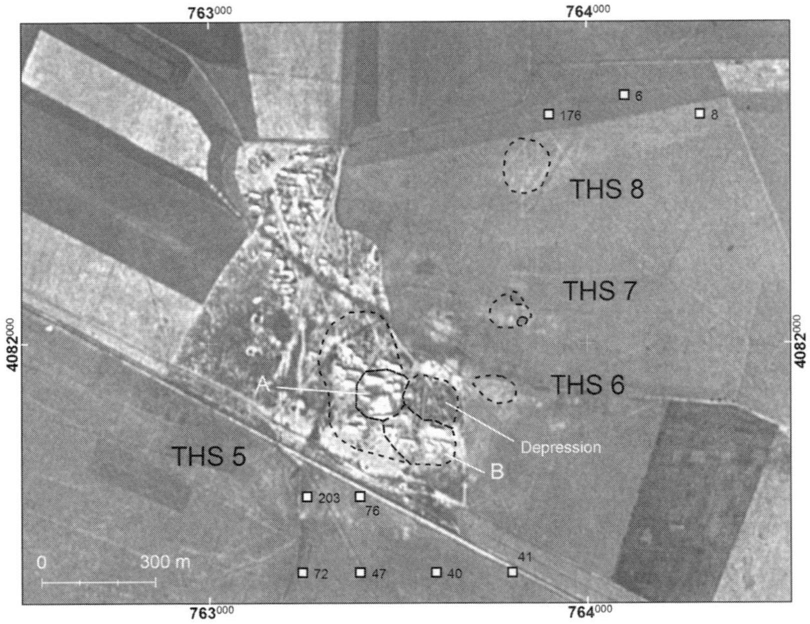

Figure A.4. THS 5, 6, 7, and 8
(CORONA 1108-1025DA005, 6 December 1969)

THS 6 (FIELD SITE NO. 23)

SITE NAME:

—

SITE POSITION:

763769 E, 4081879 N (center of mound)

SITE AREA AND MORPHOLOGY:

(fig. A.4) Small 1.5 m high oval mound, 110 m along its east–west axis × 70 m along its north–south axis. Under fallow cereal field at the time of visit, but plowed in the past; several areas of plowed-out baked brick fragments. Immediately east of enclosed depression of THS 5. Mound area 0.6 ha.

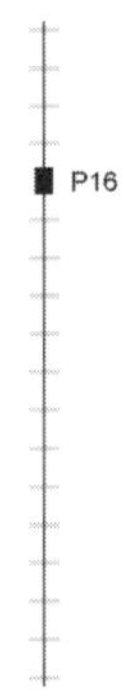

SITE SUB-AREAS AND PERIODS OF OCCUPATION:

Collected as a single unit. P16 (table C.6)

SETTLEMENT HISTORY:

This small site probably hosted only one or two structures in the late Sasanian–Early Islamic period (P16; 0.6 ha) and possibly later. It might be considered as part of the Tell al-Duwaym (THS 5) settlement complex.

THS 7 (FIELD SITE NO. 24)

SITE NAME:

—

SITE POSITION:

763787 E, 4082096 N (center of mound)

SITE AREA AND MORPHOLOGY:

(fig. A.4) Small circular mound 1.5 m above plain level, 100 m in diameter. Two small borrow pits (both 0.1 ha) at the northeastern and southeastern edges were not visible on the ground, but are apparent in December 1969 CORONA imagery. Under a fallow cereal field at the time of observation. Surface has a high concentration of baked brick fragments, clearly recently assembled. Total area 0.7 ha.

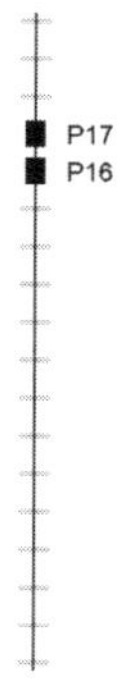

SITE SUB-AREAS AND PERIODS OF OCCUPATION:

Collected as a single unit. P16, P17 (table C.7, fig. C.3)

SETTLEMENT HISTORY:

As with THS 6, this site was a small cluster of structures in the late Sasanian–Early Islamic period (P16; 0.6 ha), but may have continued into the Abbasid period (P17; 0.6 ha). It too might be considered part of the Tell al-Duwaym (THS 5) settlement complex.

THS 8 (FIELD SITE NO. 25)

SITE NAME:

—

SITE POSITION:

763835 E, 4082461 N (location of measurement)

SITE AREA AND MORPHOLOGY:

(fig. A.4) Low mound preserved to 1 m high, under a fallow cotton field at time of observation. Approximately 125 m in diameter. Site boundaries were difficult to establish due to leveling, possibly for irrigation, but size could be approximated from coloration on December 1969 and May 1972 CORONA photographs. Estimated area 1.4 ha.

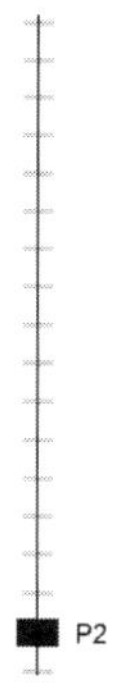

SITE SUB-AREAS AND PERIODS OF OCCUPATION:

Collected as a single unit. P2 (table C.8)

SETTLEMENT HISTORY:

This small mound was exclusively settled in the Halaf period (P2; 1.4 ha).

THS 9 (FIELD SITE NO. 13)

SITE NAME:

—

SITE POSITION:

763270 E, 4083492 N (center of mound, on east–west track)

SITE AREA AND MORPHOLOGY:

(fig. A.5) Very low (< 0.5 m) oval mound, 125 m long on its east–west axis × 80 m on the north–south axis. Under fallow field at time of visit. Total area 0.8 ha.

SITE SUB-AREAS AND PERIODS OF OCCUPATION:

Collected as a single unit. P2, P17 (table C.9)

SETTLEMENT HISTORY:

The site hosted a small Halaf village (P2; 0.8 ha) and then remained abandoned until reoccupied in the Abbasid period (P17; 0.8 ha; many untyped, but clearly Early Islamic sherds).

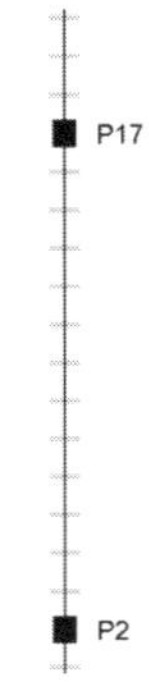

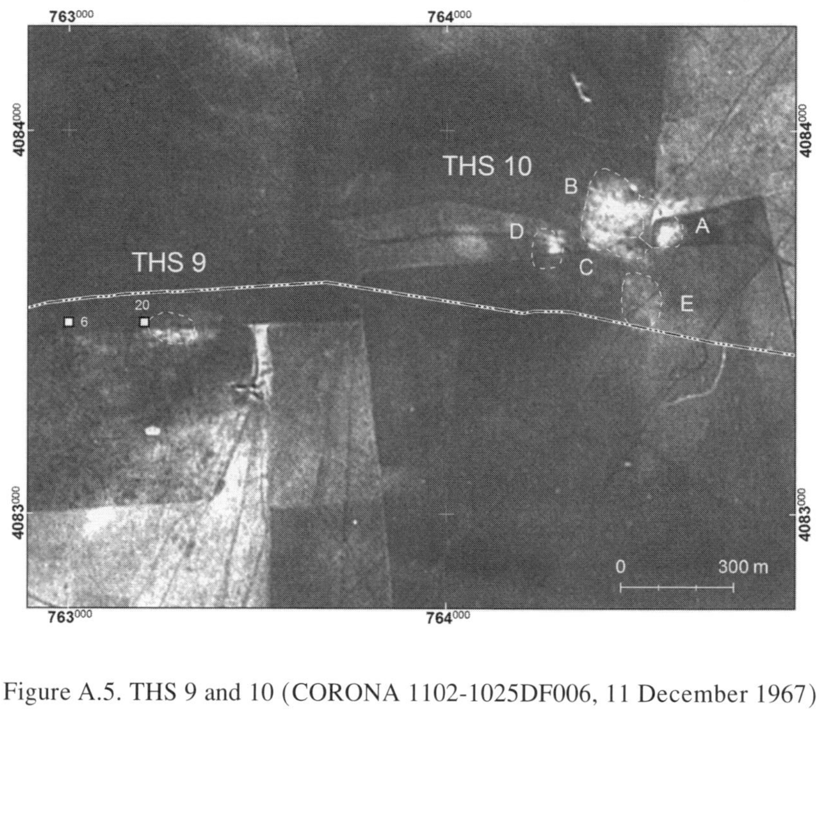

Figure A.5. THS 9 and 10 (CORONA 1102-1025DF006, 11 December 1967)

THS 10 (FIELD SITE NO. 32)

SITE NAME:

Khirbat al-Batta (source: local informant)

SITE POSITION:

764427 E, 4083796 N (midpoint of site, at boundary between Areas B and C)

SITE AREA AND MORPHOLOGY:

(fig. A.5) A set of 3 m high low mounds (A–C), 280 m on its east–west axis, around a 0.5 ha central depression, with a smaller outlying mound to the west (D) and another to the south (E). Total area 6.0 ha.

SITE SUB-AREAS AND PERIODS OF OCCUPATION:

(table C.10, fig. C.4)

Area A: 1.1 ha; P11, P13

Area B: 1.2 ha; P11, P13

Area C: 1.3 ha; P11, P13

Area D: 0.7 ha; P11

Area E: 1.2 ha; P4, P8, P11, P13

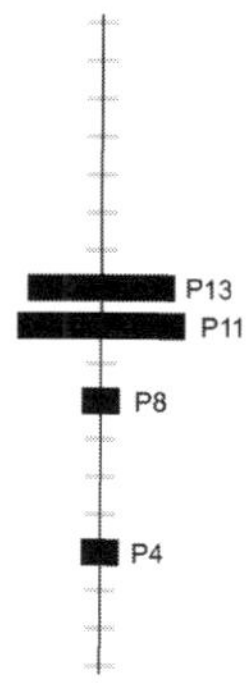

SETTLEMENT HISTORY:

The initial occupation was in Area E in the Late Chalcolithic 1–2 period (P4; 1.2 ha), and again in the Khabur period (P8; 1.2 ha). The entire site was settled in the Iron Age (P11; 5.5 ha) and again in the Hellenistic period (P13) with a slight reduction (4.8 ha).

SMALL FIND:

In Area B was found a silver-plated bronze bracelet with circles incised on its face (2 HM 35) (fig. A.21 no. 5). This object may be of recent date.

THS 11 (FIELD SITE NO. 27)

SITE NAME:

—

SITE POSITION:

765294 E, 4080144 N (center and top of mound)

SITE AREA AND MORPHOLOGY:

(fig. A.6) 2 m high low mound, 100 m long on its long northeast–southwest axis × 75 m on its short axis. Under fallow cereal field at time of observation. The site abuts the eastern side of a hollow way, which appears to have been widened and deepened into a 0.3 ha brick pit (see Section 5.3.4). A similar situation may have existed at THS 47. Total area 0.9 ha.

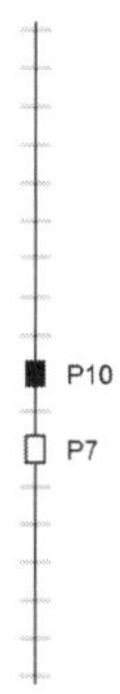

SITE SUB-AREAS AND PERIODS OF OCCUPATION:

Collected as a single unit. P7 (trace), P10 (table C.11)

SETTLEMENT HISTORY:

A trace of later third-millennium (P7) settlement might signify a temporary or seasonal occupation at that time. Sedentary occupation began in the Late Bronze Age (P10; 0.6 ha) and may have been resumed in the Islamic period.

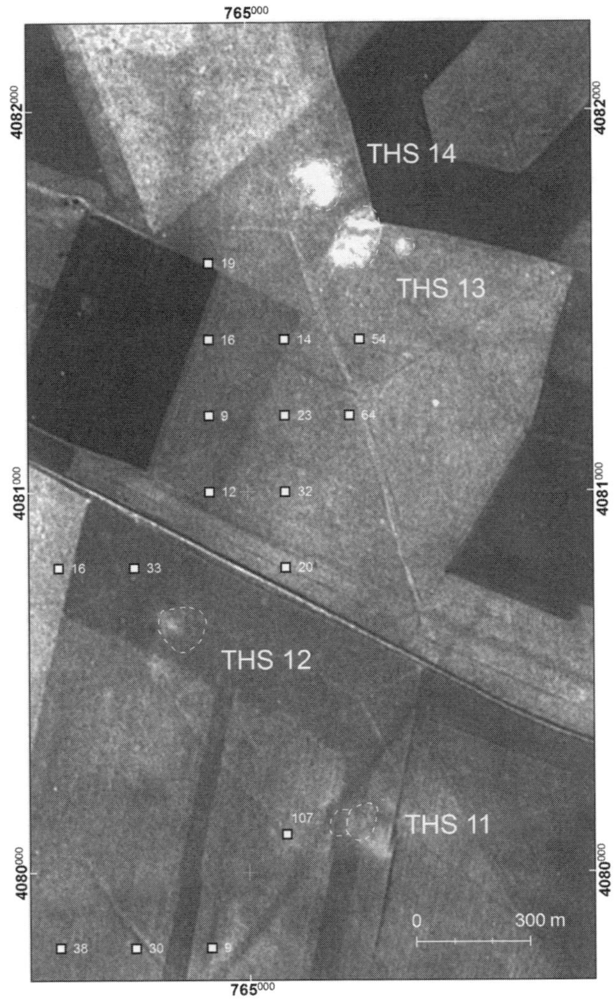

Figure A.6. THS 11, 12, 13, and 14 (CORONA 1102-1025DF006, 11 December 1967)

THS 12 (FIELD SITE NO. 10)

SITE NAME:

al-Asila (Arabic 1:50,000: الاصيلع)

SITE POSITION:

764806 E, 4080648 N (center and top of mound)

SITE AREA AND MORPHOLOGY:

(fig. A.6) A very low (ca. 1 m high) small mound under a fallow cereal field at time of observation. Total area 1.1 ha.

SITE SUB-AREAS AND PERIODS OF OCCUPATION:

Collected as a single unit. P1, P7 (trace), P10 (table C.12)

SETTLEMENT HISTORY:

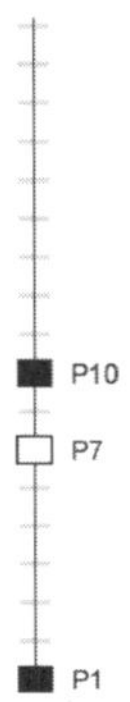

Initial settlement was during the Proto-Hassuna period (P1). It was reoccupied, probably on a temporary or seasonal basis, in the later third millennium (P7), and then settled on a permanent basis during the Late Bronze Age (P10). A concentration of baked brick fragments at the southeast edge probably derives from this latter phase of occupation.

THS 13 (FIELD SITE NO. 9)

SITE NAME:

—

SITE POSITION:

765325 E, 4081707 N (top of northern high point)

SITE AREA AND MORPHOLOGY:

(fig. A.6) A 2 m high small mound with high points at north and south, and a nearby 0.5 m high mound to its east. Both had been recently plowed for winter cereals at the time of observation. The northeastern extent of the larger western mound had been truncated by the expansion of a field. Total area 1.7 ha.

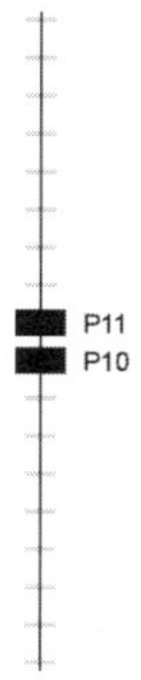

SITE SUB-AREAS AND PERIODS OF OCCUPATION:

Collected as a single unit. P10, P11 (table C.13)

SETTLEMENT HISTORY:

A small village with occupation in the Late Bronze Age (P10) and Iron Age (P11). For the Late Bronze Age, the site should possibly be considered with THS 14 as a single site.

THS 14 (FIELD SITE NO. 26)

SITE NAME:

—

SITE POSITION:

765210 E, 4081801 N (center and top of mound)

SITE AREA AND MORPHOLOGY:

(fig. A.6) 2 m high mound, irregularly shaped but roughly 130 m in diameter. Under a recently plowed cereal field at time of observation. A localized concentration of baked brick fragments at southwestern edge. Total area 1.3 ha.

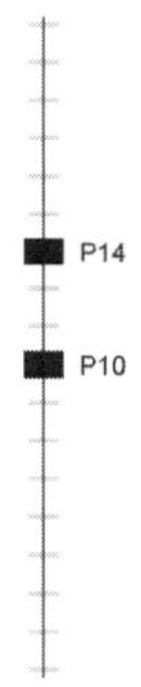

SITE SUB-AREAS AND PERIODS OF OCCUPATION:

Collected as a single unit. P10, P14 (table C.14)

SETTLEMENT HISTORY:

An initial settlement in the Late Bronze Age (P10; 1.3 ha) was followed, after an Iron Age abandonment, by a small Parthian occupation (P14; 1.3 ha).

THS 15 (FIELD SITE NO. 65)

SITE NAME:

al-'Abuda (local informant) or al-'Abadiya (Arabic 1:50,000: العباديه)

SITE POSITION:

766014 E, 4082940 N (center and top of mound)

SITE AREA AND MORPHOLOGY:

Small low mound, 3 m high, 160 m northwest–southeast × 90 m southwest–northeast. The site surface was heavily trampled; three house compounds are atop it. Area 1.2 ha.

SITE SUB-AREAS AND PERIODS OF OCCUPATION:

Collected as a single unit. P2, P4, P5b (table C.15)

SETTLEMENT HISTORY:

This site was first settled in the Halaf period (P2) and reoccupied in the Late Chalcolithic 1–2 period (P4; 1.2 ha). Settlement continued at the same scale into the Late Chalcolithic 3_4 period (P5b; 1.2 ha).

THS 16 (FIELD SITE NO. 8)

SITE NAME:

Tell al-Sara (Arabic 1:50,000: تل السرا ; French 1:200,000: Guir Tellaké)

SITE POSITION:

766126 E, 4078606 N (iron survey benchmark at top of high mound)

SITE AREA AND MORPHOLOGY:

(fig. A.7) A high (10 m) mound (A) surrounded by a flat low mounded area (ca. 1.5 m) on its north and northwest (B). High mound densely covered by recent cemetery; lower mounded area almost entirely under an extensive and densely settled modern village. Total area of settlement complex 11.3 ha.

SITE SUB-AREAS AND PERIODS OF OCCUPATION:

Area A: 0.8 ha; P2 (trace), P5b, P6, P7, P8, P13, P16, P17 (table C.16, fig. C.5)

Area B: 1.1 ha; P10, P11. Collections made only at northwest edge of Area B, beyond the extent of the village.

SETTLEMENT HISTORY:

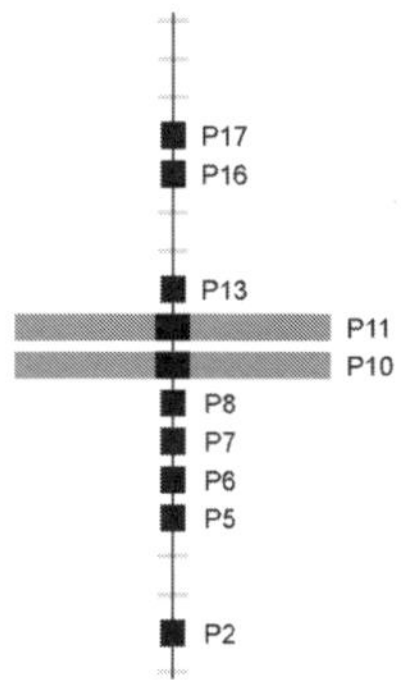

The earliest well-documented occupation on the high mound (A) is dated to the Late Chalcolithic 3–4 period (P5b; 0.8 ha), but it is likely that this settlement sat atop an earlier Halaf (P2) village. Settlement continued on the tell through the Ninevite 5 period (P6), the later third millennium B.C. (P7; including T7/4 post-Akkadian sherds), and the Khabur period (P8). Late Bronze Age and Iron Age (P10–11) occupation moved off the high mound to the lower town, which was collected in a restricted 1.1 ha area, but may have been as large as 10.5 ha. Settlement returned to the high mound in the Hellenistic (P13) and late Sasanian through Abbasid periods (P16–17).

Figure A.7. THS 16, 20, and 22 (CORONA 1102-1025DF007, 11 December 1967)

Figure A.8. THS 17, 18, 19, and 21 (CORONA 1108, 6 December 1969)

THS 17 (FIELD SITE NO. 64)

SITE NAME:

al-Masiha (Arabic 1:50,000: المسيحة)

SITE POSITION:

766824 E, 4081005 N (center and top of mound)

SITE AREA AND MORPHOLOGY:

(fig. A.8, fig. C.6) Small low site, 1 m high. 180 m east–west extent × 130 m north–south. The site is partially leveled for irrigation on the eastern side, but was under a fallow cereal field on the west at the time of observation. Site boundaries are derived from soil color on CORONA imagery. 350 m north of village of al-Siha. Estimated area 2.1 ha.

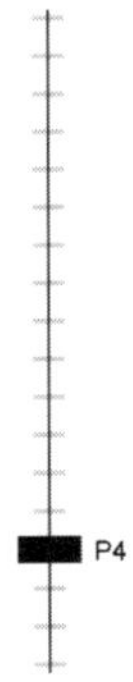

SITE SUB-AREAS AND PERIODS OF OCCUPATION:

Collected as a single unit. P4

SETTLEMENT HISTORY:

A village of the Late Chalcolithic 1–2 period (P4; 2.1 ha).

THS 18 (FIELD SITE NO. 20)

SITE NAME:

—

SITE POSITION:

767894 E, 4081880 N (center and top of northwest mound, at boundary between Areas A and B)

SITE AREA AND MORPHOLOGY:

(fig. A.8) A main complex of three small mounds around a 0.7 ha enclosed depression: a northwest mound (5 m high, collected as Areas A and B), a 3 m high mound to its east (C), and a 2 m high mound to its south (D). A small outlying mound to the northwest was difficult to measure because it now has a diesel pump and an earthen reservoir atop it. A 2.4 ha unmounded eastern extension was not collected, nor was a small outlying area to the southwest (0.3 ha). Cotton fields surrounded the site on all sides, although at the time of visit most were fallow. The site itself was either uncultivated land or had long been left fallow. Total area of the complex covers 9.8 ha.

SITE SUB-AREAS AND PERIODS OF OCCUPATION:

(table C.18)

Area A: 1.4 ha; P8, P17, P19

Area B: 1.4 ha; P8, P16, P17, P19

Area C: 1.0 ha; P4 (trace), P8, P11, P16, P17, P18, P19, P20 (common kiln slag)

Area D: 2.0 ha; P2, P4 (trace), P5b, P8, P10, P11, P17, P19

Area E: 0.6 ha; P17, P19

SETTLEMENT HISTORY:

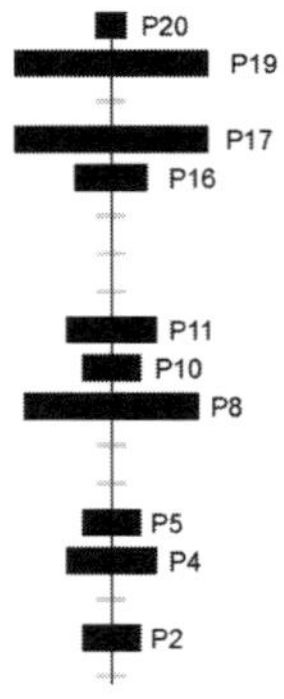

A small Halaf-period (P2) settlement first appeared in Area D (2.0 ha), followed by a trace of Late Chalcolithic 1–2 (P4) settlement on Areas C and D (3.0 ha), and substantial Late Chalcolithic 3–4 (P5b) settlement again in Area D (2.0 ha). The entire site except for Area E was settled in the Khabur period (P8; 5.8 ha), with reduced occupation in the Late Bronze Age (P10; 2.0 ha) and Iron Age (P11; 3.0 ha). Settlement resumed in the late Sasanian–Early Islamic period (P16; 2.4 ha) and expanded to cover the entire site in the Abbasid and Middle to Late Islamic periods (P17, P19–20; 6.4 ha), including the small outlying mound E. It is probable that the canal at the western edge of the main mounded area (fig. 5.31) was in use during these latter periods.

THS 19 (FIELD SITE NO. 63)

SITE NAME:

—

SITE POSITION:

767764 E, 4080807 N (approximate center of artifact scatter)

SITE AREA AND MORPHOLOGY:

(fig. A.8) Flat circular site identifiable only by soil color and slightly elevated sherd density. Approximate diameter 100 m. Recently plowed at the time of visit, very poor visibility, not collected. Estimated area 0.8 ha.

SITE SUB-AREAS AND PERIODS OF OCCUPATION:

Not collected.

SETTLEMENT HISTORY:

The site was not formally collected, but many red surface-reduced core sherds of possible Late Chalcolithic 3–4 (P5b) date.

THS 20 (FIELD SITE NO. 28)

SITE NAME:

Khirbat ʻAli (Local informant: خربت علي)

SITE POSITION:

767791 E, 4079254 N (center and top of northwest mound, at boundary between Areas A and B)

SITE AREA AND MORPHOLOGY:

(fig. A.7) Complex of low mounds around a 0.9 ha central enclosed depression, 430 m along its long north–south axis × 280 m along its short axis. Northwest of the depression is a mound 5 m high (north half collected as Area A, south half collected as Area B); to the north a lower east–west mound (C) rises 3 m. From the east side of the enclosed depression and extending to the southeast are three low mounds (D, E, and F), each 2 m high. Site sits in the middle of a cereal field, plowed at the time of observation. Soils are light in color and texture. Total area 8.2 ha.

SITE SUB-AREAS AND PERIODS OF OCCUPATION:

(table C.19)

Area A: 0.7 ha; P2, P5b, P11

Area B: 1.2 ha; P2, P5b, P7 (trace), P11

Area C: 1.7 ha; P2, P5b

Area D: 1.2 ha; P2, P10

Area E: 0.9 ha; P14

Area F: 1.8 ha; P14, P16 (trace)

SETTLEMENT HISTORY:

The northern half of the site was first settled in the Halaf (P2; 4.7 ha). The western half of the site was reoccupied in the Late Chalcolithic 3–4 period (P5b; 3.5 ha). A seasonal or temporary settlement of the later third millennium (P7) was found in Area B (1.2 ha). A small Late Bronze Age (P10) settlement on the eastern side (1.2 ha) was succeeded by a larger Iron Age (P11) village on the western mound (1.8 ha). The low southeastern mounds were settled during the Parthian period (P14; 2.7 ha). Traces of late Sasanian–Early Islamic (P16) settlement could be identified at the southern edge of the site, but was probably limited to one or two houses or nomadic occupation.

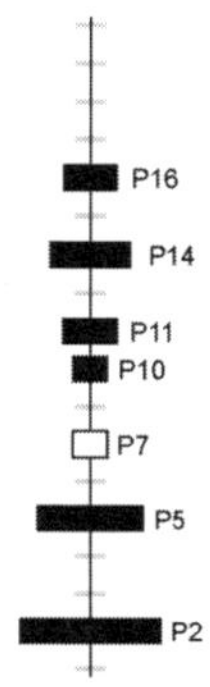

THS 21 (FIELD SITE NO. 62)

Site Name:

—

Site Position:

768197 E, 4080487 N (approximate center of artifact scatter)

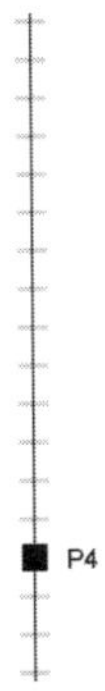

Site Area and Morphology:

(fig. A.8) Flat circular sherd scatter, entirely leveled by aggressive deep plowing; poor visibility. Approximately 100 m in diameter. Site extent estimated from sherd density and signature on CORONA imagery. Area 0.8 ha.

Site Sub-Areas and Periods of Occupation:

Collected as a single unit. P4 (table C.20)

Settlement History:

A small village of the Late Chalcolithic 1–2 period (P4; 0.8 ha).

THS 22 (FIELD SITE NO. 39)

Site Name:

—

Site Position:

768109 E, 4078294 N (approximate center of site)

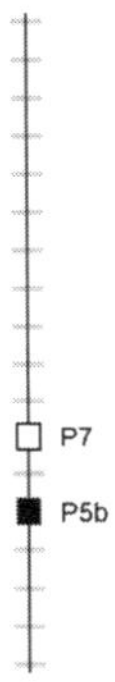

Site Area and Morphology:

(fig. A.7) Very low (< 1 m) small mound, roughly 100 m in diameter. Identified primarily by soil color on CORONA imagery. Total area 0.8 ha.

Site Sub-Areas and Periods of Occupation:

Collected as a single unit. P5b, P7 (trace) (table C.21)

Settlement History:

This very small (0.8 ha) Late Chalcolithic 3–4 (P5b) settlement was probably short lived; it was reoccupied in the later third millennium (P7), probably on a temporary basis.

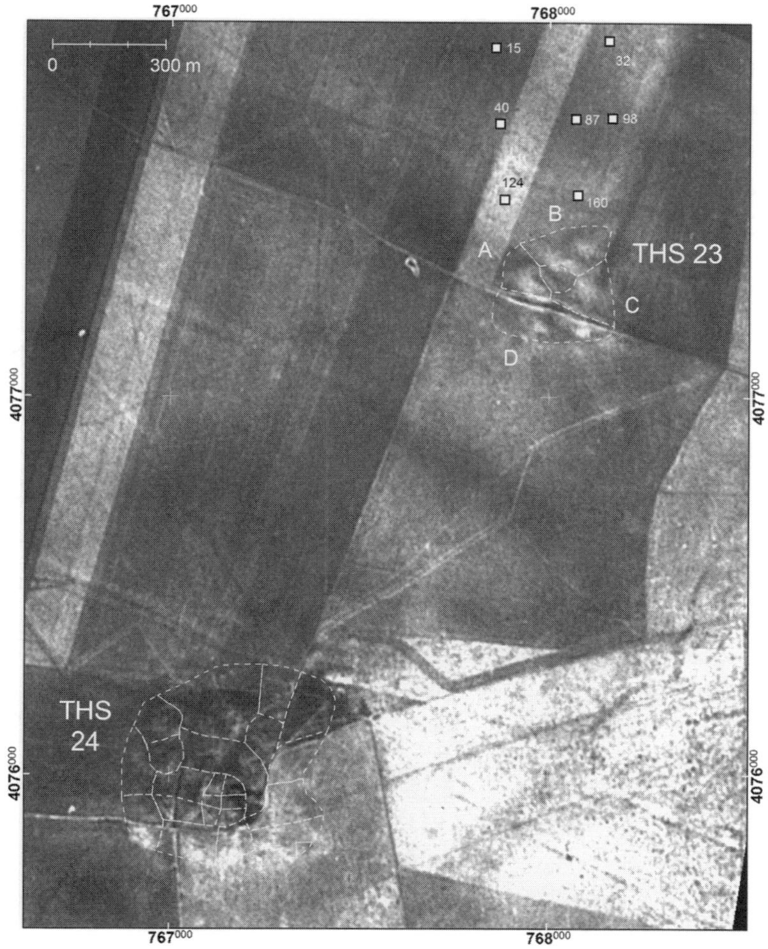

Figure A.9. THS 23 and 24 (CORONA 1102-1025DF007, 11 December 1967). For THS 24 area subdivision, see figure 4.9

THS 23 (FIELD SITE NO. 40)

SITE NAME:

Khirbat al-Trob (source: local informant)

SITE POSITION:

767792 E, 4077293 N (top of western mound, eastern part of Area A)

SITE AREA AND MORPHOLOGY:

(fig. A.9) A complex of low mounds around a 0.5 ha central enclosed depression, 300 m in diameter. The highest mound (A) is 3 m at the western side of the complex; on the eastern side of the depression is a 2 m high mound (C). A slightly mounded area (B) to the north consists of southwestern and northeastern mounds, mostly defined by soil color and sherd density. Another broad flat area (D) lies at the southern edge of the complex. The eastern part of Area D has been removed by the northwest extension of a field, but is still visible via soil coloration. Total area 8.0 ha.

SITE SUB-AREAS AND PERIODS OF OCCUPATION:

(table C.22)

Area A: 1.1 ha; P10, P11

Area B: 2.0 ha; P10, P11

Area C: 1.5 ha; P10, P11, P13, P14

Area D: 2.8 ha; P10, P13, P20 (trace)

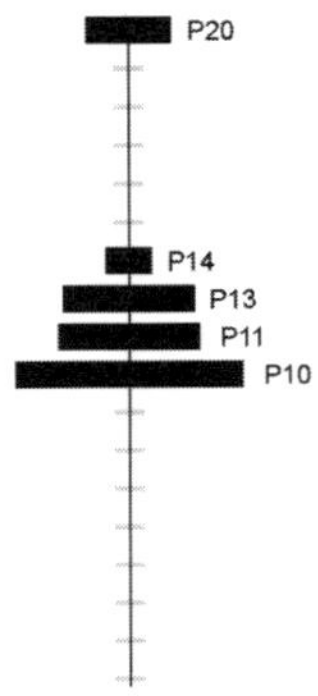

SETTLEMENT HISTORY:

Initially settled in the Late Bronze Age (P10) across all collection areas (7.5 ha). Settlement shrank slightly to the northern areas in the Iron Age (P11; 4.7 ha), and then shifted to the south and east in the Hellenistic period (P13; 4.4 ha). By the Parthian period (P14), only the eastern area was still occupied (1.5 ha). A trace of Late Islamic (P20) settlement, perhaps non-sedentary, occupied the south.

THS 24 (FIELD SITE NO. 16)

SITE NAME:

Khirbat al-'Abd (source: local informant)

SITE POSITION:

767145 E, 4075961 N (top of central mound at its north end, at boundary between Areas A and F)

SITE AREA AND MORPHOLOGY:

(figs. 4.9, A.9) A large complex of multiple mounds and enclosed depressions. At center is a 1.3 ha mound approximately 5 m high (arbitrarily subdivided into Areas A–F) with lower spurs to the south (Areas J–K) and northwest (Areas L–M, P) about 2 m above plain level. A line of three low mounds stretches along the western edge of the complex (Areas N, O, and Q, >1 m high). Two low mounds are at the eastern edge: a broad expanse (southern half collected as H, northern half collected as I, and a field cut into the southeastern edge collected separately as G) and a smaller discrete mound (S), both approximately 1 m high. Several areas at the northern periphery of the site (R, U, and T) were almost entirely unmounded and were defined by perceived declines in artifact densities. There is an enclosed depression north of the central mound and south of Area R (2.5 ha), but *Prosopis* grows densely in the troughs between most of the low mounds. With the exception of a single north–south field cutting across Areas P and N which had been plowed recently, the entire site was under fallowed cereal fields. The entire complex covers 24.0 ha.

SITE SUB-AREAS AND PERIODS OF OCCUPATION:

(figs. 4.9, C.7–C.10, and table C.23)

Area A: 0.2 ha; P2 (trace), P8, P10, P16, P17

Area B: 0.2 ha; P8, P10, P11, P16, P17, P20

Area C: 0.3 ha; P8, P10, P17, P20
Area D: 0.2 ha; P8, P10, P17
Area E: 0.2 ha; P2 (trace), P8, P10, P11, P17
Area F: 0.2 ha; P2 (trace), P8, P10, P11, P17
Area G: 0.1 ha; P8, P10
Area H: 1.2 ha; P8, P10
Area I: 1.6 ha; P8, P10
Area J: 0.9 ha; P5b, P8
Area K: 1.5 ha; P8
Area L: 0.7 ha; P2 (trace), P10, P14
Area M: 1.0 ha; P2 (trace), P8, P10, P13, P14
Area N: 1.1 ha; P10, P11, P14
Area O: 1.2 ha; P8, P10, P13
Area P: 0.7 ha; P8, P10, P13, P14
Area Q: 1.1 ha; P10, P13
Area R: 3.9 ha; P2 (trace), P10, P15, P16, P17
Area S: 1.2 ha; P10, P15, P16
Area T: 0.9 ha; P8, P10, P15, P16
Area U: 1.2 ha; P15, P16
Area V: 1.8 ha; P15, P16

SETTLEMENT HISTORY:

Halaf-period (P2) ceramics cover 6.3 ha of the central mound and the area to its west at a low density, probably because Halaf levels are obscured by subsequent occupation. A small Late Chalcolithic 3–4 occupation (P5; 0.9 ha) existed south of the central mound, but otherwise the site remained unoccupied until the Khabur period (P8), when the central mound, lower mounded areas to the east, south, and west, and an isolated area to the northeast were all settled (10.4 ha). The town grew in the Late Bronze Age (P10) to at least 16.1 ha as further areas of outer town were settled. Areas J and K, which yielded small collections, may have also been settled. In the Iron Age (P11), settlement shrank to a restricted area of the central mound and an outlying area to the southwest (1.8 ha), then shifted to the northwest part of the outer town in the Hellenistic period (P13; 4.0 ha). The western lower mounds were occupied in the Parthian period (P14; 3.6 ha). Sasanian settlement covered a broad low area of the northeastern outer town (P15; 9.0 ha) and expanded back onto the northeastern part of the central mound in the late Sasanian–Early Islamic period (P16; 9.5 ha). Abbasid settlement expanded to cover the entire central mound, but only a part of the northern outer town (P17; 5.2 ha). A small Late Islamic settlement sat on the southeastern part of the central mound (P20; 0.5 ha).

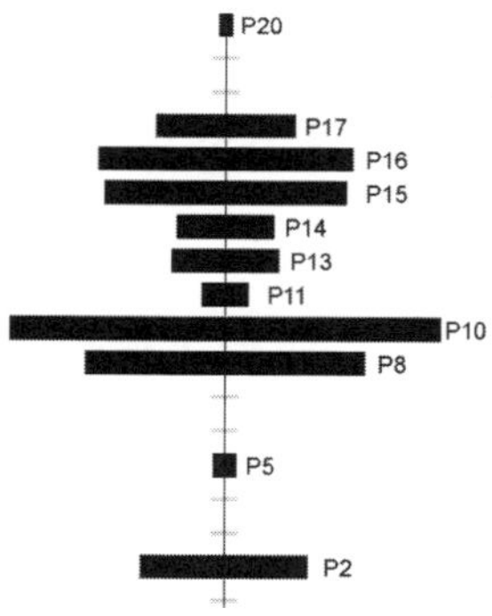

THS 25 (FIELD SITE NO. 7)

SITE NAME:

The Hamoukar Southern Extension. Known locally as Khirbat al-Fakhar (source: local informant)

SITE POSITION:

763625 E, 4076423 N (top of mound in Area B)

SITE AREA AND MORPHOLOGY:

A 31.3 ha complex central mounded area surrounded by an extensive low or unmounded outer area; the entire complex covers approximately 300 ha. For a detailed description, see Section 4.5 and figure 4.10.

SITE SUB-AREAS AND PERIODS OF OCCUPATION:

Central mounded area only; see figure 4.13 and table C.24

Area A: 1.1 ha; P4

Area B: 1.0 ha; P4, P19

Area C: 0.9 ha; P4, P16, P17, P20

Area D: 0.6 ha; P4, P16, P17, P19

Area E: 2.0 ha; P4, P16, P17

Area F: 1.2 ha; P4, P17, P19

Area G: 2.4 ha; P4, P13, P14, P17, P19

Area H: 1.7 ha; P4, P13

Area I: 3.9 ha; P4, P13, P14

Area J: 1.7 ha; P4, P14

Area K: 2.0 ha; P4

Area L: 2.3 ha; P4

Area M: 2.8 ha; P4

Area N: 1.4 ha; P4

Area O: 2.2 ha; P4, P14

Area P: 0.5 ha; P4, P14

Area Q: 3.5 ha; P4

SETTLEMENT HISTORY:

Initial settlement in the Late Chalcolithic 1–2 periods (P4) appears to have been focused on the 31.3 ha central mounded complex, which was surrounded by a 275.3 ha unmounded scatter. Whereas the central complex was probably dense village architecture, the outer scatter was an extensive area of low-density settlement clusters. The Late Chalcolithic 1–2 occupations at THS 26 and 27 should be considered as part of THS 25 as well. The interpretation of this site is discussed above in Section 8.1. After a long period of abandonment, during which the area probably served as part of the agricultural sustaining area of Hamoukar, the central part of the mounded complex was resettled in the Hellenistic period (P13; 7.9 ha) and grew in the Parthian period (P14; 10.7 ha). Settlement shifted to the western end of the central mounded complex in the late Sasanian–Early Islamic period (P16; 3.5 ha), and then expanded to the east in the Abbasid period (P17; 7.1 ha). A low scatter of Middle to Late Islamic (P19) sherds covered 6.2 ha, although it is unlikely that this entire area was occupied simultaneously. (Settlement graph does not include outer settlement.)

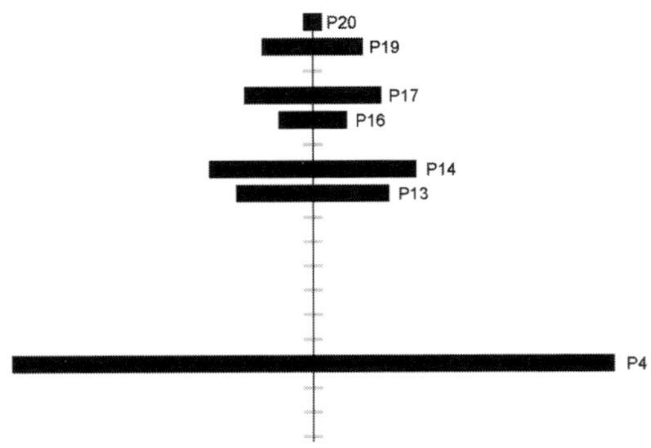

SMALL FINDS:

A fragmentary pierced basalt stamp seal with a circular design (2 HM 22) was found in Area K (fig. A.21 no. 3). Stamp seals of this size and morphology are very common in contemporary Late Chalcolithic 1–2 levels at

Tepe Gawra (Rothman 2002b). A fragmentary "hut symbol" or "spectacle idol" was found on the surface near the edge of the northern outer settlement area (1 HM 183; published in Gibson et al. 2002b: fig. 17).

THS 26 (FIELD SITE NO. 15)

SITE NAME:

Khirbat Awa'id (source: local informant)

SITE POSITION:

764495 E, 4076571 N (center and top of mound)

SITE AREA AND MORPHOLOGY:

Small oval mound approximately 2 m high. 200 m along its north–south axis × 100 m along its east–west axis. Most of the site was under a fallow cereal field at time of observation. The northeastern corner of the site has been cut into in order to expand a cotton field. Site extent is defined by mounding, since the site sits within the extensive area of Khirbat al-Fakhar (THS 25). Total area 1.6 ha. See figures 4.10 and 4.14.

SITE SUB-AREAS AND PERIODS OF OCCUPATION:

Collected as a single unit. P3, P4

SETTLEMENT HISTORY:

Initial settlement occurred in the Ubaid period (P3; 1.6 ha) and continued into the Late Chalcolithic 1–2 period (P4), at which time the site was a mounded component of the larger THS 25 settlement complex.

THS 27 (FIELD SITE NO. 14)

SITE NAME:

Tell Fakhar, part of larger Khirbat al-Fakhar; also called Khirbat Abu Lazam by local informant, after landowner

SITE POSITION:

764511 E, 4075847 N (center and top of mound)

SITE MEASUREMENTS AND MORPHOLOGY:

Circular mounded site, 6 m high and 200 m in diameter. A slight depression, now highly eroded, in the northwestern flank suggests some excavation in the distant past. Entirely under cultivated fields, fallow at the time of observation. Area 3.5 ha. See figures 4.10 and 4.14.

SITE SUB-AREAS AND PERIODS OF OCCUPATION:

Collected as a single unit. P4, P11 (table C.26, fig. C.11)

SETTLEMENT HISTORY:

This mound was initially occupied in the Late Chalcolithic 1–2 period (P4). At that time, it was a mounded area on the southeastern edge of the Khirbat al-Fakhar settlement complex (THS 25). Its sherd assemblage suggests nucleated settlement, rather than the dispersed or low-density settlement that characterizes the low areas of THS 25. Its reoccupation in the Iron Age (P11; 3.5 ha) may have extended into post-Assyrian times; the surface assemblage contained a high percentage of post-Assyrian types.

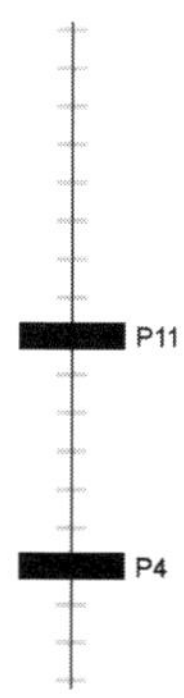

THS 28 (FIELD SITE NO. 50)

SITE NAME:

—

SITE POSITION:

765323 E, 4074977 N (center and top of mound)

SITE AREA AND MORPHOLOGY:

(fig. A.10) Small low site, <1 m high and 90 m in diameter, with a single-room structure built atop it, otherwise under a fallow cereal field. Very low-density scatter, no diagnostics. Total area 0.7 ha.

SITE SUB-AREAS AND PERIODS OF OCCUPATION:

Collected as a single unit.

SETTLEMENT HISTORY:

Undatable due to low sherd density and lack of diagnostics.

THS 29 (FIELD SITE NO. 34)

SITE NAME:

—

SITE POSITION:

765411 E, 4074507 N (center and top of mound)

SITE AREA AND MORPHOLOGY:

(fig. A.10) Oval mound 4 m high, 180 m along its long north–south axis × 130 m along its east–west axis. Lighter and finer sediments than surrounding fields. Mound slopes gradually to plain level to south, more sharply to north. Under a fallow field at the time of visit. Area 2.0 ha.

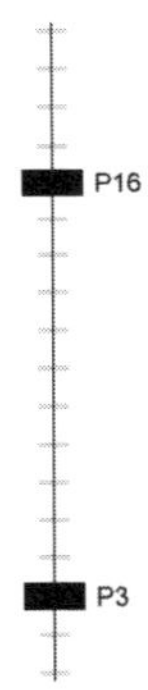

SITE SUB-AREAS AND PERIODS OF OCCUPATION:

Collected as a single unit. P3, P16 (table C.27, fig. C.12)

SETTLEMENT HISTORY:

A small Ubaid settlement (P3; 2.0 ha), the height of which suggests continuous occupation throughout the period, or perhaps an unrecognized pre-Ubaid component. The mound was reoccupied much later in the Abbasid period (P16), probably by an isolated farmstead or very small village.

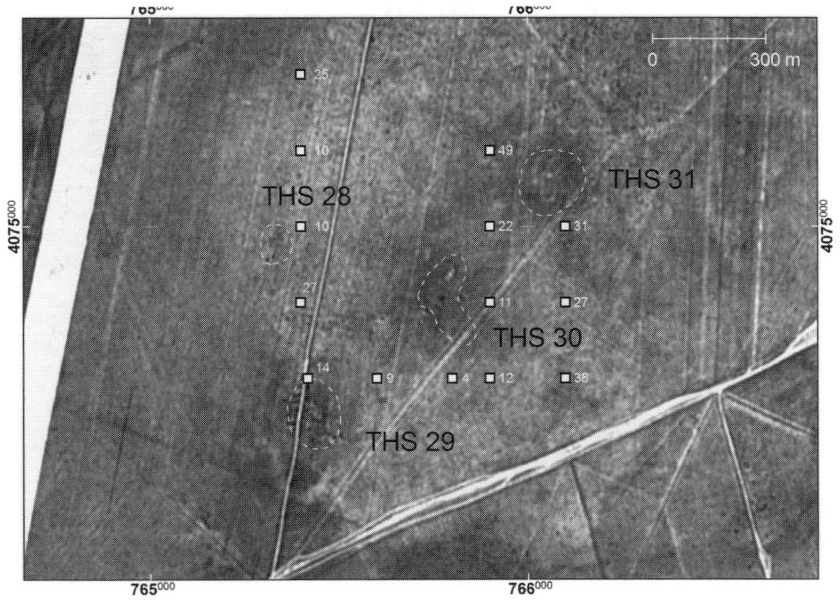

Figure A.10. THS 28, 29, 30, and 31
(CORONA 1117-1025DF147, 25 May 1972)

THS 30 (FIELD SITE NO. 49)

SITE NAME:

—

SITE POSITION:

765758 E, 4074797 N (center of central low mound)

SITE AREA AND MORPHOLOGY:

(fig. A.10) Three very low (< 1 m) mounds, 240 m along the north–south axis × 100 m along the east–west axis. Under a plowed and crusted field with low visibility. Total area 2.1 ha.

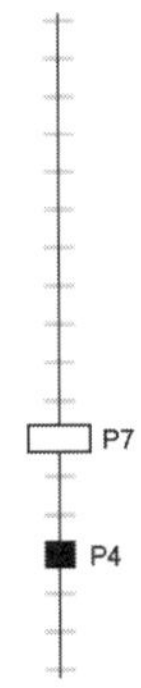

SITE SUB-AREAS AND PERIODS OF OCCUPATION:

Collected as a single unit. P4, P7 (trace) (table C.28)

SETTLEMENT HISTORY:

The site's primary occupation was in the Late Chalcolithic 1–2 period (P4; 2.1 ha) but may have been resettled on a seasonal or temporary basis in the later third millennium (P7).

THS 31 (FIELD SITE NO. 33)

SITE NAME:

—

SITE POSITION:

766088 E, 4075133 N (center of site)

SITE AREA AND MORPHOLOGY:

(fig. A.10) Small and very low circular site, 175 m in diameter. Possibly unmounded; recognizable from its lighter soil on CORONA imagery. Under a very clean fallowed cereal field at time of observation. Area 2.4 ha.

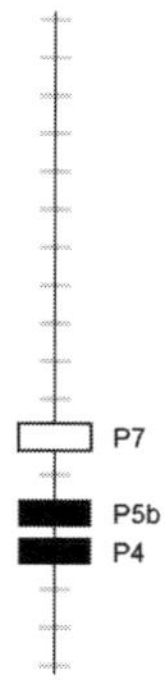

SITE SUB-AREAS AND PERIODS OF OCCUPATION:

Collected as a single unit. P4, P5b, P7 (trace) (table C.29, fig. C.13)

SETTLEMENT HISTORY:

Occupied in the Late Chalcolithic 1–2 (P4) and Late Chalcolithic 3–4 (P5b) periods (2.4 ha), perhaps continuously, although the site's low height argues against it. A trace occupation in the later third millennium (P7) may have been a seasonal or temporary settlement.

THS 32 (FIELD SITE NO. 60)

SITE NAME:

Khirbat 'Asaylan (source: local informant)

SITE POSITION:

768030 E, 4073222 N (cement benchmark at top of mound, at intersection of Areas A–D)

SITE AREA AND MORPHOLOGY:

(fig. A.11) Small conical mound, approximately 170 m in diameter, rising 7 m above the plain, with a *Prosopis*-filled depression at its southern edge. Arbitrarily subdivided along the cardinal axes into four areas (A–D). At time of visit, site was under several fallow fields. A single small structure at the base of the northwestern slope. Total area 2.6 ha.

SITE SUB-AREAS AND PERIODS OF OCCUPATION:

(table C.30)

Area A: 0.6 ha; P2, P4, P5b, P8, P11, P16

Area B: 1.0 ha; P2, P4, P5b, P8, P11, P14

Area C: 0.4 ha; P2, P5b, P8, P11

Area D: 0.6 ha; P2, P5b, P7 (trace), P8, P11

SETTLEMENT HISTORY:

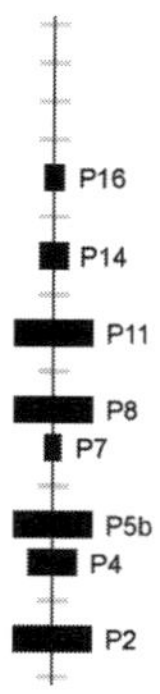

Settlement began as a Halaf (P2) village, covering the entire area of the site (2.6 ha), and was followed by a reduced Late Chalcolithic 1–2 (P4) occupation on its southern side (1.6 ha). The entire mound was again settled in the Late Chalcolithic 3–4 period (P5b; 2.6 ha, possibly to be associated with THS 33). Occupation resumed on a seasonal or temporary basis in the later third millennium (P7; 0.6 ha), but the entire mound was settled again in the Khabur period (P8) and, following a Late Bronze Age hiatus, in the Iron Age (P11; 2.6 ha). A small Parthian (P14) settlement sat on the southwestern slopes of the mound (1.0 ha), and later a late Sasanian–Early Islamic (P16) settlement sat on the southeastern slopes (0.6 ha).

SMALL FIND:

A fragmentary black limestone stamp seal with a crosshatched design (2 HM 38) was found in Area B (fig. A.21 no. 4).

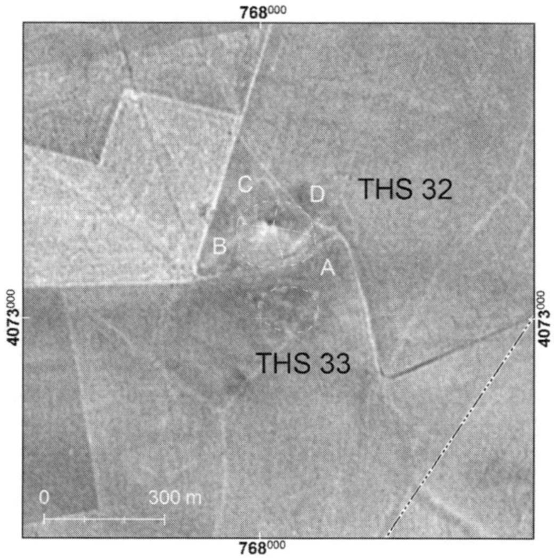

Figure A.11. THS 32 and 33
(CORONA 1108-1025DA006, 6 December 1969)

THS 33 (FIELD SITE NO. 61)

SITE NAME:

—

SITE POSITION:

768073 E, 4073028 N (location of measurement)

SITE AREA AND MORPHOLOGY:

(fig. A.11) Small low site, 1.5 m high; 145 m east–west × 110 m north–south. Recently plowed at the time of visit. Total area 1.3 ha.

SITE SUB-AREAS AND PERIODS OF OCCUPATION:

Collected as a single unit. P5b (table C.31, fig. C.14)

SETTLEMENT HISTORY:

A small Late Chalcolithic 3–4 village (P5b; 1.3 ha). Although separated by an unsettled area, this site could be considered part of THS 32.

THS 34 (FIELD SITE NO. 31)

SITE NAME:

Tell al-Fakhar (Arabic 1:50,000: تل الفخار)

SITE POSITION:

763751 E, 4074551 N (center and top of northern high point, Area A)

SITE AREA AND MORPHOLOGY:

(fig. 4.6) Circular mound 6 m high and 200 m in diameter, with two high points at the northern (collected as Area A) and southern (collected as Area B) ends. Recently plowed at the time of visit; soils very light in color with a powdery texture. CORONA imagery suggests that there were two structures atop the site in 1968–1972, but no traces of them remain. Total area 3.2 ha.

SITE SUB-AREAS AND PERIODS OF OCCUPATION:

(see table C.32)

Area A: 1.6 ha; P11

Area B: 1.6 ha; P11

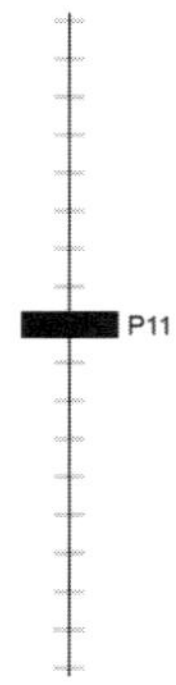

SETTLEMENT HISTORY:

Settlement was probably continuous through the early and middle first millennium B.C. (P11), including the post-Assyrian period. The height of this mound suggests that some earlier phases of occupation may not have been recognized.

THS 35 (FIELD SITE NO. 42)

SITE NAME:

—

SITE POSITION:

763916 E, 4074400 N (approximate center of site)

SITE AREA AND MORPHOLOGY:

(fig. 4.6) Small site, approximately 130 m × 90 m, completely unmounded, perhaps due to its position beneath a fallow cotton field at time of observation. Boundaries estimated from signature on December 1969 CORONA imagery. Poor surface visibility. Area 1.1 ha.

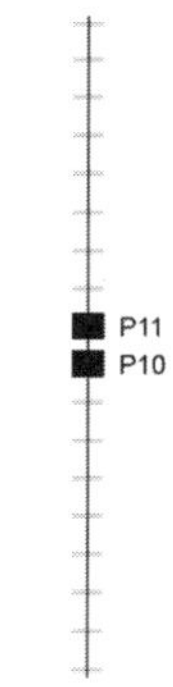

SITE SUB-AREAS AND PERIODS OF OCCUPATION:

Collected as a single unit. P10, P11 (table C.33)

SETTLEMENT HISTORY:

Settled in the Late Bronze Age (P10) and Iron Age (P11; 1.1 ha).

THS 36 (FIELD SITE NO. 41)

SITE NAME:

—

SITE POSITION:

764051 E, 4074135 N (center of mound)

SITE AREA AND MORPHOLOGY:

(fig. 4.6) Small low mound, <1 m high and 100 m in diameter. Boundaries defined primarily from signature on December 1967 and December 1969 CORONA imagery. Total area 0.8 ha.

SITE SUB-AREAS AND PERIODS OF OCCUPATION:

Collected as a single unit. P5b (table C.34)

SETTLEMENT HISTORY:

A small Late Chalcolithic 3–4 village.

THS 37 (FIELD SITE NO. 44).

SITE NAME:

Umm Adham (Arabic 1:50,000: أم العضام)

SITE POSITION:

764711 E, 4072560 N (cement benchmark at top of high mound, Area A)

SITE AREA AND MORPHOLOGY:

(fig. A.12) High mound with a broad lower mound to the south. Maximum possible dimensions 650 m on north–south axis × 420 m on east–west axis. Mound at northern end of complex is 8 m high; the lower town area is 2 m high and fades imperceptibly into the plain. Slopes of the high mound (A) are obscured by village houses, with only the top two-thirds accessible to collection on all but the north side. The mounded area to the south is undulating, with many small mounds and depressions. Almost the entire lower town is beneath the village, making the extent of the lower town very difficult to determine; the collection of this area (B) was limited and should not necessarily be considered representative of the entire lower mound. Total area, including estimated uncollected areas of the lower mound, is 20.0 ha.

SITE SUB-AREAS AND PERIODS OF OCCUPATION:

(see table C.35, figure C.15)

Area A: 2.3 ha; P7, P8, P10

Area B: 2.5 ha; P10, P16

SETTLEMENT HISTORY:

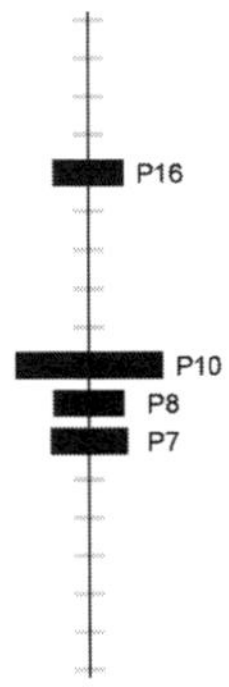

Although its height suggests an unrecognized prehistoric component, the earliest identified occupation is of the later third millennium (P7) on the high mound, including abundant post-Akkadian diagnostics (2.3 ha). Settlement continued in the Khabur period (P8; 2.3). In the Late Bronze Age (P10), the high mound continued to be occupied, and now settlement spread to the lower town to the south (at least 4.9 ha and possibly as much as 20.0 ha). Occupation may have resumed or continued into the Iron Age. After a long abandonment, the lower town was reoccupied in the late Sasanian–Early Islamic period (P16) at an indeterminate size (at least 2.5 ha, but probably much larger).

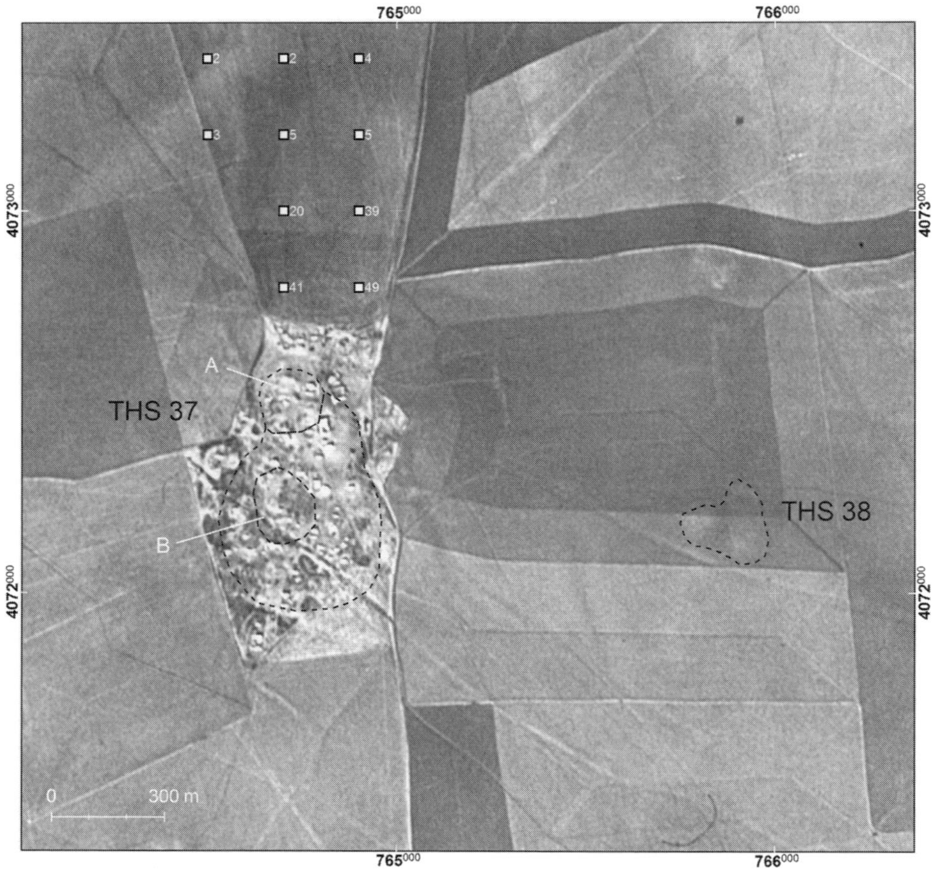

Figure A.12. THS 37 and 38
(CORONA 1108-1025DA006 6, December 1969)

THS 38 (FIELD SITE NO. 67)

SITE NAME:

—

SITE POSITION:

765884 E, 4072172 N (center of mound)

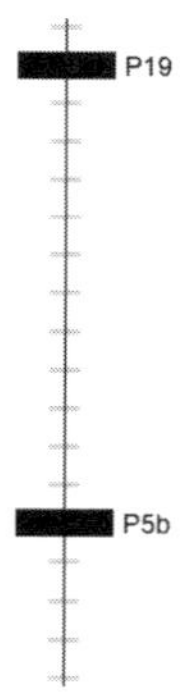

SITE AREA AND MORPHOLOGY:

(fig. A.12) Small irregularly shaped mound, 2.5 m high and 220 m in diameter. At time of visit, under harvested and densely chaff-covered cereal field, poor visibility. Area 3.2 ha.

SITE SUB-AREAS AND PERIODS OF OCCUPATION:

Collected as a single area. P5b, P19. Types not quantified for this collection.

SETTLEMENT HISTORY:

A village of the Late Chalcolithic 3–4 period (P5b; 3.2 ha) with a reoccupation in the Middle to Late Islamic period (P19; 3.2 ha).

THS 39 (FIELD SITE NO. 45)

SITE NAME:

—

SITE POSITION:

762592 E, 4073605 N (top of mound at southeastern end)

SITE AREA AND MORPHOLOGY:

(fig. 5.1) Elongated low mound, 2.5 m high, 250 m the long northwest–southeast axis × 100 m on the short axis. A single-room structure and diesel well sits at the summit. Under cereal field, which was being plowed at the time of visit. Total area 2.3 ha.

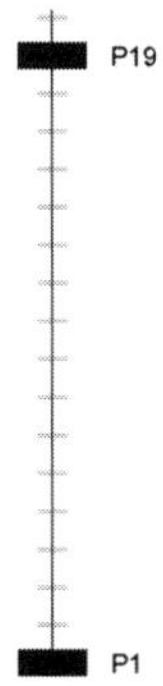

SITE SUB-AREAS AND PERIODS OF OCCUPATION:

Collected as a single unit. P1, P19 (table C.36)

SETTLEMENT HISTORY:

This small mound was first settled in the Hassuna period (P1; 2.3 ha) and reoccupied, probably on a smaller scale, in the Middle to Late Islamic period (P19). Possible occupation in the early Ninevite 5 period, but the identification of T6/1 painted decoration is questionable.

THS 40 (FIELD SITE NO. 57)

SITE NAME:

Khirbat Melhem (source: local informant)

SITE POSITION:

761557 E, 4072640 N (center and top of central mound, at intersection of Areas A–D)

SITE AREA AND MORPHOLOGY:

(fig. A.13) Broad mound with pronounced mounding at center (3 m high, arbitrarily divided into Areas A–D) and a lower mounded area surrounding it (arbitrarily subdivided into Areas E–I). Total complex dimensions 430 m east–west × 250 m north–south. Total area 8.6 ha.

SITE SUB-AREAS AND PERIODS OF OCCUPATION:

(table C.37, figs. C.16–18)

Area A: 0.4 ha; P5a, P5b, P11, P17

Area B: 0.2 ha; P5a, P5b, P11, P17

Area C: 0.3 ha; P5a, P5b, P11, P17

Area D: 0.5 ha; P5a, P5b, P11, P17

Area E: 0.9 ha; P5a, P5b, P11

Area F: 1.1 ha; P5b, P11, P17

Area G: 1.6 ha; P5a, P5b

Area H: 2.3 ha; P5a, P5b

Area I: 1.3 ha; P5a, P5b

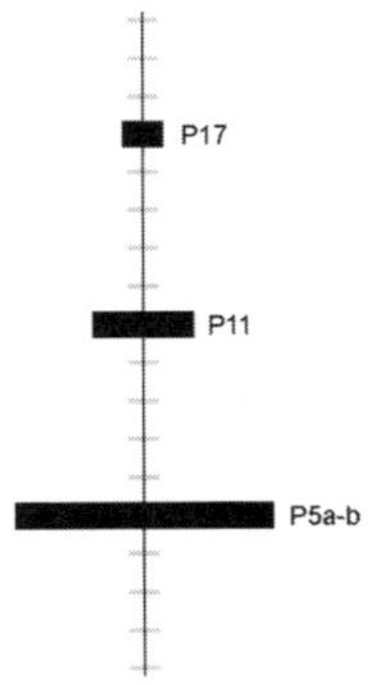

SETTLEMENT HISTORY:

A town of the middle to late fourth millennium B.C. (P5) The surface assemblage includes both local northern Mesopotamian Late Chalcolithic 3–4 types (8.6 ha) and intrusive southern Mesopotamian Late Chalcolithic 4–5 types (7.5 ha). The site was reoccupied in the Iron Age (P11), with settlement on the northern half of the site (3.4 ha) but concentrated on the central mounded areas (Areas A–D). A small Abbasid (P17) settlement also occupied this central mound (1.4 ha).

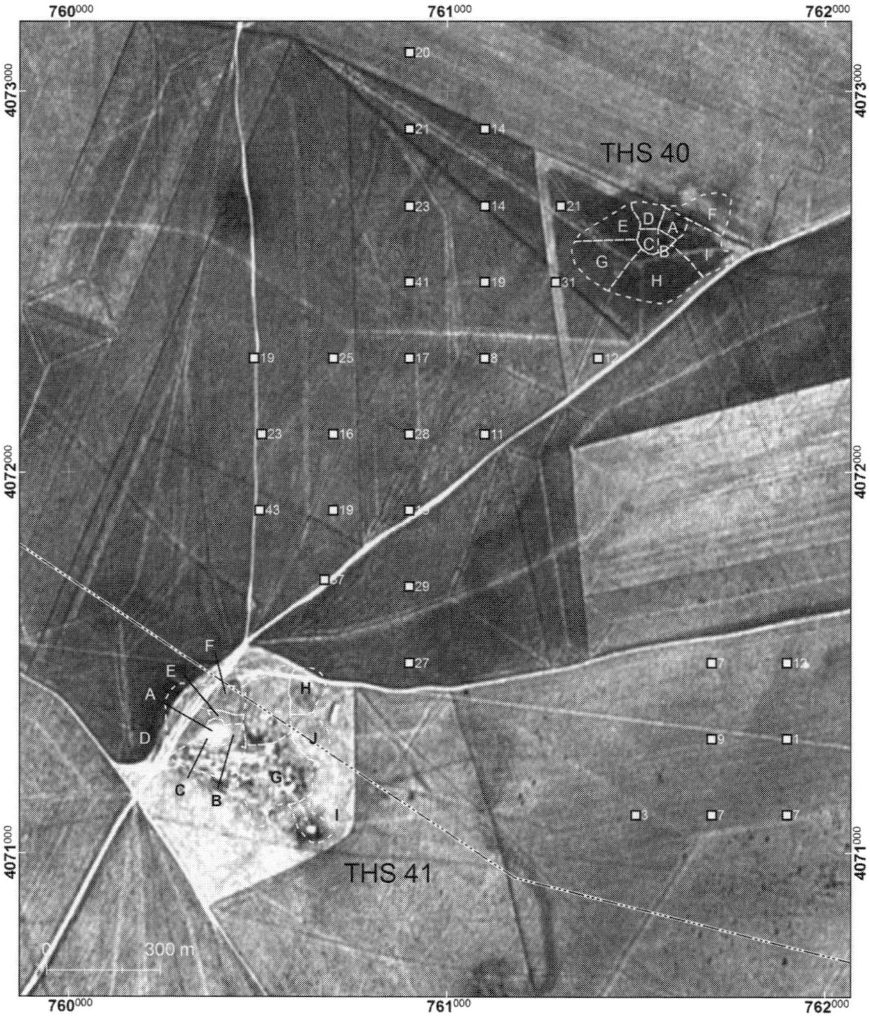

Figure A.13. THS 40 and 41
(CORONA 1117-1025DF147, 25 May 1972)

THS 41 (FIELD SITE NO. 59)

SITE NAME:

Tell Na'ur (Arabic 1:50,000: تل ناعور)

SITE POSITION:

760385 E, 4071329 N (center and top of high mound, center of Area A)

SITE AREA AND MORPHOLOGY:

(fig. A.13; see also fig. 5.2) Large site complex with a high mound at northwest and lower mounds to southeast. Conical 20 m high mound has steep northern slope and more gradual southern slope. Top 5 m collected separately (A), lower slopes collected in four equal arbitrary areas (B, C, D, E). The southern extent of Area C is presently beneath the modern village and was not collected. A low shelf (F) extends to the north from the high mound and is bisected by a paved road. The high mound is bounded to the east by a large depression with a cement well. On the eastern side of the depression is a pair of small low mounds (H and J), both 1 m high with a few dispersed modern structures. To the south of the large depression, and separated from the high mound and the eastern mounds by low saddles, is a broad low mound (G), 2 m high and presently densely covered with village houses. To its southeast is a small low mound (I) 1 m high. Total area 12.6 ha.

SITE SUB-AREAS AND PERIODS OF OCCUPATION:

(table C.38, fig. C.19)

Area A: 0.1 ha; P2, P6, P7, P8

Area B: 0.4 ha; P2, P5b, P6, P7, P8

Area C: 0.2 ha; P2, P5b, P6, P7, P8, P15

Area D: 0.7 ha; P2, P7, P8

Area E: 0.2 ha; P2, P5b, P6, P7, P8

Area F: 0.8 ha; P2, P5b, P8, P10, P13

Area G: 3.2 ha; P11, P13

Area H: 1.0 ha; P14

Area I: 0.7 ha; P13, P14, P16

Area J: 1.0 ha; P13

SETTLEMENT HISTORY:

The earliest settlement identified by the survey was a Halaf (P2) village beneath the high mound (2.4 ha). Portions of the high mound were reoccupied in the Late Chalcolithic 3–4 period (P5b; 1.5 ha) and in the Ninevite 5 period (P6; 0.7 ha). The entire high mound was settled in the later third millennium (P7; 1.6 ha) and expanded onto its northern slopes in the Khabur period (P8; 2.4 ha). Subsequently, the main mound was abandoned; Late Bronze Age (P10) settlement was on the low area north of the mound (0.8 ha) and Iron Age (P11) occupation covered a broad flat area of southeast lower town (3.2 ha). This lower town settlement expanded in the Hellenistic period (P13; 5.7 ha), but only the northeast and southeast fringes were settled in the Parthian period (P14; 1.7 ha). A small occupation returned to the high mound in the earlier Sasanian period (P15; 0.2). The southeastern lower town was resettled in the late Sasanian–Early Islamic period (P16; 3.9 ha).

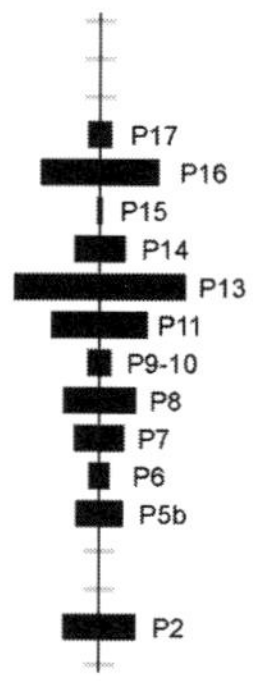

THS 42 (FIELD SITE NO. 48)

SITE NAME:

Nasiriya Sharqiya (Arabic 1:50,000: النصرية الشرقية)

SITE POSITION:

761060 E, 4074497 N (approximate center of site)

SITE AREA AND MORPHOLOGY:

(fig. A.14) Very low small mound, <1 m high and stretching 170 m along the western side of a 0.3 ha enclosed depression. Several large house compounds are atop it. The construction of the compounds seems to have involved some leveling of mounded areas. At center is a *Prosopis*-filled depression. A narrow hollow way skirts the southwestern extent of the site, but appears not to be associated with it. Total area 1.7 ha.

SITE SUB-AREAS AND PERIODS OF OCCUPATION:

Collected as a single unit. P10, P11, P19 (table C.39)

SETTLEMENT HISTORY:

After an initial Late Bronze Age (P10) through Iron Age (P11) occupation (1.7 ha), the site was resettled in the Middle to Late Islamic period (P19).

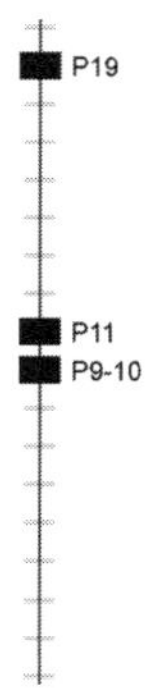

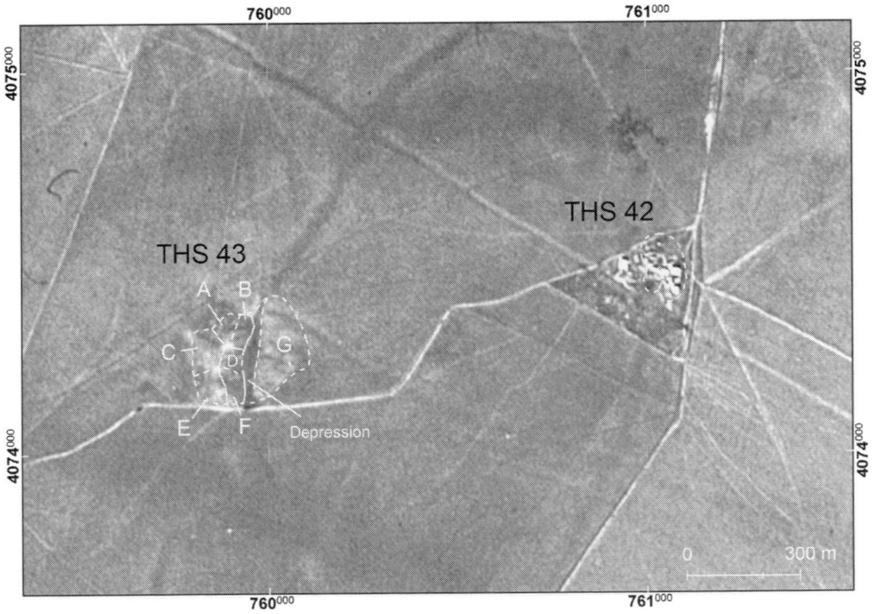

Figure A.14. THS 42 and 43
(CORONA 1108-1025DA006, 6 December 1969)

THS 43 (FIELD SITE NO. 46)

SITE NAME:

Khirbat Barjis (source: local informant)

SITE POSITION:

759874 E, 4074264 N (approximate center of western complex of mounds, at boundary between Areas C and D)

SITE AREA AND MORPHOLOGY:

(fig. A.14; see also fig. 5.3) Two north–south-oriented groups of mounds on either side of a 0.8 ha north–south elongated depression. Entire complex is 300 m in diameter. On the western side are three distinct mounds: 5 m high at north (western half collected as A, eastern half collected as B), 4 m high in the center (western slopes collected as C, eastern slopes collected as D), and a 3 m high southern mound (western slopes collected as E, eastern slopes collected as F). Each is separated by a gentle saddle. On the eastern side of the depression is a broad low area 1 m high that fades gradually into the surrounding plain (G). The north–south enclosed depression appears to have originated as a third-millennium hollow way that was deepened for mudbrick extraction; it still collects moisture and supports dense *Prosopis* growth. The entire complex was under fallow cereal fields at the time of observation. Total area of complex 6.3 ha.

SITE SUB-AREAS AND PERIODS OF OCCUPATION:

(fig. C.21, table C.40)

Area A: 0.3 ha; P2 (trace), P11, P13, P14

Area B: 0.4 ha; P2 (trace), P11, P13, P14

Area C: 0.8 ha; P2 (trace), P11, P13, P14

Area D: 0.3 ha; P2, P5b, P11, P13, P14

Area E: 0.6 ha; P2 (trace), P11

Area F: 0.5 ha; P2, P5a, P5b, P11

Area G: 2.6 ha; P14

Settlement History:

The light scatter of Halaf sherds across the areas west of the enclosed depression certainly signifies a buried Halaf core settlement (P2; 2.9 ha). The southeastern part of the mound was resettled in the Late Chalcolithic 3–4 period (P5b; 0.8 ha), with traces of southern Uruk in Area F (P5a; 0.5 ha). Given their low numbers, these Uruk sherds may have resulted from interaction with nearby "colonies" (such as THS 1 and THS 40) rather than the presence of southerners. The entire west mound was densely resettled in the Iron Age (P11; 2.9 ha) but then reduced to the north end in the Hellenistic period (P13; 1.9 ha). In the Parthian period (P14), the north end of the west mound remained fully settled but now a broad area east of the depression was also occupied (4.4 ha).

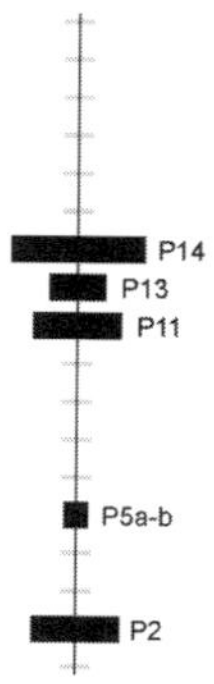

THS 44 (FIELD SITE NO. 58)

Site Name:

Khirbat Taif (source: local informant)

Site Position:

758850 E, 4072953 N (center and top of mound, at boundary between Areas A and B)

Site Area and Morphology:

(fig. A.15) Small low oval mound, 3 m high, 160 m on east–west axis × 110 m on north–south axis. Arbitrarily subdivided into a northern half (A) and a southern half (B) for collection. Two small structures at western edge. At time of visit, most of the site was under fallow cereals except the western edge, which was under a cotton field. Total area 1.5 ha.

Site Sub-areas and Periods of Occupation:

(table C.41, fig. C.20)

Area A: 0.9 ha; P1, P4, P5b, P19 (trace), P20 (trace)

Area B: 0.6 ha; P1

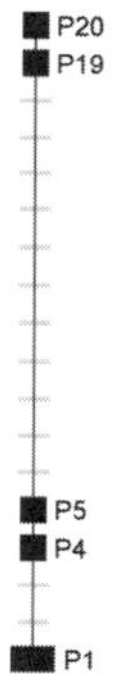

Settlement History:

A small Proto-Hassuna (P1) settlement (1.5 ha), which was partially resettled in the Late Chalcolithic 1–2 period (P4) and continued into the Late Chalcolithic 3–4 period (P5; 0.9 ha). Ephemeral traces of Middle to Late Islamic (P19–20) settlement, perhaps non-sedentary, could be identified on the northern half of the mound.

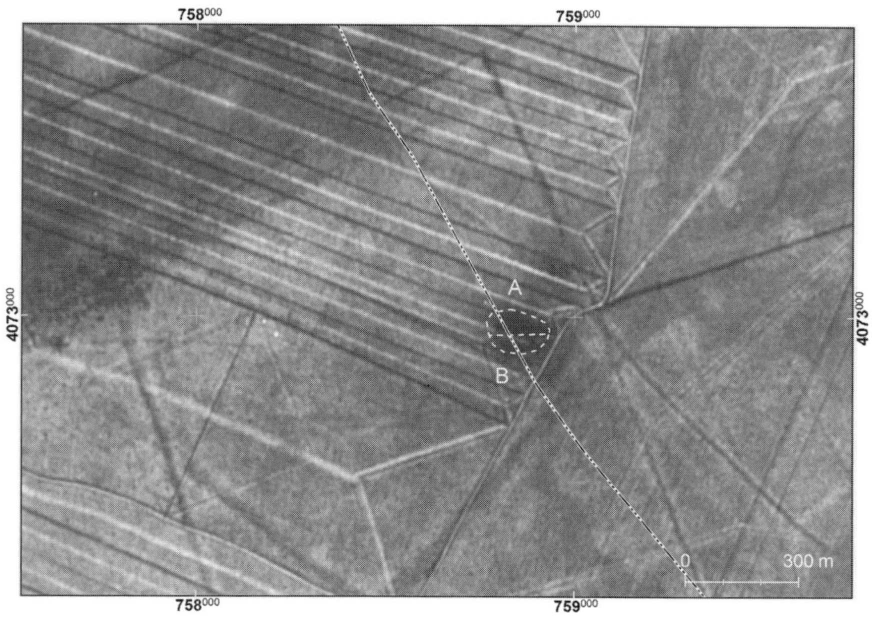

Figure A.15. THS 44 (CORONA 1117-1025DF147, 25 May 1972)

THS 45 (FIELD SITE NO. 5)

SITE NAME:

al-Saudiya (Arabic 1:50,000: السعودية)

SITE POSITION:

761703 E, 4076397 N (center and top of northern mound Areas A–B)

SITE AREA AND MORPHOLOGY:

(fig. A.16) A 6 m high mound at north (southeastern half arbitrarily collected as A, northwestern half as B) with three lower mounds: a 1 m high mound to the west (C), a 1 m high elongated east–west mound to the south (D), and a small 1.5 m high mound south of D (E). Total area of the settlement complex 8.8 ha. The top of the main mound (A–B) is now occupied by two large house compounds, the construction of which involved some terracing and excavation, and the western low mound (C) had cuts into it in two places. Most of the modern village of al-Sa'udiya sits atop the western extent of Area D, and Area E is covered by a recent cemetery. A 1.0 ha borrow pit is located between Areas A–B and the village on D, and two smaller ones are southwest of C and between the village and E. No part of the site was under cultivation at the time of visit.

SITE SUB-AREAS AND PERIODS OF OCCUPATION:

(table C.42)

Area A: 1.6 ha; P7 (trace), P10, P11, P15, P16

Area B: 1.5 ha; P7 (trace), P10, P11, P16 (single P1 sherd may indicate a prehistoric core)

Area C: 1.4 ha; P14, P15, P16

Area D: 2.2 ha; P14, P15, P16

Area E: 0.8 ha; not collected.

SETTLEMENT HISTORY:

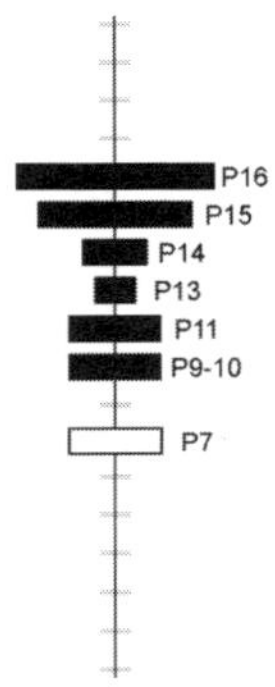

A single Hassuna sherd hints at a buried prehistoric core to the main mound (A and B), which was otherwise not recognized. This mound may have also hosted non-permanent later third-millennium settlement (P7). Certain sedentary occupation commenced in the Late Bronze Age and Iron Age (P10–11) on the main mound (3.1 ha). Settlement shifted to the western mound in the Hellenistic period (P13; 1.4 ha) and then to the south in the Parthian period (P14; 2.2 ha). The settlement grew in the earlier Sasanian period (P15; 5.1 ha) and was entirely settled in the later Sasanian–Early Islamic period (P16; 6.6 ha).

SMALL FIND:

A 40 *nummi* bronze coin of Byzantine date (2 HM 13, obverse illegible) was found on the southwestern slope of Area B (fig. A.21 no. 2).

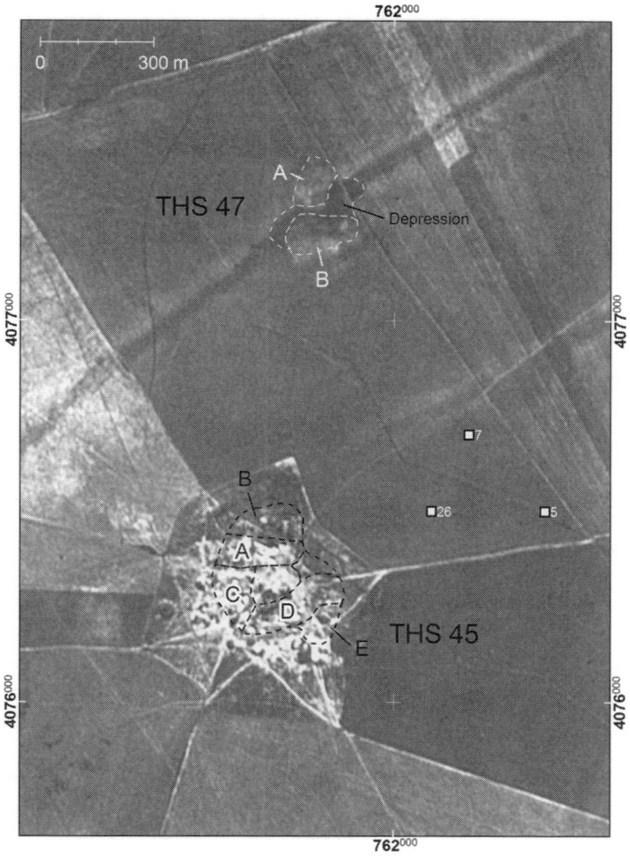

Figure A.16. THS 45 and 47 (CORONA 1108-1025DA005, 6 December 1969)

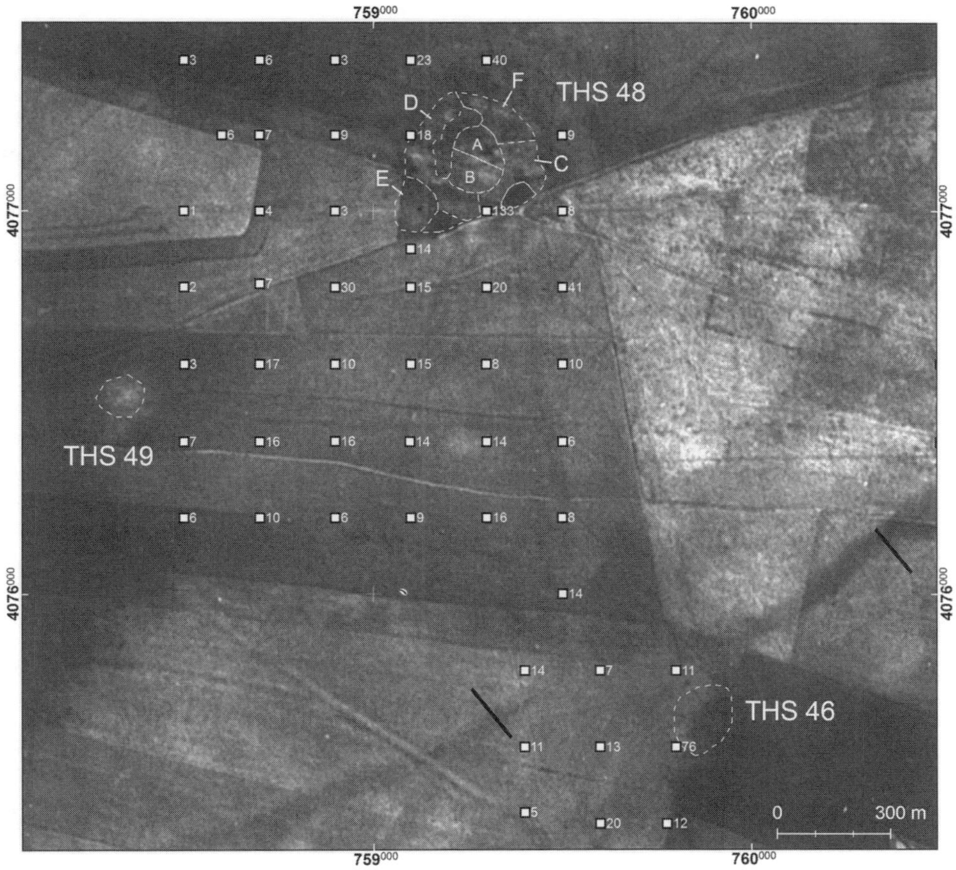

Figure A.17. THS 46, 48, and 49 (CORONA 1102-1025DF007, 11 December 1967)

THS 46 (FIELD SITE NO. 47)

SITE NAME:

—

SITE POSITION:

759900 E, 4075683 N (approximate center of mound)

SITE AREA AND MORPHOLOGY:

(fig. A.17) Circular low mound, 1.5 m high and 150 m in diameter. Bisected by a north–south dirt track, and under plowed (eastern half) and fallow (western half) cereal fields at the time of visit. Area 2.2 ha.

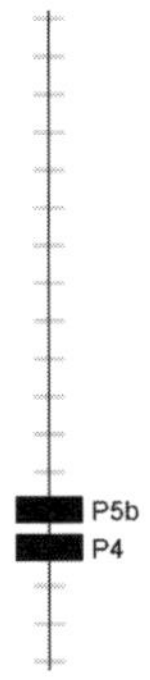

SITE SUB-AREAS AND PERIODS OF OCCUPATION:

Collected as a single unit. P4, P5b (table C.43)

SETTLEMENT HISTORY:

A small village (2.2 ha) occupied in the Late Chalcolithic 1–2 (P4) and Late Chalcolithic 3–4 (P5b) periods.

THS 47 (FIELD SITE NOS. 11 [AREA B] AND 36 [AREA A])

SITE NAME:

Khirbat al-Sukar; also called Bayt ʿAli (source: local informant)

SITE POSITION:

761809 E, 4077231 N (top and center of southern mound, Area B)

SITE AREA AND MORPHOLOGY:

(fig. A.16) A pair of low mounds on either side of a 1.4 ha linear depression. The southern mound is oval, ca. 2.5 m high and stretches 200 m along its east–west axis. Sides of the mound were plowed at time of visit, with the exception of a small uncultivated area atop the mound, where sat a single house and a diesel pump. Northern mound is 0.5 m high, 130 m along its long north–south axis × 90 m along its east–west axis. The edges are defined by more abundant *Prosopis* growth on the northern, eastern, and western sides, and signature on CORONA imagery. Under a fallow but untrodden field at the time of visit; sherd visibility low. The trough of a hollow way from THS 1 has been widened and deepened as a borrow pit between the two mounds, probably to extract building materials. Total area 2.6 ha.

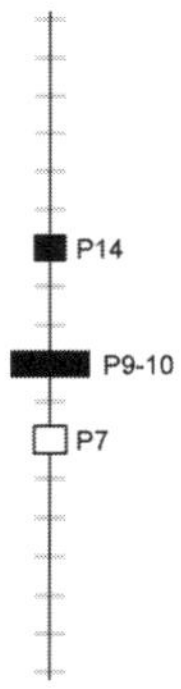

SITE SUB-AREAS AND PERIODS OF OCCUPATION:

(table C.44)

Area A: 1.1 ha; P7 (trace), P10, P14

Area B: 1.6 ha; P10

SETTLEMENT HISTORY:

Initial settlement was in the form of temporary or seasonal occupation on the southern mound in the later third millennium B.C. (P7; 1.1 ha). Both mounds were reoccupied in the Late Bronze Age (P10; 2.6 ha), but subsequent Parthian settlement (P14; 1.1 ha) was limited to the northern low mound (A).

THS 48 (FIELD SITE NO. 29)

SITE NAME:

Khirbat al-Shiha (local informant: خربت الشيهة)

SITE POSITION:

759298 E, 4077147 N (concrete survey benchmark at top of central mound, southern end of Area A)

SITE AREA AND MORPHOLOGY:

(fig. A.17) An extensive complex of low mounds and depressions, roughly 350 m in diameter. At center is a 4 m mound with a high point at its northern end (A), a gradual slope to the east (C), and a spur to the southwest (B). At the southwestern end of this spur is another small mound (E). A low north–south mound runs along the western edge of the complex (D) and is separated from the central mound by an enclosed depression. A very low area (<1 m) north of the central mound was demarcated by sherd density rather than mounding. Two smaller depressions (both 0.4 ha) sit along the site's southern edge. Total area of the complex is 10.7 ha.

SITE SUB-AREAS AND PERIODS OF OCCUPATION:

(table C.45)

Area A: 0.9 ha; P10, P11, P16 (trace)

Area B: 1.1 ha; P10, P11, P17, P19

Area C: 1.7 ha; P11, P16, P17

Area D: 2.7 ha; P11

Area E: 1.2 ha; P11, P13

Area F: 1.4 ha; P14

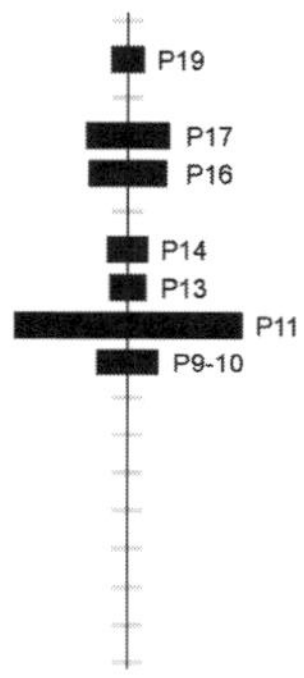

SETTLEMENT HISTORY:

The central mound was first occupied by a small village in the Late Bronze Age (P10; 2.0 ha), but expanded into an Iron Age town (P11; 7.6 ha). Thereafter settlement was restricted to the southwestern corner in the Hellenistic period (P13; 1.2 ha) and the northeastern edge in the Parthian period (P14; 1.4 ha). After a brief abandonment, settlement expanded slightly in the late Sasanian–Early Islamic period (P16; 2.6 ha) and the Abbasid period (P17; 2.8 ha). A small village of the Middle to Late Islamic period (P19) sat atop the central mound (1.1 ha).

THS 49 (FIELD SITE NO. 66)

SITE NAME:

—

SITE POSITION:

758342 E, 4076519 N (center and top of mound)

SITE AREA AND MORPHOLOGY:

(fig. A.17) Small low site, 1.5 m high, 100 m in diameter. 500 m east of village of al-Botha (THS 50). Covered by dense chaff at time of visit, very poor visibility. 1.0 ha.

SITE SUB-AREAS AND PERIODS OF OCCUPATION:

Collected as a single area. P1. Collection not quantified.

SETTLEMENT HISTORY:

A small Hassuna village (P1; 1.0 ha).

THS 50 (FIELD SITE NO. 43)

SITE NAME:

al-Botha (Arabic 1:50,000: البوثة ; French 1:200,000: Kharâb Rhannâm)

SITE POSITION:

757450 E, 4076652 N (approximate center of site complex)

SITE AREA AND MORPHOLOGY:

(fig. 5.17) Large and complex multi-mounded site. Undulating mounded area with many small intervening depressions at center, with substantial modern village atop it. Beyond the village are many small outlying mounds, probably the remains of individual house compounds, and certainly of low and fluctuating density. Two large enclosed depressions, one at northern end (0.9 ha, collected as A) and one at southeastern edge (1.1 ha, collected as B). The rest of the site was not collected. Total area, including uncollected areas of outer town, is 60.0 ha.

SITE SUB-AREAS AND PERIODS OF OCCUPATION:

(table C.46)

Area A: 0.9 ha; P16, P17

Area B: 1.1 ha; P16, P17

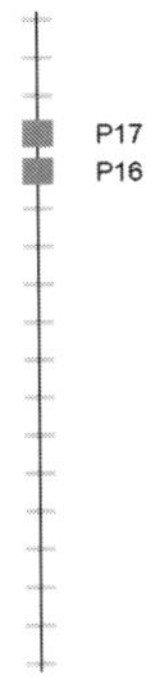

SETTLEMENT HISTORY:

A large town of the late Sasanian–Early Islamic through Abbasid period (P16–17). Its settled area is difficult to determine; the total site area (60 ha) may not have been settled simultaneously. The two collection areas were arbitrarily defined and are not necessarily representative of settlement across the entire site, although its low mounding suggests a short period of occupation.

THS 51 (FIELD SITE NO. 3)

SITE NAME:

—

SITE POSITION:

762500 E, 4078475 N (center and top of mound)

SITE AREA AND MORPHOLOGY:

(fig. 3.8) Low mound 1 m high, 1.2 ha; slight depressions to west and southeast may be traces of brick pits. The entire site is now within a cereal field.

SITE SUB-AREAS AND PERIODS OF OCCUPATION:

Collected as a single unit. P2, P6, P7, P13 (table C.47)

SETTLEMENT HISTORY:

The site was initially occupied in the Halaf period (P2). After several millennia of abandonment, it was reoccupied in the Ninevite 5 period (P6), probably late in the period and simultaneous with Hamoukar's urban expansion. It remained settled in the later third millennium (P7). At this time it sat astride several hollow ways focused on Hamoukar's likely western gate and may have had a specialized function related to the movement of goods and people in and out of the city. It was abandoned prior to the early second millennium and remained so until its final occupation in the Hellenistic period (P13). In all phases of its occupation it never exceeded 1.2 ha.

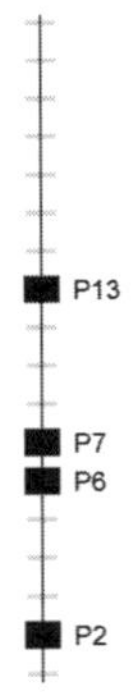

THS 52 (FIELD SITE NO. 37)

SITE NAME:

—

SITE POSITION:

759325 E, 4078269 N (center of mound, at abandoned well)

SITE AREA AND MORPHOLOGY:

(fig. A.18) Low oval mound, 0.3 m high, 200 m on north–south axis × 120 m on east–west axis. At the time of observation, an unused well sat atop it. Area 1.8 ha.

SITE SUB-AREAS AND PERIODS OF OCCUPATION:

Collected as a single unit. P2 (table C.48)

SETTLEMENT HISTORY:

A single-period Halaf village (P2; 1.8 ha).

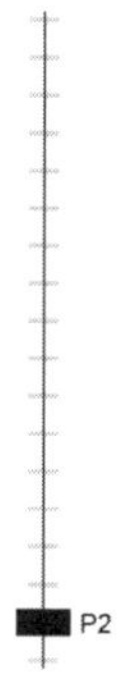

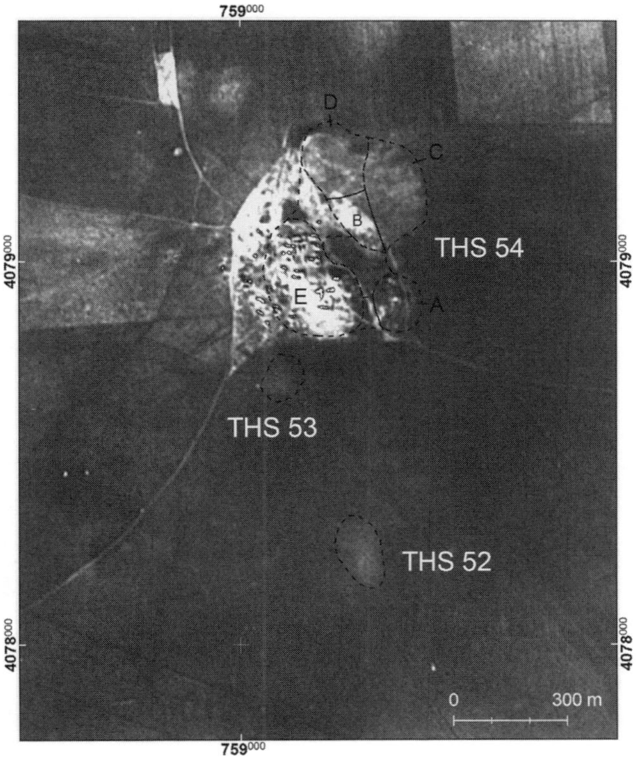

Figure A.18. THS 52, 53, and 54 (CORONA 1102-1025DF006 and F007, 11 December 1967)

THS 53 (FIELD SITE NO. 55)

SITE NAME:

—

SITE POSITION:

759118 E, 4078704 N (center and top of mound)

SITE AREA AND MORPHOLOGY:

(fig. A.18) Low circular mound, 1 m high and 100 m in diameter. Currently beneath a recently abandoned well. Area 1.0 ha.

SITE SUB-AREAS AND PERIODS OF OCCUPATION:

Collected as a single unit. P10 (table C.49)

SETTLEMENT HISTORY:

A small (1.0 ha) Late Bronze Age (P10) village, possibly to be considered as a component of Tell Tamr (THS 54).

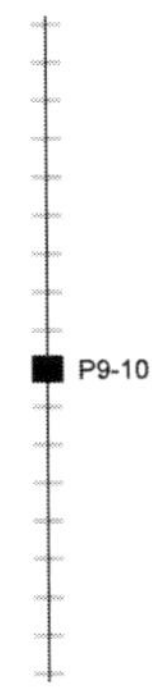

THS 54 (FIELD SITE NO. 4)

SITE NAME:

Tell Tamr (Arabic 1:50,000: تل التمر)

SITE POSITION:

759238 E, 4078931 N (center and top of Area E high mound)

SITE AREA AND MORPHOLOGY:

(fig. A.18) A settlement complex consisting of a 12 m high mound (E) with several 1–2 m high mounds to the east and northeast (A–D). In the center is a 1.5 ha enclosed depression which is full of *Prosopis* and debris from the village. The high mound (E) has been somewhat terraced for several houses that sit atop it; a more dense village obscures its northern slopes. Areas A and C have been truncated and leveled on their eastern sides by the expansion of an agricultural field, but can still be delineated by the color and texture of their soils; Area D was under a fallow cereal field at the time of collection. The entire complex covers approximately 17.8 ha.

SITE SUB-AREAS AND PERIODS OF OCCUPATION:

(table C.50)

Area A: 1.6 ha; P10, P11, P13, P16

Area B: 1.3 ha; P13, P14, P16, P17

Area C: 3.4 ha; P13, P15, P16, P17

Area D: 2.7 ha; P16, P17, P19

Area E: 5.7 ha; P7, P8, P10, P11, P15, P16

SETTLEMENT HISTORY:

Tell Tamr's earliest documented occupation was in the later third millennium (P7) on the high mound (E), although it is likely that the poor collection conditions precluded identification of earlier phases. It remained settled into the Khabur period (P8) but expanded to include the eastern lower town (A) in the Late Bronze Age and Iron Age (P10–11). During the Hellenistic period (P13), the tell (E) was abandoned, but lower town settlement expanded to 6.3 ha (A, B, and C). A reduced occupation characterized the Parthian period (P14; 1.3 ha), but settlement expanded back onto the tell in the earlier Sasanian period (P15; 9.2 ha). In late Sasanian–Early Islamic times (P16), the entire site was occupied (14.7 ha), shrank to 7.4 in the Abbasid period (P17). A small settlement (2.7 ha) existed on the northern lower town (D) in Middle to Late Islamic times (P19).

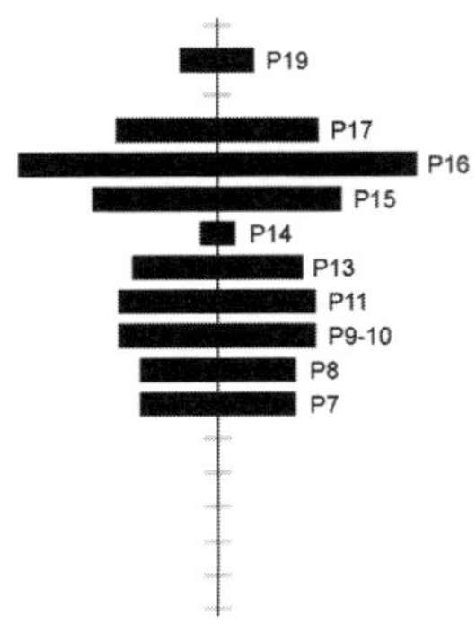

THS 55 (FIELD SITE NO. 38)

SITE NAME:

—

SITE POSITION:

760793 E, 4079853 N (approximate center)

SITE AREA AND MORPHOLOGY:

(fig. A.19) Low oval mound stretching northeast–southwest, 2 m high, 360 m on its long axis × 130 m on its short axis. Under a fallow field at time of observation, heavily trampled by animals from a nearby pastoralist encampment. Total area 3.9 ha.

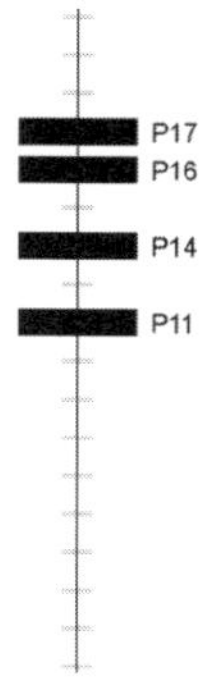

SITE SUB-AREAS AND PERIODS OF OCCUPATION:

Collected as a single unit. P11, P14, P16, P17 (table C.51, fig. C.22)

SETTLEMENT HISTORY:

This village site was first settled in the Iron Age (P11; 3.9 ha), was abandoned during the Hellenistic period (P13), and then reoccupied in the Parthian period (P14). After another hiatus, it was resettled in the late Sasanian–Early Islamic through Abbasid periods (P16–17).

Figure A.19. THS 55, 56, 57, 58, and 59 (CORONA 1108-1025DA005, 6 December 1969)

THS 56 (FIELD SITE NO. 56)

SITE NAME:

—

SITE POSITION:

760671 E, 4081141 N (center and top of mound, at intersection of Areas A–D)

SITE AREA AND MORPHOLOGY:

(fig. A.19) Low oval mound, 2 m high, 325 m north–south × 200 m east–west. Site limits were determined by sherd density and soil color. Several small depressions at the eastern edge are probably brick extraction pits. Under a plowed cereal field at the time of visit. Total area 5.2 ha.

SITE SUB-AREAS AND PERIODS OF OCCUPATION:

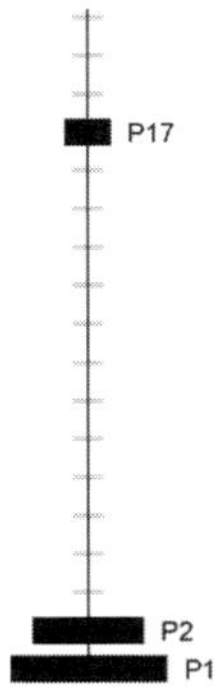

(table C.52)

Area A: 1.3 ha; P1, P2

Area B: 0.7 ha; P1, P2

Area C: 1.5 ha; P1, P17

Area D: 1.7 ha; P1, P2

SETTLEMENT HISTORY:

A substantial village of the Hassuna period (P1; 5.2 ha) and subsequent settlement in the Halaf period (P2; 3.6 ha), both with many untyped diagnostics. The southeastern corner (Area C) was resettled during the Abbasid period (P17; 1.5 ha).

THS 57 (FIELD SITE NO. 52)

SITE NAME:

—

SITE POSITION:

761473 E, 4081705 N (approximate center of artifact scatter)

SITE AREA AND MORPHOLOGY:

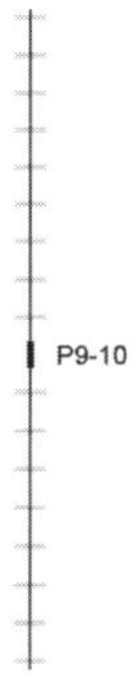

(fig. A.19) Small flat site, approximately 50 m in diameter. Completely leveled for agricultural fields; extent was determined by original signature on CORONA imagery. Recently plowed at the time of visit. Estimated area 0.2 ha.

SITE SUB-AREAS AND PERIODS OF OCCUPATION:

Collected as a single unit. P10 (table C.53)

SETTLEMENT HISTORY:

A small hamlet of the Late Bronze Age (P9–10; 0.2 ha). The even distribution of baked brick fragments across the site suggests that it may have been of some wealth, perhaps an estate (*dunnu*).

THS 58 (FIELD SITE NO. 53)

SITE NAME:

—

SITE POSITION:

761616 E, 4081812 N (approximate center of artifact scatter)

SITE AREA AND MORPHOLOGY:

(fig. A.19) Small flat site, approximately 100 m on east–west axis × 50 m on north–south axis. Completely leveled for agricultural fields; extent was determined by original signature on CORONA imagery. Recently plowed at the time of visit. Estimated area 0.5 ha.

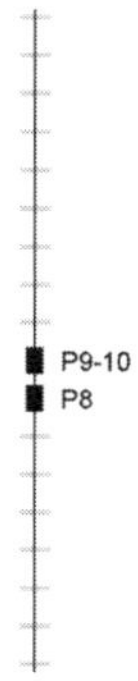

SITE SUB-AREAS AND PERIODS OF OCCUPATION:

Collected as a single unit. P8 (trace), P10 (table C.54)

SETTLEMENT HISTORY:

The trace of Khabur-period (P8) sherds might suggest a non-sedentary settlement; substantial occupation was limited to the Late Bronze Age (P9–10; 0.5 ha).

THS 59 (FIELD SITE NO. 54)

SITE NAME:

—

SITE POSITION:

761729 E, 4081938 N (approximate center of artifact scatter)

SITE AREA AND MORPHOLOGY:

(fig. A.19) Small flat site, approximately 150 m × 100 m. Completely leveled for agricultural fields; extent was determined by original signature on CORONA imagery. Western side of site deep plowed, eastern side under a fallow irrigated cereal field at time of observation. A north–south ridge of recently bulldozed cultural sediments at center of the site along field boundary, probably from leveling of the western field. Large sherds, baked brick fragments, and pieces of basalt grinding stones are abundant. Estimated area 1.1 ha.

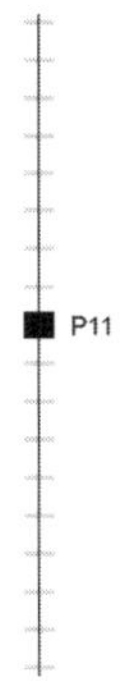

SITE SUB-AREAS AND PERIODS OF OCCUPATION:

Collected as a single site. P11 (table C.55, figs. C.23–24)

SETTLEMENT HISTORY:

Occupation was limited to the Iron Age (P11; 1.1 ha).

THS 60 (NOT NUMBERED IN FIELD)

SITE NAME:

—

SITE POSITION:

760560 E, 7082730 N (center of the southwestern mound complex)

SITE AREA AND MORPHOLOGY:

(fig. A.20) An extensive multi-mounded complex at and just beyond the northwestern edge of the survey region. From CORONA imagery analysis, the site consists of a large southwestern mound complex with an undulating topography (13.1 ha). To its northeast are four smaller and lower mounds (clockwise from southwest: 5.9 ha, 5.2 ha, 1.4 ha, and 0.2 ha). The largest of these has been cut at its southwest by the Qamishli–Mosul railway. The smallest at the north may mark the position of a weir.

SITE SUB-AREAS AND PERIODS OF OCCUPATION:

Not formally collected. During a brief visit to the large southwest complex, Parthian T14/1 sherds with diamond-stamped decoration were recognized on its southeastern mound, but occupations in other periods cannot be excluded. None of the other components of the site were visited. The entire complex appears to have been in the midst of an irrigated zone in the past (see figs. 5.30 and 5.32).

Figure A.20. THS 60 (CORONA 1108-1025DA005, 6 December 1969)

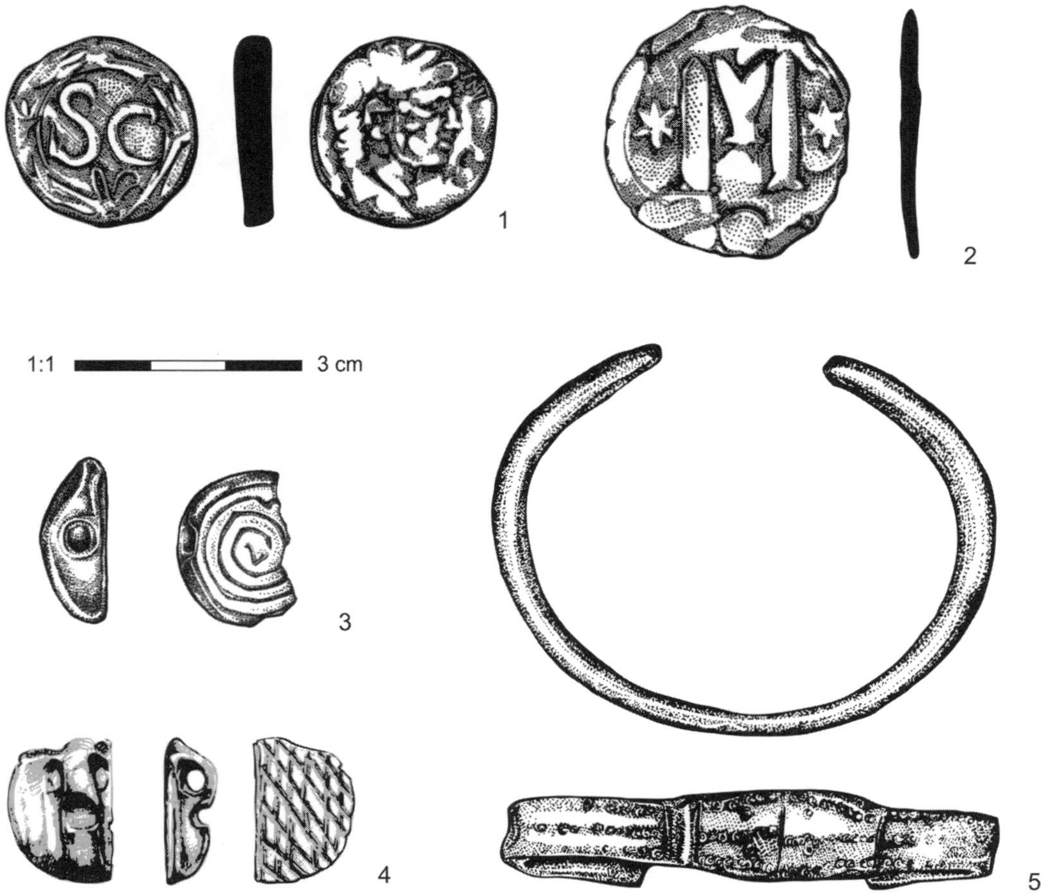

Figure A.21. Small surface finds from THS sites. 1. Bronze Roman coin from Hamoukar (2 HM 12); 2. Bronze Byzantine coin from THS 45 Area B (2 HM 13); 3. Basalt stamp seal from THS 25 Area K (2 HM 22); 4. Black limestone stamp seal from THS 32 Area B (2 HM 38); 5. Silver-plated bronze bracelet with incised circles from THS 10 Area B (2 HM 35)

APPENDIX B
CHRONOLOGY AND SURVEY CERAMIC TYPES

B.1. OVERVIEW OF THE SURVEY CERAMIC TYPES AND CHRONOLOGY

The patterns of sites and associated landscape features (*Chapters 6–7*) and broader economic, social, and political interpretations of them (*Chapter 8*) are constructs erected upon the chronological and spatial interpretation of surface artifacts. These artifacts, almost exclusively potsherds, have been assigned to types based on common variables of form, color, and fabric, and then assigned to chronological groupings with reference to excavated sequences and repetitive surface associations. The THS did not directly date sites via radiocarbon analysis, nor did it recover any historically datable artifacts such as coins or tablets. Therefore the validity of spatial patterns and of their interpretation rests upon the ceramic typology; the strengths and weaknesses of the latter must be considered in any evaluation of the former.

In this chapter, the ceramic bases for the dating of sites and features are described and evaluated. An attempt has been made to assess the relative utility of each of the types by quantifying their frequency of occurrence. As will be seen, within each period there are types that have proven to be very useful, and others whose infrequency makes them far less so.

B.1.1. THE CHARACTERISTICS OF THS CERAMIC TYPES

In the interest of making the process by which spatial patterns were reconstructed as transparent and replicable as possible, the THS attempted to adhere to clearly defined ceramic types. The survey sherd types should not be confused with vessel types. This distinction is well illustrated by a deep vessel with a knobby tripod base, a flaring rim, and comb-incised decoration, found in late third-millennium B.C. excavation contexts in Hamoukar Areas C and H (see, e.g., Gibson et al. 2002a: fig. 18 nos. 1 and 9). In the THS typology, at least three types are represented here: the rim (depending on morphology, either T7/14 or T7/15), the base (T7/12), and the decoration (T7/4). Conversely, a single survey sherd type might be found on more than one type of vessel. This situation pertains when the main variable in type definition is a distinct fabric (e.g., T7/5 stoneware, which appears in a variety of bowls, bottles, and small jars) or style of decoration (e.g., T8/1 painted Khabur ware).

An ideal survey type meets three criteria: it occurs frequently, it is morphologically robust and distinctive, and it is chronologically short-lived. Examples of high-frequency types include the bevelled-rim bowl (T5a/1) and painted Khabur ware (T8/1). In Period 5a and Period 8 assemblages respectively, these types generally represent over 50 percent of the total sherds. Except in rare instances of recent disturbance, sherds found in surface collection have long been exposed to wind, water, plowing, and trampling. Therefore, large and robust forms are well suited for survey types, such as the square jar rim (T10/12) and the double-rimmed jar (T4/4); both can sustain a great deal of abuse in the plowzone but still remain identifiable. Finally, types should have a limited span of use, preferably established stratigraphically. A form that remained in the assemblage for a long time or is similar to a type from another period is a poor type. For example, the hammerhead bowl rim of Period 5b (T5b/4) can be difficult to distinguish from the Period 11 thickened bowl rim (T11/2) when the latter is highly abraded or was poorly fired.

These three variables do not converge uniformly in all periods, unfortunately. Archaeological visibility may be well served by the ceramic assemblage for some periods, while others' assemblages make them difficult to identify via surface collection. These visibility differences can have a substantial impact on the reconstructed settlement pattern, and effort has been made to account for them in the interpretations presented here. For example, the distribution of Period 6 (early third millennium B.C.) sites relies heavily on the recognition of a series of decorated finewares that are highly distinctive, but are also not robust and occur far less frequently in the ceramic repertoire than the much less distinctive common wares. Therefore, the apparent depopulation of the plain may be the result of the relative invisibility of Period 6 ceramic survey types as much as a lack of settlement.

B.1.2. THE SUBDIVISION OF TIME IN THE ARCHAEOLOGY OF NORTHERN MESOPOTAMIA

Time in northern Mesopotamia is commonly reckoned via a complicated method of intertwining relative and absolute chronologies. Excavations at multiperiod sites have resulted in relative sequences of material culture, most commonly ceramic types and glyptic styles. These sequences have been linked to a historical chronology developed from written sources that in most cases were composed outside of the present area of interest in northern Mesopotamia. This historical chronology has in turn been associated with absolute dates based on astronomy and radiocarbon dating. All these chronologies are problematic in one way or another and must be used critically.

The least problematic periods tend to be the prehistoric ones, where closely studied and well-stratified assemblages have been dated via multiple radiocarbon determinations. Relative historical chronologies, on the other hand, are heavily debated. Mesopotamian chronologies become particularly controversial at the interface of these chronological methods. The early second and especially the later third millennia are a case in point. The historical absolute chronology in long use (the "Middle Chronology"; Brinkman in Oppenheim 1977: 335–48) was fixed by astronomical assumptions now known to be false (Gasche et al. 1998: 72–74). The Middle Chronology was never considered to be firmly established, even by its author, but it has achieved a quasi-canonical status among archaeologists because it is easier to apply it than to undertake the detailed studies necessary to revise it. Such studies have been only recently begun. Most of these reevaluations (see especially Gasche et al. 1998; Reade 2001) favor a much lower chronology that would bring periods currently placed in the early second and the third millennium B.C. forward in time. What is clear from these studies is that the absolute historical chronology in the late third and early second millennia B.C. is by no means established, and all historical designations should be heavily qualified.

Given the uncertainties about absolute historical chronology, it is not surprising that attempts to reconcile historical chronologies with relative sequences of ceramic types are speculative. In the worst cases, they extend these problems into the realm of material culture. Underlying these attempts is the assumption that political changes, in particular the rise and fall of royal dynasties or phases of political control, were coincident with shifts in ceramic-production technologies or decorative traditions. Implicit here are centralized and hierarchical views about agency and a top-down mentality regarding social change, wherein the actions of great men are the only actions that are historically significant. It is well argued that craftspersons highly specialized in the manufacture of the markers of elite status could be attached to the royal household (e.g., the Sargonic royal sealcutters; Zettler 1977), but of all the crafts in Mesopotamia, pottery production is the least likely to be tied directly to centralized political institutions (Stein and Blackman 1993; Steinkeller 1996). Pottery styles, therefore, were unlikely to have evolved in tandem with ruling houses. Nonetheless, the periodizations used by most excavation and survey projects result from attempts to shoehorn ceramic sequences into textually derived political history, which is often little more than lists of royal names and reign lengths.

In an attempt to avoid these chronological pitfalls, the THS employed a simple relative chronology which is based on major changes in ceramic traditions recognizable in surface assemblages. As a result, its chronological divisions are often much longer than those employed by excavations, where subtle changes in type frequency can be used to make dating assessments. Reference will be made to conventional historical chronologies, but without the assumption that the periods used here are coterminous with historical time divisions. For example, Period 11 certainly encompasses the span of Assyrian control over the Upper Khabur basin, but it is entirely possible that it also includes a phase of Aramean polities prior to the Assyrian conquest. It probably also includes the years following the collapse of the empire, when the region was ruled by the Neo-Babylonian empire, and perhaps the succeeding Achaemenid empire as well. Issues of historical and absolute chronology are detailed on a period-by-period basis in Section B.2.

B.1.3. THE CONSTRUCTION OF THE THS TYPOLOGY

The THS adopted its survey ceramic types (table B.1) and their periodization largely from the typology employed in the survey of the Iraqi North Jazira. The core of the typology was devised by David Tucker for the intensive surface collection of Tell al-Hawa (Ball, Tucker, and Wilkinson 1989). It was refined and expanded by Tony Wilkinson for use in the survey of Hawa's hinterland (Wilkinson and Tucker 1995). Most of their types have been adopted unchanged by the THS; while none have been eliminated from the typology described below, some could not be identified in surface assemblages based on the published description in the final report. All have been assigned new type numbers to integrate them with types defined from subsequent surveys and new published excavation assemblages.

The published version of the North Jazira Project's typology was the basis for a Working Survey Typology for the Upper Khabur basin, which was subsequently used for the Tell Beydar Survey (Wilkinson 2000a, 2002b; Ur and Wilkinson 2008; Nieuwenhuyse 2007), an intensive surface collection of Tell Brak (Ur, Karsgaard, and Oates 2007; Oates et al. 2007), and the survey of Brak's hinterland (Wright et al. 2006–07), in addition to the THS. Ultimately, more than fifty new types were added to Wilkinson and Tucker's initial 164 types, and the definitions and chronological placement of many were refined. Many of these new types were added after the final processing of THS collections and have therefore been retroactively incorporated in a non-systematic manner. Others were not used in the THS at all but have been included here in order to present the typology in its current form. For the sake of completeness, unused types are included in table B.1; but are marked with an asterisk.

The periodizations used by Tucker and Wilkinson remain largely unchanged. They assigned periods cultural ("Uruk") or historical (e.g., "Mitanni" and "Middle Assyrian") designations that can be problematic; this study has replaced them with numeric designations that are free of inappropriate cultural or historical connotations. There are, however, two major divergences with the North Jazira periodization. The "Uruk" period in the North Jazira has been split into three periods, two of which are partially overlapping (Periods 4, 5a, and 5b). The North Jazira Project's Mitanni and Middle Assyrian periods have been consolidated as the Late Bronze Age (Period 10). In the field, the THS attempted to maintain this distinction as Periods 9 and 10, but it was ultimately abandoned. Justification for these changes in the Tucker-Wilkinson periodization is provided below.

Table B.1. Northern Mesopotamian survey types. An asterisk indicates that the type was developed for another survey (Tell Beydar, Tell Brak, or Hirbemerdon Tepe) and was not used in the THS

Type	*Description*	*Field Designation*	*Illustration*
PERIOD 1: PROTO-HASSUNA			
T1/0	Untyped Proto-Hassuna	501	—
T1/1	Painted Ware	1	Figure B.4 nos. 1–12
T1/2	Husking Tray	2	(Wilkinson and Tucker 1995: fig. 62 nos. 6–9)
T1/3*	Red Burnished Ware	119	(Wilkinson and Tucker 1995: fig. 62 no. 10)
T1/4*	Coarse Chaff- or Grit-Tempered Ware	124	(Wilkinson and Tucker 1995: fig. 62 no. 11)
T1/5	Samarran Incised Ware	125.1	(Wilkinson and Tucker 1995: fig. 62. nos. 12–13)
T1/6	Samarran Stabbed Ware	125.2	Figure B.4 nos. 13–16
T1/7	Samarran Painted Ware	126	(Wilkinson and Tucker 1995: fig. 62 nos. 16–17)
PERIOD 2: HALAF			
T2/0	Untyped Halaf	502	—
T2/1	Halaf Painted Ware	3	Figure B.5 nos. 1–17
T2/2	Fingernail Rusticated Ware	137	(Wilkinson and Tucker 1995: fig. 63 no. 14)
PERIOD 3: NORTHERN UBAID			
T3/0	Untyped Ubaid	503	—
T3/1	Ubaid Painted Ware	4	Figure B.7 nos. 1–9

Table B.1. Northern Mesopotamian survey types (*cont.*)

Type	*Description*	*Field Designation*	*Illustration*
PERIOD 3: NORTHERN UBAID (*cont.*)			
T3/2	Ubaid Corrugated Ware	5	(Wilkinson and Tucker 1995: fig. 64 nos. 13–15)
T3/3	Open Bowl with Grooved Top	135	Figure B.7 nos. 10–11
T3/4	Ubaid Everted Jar Rim	147	(Wilkinson and Tucker 1995: fig. 64 nos. 18–19)
T3/5	Ubaid Incurved Rim	148	Figure B.7 nos. 12–13
PERIOD 4: LATE CHALCOLITHIC 1–2			
T4/0	Untyped Late Chalcolithic 1–2	504	—
T4/1	Coarse Shallow Bowl	7, 410	Figure B.10 nos. 1–4
T4/2	Beaded Holemouth Jar Rim	8	Figure B.10 nos. 5–7
T4/3	Sprig Ware	9	Figure B.10 nos. 17–24
T4/4	Double-Rimmed Jar	10	Figure B.10 nos. 8–10
T4/5	Flaring Jar Rim	13	Figure B.10 nos. 11–16
T4/6	Fine Beaker	16	Figure B.11 nos. 1–4
T4/7	Neckless Flaring Jar Rim	409	Figure B.11 nos. 5–8
T4/8	Deep Straight-Sided Urn	411	Figure B.11 nos. 9–11
T4/9	Early Internally Hollowed Rim	417	Figure B.11 nos. 12–18
T4/10	Clay "Hut Symbol"	419	(Tobler 1950: pl. 86a)
T4/11	Drooping Ledge Rim	422	(Matthews 2003b: fig. 3.14.12, 14)
T4/12	Blister Ware	445	(Oates 2002: 119)
T4/13*	Internally Incised Bowl	447	(Matthews 2003b: fig. 3.13.11–13)
T4/14	Clay Ladle	420	—
T4/15*	Deep Bowl	17	(Ball, Tucker, and Wilkinson 1989: fig. 28.23–24)
T4/16*	Bowl with Exterior Groove	—	—
T4/17*	Brown-Washed Ware	11	—
T4/18	Bowl with Internally Thickened Rim	21	Figure B.11 nos. 19–22
PERIOD 5B: LATE CHALCOLITHIC 3–5 INDIGENOUS TYPES			
T5b/0	Untyped Late Chalcolithic 3–5	505	—
T5b/1	Internally Hollowed Jar Rim	12	Figure B.13 nos. 1–6
T5b/2	Internally Grooved Jar Rim	14	Figure B.13 nos. 7–9
T5b/3	Late Chalcolithic Gray Ware	138	Figure B.13 nos. 10–11
T5b/4	Hammerhead Bowl Rim	152	Figure B.13 nos. 12–14
T5b/5	Casserole	153	Figure B.13 nos. 15–18
T5b/6	Carinated Fine Bowl	15, 434	Figure B.13 no. 19
T5b/7	Grooved Rim Beaker	150	Figure B.13 nos. 20–21
T5b/8	Jar with Sharp Interior Carination	406	(Pearce 2000: fig. 11d–e)
T5b/9	"Pie Plate" Rim	405	Figure B.13 nos. 22–24
T5b/10	Small Carinated Bowl	20	Figure B.13 nos. 25–26

Table B.1. Northern Mesopotamian survey types (*cont.*)

Type	*Description*	*Field Designation*	*Illustration*
T5b/11	Sharply Out-Turned Rim	121	Figure B.13 nos. 27–28
T5b/12	Internally Molded Bowl	134	Figure B.13 nos. 29–30
T5b/13*	Chaffy Hemispherical Bowl or Cup	439	—
T5b/14*	Chaffy Flat-Topped Shallow Bowl	442	(Felli 2003: fig. 4.22.2, 7)
T5b/15*	Flared Cooking Pot Rim	149	(Wilkinson and Tucker 1995: fig. 67 nos. 19–22)
T5b/16	Ceramic Ring Scraper	106	Figure B.13 nos. 31–32
T5b/17*	Double-Mouth Jar	55	(Wilkinson and Tucker 1995: fig. 65 no. 19)
Period 5a: Late Chalcolithic 4–5 Southern Mesopotamian Types			
T5a/0	Untyped Southern Uruk	521	—
T5a/1	Bevelled-Rim Bowl	6	Figure B.15 nos. 1–3
T5a/2	Nose Lug	18	Figure B.15 no. 8
T5a/3	Drooping Spout	19	Figure B.15 nos. 4–7
T5a/4	Broad Strap Handle	120	Figure B.15 no. 9
T5a/5	Oblique Bowl Rim	140	Figure B.15 nos. 10–12
T5a/6	Undercut Jar Rim	151	Figure B.15 nos. 13–15
T5a/7	Conical Cup Rim	421.1	Figure B.15 nos. 16–19
T5a/8	Conical Cup Base	421.2	Figure B.15 nos. 20–22
Period 6: Ninevite 5			
T6/0	Untyped Ninevite 5	506	—
T6/1	Painted Ware	27	(Wilkinson and Tucker 1995: fig. 68 nos. 27–30)
T6/2	Incised Gray Fineware	22	Figure B.17 no. 1
T6/3	Excised Gray Fineware	23	Figure B.17 nos. 2–5
T6/4	Vertical Grooved Fineware	25	Figure B.17 no. 6
T6/5	Ribbed Fineware	26	(Wilkinson and Tucker 1995: fig. 68 nos. 24–26)
T6/6	Pedestal Base	24	Figure B.17 nos. 7–10
T6/7	Pointed or Parabolic Fineware Base	28	Figure B.17 nos. 11–13
T6/8	Fine Beaded Rim Bowl	133	Figure B.17 nos. 14–16
T6/9	Holemouth Pot with Crescent Lug	426	Figure B.17 no. 17
Period 7: Middle to Late Third Millennium B.C.			
T7/0	Untyped Middle to Late Third Millennium	507	—
T7/1	Flat Bowl Base	29	(Wilkinson and Tucker 1995: fig. 69 nos. 1–4)
T7/2	Flat Beaker Base	30	Figure B.19 nos. 1–4
T7/3	String-Cut Flat Base	31	(Wilkinson and Tucker 1995: fig. 69 nos. 8–9)
T7/4	Comb-Incised Decoration	32	Figure B.19 nos. 5–12
T7/5	Blue-Gray Stoneware	33	Figure B.19 nos. 13–19

Table B.1. Northern Mesopotamian survey types (*cont.*)

Type	*Description*	*Field Designation*	*Illustration*
PERIOD 7: MIDDLE TO LATE THIRD MILLENNIUM B.C. (*cont.*)			
T7/6*	Non-Calcareous Stoneware	424	(Oates 2001b: fig. 185a)
T7/7	Post-Akkadian Stoneware	425	Figure B.19 no. 20
T7/8	Indented Jar Rim	103	Figure B.19 nos. 21–24
T7/9	Lugged Bowl	154	Figure B.19 nos. 25–29
T7/10	Shallow Flaring Vat Rim	401	Figure B.20 nos. 1–7
T7/11	Flat Extended-Foot Base	402	Figure B.20 nos. 8-13
T7/12	Lug-Footed Base	403	Figure B.20 nos. 14–17
T7/13	Gray Ware Round Bowl Rim	404	Figure B.20 nos. 18–23
T7/14	Folded Jar Rim	407	Figure B.21 nos. 1–5
T7/15	Folded Ridged Jar Rim	412	Figure B.21 nos. 6–10
T7/16*	Lid-Seated Jar Rim	423	(Rova 2003: pls. 30, 34)
T7/17	Triangular Cooking Pot Rim	408	Figure B.21 nos. 11–14
T7/18*	Holemouth Cooking Pot Rim with Triangular Lug	427	(Oates 2001b nos. 1665–1666)
T7/19	Beaded Cup Rim	413	Figure B.21 nos. 15–17
T7/20	Fineware Straight-Sided Cup Rim	414	Figure B.21 nos. 18–22
T7/21*	Vertical Ribbed Jar Rim	428	(Oates 2001b:176, fig. 423)
T7/22*	Collared Jar Rim with Sloping Shoulder	429	—
T7/23*	Recessed Beaker Rim	430	(Oates 2001b: fig. 414 nos. 508–511)
T7/24*	Jar with Ribbed Shoulder	431	(Oates 2001b:176, fig. 425)
PERIOD 8: KHABUR/OLD BABYLONIAN			
T8/0	Untyped Middle Bronze Age	508	—
T8/1	Khabur Painted Ware	34	Figure B.23 nos. 1–7
T8/2	Horizontally Grooved Jar Shoulder	35	Figure B.23 nos. 8–11
T8/3	Burnished Gray Ware	41	Figure B.23 nos. 12–13
T8/4	Externally Grooved Bowl	42	(Wilkinson and Tucker 1995: fig. 70 nos. 23–24)
T8/5	High Ring or Pedestal Base	39	Figure B.23 no. 14
T8/6	Channel Base	40	Figure B.23 nos. 15–16
T8/7*	(type number not used)	—	—
T8/8	Concave Fine Bowl Base	38	(Wilkinson and Tucker 1995: fig. 70 nos. 13–14)
T8/9*	Indented-Cordoned Jar	36	(Wilkinson and Tucker 1995: fig. 70 nos. 9–10)
T8/10*	Impressed Circle Decoration	37	(Wilkinson and Tucker 1995: fig. 70 nos. 11–12)
PERIOD 9: MITANNI (PERIOD DESIGNATION NOT USED)			
T9/0	Untyped Mitanni	509	—
PERIOD 10: LATE BRONZE AGE			
T10/0	Untyped Late Bronze Age	510	—

Table B.1. Northern Mesopotamian survey types (*cont.*)

Type	*Description*	*Field Designation*	*Illustration*
T10/1	Nuzi White-Painted Ware	43	(Wilkinson and Tucker 1995: fig. 71 nos. 1–5)
T10/2*	Fine Painted Goblet	44	(Wilkinson and Tucker 1995: fig. 71 nos. 6–9)
T10/3	Pedestal (Stump) Base	45	Figure B.25 nos. 1–3
T10/4	Red-Painted Plate	444	Figure B.25 no. 4
T10/5	Collared Jar Rim	47	Figure B.25 nos. 5–8
T10/6	Small Bowl	48	Figure B.25 nos. 9–11
T10/7*	Fine Beaker	49	(Wilkinson and Tucker 1995: fig. 72 no. 8)
T10/8	Nipple Base	50	Figure B.25 no. 12
T10/9	Coarse Ring Base	51	Figure B.25 nos. 13–14
T10/10	Late Bronze Age Plate	52	Figure B.25 nos. 17–20
T10/11	Pie-Crust Potstand	54	Figure B.25 nos. 15–16
T10/12	Square Jar Rim	56	Figure B.25 nos. 21–24
T10/13	Soft Carinated Bowl	416	Figure B.25 nos. 25–27
T10/14	Inwardly Bevelled Rim	443	Figure B.25 no. 28
T10/15	Incurved Ledge Rim	446	(Oates 1997: nos. 615, 624)
T10/16*	Recessed Convex Base	440	—
T10/17*	Sherds with Wavy Grooved Lines	53	(Wilkinson and Tucker 1995: fig. 72 no. 20)
PERIOD 11: IRON AGE/NEO-ASSYRIAN			
T11/0	Untyped Iron Age/Neo-Assyrian	511	—
T11/1	Ribbed Bowl Rim	57	Figure B.27 nos. 1–4
T11/2	Thickened Bowl Rim	58	Figure B.27 nos. 5–8
T11/3	Swollen Convex Base	59	Figure B.27 nos. 9–11
T11/4	Angled Ring Base	61	Figure B.27 nos. 12–14
T11/5	Button Base	63	(Wilkinson and Tucker 1995: fig. 73 nos. 14–15)
T11/6	Palace Ware	60	Figure B.27 no. 15
T11/7	Assyrian Shouldered Bowl	105	(Wilkinson and Tucker 1995: fig. 73 no. 16)
T11/8	Necked Jar Rim	114	Figure B.27 nos. 16–19
T11/9	Internally Hollowed Jar Rim	111	Figure B.27 nos. 20–22
T11/10	Folded Jar Rim	132	Figure B.27 no. 27
T11/11	Oblique T-Shaped Bowl Rim	112	Figure B.27 no. 23
T11/12	Carinated Bowl	113	Figure B.27 nos. 24–26
T11/13*	Button Ring Base	118	(Wilkinson and Tucker 1995: fig. 73 no. 23)
T11/14	Ribbed Carinated Bowl	156	Figure B.27 no. 28
T11/15*	Holemouth Cooking Pot	438	(Parker 2003: fig. 6)
PERIOD 12: POST-ASSYRIAN			
T12/0	Untyped Post-Assyrian	512	—
T12/1	Jar with Grooved Top	104	Figure B.29 no. 1

Table B.1. Northern Mesopotamian survey types (*cont.*)

Type	*Description*	*Field Designation*	*Illustration*
PERIOD 12: POST-ASSYRIAN (*cont.*)			
T12/2	Holemouth Jar with Grooved Rim	142	Figure B.29 no. 2
T12/3	Grooved-Top Bowl Rim	144	Figure B.29 nos. 3–5
T12/4	Bowl with Notched Exterior	145	Figure B.29 no. 6
T12/5	Shallow Grooved Carinated Bowl	146	Figure B.29 nos. 8–10
T12/6	Flat Bowl Rim	102	(Wilkinson and Tucker 1995: fig. 74 nos. 1–2)
T12/7	Oval Stamped Decoration	143	(Wilkinson and Tucker 1995: fig. 74 nos. 9–17)
T12/8*	Crescent Stamped Ware	157	(Wilkinson and Tucker 1995: fig. 74 nos. 26–27)
PERIOD 13: HELLENISTIC			
T13/0	Untyped Seleucid/Hellenistic	513	—
T13/1	Incurved Bowl Rim	64	Figure B.31 nos. 1–4
T13/2	Rolled-Over Jar Rim	65	Figure B.31 nos. 5–12
T13/3	Hellenistic Plate	66	Figure B.31 nos. 13–16
T13/4*	Hellenistic Fineware	67, 436	(Wilkinson and Tucker 1995: fig. 75 no. 11)
T13/5	Hellenistic Fine Ring Base	68	(Wilkinson and Tucker 1995: fig. 74 nos. 12–14)
T13/6*	Impressed Rocker Pattern on Hellenistic fabric	107.2	—
T13/7	Impressed Dog-Tooth Decoration	108	Figure B.31 nos. 17–22
T13/8	Out-Turned Bowl Rim	116	Figure B.31 nos. 23–26
T13/9	Hemispherical Bowl	117	Figure B.31 no. 27
T13/10	Amphora Base	158	(Wilkinson and Tucker 1995: fig. 75 nos. 21–23)
T13/11	Bag-Shaped Jar	159	Figure B.31 nos. 28–31
T13/12	Large Grooved Vat Rim	415	Figure B.31 nos. 32–35
T13/13	Hard Gritty Rolled Rim	435	Figure B.31 nos. 36–37
PERIOD 14: PARTHIAN TO ROMAN			
T14/0	Untyped Parthian	514	—
T14/1	Diamond Stamped Decoration	76	Figure B.33 nos. 1–3
T14/2	Straight or Grooved Jar	115	Figure B.33 nos. 4–10
T14/3	Strap Handle with Central Groove	127	Figure B.33 nos. 11–12
T14/4	Fine Strap Handle with Central Groove	163	Figure B.33 nos. 13–14
T14/5	Rod Handle	128	Figure B.33 no. 15
T14/6	Holemouth Jar with Grooved Rim	129	Figure B.33 nos. 16–23
T14/7	Flat-Collared Rim	130	(Wilkinson and Tucker 1995: fig. 76 nos. 22–23)
T14/8	Flared Concave Rim	131	Figure B.33 nos. 24–28
T14/9	Parthian/Sasanian Green Glaze	136	—
T14/10*	Fine Brittle Ware	100	(Römer-Strehl 2005: figs. 612–30)

Table B.1. Northern Mesopotamian survey types (*cont.*)

Type	*Description*	*Field Designation*	*Illustration*
T14/11	Impressed Rocker Pattern on Parthian Fabric	107.1	(Wilkinson and Tucker 1995: fig. 76 nos. 10–13)
T14/12	Coarse Red-Painted Large Bowl	418	Figure B.33 nos. 29–31
PERIOD 15: SASANIAN			
T15/0	Untyped Sasanian	515	—
T15/1	Corrugated Jar Rim	69	Figure B.35 nos. 1–3
T15/2	Simple Gritty Jar Rim	70	Figure B.35 nos. 4–5
T15/3	Sasanian Stamped Decoration	78	Figure B.35 nos. 6–7
T15/4*	Smeared Ware	77	(Lyonnet 1990:113, pl. 8.1, 6–7)
PERIOD 16: SASANIAN TO EARLY ISLAMIC			
T16/0*	Untyped Sasanian/Early Islamic	516	—
T16/1	Beaded Jar Rim	71	Figure B.35 nos. 8–14
T16/2	Coarse Brittle Strap Handle	72	Figure B.35 nos. 15–16
T16/3	Buff Grooved/Ridged Strap Handle	73	Figure B.35 nos. 17–21
T16/4	Blue-Green Glaze on Yellow Fabric	74.1	—
T16/5	Blue-Green Glaze on Fabrics of other Colors	74.2	—
T16/6	Grooved and Slashed Bowl Rim	139	Figure B.35 no. 22
T16/7*	Late Comb Incision on Green Gritty Fabric	99.1	Figure B.35 no. 23
T16/8*	Late Comb Incision on Other Fabrics	99.2	—
T16/9	Coarse Brittle Ware	75	(Bartl 1994: pls. 28–32)
T16/10	Honeycomb Ware	79	(Wilkinson and Tucker 1995: fig. 77 nos. 18–19)
PERIOD 17: ABBASID			
T17/0	Untyped Early Islamic	517	—
T17/1	Fine Eggshell Handle	80	(Wilkinson and Tucker 1995: fig. 78 no. 1)
T17/2	Band-Rimmed Jar	81	(Wilkinson and Tucker 1995: fig. 78 nos. 2–4)
T17/3	Relief-Molded Ware	83	(Wilkinson and Tucker 1995: fig. 78 nos. 5–8)
T17/4	Creamware String-Cut Base	84	Figure B.35 nos. 24–25
T17/5	Tall Slender Handle	123	Figure B.35 nos. 26–28
T17/6	Twin Rod Handle	161	Figure B.35 no. 29
T17/7*	Coarse Red Cooking Ware	160	(Wilkinson and Tucker 1995: fig. 78 no. 12)
PERIOD 18: MIDDLE ISLAMIC			
T18/0	Untyped Middle Islamic	518	—
T18/1	Sgraffito Ware	82	(Wilkinson and Tucker 1995: fig. 79 nos. 1–4)

Table B.1. Northern Mesopotamian survey types (*cont.*)

Type	*Description*	*Field Designation*	*Illustration*
PERIOD 18: MIDDLE ISLAMIC (*cont.*)			
T18/2*	Late Relief Decorated Ware	122	(Wilkinson and Tucker 1995: fig. 79 no. 24)
PERIOD 19: MIDDLE TO LATE ISLAMIC			
T19/1	Green Glaze on Reddish Brown Fabric	94.1	Figure B.35 nos. 30–31
T19/2	Yellowish Brown Splashed Glaze on Reddish Brown Fabric	94.2	—
T19/3	Other Colored Glazes on Reddish Brown Fabric	94.3	—
T19/4	Handle with Applied Knob	98	(Wilkinson and Tucker 1995: fig. 79 no. 23)
T19/5	Coarse Lid	91	(Wilkinson and Tucker 1995: fig. 79 nos. 5–6)
T19/6*	Coarse Finger-Impressed Handle	97	(Wilkinson and Tucker 1995: fig. 79 nos. 21–22)
PERIOD 20: LATE ISLAMIC			
T20/0	Untyped Late Islamic	519	—
T20/1	Rouletted Ware	92, 437	(Wilkinson and Tucker 1995: fig. 79 nos. 7–9)
T20/2	Coarse Finger-Formed Rim	95	(Wilkinson and Tucker 1995: fig. 79 nos. 17–18)
T20/3*	Coarse Impressed and Rouletted Ware	96	(Wilkinson and Tucker 1995: fig. 79 nos. 19–20)
T20/4	Fingertip-Impressed Ware	93	(Wilkinson and Tucker 1995: fig. 79 nos. 10–11)
T20/5*	Ottoman Green-Glazed Ware	101	—
PERIOD 21: GENERAL ISLAMIC			
T21/0	Untyped General Islamic	522	—
T21/1	Grooved and Slashed Bowl	85	(Wilkinson and Tucker 1995: fig. 78 nos. 15–16)
T21/2	Beaked Jar Rim	86	Figure B.35 nos. 32–34
T21/3	Islamic Flat Base	87	(Wilkinson and Tucker 1995: fig. 78 no. 20)
T21/4	Islamic Coarse Gritty Handle	89	(Wilkinson and Tucker 1995: fig. 78 nos. 21–22)
T21/5	Grooved Bowl Rim	90	(Wilkinson and Tucker 1995: fig. 78 no. 23)
T21/6	Islamic Glass Bracelet	454	(Tonghini 1998: fig. 24e–h)

B.2. THS CERAMIC TYPES BY PERIOD

In terms of the number of ceramic types for each period, the twenty-one periods are not equally represented in the THS topology. This imbalance exists for several reasons, the two most important being the uneven intensity of archaeological investigations of different historical periods in the basin and surrounding areas, and the specific chronological expertise of the researchers who constructed it. The histogram of types per THS period (fig. B.1) reveals spikes for Periods 4 and 7. Not coincidentally, the two THS sites that were most intensively and systematically investigated reached their maximum in these periods (THS 25 and THS 1, respectively); their broad areas of single-period occupation produced many distinctive and recurring forms, although not all proved to be useful elsewhere. Several Period 7 types were derived from the recent publication of third-millennium pottery from Tell Brak (Oates 2001b) in an attempt to recognize post-Akkadian (Brak phase N) settlement during the intensive survey of Brak's outer settlement (Ur, Karsgaard, and Oates 2007) and were not used in the THS. Further Period 4 types unused by the THS were also developed for the Brak survey, on the basis of surface types and the excavations in HS6 at Tell Brak (Matthews 2003b).

Other periods have fewer types on average. This is true of the early prehistoric periods (Periods 1–3) and the Middle to Late Islamic periods (Periods 17–20), but for different reasons. The most distinctive feature for the prehistoric periods are painted styles of decoration, and as a result, several different vessel forms would all be classified together on the basis of decoration (e.g., T2/1 Halaf painted decoration or T3/1 Ubaid painted decoration). Painted decoration allows otherwise non-diagnostic sherds to be typed, so the relatively small number of types per period for early prehistoric periods probably did not result in underrepresentation of early prehistoric settlement.

The same is likely not to be the case for the Islamic periods. The few types were mostly derived from surface assemblages of sites with short occupations because few substantial excavations (and fewer full publications of ceramics) exist for these periods (Wilkinson and Tucker 1995: 105). It is probable that small occupations for these periods have been overlooked by surveys in the basin.

These conclusions appear justified by comparing the number of types per period (fig. B.1) with the total number of sherds recovered per period (fig. B.2; note that this figure includes only sherds from areal collections and not those from systematic sampling units on THS 1 and THS 25). Period 2 includes only a single type used by the THS (T2/1 painted ware), but a large number of examples were typed. The low total counts for Period 3 sherds are due to the apparent abandonment of the THS region at this time, rather than to the low number of types. On the other hand, the very low quantity of Middle to Late Islamic sherds recovered is probably related to the number and quality of types for those periods, although an actual low settlement density is certainly the predominant factor.

What follows is a detailed description of each type, ordered by period. Comparisons with excavated assemblages and other survey types are not intended to be exhaustive, but rather to give a sense of the chronological range of use, variability in form, and relative frequency of occurrence in excavated contexts and in surface collections. Not all types are illustrated. The emphasis, in terms of description and illustration, is on types developed after the original Tucker-Wilkinson typology and types whose range of variation was underrepresented in that publication. Listed but not illustrated are most new types developed for the Beydar and Brak surveys; they will appear in the monographs for those surveys, currently in preparation. Likewise, the types for the late and poorly understood types are listed but not illustrated. For these types, reference is made to the original typology (Wilkinson and Tucker 1995) and other comparanda. For each period, a catchall type was created to subsume sherds of known periodization, but of types that occur too infrequently to justify the assignment of a type number. These types, which are designated as 0 (e.g., T1/0 for untyped Proto-Hassuna, T2/0 for untyped Halaf, etc.), were used as infrequently as possible and only in cases where occupations would go unrecognized in the sherd counts without their use.

For each type, sherd counts for the areal collections (survey n) and sampling units at Hamoukar (Hamoukar n) are indicated separately. Each type is described by its surface color and treatment, its fabric and temper, and any other significant traits, and some noteworthy comparanda are given. If the type was developed by Wilkinson and Tucker (1995), its type number in the North Jazira Project (NJP) typology is given.

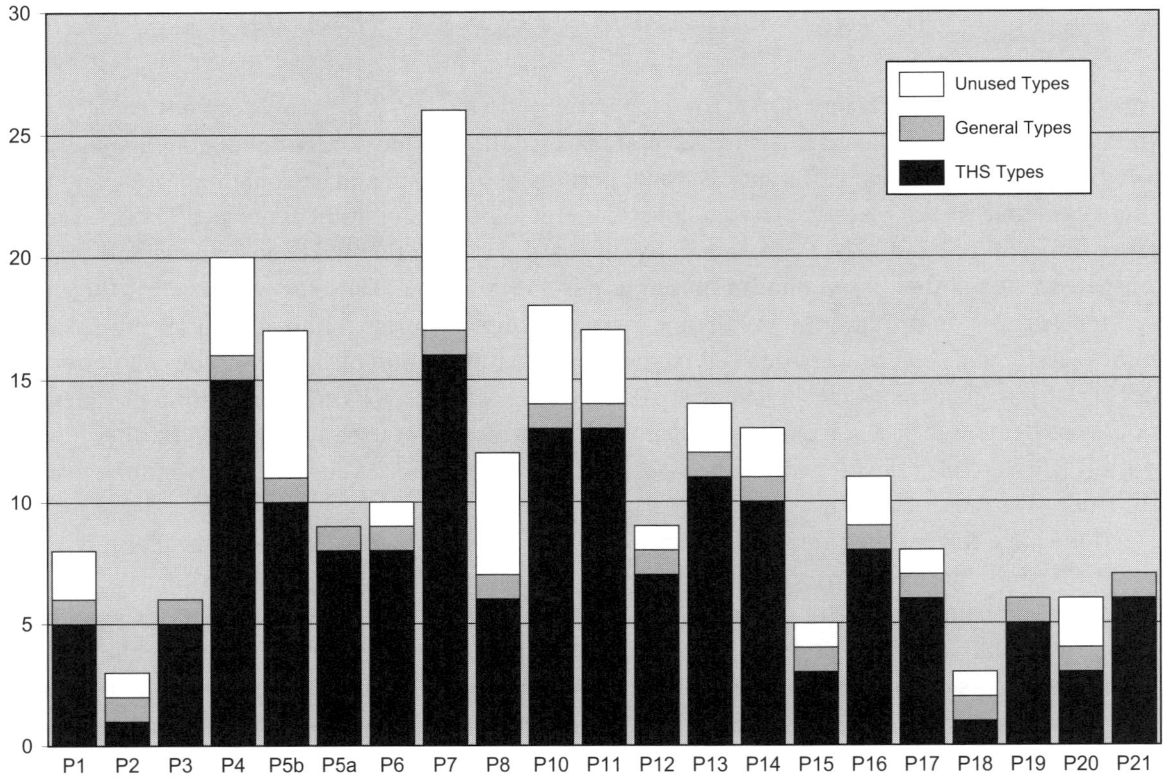

Figure B.1. Histogram of THS ceramic types by period. General types refers to Type 0 for each period (T1/0, T2/0, etc.). Unused types were defined after the completion of the survey and/or applied retroactively in a non-systematic manner

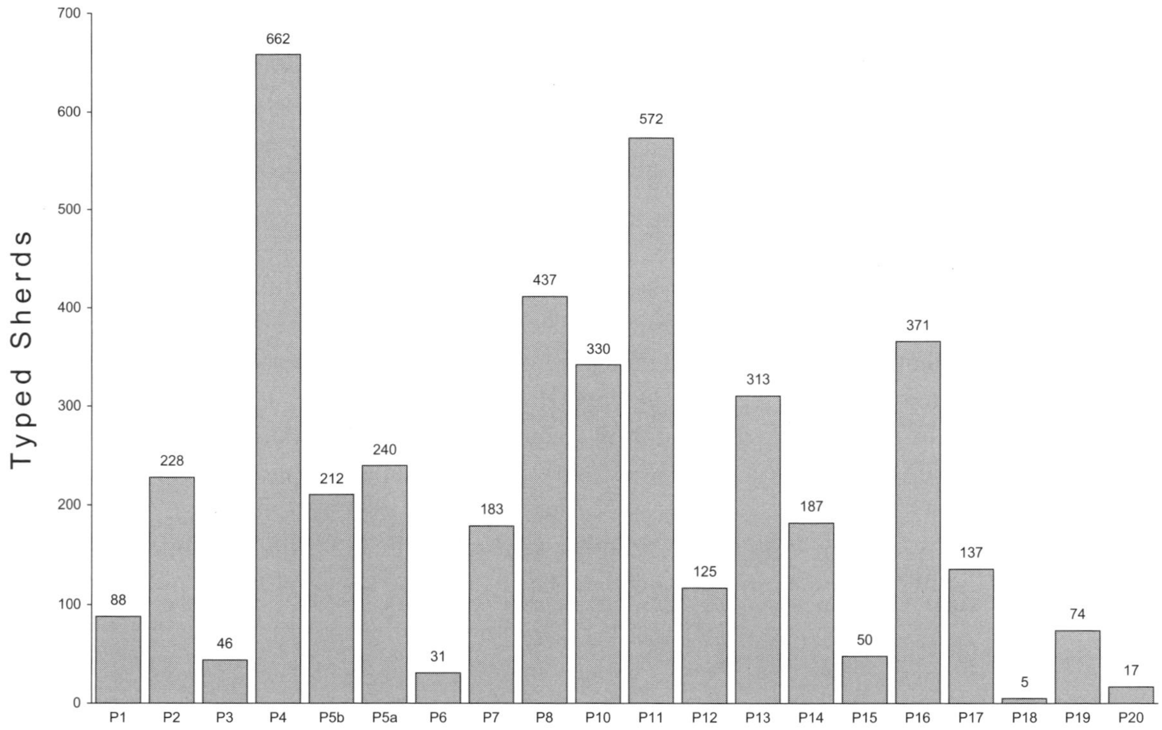

Figure B.2. Histogram of sherd frequency by THS period

B.2.1. PERIOD 1: PROTO-HASSUNA

Local comparative assemblages come from Tell Sabi Abyad (Le Mière and Nieuwenhuyse 1996), Tell Boueid II (Suleiman and Nieuwenhuyse 2002), Tell Kashkashok II (Matsutani 1991), Kharabeh Shattani (McAdam 1995), and Hassuna itself (Lloyd and Safar 1945). At the time of the survey, the THS employed the North Jazira Project types; the more recent approach to Period 1 types of Nieuwenhuyse and Wilkinson for the Tell Beydar Survey sites (2007) is better suited for surface assemblages.

Of the types employed by the THS, T1/1 painted ware was by far the most common, with lesser quantities of the Samarran types (T1/6 and T1/7) recovered (fig. B.3).

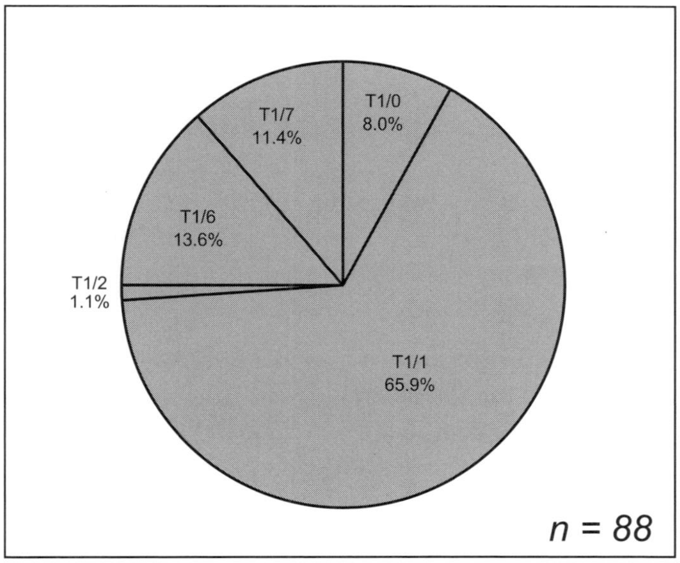

Figure B.3. Frequency of Period 1 ceramic types in THS areal collections

T1/1 Painted Ware (fig. B.4 nos. 1–12; survey n = 58). Sherds are handmade and fired for a short time in low temperatures, resulting in dark cores. Surface colors range from dark brown to pink. Surfaces are often lightly burnished, but this treatment often survives poorly in surface assemblages. Decoration takes the form of bands of dark red to black paint, often in parallel bands diagonal to the rim (as at Kashkashok II; Matsutani 1991: 25–26). Almost two-thirds of Period 1 diagnostics were of T1/1, and it was also the most common type in the Tell Beydar Survey, where it was designated as standard ware (Nieuwenhuyse 2007). NJP type 1.

1. Buff lightly smoothed or burnished surfaces; sand temper. Black-painted crisscrossing lines on interior. Rim dm ca. 17 cm. B.89.5, THS 12.
2. Buff lightly smoothed or burnished surfaces, black core; sand temper. Diagonal red-painted lines on interior and exterior. Rim dm ca. 16 cm. B.89.6, THS 12.
3. Buff surfaces; sand temper. Black-painted horizontal lines and chevrons on exterior. Rim dm ca. 15 cm. B.89.4, THS 12.
4. Light buff exterior, dark buff interior; occasional medium grit. Black vertical and horizontal painted bands on exterior. Rim dm ca. 14 cm. B.89.2, THS 12.
5. Buff interior and exterior surfaces; common fine chaff and fine white grit. Red-brown painted crosshatching on exterior. Rim dm. 19 cm. B.1055.2, THS 4.
6. Pale yellow slipped surfaces, orange-buff core; occasional sand temper. Red-brown painted decoration on interior and exterior. Rim dm 17 cm. B.1139.5, THS 44 Area B.

7. Pale yellow surfaces, gray-brown core; frequent sand temper. Black painted bands on exterior. Rim dm 15 cm. B.1138.4, THS 44 Area A.
8. Buff surfaces; sand temper. Red diagonal painted bands on exterior; black crisscrossing festoons on interior. Rim dm ca. 27 cm. B.89.3, THS 12.
9. Buff surfaces, orange core; common sand temper. Red-orange paint on exterior surface. B.1138.3, THS 44 Area A.
10. Buff surfaces, gray-brown core; frequent sand temper. Black paint on exterior and interior rim. Rim dm 15 cm. B.1139.4, THS 44 Area B.
11. Buff surfaces, red-brown core; fine sand temper. Red-brown painted lines on exterior. B.1055.1, THS 4.
12. Buff surfaces, orange core; common to frequent medium chaff. Black painted decoration on exterior. B.1139.2, THS 44 Area B.

T1/2 Husking Tray (survey n = 1). Sherds derive from a shallow ovoid tray with a flat bottom and deeply grooved on its interior surface (Le Mière 2000: 129; McAdam 1995: 37). Surface color ranges from red to brown, often with a thick reduced core. Because of its poor firing, it may not survive on the surface; the THS recognized only a single example of this type, from THS 44. NJP type 2.

T1/3 Red Burnished Ware. In the Iraqi North Jazira, sherds of this type had gray reduced cores with orange margins, fine fabric, and the characteristic red burnished surface. This type was not used by the THS, but is probably equivalent to the early mineral ware (EMW) type employed in the Tell Beydar Survey (Nieuwenhuyse 2007). NJP type 119.

T1/4 Coarse Chaff- or Grit-Tempered Ware. This type encompasses a range of poorly fired handmade sherds with dark cores, light brown surfaces, and chaff temper. This type was not used by the THS. NJP type 124.

T1/5 Samarran Incised Ware. In the North Jazira, sherds have linear incised decoration on an orange surface with a buff or cream slip, fired under well-controlled oxidizing conditions. Dark painted decoration can occur. Temper is sand or white grit. The THS did not recognize any sherds of this type. NJP type 125A.

T1/6 Samarran Stabbed Ware (fig. B.4. nos. 13–16; survey n = 12). Sherds have short incisions characterized by Wilkinson and Tucker as "stabbed." Fabric, temper, and painted decoration are identical to those of T1/5. NJP type 125B.

13. Buff surfaces; sand temper. Stabbed decoration and red painted bands and chevrons on exterior. B.89.8, THS 12.
14. Buff surfaces, gray core; abundant medium grit. Horizontal stabbed decoration on exterior. B.89.9, THS 12.
15. Dark buff exterior, green interior; abundant medium grit. Horizontal stabbed decoration on exterior. Rim dm ca. 6 cm. B.89.7, THS 12.
16. Buff surfaces, gray core; occasional sand. Evenly spaced fine punctures with traces of black paint. B.1139.6, THS 44 Area B.

T1/7 Samarran Painted Ware (survey n = 10). Sherds of this type are characterized by oxidized fabics and light surfaces heavily ornamented with dark painted designs; temper is generally a fine mineral (Nieuwenhuyse 2000: 161–62). This type, along with T1/5 and T1/6, are late in Period 1 and should be considered transitional into Period 2. NJP type 126.

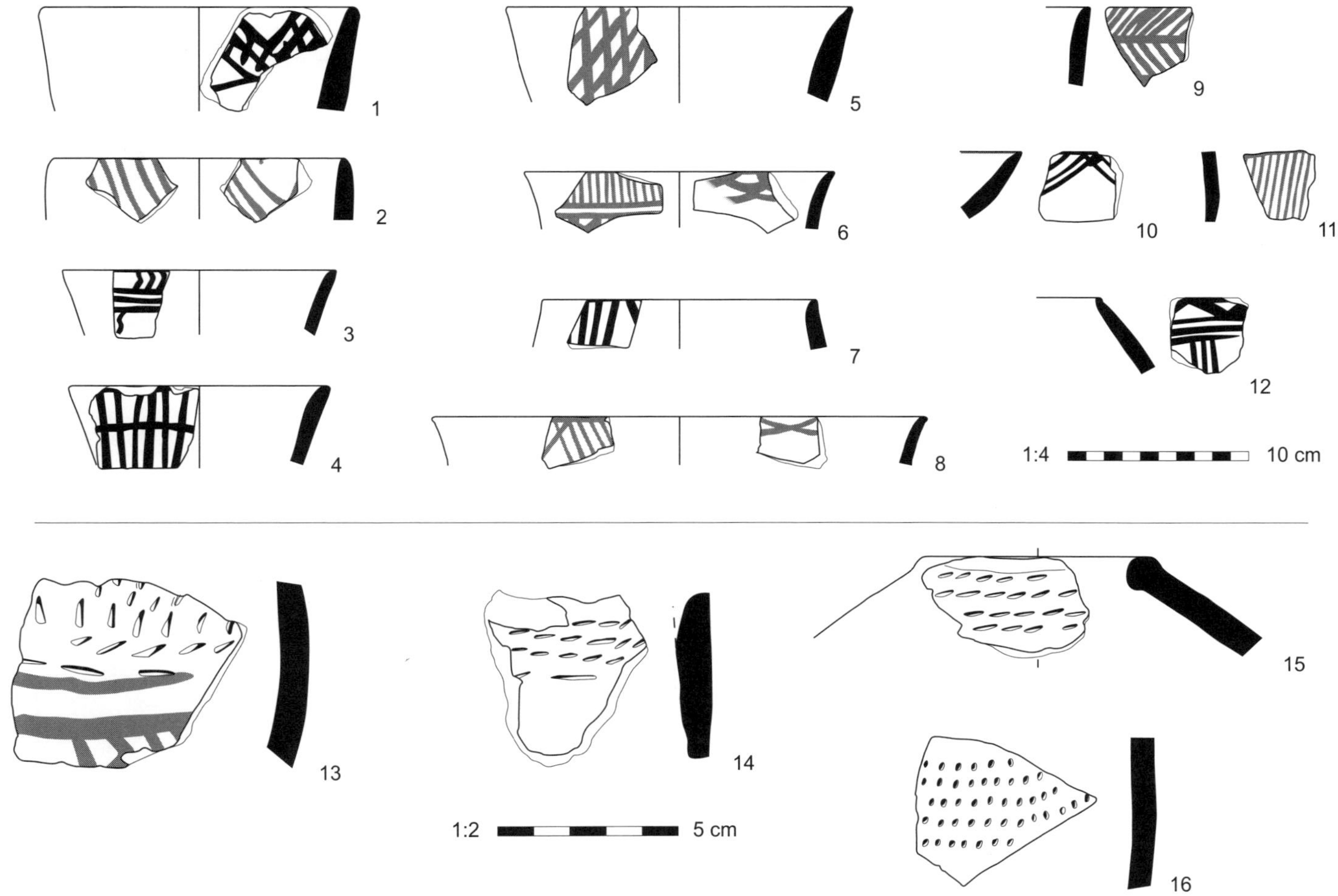

Figure B.4. Ceramic types for Period 1 (Proto-Hassuna)

B.2.2. PERIOD 2: HALAF

Much recent research has gone toward the subdivision of the Halaf period based on ceramic fabrics and decoration (Le Mière and Nieuwenhuyse 1996; Nieuwenhuyse 2007; Cruells 2006; Campbell 1995, 2007). In the North Jazira, Stuart Campbell was able to subdivide the Halaf settlement more finely for a limited area (Wilkinson and Tucker 1995: 39–40, fig. 36), as have Nieuwenhuyse and Wilkinson (Nieuwenhuyse 2000, 2007) in the western Upper Khabur basin. It has not been possible to reassess the THS Period 2 collections with these subdivisions in mind, so they are presented as a single unit here.

T2/1 Halaf Painted Ware (fig. B.5 nos. 1–17; survey n = 228). Sherds have a fine dense fabric, often with no visible temper, and are well fired throughout. Smoothed surfaces are decorated by a range of motifs in an often lustrous dark brown to reddish brown paint. Painted Halaf ware comprised 100 percent of the sherds attribed to Period 2 by the THS. NJP type 3.

1. Buff exterior, reddish interior; sand temper. Red painted festoons and black bands on exterior, red horizontal band with vertical bands on interior. Rim dm ca. 15 cm. B.66.6, THS 24 Area A.
2. Pale buff surfaces; frequent fine grit and chaff. Black paint. Rim dm 16 cm. B.183.1, THS 20 Area D.
3. Yellow-buff slipped surfaces, pink core; common fine lime temper. Black paint on interior and exterior surfaces. Rim dm 16 cm. B.67.1, THS 24 Area C.
4. Buff slipped surfaces, orange core; no visible temper. Dark red paint. Rim dm 8 cm. B.187.4, THS 24 Area L.
5. Buff surfaces and core; red-orange paint; occasional fine lime. B.94.1, THS 20 Area C.
6. Buff surfaces, orange core; no visible temper. Black paint. Rim dm 32 cm. B.1704.1, THS 41 Area F.
7. Buff slipped surfaces, orange core; no visible temper. Red painted interior and exterior surfaces. Rim dm ca. 22 cm. B.1700.10, THS 41 Area B.
8. Buff slipped surfaces, orange core; no visible temper. Dark red painted concentric circles. Rim dm 15 cm. B.1700.11, THS 41 Area B.
9. No description available; rim dm ca. 30 cm. B.115.1, THS 24 Area D.
10. Orange to buff surfaces, red-brown paint; occasional very fine chaff, frequent fine to medium grit. Rim dm 31 cm. B.93.4, THS 20 Area A.
11. Buff surfaces; occasional very fine chaff, common very fine grit. Dark brown paint on interior and exterior surfaces. Rim dm 22 cm. B.93.2, THS 20 Area A.
12. Smoothed yellow-green surfaces, gray core; occasional sand, fine fabric. Black painted surfaces. Rim dm ca. 20 cm. B.94.4, THS 20 Area C.
13. Smoothed yellow-green surfaces, gray core; occasional sand, fine fabric. Black painted surfaces. Rim dm 17 cm. B.94.2, THS 20 Area C.
14. Buff surfaces, light green core; very fine mixed grit. Dark brown paint on exterior and top of rim. Rim dm 20 cm. B.93.1, THS 20 Area A.
15. Buff surfaces; common fine chaff and fine grit. Dark brown painted decoration on exterior and interior rim. Rim dm 18 cm. B.93.3, THS 20 Area A.
16. Buff surfaces, orange core; frequent very fine lime temper. Dark red paint on exterior. Carination dm 14 cm. B.1052.6, THS 43 Area E.
17. Orange surfaces, yellow-buff core; no visible temper. Red-brown painted decoration on exterior. B.1700.12, THS 41 Area B.

T2/2: Fingernail Rusticated Ware. This uncommon type, found at Chagar Bazar and in the Eski Mosul Dam area, is characterized by horizontal rows of fingernail impressions on a pink to red lightly tempered ware (Wilkinson and Tucker 1995: 91). This type was not used by the THS. NJP type 137.

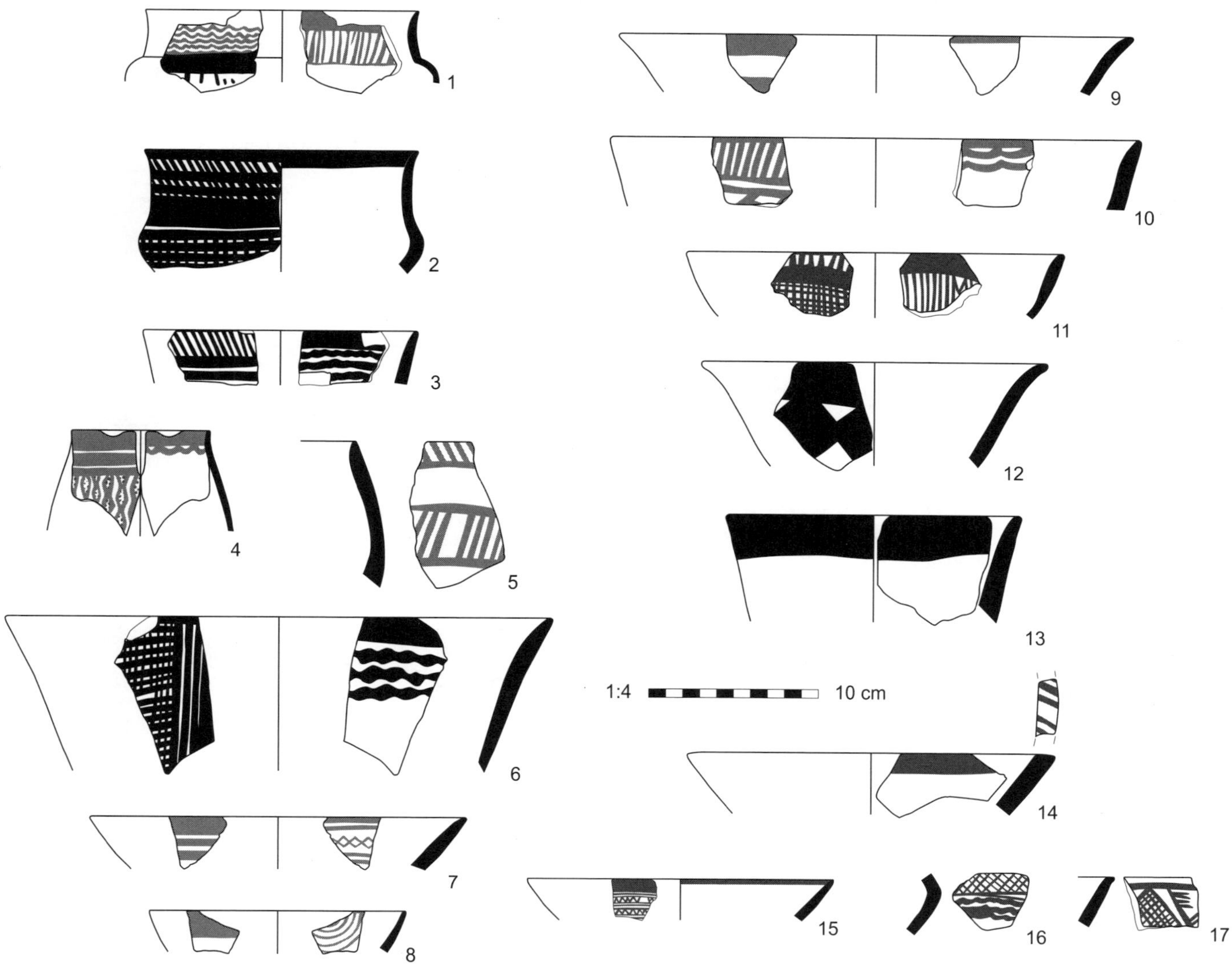

Figure B.5. Ceramic type for Period 2 (Halaf)

B.2.3. PERIOD 3: NORTHERN UBAID

Painted decoration on northern Ubaid ceramics takes the form of dark brown, black, and green painted bands, generally on a buff to green chaffy fabric. The most useful types for survey were T3/1 painted ware and the T3/5 incurved rim, which together accounted for over 80 percent of the Period 3 typed sherds (fig. B.6).

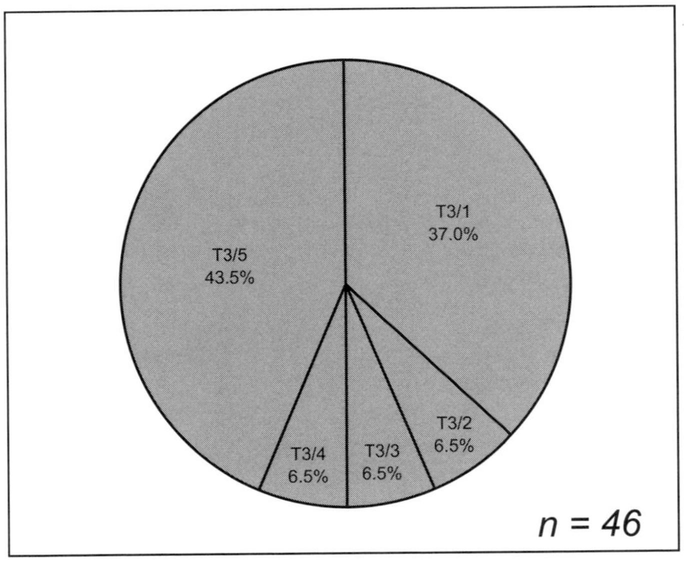

Figure B.6. Frequency of Period 3 ceramic types in THS areal collections

T3/1 Ubaid Painted Ware (fig. B.7 nos. 1–9; survey n = 17). Sherds are characterized by dark paint in bands and festoons. Surface colors are generally light (orange, buff, green) with oxidized cores; temper is generally medium to coarse chaff, sometimes with sand or white mineral. When vessel form can be distinguished, most appear to derive from small hemisperical bowls (Wilkinson, Mohahan, and Tucker 1996: fig. 7; Koizumi 1993). NJP type 4.

1. Buff surfaces; common fine to medium lime temper. Dark brown paint on exterior surface. B.1121.22, THS 29.
2. Orange-buff surfaces, brown core; occasional sand temper. Dark paint on exterior. B.1121.23, THS 29.
3. Buff surfaces, buff core; occasional fine to medium lime temper. Dark brown to black paint on exterior. B.1121.24, THS 29.
4. Yellow slipped surfaces, orange core; occasional sand temper, fine fabric. Dark brown-red paint on exterior and interior rim. Rim dm 16 cm. B.1121.18, THS 29.
5. Orange surfaces; common fine lime temper. Dark paint on exterior and interior rim. Rim dm 18 cm. B.1121.16, THS 29.
6. Orange-buff surfaces, orange core; occasional fine lime, rare medium chaff temper. Dark brown to red paint on interior and top of rim. Rim dm 15 cm. B.1121.21, THS 29.
7. Yellow slipped surfaces, orange core; occasional sand temper, fine fabric. Dark brown to red paint on interior and exterior. Rim dm 27 cm. B.1121.19, THS 29.
8. Buff surfaces with dark brown-black paint, or core; occasional fine chaff and fine lime. Rim dm 25 cm. B.1121.17, THS 29.
9. Yellow surfaces, yelow-green core; common medium chaff and fine lime temper. Dark paint on exterior and interior rims. Rim dm 19 cm. B.1121.15, THS 29.

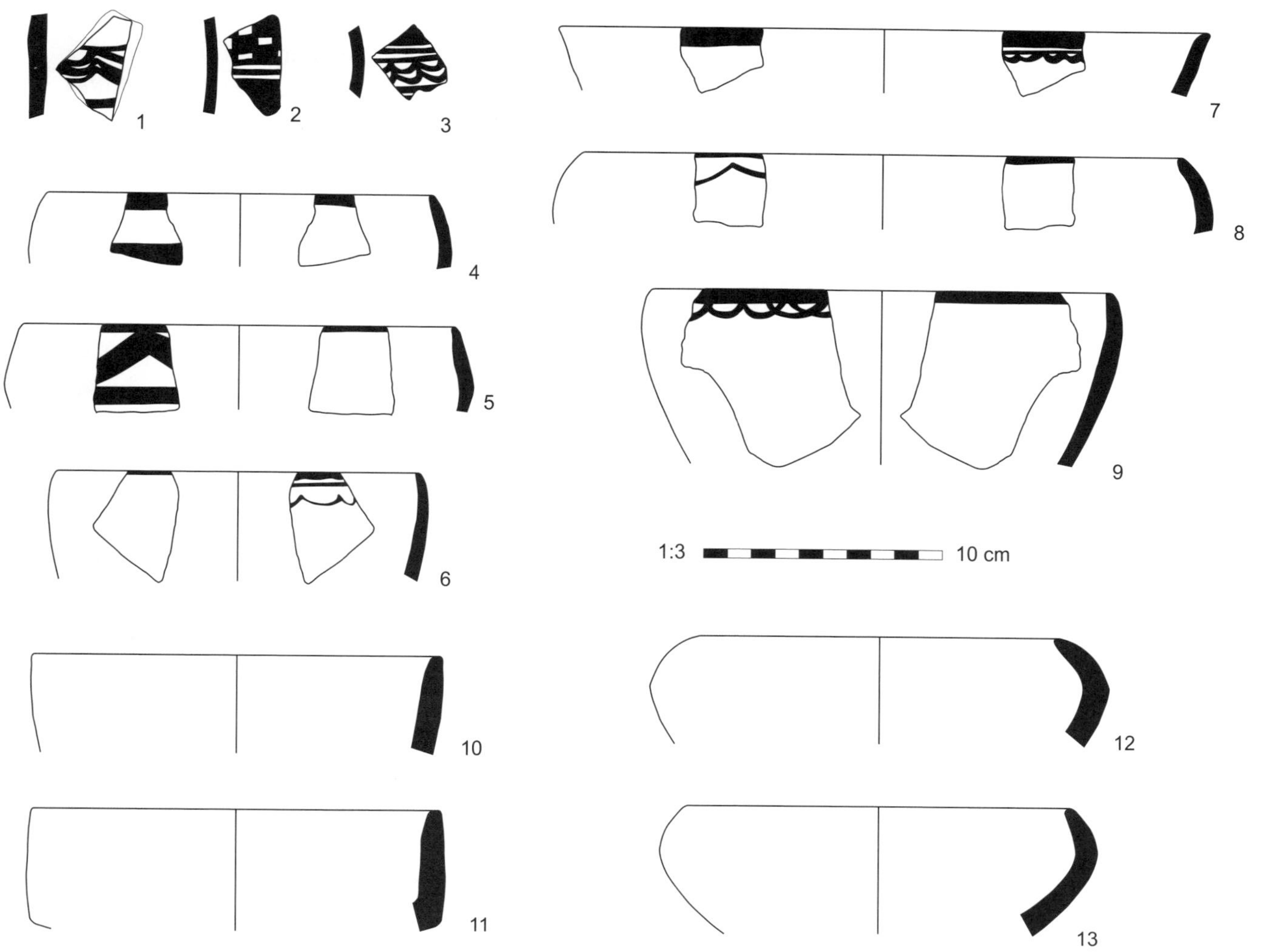

Figure B.7. Ceramic types for Period 3 (northern Ubaid)

T3/2 Ubaid Corrugated Ware (survey n = 3). These sherds have a distinctive corrugation on a buff fabric and are known from late Ubaid levels at Tepe Gawra (Tobler 1950: pls. 78c, 131, from level XIII). NJP type 5.

T3/3 Open Bowl with Grooved Top (fig. B.7 nos. 10–11; survey n = 3). These bowls have straight sides with a concave or shallow grooved rim; fabrics are brown to orange with chaff and occasional white grit temper. This type was common in the excavations at Khanijdal East (Wilkinson, Mohahan, and Tucker 1996). NJP type 135.

10. Buff surfaces, black core; common medium to coarse chaff temper. Rim dm 17 cm. B.1121.6, THS 29.
11. Buff surfaces, brown core; occasional fine lime temper in dense hard fabric. Rim dm 17 cm. B.1121.5, THS 29.

T3/4 Ubaid Everted Jar Rim (survey n = 3). This type is characterized by a robust and distinctive ledge rim, often with a slight concavity to the rim's exterior. Fabric is often heavily chaff tempered with a reduced core. At Khanijdal East, this type was considered to be a late northern Ubaid type (Khanijdal type K 26; Wilkinson, Mohahan, and Tucker 1996: fig. 10.48–49). NJP type 147.

T3/5 Ubaid Incurved Rim (fig. B.7 nos. 12–13; survey n = 20). These small convex bowls have rims that curve inward, sometimes sharply, and may be decorated with dark paint in bands and curving designs (T3/1 above; see fig. B.7 nos. 4–6, 8–9). Fabric is buff and chaff and occasionally white grit tempered. These bowls appear in later northern Ubaid contexts at Khanijdal East (Wilkinson, Mohahan, and Tucker 1996: fig. 8.27–30) and Tell Kashkashok II (Koizumi 1993). NJP type 148.

12. Yellow surfaces and core; occasional medium chaff and fine to coarse lime temper. Rim dm 19 cm. B.1121.12, THS 29.

13. Buff surfaces and core; common to frequent medium to coarse chaff, rare occasional fine lime temper. Rim dm 16 cm. B.1121.13, THS 29.

B.2.4. PERIOD 4: LATE CHALCOLITHIC 1–2

One of the most significant advances in prehistoric chronology over the last ten years has been the redefined relationships between several ceramic traditions of the late fifth and fourth millennia in northern Mesopotamia, and the development of a chronological scheme to accommodate them. For a long time, two distinct northern Mesopotamian ceramic assemblages were considered to be contemporary with the Uruk period in southern Mesopotamia. One assemblage was best known from Tepe Gawra levels XII–IX (Tobler 1950); the other was phase F in the sequence of the Amuq Plain (Braidwood and Braidwood 1960). In earlier northern Mesopotamian surveys, these ceramic traditions were analyzed together alongside southern Mesopotamia-inspired types in a generalized "Uruk" classification (Meijer 1986), although not without doubts as to their contemporaneity (Wilkinson and Tucker 1995: 92).

Following reassessments of the sequences at Nineveh (Gut 1995), Tepe Gawra (Rothman 2002a), and elsewhere (Tomita 1998a), these assemblages are now appreciated to be sequential (Helwing 2000; Rova 1999–2000; Rothman 2001b; Postgate 2002). In the new Late Chalcolithic chronology that resulted from a School of American Research Advanced Seminar, the post-Ubaid, pre-Early Dynastic/Ninevite 5 phase is subdivided into five phases (Late Chalcolithic 1–5), based on excavation sequences and radiocarbon dates (see Rothman 2001a: table 1.1; Wright and Rupley 2001). The Late Chalcolithic 1–2 periods have been variously called Early Northern Uruk (Oates and Oates 1997), Late Chalcolithic I–II (Tomita 1998a), Pre-Contact (Lupton 1996), Middle to Late Gawran (Porada et al. 1992) and post-Ubaid (Hole 2001). Material culture from this time is best known from Tepe Gawra levels XII–IX (Tobler 1950), Hammam et-Turkman (Van Loon 1988), Tell al-Hawa LP (Ball, Tucker, and Wilkinson 1989), Tell Brak HS6 (Matthews 2003b), Grai Resh (Lloyd 1940), and Qalinj Agha (Abu al-Soof 1966; Hijara 1973).

There appear to be substantial ceramic differences between Late Chalcolithic 1 and Late Chalcolithic 2, but at present they are rather qualitative. Therefore, the THS has analyzed Late Chalcolithic 1–2 together as Period 4. A preliminary subdivision of Periods 4, 5b, and 5a is presented in figure B.8. Late Chalcolithic 1 corresponds to Gawra XII and is typified by T4/3 sprig ware and T4/8 urn rims. Late Chalcolithic 2 is best represented by T4/2 beaded holemouth rims, T4/4 double-rimmed jars, and fineware of T4/6 style. The assignment of other Period 4 types to either Late Chalcolithic 1 or Late Chalcolithic 2 is at present far more speculative.

Period 4 was the THS period with the most typed sherds, the three most common being the T4/1 shallow bowl, the T4/5 flaring jar rim, and the T4/18 internally thickened rim (fig. B.9).

T4/1 Coarse Shallow Bowl (fig. B.10 nos. 1–4; survey n = 151). These shallow bowls are handmade and often irregular, with a slight thickening at the rim and toward the base. Surfaces range from buff to orange, often with a reduced core; abundantly tempered with coarse chaff also with common white grit. These forms are often labeled as Coba bowls (e.g., Matthews 2003b: 26). At Tepe Gawra, these bowls were initially found in level XII but became very common in XI-A (Tobler 1950: 151–52, pls. 141:328, 330, 144:367–71). NJP type 7.

1. Buff surfaces, gray core; frequent medium to coarse chaff temper. Rim dm 26 cm. B.1137.7, THS 25 Area K.

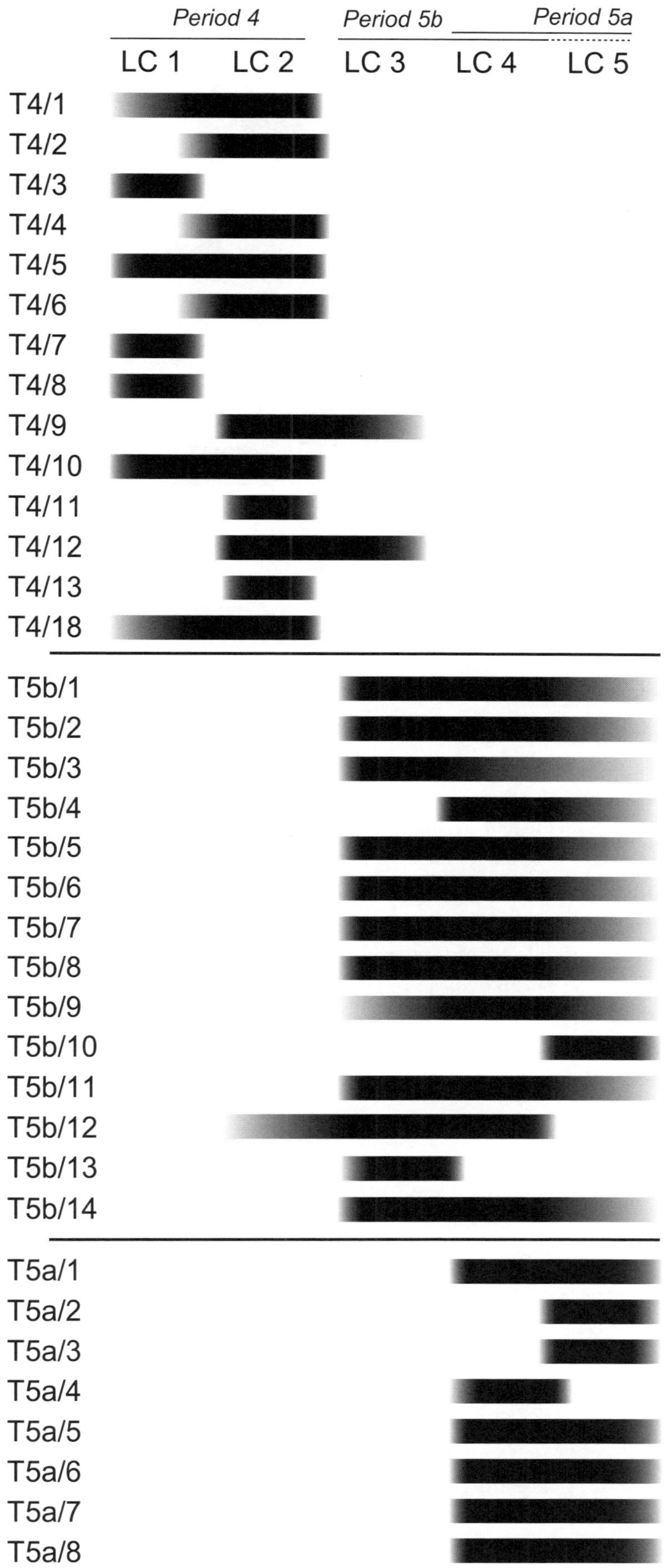

Figure B.8. Chronological longevity of ceramic types for Periods 4–5 (Late Chalcoltihic)

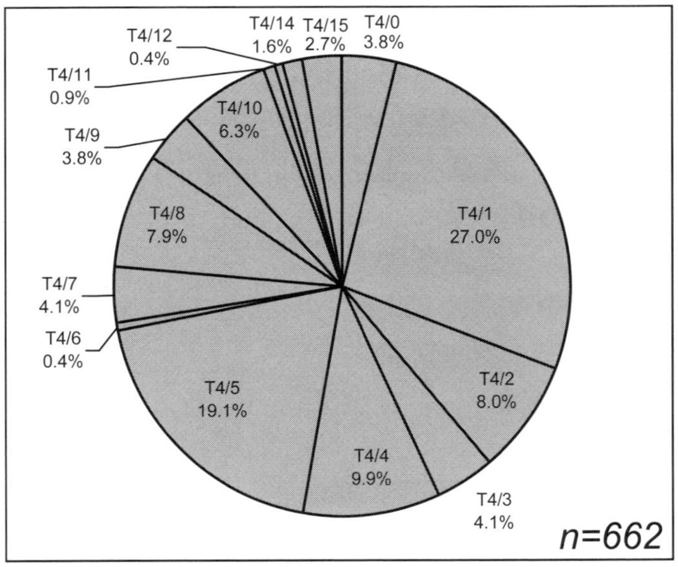

Figure B.9. Frequency of Period 4 ceramic types in THS areal collections

2. Yellow-buff surfaces, thick gray core; frequent medium to coarse chaff, common fine white grit temper. Rim dm 27 cm. A.383.22, THS 25.
3. Orange surfaces, thick gray-black core; frequent medium chaff, occasional fine white grit temper. Rim dm 21 cm. A.383.21, THS 25.
4. Orange-brown surfaces, dark orange core; frequent coarse chaff, frequent medium white grit temper; handmade and irregular. Rim dm ca. 20 cm. A.383.14, THS 25.

T4/2 Beaded Holemouth Jar Rim (fig. B.10 nos. 5–7; survey n = 45). This cooking vessel has a wide mouth with a beaded rim. The shape of the bead can vary from small and rounded to large and flattened (see the examples from Grai Resh for the full range of variation: Lloyd 1940: fig. 7.9). Surfaces are gray, burnished, and frequently show sooting; cores are dark gray to black. Temper is generally fine to medium dark and light grit. This type has been excavated at Hammam et-Turkman V (Akkermans 1988: pl. 108.102–103) and Tepe Gawra XI-A–XI, although a single specimen is known from XII (Tobler 1950: 153, 158, pls. 142:343–44, 146:402–04). NJP type 8.

5. Pale orange-buff surfaces, orange-pink core with brown margins; common to frequent fine sand, rare fine to medium chaff temper. Rim dm 18 cm. A.866.21, THS 25.
6. Blackened red-gray surfaces, thick gray core; abundant fine to medium light and dark grit temper. Rim dm 15 cm. A.383.12, THS 25.
7. Brown gray exterior, black interior and core; frequent fine to medium chaff, common fine to medium lime and grit temper. Rim dm ca. 60 cm. B.1137.6, THS 25 Area K.

T4/3 Sprig Ware (fig. B.10 nos. 17–24; survey n = 23). This type is defined by dark (red-brown to black) paint on an orange to brown surface with a pink to brown core. Fabrics are tempered with common sand and fine to medium grit and are well fired. The "classic" design consists of lines with parallel lines extending obliquely. Other geometric designs occur in the same fabric in surface assemblages; a bow tie motif is especially common. Both the sprig and geometric designs were included in this type in the North Jazira (Wilkinson and Tucker 1995: 93). Sherds of this type are most frequently body sherds, but when rims occur, they range from small bowls to necked jars. Type T4/3 is probably under-represented at THS 25 because many sherds were covered with a thick calcium carbonate accretion which obscured surface decoration. Sprig ware and

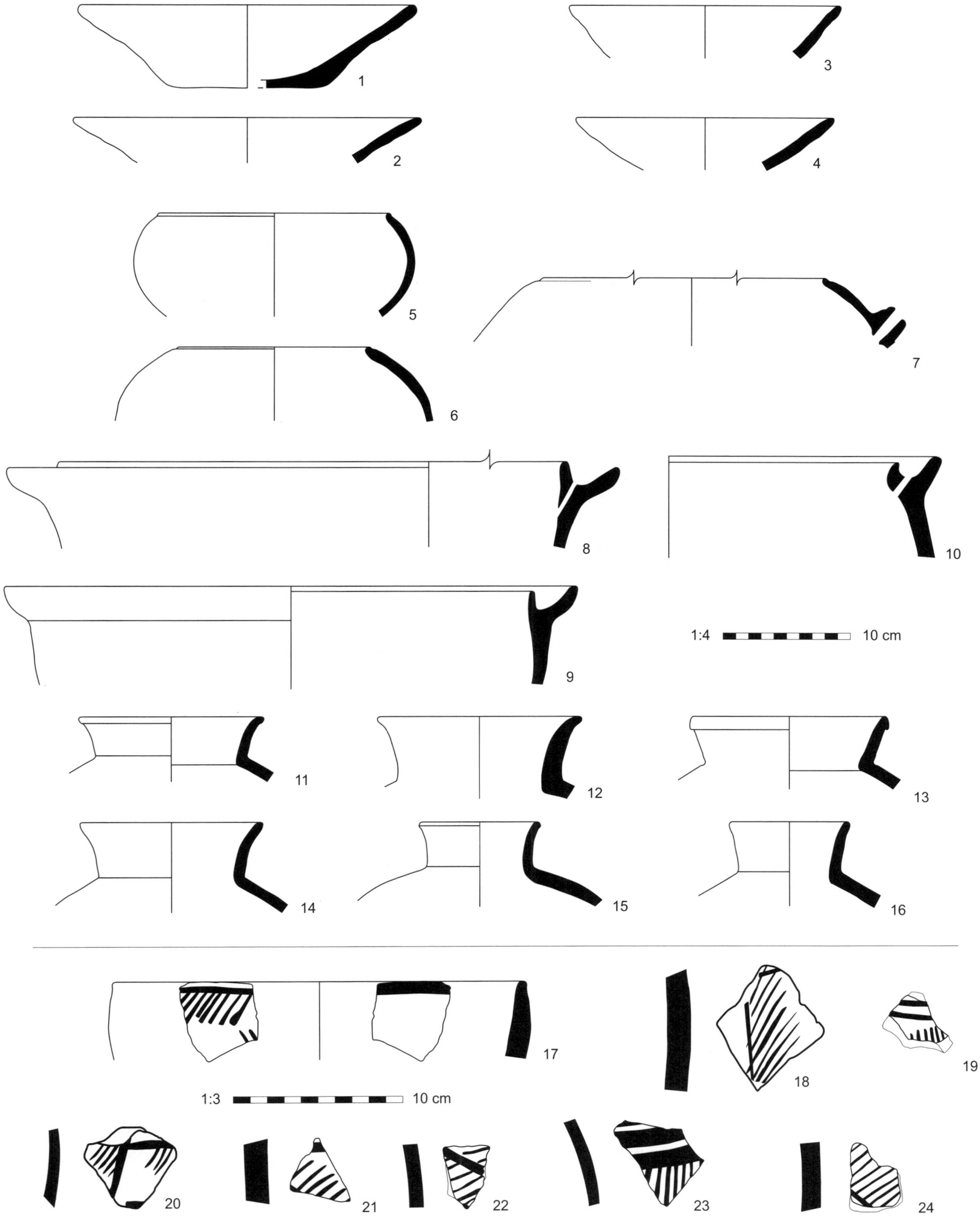

Figure B.10. Ceramic types for Period 4 (Late Chalcolithic 1–2), Types T4/1, T4/2, T4/3, T4/4, and T4/5

related Late Chalcolithic 1 painted pottery is well represented at Gawra level XII (Tobler 1950: pls. 133–39), at Umm Qseir (Tomita 1998b: fig. 64:7), and on the surface of Tell Shelgiyya (Ball 1997). Since it does not seem to continue beyond Gawra level XII, this type represents the best indicator of early Period 4 or Late Chalcolithic 1. NJP type 9.

17. Orange surfaces, orange-brown core; common sand temper. Rim dm 12 cm. B.1085.1, THS 25 Area B.
18. Buff slipped exterior, orange interior, pink core; frequent sand temper. Black painted decoration on exterior surface. B.1096, THS 25 Area O.
19. Orange-buff surfaces; common very fine dark grit and lime temper. Dark brown painted decoration on exterior surface. B.2065.1, THS 33.
20. Orange surfaces, orange-brown core; common sand temper. Dark brown painted decoration on exterior surface. B.1085.2, THS 25 Area B.
21. Orange surfaces, orange-brown core; common sand temper. Black to brown paint on exterior surface. B.2054.10, THS 40 Area C.
22. Brown surfaces; common fine grit, common sand, occasional fine chaff temper. Dark brown painted decoration on exterior surface. B.546.1, THS 25 Area F.
23. Orange-buff surfaces, red-brown core; occasional very fine chaff, common fine grit temper. Dark brown painted decoration on exterior. B.2050, THS 25 Area L.
24. Orange-buff surfaces, orange-brown core; frequent fine grit, common very fine chaff temper. Dark brown painted decoration on exterior surface. B.2051.3, THS 25 Area M.

T4/4 Double-Rimmed Jar (fig. B.10 nos. 8–10; survey n = 55). Complete vessels with this type of double or channel rim are large round-based jars; the inner rim tends to be vertical while the outer rim flares outward and curves up to create a channel. On many examples, a small hole allows liquid to drain from the channel into the vessel. Surfaces range from brown to orange to pink with generally oxidized cores. Temper is most commonly sand or grit, occasionally with some fine chaff. Vessels were well fired. Some specimens were dark painted (T4/17). Sherds were rarely found with rims intact but the robustness of its construction and the distinctiveness of its shape allowed it to be identified even when heavily plow-damaged. At Tepe Gawra, this type appeared after level XII (i.e., Late Chalcolithic 2; Tobler 1950: 152, 158, pls. 142:346, 146:405–06). Double-rimmed jars are also found at Umm Qseir (Tomita 1998b: fig. 64.1). NJP type 10.

8. Orange-buff surfaces, red-buff core; frequent fine dark grit, common fine chaff temper. Interior rim dm 58 cm. B.1137.10, THS 25 Area K.
9. Pale orange surfaces, brown core; frequent medium chaff temper; handmade and irregular. Rim dm 14 cm. A.383.13, THS 25.
10. Pale yellow surfaces, pink-orange core; frequent to abundant medium chaff, common fine white grit temper. Inner rim dm 36 cm. A.383.31, THS 25.

T4/5 Flaring Jar Rim (fig. B.10 nos. 11–16; survey n = 107). This type is characterized by a short flaring concave neck at a sharp angle from the vessel shoulder, often with a beaded or band rim. It is in general well fired but with variability in fabric: some examples occur in an orange sandy hard-fired fabric, while others are chaff tempered. This type is best used in conjunction with other Period 4 types, as it is also found in Ubaid contexts; at Hammam et-Turkman, this type occurs throughout Period V but is also found in Period IV (Akkermans 1988: 307). At Tepe Gawra it characterizes levels XI-A through IX (Tobler 1950: pls. 142:349, 351, 353, 148:430–31). NJP type 13.

11. Pale yellow slipped surfaces, brown core; abundant sand temper. Rim dm 14 cm. A.866.3, THS 25.

12. Orange-brown surfaces, orange-pink core; abundant sand temper. Rim dm 16 cm. A.866.1, THS 25.
13. Pale orange surfaces, brown core; common to frequent medium chaff, rare medium grit temper. Rim dm 15 cm. A.866.4, THS 25.
14. Buff-brown surfaces, gray core with pink margins; occasional medium chaff, occasional sand temper; hard fired. Rim dm 14 cm. B.549.2, THS 25.
15. Yellow-green surfaces and core; common sand temper. Rim dm 9 cm. B.549.3, THS 25.
16. Yellow-green surfaces and core; frequent medium to coarse chaff temper; smoothed exterior surf. Rim dm 9 cm. B.549.4, THS 25.

T4/6 Fine Beaker (fig. B.11 nos. 1–4; survey n = 3). Sherds of this type are well fired in a green to yellow fabric with common sand and fine chaff. Vessels are often decorated with panels of parallel ridges with fine notching and applied rosettes. Black paint infrequently occurs in bands on the rim, and a single specimen had rouletting on its sides. Voids within the layers of clay occasionally expanded during firing, resulting in a distinctive "blistering" (T4/12). Beakers of this type are well known from excavations at Tepe Gawra levels XI–IX (Tobler 1950: 156–57, pl. 145, photos on pls. 79–80) and at Tell Brak in CH level 13 (Oates 1987: fig. 3.6–7) and HS6 (Matthews 2003b: fig. 3.12.14, 21). In the THS region they occurred on THS 25 but only rarely on other Period 4 sites. NJP type 16.

1. Yellow-buff surfaces; common sand and fine chaff temper. Fine notched ridges and horizontal grooves on exterior. Rim dm 17 cm. B.1137.4, THS 25 Area K.
2. Buff surfaces; common medium chaff and grit temper. Incised lines and stamped rosette on exterior surface. Traces of bitumen on interior. B.2051.2, THS 25 Area M.
3. Slipped buff-yellow surfaces; common sand temper. Applique rosettes and notched ridges on exterior. B.1137.5, THS 25 Area K.
4. Pale yellow surfaces, pale yellow core with thin brown margins; occasional fine lime temper. Painted dark brown to black band on top exterior; traces of rouletting on exterior. Rim dm 11 cm. A.383.28, THS 25.

T4/7 Neckless Flaring Jar Rim (fig. B.11 nos. 5–8; survey n = 23). Jars with this type of rim have a sloping shoulder and very wide mouths. The rim itself is short and flaring, often with a very sharp interior carination. Like T4/5, this form occurs in a hard sandy fabric and in a softer chaff-tempered fabric. Some examples have black or reddish brown paint. This type was identified in single-period areas of occupation on THS 25 and appears commonly in Tepe Gawra level XII (Tobler 1950: 149, pl. 137:290).

5. Pale buff surfaces, brown core with orange margins; common fine to medium chaff temper. Brown-black paint on rim. Rim dm 18 cm. A.866.11, THS 25.
6. Pale yellow surfaces, light brown core; common fine chaff temper. Rim dm 19 cm. A.866.10, THS 25.
7. Pink-buff surfaces, brown core with orange margins; rare fine chaff, frequent fine sand temper. Rim dm 36 cm. A.383.6, THS 25.
8. Pale orange surfaces, brown core; common fine to medium chaff, rare sand temper. Faint traces of red-brown paint on exterior. Rim dm 16 cm. A.383.4, THS 25.

T4/8 Deep Straight-Sided Urn (fig. B.11 nos. 9–11; survey n = 44). This rim type occurs on very large straight-sided vessels with round bases. The rims, which appear banded in profile, could be characterized as either inwardly bevelled or slightly flaring. Most examples occur in an oxidized and hard-fired sandy fabric, but a few were chaff tempered with a dark core. This type was identified in single-period areas of occupation on THS 25, but is very common in Tepe Gawra level XII burials, where it sometimes occurs with T4/3 sprig ware decoration (Tobler 1950: 148–49,

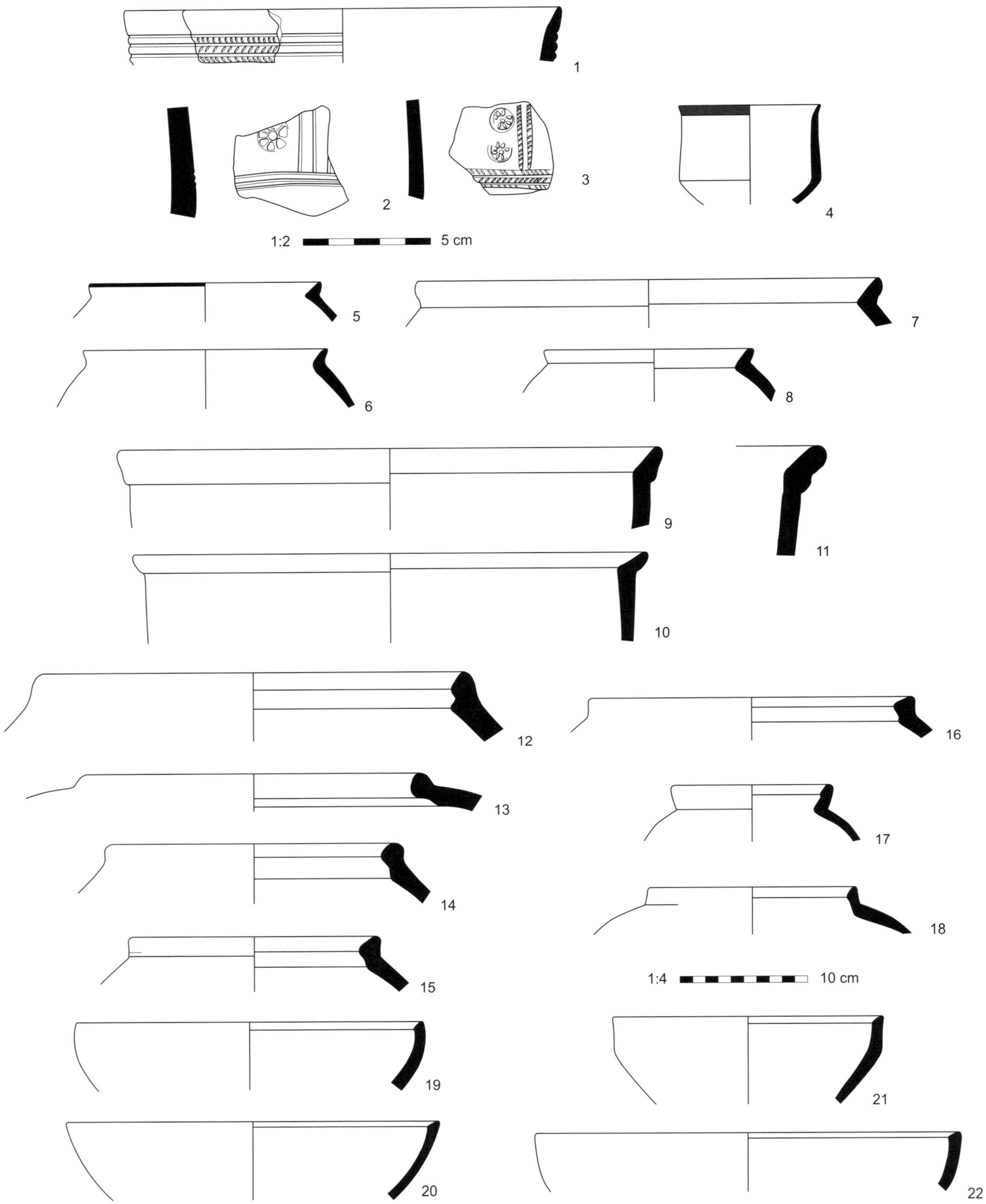

Figure B.11. Ceramic types for Period 4 (Late Chalcolithic 1–2), Types T4/6, T4/7, T4/8, T4/9, and T4/18

pl. 136:275). Examples from Tell Shelgiyya were also painted (Ball 1997: figs. 3.1–2, 4.7–8). With T4/3 sprig ware, this type is an early Period 4 (Late Chalcolithic 1) indicator.

9. Orange surfaces, black core; fine to common chaff temper. Rim dm 42 cm. B.149, THS 26.
10. Pale yellow-green surfaces and core; frequent medium chaff, frequent fine to medium light and dark grit temper. Rim dm ca. 40 cm. A.383.7, THS 25.
11. Orange surfaces, red-pink core; abundant fine sand temper; hard fired. Rim dm >51 cm. A.383.2, THS 25.

T4/9 Early Internally Hollowed Rim (fig. B.11 nos. 12–18; survey n = 21). Surfaces are yellow to brown, often with a reduced core, and heavily chaff tempered. Rim morphology is variable, but all examples have a groove or hollow on the interior. This rim form was included as part of T5b/1 in the North Jazira, but is morphologically distinct and occurs in association with other Period 4 types in single-period areas of occupation on THS 25 and at Umm Qseir (Tomita 1998b: fig. 64.3), Tell Brak HS6 (Matthews 2003b: figs. 3.12.11, 13, 3.13.7) and Hammam et-Turkman Vb, where it is the most common jar rim type (Akkermans 1988: 309, pl. 110:120–21).

12. Orange exterior, yellow interior, thick black core; frequent to abundant fine to medium chaff, common sand temper. Rim dm ca. 33 cm. B.165.3, THS 31.
13. Orange exterior, gray interior, thick black core; frequent medium chaff, common fine lime temper. Rim dm 26 cm. B.165.4, THS 31.
14. Pale yellow-green surfaces, gray-green core; common fine to medium chaff, common sand temper. Rim dm 22 cm. B.165.2, THS 31.
15. Yellow exterior, pale orange interior, brown core; common to frequent fine to medium chaff, occasional sand temper. Rim dm 19 cm. B.165.5, THS 31.
16. Pale yellow surfaces, yellow-green core; frequent medium to coarse chaff temper. Rim dm 25 cm. B.165.1, THS 31.
17. Orange-buff surfaces, light gray core; common fine grit, common fine chaff temper. Rim dm 12 cm. B.1137.1, THS 25 Area K.
18. Yellow-buff surfaces, brown core; frequent fine to medium chaff temper. Rim dm 16 cm. B.1137.2, THS 25 Area K.

T4/10 Clay "Hut Symbol" (survey n = 35). Clay objects of this type have two large loops atop a hollow, bell-like base. It is often considered to be an early version of the later "eye idol," but is also interpreted as a twining device (Fortin 1999: 29, 183). Its shape is distinctive even when heavily damaged by plowing, particularly the durable junction between the "eyes" and the base. This type was identified in single-period areas of occupation on THS 25, but also occurs in Period 4 levels at Grai Resh (Lloyd 1940: fig. 7.1), Tepe Gawra (Tobler 1950: pl. 86a), and Tell Musharifa (Oguchi 1987: pl. 1.4).

T4/11 Drooping Ledge Rim (survey n = 5). This large storage jar rim is characterized by a slightly incurving shoulder with a sharp interior angle. THS specimens had a wide drooping ledge rim, but examples from Tell Brak HS6 are straight (Matthews 2003b: fig. 3.14.12, 14). Surfaces are buff to orange with reduced cores and frequent sand temper, occasionally also with chaff. Some examples have T4/17 wash or paint. This type was identified in single-period areas of occupation on THS 25.

T4/12 Blister Ware (survey n = 2). Sherds of this type come from vessels made with a slab technique; during firing, voids expand to create the characteristic "blistered" appearance of the surfaces. Blister ware is common on finewares of T4/6, but can also occur on finewares of Period 5b (Oates 2002: 119). This type was developed during the Tell Brak suburban survey and was retroactively and non-systematically applied to THS collections.

T4/13 Internally Incised Bowl. These handmade chaff- and grit-tempered bowls have a distinctive crosshatched incised pattern on their interiors that allows them to be identified from body sherds. Examples are known from Tell Brak at HS6 (Matthews 2003b: fig. 3.13.11–13) and in Period 4 areas of the outer town (Hole 2001: fig. 7.5). This type was developed during the Brak suburban survey and was not used in the THS.

T4/14 Clay Ladle (survey n = 9). This type was identified in single-period areas of occupation on THS 25 and may be geographically limited to the eastern Upper Khabur basin.

T4/15 Deep Bowl (survey n = 15). These chaff-tempered deep open forms were defined by Wilkinson and Tucker based on excavations at trench LP at Tell al-Hawa (Ball, Tucker, and Wilkinson 1989: fig. 28.23–24). Because of their simple form, which occurs throughout the prehistoric period, this type was only used in association with other Period 4 sherds in the THS. NJP type 17.

T4/16 Bowl with Exterior Groove. Bowl rims similar in form to T4/1 but with a distinctive groove along the rim exterior are considered to be diagnostic of Late Chalcolithic 1 at Tell Brak (Joan Oates, pers. comm.). This type was developed during the Brak suburban survey and was not used in the THS.

T4/17 Brown Washed Ware. This type encompasses sherds with dark (red to brown) paint or wash on a hard-fired sandy fabric, in a range of forms of other types (e.g., T4/4, T4/5, T4/7, and T4/8). This type was not used by the THS. NJP type 11.

T4/18 Bowl with Internally Thickened Rim (fig. B.11 nos. 19–22; survey n = 104). A chaff-tempered convex bowl rim with buff surfaces and an often-reduced core. The relatively fine and angular Period 4 version of this bowl appears to evolve smoothly into a coarser Period 5b version (T5b/13). This bowl is well represented at Tell Brak HS6 (Matthews 2003b: figs. 3.13.2, 3.15.31), but appears infrequently at Tepe Gawra. The distinction between Period 4 and Period 5b versions was not uniformly made during the THS, and therefore this type has been excluded from analysis. NJP type 21.

19. Pale yellow surfaces, yellow-gray core; frequent medium chaff temper. Lower exterior scraped. Rim dm 27 cm. A.383.15, THS 25.
20. Pale yellow surfaces, yellow-gray core; frequent medium chaff temper. Lower exterior scraped. Rim dm 27 cm. A.866.14, THS 25.
21. Pale yellow surfaces, thin black core; frequent medium chaff, occasional fine white grit temper. Rim dm 21 cm. A383.9, THS 25.
22. Pale orange surfaces with traces of buff slip on exterior, thick black core; frequent to abundant medium chaff temper. Rim dm 33 cm. A.383.10, THS 25.

B.2.5. PERIOD 5B: LATE CHALCOLITHIC 3–5 INDIGENOUS TYPES

The best sequences for indigenous northern Mesopotamian ceramics come from Tell Brak Area TW (Oates and Oates 1991, 2002, Oates 2002) and further afield at Hacinebi Tepe on the Turkish Euphrates (Pearce 2000, Pollock and Coursey 1995). In the THS, Period 5b includes Late Chalcolithic 3 and 4, but because the definition of Late Chalcolithic 5 is based on the presence of particular southern Uruk types, it is uncertain whether the manufacture and consumption of the chaff tempered types of the indigenous assemblage continued into Late Chalcolithic 5. Excavations are of no help in this matter: Late Uruk Habuba Kabira and the Late Uruk levels in Brak TW are exclusively southern in their ceramics (Sürenhagen 1978, 1986, Oates and Oates 1991, Oates 2002: 114–15). Was this because local ceramic techniques were no longer in use, or was it because these southern Uruk communities were not using pots of the local tradition? It is assumed here that local communities, people of southern origin, and their pots continued to coexist, as they had in the Late Chalcolithic 4 period, and that the few sequences and sites excavated to date are non-representative of all ceramic use and discard; therefore Period 5b encompasses Late Chalcolithic 3–5. However, it must be remembered that there is no stratigraphic justification for this assumption at present.

Period 5b types are found in two main fabrics. The first is a coarsely made, heavily chaff tempered ware with brown to reddish-orange surfaces and a thick reduced core. At Hacinebi, the former color is predominantly Late Chalcolithic 3, whereas the latter characterizes Late Chalcolithic 4 pottery (Pearce 2000); the surface colors of sherds collected from short occupation areas of Tell Brak's outer town appear to be in agreement. The second fabric is a fineware with yellow, pink, or orange smoothed or slipped surfaces and most frequently without visible temper. It is occasionally possible to position types chronologically within Period 5b; see fig. B.8.

The most common types on the survey (fig. B.12) were the T5b/4 hammerhead bowl rim (31.1%) and the T5b/11 sharply out-turned rim (22.6%). At Hamoukar, both of these types were far less frequent; the T5b/9 "Pie Plate" rim was by far the most common (40.1%), followed by the T5b/1 internally hollowed jar rim.

T5b/1 Internally Hollowed Jar Rim (fig. B.13 nos. 1–6; survey n = 28, Hamoukar n = 41). This type has a variable rim, most commonly triangular in section, with a distinctive concavity behind it.

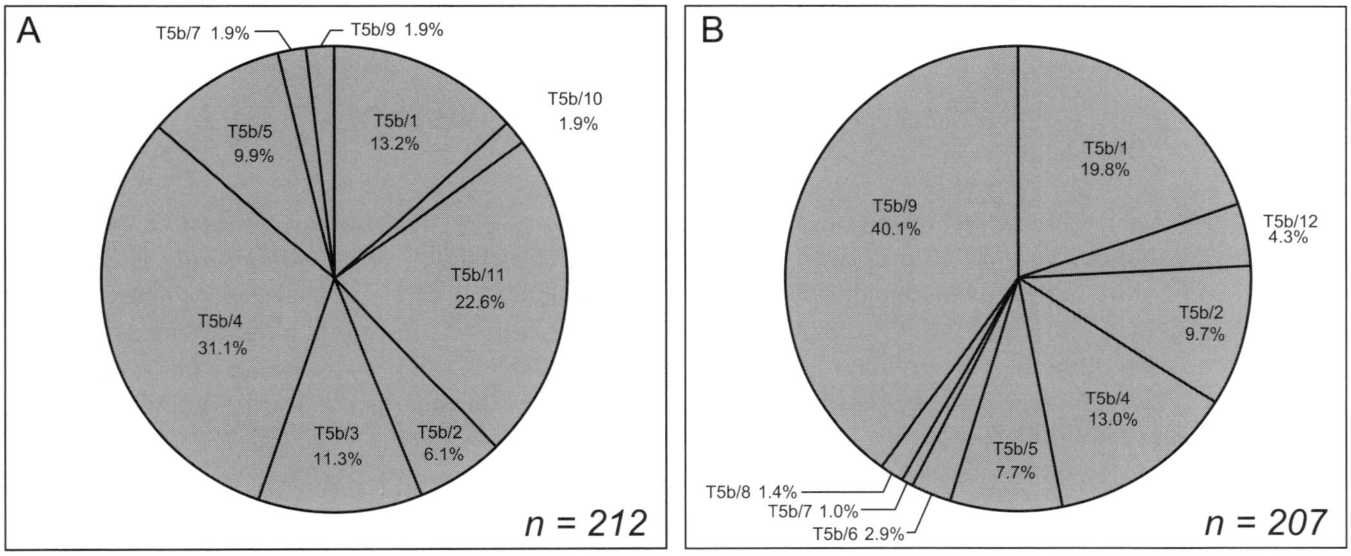

Figure B.12. Frequency of Period 5b ceramic types (*A*) in THS areal collections and (*B*) in Hamoukar sampling units

Surfaces range from brown to red; fabrics are the standard chaff temper with a thick reduced core. T5b/1 is probably an evolved form of T4/9; the two types were not distinguished in the North Jazira. Many examples were excavated in Area B at Hamoukar (Gibson et al. 2002b: fig. 20.1–3). It occurs in TW level 16 at Tell Brak (Oates and Oates 1993: 193, fig. 53.56). NJP type 12.

1. Orange surfaces, brown core with red-orange margins; frequent medium chaff temper. Rim dm 28 cm. B.2052.2, THS 40 Area A.
2. Orange surfaces, black core; frequent medium chaff, occasional fine dark grit temper. Rim dm 24 cm. B.2052.1, THS 40 Area A.
3. Orange surfaces, thick black core; frequent medium chaff temper. Rim dm 29 cm. B.2052.3, THS 40 Area A.

4. Orange surfaces, brown core; common to frequent medium chaff temper. Rim dm 19 cm. B.2052.4, THS 40 Area A.

5. Orange surfaces, thick black core; frequent medium chaff temper. Rim dm 32 cm. B.1050.1, THS 36.

6. Orange-buff surfaces, brown core; common fine chaff, common fine to medium grit temper. Rim dm 24 cm. B.93.5, THS 20 Area A.

T5b/2 Internally Grooved Jar Rim (fig. B.13 nos. 7–9; survey n = 13, Hamoukar n = 20). This type has a variable rim morphology, but all examples are characterized by a horizontally grooved rim interior. In some cases these might be two or three wide grooves; in other cases, they might be better described as incisions. The type encompasses large storage jars in the standard red-brown chaff-tempered ware and yellow to orange fineware jars with no visible temper. This type may also be related to the earlier T4/9; the rim variation may ultimately prove to be chronologically significant. Early versions appear to have few large grooves (e.g., Pearce 2000: fig. 4e–g in Hacinebi phase A), whereas later examples have more finer grooves or even incisions. The latter were common in TW level 16 at Tell Brak (Oates and Oates 1993: figs. 51.20, 53.57). NJP type 14.

7. Orange surfaces, thick gray core; common medium chaff, occasional sand temper. Rim dm 20 cm. B.2052.7, THS 40 Area A.

8. Pale orange surfaces, gray core with orange margins; frequent medium chaff temper. Rim dm 23 cm. B.2052.8, THS 40 Area A.

9. Buff surfaces, dark gray core; frequent medium chaff temper. Rim dm 20 cm. B.2065.2, THS 33.

T5b/3 Late Chalcolithic Gray Ware (fig. B.13 nos. 10–11; survey n = 24). This is a common fabric type that occurs in a range of forms, mostly bowls. THS examples were predominantly gray and lightly burnished on one or both surfaces, with abundant chaff and a thick reduced core; some examples also have occasional to common white grit temper. The morphological range of variation is chronologically relevant: an angular flat-topped bowl form is earlier than the more common form with a large beaded rim. The latter peaks in frequency early in Hacinebi phase A (Pearce 2000: 117, fig. 5a–e). NJP type 138.

10. Buff-brown surfaces, black core; frequent medium chaff, occasional fine to medium lime temper. Rim dm 34 cm. B.2065.12, THS 33.

11. Buff-green surfaces; common fine chaff temper. Rim dm 34 cm. B.2065.7, THS 33.

T5b/4 Hammerhead Bowl Rim (fig. B.13 nos. 12–14; survey n = 66, Hamoukar n = 27). This distinctive T-shaped rim occurs on large shallow bowls in the standard red-bown chaff tempered fabric. The classic T-rimmed hammerhead bowl is characteristic of phase B (Late Chalcolithic 4) at Hacinebi Tepe (Pearce 2000: fig. 9). The hammerhead bowl rim was the most frequent Period 5b type in the THS excluding Hamoukar. NJP type 152.

12. Gray surfaces, dark gray core; frequent medium chaff temper. Rim dm 29 cm. B.1095.6, THS 40 Area I.

13. Yellow (slipped?) surfaces, buff core; frequent medium chaff temper. Rim dm ca. 38 cm. B.2052.23, THS 40 Area A.

14. Orange surfaces, thick black core; frequent to abundant medium chaff temper. Rim dm 45 cm. B.1050.2, THS 36.

T5b/5 Casserole (fig. B.13 nos. 15–18; survey n = 21, Hamoukar n = 16). This type can be recognized by its simple out-turned rim on an inward-sloping body, or by its irregular carination. Surface colors range from gray-brown to orange-red and are most often burnished. Cores are reduced,

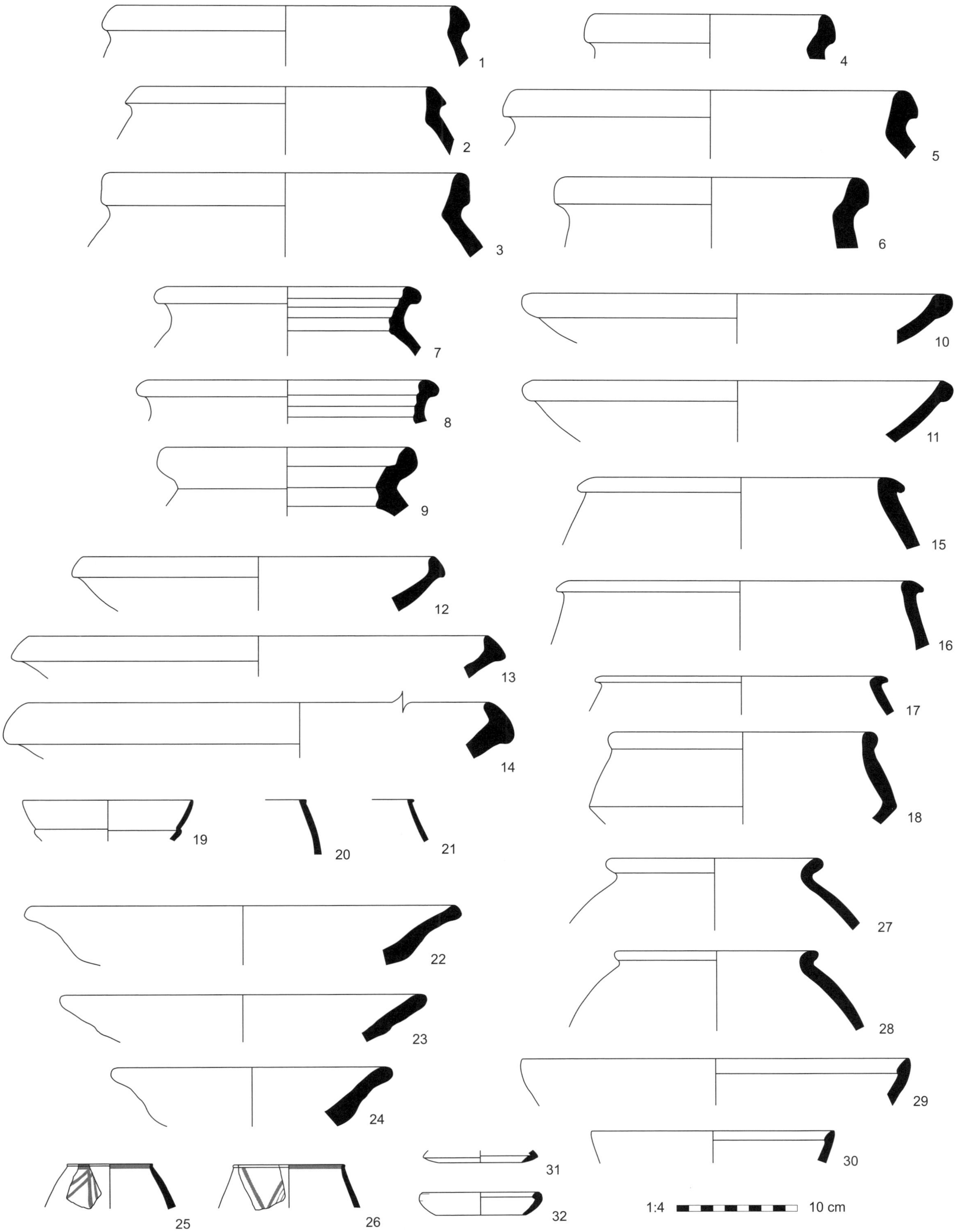

Figure B.13. Ceramic types for Period 5b (indigenous Late Chalcolithic 3–5)

with abundant chaff and common grit. Some examples from the Hamoukar Area B excavations have deep crescent-shaped scoring on the exterior below the carination. Many examples also have sooting on the exterior. If the fabric is considered, it is possible to identify this type from the carination alone. At Hacinebi Tepe and Tell Brak HS1, there is variation between Late Chalcolithic 3 and Late Chalcolithic 4 casseroles (Pearce 2000; Felli 2003: 69–70). Late Chalcolithic 3 examples are predominantly gray with simple slightly thickened and everted rims (Pearce 2000: figs. 3e–f, 8a–c), whereas those from phase B are reddish with a sharply everted rim (Pearce 2000: 117–18, fig. 10). The former type occurs frequently at the bottom of the Area A step trench at Hamoukar (Gibson et al. 2002b: fig. 19.11) and in HS1 at Brak (Felli 2003: fig. 19.1–9); the latter form is the most common casserole type in Late Chalcolithic 4 levels at Brak TW (Oates and Oates 1993: 197, fig. 196.60–70) and at Hamoukar Area B (Gibson et al. 2002b: fig. 20.4–5). These two variations were included in T5b/5 in the THS, but should be distinguishable in future surface collections. NJP type 153.

15. Orange surfaces, brown core; frequent medium to coarse chaff. Rim dm 24 cm. B.1095.8, THS 40 Area I.
16. Orange surfaces, thick brown core; frequent medium chaff, common fine dark grit temper. Rim dm 28 cm. B.2052.9, THS 40 Area A.
17. Orange surfaces, brown core; common fine to medium chaff temper. Rim dm 26 cm. B.2052.11, THS 40 Area A.
18. Gray-brown surfaces, black core; frequent medium chaff, common medium dark grit temper. Rim dm 21 cm. B.75.4, THS 2.

T5b/6 Carinated Fine Bowl (fig. B.18 no. 19; Hamoukar n = 6). This bowl has thin walls with a distinctively shaped carination in the vessel profile. Surfaces are smoothed, yellow to orange or pink, and often variable on the same vessel as a result of stacking in the kiln. Fabrics are fine, often with no visible temper. The more obtuse-angled carinations are chronologically later (Felli 2003: 71). Early forms are well represented at Tell Brak HS1 level 6 (Felli 2003: fig. 4.21.1–2, 5–8). This type was found only at Hamoukar. NJP type 15.

19. Orange-brown surfaces, gray core; no visible temper. Rim dm 14 cm. A.94.10, THS 1 Unit 44.

T5b/7 Grooved-Rim Beaker (fig. B.13 nos. 20–21; survey n = 4, Hamoukar n = 2). These rims occur on a small fineware vessel with yellow to orange surfaces, oxidized cores, and fine fabric, sometimes sand tempered. The vessel sides slope inward to a flat top, which often (but not always) has a groove in the top. Excavated examples come from Tell Brak HS1 level 6 (Felli 2003: fig. 4.21.19). This type is distinctive but infrequent. NJP type 150.

20. Buff-brown surfaces; frequent sand temper. B.2065.6, THS 33.
21. Orange-buff surfaces, red-orange core; rare sand temper. B.2065.5, THS 33.

T5b/8 Jar with Sharp Interior Carination (Hamoukar n = 3). Rims of this type have a range of shapes, but all are characterized by a very sharp interior carination at a seemingly ill-fitting junction between neck and body. Rims are flat with a slight thickening on the interior. Fabrics are of the standard Period 5b fineware variety. Complete examples have irregular bag-shaped bodies. This type is characteristic of Hacinebi phase B (Pearce 2000: fig. 11d–e). This type is uncommon in the THS and at Hamoukar.

T5b/9 "Pie Plate" Rim (fig. B.13 nos. 22–24; survey n = 4, Hamoukar n = 83). This large shallow bowl or plate is handmade and irregular, with coarse chaff and grit temper and a thick reduced core. The base is roughly scraped. This type was defined based on its frequency on the surface of Hamoukar's high mound; it is also very common at Tell Brak TW level 16, but occurs as late as level 12 (Oates and Oates 1993: 197, fig. 54.66). Rims of this type were rare elsewhere, but they were the most abundant of all Period 5b types at Hamoukar.

22. Orange surfaces, brown core; frequent to abundant medium to coarse chaff; scraped and scored exterior bottom. Rim dm 35 cm. A.373.2, THS 1 Unit 108.

23. Pale orange surfaces, gray-brown core; abundant medium to coarse chaff; scraped exterior base. Rim dm 30 cm. A.81.2, THS 1 Unit 31.

24. Pale orange surfaces, gray-brown core; abundant medium to coarse chaff; scraped exterior base. Rim dm 23 cm. A.82.2, THS 1 Unit 32.

T5b/10 Small Carinated Bowl (fig. B.13 nos. 25–26; survey n = 4). These small plain bowls are found in common ware and in finer fabrics with fine chaff and sand temper. Reddish brown to black painted decoration takes the form of simple linear designs, especially triangles. Unpainted examples are known, but only painted specimens were considered diagnostic by the THS. This bowl appears to be late in the fourth millennium (e.g., Late Chalcolithic 5) at Tell Mohammad Arab period 1 (Roaf and Killick 1987: fig. 2) and Tell Brak TW. NJP type 20.

25. Pale green smoothed surfaces and core; no visible temper. Reddish brown painted decoration. Rim dm 7 cm. B.1700.8, THS 41 Area B.

26. Buff surfaces and core; no visible temper. Reddish brown painted decoration. Rim dm 9 cm. B.1700.7, THS 41 Area B.

T5b/11 Sharply Out-Turned Rim (fig. B.13 nos. 27–28; survey n = 48). This storage jar is characterized by a rounded shoulder and a simple out-turned run. In the North Jazira, it was considered to be a local northern type, but examples found in the THS appear to be of the southern Mesopotamian manufacturing tradition: well fired (yellow to orange surfaces, oxidized cores) and tempered with abundant sand or fine grit. NJP type 121.

27. Pale yellow surfaces, buff core; frequent sand temper. Rim dm 17 cm. B.1091.1, THS 40 Area D.

28. Yellow surfaces, orange core; frequent sand temper. Rim dm 16 cm. B.1094.7, THS 40 Area H.

T5b/12 Internally Molded Bowl (fig. B.13 nos. 29–30; Hamoukar n = 9). This chaff- and grit-tempered, unevenly fired bowl appears to be a later and coarser version of the Period 4 T4/18, made out of standard Period 5b fabric. During the THS, these two chronologically distinct types were not distinguished, therefore they have not been used in analysis. Parallel examples come from Hacinebi phase A (Pearce 2000: fig. 2f–i). NJP type 134.

29. Buff surfaces, brown core with orange margins; common fine to medium chaff, occasional sand temper. Rim dm 32 cm. B.526.6, THS 16 Area A.

30. Yellow-buff surfaces, green core; sandy near-overfired fabric. Rim dm 23 cm. B.526.7, THS 16 Area A.

T5b/13 Chaffy Hemispherical Bowl or Cup. This type is a simple convex bowl with chaff temper and a reduced core. Its simple shape makes it a poor diagnostic type when found in isolation. In the Tell Brak TW sequence, this form is most characteristic of Late Chalcolithic 3 levels (J. Oates, pers. comm.). It was defined from surface associations on Brak's outer town and was not used in the THS.

T5b/14 Chaffy Flat-Topped Shallow Bowl. This bowl has a rim with a flat top, often with a faint groove or concavity. It is heavily chaff tempered and poorly fired. This type was defined from surface associations on Tell Brak's outer town and was not used in the THS. This bowl type occurs throughout Hacinebi phase A (Pearce 2000: figs. 2d–e, 7f–h) and in Brak HS1 (Felli 2003: fig. 4.22.2, 7).

T5b/15 Flared Cooking Pot Rim. This type was not recognized in THS surface collections. NJP type 149.

T5b/16 Ceramic Ring Scraper (fig. B.13 nos. 31–32; survey n = 4). This distinctive object is best interpreted as a tool for thinning the walls of ceramic vessels by scraping off excess clay in a controlled manner (Alden 1988). They are made from fine and dense clay, often fired almost to the point of vitrification. Examples are also found in the third millennium (e.g., Tell Brak phases M–N; Oates 2001b: nos. 416–20), so they should be used as an indicator of ceramic manufacture in association with other more chronologically sensitive types. Although it has been given a type designation within Period 5b, this type has not been used for chronological analysis. NJP type 106.

31. Pale green surfaces and core; no visible temper. Dm 9.5 cm. A.362.1, THS 1 Unit 98.
32. Olive green surfaces and core; no visible temper, very fine fabric. Rim dm 9.5 cm. B.1095.16, THS 40 Area I.

T5b/17 Double-Mouth Jar. Although a distinctive shape, this type occurs from Period 3 to Period 7 and cannot be used for chronological analysis without careful attention to fabric. This type was not used by the THS. NJP type 55.

B.2.6. PERIOD 5A: LATE CHALCOLITHIC 4–5 SOUTHERN MESOPOTAMIAN TYPES

As a result of an almost exclusively architectural and art historical focus in the excavations at Uruk, the pottery chronology of the period is poorly understood (Nissen 2002). Most of what is known, therefore, comes from sites of the Uruk Expansion phenomenon in Syria, Turkey, and Iran. There exist almost no fourth-millennium radiocarbon dates from southern Mesopotamia, but extensive datings from expansion sites in the "periphery" have now demonstrated that the phenomenon lasted much longer than previously suspected (compiled in Wright and Rupley 2001). As a result, it is possible to define assemblages for the Middle Uruk period from Tell Sheikh Hassan and Hacinebi Tepe (Boese 1995; Bachmann 1998; Pollock and Coursey 1995; Stein 2001) and Late Uruk assemblages from Habuba Kabira (Sürenhagen 1978) and Jebel Aruda. Both Middle and Late Uruk types are present at Tell Brak Area TW (Oates and Oates 1991).

Unfortunately, these excavations demonstrate that the southern Uruk pottery assemblage remained largely unchanged from the middle to late fourth millennium B.C. There are few exceptions: a pinched lip on the rim of a conical cup (T5a/7) is a Middle Uruk characteristic, while the tall bottle with drooping spout (T5a/3) is a Late Uruk indicator. Southern Uruk types tend to be made of an evenly fired yellow to orange sandy fabric, which stands out strongly from the low-fired and heavily chaff-tempered ware of the local tradition.

It is unsurprising that the T5a/1 bevelled-rim bowl is the most common Period 5a type at Hamoukar and throughout the survey (fig. B.14). At Hamoukar it constituted almost 80 percent of identifiable Period 5a sherds. Its lower percentage at other sites (36.3%) is almost certainly due to methodological differences: after a few examples had been collected, collectors discontinued collecting them in areal collections to avoid overwhelming the subsequent processing program. For this period, the survey made particularly heavy use of the untyped designation (T5a/0, n = 42). Untyped forms under this designation include chaff-tempered oval trays, non-drooping conical spouts, bottle tops, twisted handles, decorated slips, and incised shoulders.

T5a/1 Bevelled-Rim Bowl (fig. B.15 nos. 1–3; survey n = 87, Hamoukar n = 75). Bevelled-rim bowls can be recognized by their trademark outwardly bevelled rim, coarse grit temper, and crude manufacture. Exterior surfaces are rough and uneven; interior surfaces are smooth from the use of a mold in the production process. Many examples have finger or fist marks on the interior base. Because of the distinctive manufacturing method, almost every sherd of a bevelled-rim

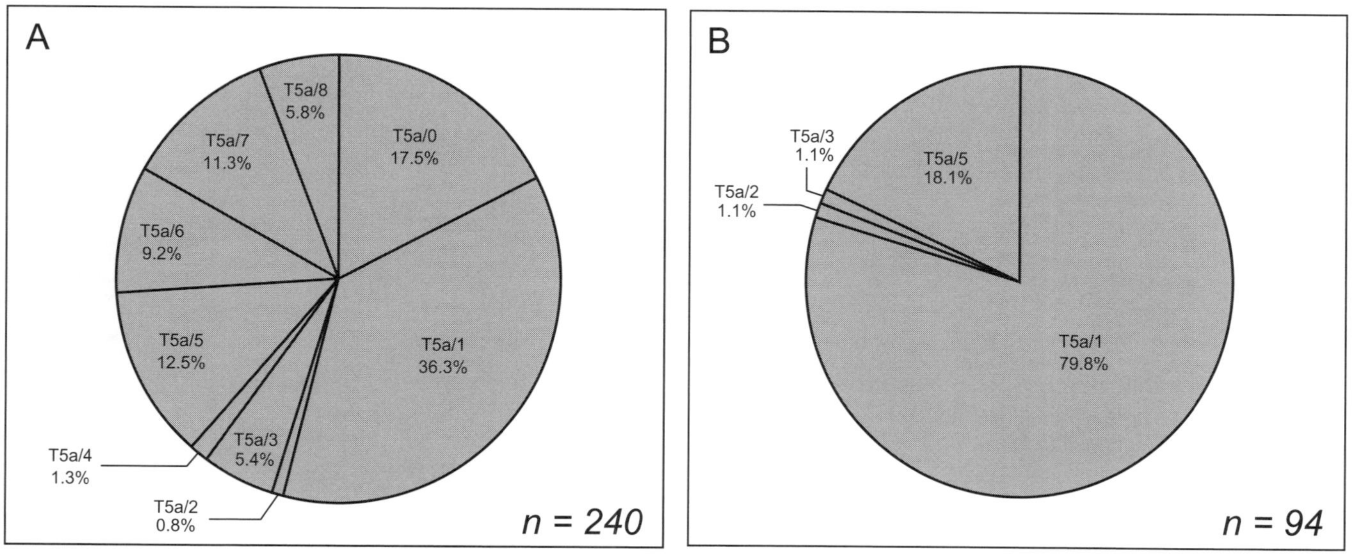

Figure B.14. Frequency of Period 5a ceramic types (*A*) in THS areal collections and (*B*) in Hamoukar sampling units

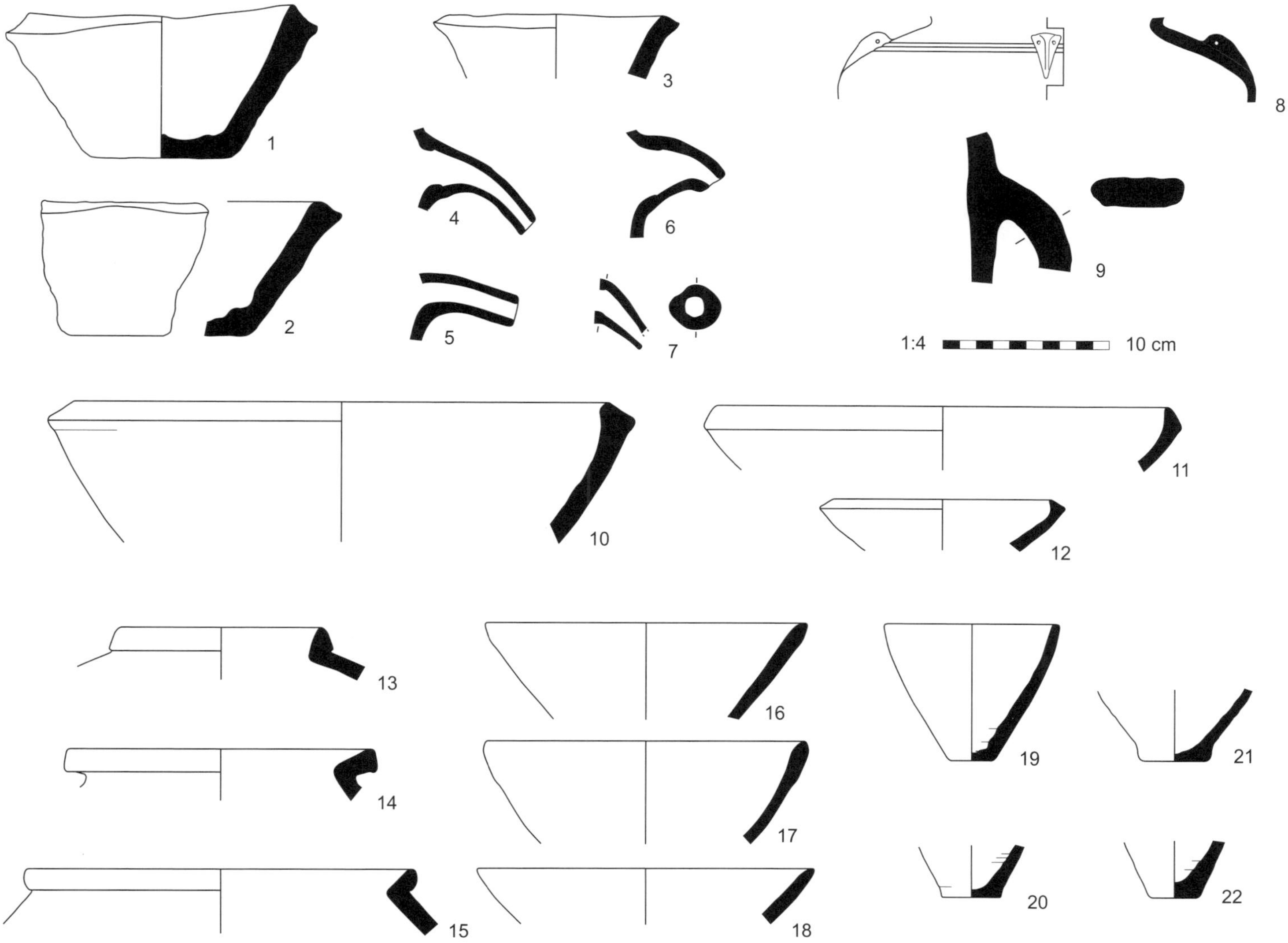

Figure B.15. Ceramic types for Period 5a (Southern Uruk Late Chalcolithic 4–5)

bowl is diagnostic. In chronological terms, this type occurs in both Middle (Late Chalcolithic 4) and Late (Late Chalcolithic 5) contexts, but is also found stratified into the "proto-Ninevite 5" levels at Tell Brak Area TW (Oates 2002: 114). Uruk bevelled-rim bowls were even more common than the sherd count suggests; at several sites, collectors discontinued collecting them after five to ten had been picked up. NJP type 6.

1. Orange exterior, orange-brown interior, brown core; frequent coarse chaff, common fine to medium lime temper; mold-made. Base dm 8 cm. B.1092.7, THS 40 Area G.
2. Orange-red surfaces, black core with orange margins; frequent medium to coarse chaff, common sand temper; mold-made. B.1092.6, THS 40 Area G.
3. Pale orange surfaces and core; common fine to medium chaff, frequent fine white grit temper. Rim dm ca. 16 cm. A.385.26, THS 1 Unit 117.

T5a/2 Nose Lug (fig. B.15 no. 8; survey n = 2, Hamoukar n = 1). These apparently non-functional pierced lugs occur in groups of four on the flat shoulders of abundantly grit-tempered southern Uruk jars, often with short straight necks (Sürenhagen 1978: pls. 6–12). Nose lugs can occur in association with incised decoration. They occurred infrequently in the THS. NJP type 18.

8. Yellow slipped exterior, orange surfaces and core; occasional fine to medium lime temper. B.75.7, THS 2.

T5a/3 Drooping Spout (fig. B.15 nos. 4–7; survey n = 13, Hamoukar n = 1). These sand-tempered spouts have a thick base which tapers and curves downward. They can occur on tall bottles (e.g., Sürenhagen 1978: pl. 17) or on shorter jars (e.g., Sürenhagen 1978: pl. 12:76). Drooping spouts are one of the very few firm indicators of the Late Uruk/Late Chalcolithic 5 period (Schwartz 2001: 242). In the Tell Brak TW sequence, they occur in level 12 (Oates and Oates 1993: fig. 49:3). NJP type 19A.

4. Pale orange surfaces, orange core; common sand, occasional medium lime. B.1095.14, THS 40 Area I.
5. Yellow-green surfaces and core; common sand, occasional medium lime. B.1095.15, THS 40 Area I.
6. Pale orange surfaces, orange core; common sand, occasional medium lime. B.1095.13, THS 40 Area I.
7. Buff-brown surfaces, orange core; sand and light grit temper. A.158.7, THS 1 Unit 57.

T5a/4 Broad Strap Handle (fig. B.15 no. 9; survey n = 3). This uncommon type is identifiable by its broad section and typical Period 5a abundant grit temper. It occurs in Middle Uruk levels at Hacinebi Tepe (Pearce 2000: fig. 14) and at Late Uruk Habuba Kabira (Sürenhagen 1978: types F1–2, 5). NJP type 120.

9. Yellow surfaces, buff core; frequent sand, frequent fine to medium lime. B.1094.13, THS 40 Area H.

T5a/5 Oblique Bowl Rim (fig. B.15 nos. 10–12; survey n = 30, Hamoukar n = 17). Sherds of this type are similar in shape to Period 11 bowls but are easily distinguished by their typical Period 5a fabric: yellow to orange surfaces, oxidized core, and frequent to abundant sand or grit. NJP type 140.

11. Orange surfaces, orange-brown core; occasional sand, occasional fine lime. Rim dm 27 cm. B.1094.5, THS 40 Area H.
12. Yellow surfaces, buff core; occasional sand, sandy fabric. Rim dm 13 cm. B.2052.14, THS 40 Area A.

T5a/6 Undercut Jar Rim (fig. B.15 nos. 13–15; survey n = 22). This rim type includes a range of short-necked rims on standard heavily grit-tempered southern Uruk fabric. NJP type 151.

13. Pale yellow exterior, buff interior, orange-brown core; common sand temper. Rim dm 12 cm. B.1092.3, THS 40 Area G.
14. Buff to orange surfaces, orange core; frequent fine lime, common sand temper. Rim dm 18 cm. B.1072.2, THS 3 Area B.
15. Pale orange surfaces, brown core; common sand temper. Rim dm 23 cm. B.2052.24, THS 40 Area A.

T5a/7 Conical Cup Rim (fig. B.15 nos. 16–19; survey n = 27). Uruk conical cups have straight or slightly convex sides and a round, sometimes slightly thickened rim. Surfaces are yellow to orange with oxidized cores and common to abundant sand or grit temper. The form itself is not distinctive; only when it occurs in the standard Period 5a fabric can a sherd be assigned to this type. A small pinched lip is diagnostic of the Middle Uruk period, or Late Chalcolithic 4 (Oates and Oates 1993: 192, fig. 51.33–35; Schwartz 2001: 241; Pearce 2000: 118). Whole conical cups have T5a/8 bases.

16. Buff (slipped?) surfaces, brown core with pink margins; common to frequent sand temper. Rim dm 19 cm. B.2052.13, THS 40 Area A.
17. Orange surfaces and core; common sand temper. Rim dm 19 cm. B.1094.12, THS 40 Area H.
18. Buff surfaces and core; occasional sand temper; fine fabric. Rim dm 20 cm. B.2054.6, THS 40 Area C.
19. Orange surfaces and core; frequent sand, frequent fine lime temper. Rim dm 10 cm, base dm 2.4 cm. B.1095.9, THS 40 Area I.

T5a/8 Conical Cup Base (fig. B.15 nos. 20–22; survey n = 14). Bases of this type derive from the same cup form as T5a/7 and are identical in fabric. Some examples show slight thickening of the vessel walls toward the base. Base bottoms are string-cut (Sürenhagen 1978: 89).

20. Orange surfaces, brown core; common sand, common fine lime temper. Base dm 3.4 cm. B.1095.10, THS 40 Area I.
21. Orange surfaces and core; frequent to abundant fine dark grit temper; string-cut base. Base dm 4 cm. B.75.6, THS 3.
22. Orange exterior, gray interior and core; common sand temper; string-cut base. Base dm 3.2 cm. B.1095.11, THS 40 Area I.

B.2.7. PERIOD 6: NINEVITE 5

The first half of the third millennium B.C. remains difficult to study from surface collections due to the nature of the ceramic assemblage. The most robust and frequently occurring types, such as pedestal (T6/6) and parabolic (T6/7) bases, crescent lug handles (T6/9), and fine beaded-rim cups (T6/8), all remain in use for the entire Ninevite 5 period (Schwartz 1988a), whereas the chronologically sensitive decorated types (see discussion in Roaf and Killick 1987) survive poorly on the surface of sites and are uncommon, perhaps because they were specialized finewares (Stein and Wattenmaker 1990, 2003). Painted Ninevite 5 sherds (T6/1), the best indicator of early Ninevite 5 occupation, are exceedingly rare in surface assemblages (Buccellati and Kelly-Buccellati 1988: 44–45; Wilkinson and Tucker 1995: 49). As a result, it is difficult to subdivide the Ninevite 5 period in surface assemblages; the distribution of Ninevite 5 sherds at Hamoukar and in the survey region (figs. 6.13–14) represents sherds of all phases of Ninevite 5.

The distinctions between decorated Ninevite 5 types are the basis for the subdivision of the first half of the third millennium in the Early Jazira sequence (Lebeau 2000) and have been used in survey around Tell Leilan (Weiss 2003). In the THS region, however, their infrequent occurrence in surface collections rendered it infeasible to use them to subdivide Period 6 in this manner. Decorated Ninevite 5 wares appear to be a Tigridian form (Rova 1988) which is increasingly uncommon as one moves farther west. These types are rare in the Tell Beydar Survey region (Ur and Wilkinson 2008) and almost completely absent in the western basin and along the Khabur River (Lyonnet 1998). This distribution dropoff is already apparent in the eastern basin around Hamoukar.

The THS ceramic typology does not include types from the recently identified "proto-Ninevite 5" horizon falling between the Late Uruk and Ninevite 5 periods, which has been introduced into the third millennium B.C. Early Jazira sequence as Early Jazira 0. Sherds from this phase have been excavated in the uppermost levels of Tell Brak TW (Oates and Oates 1991: fig. 8; Emberling et al. 1999: fig. 6) and on the HS spur (Matthews 2003a).

The most frequent type in the survey was the T6/8 fine beaded rim, which was also common at Hamoukar (fig. B.16). Most frequently found at Hamoukar was the T6/7 parabolic base, a figure skewed by a single unit (see below). In both cases, however, the total number of recovered Period 6 sherds (survey n = 31, Hamoukar n = 114) is very low. Very few were worthy of illustration, and the examples presented here should be supplemented by the North Jazira typology (Wilkinson and Tucker 1995: fig. 68) and the cited comparisons.

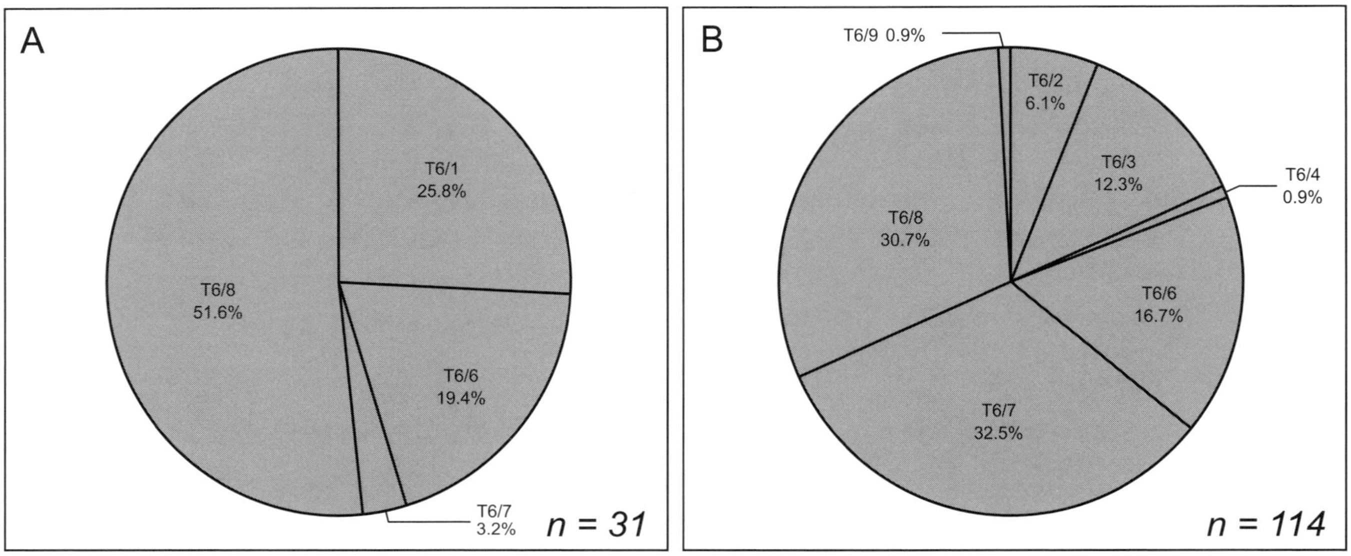

Figure B.16. Frequency of Period 6 ceramic types (*A*) in THS areal collections and (*B*) in Hamoukar sampling units

T6/1 Painted Ware (survey n = 8). Fabrics are sand- or chaff-tempered with oxidized surfaces. Paint is a reddish brown or plum in geometric and occasionally naturalistic designs, although the THS sherds of this type were all too small to describe adequately their motifs. When complete, T6/1 vessels are stemmed jars or bowls on T6/6 pedestal bases (Schwartz 1988a). Painted Ninevite 5 wares are to be placed at the start of the Ninevite 5 sequence (Roaf and Killick 1987). Although it is a very distinctive painted type, it occurs rarely in surface assemblages, perhaps because its painted designs survive poorly when exposed on the surface. All THS examples of this type were too fragmentary for illustration. NJP type 27.

T6/2 Incised Gray Fineware (fig. B.17 no. 1; Hamoukar n = 7). Vessels are fine, slightly closed cups or bowls in a greenish gray ware with smoothed surfaces and no visible temper. Decoration consists of patterns of wavy lines and dots. In the THS, this type was found only at Hamoukar itself. NJP type 22.

1. Pale yellow-green exterior, pale orange interior and core; no visible temper. Wide horizontal grooves, diagonal incisons, and parallel vertical notched incisions. A.54.3, THS 1 Unit 4.

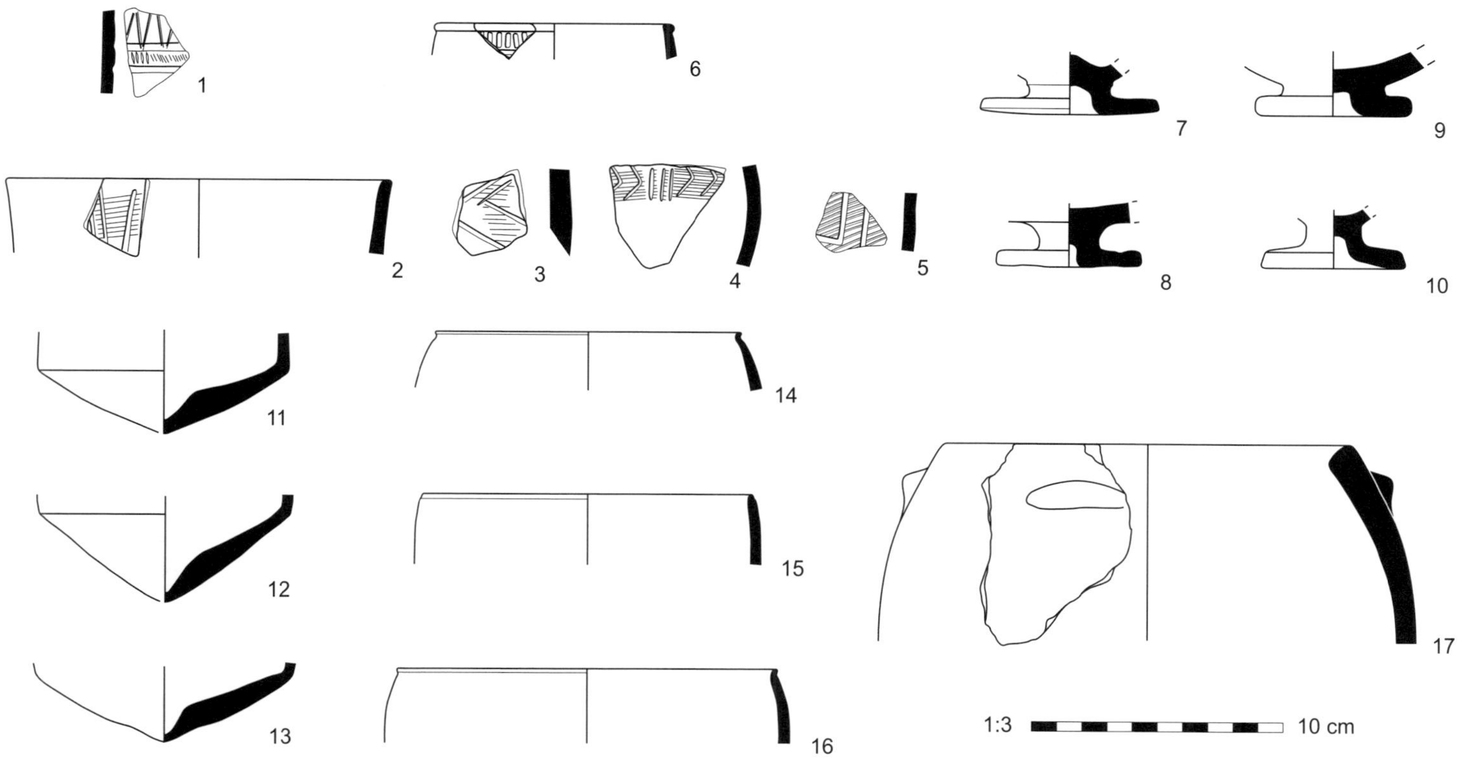

Figure B.17. Ceramic types for Period 6 (Ninevite 5)

T6/3 Excised Gray Fineware (fig. B.17 nos. 2–5; Hamoukar n = 14). Fabric similar to T6/2. Decoration takes the form of broad horizontal and vertical excisions which create the appearance of raised panels between them. On many examples, these panels are incised with parallel vertical or oblique lines, or even more complex designs. In the THS, this type was found only at Hamoukar itself, and only in the very late version characteristic of Tell Leilan IIId. NJP type 23.

2. Pale green surfaces and core; rare fine sand temper. Vertical grooves over fine horizontal parallel incisions. Rim dm ca. 12 cm. A.54.2, THS 1 Unit 4.
3. Pale green surfaces, green-gray core; occasional fine sand temper. Grooved chevrons over fine horizontal incisions. A.70.6, THS 1 Unit 20.
4. Pale yellow surfaces and core; no visible temper. Sandy fabric. A.167.3, THS 1 Unit 66.
5. Green-gray surfaces, dark core; sandy fabric without visible temper. A.167.4, THS 1 Unit 66.

T6/4 Vertical Grooved Fineware (fig. B.17 no. 6; Hamoukar =1). This greenish-gray fineware is possibly an early form of T6/3 excised ware (Roaf and Killick 1987: 219). It is similar to T6/2 and T6/3 in form and fabric. A single specimen was found in the THS, at Hamoukar itself. NJP type 25.

6. Pale yellow surfaces and core; no visible temper. Broad vertical grooves. A.75.1, THS 1 Unit 25.

T6/5 Ribbed Fineware. Sherds of this type are distinguished by horizontal ribs or grooves on a gray to greenish gray fine fabric. Complete versions have pedestal (T6/6) or parabolic (T6/7) bases. No sherds of this type were recognized by the THS. NJP type 26.

T6/6 Pedestal Base (fig. B.17 nos. 7–10; survey n = 6, Hamoukar n = 19). A robust green to gray base in the form of a flat disc with a central depression. Despite the name, most T6/6 bases are rather squat. In the production sequence, they are coarse later additions (often with visible chaff temper) to fineware upper bodies. T6/6 is a common type at Hamoukar and elsewhere in the THS in Period 6. NJP type 24.

7. A.118.2, Hamoukar Area A.
8. A.118.1, Hamoukar Area A.
9. Green-gray surfaces and core; common fine sand. Base dm 6.2 cm. A.154.4, THS 1 Unit 53.
10. A.437.9, Hamoukar Area A.

T6/7 Pointed or Parabolic Fineware Base (fig. B.17 nos. 11–13; survey n = 1, Hamoukar n = 37). This type is the base associated with, and identical in fabric to, rims of the various fineware cup types (T6/2, T6/3, T6/4, and T6/5). In form, it is characterized by a pointed base, with slight thickening toward the point, below a carination. Although uncommon elsewhere in the THS, examples were collected at Hamoukar, including thirty specimens from a single spot (Unit 68) on the lower town. NJP type 28.

11. Green-buff surfaces, buff core; no visible temper. Dm at carination 10 cm. A.169.2, THS 1 Unit 68.
12. Buff surfaces and core; common medium chaff below carination, no visible temper above carination. Dm at carination 10 cm. A.169.3, THS 1 Unit 68.
13. Gray-green surfaces and core; common fine to medium chaff on interior surface, elsewhere no visible temper. Dm at carination 11 cm. A.169.1, THS 1 Unit 68.

T6/8 Fine Beaded-Rim Bowl (fig. B.17 nos. 14–16; survey n = 16, Hamoukar n = 35). This type is a plain cup or bowl in a fine fabric similar to the previous types, but without decoration. Its defining feature is a very small and fine beaded rim. It is distinguished from the post-Akkadian T7/23 recessed beaker rim by its fabric and the slight convexity of its sides. NJP type 133.

14. Gray-green surfaces and core; no visible temper. Fine horizontal striations on exterior. Rim dm 12 cm. A.60.1, THS 1 Unit 10.
15. Pale green surfaces and core; no visible temper. Rim dm 13 cm. A.160.1, THS 1 Unit 59.
16. Yellow-green surfaces, green core; sand temper. Near-vitrified surfaces. Rim dm 15 cm. B.526.9, THS 16 Area A.

T6/9 Holemouth Pot with Crescent Lug (fig. B.17 no. 17; Hamoukar n = 1). This rim type comes from a handmade cooking pot with brown to gray, often burnished surfaces and a dark core with abundant grit temper. Its distinguishing feature is an applied handle in a crescent or horseshoe shape. This type was not used systematically in the THS. NJP type 18C.

17. Red-brown surfaces with burnished exterior; abundant medium to coarse dark grit temper. Horizontal lug handle. Rim dm 16 cm. A.371.2, THS 1 Unit 106.

B.2.8. PERIOD 7: MID- TO LATE THIRD MILLENNIUM B.C.

Because of the important political and social changes (Steinkeller 1998; Sallaberger 2007) as well as climatic events (Weiss and Courty 1993) that have been proposed, heroic efforts have been made toward subdividing the ceramic chronology of the later third millennium B.C. Chronological schemes take the form of site-specific sequences, for example Tell Leilan (Weiss and Courty 1993), Tell Brak (Oates, Oates, and McDonald 2001), and Tell Mohammed Diyab (Nicolle 2006), and most recently, the Early Jazira I–V sequence for the Upper Khabur basin and surrounding regions (Pfälzner 1997, 1998; Lebeau 2000; Lebeau and Rova 2003). Although they use neutral terminology, all are ultimately tied to the southern Mesopotamian historical chronology; all have a phase which is considered to be coterminous with the Akkadian dynasty, for example (e.g., Brak phase M, Leilan IIb, Early Jazira IV).

These high-resolution chronological schemes have proven difficult to apply in practice to excavation contexts, not to mention surface assemblages. The "sila bowl," which is considered to be an Akkadian-period rationing standard at Tell Leilan (Senior and Weiss 1992), appears in both Early Dynastic III and Akkadian contexts at Tell Brak and Tell Barri (Oates 2001b: 193–94; Valentini 2005: 183); it is better interpreted as a product of the increasing mass production and craft specialization of potters at the time of urban expansion in the mid-third millennium B.C. (Stein and Blackman 1993). Lyonnet attempted to make a ceramic differentiation between Leilan phases IIa (Early Dynastic III) and IIb (Akkadian) for the Mohammed Diyab surface collection, but noted that most of her types occurred in both periods; in her survey of the western Upper Khabur basin she includes them in a single phase (Lyonnet 1990: 74–75; 2000: 18–19), as do Stein and Wattenmaker (2003). At Tell Brak, the only site in the basin with a ceramic sequence that can be connected stratigraphically to a historical southern Mesopotamian ruler, it has been demonstrated that most types span two or more phases of the third millennium B.C. (Oates 2001b), and the same is true at Tell Beydar (Rova 2003) and Tell Mozan (Pfälzner, Wissing, and Hubner 2004). This includes all of the most common Period 7 ceramic types. Pottery production was decentralized under independent specialists and not controlled by large institutions via attached specialists (Stein and Blackman 1993: 53–55; Steinkeller 1996). It is therefore not surprising that existing ceramic traditions would continue unchanged by political shifts. Therefore, the THS followed Lyonnet, Wilkinson and Tucker, and Stein and Wattenmaker in treating the later third millennium B.C. as a single entity.

The THS was able to expand substantially the number of Period 7 survey types on the basis of large collections of diagnostics from Hamoukar's lower town. Subsequent lower town excavations in Areas C, E, and H may explain why this was the case: in these excavations, the final level was a late third-millennium occupation in which whole or restorable vessels had been left on floors, probably as the result of a sudden citywide abandonment (Colantoni and Ur in press). In areas of the lower town which are today cultivated, recent plowing has brought sherds from these vessels to the surface (and in some cases may be responsible for breaking them), but has yet to pulverize them into the more fragmentary state typical of surface assemblages in general. The majority of these new types probably derive from this latest phase of Period 7, but it must be remembered that the lower town was also settled at the end of Period 6 (see Section 6.4.1). We have, therefore, tried to specify their chronological range when possible, especially with reference to the very complete and well-published Tell Brak sequence (Oates 2001b).

Proposed climatic catastrophes aside, conclusively identified "post-Akkadian" levels are now known from Tell Brak, Tell Mozan, Tell Arbid, Tell Mohammed Diyab, Tell al-Rimah, Tell Taya, and Nineveh (McMahon 1998: 27–28; McMahon and Quenet 2007; Oates 2001b; Oates and Oates 2001b; Postgate, Oates, and Oates 1997; Nicolle 2006; Koliński 2007; Dohmann-Pfälzner and Pfälzner 2001). It is therefore possible to propose some preliminary post-Akkadian types, some of which appear to follow the Akkadian period immediately (Early Jazira V, Ur III) and others that are later but still pre-Period 8 (Middle Bronze Age I, Isin-Larsa). With the exception of comb incision (T7/4), none occur commonly enough to be suitable survey types at present; unfortunately it appears that the most common post-Akkadian types were also common in earlier phases of Period 7.

The most common Period 7 types on survey were comb-incised decoration (T7/4), stonewares (T7/5), and the lugged bowl rim (T7/9), each comprising just under 20 percent of the identified types (fig. B.18). These types were also among the most common at Hamoukar, alongside the folded jar rim (T7/14).

T7/1 Flat Bowl Base (survey n = 18, Hamoukar n = 71). This type is a simple flat base with gently curving sides, often with visible wheel striations. Surface colors are variable, but most commonly are green to yellow. Most fabrics are well fired to the hardness of a near-stoneware; others are tempered with sand and fine chaff. This type is not very distinctive and must be used with caution in isolation. NJP type 29.

T7/2 Flat Beaker Base (fig. B.19 nos. 1–4; survey n = 13, Hamoukar n = 36). Sherds of this type derive from a tall straight-sided or slightly convex beaker. Externally, the base is flat or slightly concave, with a sharp edge and visible wheel striations; on the interior, the potter's fingers have

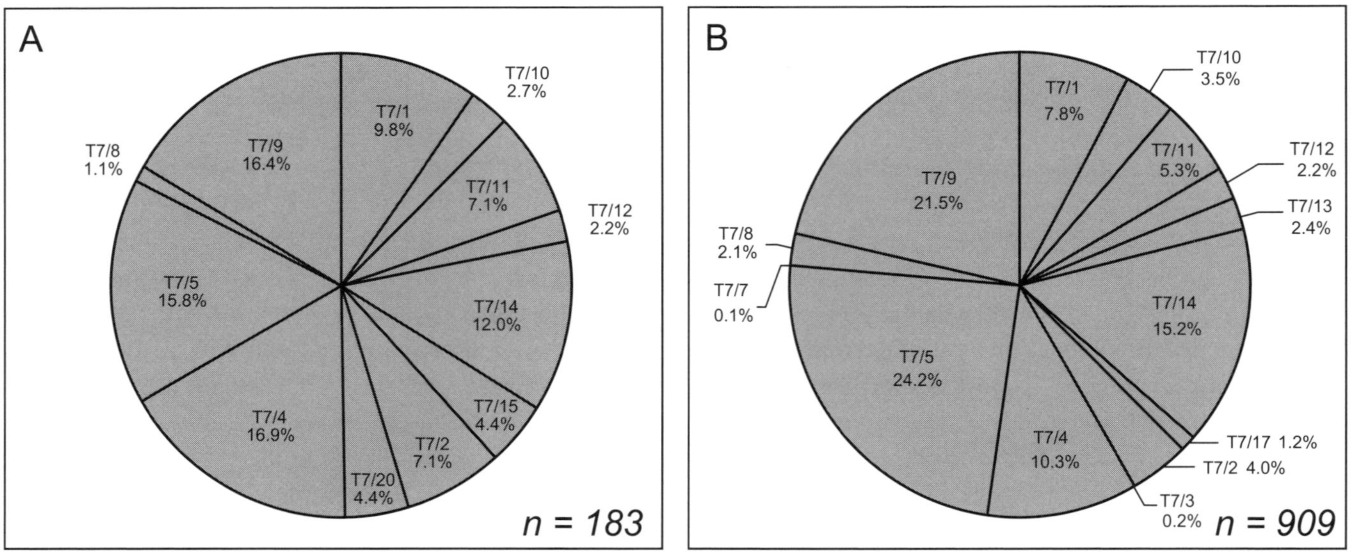

Figure B.18. Frequency of Period 7 ceramic types (*A*) in THS areal collections and (*B*) in Hamoukar sampling units

often left a series of horizontal grooves or steps (see especially fig. B.19 no. 1). Fabrics range from a fine version of the standard yellow-green common ware to a fine greenish near-stoneware. The latter are well fired and survive well on the surface; they make up the majority of identifiable diagnostics in field-scatter collections. Beakers are the most common vessel type in Akkadian levels at Tell Brak (Oates 2001b: 178–79). NJP type 30.

1. Green-gray surfaces and core; occasional fine sand temper, sandy fabric; hard fired. Base dm 6 cm. A.376.10, THS 1 Unit 103.
2. Gray-green surfaces, green core; occasional fine lime temper, sandy fabric. Base dm 7 cm. A.69.6, THS 1 Unit 19.
3. Pale green surfaces and core; rare fine sand temper; fine fabric; fine horizontal striations on exterior. Base dm 7 cm. A.165.12, THS 1 Unit 64.
4. Pale green surfaces and core; occasional to common fine sand temper, sandy fabric. Base dm 7 cm. A.376.12, THS 1 Unit 103.

T7/3 String-Cut Flat Base (Hamoukar n = 2). This base type was made of the standard Period 7 yellow-green fabric, with whorled incisions on the base from the use of a string to remove it from the hump. Wilkinson intended it to be a post-Akkadian indicator, but did not find it effective in surface collections (Wilkinson and Tucker 1995: 96). Nonetheless, it is one of the most common post-Akkadian diagnostic forms at Tell Brak, where it appears on a straight-sided open plate or bowl (Oates 2001b: 174 and nos. 635–40), but this type does appear to begin in Akkadian levels at Brak (Oates 2001b: 178, fig. 435.1019–33). As with so many of the post-Akkadian forms known from Brak, this type is difficult to distinguish from earlier types; in the THS, only a few sherds could be confidently assigned to this type, all from Hamoukar itself. NJP type 31.

T7/4 Comb-Incised Decoration (fig. B.19 nos. 5–12; survey n = 31, Hamoukar n = 94). This type of decoration appears on the sides of large storage vessels of the standard Period 7 common ware. The incisions are made with a comb with usually three to six prongs, and occur in straight and wavy bands. The most common pattern is one of two parallel horizontal bands with a single wavy band in between them. Combs are were also used to produce punctate designs in vertical, diagonal, and chevron motifs. These different patterns are chronologically significant. At Tell

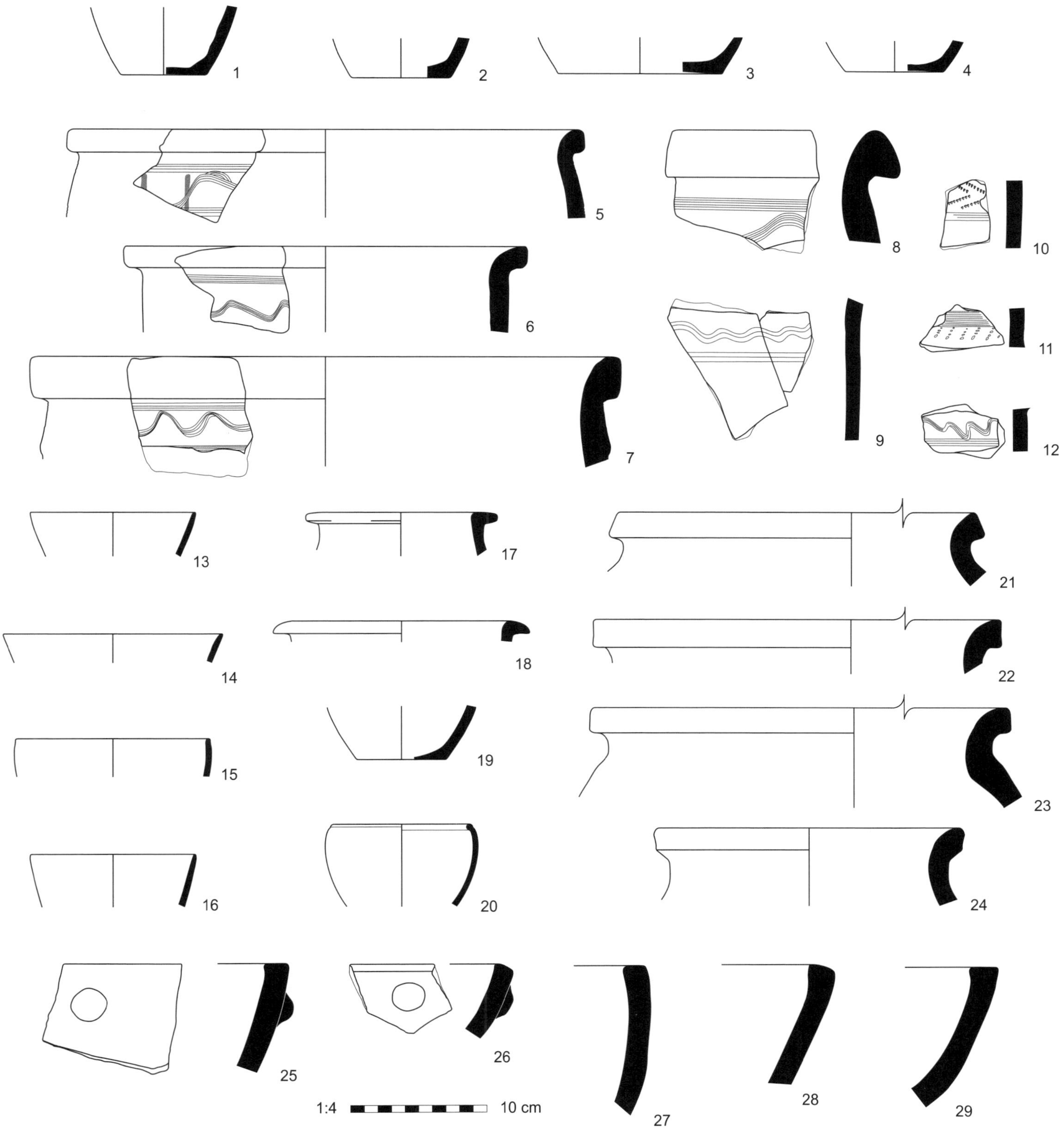

Figure B.19. Ceramic types for Period 7 (mid- to late third millennium), Types T7/2, T7/4, T7/5, T7/7, T7/8, and T7/9

Brak comb-incised decoration occurs in phase M (Akkadian) and phase N (post-Akkadian) levels, although at low frequency in both. However, Joan Oates (2001b: 164–65) distinguishes an elaborated Akkadian variety from a simpler post-Akkadian version which normally consists of a wavy band framed by two horizontal bands (see also Postgate, Oates, and Oates 1997: 27; Reade 1968: pl. 85:20). This latter version predominates in the final levels of Hamoukar lower town trenches (Gibson et al. 2002a: fig. 18), across the lower town (fig. 6.19) and elsewhere on the surfaces of sites in the THS region. Comb-incised sherds of this type are also known from excavations at Nineveh (McMahon 1998), Tell Taya (Reade 1968), Tell Jigan in the Eski Mosul region (Oguchi 2003), and the high mound at Tell Leilan (Frane 1996: fig. 84.2). Its relatively high frequency makes T7/4 the best indicator of post-Akkadian or Early Jazira V settlement for northern Mesopotamia. If attention is not paid to fabric and number of comb prongs, this type can be confused with comb-incised decoration of Sasanian and Islamic date (T16/7 and T16/8). Comb incision is often found on vessels with T7/14 or T7/15 rims and T7/12 lug-footed bases. NJP type 32.

5. Buff surfaces, gray core; frequent fine to medium chaff temper. Four-prong bands of comb incision, with two vertical smears of black paint or bitumen. Rim dm 37 cm. B.1701.1, THS 41 Area C.
6. Yellow-green surfaces, pale green core; frequent fine chaff, occasional fine lime temper. Four-prong horizontal and wavy comb incision bands. B.526.24, THS 16 Area A.
7. Green to buff surfaces; frequent fine chaff, common medium to coarse grit temper. Four-prong horizontal and wavy comb incision bands. Rim dm 40 cm. B.1106.22, THS 37 Area A.
8. Buff surfaces, brown core; common fine chaff and fine grit temper. Six-prong horizontal and wavy comb incision bands. B.1106.24, THS 37 Area A.
9. Pale green surfaces, light brown core; common medium chaff, rare fine sand temper. Three-prong comb incision. Interior scraped vertically. A.74.1, THS 1 Unit 24.
10. Pale yellow surfaces, buff core; common fine chaff temper. Four-prong horizontal band of comb incision and punctate wedges in chevron pattern. A.93.2, THS 1 Unit 43.
11. Yellow-buff surfaces and core; common fine chaff temper. Nine-prong band of comb incision with diagonal punctate. B.526.33, THS 16 Area A
12. Buff surfaces and core; common fine chaff temper. Four-prong horizontal and wavy comb incision bands. B.526.34, THS 16 Area A.

T7/5 Blue-Gray Stoneware (fig. B.19 nos. 13–19; survey n = 29, Hamoukar n = 220). Sherds of this fabric type are extremely dense and hard fired, predominantly without temper or inclusions; the high-firing temperature results in a characteristic slightly vitrified surface (Schneider 1989: 31–34; Oates 2001b: 151–53). Surfaces and cores are light gray, blue-gray, or green in color; the surfaces often have yellow horizontal streaking. These stonewares were made of locally available clays in the basin (Schneider and Daszkiewicz 2001), and were the most common variety at Tell Brak and Hamoukar. Bowls, beakers, bottles, and even jars occur in stoneware (see especially Oates 2001b: figs. 392–97), however it is the fabric that is the defining characteristic of this type. Because of its distinctiveness, and the fact that every sherd from a vessel is diagnostic, it is a very common and effective survey diagnostic. NJP type 33.

13. Yellow-green surfaces with blue-gray horizontal streaks, blue-gray core; no visible temper. Very hard fired. Rim dm 12 cm. A.53.5, THS 1 Unit 3.
14. Pale gray surfaces with pink-orange horizontal striations (exterior) and yellow striations (interior), gray core; no visible temper. Rim dm 16 cm. A.87.1, THS 1 Unit 37.
15. Yellow horizontal striations on blue-gray surfaces, blue-gray core; no visible temper. hard fired. Rim dm 14 cm. A.78.4, THS 1 Unit 28.

16. Blue-gray surfaces with yellow horizontal streaks, blue-gray core; no visible temper. Rim dm 12 cm. A.370.7, THS 1 Unit 105.
17. Dark red surfaces with horizontal black-gray streaks, gray core; no visible temper; fine hard fabric. Rim dm 14 cm. A.181.1, THS 1 Unit 80.
18. Pale gray surfaces, gray core; no visible temper. Rim dm 16 cm. A.86.1, THS 1 Unit 36.
19. Blue-gray surfaces with yellow horizontal streaks, blue-gray core; no visible temper. Base dm. 6.5 cm. A.194.3, THS 1 Unit 92.

T7/6 Non-Calcareous Stoneware. This stoneware fabric type employs clays from sources north of the basin, and may often (but not always) be macroscopically differentiated from T7/5 calcareous stoneware by its dark gray color and frequency of orange streaking (Schneider and Daszkiewicz 2001). Sherds of this type derive from a wide range of vessel forms and as with the previous type, it is the fabric that is characteristic. This type was defined for the Tell Brak surface collection and was not used in the THS; however, a non-systematic reassessment of collections did not recognize stonewares of this type.

T7/7 Post-Akkadian Stoneware (fig. B.19 no. 20; Hamoukar n = 1). A third type of stoneware can be identified from post-Akkadian levels at Tell Brak, Tell al-Rimah, and Tell Taya (Oates 2001b: 171–73; Oates and Oates 2001b; Reade 1982: pl. 5 bottom row). Post-Akkadian stoneware is gray to green and often vertically burnished in a way that leaves a pinkish streaking. This type was created after THS ceramic processing had been completed and was therefore not systematically utilized. One T7/7 sherd from Hamoukar's lower town could be retroactively assigned to this type. Although distinctive, it is not a very common type in the late Period 7 ceramic repertoire.

20. Pale yellow-green surfaces with thick horizontal red streaks, red-brown core; no visible temper, very hard fired. Surfaces almost vitrified. Rim dm 10 cm. A.158.8, THS 1 Unit 57.

T7/8 Indented Jar Rim (fig. B.19 nos. 21–24; survey n = 2, Hamoukar n = 19). This simple band-rim type often features a groove or slight concavity. It is generally composed of the standard Period 7 yellow-green fabric. It was common at Tell al-Hawa but not elsewhere in the North Jazira (Wilkinson and Tucker 1995: 97). At Tell Beydar, it is most characteristic of Early Jazira IIIa (i.e., early Period 7; P. Quenet, pers. comm.) and is assigned a similarly early date at Tell al-Raqa'i (Curvers and Schwartz 1990: figs. 6, 18). Most examples from Tell Brak derive from phase L (pre-Akkadian) levels (e.g., Oates 2001b nos. 1544, 1547–48). Almost all THS examples were found at Hamoukar itself. NJP type 103.

21. Yellow-green surfaces and core; frequent medium chaff, occasional fine dark grit. Possible traces of comb incision on exterior. Rim dm 34 cm. B.1700.6, THS 41 Area B.
22. Pale yellow surfaces, orange-pink core; common fine chaff, occasional fine sand temper. Rim dm 28 cm. A.167.1, THS 1 Unit 66.
23. Pale yellow surfaces, yellow-gray core; common sand temper; sandy fabric. Rim dm 38 cm. A.73.1, THS 1 Unit 23.
24. Pale green surfaces, green core; common fine chaff temper, sandy fabric. Rim dm 22 cm. A.166.2, THS 1 Unit 65.

T7/9 Lugged Bowl (fig. B.19 nos. 25–29; survey n = 30, Hamoukar n = 195). Rim sherds of this type have a rounded flat top and are very robust. Some examples feature a horizontal lug. Fabrics are slightly more chaff tempered than the standard Period 7 common ware. Intact vessels with this type of rim from Hamoukar Area H are very large oval basins (Ur 2002a: fig. 12.20; Colantoni and Ur in press; see also Oates 2001b nos. 1699–1700); therefore rim diameters of illustrated sherds are listed below, although these measurements may not have applied to the entire vessel. This type was also used as an Early Dynastic III–Akkadian diagnostic in the Tell Mohammed Diyab surface collection (Lyonnet 1990: figs. 9–10) and continues in use into the post-Akkadian period at that site (Nicolle 2006: fig. 7–18.3, 8). NJP type 154.

25. Pale yellow surfaces, orange-brown core; common fine chaff temper. Rim dm 46 cm. A.174.1, THS 1 Unit 73.
26. Pale green surfaces and core; common to frequent medium chaff temper. Rim dm 30–40 cm. A.160.3, THS 1 Unit 59.
27. Pale yellow-green surfaces, green core; frequent to abundant medium chaff temper. Rim dm 50 cm. A.165.1, THS 1 Unit 64.
28. Pale yellow surfaces, buff-orange core; frequent fine to medium chaff, occasional sand temper. Rim dm 40 cm. A.185.5, THS 1 Unit 83.
29. Pale yellow-green surfaces and core; common fine chaff temper. Rim dm >51 cm. A.185.4, THS 1 Unit 83.

T7/10 Shallow Flaring Vat Rim (fig. B.20 nos. 1–7; survey n = 5, Hamoukar n = 32). This type is characterized by a rim of variable morphology but generally bevelled outwardly, in standard Period 7 common ware fabric. Its most distinctive feature is its flaring and slightly concave sides. It was defined by its abundance on the Hamoukar lower town and confirmed via excavations in Area H (Ur 2002a: fig. 12.22). The vessel on which this rim occurs can have a simple flat base, but excavated examples from Hamoukar Area H have an extended footing (see T7/11 below). Excavated parallels range from Akkadian levels at Tell Brak (Oates 2001b: figs. 435 nos. 1038–44, 436 nos. 1046–55) to Middle Bronze Age I levels at Tell Mohammed Diyab (Nicolle 2006: fig. 7–23.6).

1. Pale yellow surfaces, pink-buff core; common to frequent medium chaff, occasional medium to coarse lime temper. Rim dm 41 cm. A.370.10, THS 1 Unit 105.
2. Pale yellow exterior, orange-brown interior, orange-pink core; common to frequent fine chaff temper. Rim dm 47 cm. A.185.3, THS 1 Unit 83.
3. Pale orange surfaces, brown core; frequent medium chaff temper. Rim dm 36 cm. A.184.3, THS 1 Unit 83.
4. Pale yellow smoothed surfaces, thick black core with orange margins; occasional fine chaff, occasional sand temper. Rim dm 33 cm. A176.2, THS 1 Unit 75.
5. Pale green surfaces and core; common fine to medium chaff, occasional sand temper. Rim dm 51 cm. A.68.1, THS 1 Unit 18.
6. Pale green surfaces and core; frequent sand, medium fine chaff temper. Rim dm 33 cm. A.151.14, THS 1 Unit 50.
7. Pale yellow-green surfaces, gray-green core; frequent medium chaff temper. Rim dm ca. 36 cm. A165.7, THS 1 Unit 64.

T7/11 Flat Extended-Foot Base (fig. B.20 nos. 8–13; survey n = 13, Hamoukar n = 48). The distinctive characteristic of this type is a flat base that extends slightly beyond its walls, presumably to offer the vessel additional stability. The extension ranges from square in section to slightly outwardly bevelled. The join between the vessel wall and base is particularly robust, making the type more likely to survive on plowed surfaces. Complete excavated examples have a T7/10 flaring rim. This type was defined by its abundance on the Hamoukar lower town and confirmed via excavations in Hamoukar Area H and Tell Brak phases L–M (Oates 2001b: nos. 1053–54, 1573). It also occurred frequently on the surface of Tell Mohammed Diyab (Lyonnet 1990: fig. 14.1).

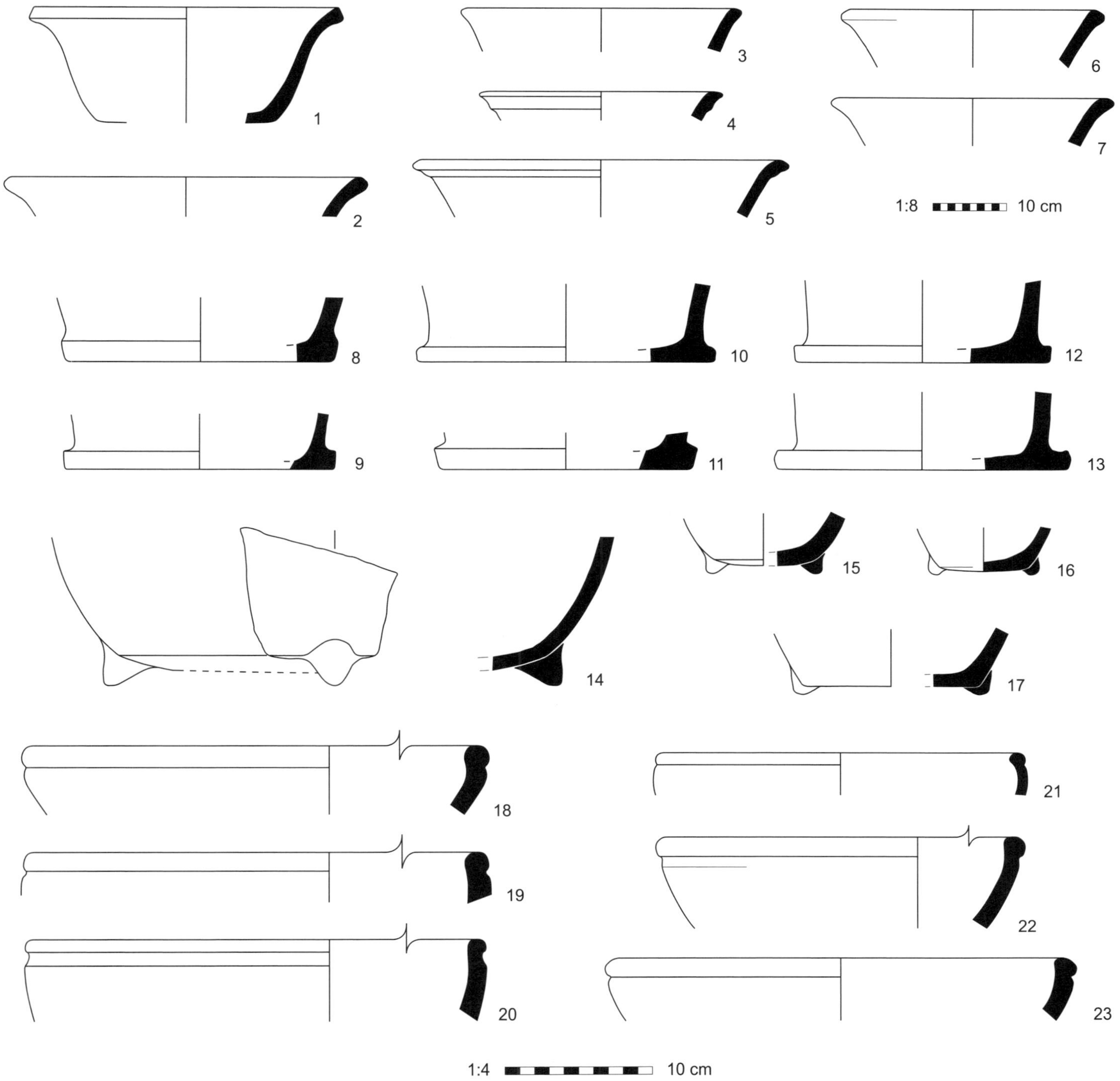

Figure B.20. Ceramic types for Period 7 (mid- to late third millennium), Types T7/10, T7/11, T7/12, and T7/13

8. Pale yellow-green surfaces, green core; common to frequent fine chaff, occasional sand temper, sandy fabric. Base dm 24 cm. A.385.30, THS 1 Unit 117.

9. Pale yellow-green surfaces, yellow-gray core; common fine chaff temper, sandy fabric. Base dm 24 cm. A.385.31, THS 1 Unit 117.

10. Pink to yellow surfaces, pink-orange core; common sand and occasional fine lime temper. Base dm 26 cm. A.53.1, THS 1 Unit 3.

11. Pale yellow-green surfaces, buff-brown core; frequent fine to medium chaff, occasional sand temper. Base dm 22 cm. A.64.1, THS 1 Unit 14.

12. Pale yellow surfaces, orange-pink core; common fine chaff, common fine to medium lime temper. Base dm 23 cm. A.366.1, THS 1 Unit 102.
13. Buff exterior, gray-green interior, pink-buff core; occasional fine chaff, common sand temper. Base dm. 21 cm. A.154.1, THS 1 Unit 53.

T7/12 Lug-Footed Base (fig. B.20 nos. 14–17; survey n = 4, Hamoukar n = 20). This base is slightly convex with three firmly applied knobs, in the standard Period 7 common ware fabric. Whole vessels with this base type from Areas C and H at Hamoukar have tall straight sides with T7/4 comb-incised decoration and T7/14 or T7/15 flaring rims (Gibson et al. 2002a: fig. 18). This type was defined by its abundance on the Hamoukar lower town and confirmed via excavations in Area H. It is common at Hamoukar and also attested at Tell Fisna (Numoto 1988: fig. 25 nos. 216–17), but absent at Tell Brak and unreported at Tell Leilan. It therefore may be restricted geographically to northern Iraq and the eastern Upper Khabur basin.

14. Pale green surfaces and core; common chaff, common sand temper. Base dm at carination 39 cm. A.151.16, THS 1 Unit 50.
15. Pale yellow-green surfaces, gray-green core; common to frequent fine chaff, occasional sand temper. Base dm at carination 9 cm. A154.2, THS 1 Unit 53.
16. Pale yellow surfaces, pale orange core; common fine chaff and occasional sand temper. Base dm at carination 8 cm. A.165.15, THS 1 Unit 64.
17. Pale yellow-green exterior, buff interior, buff-gray core; frequent sand, occasional fine chaff temper. Base dm at carination 16 cm. A.161.6, THS 1 Unit 60.

T7/13 Gray Ware Round Bowl Rim (fig. B.20 nos. 18–23; Hamoukar n = 22). This bowl rim has a gray to brown burnished surface and a reduced core. The rim is rounded and distinguished from the bowl edges by a horizontal groove. This type occurred on the Hamoukar lower town and in the Area H excavations, but was not recognized on the surface of sites elsewhere in the THS region. It is also a common type for the later third millennium in the Tell Mohammed Diyab surface collection (Lyonnet 1990: fig. 11).

18. Pale green-gray surfaces, gray core; occasional fine sand temper, sandy fabric. Rim dm ca. 40 cm. A.172.6, THS 1 Unit 71.
19. Pale gray surfaces, thick black core; common medium chaff temper; lightly burnished. Rim dm 40 cm. A.174.2, THS 1 Unit 73.
20. Pale gray surfaces, dark gray core; frequent medium chaff temper. Rim dm 30 cm. A.389.14, THS 1 Unit 127.
21. Dull gray surfaces and core; common fine sand temper. Rim dm 24 cm. A.62.3, THS 1 Unit 12.
22. Gray burnished exterior, green-gray interior, thick gray core with brown margins; common fine chaff temper; micaceous fabric. Rim dm 34 cm. A.370.8, THS 1 Unit 105.
23. Gray surfaces and core; common sand temper. Rim dm 30 cm. A.66.1, THS 1 Unit 16.

T7/14 Folded Jar Rim (fig. B.21 nos. 1–5; survey n = 22, Hamoukar n = 138). This type is characterized by an outward-leaning folded rim on a large straight-sided vessel with a very wide mouth. Surface colors range from yellow to green. Fabrics are evenly fired throughout and tempered with common fine chaff and sand. This type survives well on the surface and is very common at Hamoukar. It was used as an Early Dynastic III–Akkadian indicator at Tell Mohammed Diyab (Lyonnet 1990: fig. 2.1–2) and is found in Akkadian levels at Tell Brak (Oates 2001b: no. 1414). At the time of the Hamoukar surface collection, rims of T7/15 were included as part of this type. The morphological differences between these two types are slight and may prove not to be chronologically significant.

Figure B.21. Ceramic types for Period 7 (mid- to late third millennium), Types T7/14, T7/15, T7/17, T7/19, and T7/20

1. Pale yellow-green surfaces, gray-green core; common to frequent fine chaff temper, sandy fabric. Rim dm 48 cm. A.178.1, THS 1 Unit 77.
2. Pale yellow-green surfaces and core; frequent to abundant medium chaff temper. Rim dm 40 cm. A.376.4, THS 1 Unit 103.
3. Pale green surfaces, buff core; common to frequent medium chaff temper. Rim dm 38 cm. A.376.7, THS 1 Unit 103.
4. Pale yellow-green surfaces and core; frequent sand, frequent fine chaff temper. Rim dm 46 cm. A.151.5, THS 1 Unit 50.
5. Pale yellow exterior, pale orange interior and core; common fine chaff, common fine to medium lime temper. Rim dm 42 cm. A.172.1, THS 1 Unit 71.

T7/15 Folded Ridged Jar Rim (fig. B.21 nos. 6–10; survey n = 8). This rim type is closely related to T7/14 and occurs on the same vessel types and in the identical fabric. The primary difference is that the fold beneath the rim is extended into a ridge. It was an Early Dynastic III–Akkadian diagnostic type for the Tell Mohammed Diyab surface collection (Lyonnet 1990: fig. 2.3–4). T7/14 and T7/15 appear to be characteristic of the eastern basin and the Iraqi North Jazira; similarly folded or ridged rims do occur at Tell Brak and Tell Beydar but on storage jars with more closed profiles (Oates 2001b; Rova 2003). This rim type was used during the 2000 field survey but not for the 1999 Hamoukar surface collection.

6. Pale yellow surfaces, brown core; frequent fine chaff temper. Rim dm 35 cm. A.370.3, THS 1 Unit 105.
7. Pale yellow surfaces, orange-brown core; frequent fine to medium chaff, occasional red-brown fine grit temper. Rim dm 36 cm. A.184.1, THS 1 Unit 83.
8. Pale yellow surfaces, orange core; frequent fine chaff and fine sand temper. Rim dm 34 cm. A.376.5, THS 1 Unit 103.
9. Pale yellow-green surfaces and core; common to frequent medium chaff, occasional fine grit temper. Rim dm 38 cm. A.178.2, THS 1 Unit 77.
10. Pale yellow surfaces, pink-buff core; common medium chaff temper. Rim dm 28 cm. A.161.5, THS 1 Unit 60.

T7/16 Lid-Seated Jar Rim. The distinctive sinuous profile of this rim type was very common on third-millennium sites in the Tell Beydar Survey region, and was defined on this basis and on its frequency in the Beydar excavations (Rova 2003: pls. 30, 34). It was not used during the THS and may be restricted geographically to the western basin.

T7/17 Triangular Cooking Pot Rim (fig. B.21 nos. 11–14; Hamoukar n = 11). Period 7 cooking pots in the THS region are characterized by short necks and triangular rims. Surfaces are often burnished and range in color from orange to dark brown; cores are brown to black. Temper is frequent to abundant dark grit. This type was defined in the surface collection at Hamoukar; examples were later found in the excavations in Area H. The THS cooking pot differs in rim shape from the most common types at Tell Brak and Tell Beydar (see T7/18 below). The distinction between T7/17 and T7/18 could thus be geographic, but as parallel forms were found in post-Akkadian contexts at Brak (Oates 2001b: no. 841) and Tell Mohammed Diyab (Nicolle 2006: fig. 7–22.3), it may be chronological.

11. Orange surfaces with pink-buff exterior slip; frequent chaff and medium to coarse dark grit temper. Rim dm ca. 43 cm. A.78.1, THS 1 Unit 28.
12. Orange-brown burnished surfaces, black core; occasional fine chaff, abundant fine to medium dark grit temper. Rim dm 29 cm. A.189.6, THS 1 Unit 87.
13. Pale orange surfaces, red-brown core; abundant medium to coarse dark grit temper. Rim dm 26 cm. A.158.4, THS 1 Unit 57.

14. Pale buff (slipped?) exterior, orange interior, brown-gray core; abundant medium dark grit temper. Rim dm 22 cm. A.385.18, THS 1 Unit 117.

T7/18 Holemouth Cooking Pot Rim with Triangular Lug. This rim type characterizes the most common cooking pot type for the western and central Upper Khabur basin. It is identical to T7/17 in color and fabric, but is a holemouth with a thickened or club rim. Attached to the rim are handles which are triangular when viewed from above. At Tell Brak these rims are found in phase M (Oates 2001b nos. 1665–66). At Tell Beydar they are considered Early Jazira IIIb and later (Rova 2003: 434–35, types R.CP.04–06).

T7/19 Beaded Cup Rim (fig. B.21 nos. 15–17). Rim sherds of this type are known from Tell Leilan (Weiss 1983: fig. 10.7) and Hamoukar Area A (Gibson et al. 2002b: fig. 22.20–26). It was defined after collections processing and is therefore not quantified here, but it was common on the surface of Hamoukar. It can be distinguished from its Period 6 predecessor T6/8 by its smaller rim diameter and coarser fabric.

15. Pale yellow surfaces, buff core; rare fine lime temper. Rim dm 8 cm. A.160.2, THS 1 Unit 59.
16. Pale yellow surfaces and core; no visible temper, sandy fabric. Rim dm 14 cm. A.371.1, THS 1 Unit 106.
17. Pale yellow-green surfaces and core; rare sand temper, sandy fabric. Rim dm 12 cm. A.193.1, THS 1 Unit 91.

T7/20 Fine Straight-Sided Cup Rim (fig. B.21 nos. 18–22; survey n = 8). This fine or near-stoneware rim derives from the same straight-sided cup or beaker at the base T7/2 and occurs in the same fabrics. This type was defined after the 1999 season and was not used in processing the Hamoukar collection units.

18. Pale yellow surfaces, green core; no visible temper, sandy fabric. Rim dm ca. 25 cm. A.165.9, THS 1 Unit 64.
19. Pale buff surfaces and core; fine sand temper, sandy fabric. Rim dm 19 cm. A.73.8, THS 1 Unit 23.
20. Pale yellow surfaces, buff core; no visible temper. Rim dm 18 cm. A.79.6, THS 1 Unit 29.
21. Pale green surfaces and core; occasional sand. Rim dm 15 cm. A.158.6, THS 1 Unit 57.
22. Pale yellow-green surfaces and core; no visible temper, sandy fabric. Rim dm 18 cm. A.189.4, THS 1 Unit 87.

T7/21 Vertical Ribbed Jar Rim. Rims of this type are known from post-Akkadian Tell Brak (Oates 2001b: 176, fig. 423) and Middle Bronze Age I levels at Chagar Bazar and Lidar Höyük (McMahon and Quenet 2007: pl. 3.45 nos. 207–08; Kaschau 1999). Brak examples are buff to orange with grit and chaff temper. This type was defined for the Brak surface collection and was not used at Hamoukar.

T7/22 Collared Jar Rim with Sloping Shoulder. This storage jar rim occurs in Middle Bronze Age I levels at Lidar Höyük (Kaschau 1999). It occurs rarely on the surface of Period 7 sites in the Tell Beydar region but was not identified on THS sites.

T7/23 Recessed Beaker Rim. This distinct rim type is found on tall beakers in post-Akkadian levels at Tell Brak (Oates 2001b), Tell al-Rimah (Postgate, Oates, and Oates 1997; Oates and Oates 2001b), and a rich burial at Tell Beydar (Debruyne 1997); however, it is uncommon in excavated contexts and has not been identified in surface assemblages either. At Brak it occurs in a grit-tempered fine buff fabric. This type was defined for the Brak surface collection and was not used at Hamoukar.

T7/24 Jar with Ribbed Shoulder. This type of shoulder appears on large storage jars in phase N (post-Akkadian) contexts at Tell Brak (Oates 2001b: 176, fig. 425). It was created for the Tell Brak surface collection and was not used by the THS. Brak examples have buff to orange fabrics with grit and chaff temper. This type was defined for the Brak surface collection and was not used at Hamoukar.

B.2.9. PERIOD 8: KHABUR/OLD BABYLONIAN

The early second-millennium northern Mesopotamian ceramic assemblage was first defined by Mallowan's excavations at Chagar Bazar and has a long history of scholarship (reviewed in Frane 1996). Our understanding of this assemblage has been recently expanded by thorough presentations of pottery from Tell Brak (Oates, Oates, and McDonald 1997), Tell al-Rimah (Postgate, Oates, and Oates 1997), and Tell Leilan (Frane 1996). The most significant new finding from the long sequences at Brak and Rimah is that many "Old Babylonian" forms, painted Khabur ware included, continue into the early part of the Mitanni period. Therefore, Period 8, as defined by the following survey types, should be considered as early second millennium, and great caution must be used when attempting to correlate these types with political events.

The most frequently occurring Period 8 type, and indeed the most common type for all periods, is T8/1 Khabur painted ware (fig. B.22). Also commonly occurring are T8/2 grooved jar shoulders and T8/6 channel bases; other types are each less than 3 percent of the Period 8 assemblage.

T8/1 Khabur Painted Ware (fig. B.23 nos. 1–7; survey n = 297). This type of decoration consists of simple bands that appear as red to reddish brown paint on buff surfaces under typical firing conditions, but that sometimes appear as black bands on a yellow to green surface. Sherds can be tempered with dark grit or medium to coarse chaff. T8/1 decoration appears on many vessel shapes; the combination of painted decoration and fabric defines the type. The long history of scholarship on Khabur ware need not be repeated here (see Oguchi 2000). Khabur painted ware has been considered as diagnostic of the Old Babylonian period, in political terms, but it continued in use into the early Mitanni period at Tell Brak and Tell al-Rimah (Oates, Oates, and McDonald 2001: 67; Postgate, Oates, and Oates 1997). It was the most common survey type

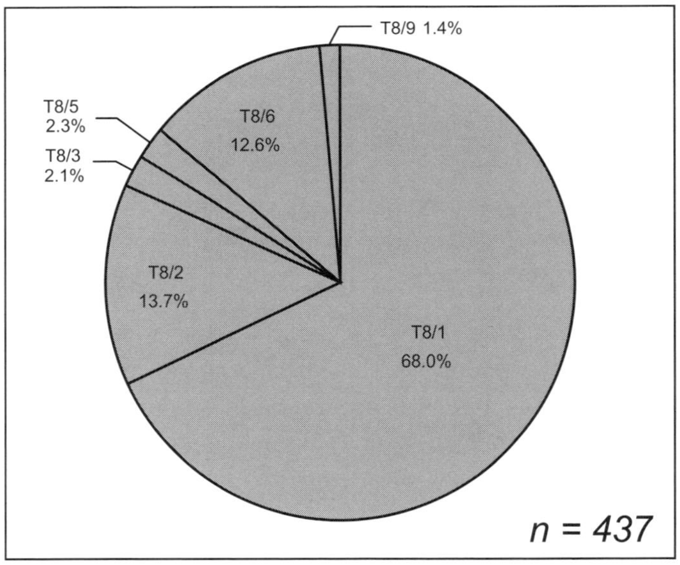

Figure B.22. Frequency of Period 8 ceramic types in THS areal collections

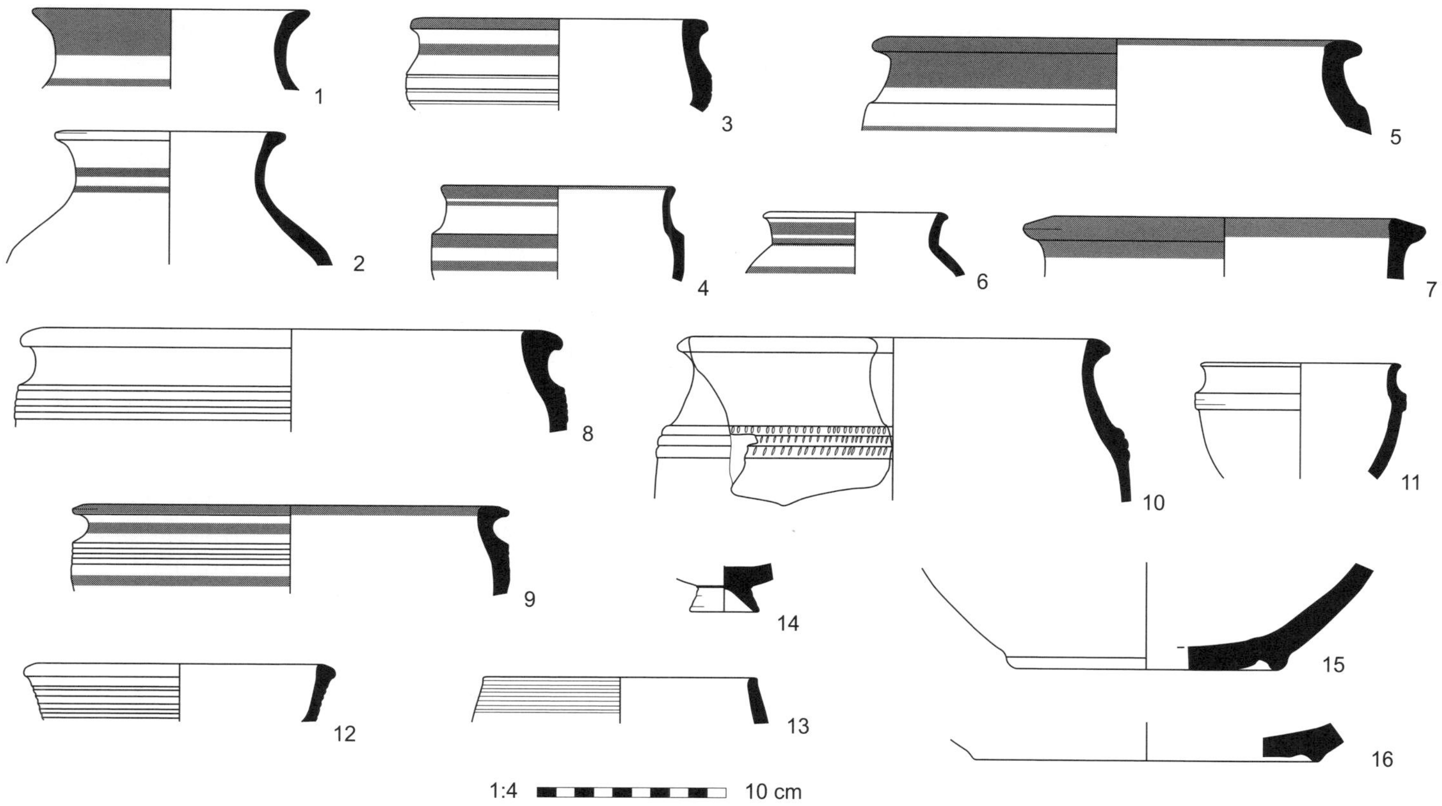

Figure B.23. Ceramic types for Period 8 (early second millennium)

in the THS and completely dominated the collections for all sites where it was present. Painted Hellenistic types can appear superficially similar, but are distinguishable by their characteristic abundant grit temper. NJP type 34.

1. Buff surfaces; frequent fine to medium chaff, occasional lime temper. Dark brown painted bands. Rim dm 14 cm. B.1106.18, THS 37 Area A.
2. Pink exterior, red interior, dark brown core; common very fine lime temper. Red painted bands. Rim dm 11 cm. B.526.1, THS 16 Area A.
3. Orange-buff surfaces; abundant fine chaff, occasional fine grit temper. Light brown painted bands and three horizontal grooves. Rim dm 14 cm. B.66.2, THS 24 Area A.
4. Buff surfaces and core; occasional sand, occasional fine lime temper. Red-brown painted bands. Rim dm 12 cm. B.1700.3, THS 41 Area B.
5. Orange-buff surfaces; frequent fine grit temper. Red-brown painted bands. Rim dm 24 cm. B.1106.19, THS 37 Area A.
6. Buff surfaces; common fine chaff, occasional fine to medium lime temper. Reddish brown painted bands. Rim dm 9 cm. B.66.1, THS 24 Area A.
7. Buff surfaces, orange-brown core; common medium chaff temper. Dark red painted bands. Rim dm 18 cm. B.161.2, THS 24 Area H.

T8/2 Horizontally Grooved Jar Shoulder (fig. B.23 nos. 8–11; survey n = 60). The defining characteristic of these sherds is a flat band of ridges, often slightly raised, below a concave shoulder. This feature appears on open vessels in a range of sizes, some with T8/1 painted decoration. It occurs in the same fabric as T8/1. This type is common at Tell Leilan (Frane 1996: figs. 71–77) and Tell Mohammed Diyab (Nicolle 2006: figs. 7–26). Wilkinson assumed this type to be early in the second millennium (Wilkinson and Tucker 1995: 97), but this is not supported at Brak, Tell al-Rimah, or Leilan. NJP type 35.

8. Pale yellow (slipped?) exterior, buff interior, orange-brown core; frequent medium chaff temper. Rim dm 26 cm. B.1703.1, THS 41 Area E.

9. Yellow-buff surfaces, buff core; common medium chaff temper. Raised band of grooves and dark red painted bands. Rim dm 20 cm. B.141.5, THS 24 Area J.

10. Light pink surfaces, orange-pink core; frequent fine lime temper. Three notched ridges. Rim dm 21 cm. B.526.22, THS 16 Area A.

11. Buff surfaces, orange core; occasional sand temper. Rim dm 10 cm. B.1700.2, THS 41 Area B.

T8/3 Burnished Gray Ware (fig. B.23 nos. 12–13; n = 9). Bowl sherds of this type are lightly burnished dark gray with reduced cores. They occur in several different open vessel forms at Tell Brak (Oates 1997: fig. 189), Tell al-Rimah (Postgate, Oates, and Oates 1997: 64), and Tell Leilan (Frane 1996: fig. 25.1–2). They can be distinguished from the heavily chaff-tempered Period 5b gray ware (T5b/3) by their sand temper. This type continues into Period 10 in excavated contexts. NJP type 41.

12. Pale gray surfaces, gray core; rare sand, rare fine chaff temper, fine fabric. Rim dm 15 cm. B.1701.19, THS 41 Area C.

13. Pale gray surfaces, gray core; rare sand, rare fine chaff temper, fine fabric. Rim dm 14 cm. B.1701.20, THS 41 Area C.

T8/4 Externally Grooved Bowl. This bowl type has an incurved rim with several horizontal grooves on its exterior. They are found in buff to pink fabrics and also in a burnished gray ware. Excavated contexts include Tell Brak Area HH (Oates 1997: nos. 170–71) and the Tell Leilan Acropolis Temple (Frane 1996: fig. 45). This type was not used by the THS. NJP type 42.

T8/5 High Ring or Pedestal Base (fig. B.23 no. 14; survey n = 10). This base type is characterized by a small and relatively high ring base in a buff fineware with occasional sand temper. Wilkinson proposed it to be a late Old Babylonian form with possible overlap with the beginning of the Mitanni period (Wilkinson and Tucker 1995: 97). Excavated examples are known from Tell Leilan (Frane 1996: figs. 117–19) and Tell Mohammed Diyab (Nicolle 2006: fig. 7–27.4–6). NJP type 39.

14. Buff surfaces; fine sand, occasional fine lime. Base dm 4 cm. B.1080.3, THS 54 Area E.

T8/6 Channel Base (fig. B.23 nos. 15–16; survey n = 55). This flat base has a groove around its outer edge which is often nothing more than a large incision on some specimens. Fabrics are buff to orange and fired evenly throughout; temper is common to frequent chaff. Excavated channel bases come from Tell Brak HN (McDonald and Jackson 2003: figs. 7.25.7–8, 7.26.13–14). This base type is common at Tell al-Rimah (Postgate, Oates, and Oates 1997: pl. 88), where forty-three of fifty-five published examples come from Old Babylonian levels (Ur 2005a: 67). It is considered to be highly diagnostic for Leilan period 1 (Frane 1996: 126–27). This distinctive base type was common in the THS region (12.6% of identified Period 8 sherds). NJP type 40.

15. Orange surfaces, brown core; common medium chaff temper. Base dm 13 cm. B.160.15, THS 24 Area G.

16. Buff surfaces, orange core; common fine to medium chaff, rare fine lime temper. Base dm 18 cm. B.161.5, THS 24 Area H.

T8/7 This type number was not used by the THS.

T8/8 Concave Fine Bowl Base. This base type can be similar in shape to T8/6, but is much smaller and of finer fabric. The THS did not use this type. NJP type 38.

T8/9 Indented-Cordoned Jar (survey n = 6). Body sherds of this type have a thick raised band with a groove or indentation. This type was not used consistently by the THS. NJP type 36.

T8/10 Impressed Circle Decoration. Sherds of this type have small impressed rings or squares, often on T8/2 jars. Wilkinson notes its rarity outside of the North Jazira (Wilkinson and Tucker 1995: 97), and no sherds of this type were recognized by the THS. NJP type 37.

B.2.10. PERIOD 10: LATE BRONZE AGE

In the field and in preliminary reports, Period 9 was used to designate settlement of the period of Mitanni control. Despite the detailed recent ceramic publications from Tell Brak (Oates 1997), Tell al-Rimah (Postgate, Oates, and Oates 1997), and sites on the Khabur River (Pfälzner 1995), it remains difficult to distinguish "Mitanni" ceramics from "Middle Assyrian" ones in surface assemblages. The problem is complicated by geographical variation in the timing of the shift in political control. For example, the "Middle Assyrian" period begins at Rimah earlier than it does at Brak, which remains under Mitannian control after the Sinjar Plain has been lost to the Assyrians. Thus, a fourteenth-century vessel form at Brak is "Mitannian," but at Rimah it would be "Middle Assyrian" (Postgate, Oates, and Oates 1997: 56). When faced with such a disjuncture between the politically defined chronological periodization and the evolution of ceramic traditions, the THS took the safest course of action and based this period on the latter, opting for a general Late Bronze Age survey period. Types of Wilkinson and Tucker's Mitanni period (formerly THS Period 9) are thus included in Period 10. The survey of the Cizre Plain used a similar combination of types (Parker 2001: fig. 3.5).

Nonetheless, it is possible to suggest some Period 10 types which are earlier in the Late Bronze Age. Most obviously this includes T10/1 Nuzi white-painted ware, which, despite its ubiquity in the literature, is a very poor survey type. Also early is the T10/2 fine painted goblet, which survives poorly on the surface. Only slightly more useful as early indicators are the T10/3 pedestal base and the T10/4 red-painted plate, which together comprise just over 2 percent of the Period 10 assemblage (although T10/4 was not applied systematically; see below).

The most common Period 10 types were the T10/10 plate and the T10/12 square jar rim, together making up almost 60 percent of identified examples (fig. B.24). The frequency of the latter is a surprise, given its infrequency in the published corpora from Tell Brak and Tell al-Rimah, and is probably related to its surface durability. Other useful types were the T10/13 soft carinated bowl and the T10/5 collared jar rim, each of which comprised about 10 percent of Period 10 types. The most common Period 10 fabric is buff to pale green and heavily chaff tempered. In quantified assemblages, as much as 83 percent of all sherds are made from such fabrics (Pfälzner 1995: 33–41 and fig. 55).

T10/1 Nuzi White-Painted Ware. Geometric, floral, and animal designs are painted in white on a red or brown painted background. Fabrics are yellow to buff with fine chaff temper. Most frequently, this painted decoration occurs on tall cups with T10/3 pedestal bases. This type is rare in both surface collections and in excavations (Oates 1997: fig. 92). In the Iraqi North Jazira, it was found only at Tell Hamida (Zimansky 1995) and at Tell al-Hawa itself; no examples were found on any THS site. NJP type 43.

T10/2 Fine Painted Goblet. Sherds of this type generally come from the rims of fine goblets and have bands of red or brown paint. One band often runs along the rim. Complete examples can have T10/8 or more often T10/3 bases. The THS did not identify any sherds of this type. NJP type 44.

T10/3 Pedestal (Stump) Base (fig. B.25 nos. 1–3; survey n = 6). This robust base type consists of a solid piece of clay which occasionally flares out to a flat base. Specimens from Tell Brak were

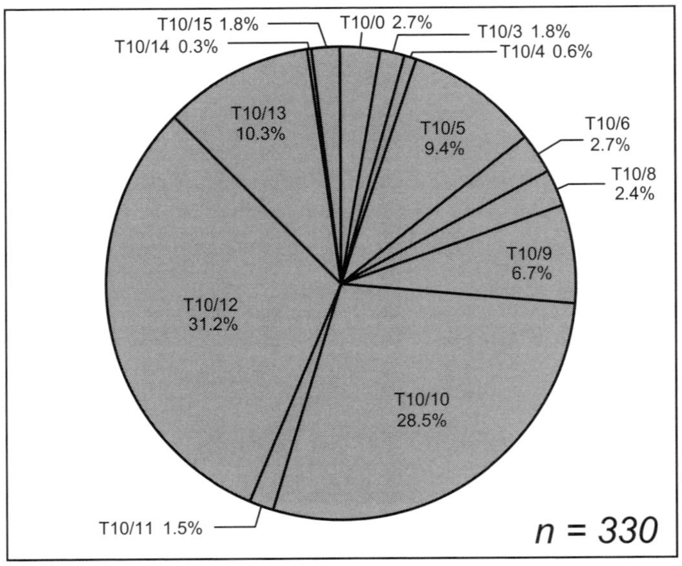

Figure B.24. Frequency of Period 10 ceramic types in THS areal collection

in a buff gritty fabric with little or no chaff temper. Its solid construction enables it to survive well on the surface. At Brak, the pedestal base does appear to be an earlier Period 10 type, found almost entirely in level 2 and earlier (Oates 1997: fig. 194). Unfortunately, it occurs rarely in surface collections. NJP type 45.

1. Buff exterior, red interior. Common grit temper. Base dm 1.7 cm. B.1077.1, THS 18 Area D.
2. Buff surfaces; common medium grit temper. Base dm 4 cm. B.1077.2, THS 18 Area D.
3. Pale yellow surfaces, exterior lightly burnished, buff core; rare chaff temper, fine fabric. Base dm 2.2 cm. B.189.10, THS 24 Area R.

T10/4 Red-Painted Plate (fig. B.25 no. 4; survey n = 2). This shallow plate is defined by its distinctive red-painted rim and upper edges. Surfaces are orange to brown and often burnished. Temper is grit and chaff; cores are slightly reduced. At Tell Brak, red-painted plates are most common in the level of the Mitanni Palace (Area HH level 2; Oates 1997: 73), but continue in use in the Middle Assyrian period at Tell al-Rimah (Postgate, Oates, and Oates 1997: pl. 34). It is related to a series of other unpainted Late Bronze Age plates that are designated as T10/10. At the time of processing, red-painted plates were included with unpainted Late Bronze Age plates (T10/10) and could not be retroactively split out in the counts, with the exception of two. Although not a common type, it occurred much more frequently than the count number suggests. NJP type 52.

4. Orange burnished surfaces with red horizontally applied paint; common fine chaff, occasional fine dark grit temper. Rim dm 41 cm. B.98.1, THS 23 Area B.

T10/5 Collared Jar Rim (fig. B.25 nos. 5–8; survey n = 31). These storage-jar rims have a simple rounded oval shape in section on sloping shoulders. They are found at Tell Brak, Tell al-Rimah, Tell Sheikh Ahmed, and Tell Sabi Abyad (Rossmeisl 1989). This type is considered characteristic of Middle Assyrian levels at Tell Sheikh Hamad (Pfälzner 1995: 136, pls. 120–21). Based on its occurrence at Tell Mohammed Arab, Wilkinson interpreted it as a mid- to late Middle Assyrian form (Wilkinson and Tucker 1995: 99) and its common occurrence only in level 1 at Tell Brak Area HH (Oates 1997: no. 45) appears to support this interpretation. THS examples have buff

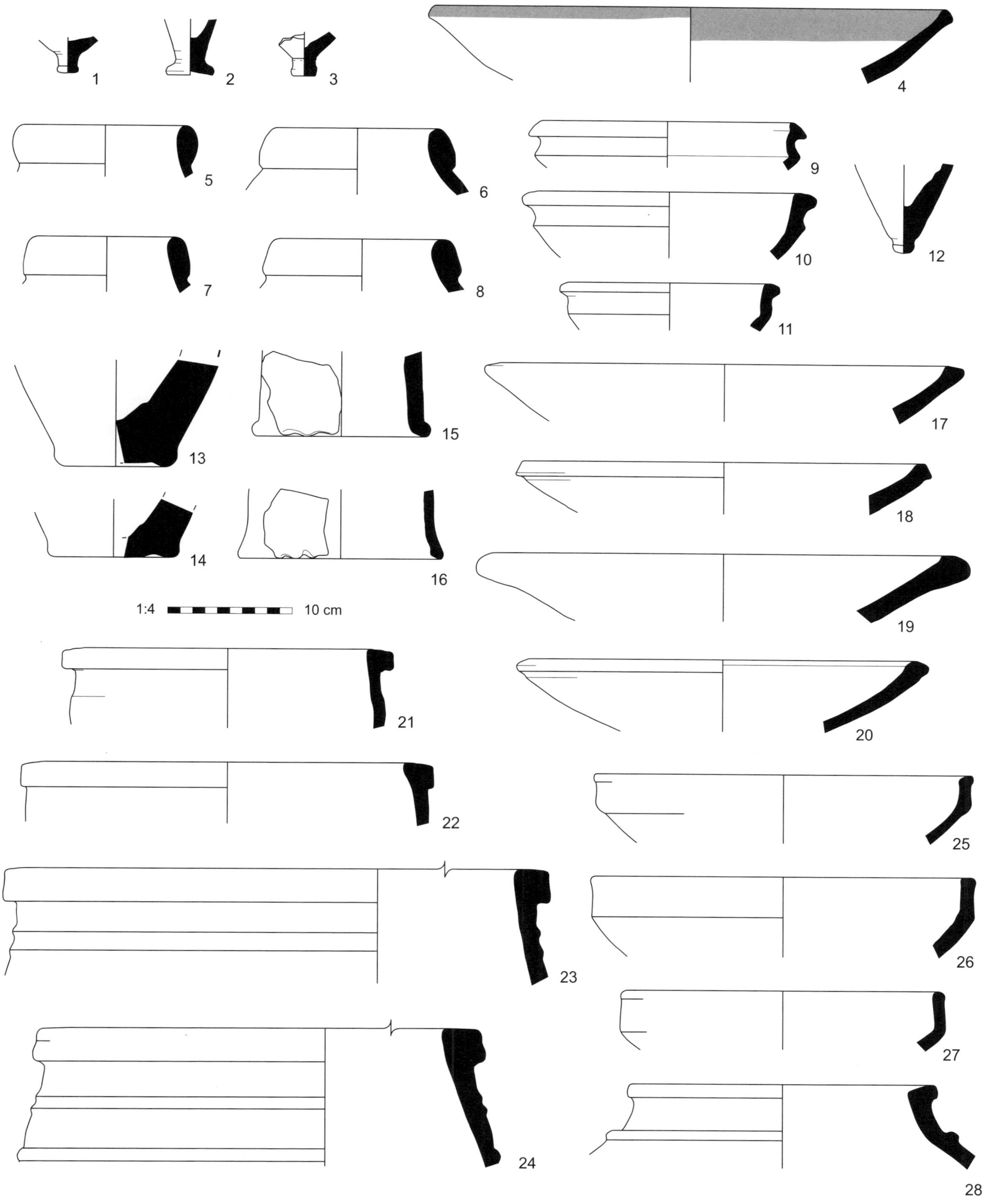

Figure B.25. Ceramic types for Period 10 (Late Bronze Age)

to green surfaces, slightly darker (reduced) cores, and common to frequent chaff temper. NJP type 47.

5. Pale yellow-green surfaces, gray-green core; frequent medium chaff temper. Rim dm 13 cm. B.142.4, THS 24 Area N.
6. Buff surfaces, pale green core; frequent fine sand temper. Rim dm 13 cm. B.2065.9, THS 33.
7. Buff surfaces and core; common fine grit, common fine chaff temper. Rim dm 11 cm. B.86.2, THS 11.
8. Yellow-green surfaces and core; common to frequent medium chaff temper. Rim dm 13 cm. B.161.1, THS 24 Area H.

T10/6 Small Bowl (fig. B.25 nos. 9–11; survey n = 9). These carinated bowl sherds have a sharp carination on the standard green to buff chaff-tempered fabric. The type includes a high degree of morphological variability. Their frequency at Tell al-Rimah in Middle Assyrian levels (Postgate, Oates, and Oates 1997: 61–62, pls. 28–32) and absence from all but Tell Brak HH level 1 (e.g., Oates 1997: nos. 2, 9–10) suggests that this type should be placed later in Period 10. Carinated bowls are common in Period 8 and Period 10, so this type was applied very conservatively on the THS. NJP type 48.

9. Pale yellow exterior, orange interior and core; occasional fine chaff and sand temper. Rim dm 20 cm. B.160.21, THS 24 Area G.
10. Buff surfaces and core; frequent to abundant medium chaff. Rim dm 21 cm. B.160.6, THS 24 Area G.
11. Pale yellow surfaces; common to frequent medium chaff, rare fine lime temper. Rim dm 16 cm. B.161.4, THS 24 Area H.

T10/7 Fine Beaker. In the North Jazira, this beaker rim occurred in a fine green to buff fabric and probably derived from tall straight-sided cups (Wilkinson and Tucker 1995: 99). The THS did not use this type. NJP type 49.

T10/8 Nipple Base (fig. B.25 no. 12; survey n = 8). This distinctive base type occurs in a green to buff gritty fabric. It survives well on the surface due to its thick construction. At Tell Brak and Tell al-Rimah, it is most frequent in later Period 10 levels (Oates 1997: nos. 316–20; Postgate, Oates, and Oates 1997: 56), whereas the pedestal base T10/3 is the predominant Mitanni form (see above). NJP type 50.

12. Buff exterior, orange interior and core; common medium chaff, occasional sand temper. B.138.1, THS 23 Area D.

T10/9 Coarse Ring Base (fig. B.25 nos. 13–14; survey n = 22). This robust base type is characterized by a thickly constructed ring on a coarse storage jar (possibly with rims of types T10/5, T10/12, or T10/14). Surfaces are light green to buff and generally heavily tempered with medium to coarse chaff. NJP type 51.

13. Buff surfaces; abundant medium chaff, occasional medium grit temper. Base dm 8 cm. B.1069.9, THS 59.
14. Light green surfaces, green-gray core; frequent medium chaff temper. Base dm 9 cm. B.179.4, THS 11.

T10/10 Late Bronze Age Plate (fig. B.25 nos. 17–20; survey n = 94). This type encompasses a range of rim shapes. Surfaces are orange to brown with occasional chaff or grit temper. THS examples have slightly convex sides and thickened rims. Many diverse examples were found in Tell Brak

HH (Oates 1997: figs. 181, 184–85) and at Tell al-Rimah (Postgate, Oates, and Oates 1997: pls. 36–38). The counts for this type include some red-painted plates (T10/4), which were initially included as part of T10/10 (see above). NJP type 52.

17. Pale orange surfaces and core; common medium chaff and fine lime temper. Rim dm 36 cm. B.189.8, THS 24 Area R.
18. Buff surfaces, orange-brown core; frequent fine to medium chaff temper. Rim dm 32 cm. B.187, THS 24 Area L.
19. Buff surfaces and core; common medium to coarse chaff, occasional fine to medium lime temper. Rim dm 36 cm. B.144.1, THS 24 Area S.
20. Pale orange surfaces, orange-brown core; common medium chaff, occasional medium dark grit temper. Rim dm 31 cm. B.1140.3, THS 41 Area A.

T10/11 Pie-Crust Potstand (fig. B.25 nos. 15–16; survey n = 5). The edges of these short potstands have an distinctive undulating, finger-impressed morphology. They occur in the standard Period 10 green to buff chaff-tempered ware. Excavated examples at Tell Brak come from HH levels 2–1 (ca. early to mid-thirteenth century B.C.; Oates 1997: figs. 215–16). Wilkinson and Tucker (NJP type 109) also recognized an Old Babylonian version of this stand. At Tell al-Rimah a few examples do come from earlier levels but in general the pie-crust potstand is a Mitanni type there (Postgate, Oates, and Oates 1997: 73, pls. 93–94) and also occurs in fourteenth-century levels at Tell Bderi (Pfälzner 1995: 83, pl. 57b). In the THS, this type was considered as a Period 10 diagnostic. NJP type 54.

15. Yellow surfaces, buff core; common to frequent medium chaff temper. Finger-impressed lower edge. Rim dm 13 cm. B.114.11, THS 24 Area B.
16. Buff surfaces, brown core; common sand temper. Finger-impressed lower edge. Rim dm ca. 16 cm. B.89, THS 12.

T10/12 Square Jar Rim (fig. B.25 nos. 21–24; survey n = 103). This common and robust rim type appears square in section and may have a slight concavity in its outer edge. Complete vessel forms are large open jars, often with horizontal ribs below the rim. They occur in the standard Period 10 green to buff chaff-tempered ware. Excavated examples come from HH level 2 at Tell Brak (Oates 1997: no. 614) and Tell al-Rimah (Postgate, Oates, and Oates 1997: nos. 616, 623). NJP type 56.

21. Orange-brown surfaces, brown core; common fine to medium chaff temper. Rim dm 23 cm. B.160.8, THS 24 Area G.
22. Yellow surfaces and core; common to frequent medium chaff temper. Rim dm 29 cm. B.160.14, THS 24 Area G.
23. Yellow-green surfaces and core; frequent medium to coarse chaff temper. Rim dm 60 cm. B.160.2, THS 24 Area G.
24. Yellow surfaces, yellow-green core; frequent medium chaff temper. Rim dm 46 cm. B.160.3, THS 24 Area G.

T10/13 Soft Carinated Bowl (fig. B.25 nos. 25–27; survey n = 34). Sherds of this rim type have vertical sides above a discrete but not very angular carination with a slight thickening. THS examples had orange, buff, and yellow surfaces with oxidized cores and common medium to fine chaff temper, occasionally with some sand or fine grit as well. It was recognized in THS surface collections; excavations at Tell Brak HH level 1 (Oates 1997: no. 54) and Mitanni and Middle Assyrian levels at Tell al-Rimah (Postgate, Oates, and Oates 1997: pls. 31–33) have produced similar types. This type was also recognized on the surface of Tell Mohammed Diyab (Lyonnet 1990: fig. 26).

25. Pale orange surfaces, brown core with pink margins; common fine to medium chaff and fine lime temper. Rim dm 30 cm. B.189.7, THS 24 Area R.

26. Red-buff surfaces, buff core; abundant medium to coarse chaff, occasional grit temper. Rim dm 30 cm. B.144.5, THS 24 Area S.

27. Red-orange surfaces and core; common medium chaff, rare fine dark grit temper. Rim dm 25 cm. B.160.9, THS 24 Area G.

T10/14 Inwardly Bevelled Rim (fig. B.25 no. 28; survey n = 1). This large storage jar rim has a distinct inward bevelling on typical Late Bronze Age common ware fabric (light green to buff surfaces and core; chaff tempered with some grit). As with T10/12 and T10/15, it is robust and survives well in surface assemblages. Complete vessels with this rim type are large ovoid storage jars, sometimes with T10/9 bases. Illustrated examples from Tell al-Rimah come from Mitanni levels (e.g., Postgate, Oates, and Oates 1997: nos. 988, 990–91, 995), HH level 2 at Tell Brak (Oates 1997: no. 629), and Mitanni levels at Tell Bderi (Pfälzner 1995: pls. 40–42). This type was developed during the Brak suburban survey, where it was common on the surface of the outer town; its relative infrequency in the THS is the result of retroactive and non-systematic assignment of sherds to this type.

28. Pale yellow surfaces, buff core; common to frequent medium chaff, rare medium lime temper. Rim dm 24 cm. B.189.4, THS 24 Area R.

T10/15 Incurved-Ledge Rim (survey n = 6). Rims of this type are flat or slightly downcurving and occur on large storage jars with slightly closed profiles. With T10/12 and T10/14, this robust storage jar occurs in a green to buff heavily chaff-tempered fabric and is often decorated with horizontal notched ridges and wavy grooves. This type was developed during the Tell Brak suburban survey, where it was common on the surface of the outer town, and was retroactively applied in a non-systematic manner in the THS. Vessels of this type come from Brak HH levels 4–1 (Oates 1997: nos. 615, 624).

T10/16 Recessed Convex Base. This type was developed during the Tell Brak suburban survey and was not used in the THS.

T10/17 Sherds with Wavy Grooved Lines. Decorated sherds of this type have broad and shallow grooves in a horizontal wavy pattern. Similar decoration can also be found on Period 8 sherds in the Upper Khabur basin and in fact appears to be more common on Period 8 vessels at Tell al-Rimah (Ur 2005a: 67). In the North Jazira, this type was used as a Middle Assyrian indicator only when sherds had the standard green to buff chaffy fabric; it was not used by the THS. NJP type 53.

B.2.11. PERIOD 11: IRON AGE/NEO-ASSYRIAN

During Period 11, the THS and adjacent areas were incorporated into the vast Assyrian empire (Wilkinson et al. 2005). On the basis of excavations in the imperial capitals (e.g., Lines [Oates] 1954; Oates 1959; Lumsden 1999), rural towns and villages in the northwestern hinterland of Nineveh (Green 1999), and more distant provincial centers (Jamieson 1999; Matney et al. 2007: 45–47), it has been possible to define a set of "imperial types" (Parker 2001: 283–85; 2003) with a broad geographic distribution.

The assemblage of the seventh century B.C. is well established, but difficulties abound in understanding what constitutes earlier and later Iron Age pottery. A series of grooved ceramics (T11/15) seem to immediately predate Assyrian control in the Upper Tigris region around Bismil, but these types do not appear to the south in the Cizre Plain region (Parker 2003; see also Blaylock 1999: 267–69). The question, therefore, remains as to whether the infrequency of this type in the Upper Khabur basin is due to a lack of pre-ninth-century settlement or because its manufacture and distribution was limited to areas north of the Tur Abdin.

The issue of what types might indicate post-Assyrian settlement is just as thorny. John Curtis (1989) has argued that the Khirbat Qasrij pottery is to be dated to the period following the collapse of the Assyrian empire, perhaps the first half of the sixth century B.C., on the basis of two types and an overall shift from chaff temper, characteristic of seventh-century Neo-Assyrian pottery, to grit tempering, characteristic of the Seleucid/Hellenistic assemblage of the third–second centuries (see below). Nonetheless, the proposed sixth-century assemblage appears remarkably similar to that of the seventh century (Green 1999: 115–16). Unless otherwise noted, the Period 11 THS ceramic types were being manufactured in the seventh century B.C., at the height of Neo-Assyrian imperial control.

The most common Period 11 type was the T11/8 necked jar rim, which accounted for almost half of the Hamoukar types and 30.4 percent of examples from elsewhere on the survey (fig. B.26). Also common were the T11/2 thickened bowl rim and the T11/4 angled ring base and, to a lesser extent, the T11/1 ribbed bowl rim.

T11/1 Ribbed Bowl Rim (fig. B.27 nos. 1–4; survey n = 68, Hamoukar n = 2). The defining feature of

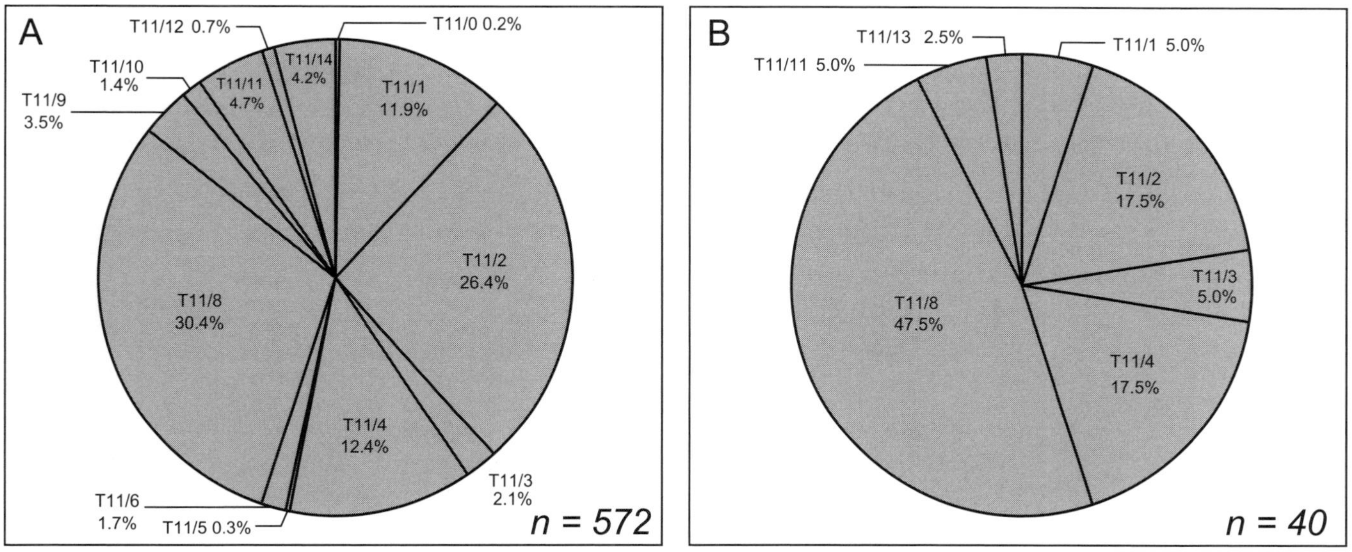

Figure B.26. Frequency of Period 11 ceramic types (*A*) in THS areal collections and (*B*) in Hamoukar sampling units

this rim type can be characterized as either a rounded rib on the edge of the rim, or as a groove set back from the rim edge. Colors range from yellow to buff to orange with a slightly darker core; temper is medium chaff and often also fine grit or sand. This type is well known from seventh-century B.C. contexts at Nineveh and Nimrud (Lines [Oates] 1954; Oates 1959; Lumsden 1999) and possibly continuing into the early sixth century at Khirbat Qasrij (Curtis 1989: fig. 27). It was used as an Assyrian type fossil in the Cizre Survey (Parker 2001: 281). NJP type 57.

1. Orange surfaces, thin brown core; frequent medium chaff, occasional fine lime temper. Rim dm 26 cm. B.1068.21, THS 59.
2. Buff surfaces and core; common fine grit temper. Rim dm 25 cm. B.1068.3, THS 59.
3. Orange-brown burnished surfaces, exterior vertically burnished, brown core; common medium chaff temper. Rim dm 24 cm. B.1068.20, THS 59.
4. Yellow exterior, buff interior, pink core; common to frequent fine to medium chaff, common medium lime temper. Rim dm 27 cm. B.1068.19, THS 59.

T11/2 Thickened Bowl Rim (fig. B.27 nos. 5–8; survey n = 151, Hamoukar n = 7). This rim type is also very common and comes from a bowl form related to T11/1; it occurs in the same range for colors and fabrics. It is possible that this form evolved into a more rounded, more sand-tempered post-Assyrian form (T12/5). Eroded specimens can be confused with the T5b/4 hammerhead bowl rim, but are generally more evenly fired than the reduced-core Period 5b type. NJP type 58.

5. Buff exterior, orange interior and core; frequent to abundant sand temper. Rim dm 27 cm. B.1068.29, THS 59.
6. Buff surfaces and core; frequent to abundant sand temper. Rim dm 21 cm. B.199.4, THS 43 Area C.
7. Orange surfaces, thin black core; common to frequent medium chaff temper. Rim dm 26 cm. B.1068.27, THS 59.
8. Orange surfaces, orange-brown core; occasional fine chaff, occasional sand, occasional fine lime temper. Rim dm 16 cm. B.1068.25, THS 59.

T11/3 Swollen Convex Base (fig. B.27 nos. 9–11; survey n = 12, Hamoukar n = 2). These distinctive bases have a slight thickening, often offset by a carination, that make them resilient in surface collections. Surface colors range from yellow to green to orange-brown; temper is common fine chaff. This base occurs on large storage jars with T11/8 rims. A range of excavated specimens is known from Khirbat Qasrij (Curtis 1989: fig. 43.305–15). NJP type 59.

9. Gray-green exterior, buff interior and core; abundant fine grit, occasional fine chaff temper. Base dm at carination 4 cm. B.1069.2, THS 59.
10. Red-orange surfaces, brown core; common fine chaff, occasional sand temper. Base dm at carination 6 cm. A.70.8, THS 1 Unit 20.
11. Buff surfaces, yellow-green core; common to frequent medium chaff temper. Base dm at carination 2.0 cm. B.1102.4, THS 27.

T11/4 Angled Ring Base (fig. B.27 nos. 12–14; survey n = 71, Hamoukar n = 7). This ring-base type is distinguished by a sharp angle in section; often there is a groove between the inside of the ring and the flat part of the base, which makes the latter appear as a raised disc (fig. B.27 no. 13). In complete examples it is attached to bowls with T11/1 and T11/2 rims, and it occurs in identical fabrics (e.g., Oates 1959: pl. 35). The range of variation within this base type is well illustrated by the Qasrij Cliff examples (Curtis 1989: fig. 14.84–91). NJP type 61.

12. Pale yellow surfaces and core; rare fine sand. Base dm 8 cm. A.70.4, THS 1 Unit 20.
13. Buff exterior, pink interior; abundant fine chaff and fine grit temper. Base dm 7 cm. B.1069.5, THS 59.
14. Buff surfaces; abundant medium chaff, occasional fine grit temper. Base dm 7 cm. B.1069.4, THS 59.

T11/5 Button Base (survey n = 2). This very small button or convex disc base occurs in medium to fine wares. It was uncommon in the THS. NJP type 63.

T11/6 Palace Ware (fig. B.27 no. 15; survey n = 10). Beakers of this type have high flaring necks in a very fine orange to buff fabric. Three components were considered diagnostic: flaring rims, the carination between neck and globular body, and body sherds with the distinctive dented appearance. This luxury tableware has been found not only in the Assyrian capitals (Oates 1959: nos. 60–69; Oates and Oates 2001c: fig. 158), but also in rural places like Hamoukar Area C and Khirbat Qasrij (Curtis 1989: fig. 31). Only a single palace ware sherd was found in the survey of the western basin (Anastasio 1999: 175), but this may have resulted from the methodological decision to target high mounds at the expense of the lower towns and small low mounds that seem to be the most common loci of Period 11 settlement in the THS and Iraqi North Jazira regions. NJP type 60.

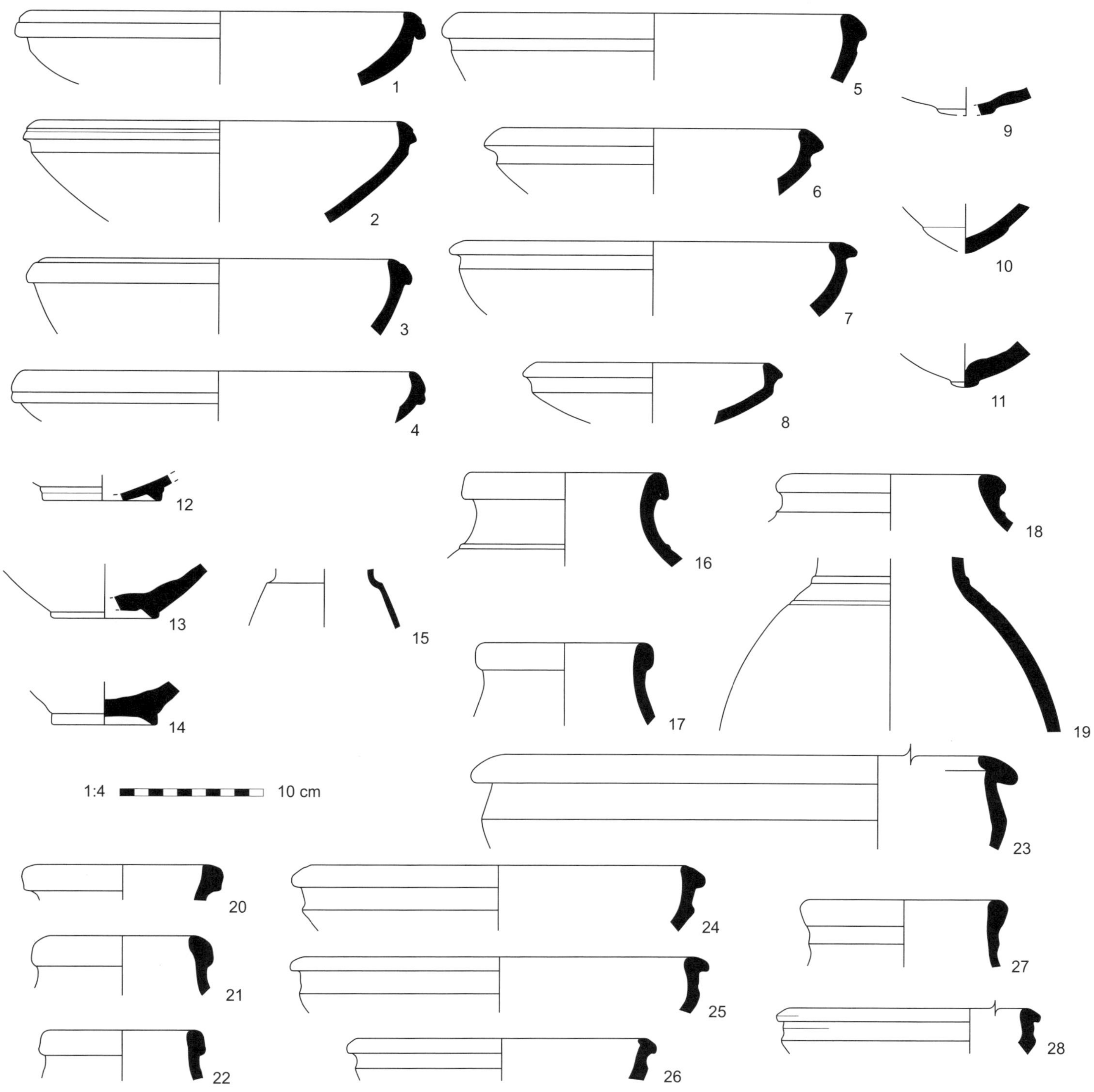

Figure B.27. Ceramic types for Period 11 (Iron Age/Neo-Assyrian)

15. Buff surfaces, orange core; no visible temper. Dm 8 cm at carination. B.199.7, THS 43 Area C.

T11/7 Assyrian Shouldered Bowl. This carinated bowl type comes from a general class of Period 11 carinated bowls (T11/12), but was not distinct enough in its presentation in the North Jazira typology (Wilkinson and Tucker 1995: 101) for use in the THS. This form could also belong to a potstand (Schneider 1999: type 20 nos. 1–2). NJP type 105.

T11/8 Necked Jar Rim (fig. B.27 nos. 16–19; survey n = 174, Hamoukar n = 19). This common rim type is characterized by a simple round rim on a slightly concave neck, often with a ridge at the junction of neck and body (Lines [Oates] 1954: pl. 39.1–3). Fabrics are buff to orange throughout, with frequent fine to medium chaff and sometimes also fine white grit in lesser amounts. It can be distinguished from the earlier Period 10 form (T10/5) by its smaller rounded rim, longer neck, and finer chaff temper. In the THS, this type was the most common for Period 11. The necked jar particularly common on Neo-Assyrian sites on the Cizre Plain (Parker 2001: 284). NJP type 114.

16. Orange surfaces and core; common fine to medium chaff temper. Rim dm 13 cm. B.199.2, THS 43 C.

17. Buff surfaces and core; common medium chaff, occasional medium lime temper. Rim dm 11 cm. B.1068.8, THS 59.

18. Yellow surfaces and core; common medium chaff, common fine lime temper. Rim dm 16 cm. B.1068.1, THS 59.

19. Green surfaces and core; common fine to medium chaff, occasional sand temper. Dm at ridge 11 cm. B.1068.32, THS 59.

T11/9 Internally Hollowed Jar Rim (fig. B.27 nos. 20–22; survey n = 20). This rim type occurs in similar fabrics and on the same vessels as the related rim T11/8, but has a distinctive convexity behind the rim. Sherds of this type have been excavated in the Eski Mosul region at Qasrij Cliff (Curtis 1989: fig. 11.58–59) and Khirbat Qasrij (Curtis 1989: fig. 33.168, 171–73, 180–81). NJP type 111.

20. Pale buff surfaces, thin gray core; common to frequent medium chaff, occasional fine sand temper. Rim dm 14 cm. A.68.4, THS 1 Unit 18.

21. Pale buff surfaces, orange core; common medium chaff. Rim dm 10 cm. B.1104.3, THS 34.

22. Pink-buff surfaces, pale orange core; common to frequent medium chaff temper. Rim dm 10 cm. A.71.1, THS 1 Unit 21.

T11/10 Folded Jar Rim (fig. B.27 no. 27; survey n = 8). As with T11/8 and T11/9, this rim type is buff to orange and predominantly chaff tempered. It is particularly well known from seventh-century contexts and may therefore serve as an indicator of later Neo-Assyrian settlement (Wilkinson and Tucker 1995: 101). These jar rims were well represented at Khirbat Qasrij, where the excavator argues for a short occupation in the first half of the sixth century B.C. (Curtis 1989: 48–49, nos. 227–40). NJP type 132.

27. Buff surfaces, orange core; common medium chaff, occasional fine lime temper. Rim dm 10 cm. B.1068, THS 59.

T11/11 Oblique T-Shaped Bowl Rim (fig. B.27 no. 23; survey n = 27, Hamoukar n = 2). This bowl rim has an inner rim that gives it a T shape in section. It occurs in the standard Period 11 chaff-tempered fabric. NJP type 112.

23. Buff surfaces, orange core; common to frequent medium chaff, occasional fine dark grit temper. Rim dm 52 cm. B.1068.5, THS 59.

T11/12 Carinated Bowl (fig. B.27 nos. 24–26; survey n = 4). This type has a simple thickened or everted rim on a carinated vertical-sided bowl. The carination occasionally takes the form of an exterior rib. It is probably descended from the Period 10 type T10/6 but can be distinguished by its buff to orange color and finer chaff temper. Excavated examples come from Nimrud (Oates 1959: pl. 35.26). NJP type 113.

24. Buff surfaces and core; common medium chaff, common sand temper. Rim dm 26 cm. B.170.9, THS 55.

25. Buff surfaces and core; common medium chaff, occasional medium lime temper. Rim dm 27 cm. B.1068.6, THS 59.

26. Buff surfaces, orange core; frequent sand temper. Rim dm 20 cm. B.198.2, THS 43 Area D.

T11/13 Button Ring Base (Hamoukar n = 1). This base appears similar to T11/5 but has a very fine ring which in some cases does not extend down as far as the center of the base. It occurs in a buff to brown fine or slightly chaff-tempered fabric in the excavations at Hamoukar Area C (Ur 2002b: fig. 14.17). NJP type 118.

T11/14 Ribbed Carinated Bowl (fig. B.27 no. 28; survey n = 24). This type is very similar in shape and fabric to T11/12 but with the addition of a horizontal rib or ridge between the rim and carination. Because of its presence at Qasrij Cliff, but its absence at Khirbat Qasrij and the lower town of Nineveh, Wilkinson uses it as an indicator of tenth- to eighth-century settlement (Wilkinson and Tucker 1995: 101). NJP type 156.

28. Buff surfaces and core; frequent medium chaff. Rim dm 25 cm. B.199.3, THS 43 Area C.

T11/15 Holemouth Cooking Pot. This holemouth cooking pot rim is heavily grit tempered and features incised horizontal lines below the rim. It serves as an early Iron Age indicator in the Upper Tigris region (Blaylock 1999: 267–69, fig. 3; Parker 2003: fig. 6). It was used as a diagnostic type in the Wadi Agig survey (Bernbeck 1993: figs. 118–19). This type was created during the Tell Brak suburban survey and was not used by the THS.

B.2.12. PERIOD 12: POST-ASSYRIAN

The middle of the first millennium B.C. is a poorly understood period in northern Mesopotamia, both historically and archaeologically. The seventh-century B.C. ceramic assemblage is well documented (see Section B.2.11) and the post-fourth-century Hellenistic repertoire is also established. The intervening time (the time of the Neo-Babylonian and Archaemenid empires) remains archaeologically vague, despite great historical events such as the collapse of Assyria, the rise and fall of the Neo-Babylonian empire, and the coming of the Achaemenids. Three sites can potentially contribute to a solution to this problem. The small site of Khirbat Qasrij in the Eski Mosul region (Curtis 1989) and the former Assyrian provincial capital at Tell Sheikh Hamad (Kühne 2005) appear to offer assemblages for the Neo-Babylonian period, the latter confirmed by epigraphic evidence. At the other end of this span, an assemblage from Kharabeh Shattani, also in the Eski Mosul region, has been dated to the late Achaemenid period (Goodwin 1995).

For the North Jazira Project, Wilkinson and Tucker devised a set of provisional "post-Assyrian" types (Wilkinson and Tucker 1995: 102, fig. 74). The eight types were assigned to this span on the basis of parallels with local (Khirbat Qasrij and Kharabeh Shattani) and distant (e.g., Pasargadae in Fars and Abu Qubur in southern Iraq) assemblages or because they appeared to have both Neo-Assyrian and Hellenistic characteristics (frequently Hellenistic-style abundant grit temper in a morphologically Assyrian form). The transition from the Assyrian level 4 and the post-Assyrian level 3 at Khirbat Khatuniyeh appears to offer stratigraphic confirmation of this proposed shift in temper in the century following the collapse of the Assyrian empire (Curtis and Green 1997: 81).

The THS adopted the provisional North Jazira Project types with a mind toward further testing. They are not common; only 125 Period 12 sherds were identified, compared to 572 typed Period 11 sherds and 313 typed Period 13 sherds. Almost half were the T12/5 shallow grooved carinated bowl (fig. B.28). Also frequent in the assemblage were T12/3 grooved-top bowl rims (22.4%). Perhaps the most distinctive form, T12/7 oval stamped decoration, is very uncommon.

T12/1 Jar with Grooved Top (fig. B.29 no. 1; survey n = 17). In the North Jazira, this type designated a range of thick-rimmed storage jar rims with large grooves. Sherds are green to buff or brown with chaff and occasionally grit temper. NJP type 104.

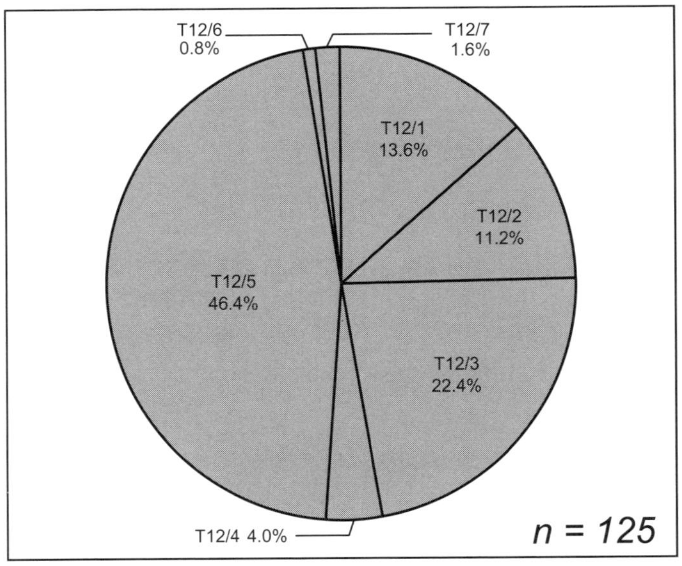

Figure B.28. Frequency of Period 12 ceramic types in THS areal collections

1. Pale orange surfaces, brown core; frequent sand and fine lime temper. Rim dm 14 cm. B.1103.2, THS 27.

T12/2 Holemouth Jar with Grooved Rim (fig. B.29 no. 2; survey n = 14). This rim type describes thickened holemouth rims with large exterior grooves, sometimes also notched or with T13/7 dog-tooth decoration. Their predominant grit temper aligns them more closely with Period 13 (Hellenistic) manufacturing techniques than with Period 11 (Iron Age/Neo-Assyrian) ones. NJP type 142.

2. Orange surfaces, brown core; frequent fine to medium grit and lime temper. Impressed triangles and stamped decoration. Rim dm 23 cm. B.158.1, THS 51.

T12/3 Grooved-Top Bowl Rim (fig. B.29 nos. 3–5; survey n = 28). The defining characteristics of this type are a multiply-grooved rim with a notched carination beneath it. Examples from the THS tend to be brown to buff and sand or grit tempered. NJP type 144.

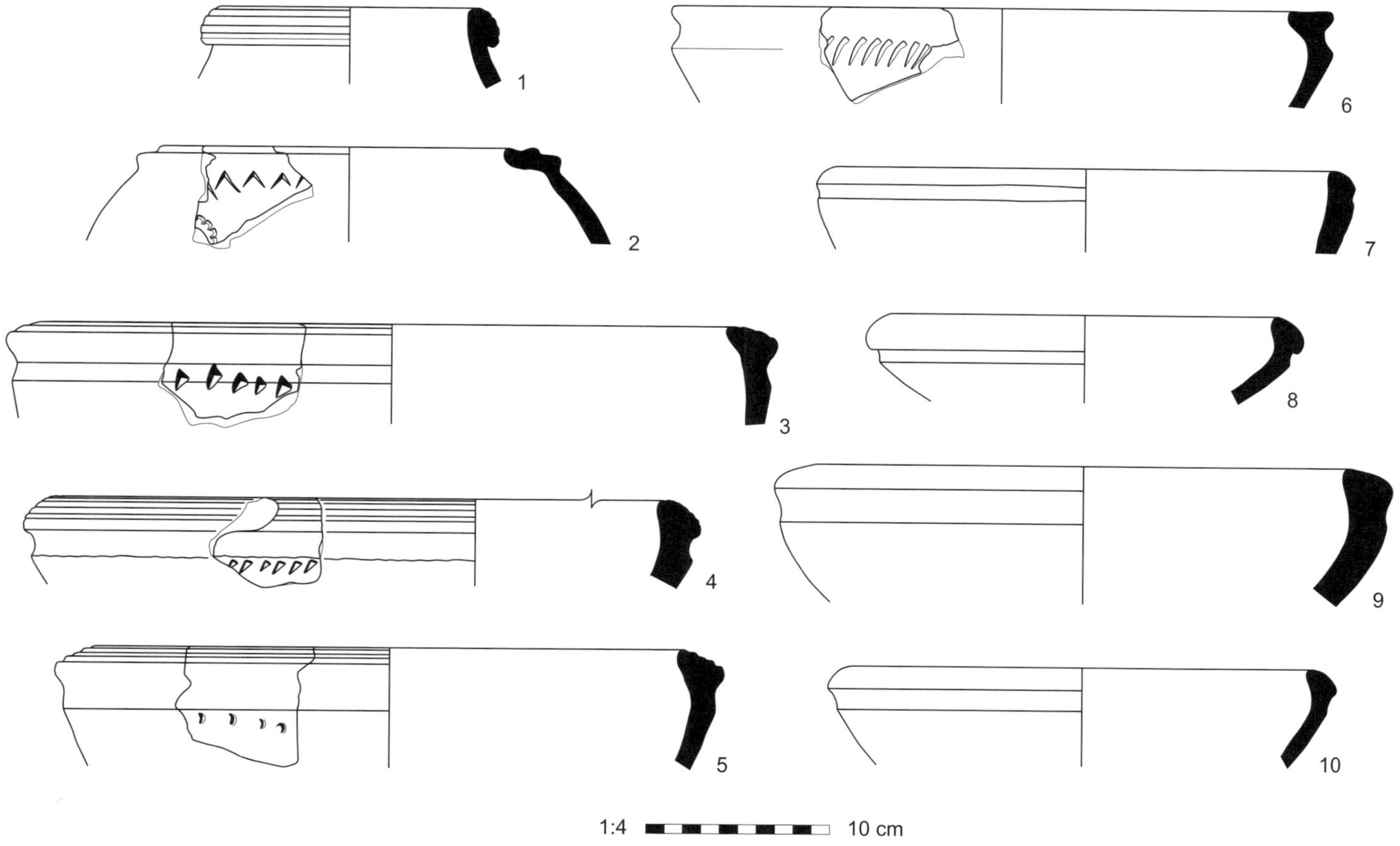

Figure B.29. Ceramic types for Period 12 (post-Assyrian)

3. Pale cream slipped surfaces, orange-red core; common to frequent sand and fine dark grit temper. Grooved rim and notched horizontal ridge. Rim dm 37 cm. B.1057.1, THS 5 Area A.
4. Gray exterior, orange interior, gray-brown core; common dark grit temper. Grooved rim, notched horizontal ridge. Rim dm ca. 45 cm. A.77.1, THS 1 Unit 27.
5. Buff-cream slipped surfaces, pink-orange core; common sand temper. Grooved rim, notched horizontal ridge. Rim dm 32 cm. B.1072.1, THS 3 Area B.

T12/4 Bowl with Notched Exterior (fig. B.29 no. 6; survey n = 5). This rim type appears on bowls with a rounded thickened rim and a notched carination beneath it. It has an evenly fired brown fabric with sand and occasionally fine chaff temper in lesser quantities. Like T12/3 and T12/5, this form was tentatively assigned to the post-Assyrian period primarily on its "evolved" resemblance to Assyrian types, in this case, T11/2 (Wilkinson and Tucker 1995: 102). This type was also recognized by the western basin survey (Anastasio 1999: fig. 4). NJP type 145.

6. Buff to brown surfaces; common fine chaff and medium grit temper. Notched horizontal ridge. Rim dm 36 cm. B.1069.13, THS 59.

T12/5 Shallow Grooved Carinated Bowl (fig. B.29 nos. 8–10; survey n = 58). This bowl type is similar in shape to the T11/2 carinated bowl of Period 11, but with a generally softer profile; the space between the carination and rim is often shorter and the carination less pronounced. Surfaces are brown to buff in a well-fired sandy fabric. NJP type 146.

8. Pale orange surfaces, dark brown core; frequent sand and fine dark grit temper. Rim dm 21 cm. B.1103.8, THS 27.
9. Orange surfaces, orange-brown core; frequent sand temper. Rim dm 29 cm. B.1103.5, THS 27.
10. Yellow (slipped ?) surfaces, pink-buff core; common sand and fine lime temper. Rim dm 25 cm. B.2054.1, THS 40 Area C.

T12/6 Flat Bowl Rim (survey n = 1). In the North Jazira, this type was defined as a shallow bowl with a flat thickened rim; based on geographically broad parallels (Wilkinson and Tucker 1995: 102). It was not used systematically in the THS. NJP type 102.

T12/7 Oval-Stamped Decoration (survey n = 2). Sherds of this decorative type featured oval embossed stamps, often with a serrated edge. At Nimrud, sherds of this type were considered Hellenistic, but in the Iraqi North Jazira, they occurred on chaff-tempered Neo-Assyrian forms as well (Wilkinson and Tucker 1995: 102). Oval stamped decoration was very rare in the THS, although circular stamped decoration occurred on other Period 12 types (see, e.g., fig. B.29 no. 2). NJP type 143.

T12/8 Crescent-Stamped Ware. The defining characteristic of this decoration type in the Iraqi North Jazira was a row of shallow impressed stamps in crescent form on a sandy fabric. No sherds of this type were identified in the THS region. NJP type 157.

B.2.13. PERIOD 13: HELLENISTIC

The Period 13 ceramic repertoire is well understood and clearly represented in the THS and adjacent areas of northern Mesopotamia. The homogeneity of Hellenistic pottery across southeastern Turkey, northern Syria, and northern Iraq means that types well known from Nimrud, Hammam et-Turkman, Sultantepe, and Tell Sweyhat are clearly identifable (Lloyd 1954; Oates and Oates 1958; Holland 2006; Lázaro 1988).

Many Period 13 types are made of a fabric that allows otherwise indistinct rim and base sherds to be identified. Although there is variation, the standard Hellenistic common ware fabric was tempered with abundant fine to medium sand or dark grit and evenly fired to buff, orange, or brown surface and core; very often these fabrics are partially covered with a red paint or a thin slip applied only to the rim or the most visible areas of the vessel (Dorna-Metzger 1996: 363–65).

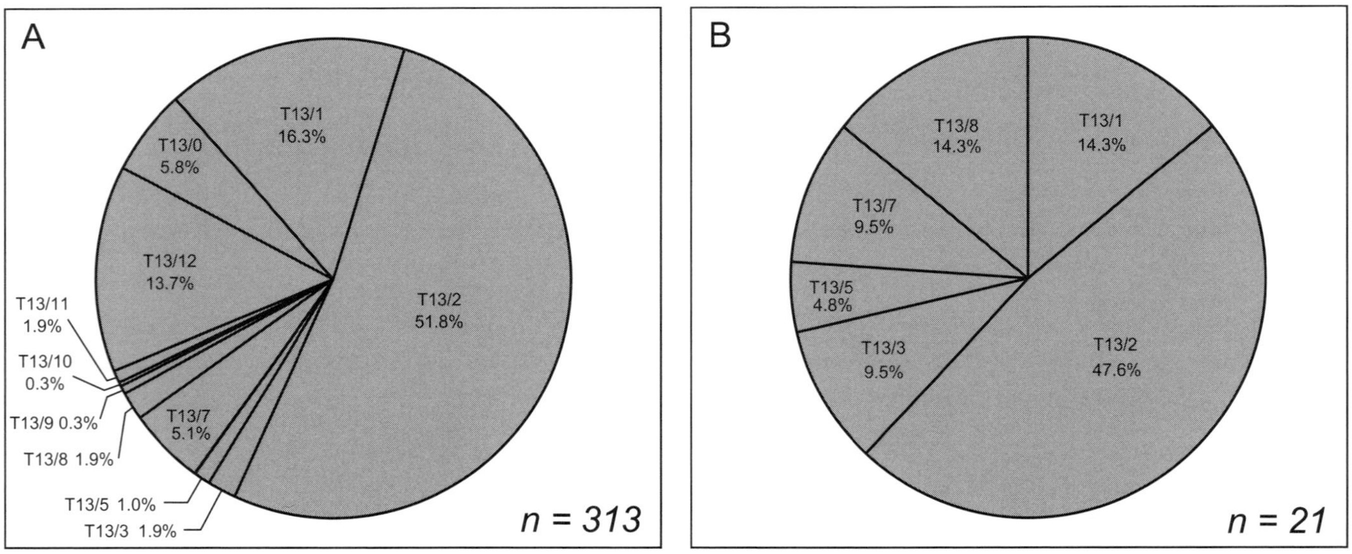

Figure B.30. Frequency of Period 13 ceramic types (*A*) in THS areal collections and (*B*) in Hamoukar sampling units

The most common Period 13 type, comprising almost 50 percent of all identified sherds on the survey, is the T13/2 rolled-over jar rim (fig. B.30). It was equally common in Hamoukar collection units. The other commonly occurring types on survey sites are the T13/1 incurved bowl rim (16.3%) and the T13/12 large grooved vat rim (13.7%)

T13/1 Incurved Bowl Rim (fig. B.31 nos. 1–4; survey n = 51, Hamoukar n = 3). This common incurving rim form derives from a small convex bowl. The upper exterior and interior are often red painted in a careless manner. Surfaces are buff to orange with a slightly darker core; fabrics are tempered with common to abundant sand. This type was also very common in the survey of the western basin (Dorna-Metzger 1996: 364, figs. 5–6) and is known from Nimrud and Sultantepe (Oates and Oates 1958: pl. 23:14–16; Lloyd 1954: fig. 1:28–30) NJP type 64.

1. Buff surfaces; occasional sand temper, fine fabric. Dark red paint on exterior and rim interior. Rim dm 10 cm. B.173.22, THS 10 Area A.
2. Buff surfaces, brown core; common sand, occasional medium lime temper. Dark red paint on interior and exterior surfaces. Rim dm 13 cm. B.143.1, THS 24 Area Q.
3. Pale orange surfaces, orange core; frequent sand, frequent fine to medium lime temper. Rim dm 20 cm. B.526.16, THS 16 Area A.
4. Buff surfaces, buff core; frequent to abundant sand temper. Dark red paint on interior and exterior surfaces. Rim dm 23 cm. B.173, THS 10 Area A.

T13/2 Rolled-Over Jar Rim (fig. B.31 nos. 5–12; survey n = 162; Hamoukar n = 10). This distinctive jar rim type was the most common Period 13 diagnostic type in the THS. Although the type encompasses substantial morphological variability, all rims are everted and rolled over with a pronounced ridge beneath the rim. It is possible that this variation is chronologically significant; for example, the inwardly beveled rims (fig. B.31 nos. 5–7, 11) are strongly similar to a form in the Achaemenid assemblage at Kharabeh Shattani (Goodwin 1995: fig. 48:2). Rims can be painted red, often in an uneven manner. Surfaces are yellow to orange with a slightly darker sand tempered core. This type was also found in great abundance in Hammam et-Turkman XA (Lázaro 1988: 515–16, pls. 165–67) and was present in Hellenistic levels at Nimrud (Oates and Oates 1958: pls. 25:14, 27:10–11). It may be a descendant of the Period 11 folded jar rim (T11/10). NJP type 65.

5. Yellow exterior, buff interior, orange-brown core; abundant sand, abundant fine lime temper. Rim dm 22 cm. B.171.4, THS 10 Area B.
6. Buff surfaces and core; frequent sand, frequent fine lime temper. Rim dm 17 cm. B.143, THS 24 Area Q.
7. Buff surfaces, brown core; frequent sand temper. Red-painted exterior rim. Rim dm 17 cm. B.173.16, THS 10 Area A.
8. Yellow exterior, buff interior, orange-brown core; abundant sand, abundant fine lime temper. Rim dm 19 cm. B.171.3, THS 10 Area B.
9. Orange surfaces, orange-red core; abundant sand, abundant fine lime temper. Rim dm 15 cm. B.171.1, THS 10 Area B.
10. Orange surfaces, orange-brown core; frequent sand temper. Red-painted exterior rim. Rim dm 12 cm. B.143, THS 24 Area Q.
11. Buff exterior, orange interior and core; abundant sand temper. Rim dm 10 cm. B.173.10, THS 10 Area A.
12. Pale green-gray surfaces and core; frequent to abundant fine grit temper. Rim dm 12 cm. A.97.3, THS 1 Unit 47.

T13/3 Hellenistic Plate (fig. B.31 nos. 13–16; survey n = 6, Hamoukar n = 2). This rim type encompasses a range of shallow plate types, including the classic "fish plate" with sharply downturned outer rim. Examples in the Iraqi North Jazira had a fine gray fabric; THS specimens tended to

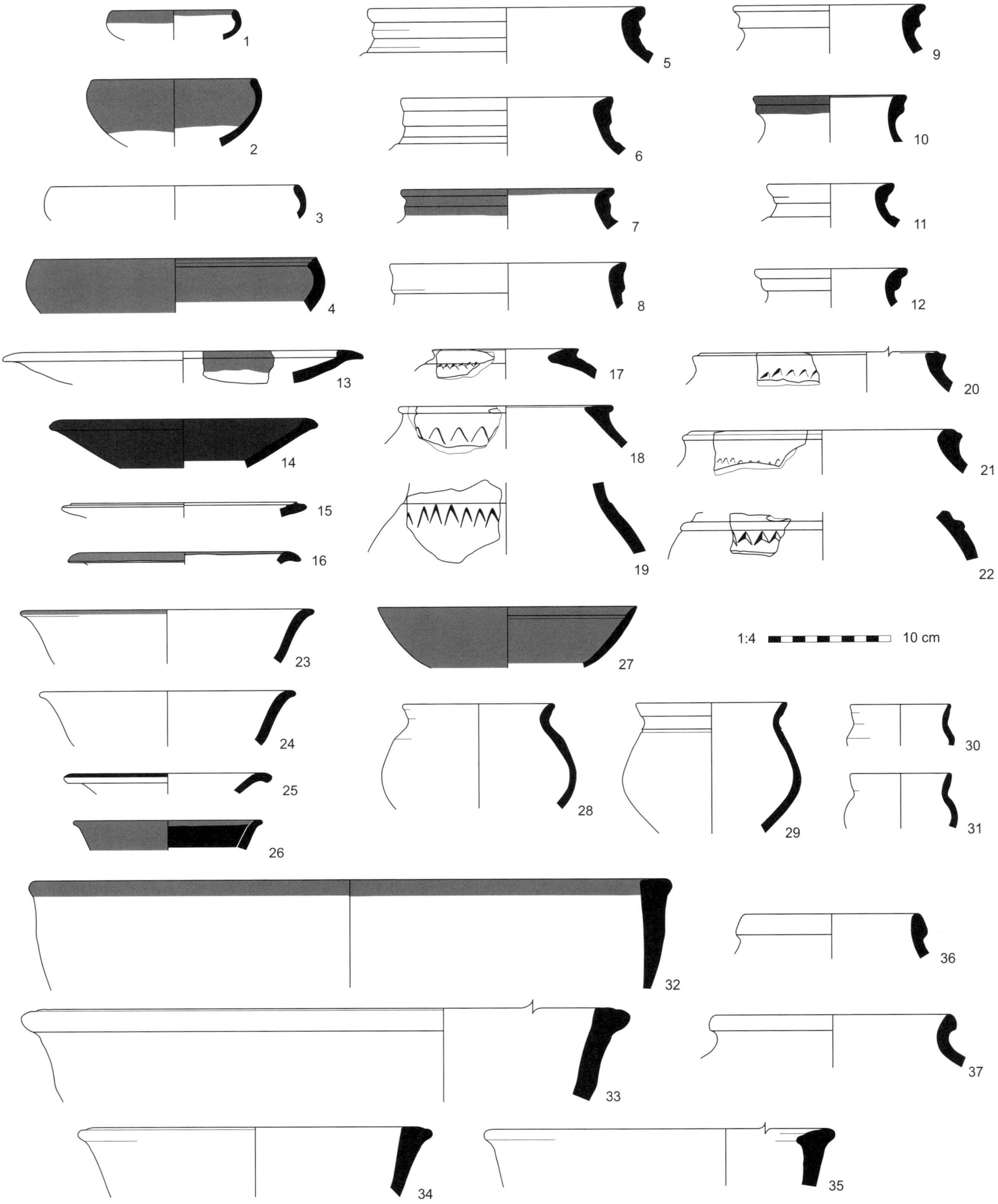

Figure B.31. Ceramic types for Period 13 (Hellenistic)

be coarser, in a sandy buff fabric. Many examples were painted, perhaps to emulate imported black-glazed finewares (e.g., fig. B.31 no. 14). This type was also a common diagnostic in the western basin (Dorna-Metzger 1996: figs. 1–4) and in Hellenistic Nimrud (Oates and Oates 1958: pl. 23:1–6). NJP type 66.

13. Buff surfaces, brown core; common sand, occasional medium lime temper. Red to black paint on interior. Rim dm. 26 cm. B.143.2, THS 24 Area Q.

14. Buff surfaces, pink core; common sand temper. Black-painted surfaces. Rim dm 20 cm. B.173.5, THS 10 Area A.

15. Buff surfaces, orange core; frequent fine lime temper. Rim dm 20 cm. A.97.9, THS 1 Unit 47.

16. Pale orange slipped surfaces, brown core; common sand and fine white grit temper. Red-painted rim and interior. Rim dm 19 cm. A.389.17, THS 1 Unit 127.

T13/4 Hellenistic Fineware. This fabric type serves as a catchall for a range of Hellenistic finewares. True Attic glossy sherds were entirely absent, but finewares of Eastern Sigillata A and B varieties did occur, albeit rarely. Sherds have a thick red or black slip on a well-fired orange or gray fabric, and show no temper or rare sand. T13/6 rocker pattern decoration occurs in these fabrics. This type was not used by the THS. NJP type 67.

T13/5 Hellenistic Fine Ring Base (survey n = 3, Hamoukar n = 1). This base type is characterized by a high ring which can occur in T13/4 fineware fabrics or in a finer version of the standard Period 13 common ware. Some examples have an incised ring on the interior opposite the ring. NJP type 68.

T13/6 Impressed Rocker Pattern on Hellenistic Fabric. A curved zigzag pattern is the defining characteristic of this decorative type. In the Tell Brak survey region, this decoration occurs almost exclusively on T13/4 fabrics of the Eastern Sigillata A variety (J. Gates-Foster, pers. comm.). NJP type 107B.

T13/7 Impressed Dog-Tooth Decoration (fig. B.31 nos. 17–22; survey n = 16, Hamoukar n = 2). This distinctive decorative technique involves rows of often overlapping stamped triangles. On THS sites, it most frequently occurs below the rims of large storage jars with orange to brown sandy fabrics. Several examples of this decoration occur on T12/1 and T12/2 post-Assyrian jars (see, e.g., fig. B.29 no. 2). NJP type 108.

17. Red-buff surfaces; occasional fine chaff, common fine to medium grit temper. Impressed wedges. Rim dm 11 cm. B.144.2, THS 24 Area S.

18. Pink-cream slipped rim and exterior, pale orange interior; red-orange core; common-frequent fine lime temper. Impressed wedges. Rim dm 17 cm. A.389.19, THS 1 Unit 127.

19. Buff exterior, orange interior, brown core; frequent fine to medium dark grit temper. Impressed wedges. Dm at ridge 17 cm. B.158.3, Site 51.

20. Orange surfaces, brown core; common fine to medium dark grit temper. Impressed wedges. Rim dm 27 cm. B.143.5, THS 24 Area Q.

21. Orange surfaces, brown core; common fine to medium dark grit temper. Impressed wedges. Rim dm 21 cm. B.143.4, THS 24 Area Q.

22. Orange surfaces, buff core; frequent to abundant sand, frequent fine to medium lime temper. Impressed wedges and traces of red paint. Dm at ridge 23 cm. B.158.4, Site 51.

T13/8 Out-Turned Bowl Rim (fig. B.31 nos. 23–26; survey n = 6, Hamoukar n = 3). The rim of this bowl turns outward, giving it a slightly sinuous profile. Examples are red or black painted, and in several examples, painted with both. Surfaces are yellow to brown with orange cores and common sand, although some have a fine fabric. Solid parallels are to be found at Hellenistic Nimrud (Oates and Oates 1958: pl. 23:8–11). NJP type 116.

23. Buff surfaces, brown core; occasional fine dark grit temper. Traces of red and black paint. Rim dm 23 cm. A.97.4, THS 1 Unit 47.
24. Buff surfaces, brown core; occasional fine dark grit temper. Traces of red and black paint. Rim dm 20 cm. A.97.5, THS 1 Unit 47.
25. Pale yellow surfaces and core; common-frequent sand temper. Black-painted rim. Rim dm 17 cm. A.97.7, THS 1 Unit 47.
26. Buff surfaces, orange core; common sand temper. Red and black paint. Rim dm 15 cm. B.173.11, THS 10 Area A.

T13/9 Hemispherical Bowl (fig. B.31 no. 27; survey n = 1). This small bowl is characterized by incised lines on the interior and exterior. It occurs in a grit-tempered fabric with brown surfaces and orange cores. Some examples have the standard Hellenistic red or brown paint. Whole examples are hemispherical. In the THS, this type was rare. NJP type 117.

27. Pink surfaces and core; common sand and fine lime temper. Dark red paint on all surfaces. Rim dm 21 cm. B.173.6, THS 10 Area A.

T13/10 Amphora Base (survey n = 1). Sherds of this type occur in the standard Hellenistic grit-tempered ware and are very durable because of their thick construction. They are, however, not very common in the THS. Excavated examples come from Hammam et-Turkman period X-A (Lázaro 1988: pl. 169:145–48). NJP type 158.

T13/11 Bag-Shaped Jar (fig. B.31 nos. 28–31; survey n = 4). This small jar has a rounded shoulder and a simple rim on a short vertical neck. Examples from THS sites had orange to brown surfaces and cores and were tempered with fine dark grit or sand. Examples were recovered from the Ezida excavations at Nimrud (Oates and Oates 1958: pl. 24:21). This type may be related to, or descended from, proposed Achaemenid forms from Kharabeh Shattani (Goodwin 1995: fig. 58). NJP type 159.

28. Orange surfaces, orange-brown core; common to frequent sand, common to frequent sand, common dark grit temper. Rim dm 12 cm. B.187, THS 24 Area L.
29. Orange-red surfaces, brown core; common sand temper. Rim dm 12 cm. B.199.1, THS 43 Area C.
30. Yellow (slipped?) exterior, orange interior and core; abundant sand, abundant fine lime temper. Rim dm 8 cm. B.539, THS 54 Area B.
31. Orange surfaces and core; abundant sand temper. Rim dm 8 cm. B.171.17, THS 10 Area B.

T13/12 Large Grooved Vat Rim (fig. B.31 nos. 32–35; survey n = 43). Sherds from these large open vessels have thickened rims with large grooved tops. Fabric is buff to orange-red and heavily tempered with dark grit. Most examples have a carelessly and unevenly applied red wash on the rims and the upper body. It is probably related to the grooved rim vessels provisionally assigned to the post-Assyrian period (see T12/1 and T12/3 above). This type is also common in the Tell Brak region (J. Gates-Foster, pers. comm.).

32. Pale orange surfaces, orange core; common fine to medium grit. Red-painted rim and interior, traces on exterior. Rim dm 51 cm. A.97.2, THS 1 Unit 47.

33. Orange-red surfaces with traces of red paint on top of rim, brown core with orange-red margins; abundant sand, abundant fine dark grit. Rim dm 64 cm. B.171.10, THS 10 Area B.

34. Buff surfaces with traces of red paint on top of rim, orange-buff core; frequent sand. Rim dm 25 cm. B.171.8, THS 10 Area B.

35. Buff surfaces with traces of red paint on top of rim, brown core; frequent fine to medium dark grit. Rim dm 38 cm. B.171.11, THS 10 Area B.

T13/13 Hard Gritty Rolled Rim (fig. B.31 nos. 36–37). This type is a simple elongated round storage jar rim that is oval in section. It is not a distinctive form but it occurs in Hellenistic standard common ware in large numbers on sites in the Tell Brak region. It was defined for the Brak suburban survey and was not used in the THS. It may have parallels at Hellenistic Nimrud (Oates and Oates 1958: pl. 25:18 "Toureen," pl. 27:12).

36. Pale yellow-buff (slipped?) exterior, orange interior, pink core; common fine to medium grit. A.389.20, THS 1 Unit 127.

37. Pale yellow-buff surfaces, gray core; frequent medium grit. Rim dm 19 cm. A.69.2, THS 1 Unit 19.

B.2.14. PERIOD 14: PARTHIAN–ROMAN

Exposures of Period 14 levels at sites in the Upper Khabur basin and adjacent areas have been very limited and generally with the intention of reaching the earlier levels beneath them. The major exception is the excavations at the Roman military camp at Ain Sinu in northern Iraq (Oates 1968; Oates and Oates 1959). Ain Sinu, however, appears to be very late Parthian; the excavators date it to the early third century A.D. (Oates 1968: 89–92). There are also some sherds illustrated of recent excavations in Parthian Ashur from levels dated to the second and third centuries (Hauser 1996). Several Period 14 types appear in one of the assemblages but not the other.

Many Period 14 types occur in what appears to be a typical Parthian fabric. The surfaces and cores are well fired pink to buff with slight sand temper or none at all. Surfaces are slipped in light pink, light orange, or cream.

The most common Period 14 type is the T14/2 straight or grooved jar, which represents almost a quarter of all identified Parthian sherds (fig. B.32). Also common is the T14/3 strap handle. The other types all occur with surprising consistency at 6–7 percent of the Period 14 surface assemblage. The catchall type T14/0 was employed to account for a range of infrequently occurring bowl rims in the distinctive slipped Parthian fabric.

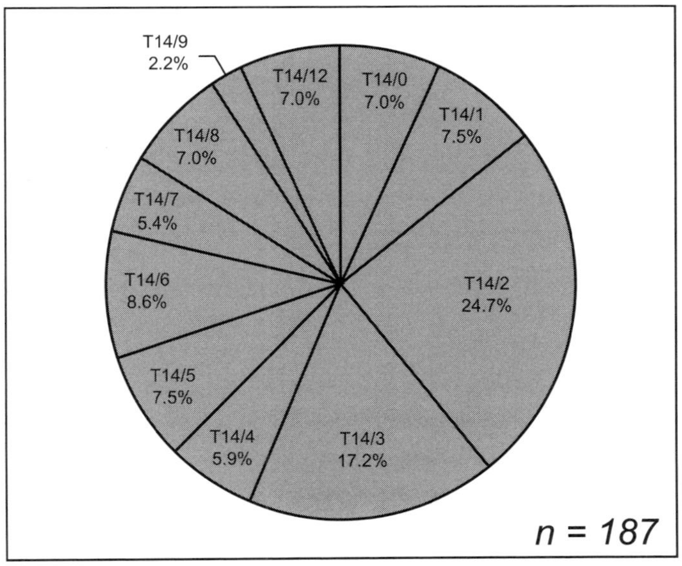

Figure B.32. Frequency of Period 14 ceramic types in THS areal collections

T14/1 Diamond-Stamped Decoration (fig. B.33 nos. 1–3; survey n = 14). Sherds with this decorated type are the most distinctive Period 14 indicator. The decoration consists of diamond-shaped depressions with raised dots. The dots most often occur in fours, but other numbers are known (Oates 1968: 148). The diamond stamps are themselves often arranged into diamond patterns on the shoulders of necked vessels with T14/3 handles and T14/2 rims. Fabric is most often the fine yellow or cream Period 14 ware with no visible temper. At Ain Sinu this decoration is considered to be late Parthian (early third century; Oates 1968: fig. 22:49–50, 54–55). It also occurs at Hatra (Ibrahim 1986: pls. 187–92) and Tell Barri (Pierobon-Benoit 1998: fig. 34). NJP type 76.

1. Yellow surfaces, orange core; no visible temper, fine fabric. Impressed diamond stamps. B.170.21, THS 55.
2. Pale yellow surfaces, pale yellow core; no visible temper, fine fabric. Impressed diamond stamps. B.170.20, THS 55.
3. Pale yellow-green surfaces and core; sandy fabric with no visible temper. Impressed diamond stamps. B.170.22, THS 55.

T14/2 Straight or Grooved Jar (fig. B.33 nos. 4–10; survey n = 46). Rims of this straight-necked jar type can be plain but often have a pronounced groove on the exterior. They occur frequently in the standard fine fabric, but some examples were more heavily sand or grit tempered. Many T14/2 sherds had handle fragments, probably of T14/3 type. Rims of this type were also commonly found on Period 14 sites in the western basin (Dorna-Metzger 1996: figs. 20–21). Excavated rims from Ain Sinu are elaborately excised and appear on handled jars with T14/1 decoration (Oates 1968: fig. 22). NJP type 115.

4. Yellow slipped surfaces and core; occasional sand, occasional fine lime temper, fine fabric. Rim dm 11 cm. B.187, THS 24 Area L.
5. Orange surfaces, brown core; occasional fine lime temper. Rim dm 11 cm. B.521.2, THS 43 Area G.
6. Pale greenish buff surfaces, pale green core; common sand, common fine grit temper. Rim dm 12 cm. B.548.2, THS 25 Area J.
7. Pale yellow surfaces, yellow-green core; rare sand temper, fine fabric. Rim dm 12 cm. B.521.1, THS 43 Area G.
8. Pale yellow surfaces, orange core; no visible temper, fine fabric. Rim dm 11 cm. B.100.3, THS 47 Area A.
9. Red-buff surfaces, red-brown core; frequent fine dark grit, frequent fine to medium lime temper. Rim dm 12 cm. B.185.1, Site 20 Area F.
10. Pale yellow surfaces and core; rare sand temper, fine fabric. Rim dm 13 cm. B.100.4, THS 47 Area A.

T14/3 Strap Handle with Central Groove (fig. B.33 nos. 11–12; survey n = 32). These slender handles have a very distinctive non-symmetrical grooved cross section and occur most frequently in the standard fine Period 14 fabric. NJP type 127.

11. Pale yellow surfaces, yellow-green core; occasional fine voids, no visible temper, fine fabric. B.170.18, THS 55.
12. Pale yellow slipped surfaces, orange core; rare fine to medium lime temper, fine fabric. B.170.17, THS 55.

T14/4 Fine Strap Handle with Central Groove (fig. B.33 nos. 13–14; survey n = 11). This handle type is a smaller and even finer version of T14/3. It occurs in the same fabric. NJP type 163.

13. Pale yellow surfaces, orange core; no visible temper, fine fabric. B.521.10, THS 43 Area G.
14. Pale yellow surfaces, orange core; no visible temper, fine fabric. B.521.9, THS 43 Area G.

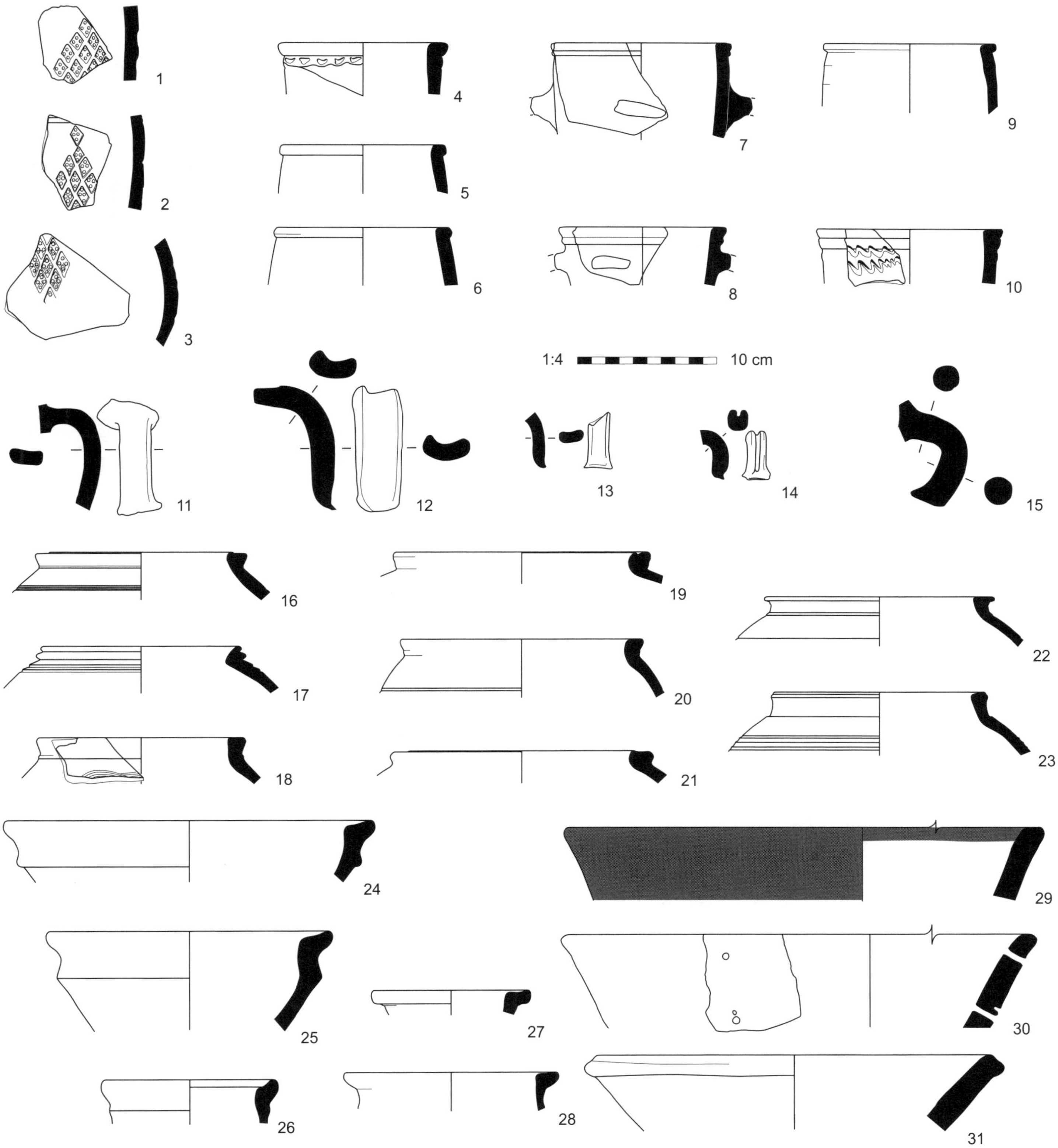

Figure B.33. Ceramic types for Period 14 (Parthian–Roman)

T14/5 Rod Handle (fig. B.33 no. 15; survey n = 14). This handle type is circular in section and manufactured in the standard fine Period 14 fabric. It derives its date from surface associations in the THS and the Iraqi North Jazira (Wilkinson and Tucker 1995: 104) and excavations at Tell Mahuz (Venco Riccardi 1970–71). NJP type 128.

15. Pale yellow surfaces, buff core; occasional sand, fine fabric. B.521.11, THS 43 Area G.

T14/6 Holemouth Jar with Grooved Rim (fig. B.33 nos. 16–23; survey n = 16). This type is known from excavations in second- and third-century Ashur (Hauser 1996: figs. 6e, 7h), but appears to be absent from third-century Ain Sinu. In the North Jazira, two Period 14 holemouth jar rims were distinguished (NJP types 129 and 164). The THS found these difficult to differentiate in practice, and included their full range of variation as a single rim type.

16. Pale green surfaces; occasional fine chaff, occasional coarse grit temper. Seven-prong band of comb incision. Rim dm 13 cm. B.548.6, THS 25 Area J.
17. Pale yellow surfaces, yellow-green core; occasional fine voids, rare medium lime temper, fine fabric. Rim dm 14 cm. B.170.14, THS 55.
18. Yellow surfaces; common medium chaff and fine grit temper. Wavy and horizontal bands of comb incision. Rim dm 13 cm. B.502.1, THS 24 Area P.
19. Gray exterior, orange interior, red-brown core; occasional sand temper. Rim dm 18 cm. B.170.10, THS 55.
20. Yellow exterior, orange interior and core; occasional to common sand temper. Rim dm 17 cm. B.170.11, THS 55.
21. Orange surfaces, red-orange core; frequent sand and fine lime temper. Rim dm 16 cm. B.142.3, THS 24 Area N.
22. Pale yellow slipped surfaces, orange core; rare fine lime temper, fine fabric. Rim dm 14 cm. B.170.12, THS 55.
23. Yellow surfaces, buff core; common sand temper, sandy fabric. Rim dm 15 cm. B.170.13, THS 55.

T14/7 Flat Collared Rim (survey n = 10). This rim type is characterized by a squared flat top with a ridge beneath; rims have a duck bill-like shape in profile. THS examples occur in the standard Period 14 fabric. T14/7 appears to be related to but not identical with the NJP jar rim type 130, which has a less pronounced lower ridge (see Wilkinson and Tucker 1995: fig. 76:22–23).

T14/8 Flared Concave Rim (fig. B.33 nos. 24–28; survey n = 13). The defining feature of this distinctive rim type is a gentle outward flaring with a slight concavity. The rim itself can occur on a range of bowls and jar necks, but always in the typical Period 14 fine fabric. This form is related to and probably encompasses NJP type 131, but the distinctive pie-crust decoration of that type was entirely absent on THS sites. T14/8 was defined based on its fabric and its surface associations on THS sites. Similar rims excavated at Ain Sinu are glazed (Oates 1968: fig. 21:10–13).

24. Gray surfaces, brown core; common sand, common medium to coarse dark grit temper. Rim dm 26 cm. B.521.7, THS 43 Area G.
25. Gray surfaces, brown core; common sand, common medium to coarse dark grit temper. Rim dm 20 cm. B.521.8, THS 43 Area G.
26. Pale orange surfaces, brown core; common sand temper. Rim dm 12 cm. B.521.4, THS 43 Area G.
27. Buff surfaces, orange-brown core; no visible temper. Rim dm 11 cm. B.521.6, THS 43 Area G.
28. Buff surfaces, brown core; common sand temper. Rim dm 15 cm. B.521.5, THS 43 Area G.

T14/9 Parthian–Sasanian Green Glaze (survey n = 4). The glazes of this type have a pale green color and a finely crazed appearance. Their fabrics are well-fired pink or yellow and sand tempered. They are much harder than the later Sasanian–Early Islamic types T16/4 and T16/5. Although this type is listed here with other Period 14 types, it is a long-lasting glazing technique and can also appear on Sasanian forms. NJP type 136.

T14/10 Fine Brittle Ware. This fabric type is very thin and hard fired; it tends to fragment into very small pieces. The often corrugated surfaces are red to dark red with orange cores and grit temper. It is often taken as an indicator of Roman military presence, based on its frequency at Roman camps (Oates 1968: 150; Campbell 1989) and in western Syria (Harper 1980). No sherds of this type were recovered by the THS. T14/10 fine brittle ware evolves into the coarser and softer Sasanian–Early Islamic version (T16/9 and handle T16/2); for this reason, in the western basin it was only considered diagnostic on specific rim shapes (Dorna-Metzger 1996: 368, figs. 23–24; Römer-Strehl 2005: figs. 612–30). NJP type 100.

T14/11 Impressed Rocker Pattern on Parthian Fabric (survey n = 1). The decoration itself is identical to the Period 13 version (T13/6), but occurs on the standard Period 14 fine fabric. Occurs on sites in the Iraqi Jazira (Ibrahim 1986: pl. 222). NJP type 107A.

T14/12 Coarse Red-Painted Large Bowl (fig. B.33 nos. 29–31; survey n = 13). Unlike most Period 14 types, this large bowl rim type is coarsely made with abundant sand and dark grit and carelessly painted in red. The fabric is orange to brown with a slightly darker core. This type was defined based on surface associations on predominantly Period 14 THS sites; it is probably related to a similar Period 13 large bowl (T13/12).

29. Orange surfaces with all-over red paint, orange-brown core; abundant sand, abundant medium dark grit temper. Coarsely made. Rim dm 42 cm. B.170.1, THS 55.

30. Orange surfaces with all-over red paint, orange-brown core; abundant sand, abundant medium dark grit temper. Three drilled holes; coarsely made. Rim dm 43 cm. B.170.2, THS 55.

31. Red-painted exterior, bitumen-smeared interior, brown core; abundant sand, abundant fine to medium dark grit temper. Coarsely made. Rim dm ca. 28 cm. B.170.3, THS 55.

B.2.15. PERIOD 15: SASANIAN

Starting with the Sasanian period, northern Mesopotamian surveys can no longer rely on substantial excavated local assemblages; with a few exceptions (Venco Riccardi 1970–71; Mahmoud et al. 1988; Boehmer 1974), one must go farther afield (e.g., to Ctesiphon; Venco Riccardi 1984), accepting all the problems that come with long-distance comparanda. Despite the major social and economic changes of the Sasanian period, chronological studies tend to focus on coins and luxury crafts, the types of material culture least likely to be found on the surfaces of archaeological sites (see reviews in Simpson 1996, 2000). As a result, survey types have been developed from surface associations, which is always risky, given the historical tendency toward settlement continuity and resettlement. The THS relied almost entirely on the surface association-based types used in the North Jazira (Wilkinson and Tucker 1995: 105–06, fig. 77).

Only fifty sherds of Period 15 types were recovered by the THS. Just over half were T15/1 corrugated jar rims (fig. B.34). The most distinctive type, body sherds with T15/3 stamped decoration, accounted for 24 percent of sherds.

T15/1 Corrugated Jar Rim (fig. B.35 nos. 1–3; survey n = 28). This thick sand-tempered jar rim is characterized by two or more deep grooves on a hard-fired buff to yellow fabric. Some examples have bands of comb incision. Sherds of this type were Sasanian indicators for the Tell Mohammed Diyab surface collection (Lyonnet 1990: fig. 29:2–4). NJP type 69.

1. Buff surfaces, orange-brown core; frequent sand temper. Rim dm 18 cm. B.190.7, THS 24 Area V.
2. Yellow surfaces and core; frequent sand temper. Rim dm 23 cm. B.190.8, THS 24 Area V.
3. Buff surfaces, red-brown core; common sand temper. Rim dm 23 cm. B.190.13, THS 24 Area V.

T15/2 Simple Gritty Jar Rim (fig. B.35 nos. 4–5; survey n = 10). The rim of this type is indistinct, but

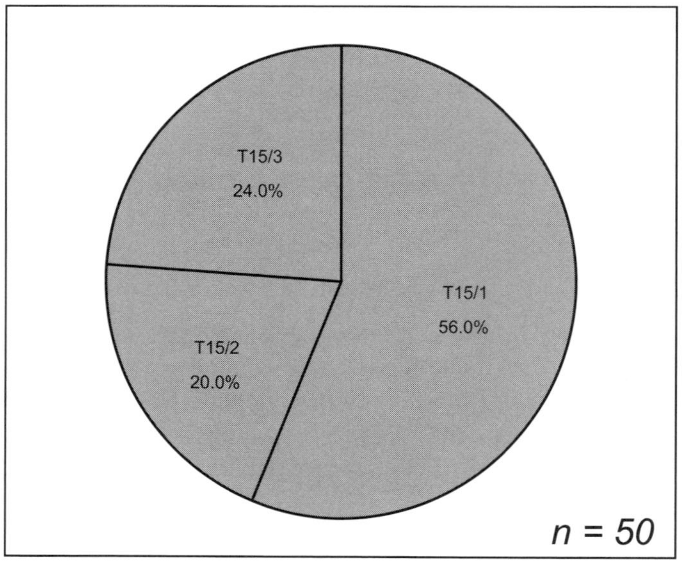

Figure B.34. Frequency of Period 15 ceramic types in THS areal collections

when found in a hard-fired sand-tempered fabric and in association with other Period 15 or 16 diagnostic types, it is useful for confirming Sasanian–Early Islamic occupation. NJP type 70.

4. Buff exterior, pink interior and core; frequent-abundant sand and fine lime temper. Rim dm 20 cm. B.190.6, THS 24 Area V.
5. Orange-brown surfaces and core; common sand, occasional coarse lime temper. Rim dm 19 cm. B.190.11, THS 24 Area V.

T15/3 Sasanian Stamped Decoration (fig. B.35 nos. 6–7; survey n = 12). These oval or circular stamps have raised figures of animals or humans, generally on a hard sandy fabric. This very distinctive type is unfortunately not very common in surface assemblages. Found at Tell Barri (Pierobon-Benoit 1998: figs. 30–31), Nineveh (Simpson 1996: fig. 1), and in the Eski Mosul Dam area (Sürenhagen 1987: fig. 3). NJP type 78.

6. Reddish buff surfaces, red core; frequent fine grit temper. Stamped decoration. B.2069.4, THS 15.
7. Buff slipped exterior, orange-brown interior and core; common to frequent sand temper. Stamped decoration. B.1701.21, THS 41 Area C.

T15/4 Smeared Ware. Sherds of this type come from large storage jars that were rusticated with a coarse sandy slip, perhaps in order to enhance porosity (Simpson 1996: 100). Parallels come from Tell Batas (Boehmer 1974: 101–02, 106, fig. 3, 5) and the surface of Tell Mohammed Diyab (Lyonnet 1990: 113, pl. 8:1, 6–7). Sherds of this type were not recognized by the THS. NJP type 77.

Figure B.35. Ceramic types for Periods 15–21 (Sasanian–Late Islamic)

B.2.16. PERIOD 16: SASANIAN–EARLY ISLAMIC

This ceramic period includes types that appear, primarily from surface associations, to have been in use at the end of the period of Sasanian political control and into the early centuries of Islam. Periods 15 and 16 should be considered in part overlapping rather than entirely sequential. Until recently, publications of Early Islamic pottery focused exclusively on glazed vessels from an art-historical perspective, and often dealt with unprovenanced pieces from collections. Recently, publications of well-excavated Early Islamic collections have appeared, particularly from Raqqa (Miglus 1999) and Madinat al-Far (Bartl 1994).

The most frequent Period 16 type was the T16/3 grooved or ridged strap handle (fig. B.36). This type was second only to painted Khabur ware (T8/1) in frequency among types of all periods, almost certainly due to its durable construction. The most distinctive glazed type, T16/4 blue-green glaze, was far less common (5.9%).

T16/1 Beaded Jar Rim (fig. B.35 nos. 8–14; survey n = 63). This rim type has a large bead or bulge on the side, in a yellow to buff, sand or grit tempered fabric. THS examples are hard fired. NJP type 71.

8. Orange-brown surfaces, red-brown core; frequent sand and fine lime temper. Rim dm 11 cm. B.190.5, THS 24 Area V.
9. Yellow surfaces, buff core; frequent sand temper. Rim dm 14 cm. B.190.2, THS 24 Area V.
10. Pale yellow surfaces, buff core; common-frequent sand temper, hard fired. Rim dm 13 cm. B.190.3, THS 24 Area V.
11. Orange-brown surfaces, red-brown core; frequent sand temper. Rim dm 13 cm. B.190.4, THS 24 Area V.
12. Buff surfaces, orange-brown core; common sand temper, hard fired. Rim dm 20 cm. B.190.1, THS 24 Area V.
13. Buff surfaces; common fine sand temper. Rim dm 17 cm. B.144.4, THS 24 Area S.
14. Buff surfaces; occasional fine chaff, common fine grit temper. Rim dm 18 cm. B.144, THS 24 Area S.

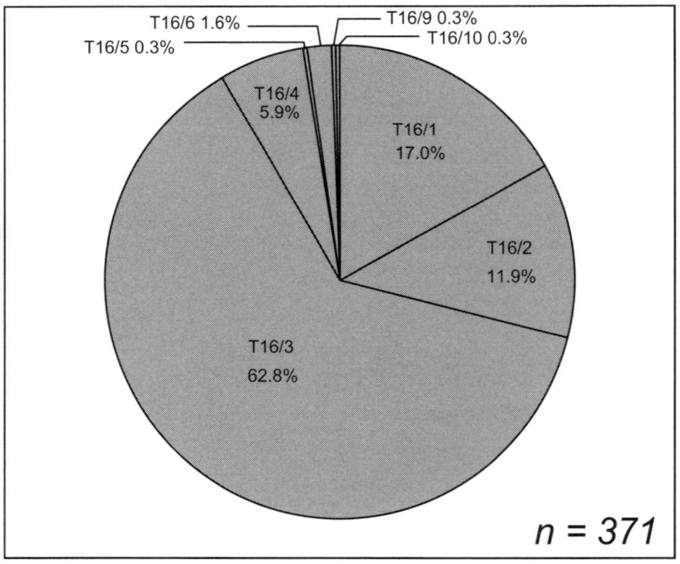

Figure B.36.Frequency of Period 16 ceramic types in THS areal collections

T16/2 Coarse Brittle Strap Handle (fig. B.35 nos. 15–16; survey n = 44). This cooking-ware handle type has a cross section with either a longitudinal groove or a raised flat ridge. Surfaces are red to brown on a reduced core tempered with coarse white grit. These handles were attached to club-rimmed cooking vessels of T16/9 fabric. This type was defined by surface associations in the Iraqi North Jazira. It has been dated to the sixth–seventh centuries at Halabiye (Orssaud 1991: 263–64, fig. 122:21) and occurs in Abbasid levels at Raqqa (Miglus and Stępniowski 1999: 52, pl. 31p, 32l–m). NJP type 72.

15. Red surfaces; abundant medium grit temper. Broad shallow longitudinal groove. B.190.28, THS 24 Area V.

16. Red-brown exterior, buff interior; abundant grit temper. Two broad longitudinal grooves on handle exterior. B.190.29, THS 24 Area V.

T16/3 Buff Grooved/Ridged Strap Handle (fig. B.35 nos. 17–21; survey n = 233). This handle is identical in form to T16/2, but in a buff to yellow sandy fabric, often wet-smoothed. Its durable construction makes it nearly indestructible in surface assemblages. This type was defined by surface associations in the Iraqi North Jazira and excavated in Abbasid contexts at Tell Aswad (Miglus and Stępniowski 1999: 52, pl. 66). NJP type 73.

17. Buff surfaces; abundant grit temper. B.190.24, THS 24 Area V.

18. Buff surfaces; abundant grit temper. Broad longitudinal groove on handle exterior. B.190.25, THS 24 Area V.

19. Pale yellow-green surfaces and core; common fine chaff, occasional medium grit temper. Longitudinal ridge on handle exterior. A.385.34, THS 1 Unit 117.

20. Pale yellow-green surfaces and core; rare to occasional fine chaff, common medium lime temper. Longitudinal ridge on handle exterior. A.76.1, THS 1 Unit 28.

21. Pale yellow-green surfaces and core; common sand temper. Neck dm 18 cm. B.190, THS 24 Area V.

T16/4 Blue-Green Glaze on Yellow Fabric (n = 22). This glaze has a distinctive combination of blue color on a soft yellow fabric. Glazes of this type have a wide distribution but were probably produced in workshops in Basra (Whitehouse 1979; Mason 1995). NJP type 74A.

T16/5 Blue-Green Glaze on Fabrics of Other Colors (n = 1). The glaze of this type is identical to T16/4 but occurs on reddish and other color fabrics. NJP 74B.

T16/6 Grooved and Slashed Bowl Rim (fig. B.35 no. 22; survey n = 6). This flat rim has a small vertical flange on its inner edge and a series of parallel grooves or incisions. In many examples, larger incisions have been subsequently made across them obliquely at even intervals. The vessel form itself is either a small bowl or a jar lid. This type is generally dated to the sixth–seventh centuries (Sodini and Villeneuve 1992: 209; Orssaud 1991: 267, fig. 124:56–61; Bartl 1996: 333, fig. 2:7–9). This rim type is part of the more inclusive NJP type 139.

22. Red-brown to buff surfaces, brown core; common fine chaff and grit temper. Rim dm 14 cm. Grooved and slashed decoration, partially abraded. B.540.1, THS 54 Area D.

T16/7 Late Comb Incision on Green Gritty Fabric (fig. B.35 no. 23). This decorated type includes late comb-incised sherds that occur on a green grit-tempered fabric. It differs from the Period 7 type in the much wider comb, often with ten or more prongs, and its distinct light green gritty fabric. Based on surface associations, it has been assigned to Period 16, but could continue later. This type has not been used for quantified chronological analysis.

23. Yellow slipped surfaces, green-gray core; frequent sand temper. Twelve-prong wavy band of comb incision. Rim dm 20 cm. B.2052.25, THS 40 Area A.

T16/8 Late Comb Incision on Other Fabrics. Like T16/7, this type encompasses later forms of comb incision. In the THS, this type was not used; instead, when fabrics offered clues to dating, the sherd was assigned the general period type (e.g., for comb incision on the standard Period 14 fineware, T14/0). Combed decoration lasts at least until the Middle Islamic period (e.g., Tonghini 1998: figs. 135–39).

T16/9 Coarse Brittle Ware (survey n = 1). This fabric type is red to reddish brown with a reduced core and coarse grit temper. The fabric is the diagnostic characteristic, although it occurs on straight-sided slightly closed pots with small club rims (Bartl 1994: pls. 28–31) and round pots with short straight corrugated necks (Bartl 1994: pl. 32:1, 4–6). At Madinat al-Far, these types are dated to the Early Islamic period (ca. A.D. 750–900; Bartl 1994: 113); the former are found throughout Abbasid areas of Samarra (Northedge and Falkner 1987: 163, fig. 11:44) at at Tell Aswad (Miglus and Stępniowski 1999: pls. 31–33), and on Early Islamic sites in the Qoueiq River survey (Northedge 1981: fig. 245:8–11). This type was not used consistently by the THS. NJP type 75.

T16/10 Honeycomb Ware (survey n = 1). This decoration type is characterized by a heavily sand-tempered green to buff slip which has been patterned into channels or honeycombs with a thumb before firing. In the Eski Mosul region, honeycomb ware sherds are found with primarily Early Islamic assemblages (Simpson 1996: 100). NJP type 79.

B.2.17. PERIOD 17: ABBASID

Understanding of Abbasid-period pottery has expanded greatly with recent publications of ceramics from Tell Aswad in Raqqa (Miglus 1999) and Madinat al-Far (Bartl 1994; Haase 1996). As with Periods 15 and 16, Periods 16 and 17 should be seen as overlapping rather than sequential.

The most common Period 17 type was the T17/4 creamware string-cut base, which accounted for over half of all typed sherds for this period (fig. B.37). T17/3 relief-molded ware was also common, due to its distinctive appearance on even very small body sherds. Likewise, the T17/5 slender handle could be recognized from small fragments and was a common type in this assemblage.

T17/1 Fine Eggshell Handle (survey n = 1). Thin handles of this type are found in a light yellow or yellowish green sand-tempered fabric. They often have an applied knob at the top near the juncture with the vessel neck. Only a single certain specimen was recovered by the THS. This type comes from excavated contexts at Tell Aswad (Miglus and Stępniowski 1999: pl. 67–68) and is also known from the Samarra surface collection (Northedge and Falkner 1987: fig. 11:42). NJP type 80.

T17/2 Band-Rimmed Jar (survey n = 8). These rims have a rounded and slightly incurved band on a tall neck. Fabrics are light green to yellow and often without visible temper. This type was assigned to Period 17 based on surface associations in the North Jazira, but it probably is a long-lasting form: similar rims are dated to the eleventh–fourteenth centuries at Qalat Jabar (Tonghini 1998: fig. 123) and even later examples are rouletted (T20/1). NJP type 81.

T17/3 Relief-Molded Ware (survey n = 24). Sherds of this decorated type have broad areas covered by fine geometric and floral designs in relief. The designs, and the vessels themselves, are made in molds (see Fortin 1999: 196 no. 163). The fabric is a fine buff or green with occasional sand temper. Excavated examples come from late eighth-century levels of Tell Aswad in Raqqa (Gonnella 1999). NJP type 83.

T17/4 Creamware String-Cut Base (fig. B.35 nos. 24–25; survey n = 70). This base type is characterized by a slightly extended foot with string marks and deep finger grooves on the interior. The fabric is a lightly sand-tempered yellow or cream color throughout. Bases of this type may derive from the same vessels as the T17/1 handle. NJP type 84.

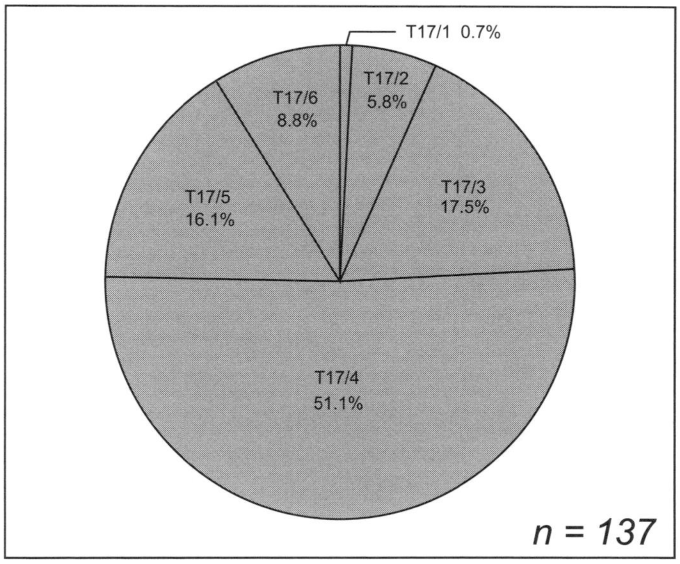

Figure B.37. Frequency of Period 17 ceramic types in THS areal collections

24. Yellow-green slipped surfaces, yellow-green core; common sand and fine to medium grit temper. Base dm 9 cm. B.114.9, THS 24 Area B.

25. Yellow-green slipped surfaces, yellow-green core; common sand and fine to medium grit temper. Base dm 16 cm. B.114.10, THS 24 Area B.

T17/5 Tall Slender Handle (fig. B.35 nos. 26–28; survey n = 22). These tall handles often have a slight longitudinal groove. Fabric is buff to light green with light sand temper. NJP type 123.

26. Yellow to buff surfaces; frequent fine grit, occasional fine chaff temper. Parallel longitudinal incised lines. B.540.8, THS 54 Area D.

27. Yellow to buff surfaces, yellow-green core; frequent fine grit, occasional fine chaff temper. Parallel longitudinal incised lines. B.540.9, THS 54 Area D.

28. Yellow to buff surfaces; common fine grit, occasional fine chaff temper. Deep longitudinal groove. B.540.10, THS 54 Area D.

T17/6 Twin Rod Handle (fig. B.35 no. 29; survey n = 12). This straight handle type is a larger version of T17/5 with two rods. It also occurs in a lightly sand-tempered light green to buff ware. NJP type 161.

29. Pale yellow slipped surfaces, orange-pink core; no visible temper, fine fabric. B.170.19, THS 55.

T17/7 Coarse Red Cooking Ware. This fabric type is a thicker and more coarsely manufactured version of T16/9. It was not used by the THS. NJP type 160.

B.2.18. PERIOD 18: MIDDLE ISLAMIC

We have become better informed about Middle Islamic pottery from recent publications from Qalat Jabar (Tonghini 1998) and sites on the Turkish Upper Tigris (Moore 1993; Redford 1998). These studies go a long way toward illustrating the non-glazed component of the assemblage, which has traditionally been overlooked in publications of museum collections (Porter 1981). Also helpful is the large collection of high-resolution, full-color photographs of eleventh- to thirteenth-century glazed sherds on the Tell Tuneinir Web site (http://users.stlcc.edu/mfuller/tuneinir/).

The two types assigned this period were both very rare; the five identifiable sherds of sgraffito ware make up the entire Period 18 assemblage in the THS region.

T18/1 Sgraffito Ware (survey n = 5). In the Balikh Valley survey, this was the only certain type for the eleventh century (Bartl 1994: 187), although it was considered to cover the eleventh through thirteenth centuries in the North Jazira (Wilkinson and Tucker 1995: 107). This glazed type was very rare in the THS. NJP type 82.

T18/2 Late Relief-Decorated Ware. This type of decoration is similar to T17/3 relief-molded ware except the relief is lower and vacant space is infilled with small dots. Such decoration is found in Ayyubid assemblages at Tell Tuneinir (see Tell Tuneinir Web site). No sherds of this type were recognized by the THS. NJP type 122.

B.2.19. PERIOD 19: MIDDLE–LATE ISLAMIC

As with Period 18, the THS relied almost entirely on the types and periodizations of Wilkinson and Tucker without modification. Although the types have been given new designations, they are otherwise identical. The reader is referred to the publication of the North Jazira Project for type descriptions (Wilkinson and Tucker 1995: 107–08, figs. 78–79).

The most common type was the distinctive T19/1 green glaze which comprised 73 percent of all Period 19 sherds, and the three glazed types together make up almost 90 percent of the assemblage (fig. B.38). Until detailed publications of non-glazed common wares appear, Middle to Late Islamic-period settlement will be difficult to establish on survey.

T19/1 Green Glaze on Reddish Brown Fabric (fig. B.35 nos. 30–31; survey n = 54). Sherds of this glazed type are common in Ayyubid levels at Tell Tuneinir (see Tell Tuneinir Web site). NJP type 94A.

30. Dark green glazed surfaces, red-orange fabric. Rare sand temper. Rim dm 11 cm. B.114.7, THS 24 Area B.

31. Dark green glazed surfaces, red-orange fabric. Rare-occasional sand temper. Rim dm 11 cm. B.114.8, THS 24 Area B.

T19/2 Yellowish-Brown Glaze on Reddish Brown Fabric (survey n = 9). NJP type 94B.

T19/3 Other Colored Glazes on Reddish Brown Fabric (survey n = 3). NJP type 94C.

T19/4 Handle with Applied Knob (survey n = 4). NJP type 98.

T19/5 Coarse Lid (survey n = 1). A range of these lids have recently been published from Gritille (Redford 1998: fig. 3:13–14) and Tille Höyük (Moore 1993: figs. 44–45). NJP type 91.

T19/6 Coarse Finger-Impressed Handle. No sherds of this type were recognized by the THS. NJP type 97.

B.2.20. PERIOD 20: LATE ISLAMIC

Period 20 encompasses the post-Mongol Ottoman period up to the end of the nineteenth century. Some Period 19 types probably continued in use into this period. Historical accounts indicate the almost complete abandonment of the basin by sedentary agriculturalists (see Section 2.2), so it comes as little surprise that the sherds assigned to this period occur so infrequently; only seventeen sherds could be identified. The meager collections have little to add to the North Jazira typology, where full descriptions of these types can be found (Wilkinson and Tucker 1995: 107–08, 122, fig. 79).

T20/1 Rouletted Ware (survey n = 5). NJP type 92.

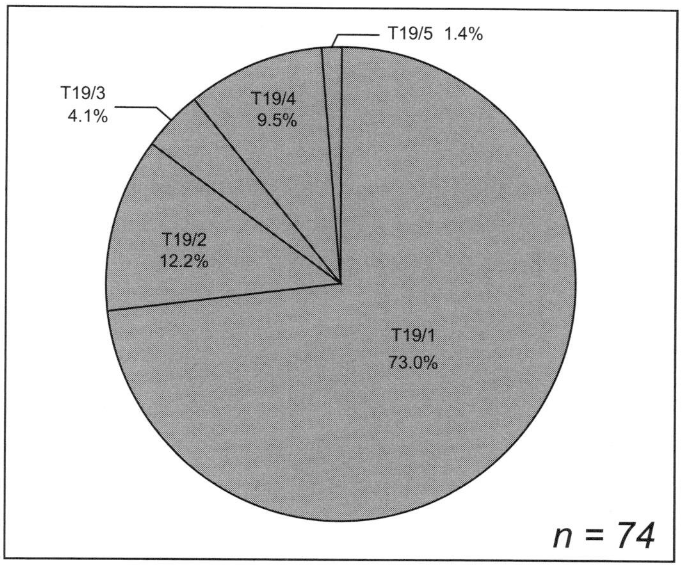

Figure B.38. Frequency of Period 19 ceramic types in THS areal collections

T20/2 Coarse Finger-Formed Rim (survey n = 4). NJP type 95.

T20/3 Coarse Impressed and Rouletted Ware. Sherds of this type were not recognized by the THS. NJP type 96.

T20/4 Fingertip-Impressed Ware (survey n = 5). NJP type 93.

T20/5 Ottoman Green Glazed Ware. Sherds of this type were not recognized by the THS. NJP type 101.

B.2.21. PERIOD 21: GENERAL ISLAMIC

Wilkinson and Tucker (1995: 108) recognized five recurring types in surface assemblages that could be placed in the Islamic period but not confidently assigned to any single sub-phase. The THS added one type to this list, the T21/6 glass bracelet. Otherwise, the THS did not modify the North Jazira Project types and the reader is referred to its publication for full type descriptions (Wilkinson and Tucker 1995: 108, 121–22, fig. 78). The types of this "Period" 21 were not used for analysis, other than to confirm Islamic settlement when few or no other diagnostics had been recovered.

T21/1 Grooved and Slashed Bowl (survey n = 1). NJP type 85.

T21/2 Beaked Jar Rim (fig. B.35 nos. 32–34; survey n = 45). NJP type 86.

32. Yellow-green slipped surfaces, yellow-green core; common sand and fine to medium grit temper. Rim dm 7.5 cm. B.114.1, THS 24 Area B.
33. Yellow-green slipped surfaces, yellow-green core; common sand and fine to medium grit temper. Rim dm 7 cm. B.114.2, THS 24 Area B.
34. Yellow-green slipped surfaces, yellow-green core; common sand and fine to medium grit temper. Rim dm 8 cm. B.114.4, THS 24 Area B.

T21/3 Islamic Flat Base (survey n = 1). This rather indistinct type was not used consistently in the THS. NJP type 87.

T21/4 Islamic Coarse Gritty Handle (survey n = 2). NJP type 89.

T21/5 Grooved Bowl Rim (survey n = 7). NJP type 90.

T21/6 Islamic Glass Bracelet (survey n = 18). Fragments of glass bracelets (Spaer 1992) were often found on Islamic-period sites in a wide variety of colors, including some polychrome examples. They are also found at Qalat Jabar (Tonghini 1998: fig. 24e–h).

APPENDIX C

SURFACE CERAMICS FROM THS SITES

C.1. QUANTIFICATION OF SURFACE CERAMICS ON THS SITES

This appendix presents the surface finds from THS sites in tabular form and, at certain sites, by pottery drawings. For each site that received a formal collection, the number of sherds of each survey type (see *Appendix B*) is presented, ordered by site collection area and chronological period. The reader will note that these raw counts may appear to diverge in some cases from the attributions of settlement periods found for each site in *Appendix A*. There are several reasons for such cases. Often, low quantities of sherds from deeply buried prehistoric phases of multiperiod mounds are given greater weight than periods whose remains presumably are found closer to the surface. Similar weight was given to sherds from periods that are characterized by few or non-distinctive survey types (e.g., Period 6). Often, settlement in a given period was attributed to sites or areas that produced relatively few typed sherds but many body sherds of a particularly distinctive fabric or diagnostics that, for one reason or another, have not been included in the survey typology. These latter outliers were retroactively placed in catchall types for each period (e.g., T1/0 for untyped Proto-Hassuna, T2/0 for untyped Halaf, etc.). These types were not used systematically, so their absence in the tables below does not mean that untyped but chronologically sensitive sherds were not present.

Low numbers of diagnostic sherds for any given period were likely to be disregarded, with the occasional exception of prehistoric sherds from presumably deeply buried levels (see above). Unique occurrences of a sherd from a particular period were almost always disregarded. On the other hand, relatively high quantities of Period 7 typed sherds were in many cases not considered to be a result of former settlement, but rather a result of the ancient manuring practices that have covered the terrain around Hamoukar with a nearly continuous carpet of sherds (see Section 5.2). In these instances, the Period 7 sherds were uniformly small and heavily battered. Certain types are listed in the tables, but were disregarded for the purposes of chronological analysis, generally because of concerns that the type's duration of use extended over more than one period (e.g., T4/18, which was often difficult to distinguish from the later T5b/12 version).

Finally, natural or cultural taphonomic processes, rather than ancient settlement, may have explained the density of surface materials. These factors were evaluated on a collection by collection basis.

C.2. ILLUSTRATED CERAMIC COLLECTIONS FROM THS SITES

This appendix also includes illustrations of selected collections from selected THS sites. Because the survey's field typology was based on the already well-developed typology of Wilkinson and Tucker (1995; see Section B.1.3 above), no attempt was made to draw a representative sample of all types in the field. Collections were likely to be drawn if they included potential new types, illustrated a range of variation within a type that was not represented in the North Jazira Project publication, or contained distinctive but unknown forms. Therefore, the figures in this appendix should not be considered representative of any given collection area or site; they should be considered along with the collection data in the accompanying tables and the final interpretation of settlement found in *Appendix A*.

Figure C.1. Surface ceramics from THS 2

1.	Pale yellow slipped exterior, orange surfaces and core; frequent sand and fine to medium grit temper. Rim dm 8 cm. B.75.1.
2.	Orange surfaces and core; occasional sand and fine to medium lime temper. Rim dm 13 cm. B.75.2.
3.	Pale orange surfaces and core; occasional fine sand. Rim dm 19 cm. B.75.3.
4.	Gray-brown surfaces, black core; frequent medium chaff, common medium dark grit. Rim dm 21 cm. T5b/5. B.75.4.
5.	Yellow slipped surfaces, orange core; frequent fine to medium lime and sand temper. Rim dm 25 cm. B.75.5.
6.	Yellow slipped exterior, orange surfaces and core; occasional fine to medium lime temper. Pierced nose lug and horizontal incised lines. T5a/2. B.75.7.
7.	Orange surfaces and core; frequent to abundant fine dark grit. String-cut base. Base dm 4 cm. T5a/8. B.75.6.

Figure C.2. Surface ceramics from THS 4

1.	Buff surfaces with brown paint, red-brown core; very fine sand temper. T1/1. B.1055.1.
2.	Buff surfaces with light brown paint; common fine chaff, common fine white grit temper. Rim dm 19 cm. T1/1. B.1055.2.
3.	Pink-buff interior and exterior, slipped or burnished; abundant fine to medium mixed grit, common fine chaff temper. Rim dm ca. 20 cm. B.1055.5.
4.	Gray burnished surfaces, dark gray core; frequent medium chaff, common fine grit temper. Rim dm 15 cm. B.1055.4.
5.	Green-buff surfaces, reddish buff core; common fine chaff and fine white grit. B.1055.3.

Figure C.3. Surface ceramics from THS 7

1.	Pale yellow surfaces, possibly slipped, brown core with orange margins; frequent sand temper. Rim dm 14 cm. B.1060.1.
2.	Pale yellow-green surfaces, gray-green core; common to frequent sand temper. Rim dm 11 cm. B.1060.2.
3.	Pale yellow-green surfaces, gray-green core; common to frequent sand temper. Rim dm 11 cm. B.1060.3.
4.	Pale yellow-green surfaces, gray-green core; common to frequent sand temper. Rim dm 9 cm. B.1060.4.
5.	Orange-red surfaces, orange core; common to frequent sand temper. Rim dm 13 cm. T16/9. B.1060.5.

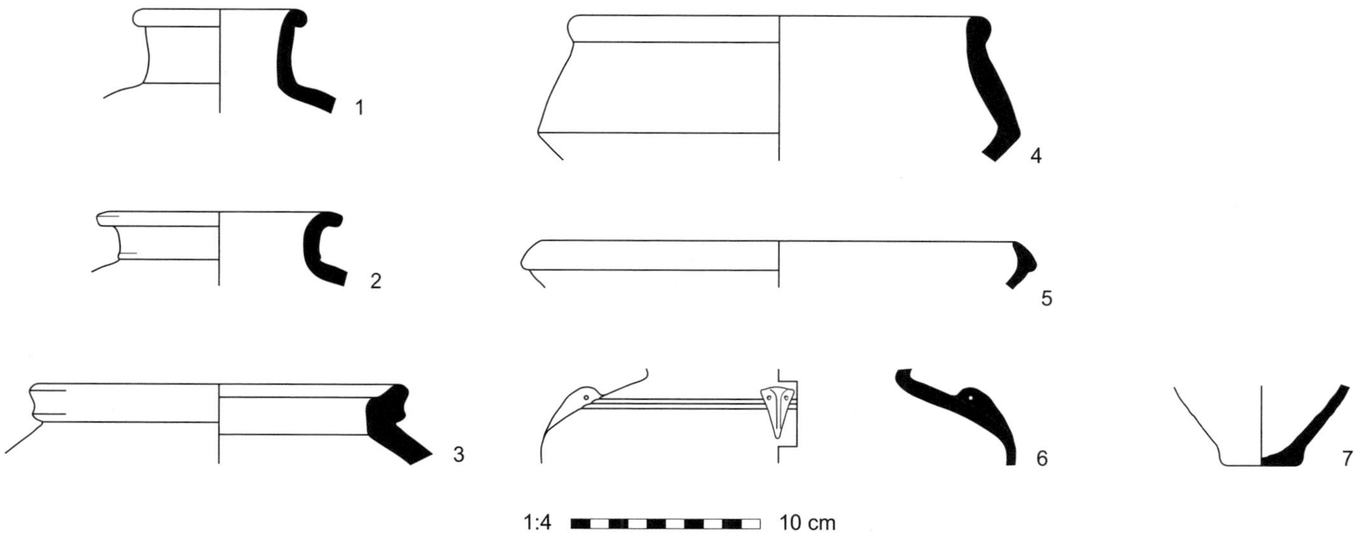

Figure C.1. Surface ceramics from THS 2

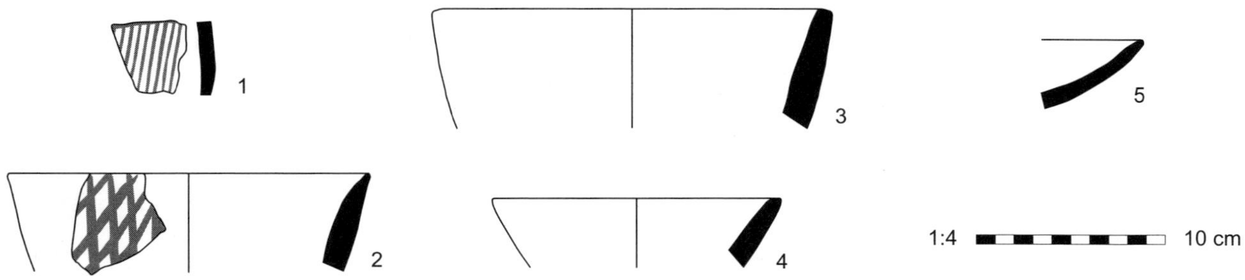

Figure C.2. Surface ceramics from THS 4

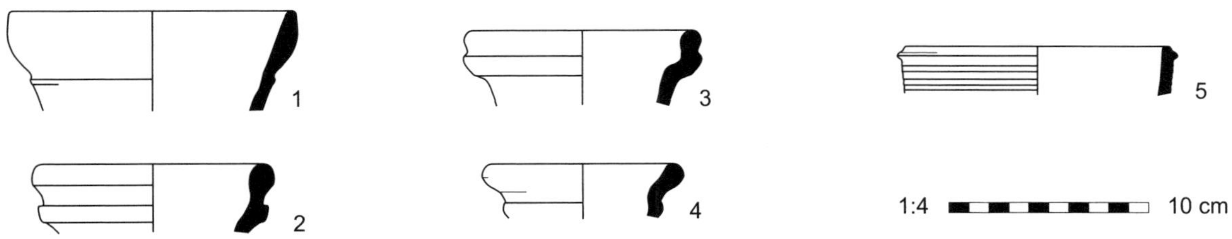

Figure C.3. Surface ceramics from THS 7

Figure C.4. Surface ceramics from THS 10

1. Buff exterior, orange interior and core; abundant sand temper. Rim dm 10 cm. T13/2. Area A. B.173.10.
2. Orange exterior, buff interior, gray-brown core; frequent fine dark grit. Rim dm 12 cm. T13/2. Area A. B.173.
3. Buff exterior, orange interior and core; abundant sand temper. Rim dm 20 cm. T13/2. Area A. B.173.4.
4. Buff surfaces, brown core; frequent sand temper. Red painted exterior rim. Rim dm 17 cm. T13/2. Area A. B.173.16.
5. Yellow exterior, buff interior, orange-brown core; abundant sand and fine lime temper. Rim dm 22 cm. Area B. B.171.4.
6. Buff exterior, orange interior and core; frequent to abundant fine dark grit. Rim dm 24 cm. Area B. B.171.7.
7. Orange surfaces, orange-red core; abundant sand, abundant fine lime temper. Rim dm 15 cm. T13/2. Area B. B.171.1.
8. Buff surfaces, orange core; frequent sand and fine lime temper. Rim dm 16 cm. T13/2. Area B. B.171.2.
9. Yellow exterior, buff interior, orange-brown core; abundant sand, abundant fine lime temper. Rim dm 19 cm. T13/2. Area B. B.171.3.
10. Gray surfaces and core; occasional sand temper. Rim dm 14 cm. Area A. B.173.17.
11. Orange surfaces and core; abundant sand temper. Rim dm 8 cm. Area B. B.171.17.
12. Orange surfaces with red paint, brown core; frequent fine dark grit. Rim dm 12 cm. Area B. B.171.6.
13. Buff surfaces, gray core; abundant sand and fine dark grit. Rim dm 15 cm. Area B. B.171.5.
14. Yellow slipped surfaces, orange core; occasional fine lime temper. Rim dm 9 cm. Area B. B.171.16.
15. Crazed yellow-white glaze on yellow fabric; no visible temper. Rim dm 21 cm. Area B. B.171.18.
16. Orange surfaces, brown core; frequent abundant fine dark grit. Rim dm 30 cm. Area B. B.171.19.
17. Buff surfaces; occasional sand temper, fine fabric. Dark red paint on exterior and rim interior. Rim dm 10 cm. T13/1. Area A. B.173.22.
18. Orange surfaces with red paint, orange-brown core; frequent sand and fine lime temper. Rim dm 29 cm. T13/1. Area B. B.171.14.
19. Buff surfaces, brown core; frequent dark fine to medium grit temper. Rim dm 22 cm. T13/1. Area B. B.171.13.
20. Buff surfaces with dark paint, brown core; frequent sand temper. Rim dm 25 cm. T13/1. Area B. B.171.15.
21. Pink surfaces and core; common sand and fine lime temper. Dark red paint on all surfaces. Rim dm 21 cm. T13/9. Area A. B.173.6.
22. Buff surfaces, pink core; common sand temper. Black painted surfaces. Rim dm 20 cm. T13/3. Area A. B.173.5.
23. Buff surfaces; occasional sand temper, fine fabric. Dark red paint on exterior and rim interior. Rim dm 10 cm. T13/1. Area A. B.173.22.
24. Buff surfaces, orange core; common sand temper. Red and black paint. Rim dm 15 cm. T13/8. Area A. B.173.11.
25. Buff surfaces and core; abundant sand temper. Rim dm 38 cm. T13/12. Area B. B.171.9.
26. Buff surfaces with traces of red paint on top of rim, brown core; frequent fine to medium dark grit. Rim dm 38 cm. T13/12. Area B. B.171.11.
27. Buff surfaces, orange core; traces of red paint on top of rim; abundant sand and medium to coarse grit temper. Rim dm 30 cm. T13/12. Area B. B.171.12.
28. Buff surfaces with traces of red paint on top of rim, orange-buff core; frequent sand. Rim dm 25 cm. T13/12. Area B. B.171.8.
29. Orange-red surfaces with traces of red paint on top of rim, brown core with orange-red margins; abundant sand, abundant fine dark grit. Rim dm 64 cm. T13/12. Area B. B.171.10.
30. Orange surfaces, brown core with orange margins; frequent fine dark grit. Rim dm 27 cm. Area A. B.173.4.

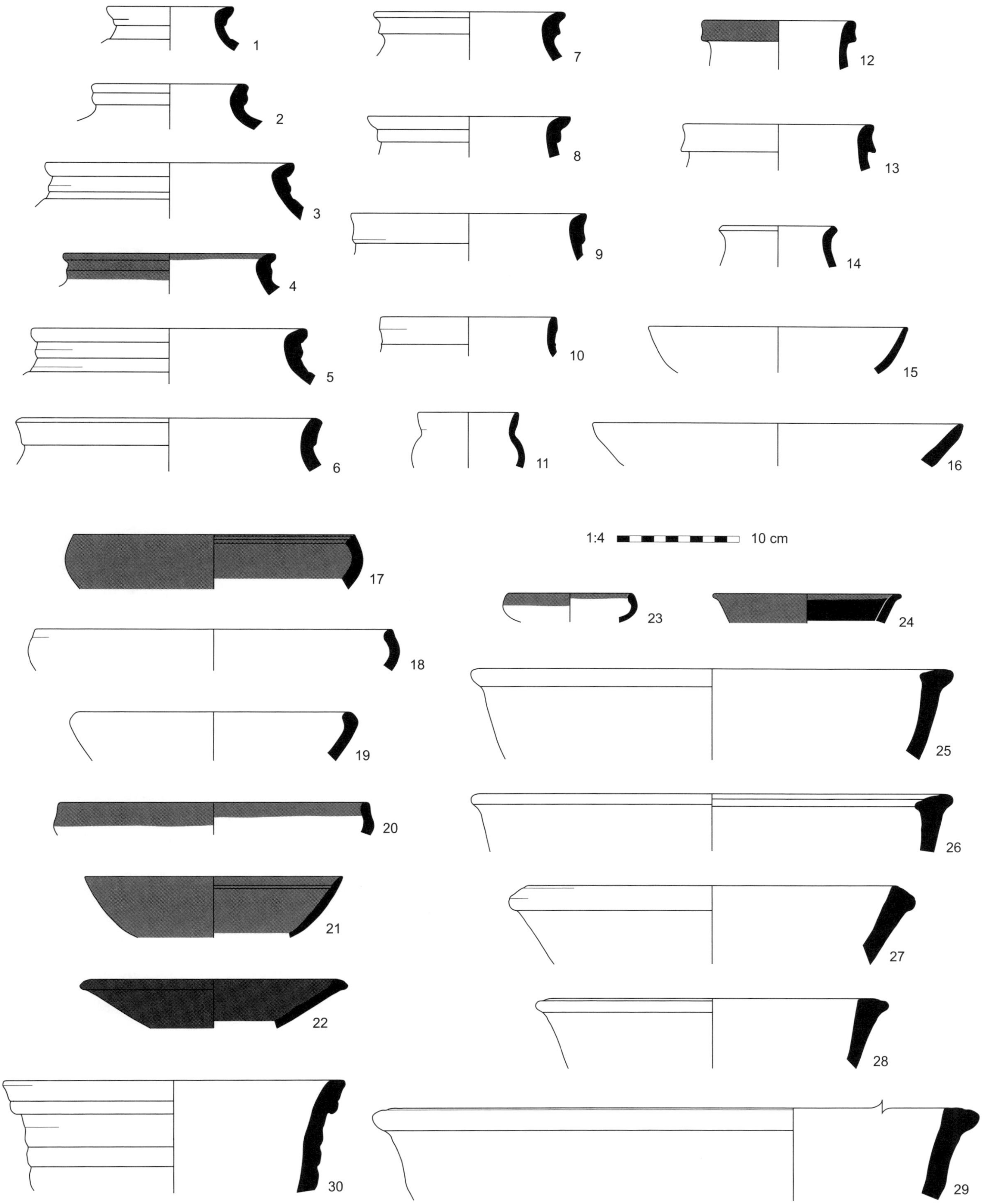

Figure C.4. Surface ceramics from THS 10

Figure C.5. Surface ceramics from THS 16

1. Pale orange smoothed surfaces, dark orange core; fine voids, no visible temper. Rim dm 19 cm. Area A. B.526.19.
2. Yellow surfaces, green core; no visible temper. Rim dm 18 cm. Area A. B.526.18.
3. Pale buff surfaces, orange core; occasional sand temper. Rim dm 17 cm. Area A. B.526.17.
4. Pale orange surfaces, orange core; frequent sand, frequent fine to medium lime temper. Rim dm 20 cm. T13/1. Area A. B.526.16.
5. Gray surfaces, black core; no visible temper. Rim dm 11 cm. Area A. B.526.11.
6. Yellow-green surfaces, green core; sand temper. Near-vitrified surfaces. Rim dm 7 cm. T6/8. Area A. B.526.10.
7. Yellow-green surfaces, green core; sand temper. Near-vitrified surfaces. Rim dm 15 cm. T6/8. Area A. B.526.9.
8. Pink exterior, red interior, dark brown core; common very fine lime temper. Red painted bands. Rim dm 11 cm. T8/1. Area A. B.526.1.
9. Light pink surfaces, orange-pink core; frequent fine lime temper. Three notched ridges. Rim dm 21 cm. T8/2. Area A. B.526.22.
10. Buff surfaces, brown core with orange margins; common fine to medium chaff, occasional sand temper. Rim dm 32 cm. T5b/12. Area A. B.526.6.
11. Yellow-buff surfaces, green core; sandy near-overfired fabric. Rim dm 23 cm. T5b/12. Area A. B.526.7.
12. Buff surfaces, thin black core with orange margins; frequent fine chaff, common fine lime temper. Rim dm 31 cm. Area A. B.526.4.
13. Orange surfaces, thick black core; frequent to abundant coarse chaff. Rim dm 33 cm. T5b/4. Area A. B.526.14.
14. Buff surfaces, gray core; common sand temper. Traces of paint on rim. Rim dm 26 cm. Area A. B.526.2.
15. Buff surfaces, pink core; occasional coarse chaff, frequent very fine lime temper. Rim dm 25 cm. Area A. B.526.21.
16. Orange surfaces, brown core; frequent fine grit and sand, occasional fine chaff temper. Rim dm 20 cm. Area A. B.526.13.
17. Orange surfaces and core with brown margins; frequent fine to medium chaff temper. Rim dm 20 cm. Area A. B.526.20.
18. Buff surfaces with faint black paint; sandy fabric. Rim dm 17 cm. Area A. B.526.12.
19. Orange lightly burnished surfaces, black core; common medium chaff temper. Rim dm 18 cm. Area A. B.526.3.
20. Buff surfaces, black core with orange margins; frequent fine to medium chaff temper. Rim dm 43 cm. Area A. B.526.5.
21. Orange surfaces and core; common to frequent medium chaff. Rim dm 32 cm. T10/10. Area A. B.526.31.
22. Yellow-green surfaces, green core; sandy near-overfired fabric. Rim dm 23 cm. Area A. B.526.8.
23. Buff surfaces and core; fine sandy fabric. Base dm 5 cm. Area A. B.526.28.
24. Buff surfaces, orange core; frequent sand and fine to medium lime temper. Rim dm 15 cm. Area A. B.526.15.
25. Yellow surfaces and core; no visible temper. Scraper edge dm 7 cm. T5b/16. Area A. B.526.30.
26. Yellow-green surfaces, pale green core; frequent fine chaff, occasional fine lime temper. Four-prong horizontal and wavy comb-incision bands. T7/4. Area A. B.526.24.
27. Buff surfaces and core; common fine chaff temper. Four-prong horizontal and wavy comb incision bands. T7/4. Area A. B.526.34.
28. Yellow to buff surfaces and core; common fine chaff temper. Nine-prong band of comb incision with diagonal punctate. T7/4. Area A. B.526.33.

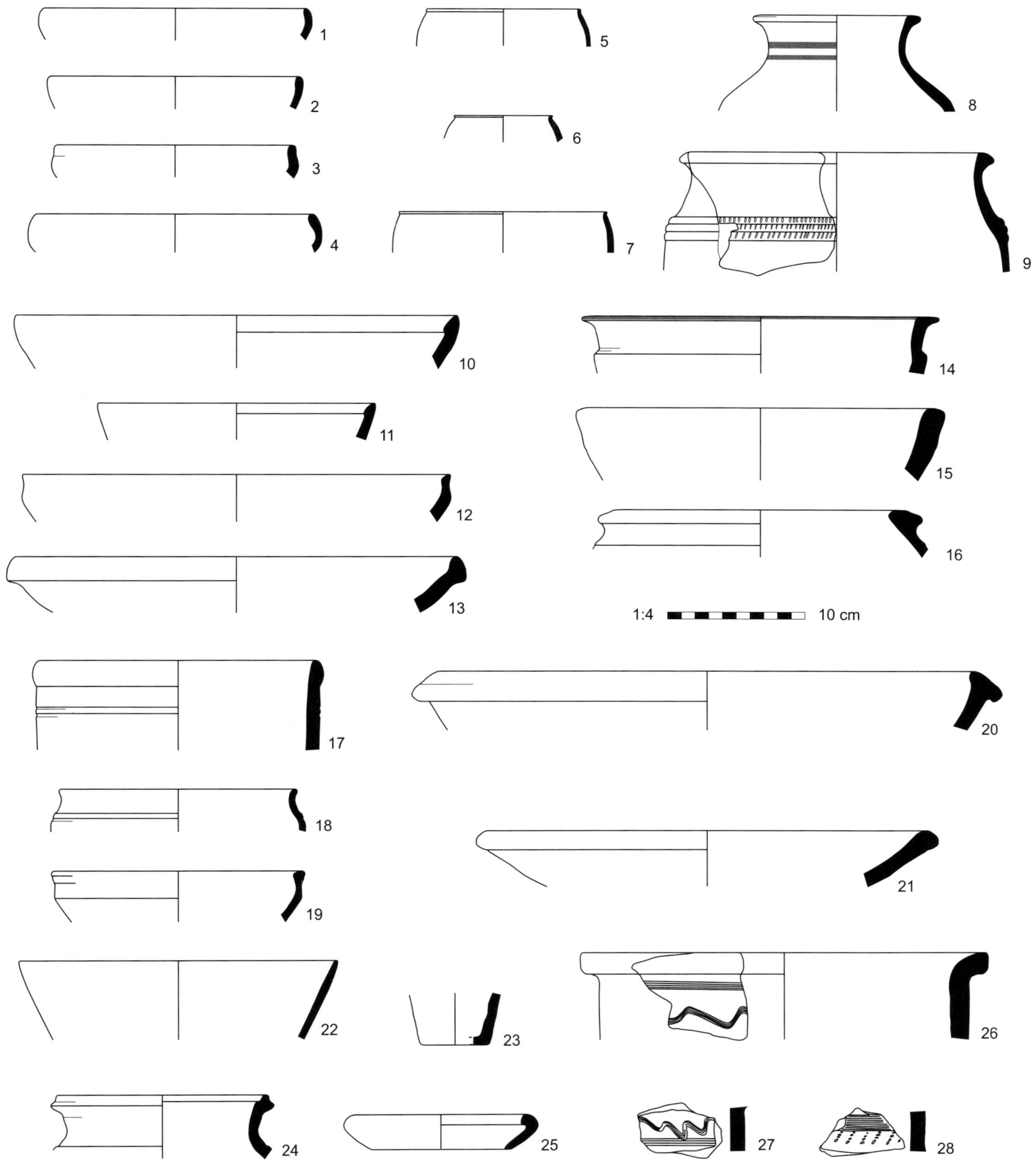

Figure C.5. Surface ceramics from THS 16

Figure C.6. Surface ceramics from THS 17

1.	Reddish buff surfaces; fine to medium chaff, common to frequent fine grit temper. Rim dm 34 cm. B.2068.3.
2.	Buff surfaces; lime and frequent medium chaff temper. Orange paint on exterior. Rim dm 24 cm. B.2068.2.
3.	Buff surfaces; fine sand temper. Dark brown painted surfaces. Rim dm 20 cm. B.2068.6.
4.	Reddish brown surfaces; common fine grit temper. Dark brown painted decoration on exterior. B.2068.5.
5.	Brown surfaces; fine dark grit temper. Black painted decoration on exterior. Rim dm 22 cm. B.2068.4.
6.	Buff surfaces; occasional fine chaff, common fine dark grit temper. Brown paint on exterior. Rim dm 18 cm. B.2068.1.

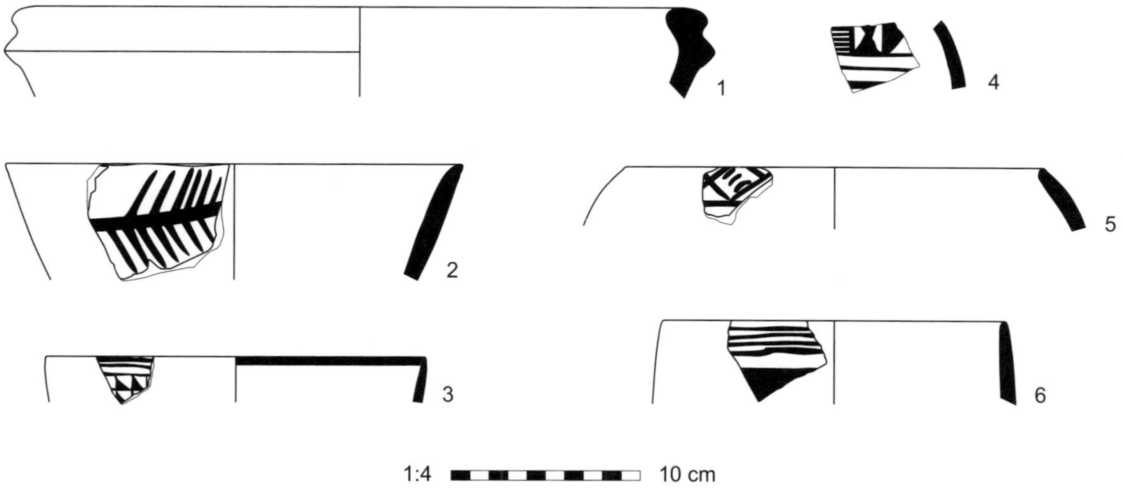

Figure C.6. Surface ceramics from THS 17

Figure C.7. Surface ceramics from the central mound of THS 24 (Areas A–F)

1. Yellow-buff slipped surfaces, pink core; common fine lime temper. Black paint on interior and exterior surfaces. Rim dm 16 cm. T2/1. Area C. B.67.1.
2. Buff exterior, reddish interior; sand temper. Red painted festoons and black bands on exterior, red horizontal band with vertical bands on interior. Rim dm ca. 15 cm. T2/1. Area A. B.66.6.
3. No description available. Rim dm ca. 30 cm. T2/1. Area D. B.115.1.
4. Yellow-green slipped surfaces and core; common to frequent medium chaff temper. Rim dm 36 cm. Area E. B.159.3.
5. Buff surfaces with red painted bands, pale orange core; occasional fine lime, rare medium chaff temper. Dm at carination 27 cm. T8/1. Area E. B.159.1.
6. Buff surfaces; common fine chaff, occasional fine to medium lime temper. Reddish brown painted bands. Rim dm 9 cm. T8/1. Area A. B.66.1.
7. Orange-buff surfaces; abundant fine chaff, occasional fine grit temper. Light brown painted bands and three horizontal grooves. Rim dm 14 cm. T8/1. Area A. B.66.2.
8. Yellow surfaces, buff core; common to frequent medium chaff temper. Finger-impressed lower edge. Rim dm 13 cm. T10/11. Area B. B.114.11.
9. Pale yellow slipped surfaces, pink-orange core; common sand temper. Rim dm 9 cm. T21/2. Area E. B.159.2.
10. Yellow-green slipped surfaces, yellow-green core; common sand and fine to medium grit temper. Rim dm 7.5 cm. T21/2. Area B. B.114.1.
11. Yellow-green slipped surfaces, yellow-green core; common sand and fine to medium grit temper. Rim dm 8 cm. T21/2. Area B. B.114.4.
12. Yellow-green slipped surfaces, yellow-green core; common sand and fine to medium grit temper. Rim dm 7 cm. T21/2. Area B. B.114.2.
13. Yellow-green slipped surfaces, yellow-green core; common sand and fine to medium grit temper. Rim dm 13 cm. Area B. B.114.3.
14. Yellow-green slipped surfaces, yellow-green core; common sand and fine to medium grit temper. Rim dm 13 cm. Area B. B.114.5.
15. Pale green exterior, buff interior; common fine chaff and medium grit temper. Rim dm ca. 14 cm. Area A. B.66.
16. Black burnished surfaces, brown core; frequent sand temper. Shallow wavy incision. Rim dm 19 cm. Area C. B.67.
17. Olive green surfaces and core; occasional fine to medium lime temper. Overfired. Rim dm 15 cm. Area C. B.67.
18. Gray surfaces, brown core; common to frequent sand; hard fired. Rim dm 23 cm. Area B. B.114.6.
19. Pale yellow smoothed surfaces, buff core; occasional fine sand temper. Rim dm 21 cm. Area C. B.67.
20. No description available. Rim dm 17 cm. Area D. B.115.
21. Dark green glazed surfaces, red-orange fabric. Rare to occasional sand temper. Rim dm 11 cm. T19/1. Area B. B.114.8.
22. Dark green glazed surfaces, red-orange fabric. Rare sand temper. Rim dm 11 cm. T19/1. Area B. B.114.7.
23. Yellow-green slipped surfaces, yellow-green core; common sand and fine to medium grit temper. Base dm 9 cm. T17/4. Area B. B.114.9.
24. Yellow-green slipped surfaces, yellow-green core; common sand and fine to medium grit temper. Base dm 16 cm. T17/4. Area B. B.114.10.
25. No description available. Impressed notches on rim; shallow wavy groove below rim. Rim dm 12 cm. Area D. B.115.
26. No description available. Rim dm 8 cm. Area D. B.115.

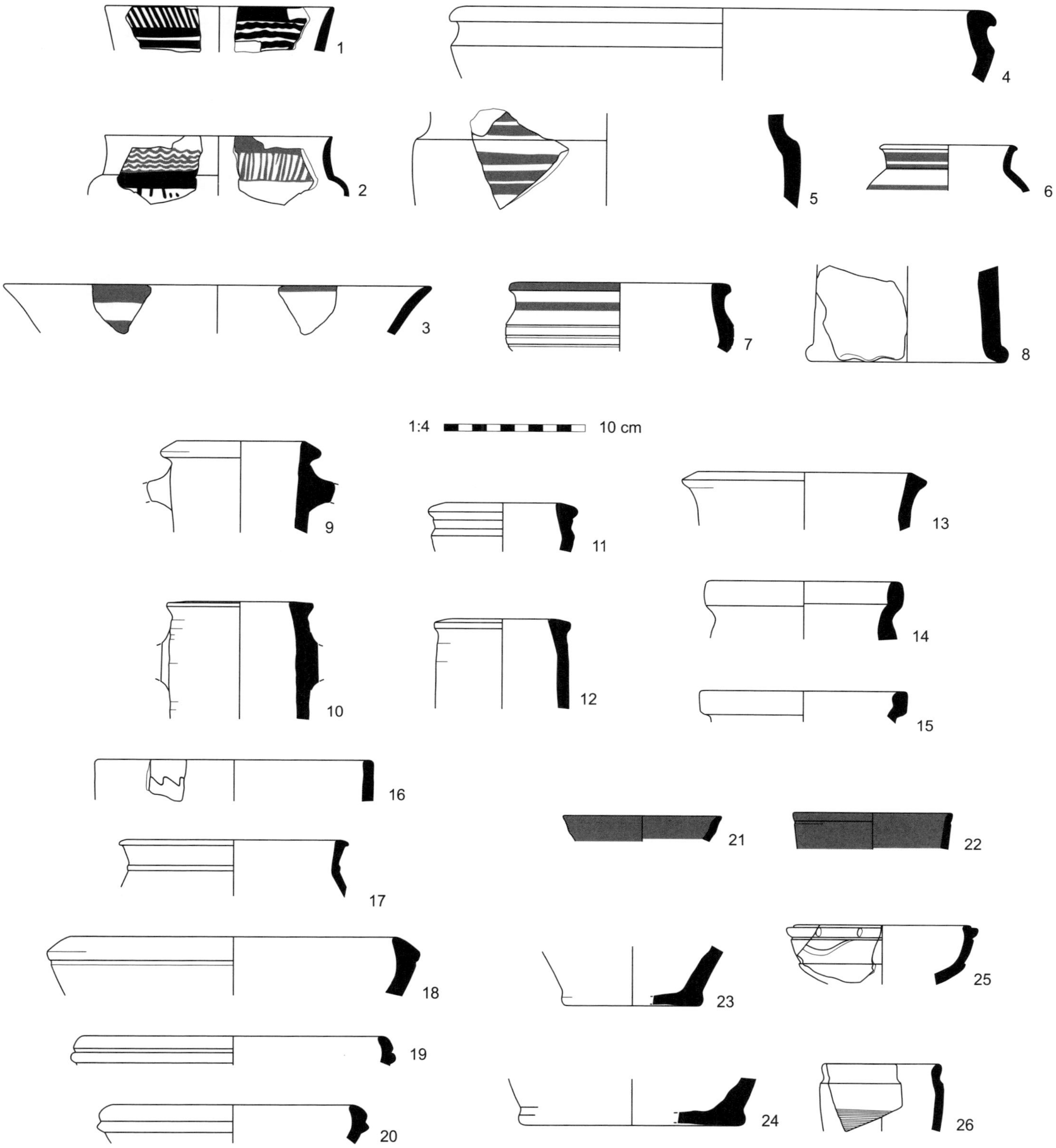

Figure C.7.Surface ceramics from the central mound of THS 24 (Areas A–F)

Figure C.8. Surface ceramics from the southeastern edge of THS 24 (Area G)

1. Yellow-green surfaces and core; frequent medium to coarse chaff temper. Rim dm 60 cm. T10/12. B.160.2.
2. Yellow surfaces, yellow-green core; frequent medium chaff temper. Rim dm 46 cm. T10/12. B.160.3.
3. Buff surfaces, brown core; common medium chaff, occasional fine lime temper. Rim dm 32 cm. T10/12. B.160.4.
4. Orange-brown surfaces, brown core; common fine to medium chaff temper. Rim dm 23 cm. T10/12. B.160.8.
5. Yellow surfaces and core; common to frequent medium chaff temper. Rim dm 29 cm. T10/12. B.160.14.
6. Pale yellow exterior, orange interior and core; occasional fine chaff and sand temper. Rim dm 20 cm. T10/6. B.160.21.
7. Buff surfaces and core; frequent to abundant medium chaff. Rim dm 21 cm. T10/6. B.160.6.
8. Orange surfaces, brown core; common medium chaff temper. Base dm 13 cm. T8/6. B.160.15.
9. Yellow-green surfaces and core; frequent medium to coarse chaff temper. Rim dm 41 cm. T10/15. B.160.19.
10. Pale yellow slipped surfaces, orange core; common fine to medium chaff temper. Rim dm 38 cm. B.160.16.
11. Yellow-green surfaces, green core; occasional medium chaff, common sand temper. Raised band of grooves. Rim dm 21 cm. T10/15. B.160.10.
12. Orange surfaces, brown core; common fine to medium chaff, occasional sand temper. Rim dm 22 cm. B.160.12.
13. Orange surfaces and core; frequent medium chaff temper. Base dm 14 cm. T10/11. B.160.13.
14. Buff slipped surfaces with red painted bands, orange core; occasional to common medium to fine chaff, occasional fine lime temper. Rim dm 17 cm. T8/1. B.160.16.
15. Pale yellow surfaces, orange-buff core; common medium chaff, occasional sand temper. Rim dm 26 cm. T10/13. B.160.5.
16. Red-orange surfaces and core; common medium chaff, rare fine dark grit temper. Rim dm 25 cm. T10/13. B.160.9.

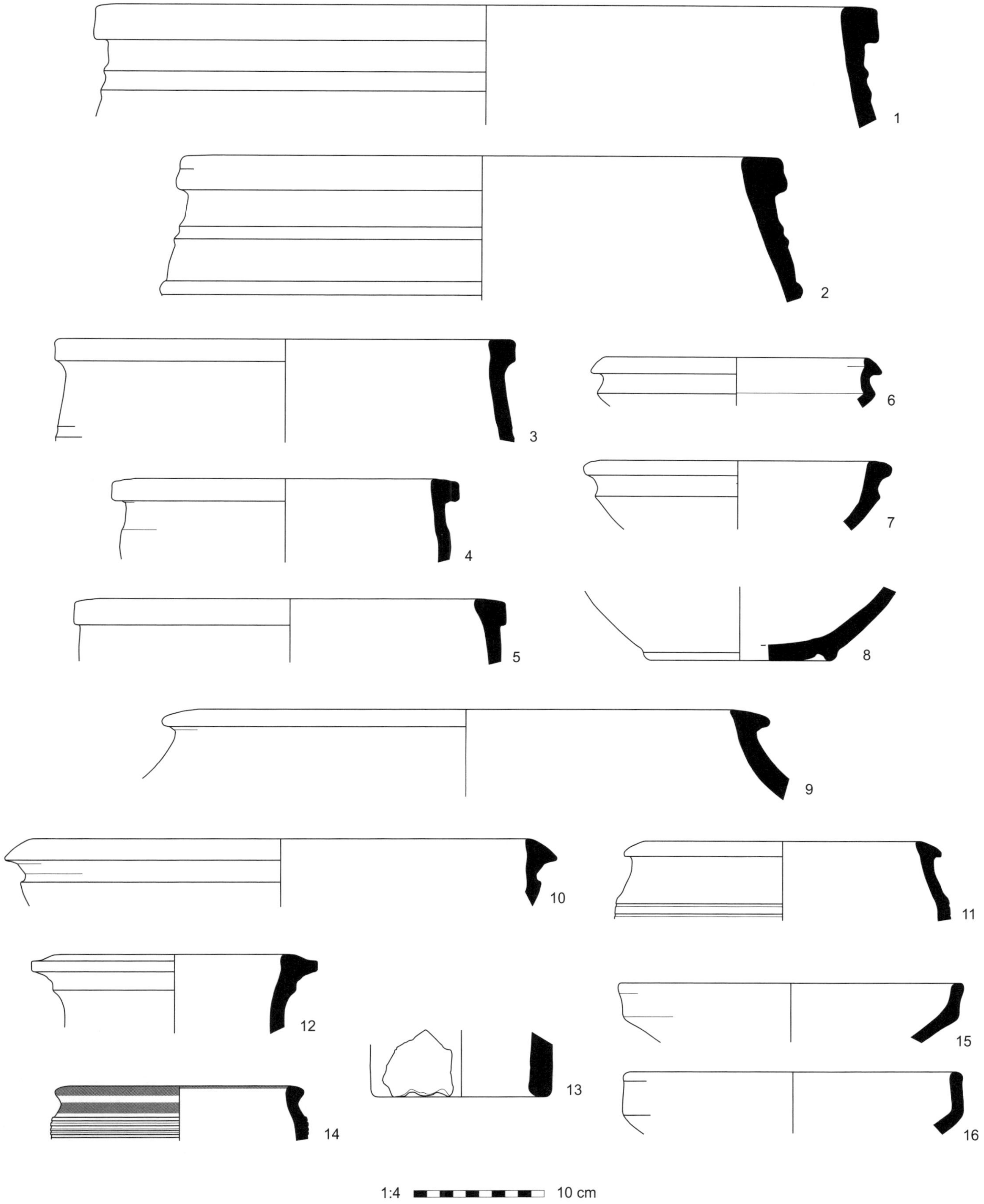

Figure C.8. Surface ceramics from the southeastern edge of THS 24 (Area G)

Figure C.9. Surface ceramics from the southwestern lower town at THS 24 (Areas H–Q)

1. Buff slipped surfaces, orange core; no visible temper. Dark red paint. Rim dm 8 cm. T2/1. Area L. B.187.4.
2. Buff surfaces with red-brown paint; rare sand temper, dense fabric. Smoothed interior. T1/1. Area J. B.141.4.
3. Orange surfaces, thick black core; frequent medium to coarse chaff temper. Rim dm 15 cm. Area L. B.187.
4. Buff surfaces with red-brown paint, smoothed interior; rare sand, dense fabric. Buff surfaces, orange core; common to frequent medium chaff temper. Rim dm 21 cm. Area J. B.141.1.
5. Pale yellow surfaces; common to frequent medium chaff and rare fine lime temper. Rim dm 16 cm. T10/6. Area H. B.161.4.
6. Pale yellow-green (slipped?) surfaces, buff core; frequent medium chaff, occasional sand temper. Rim dm 23 cm. Area H. B.161.3.
7. Buff surfaces, orange-brown core; frequent fine to medium chaff temper. Rim dm 32 cm. T10/10. Area L. B.187.
8. Buff surfaces with dark red to black paint, orange-brown core; common chaff temper. Rim dm 18 cm. T8/1. Area H. B.161.2.
9. Yellow-buff surfaces, buff core; common medium chaff temper. Raised band of grooves and dark red painted bands. Rim dm 20 cm. T8/2. Area J. B.141.5.
10. Yellow-green surfaces and core; common to frequent medium chaff. Rim dm 13 cm. T10/5. Area H. B.161.1.
11. Pale yellow-green surfaces, gray-green core; frequent medium chaff temper. Rim dm 13 cm. T10/5. Area N. B.142.4.
12. Buff surfaces, orange core; common fine to medium chaff, rare fine lime temper. Base dm 18 cm. T8/6. Area H. B.161.5.
13. Orange surfaces, brown core; abundant medium to coarse chaff. Handmade and uneven. Rim dm ca. 34 cm. T3/5. Area J. B.141.2.
14. Pale yellow surfaces, yellow-green core; sandy fabric. Rim dm 15 cm. Area Q. B.143.6.
15. Buff surfaces with red to black paint; brown core; common sand, occasional medium lime temper. Rim dm 13 cm. T13/1. Area Q. B.143.1.
16. Orange surfaces, orange-brown core; common to frequent sand, common dark grit temper. Rim dm 12 cm. T13/11. Area L. B.187.
17. Buff exterior, orange interior, brown core; common to frequent sand temper. Rim dm 16 cm. Area Q. B.143.3.
18. Orange-buff surfaces, orange core; occasional medium chaff and fine lime temper. Rim dm 15 cm. T13/13. Area J. B.141.3.
19. Orange surfaces with red paint, orange-brown core; frequent sand temper. Rim dm 12 cm. T13/2. Area Q. B.143.
20. Buff surfaces and core; frequent sand and fine lime temper. Rim dm 17 cm. T13/2. Area Q. B.143.
21. Yellow slipped surfaces and core; occasional sand, occasional fine lime temper, fine fabric. Rim dm 11 cm. T14/2. Area L. B.187.
22. Orange surfaces, brown core; common fine to medium dark grit. Row of triangular impressed wedges beneath rim. Rim dm 27 cm. T13/7. Area Q. B.143.5.
23. Orange surfaces, brown core; common fine to medium dark grit. Row of triangular impressed wedges beneath rim. Rim dm 21 cm. T13/7. Area Q. B.143.4.
24. Pale orange surfaces, orange-brown core; common sand, fine fabric. Rim dm 18 cm. T14/6. Area N. B.142.1.
25. Orange surfaces, red-orange core; frequent sand and fine lime temper. Rim dm 16 cm. T14/6. Area N. B142.3.
26. Yellow surfaces; common medium chaff and fine grit temper. Wavy and horizontal bands of comb incision. Rim dm 13 cm. B.502.1. T14/6. Area P. B.502.1.
27. Buff surfaces with red to black paint; brown core; common sand, occasional medium lime temper. Rim dm 26 cm. T13/3. Area Q. B.143.2.

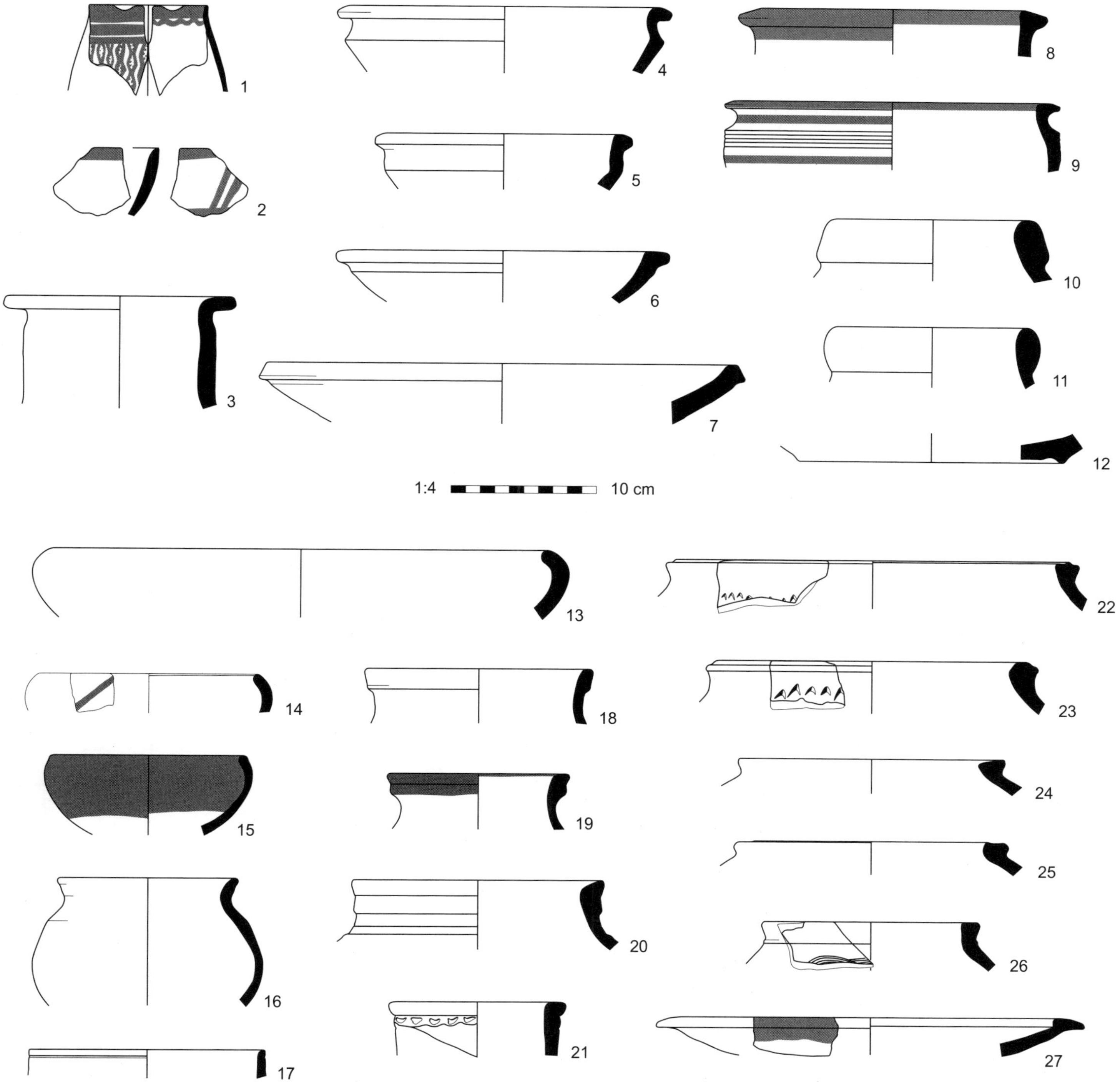

Figure C.9. Surface ceramics from the southwestern lower town at THS 24 (Areas H–Q)

Figure C.10. Surface ceramics from the northeastern lower town at THS 24 (Areas R–V)

1. Buff exterior, pink interior and core; frequent to abundant sand and fine lime temper. Rim dm 20 cm. T15/2. Area V. B.190.6.
2. Sooted buff surfaces, orange-brown core; frequent sand and fine lime temper. Rim dm 22 cm. Area V. B.190.9.
3. Orange-brown surfaces, red-brown core; frequent sand and fine lime temper. Rim dm 20 cm. Area V. B.190.10.
4. Orange-brown surfaces and core; common sand, occasional coarse lime temper. Rim dm 19 cm. T15/2. Area V. B.190.16.
5. Orange-brown surfaces and core; common sand, occasional coarse lime temper. Rim dm 19 cm. T15/2. Area V. B.190.11.
6. Buff surfaces; common fine sand temper. Rim dm 17 cm. T16/1. Area S. B.144.4.
7. Buff smoothed surfaces, buff core; common sand temper. Rim dm 20 cm. Area V. B.190.14.
8. No description available. Rim dm 18 cm. Area V. B.190.15.
9. Yellow surfaces, buff core; frequent sand temper. Rim dm 14 cm. T16/1. Area V. B.190.2.
10. Buff surfaces; occasional fine chaff, common fine grit temper. Rim dm 18 cm. T16/1. Area S. B.144.
11. Buff surfaces, orange-brown core; common sand temper, hard fired. Rim dm 20 cm. T16/1. Area V. B.190.1.
12. Yellow-green surfaces and core; common sand temper. Rim dm 20 cm. T16/1. Area R. B.189.3.
13. Orange-brown surfaces, red-brown core; frequent sand and fine lime temper. Rim dm 11 cm. T16/1. Area V. B.190.5.
14. Orange-brown surfaces, red-brown core; frequent sand temper. Rim dm 13 cm. T16/1. Area V. B.190.4.
15. Pale yellow surfaces, buff core; common to frequent sand temper, hard fired. Rim dm 13 cm. T16/1. Area V. B.190.3.
16. Buff surfaces, orange-brown core; frequent sand temper. Rim dm 18 cm. T15/1. Area V. B.190.7.
17. Yellow surfaces and core; frequent sand temper. Rim dm 23 cm. T15/1. Area V. B.190.8.
18. Buff surfaces, red-brown core; common sand temper. Comb-incised decoration. Rim dm 23 cm. T15/1. Area V. B.190.13.
19. Pale yellow-green surfaces, green core; frequent medium chaff. Rim dm 10 cm. Area V. B.190.12.
20. Red-brown exterior, buff interior; abundant grit temper. Two broad longitudinal grooves on handle exterior. T16/2. Area V. B.190.29.
21. Red surfaces; abundant medium grit temper. Broad shallow longitudinal groove. T16/2. Area V. B.190.28.
22. Pale yellow-green surfaces and core; common sand temper. Neck dm 18 cm. T16/3. Area V. B.190.
23. Green surfaces, buff core; abundant grit temper. Area V. B.190.27.
24. Buff surfaces; abundant grit temper. T16/3. Area V. B.190.24.
25. Buff surfaces; abundant grit temper. Broad longitudinal groove on handle exterior. T16/3. Area V. B.190.25.
26. Pale yellow-green slipped surfaces, pink-orange core; common medium chaff temper. Possibly a Late Bronze Age potstand. Rim dm 29 cm. Area R. B.189.2.
27. Buff surfaces, orange-brown core; common medium chaff temper. Possibly a Late Bronze Age potstand. Rim dm 25 cm. Area R. B.189.1.
28. Pale orange surfaces, brown core with pink margins; common fine to medium chaff and fine lime temper. Rim dm 30 cm. T10/13. Area R. B.189.7.
29. Red-buff surfaces, buff core; abundant medium to coarse chaff, occasional grit temper. Rim dm 30 cm. T10/13. Area S. B.144.5.
30. Red-buff surfaces; occasional fine chaff, common fine to medium grit temper. Impressed wedges. Rim dm 11 cm. T13/7. Area S. B.144.2.
31. Yellow-green surfaces and core; common sand temper. Rim dm 17 cm. Area R. B.189.5.
32. Pale yellow surfaces, buff core; common to frequent medium chaff, rare medium lime temper. Rim dm 24 cm. T10/14. Area R. B.189.4.
33. Orange surfaces, orange-brown core; frequent medium chaff temper. Base dm 7 cm. T10/9. Area R. B.189.11.
34. Pale yellow surfaces, exterior lightly burnished, buff core; rare chaff temper, fine fabric. Base dm 2.2 cm. T10/3. Area R. B.189.10.
35. Pale orange surfaces and core; common medium chaff and fine lime temper. Rim dm 36 cm. T10/10. Area R. B.189.8.
36. Pale orange surfaces and core; common medium chaff and fine lime temper. Rim dm 38 cm. T10/10. Area R. B.189.9.
37. Buff surfaces and core; common medium to coarse chaff, occasional fine to medium lime temper. Rim dm 36 cm. T10/10. Area S. B.144.1.

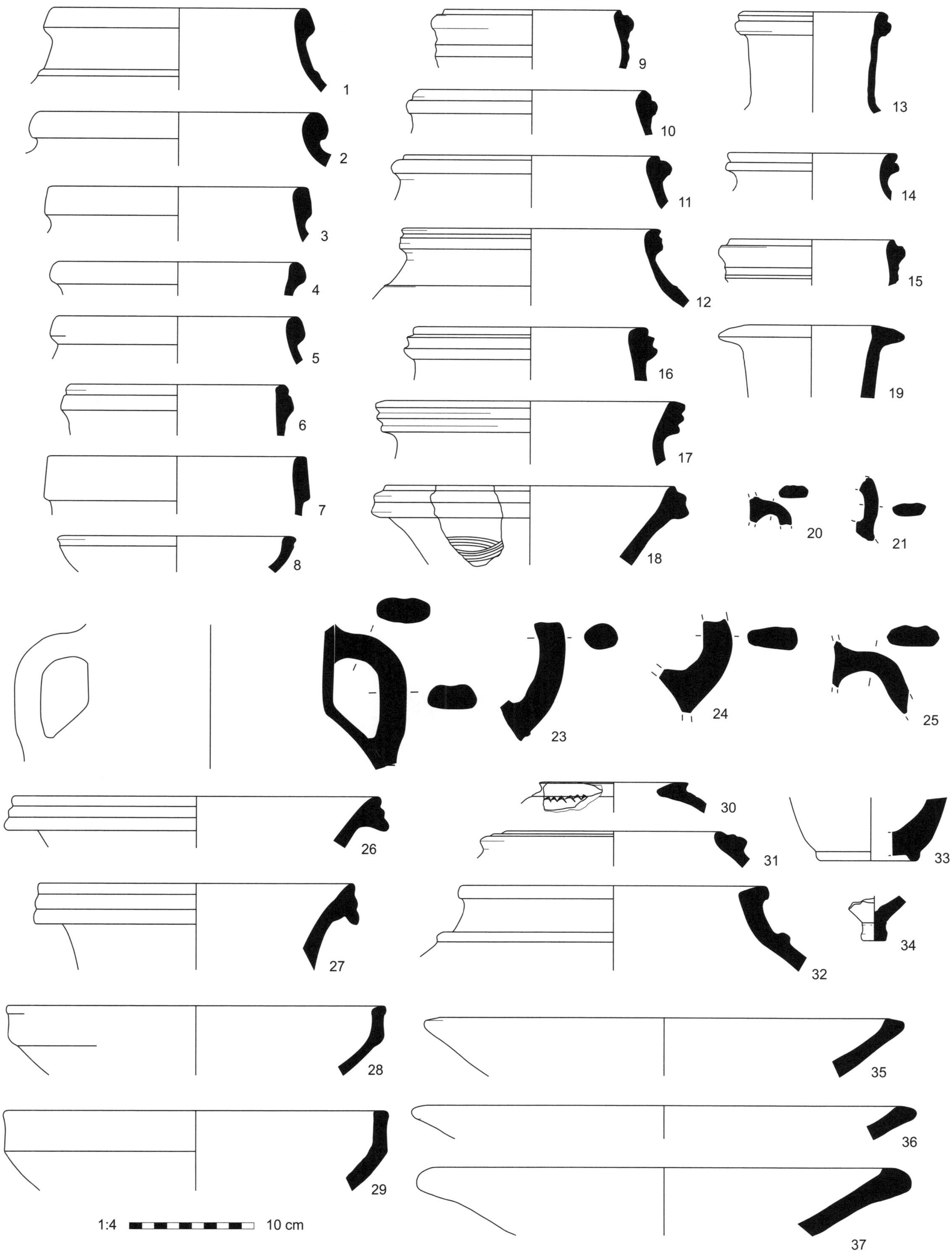

Figure C.10. Surface ceramics from the northeastern lower town at THS 24 (Areas R–V)

Figure C.11. Surface ceramics from THS 27

1. Pale orange surfaces, dark brown core; frequent sand and fine dark grit temper. Rim dm 21 cm. T12/5. B.1103.8.
2. Buff exterior, orange interior and core; frequent sand temper. Notched ridge. Rim dm 20 cm. B.1103.1.
3. Orange surfaces, orange-brown core; frequent sand temper. Rim dm 29 cm. T12/5. B.1103.5.
4. Pale yellow surfaces and core; common medium chaff temper. Rim dm 12 cm. T11/1. B.1103.7.
5. Buff surfaces, yellow-green core; common to frequent medium chaff temper. Base dm at carination 2.0 cm. T11/3. B.1102.4.
6. Buff surfaces, orange core; frequent to abundant sand, rare coarse lime temper. Rim dm 10 cm. B.1102.1.
7. Buff surfaces, orange core; frequent to abundant sand, rare coarse lime temper. Rim dm 12 cm. B.1102.2.
8. Buff smoothed surfaces, orange core; frequent to abundant sand, rare coarse lime temper. Rim dm 11 cm. B.1102.3.
9. Buff surfaces, orange core; frequent medium chaff, occasional fine lime temper. Rim dm 13 cm. B.1103.3.
10. Pale orange surfaces, black core with orange margins; common to frequent medium chaff. Rim dm 12 cm. B.1103.4.
11. Pale orange surfaces, brown core; frequent sand and fine lime temper. Rim dm 14 cm. T12/1. B.1103.2.

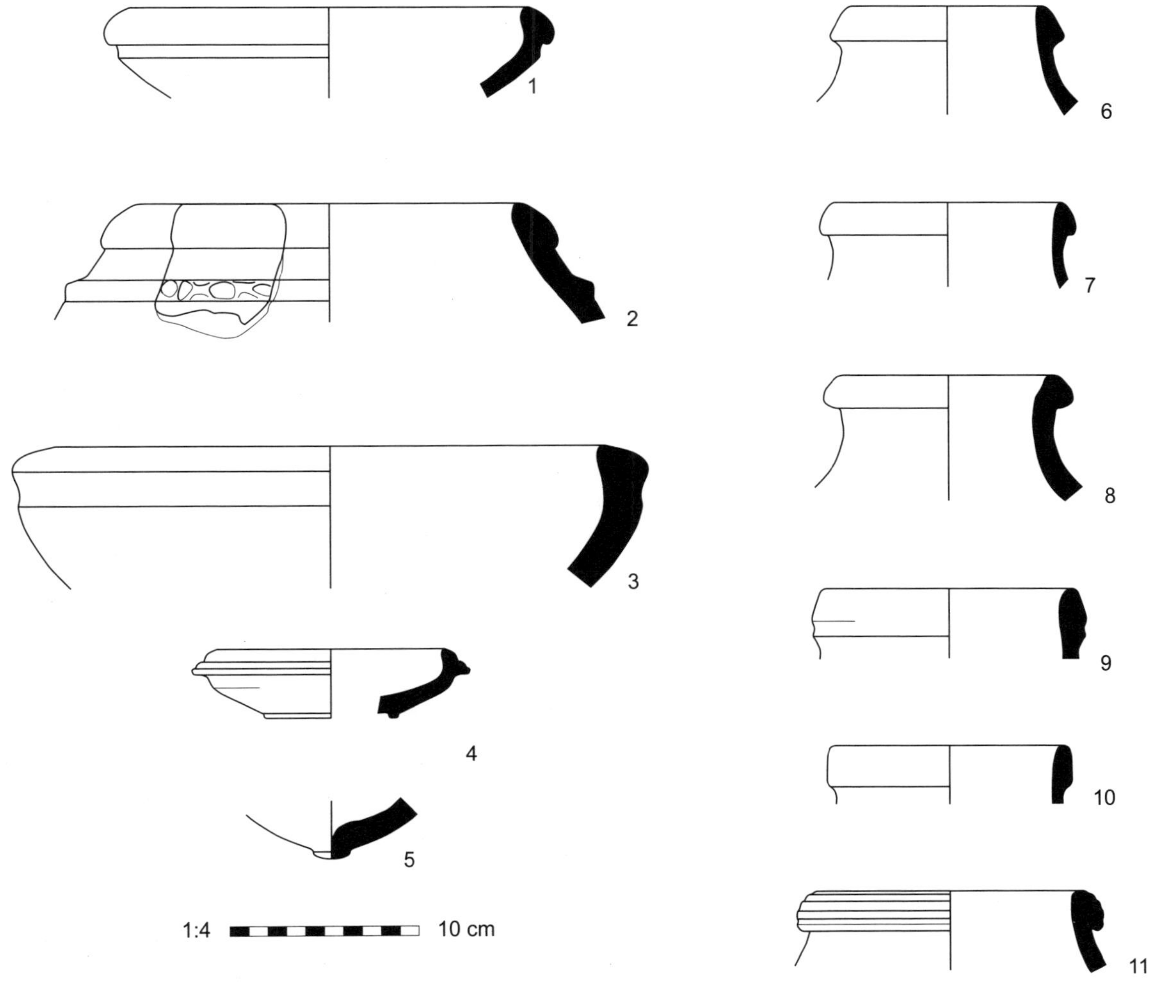

Figure C.11. Surface ceramics from THS 27

Figure C.12. Surface ceramics from THS 29

1. Orange surfaces, brown core; common medium to coarse chaff, occasional fine lime temper. Uneven. Rim dm 28 cm. B.1121.7
2. Yellow surfaces, yellow-green core; frequent medium chaff, occasional medium lime. Handmade. Rim dm 20 cm. B.1121.8.
3. Green surfaces and core; common coarse chaff temper. Rim dm 8 cm. B.1121.25.
4. Buff surfaces, black core; common medium to coarse chaff temper. Rim dm 17 cm. T3/3. B.1121.6.
5. Buff surfaces, brown core; occasional fine lime temper in dense hard fabric. Rim dm 17 cm. T3/3. B.1121.5.
6. Yellow surfaces and core; occasional medium chaff and fine to coarse lime temper. Rim dm 19 cm. T3/5. B.1121.12.
7. Buff surfaces and core; common to frequent medium to coarse chaff, rare occasional fine lime temper. Rim dm 16 cm. T3/5. B.1121.13.
8. Orange exterior, buff interior and core; occasional fine chaff, dense handmade fabric. Rim dm 31 cm. B.1121.10.
9. Orange surfaces with black painted rim, black core with orange margins; frequent medium chaff. Handmade. Rim dm 26 cm. B.1121.9.
10. Yellow-buff surfaces, orange core; occasional coarse chaff, occasional medium to coarse grit temper. Handmade. Rim dm 26 cm. B.1121.11.
11. Buff surfaces, green core; rare fine chaff, rare medium lime temper. Rim dm 12 cm. B.1121.14.
12. Yellow surfaces, buff core; common fine to medium chaff. Handmade and uneven. Rim dm 8 cm. B.1121.1.
13. Yellow surfaces and core; frequent to abundant medium chaff, occasional fine to medium lime temper. Handmade and uneven. Rim dm 18 cm. B.1121.2.
14. Buff surfaces with black paint, buff core; dense fabric with rare fine lime temper. Rim dm 16 cm. B.1121.4.
15. Buff surfaces with black paint, buff core; dense fabric with rare fine lime temper. Rim dm 20 cm. B.1121.3.
16. Buff surfaces; common fine to medium lime temper. Dark brown paint on exterior surface. T3/1. B.1121.22.
17. Orange-buff surfaces, brown core; occasional sand temper. Dark paint on exterior. T3/1. B.1121.23.
18. Buff surfaces, buff core; occasional fine to medium lime temper. Dark brown to black paint on exterior. T3/1. B.1121.24.
19. Yellow slipped surfaces, orange core; occasional sand temper, fine fabric. Dark brown-red paint on exterior and interior rim. Rim dm 16 cm. T3/1. B.1121.18.
20. Orange surfaces; common fine lime temper. Dark paint on exterior and interior rim. Rim dm 18 cm. T3/1. B.1121.16.
21. Orange-buff surfaces, orange core; occasional fine lime, rare medium chaff temper. Dark brown to red paint on interior and top of rim. Rim dm 15 cm. T3/1. B.1121.21.
22. Yellow slipped surfaces, orange core; occasional sand temper, fine fabric. Dark brown to red paint on interior and exterior. Rim dm 27 cm. T3/1. B.1121.19.
23. Buff surfaces with dark brown-black paint, orange core; occasional fine chaff and fine lime. Rim dm 25 cm. T3/1. B.1121.17.
24. Yellow surfaces, yelow-green core; common medium chaff and fine lime temper. Dark paint on exterior and interior rims. Rim dm 19 cm. T3/1. B.1121.15.

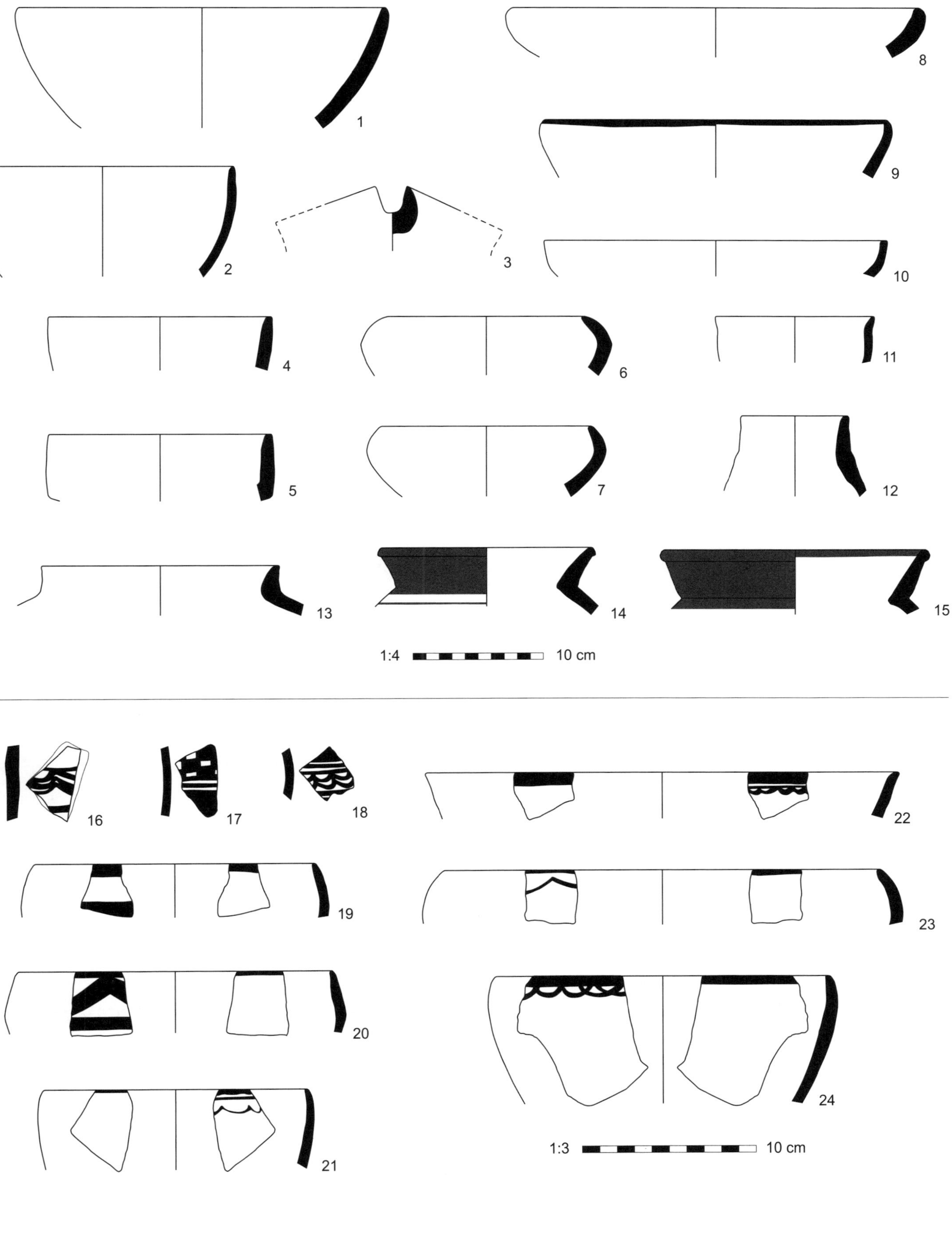

Figure C.12. Surface ceramics from THS 29

Figure C.13. Surface ceramics from THS 31

1. Orange exterior, yellow interior, thick black core; frequent to abundant fine to medium chaff, common sand temper. Rim dm ca. 33 cm. T4/9. B.165.3.
2. Orange exterior, gray interior, thick black core; frequent medium chaff, common fine lime temper. Rim dm 26 cm. T4/9. B.165.4
3. Pale yellow-green surfaces, gray-green core; common fine to medium chaff, common sand temper. Rim dm 22 cm. T4/9. B.165.2.
4. Pale yellow surfaces, yellow-green core; frequent medium to coarse chaff temper. Rim dm 25 cm. T4/9. B.165.1.
5. Yellow exterior, pale orange interior, brown core; common to frequent fine to medium chaff, occasional sand temper. Rim dm 19 cm. T4/9. B.165.5.
6. Lightly burnished gray exterior, gray interior, black core; common to frequent fine to medium chaff and fine lime temper. Rim dm 15 cm. T4/2. B.165.6.
7. Pale orange smoothed surfaces, thick black core; common to frequent medium chaff and sand. Rim dm 29 cm. B.165.7.

Figure C.14. Surface ceramics from THS 33

1. Buff-brown surfaces; frequent sand temper. T5b/7. B.2065.6.
2. Orange-buff surfaces, red-orange core; rare sand temper. T5b/7. B.2065.5.
3. Orange-buff surfaces; common very fine dark grit and lime temper. Dark brown painted decoration on exterior surface. T4/3. B.2065.1.
4. Buff-brown surfaces, black core; frequent medium chaff, occasional fine to medium lime temper. Rim dm 34 cm. T5b/3. B.2065.12.
5. Buff-green surfaces; common fine chaff temper. Rim dm 34 cm. T5b/3. B.2065.7.
6. Buff surfaces, dark gray core; frequent medium chaff temper. Rim dm 20 cm. T5b/2. B.2065.2.
7. Buff surfaces, pale green core; frequent fine sand temper. Rim dm 13 cm. T10/5. B.2065.9.

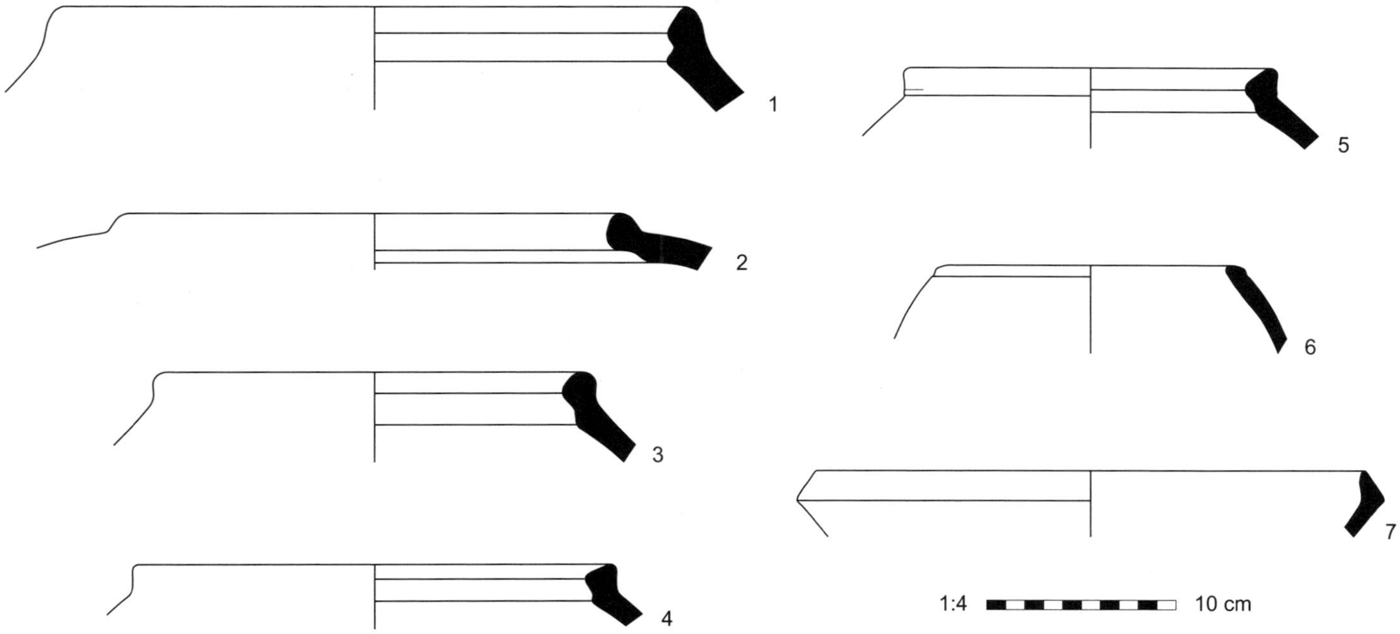

Figure C.13. Surface ceramics from THS 31

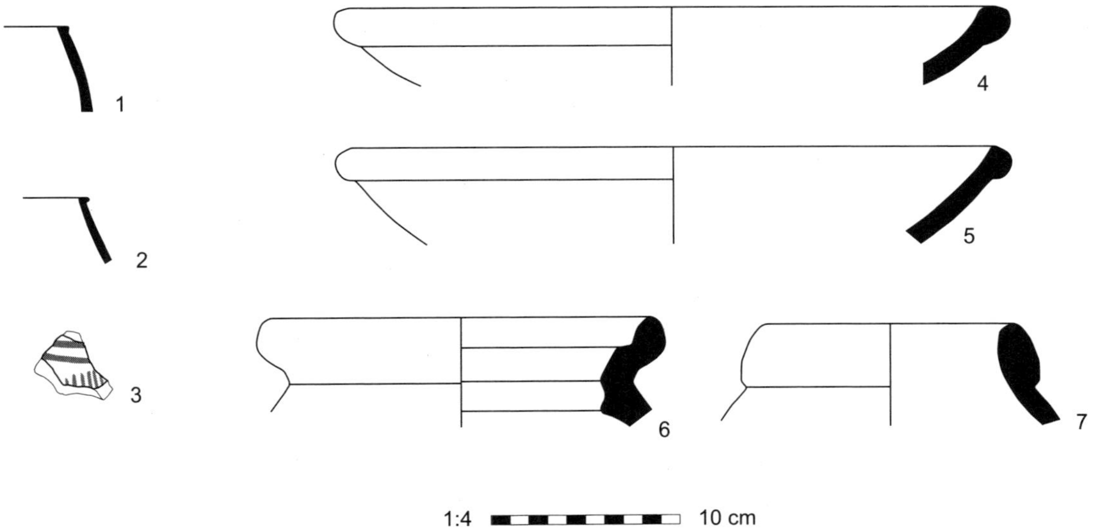

Figure C.14. Surface ceramics from THS 33

Figure C.15. Surface ceramics from the central mound at THS 37 (Area A)

1. Green exterior, buff interior; common fine grit and chaff temper. Rim dm 48 cm. B.1106.9.
2. Buff surface, reddish buff core; common fine grit temper. Rim dm 45 cm. B.1106.13.
3. Buff surfaces, orange core; common medium chaff, rare fine grit temper. Rim dm 36 cm. B.1106.5.
4. Green surfaces, brown core; frequent fine chaff and fine grit temper. Rim dm 35 cm. B.1106.7.
5. Green surfaces and core; frequent fine chaff temper. Rim dm 39 cm. B.1106.8.
6. Green surfaces; abundant fine to medium chaff, rare grit temper. Rim dm 15 cm. B.1106.4.
7. Gray burnished surfaces; chaff and common fine grit temper. Rim dm 16 cm. T8/4. B.1106.25.
8. Buff surfaces; frequent fine to medium chaff, occasional lime temper. Dark brown painted bands. Rim dm 14 cm. T8/1. B.1106.18.
9. Orange-buff surfaces; frequent fine grit temper. Red-brown painted bands. Rim dm 24 cm. T8/1. B.1106.19.
10. Green surfaces; occasional medium chaff, frequent sand temper. Rim dm 25 cm. B.1106.11.
11. Buff surfaces, brown core; common fine grit, frequent medium chaff temper. Rim dm 57 cm. B.1106.14.
12. Buff surfaces; abundant medium chaff, occasional medium grit temper. Rim dm 56 cm. T7/4. B.1106.23.
13. Green to buff surfaces; frequent fine chaff, common medium to coarse grit temper. Four-prong horizontal and wavy comb-incision bands. Rim dm 40 cm. T7/4. B.1106.22.
14. Green exterior, buff interior, brown core; frequent chaff, occasional medium grit. Comb-incised bands and diagonal punctate decoration. T7/4. B.1106.1.
15. Buff surfaces, brown core; common fine chaff and fine grit temper. Six-prong horizontal and wavy comb-incision bands. T7/4. B.1106.24.
16. Green surfaces; frequent fine chaff, common medium to coarse grit temper. Bands of comb incisions. T7/4. B.1106.21.
17. Buff surfaces; abundant medium chaff temper. Comb-incised bands and impressed circles. T7/4. B.1106.20.
18. Orange-buff surfaces and core; occasional fine grit and common fine chaff temper. Base dm 5.5 cm. B.1106.15.
19. Buff surfaces and core; rare grit, common medium chaff temper. Base dm 4.5 cm. B.1106.17.
20. Buff surfaces; fine sand and rare fine chaff temper. Wheel striations on exterior. Base dm 6 cm. T7/2. B.1106.16.
21. Brown surfaces; common fine lime, occasional fine chaff temper. Rim dm 12 cm. B.1106.12.
22. Green surfaces; frequent medium chaff, common fine grit temper. Rim dm 19 cm. B.1106.10.

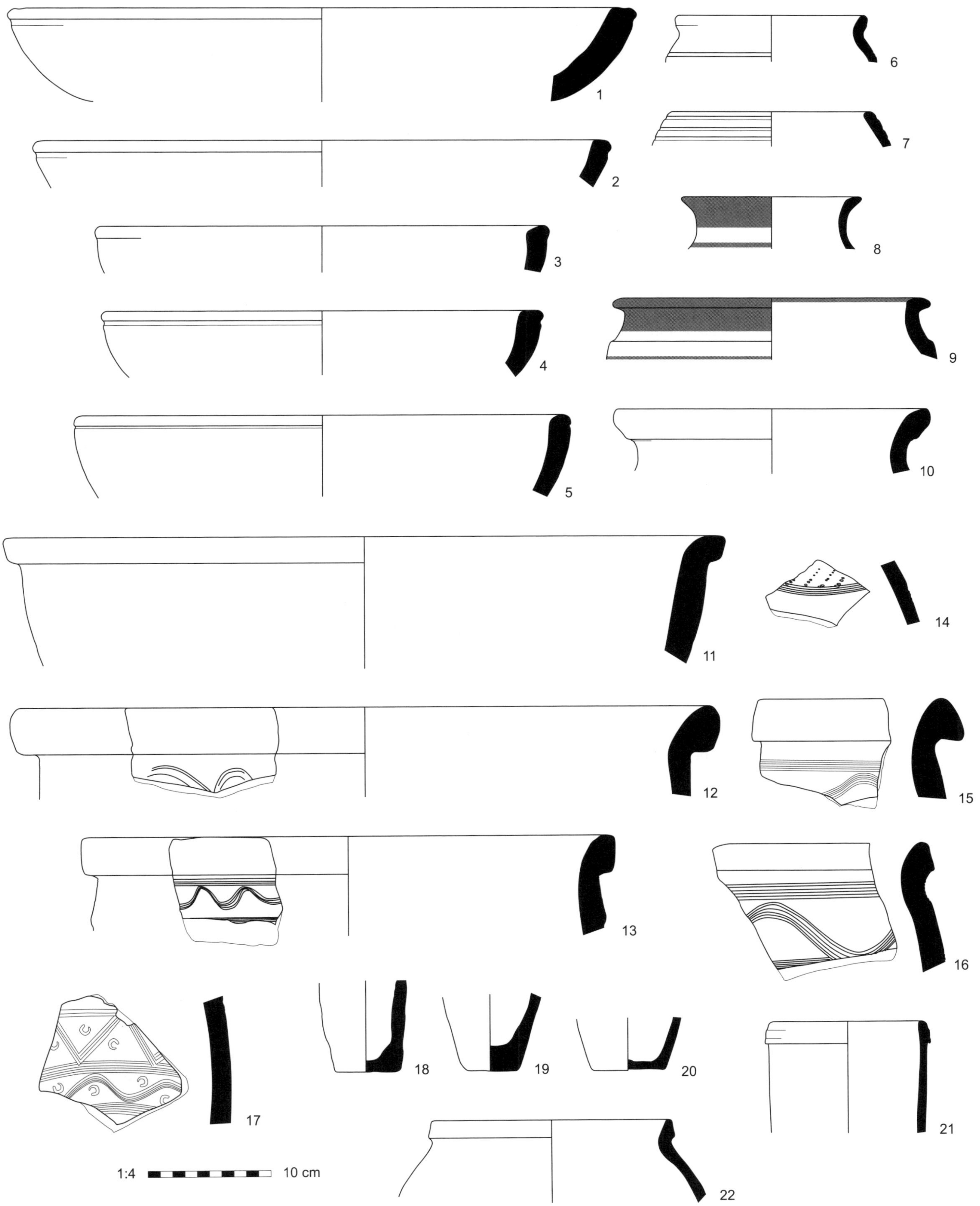

Figure C.15. Surface ceramics from the central mound at THS 37 (Area A)

Figure C.16. Surface ceramics from THS 40: grit-tempered closed forms

1. Orange surfaces and core; frequent sand and fine to medium dark grit temper. Rim dm 16 cm. Area H. B.1094.9.
2. Orange-red surfaces, brown core; frequent sand and fine dark grit temper. Rim dm 20 cm. Area A. B.2052.21.
3. Buff (slipped?) surfaces, brown core with pink margins. Frequent sand temper. Rim dm 19 cm. Area A. B.2052.6.
4. Pale yellow surfaces, buff-orange core; common sand, occasional medium lime temper. Rim dm 19 cm. Area A. B.2052.5.
5. Pale orange surfaces, red-orange core; common sand temper. Rim dm 14 cm. Area A. B.2052.20.
6. Pale orange surfaces, orange-brown core; common sand and fine lime temper. Rim dm 13 cm. Area C. B.2054.7.
7. Orange surfaces and core; common to frequent sand and fine lime temper. Rim dm 10 cm. Area H. B.1094.10.
8. Pale yellow exterior, buff interior, orange-brown core; common sand temper. Rim dm 12 cm. T5a/6. Area G. B.1092.3.
9. Pale orange surfaces, brown core; common sand temper. Rim dm 23 cm. T5a/6. Area A. B.2052.24.
10. Pale yellow (slipped?) surfaces, orange core; occasional to common sand, rare to occasional fine to medium lime temper. Rim dm 23 cm. Area G. B.1092.4.
11. Yellow (slipped?) surfaces, orange core; frequent sand and fine lime temper. Rim dm 9 cm. T5b/11. Area H. B.1094.8.
12. Buff smoothed or lightly burnished surfaces, thin black core; occasional to rare fine grit. Unevenly made. Rim dm 9 cm. Area D. B.1091.3.
13. Pale yellow surfaces, buff core; frequent sand temper. Rim dm 17 cm. T5b/11. Area D. B.1091.1.
14. Pale orange surfaces, buff core; common sand temper. Rim dm 13 cm. T5b/11. Area A. B.2052.19.
15. Yellow surfaces, orange core; frequent sand temper. Rim dm 16 cm. T5b/11. Area H. B.1094.7.
16. Yellow surfaces, buff-orange core; common sand temper. Rim dm 15 cm. T5b/11. Area H. B.1094.6.
17. Orange surfaces, pink-orange core; common to frequent sand and fine lime temper. Rim dm 16 cm. T5b/11. Area G. B.1092.1.
18. Pale orange surfaces, orange-brown core; common sand temper. Rim dm 16 cm. T5b/11. Area G. B.1092.2.
19. Yellow slipped exterior with black paint, yellow interior, orange-brown core; abundant sand and fine to medium dark grit temper. Area D. B.1091.6.
20. Green surfaces, gray-green core; frequent sand temper. Rim dm 5 cm. Area I. B.1095.2.
21. Pale orange surfaces, orange core; frequent sand and fine lime temper. Rim dm 4.5 cm. Area I. B.1095.3.
22. Pale yellow surfaces, green-gray core; common sand temper. Rim dm 17 cm. Area D. B.1091.2.
23. Pale orange surfaces, orange core; common sand, occasional medium lime. T5a/3. Area I. B.1095.14.
24. Pale orange surfaces, orange core; common sand, occasional medium lime. T5a/3. Area I. B.1095.13.
25. Yellow-green surfaces and core; common sand, occasional medium lime. T5a/3. Area I. B.1095.15.
26. Orange-pink surfaces, orange-brown core; frequent sand and fine lime temper. T5a/3. Area H. B.1094.14.
27. Pale orange surfaces, orange-brown core; abundant sand temper. Rim dm 6 cm. Area I. B.1095.12.

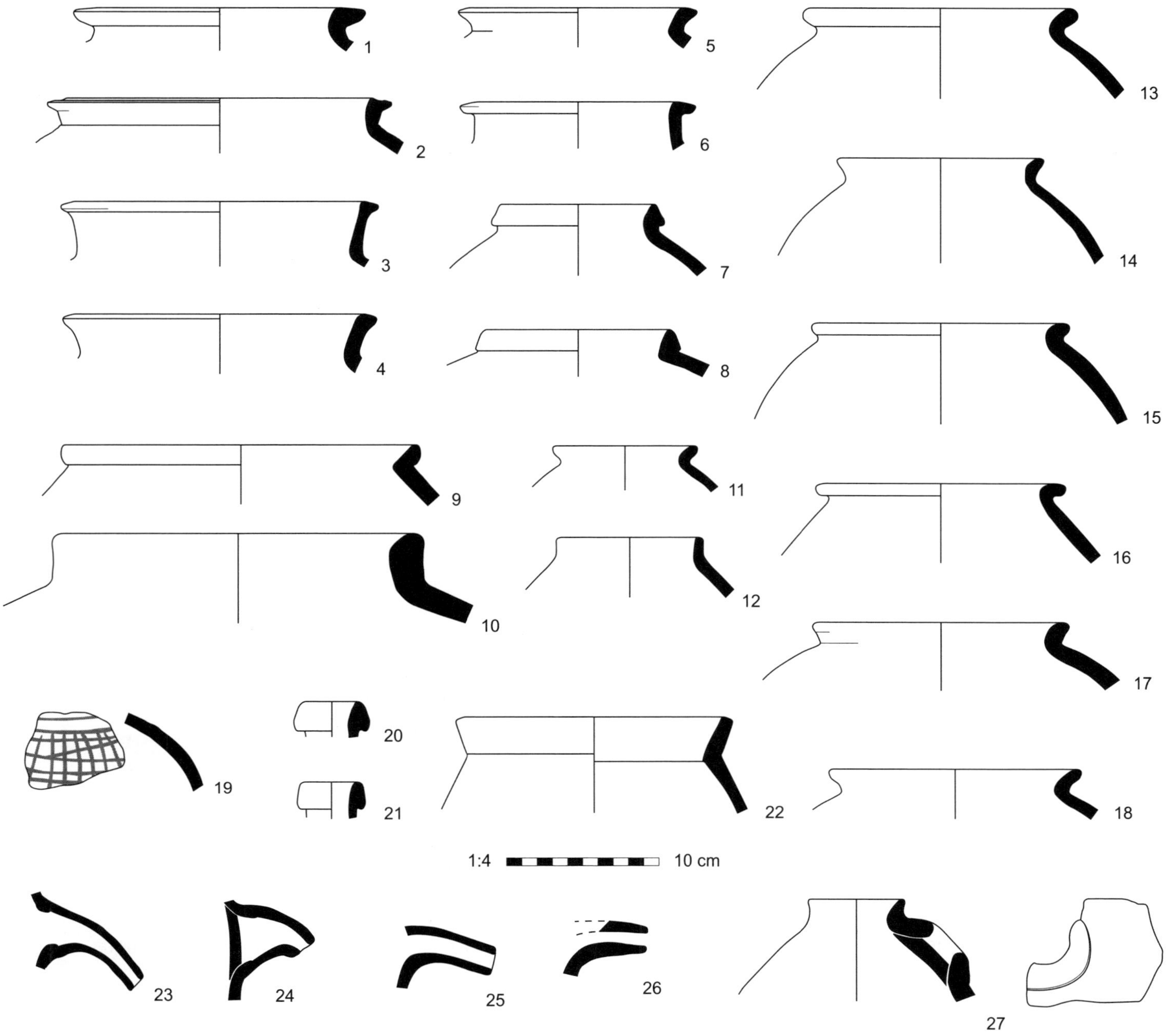

Figure C.16. Surface ceramics from THS 40: grit-tempered closed forms

Figure C.17. Surface ceramics from THS 40: grit-tempered open forms and southern Mesopotamian chaff-tempered types

1. Orange surfaces, orange-red core; common fine chaff, sand, and lime temper. Rim dm 21 cm. Area H. B.1094.3.
2. Yellow surfaces, buff core; occasional sand, sandy fabric. Rim dm 13 cm. T5a/5. Area A. B.2052.14.
3. Orange surfaces, orange-brown core; occasional sand, occasional fine lime. Rim dm 27 cm. T5a/5. Area H. B.1094.5.
4. Orange-brown surfaces, thin gray core; common sand temper. Rim dm 36 cm. T5a/5. Area G. B.1092.5.
5. Yellow surfaces, orange core; occasional fine lime and sand temper. Rim dm 38 cm. T5a/5. Area H. B.1094.4.
6. No description available. Rim dm 42 cm. T5a/5. Area F. B.1093.1.
7. Yellow slipped exterior, orange interior and core; frequent sand. Rim dm ca. 48 cm. T5a/5. Area A. B.2052.15.
8. Pale orange surfaces, thick gray core; common sand temper. Rim dm 28 cm. Area A. B.2052.16.
9. Green surfaces, gray-green core; frequent sand temper. Rim dm 15 cm. Area I. B.1095.4.
10. Yellow (slipped?) surfaces, brown core; frequent sand. Black painted band at rim. Rim dm 19 cm. Area D. B.1091.4.
11. Buff exterior, yellow interior, orange core; black painted band at rim. Rim dm 24 cm. Area D. B.1091.5.
12. Pink-orange surfaces, brown core; common sand temper. Rim dm 28 cm. Area I. B.1095.7.
13. Buff (slipped?) surfaces, brown core with pink margins; common to frequent sand temper. Rim dm 19 cm. T5a/7. Area A. B.2052.13.
14. Buff surfaces and core; occasional sand temper; fine fabric. Rim dm 20 cm. T5a/7. Area C. B.2054.6.
15. Orange surfaces and core; common sand temper. Rim dm 19 cm. T5a/7. Area H. B.1094.12.
16. Yellow-green surfaces and core; occasional sand. Rim dm 20 cm. T5a/7. Area I. B.1095.5.
17. Orange surfaces and core; frequent sand, frequent fine lime temper. Rim dm 10 cm, base dm 2.4 cm. T5a/7 and T5a/8. Area I. B.1095.9.
18. Orange surfaces, brown core; common sand, common fine lime temper. Base dm 3.4 cm. T5a/8. Area I. B.1095.10.
19. Orange exterior, gray interior and core; common sand temper; string-cut base. Base dm 3.2 cm. T5a/8. Area I. B.1095.11.
20. Orange exterior, orange-brown interior, brown core; frequent coarse chaff, common fine to medium lime temper; mold made. Base dm 8 cm. T5a/1. Area G. B.1092.7.
21. Orange-red surfaces, black core with orange margins; frequent medium to coarse chaff, common sand temper; mold made. T5a/1. Area G. B.1092.6.
22. Orange-brown surface, dark brown to black core; frequent to abundant coarse chaff, occasional fine to medium lime and sand temper. Probably oval. Area G. B.1092.8.
23. Orange surfaces, thick black core; frequent to abundant very coarse chaff, occasional medium grit temper. Probably oval. Area F. B.1093.2.
24. Yellow surfaces, buff core; frequent sand, frequent fine to medium lime. T5a/4. Area H. B.1094.13.

Figure C.17. Surface ceramics from THS 40: grit-tempered open forms and southern Mesopotamian chaff-tempered types

Figure C.18. Surface ceramics from THS 40: chaff-tempered and post–fourth-millennium forms

1. Light gray surfaces, dark gray core; frequent medium chaff and sand temper. Rim dm ca. 50 cm. T5b/3. Area C. B.2054.4.
2. Yellow (slipped?) surfaces, buff core; frequent medium chaff temper. Rim dm ca. 38 cm. T5b/4. Area A. B.2052.23.
3. Orange surfaces, orange-brown core; frequent medium chaff. Rim dm 37 cm. T5b/4. Area A. B.2052.12.
4. Orange surfaces, thick black core; frequent medium chaff, rare fine lime temper. Rim dm 33 cm. T5b/4. Area C. B.2054.2.
5. Gray surfaces, dark gray core; frequent medium chaff temper. Rim dm 29 cm. T5b/4. Area I. B.1095.6.
6. Orange surfaces, thick brown core; frequent medium chaff, common fine dark grit temper. Rim dm 28 cm. T5b/5. Area A. B.2052.9.
7. Buff surfaces, yellow core; frequent medium chaff. Rim dm 23 cm. T5b/5. Area A. B.2052.10.
8. Orange surfaces, brown core; common fine to medium chaff temper. Rim dm 26 cm. T5b/5. Area A. B.2052.11.
9. Orange surfaces, brown core; frequent medium to coarse chaff. Rim dm 24 cm. T5b/5. Area I. B.1095.8.
10. Orange surfaces, brown core with red-orange margins; frequent medium chaff temper. Rim dm 28 cm. T5b/1. Area A. B.2052.2.
11. Orange surfaces, black core; frequent medium chaff, occasional fine dark grit temper. Rim dm 24 cm. T5b/1. Area A. B.2052.1.
12. Orange surfaces, thick black core; frequent medium chaff temper. Rim dm 29 cm. T5b/1. Area A. B.2052.3.
13. Orange surfaces, brown core; common to frequent medium chaff temper. Rim dm 19 cm. T5b/1. Area A. B.2052.4.
14. Orange surfaces, thick gray core; common medium chaff, occasional sand temper. Rim dm 20 cm. T5b/2. Area A. B.2052.7.
15. Pale orange surfaces, gray core with orange margins; frequent medium chaff temper. Rim dm 23 cm. T5b/2. Area A. B.2052.8.
16. Orange-buff surfaces, thick black core; frequent chaff temper. Rim dm 16 cm. Area C. B.2054.8.
17. Yellow surfaces, orange-buff core; rare fine lime and sand temper. Rim dm 9 cm. T5b/10. Area H. B.1094.11.
18. Pale pink-orange surfaces, pink core; common sand temper. Rim dm 10 cm. Area A. T5b/10. B.2052.17.
19. Olive green surfaces and core; no visible temper, very fine fabric. Rim dm 9.5 cm. T5b/16. Area I. B.1095.16.
20. Orange surfaces, orange-brown core; common sand temper. Black to brown paint on exterior surface. T4/3. Area C. B.2054.10.
21. Orange surfaces, thick black core; frequent to abundant medium to coarse chaff temper. Rim dm 34 cm. Area A. B.2052.18.
22. Yellow-green surfaces and core; frequent sand temper. Rim dm 6 cm. Area C. B.2054.5.
23. Buff burnished surfaces, gray core; no visible temper. Rim dm 13 cm. Area C. B.2054.9.
24. Pink-orange surfaces, buff core; common sand, occasional fine chaff temper. Rim dm 24 cm. Area C. B.2054.3.
25. Yellow (slipped?) surfaces, pink-buff core; common sand and fine lime temper. Rim dm 25 cm. T12/5. Area C. B.2054.1.

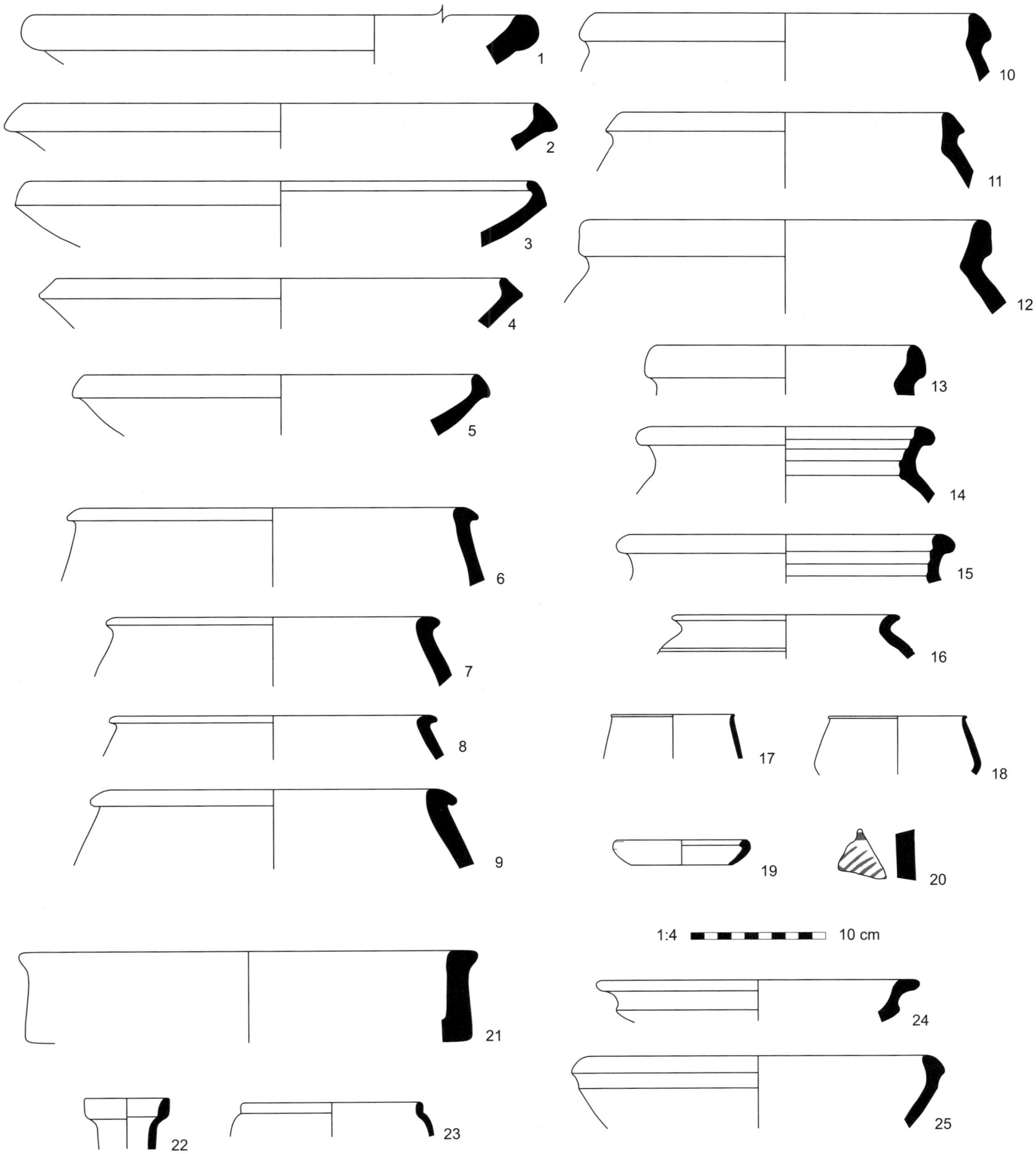

Figure C.18. Surface ceramics from THS 40: chaff-tempered and post–fourth-millennium forms

Figure C.19. Surface ceramics from THS 41

1. Pale yellow surfaces, yellow-green core; frequent medium chaff temper. Eight-prong band of comb-incised decoration. Rim dm 56 cm. T7/4. Area E. B.1703.2.
2. Buff surfaces, gray core; frequent fine to medium chaff temper. Four-prong bands of comb incision, with two vertical smears of black paint or bitumen. Rim dm 37 cm. T7/4. Area C. B.1701.1.
3. Yellow-green surfaces and core; frequent medium chaff, occasional fine dark grit. Possible traces of comb incision on exterior. Rim dm 34 cm. T7/8. Area B. B.1700.6.
4. Yellow surfaces, orange core; frequent fine chaff, rare coarse grit temper. Faint traces of comb-incised decoration on exterior. Rim dm 39 cm. Area C. B.1701.2.
5. Yellow-green surfaces and core; common sand, fine grit, and medium chaff. Rim dm 11 cm. Area B. B.1700.5.
6. Pale yellow surfaces, pale green core; frequent medium chaff, rare fine lime temper. Rim dm 18 cm. Area C. B.1701.3.
7. Pale yellow-green surfaces and core; no visible temper. Wheel striation on exterior. Base dm 6 cm. T7/2. Area C. B.1701.22.
8. Buff surfaces, orange core; common fine to medium chaff temper. Base dm 5 cm. Area C. B.1701.5.
9. Yellow-green smoothed exterior, yellow-green interior, orange core; common medium chaff, occasional fine lime temper. Rim dm 27 cm. Area C. B.1701.4.
10. Yellow-green surfaces, pale green core; no visible temper. Rim dm 19 cm. Area C. B.1701.6.
11. Pale green lightly burnished surfaces, pale green core; slightly sandy fabric. Rim dm 18 cm. Area A. B.1140.1.
12. Yellow-green surfaces, green core; slightly sandy fabric. Rim dm 16 cm. Area C. B.1701.10.
13. Yellow-green surfaces, green core; slightly sandy fabric. Rim dm 14 cm. Area C. B.1701.11.
14. Yellow-green surfaces, green core; slightly sandy fabric. Rim dm 16 cm. Area C. B.1701.12.
15. Pale gray surfaces, gray core; rare sand, rare fine chaff temper, fine fabric. Rim dm 15 cm. T8/3. Area C. B.1701.19.
16. Pale gray surfaces, gray core; rare sand, rare fine chaff temper, fine fabric. Rim dm 14 cm. T8/3. Area C. B.1701.20.
17. Pale green smoothed surfaces and core; sandy fabric. Rim dm 10 cm. Area C. B.1701.7.
18. Buff surfaces, pale orange core; no visible temper. Rim dm 11 cm. Area A. B.1140.4.
19. Yellow surfaces, orange core; rare fine chaff temper. Red band of paint on rim. Rim dm 10 cm. Area C. B.1701.9.
20. Pale green smoothed surfaces and core; sandy fabric. Rim dm 10 cm. Area C. B.1701.8.
21. Buff smoothed surfaces, orange core; no visible temper. Rim dm 14 cm. Area C. B.1701.16.
22. Pale green smoothed surfaces, green core; no visible temper. Black painted decoration. Rim dm 8 cm. T5b/10. Area C. B.1701.13.
23. Buff surfaces and core; no visible temper. Reddish brown painted decoration. Rim dm 9 cm. T5b/10. Area B. B.1700.7.
24. Pale green smoothed surfaces and core; no visible temper. Reddish brown painted decoration. Rim dm 7 cm. T5b/10. Area B. B.1700.8.
25. Buff (slipped?) exterior with dark red painted lines, orange core; occasional fine lime temper. Dm at carination 10 cm. Area B. B.1700.9.
26. Pale yellow surfaces, green core; sandy fabric. Rim dm 17 cm. Area C. B.1701.15.
27. Pale green surfaces and core; no visible temper. Wheel striations on exterior. Rim dm 20 cm. Area B. B.1700.4.
28. Yellow-green slipped surfaces and core; no visible temper. Rim dm 14 cm. Area A. B.1140.5.
29. Pale yellow surfaces and core; no visible temper. Rim dm 15 cm. Area C. B.1701.18.

30 Yellow surfaces and core; occasional fine lime temper. Rim dm 16 cm. Area C. B.1701.14.

31 Yellow-green surfaces, green core; sandy fabric. Rim dm 13 cm. Area C. B.1701.17.

32 Pale yellow surfaces, yellow-gray core; no visible temper. Rim dm 16 cm. Area F. B.1704.2.

33 Pale yellow (slipped?) exterior, buff interior, orange-brown core; frequent medium chaff temper. Rim dm 26 cm. T8/2. Area E. B.1703.1.

34 Buff surfaces, orange core; occasional sand temper. Rim dm 10 cm. T8/2. Area B. B.1700.2.

35 Buff surfaces and core; occasional sand, occasional fine lime temper. Red-brown painted bands. Rim dm 12 cm. T8/1. Area B. B.1700.3.

36 Buff surfaces, orange core; no visible temper. Black paint. Rim dm 32 cm. T2/1. Area F. B.1704.1.

37 Buff slipped surfaces, orange core; no visible temper. Red painted interior and exterior surfaces. Rim dm ca. 22 cm. T2/1. Area B. B.1700.10.

38 Buff slipped surfaces, orange core; no visible temper. Dark red painted concentric circles. Rim dm 15 cm. T2/1. Area B. B.1700.11.

39 Yellow and reddish brown streaked and slightly vitrified surfaces, gray core; common very fine voids. Rim dm 12 cm. T7/5. Area B. B.1700.1.

40 Buff surfaces, yellow core; no visible temper. Rim dm 13 cm. T7/20. Area A. B.1140.2.

41 Buff slipped exterior, orange-brown interior and core; common to frequent sand temper. Stamped decoration. T15/3. Area C. B.1701.21.

42 Pale orange surfaces, orange-brown core; common medium chaff, occasional medium dark grit temper. Rim dm 31 cm. T10/10. Area A. B.1140.3.

43 Pale orange surfaces, brown core; common medium chaff. Rim dm ca. 40 cm. T5b/4. Area E. B.1703.3.

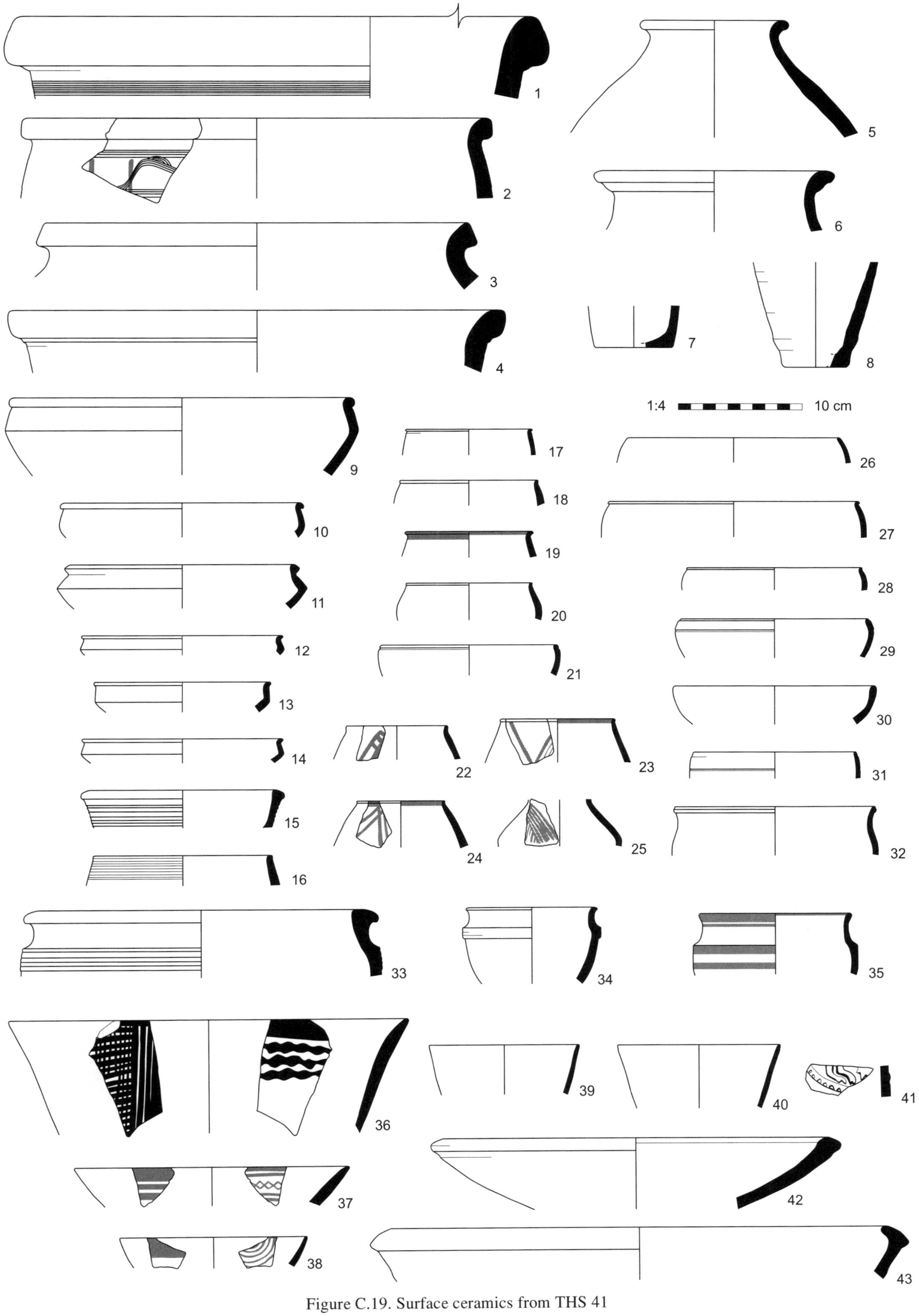

Figure C.19. Surface ceramics from THS 41

Figure C.20. Surface ceramics from THS 43

1. Buff surfaces, orange core; frequent very fine lime temper. Dark red paint on exterior. Dm 14 cm at carination. T2/1. Area E. B.1052.6.
2. Buff surfaces, orange core; no visible temper. Dm 8 cm at carination. T11/6. Area C. B.199.7.
3. Orange-red surfaces, brown core; common sand temper. Rim dm 12 cm. T13/11. Area C. B.199.1.
4. Buff surfaces, gray core; no visible temper. Rim dm 12 cm. Area E. B.1052.4.
5. Orange surfaces and core; common fine to medium chaff temper. Rim dm 13 cm. T11/8. Area C. B.199.2.
6. Buff surfaces and core; frequent fine dark grit. Rim dm 11 cm. Area E. B.1052.1.
7. Orange surfaces and core; frequent to abundant sand and fine to medium grit temper. Rim dm 15 cm. Area E. B.1052.2.
8. Red smoothed surfaces, brown core; occasional fine chaff temper. Rim dm 19 cm. Area C. B.199.6.
9. Pink surfaces, buff-brown core; occasional medium chaff temper. Rim dm 23 cm. T11/12. Area E. B.1052.3.
10. Buff surfaces and core; frequent medium chaff. Rim dm 25 cm. T11/14. Area C. B.199.3.
11. Yellow smoothed surfaces, orange core; frequent medium chaff temper. Rim dm 26 cm. Area C. B.199.5.
12. Buff surfaces, orange core; frequent sand temper. Rim dm 28 cm. T11/12. Area D. B.198.3.
13. Orange surfaces; common chaff and sand temper. Rim dm 24 cm. Area D. B.198.1.
14. Buff surfaces, orange core; frequent sand temper. Rim dm 20 cm. T11/12. Area D. B.198.2.
15. Buff surfaces and core; frequent to abundant sand temper. Rim dm 21 cm. T11/2. Area C. B.199.4.
16. Gray surfaces, brown core; common sand, common medium to coarse dark grit temper. Rim dm 26 cm. T14/8. Area G. B.521.7.
17. Gray surfaces, brown core; common sand, common medium to coarse dark grit temper. Rim dm 20 cm. T14/8. Area G. B.521.8.
18. Pale yellow surfaces, yellow-green core; rare sand temper, fine fabric. Rim dm 12 cm. T14/2. Area G. B.521.1.
19. Orange surfaces, brown core; occasional fine lime temper. Rim dm 11 cm. T14/2. Area G. B.521.2.
20. Buff surfaces, brown core; common sand temper. Rim dm 15 cm. T14/8. Area G. B.521.5.
21. Pale orange surfaces, brown core; common sand temper. Rim dm 12 cm. T14/8. Area G. B.521.4.
22. Buff surfaces, orange-brown core; no visible temper. Rim dm 11 cm. T14/8. Area G. B.521.6.
23. Pale yellow surfaces, orange core; no visible temper, fine fabric. T14/4. Area G. B.521.10.
24. Pale yellow surfaces, orange core; no visible temper, fine fabric. T14/4. Area G. B.521.9.
25. Pale yellow surfaces, buff core; occasional sand, fine fabric. T14/5. Area G. B.521.11.
26. No description available. Area G. B.521.3.
27. Orange surfaces with red and black paint, brown core; common sand and fine lime temper. Rim dm 21 cm. Area D. B.198.4.
28. Orange surfaces, buff core; common medium chaff, rare coarse lime temper. Rim dm 19 cm. Area E. B.1052.5.

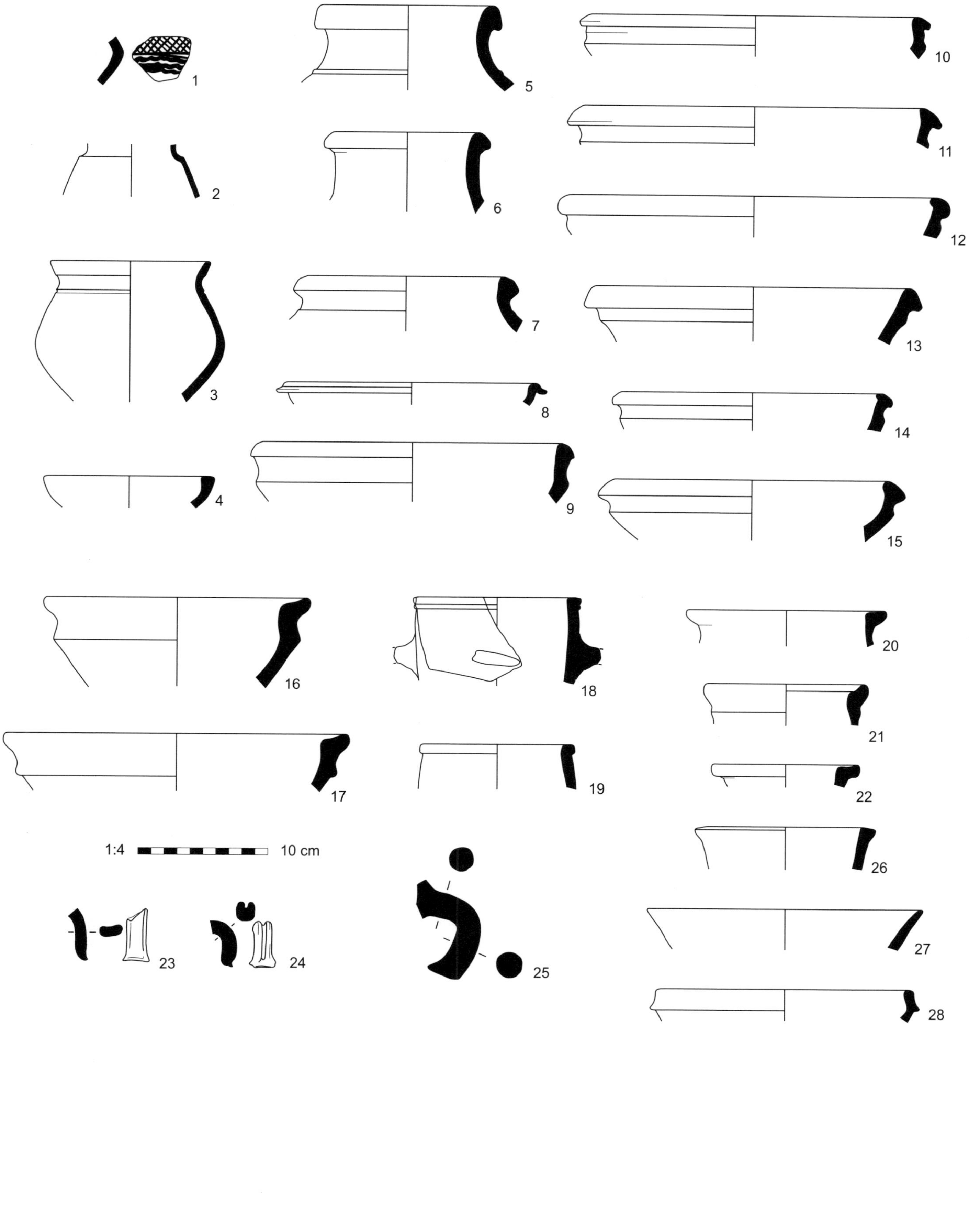

Figure C.20. Surface ceramics from THS 43

Figure C.21. Surface ceramics from THS 44

1. Pale yellow surfaces, gray-brown core; frequent sand temper. Black painted bands on exterior. Rim dm 15 cm. T1/1. Area A. B.1138.4.
2. Pale yellow slipped surfaces, orange-buff core; occasional sand temper. Red-brown painted decoration on interior and exterior. Rim dm 17 cm. T1/1. Area B. B.1139.5.
3. Pale orange surfaces with dark red paint, thick black core; frequent medium chaff temper. Handmade. T1/1. Area B. B.1139.3.
4. Buff surfaces, gray-brown core; frequent sand temper. Black paint on exterior and interior rim. T1/1. Area B. B.1139.4.
5. Buff surfaces, orange core; common sand temper. Red-orange paint on exterior surface. T1/1. Area A. B.1138.3.
6. Buff surfaces, gray core; occasional sand. Evenly spaced fine punctures with traces of black paint. T1/6. Area B. B.1139.6.
7. Buff surfaces, orange core; common to frequent medium chaff. Black painted decoration on exterior. T1/1. Area B. B.1139.2.
8. Pale orange surfaces, gray core with orange margins; common to frequent sand and fine lime temper. Handmade. Rim dm 26 cm. Area B. B.1139.1.
9. Buff surfaces, brown core; common fine to medium chaff temper. Shallow incisions below rim. Handmade. Rim dm 18 cm. Area A. B.1138.1.
10. Orange-red surfaces, brown core; frequent sand temper. Rim dm 14 cm. Area A. B.1138.2.

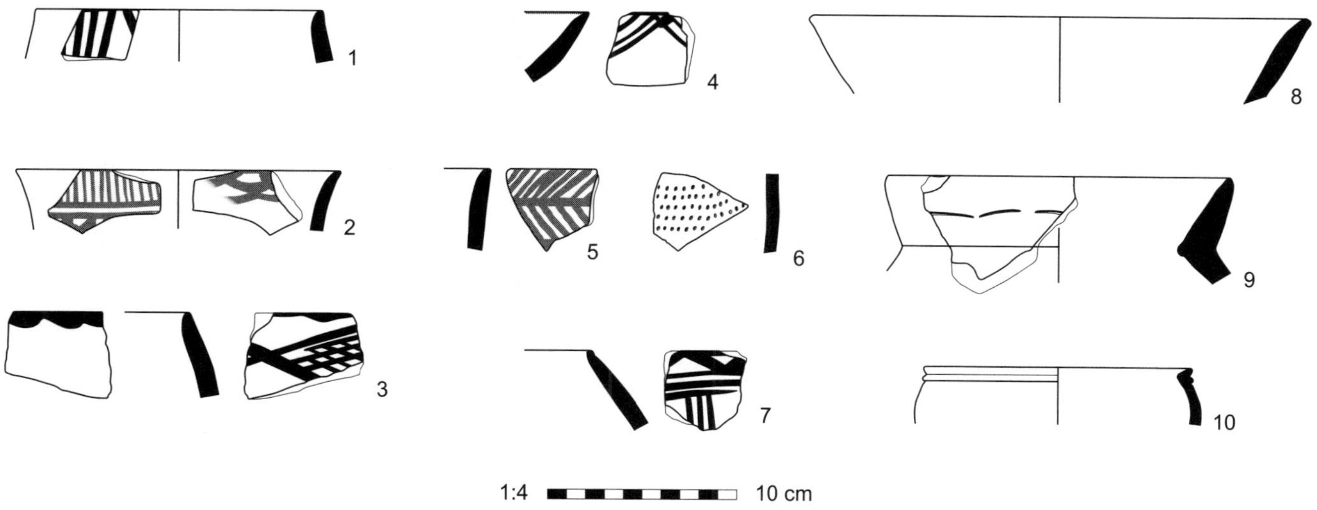

Figure C.21. Surface ceramics from THS 44

Figure C.22. Surface ceramics from THS 55

1. Yellow surfaces, buff core; common sand temper, sandy fabric. Rim dm 15 cm. T14/6. B.170.13.
2. Gray exterior, orange interior, red-brown core; occasional sand temper. Rim dm 18 cm. T14/6. B.170.10.
3. Yellow exterior, orange interior and core; occasional to common sand temper. Rim dm 17 cm. T14/6. B.170.11.
4. Pale yellow slipped surfaces, orange core; rare fine lime temper, fine fabric. Rim dm 14 cm. T14/6. B.170.12.
5. Pale yellow surfaces, yellow-green core; occasional fine voids, rare medium lime temper, fine fabric. Rim dm 14 cm. T14/6. B.170.14.
6. Orange surfaces with allover red paint, orange-brown core; abundant sand, abundant medium dark grit temper. Coarsely made. Rim dm 42 cm. T14/12. B.170.1.
7. Orange surfaces with allover red paint, orange-brown core; abundant sand, abundant medium dark grit temper. Three drilled holes; coarsely made. Rim dm 43 cm. T14/12. B.170.2.
8. Red painted exterior, bitumen-smeared interior, brown core; abundant sand, abundant fine to medium dark grit temper. Coarsely made. Rim dm ca. 28 cm. T14/12. B.170.3.
9. Buff surfaces and core; common medium chaff, common sand temper. Rim dm 26 cm. T11/12. B.170.9.
10. Red slipped or painted exterior, orange-brown interior with band of black paint or bitumen at rim; brown core with orange-red margins; frequent to abundant sand and fine to medium grit temper. Rim dm 18 cm. B.170.5.
11. Red-orange smoothed or slipped surfaces, brown core; frequent medium grit, rare coarse medium lime temper. Rim dm 15 cm. B.170.6.
12. Pale orange surfaces with bitumen smeared on rim, orange-brown core; common sand temper. Rim dm 13 cm. B.170.7.
13. Pale orange surfaces, brown core; frequent sand, occasional medium grit. Rim dm 15 cm. B.170.8.
14. Pale yellow surfaces, yellow-green core; occasional fine voids, no visible temper, fine fabric. T14/3. B.170.18.
15. Pale yellow slipped surfaces, orange core; rare fine to medium lime temper, fine fabric. T14/3. B.170.17.
16. Pale yellow slipped surfaces, orange-pink core; no visible temper, fine fabric. T17/6. B.170.19.
17. Yellow surfaces, orange core; no visible temper, fine fabric. Impressed diamond stamps. T14/1. B.170.21.
18. Pale yellow surfaces, pale yellow core; no visible temper, fine fabric. Impressed diamond stamps. T14/1. B.170.20.
19. Pale yellow-green surfaces and core; sandy fabric with no visible temper. Impressed diamond stamps. T14/1. B.170.22.

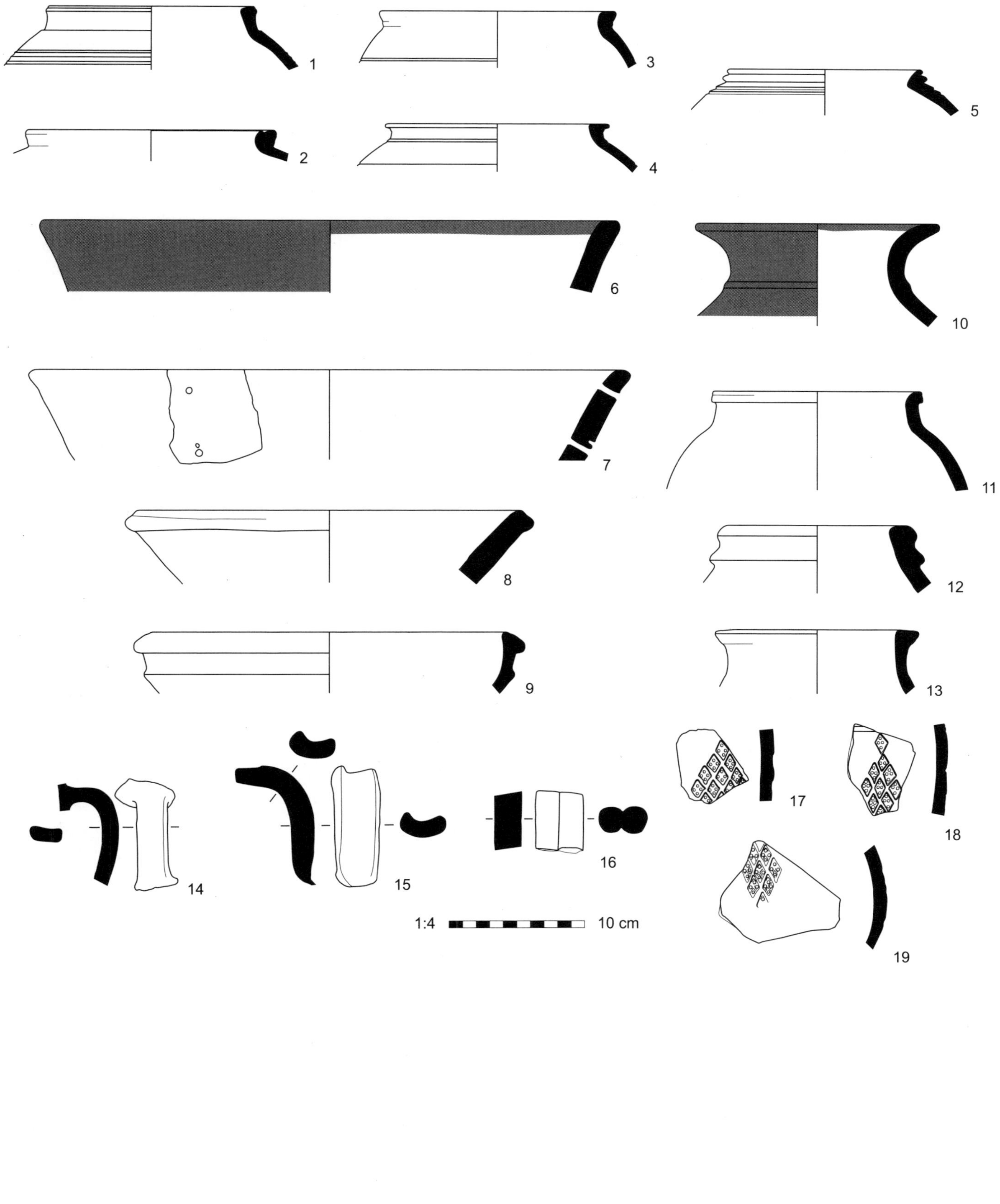

Figure C.22. Surface ceramics from THS 55

Figure C.23. Surface ceramics from THS 59: closed forms

1. Yellow surfaces and core; common medium chaff, common fine lime temper. Rim dm 16 cm. T11/8. B.1068.1.
2. Yellow surfaces, green core; common fine to medium chaff temper. Rim dm 14 cm. B.1068.11.
3. Buff surfaces, orange core; common medium chaff, occasional fine lime temper. Rim dm 10 cm. T11/10. B.1068.
4. Buff surfaces, orange core; common medium chaff, occasional fine lime temper. Rim dm 10 cm. T11/8. B.1068.7.
5. Buff surfaces, orange core; occasional fine chaff, frequent sand and fine lime temper. Rim dm 11 cm. T11/8. B.1068.10.
6. Orange surfaces, brown core; common fine chaff, occasional sand temper. Rim dm 13 cm. T11/8. B.1068.9.
7. Buff surfaces and core; common medium chaff, occasional medium lime temper. Rim dm 11 cm. T11/8. B.1068.8.
8. Green surfaces and core; common fine to medium chaff, occasional sand temper. Dm 11 cm at ridge. T11/8. B.1068.32.
9. Yellow exterior, buff interior and core; frequent medium chaff, common sand. Dm 18 cm at raised ridge. B.1068.33.
10. Yellow surfaces, buff core; common medium chaff, occasional fine lime and sand temper. Rim dm 19 cm. B.1068.3.
11. Yellow surfaces and core; common fine to medium chaff. Rim dm 24 cm. B.1068.2.
12. Yellow surfaces, buff core; common fine chaff, occasional sand temper. Rim dm 16 cm. B.1068.4.
13. Green exterior, pink-buff interior; medium to coarse chaff, occasional medium to coarse lime temper. Irregular row of circular impressions. Rim dm 20 cm. B.1069.14.
14. Red exterior, buff interior; common medium chaff and fine grit. Rim dm 16 cm. B.1068.
15. Pink exterior, reddish brown interior; frequent chaff, occasional fine to medium grit temper. Raised notched ridge. Rim dm 22 cm. B.1069.15.
16. Yellow surfaces, buff core; frequent fine lime temper. Rim dm 14 cm. B.1068.14.
17. Buff surfaces, orange core; common fine lime temper. Rim dm 11 cm. B.1068.13.
18. Brown surfaces, black core; abundant medium chaff and grit. Rim dm ca. 15 cm. B.1068.
19. Buff surfaces, brown core; common fine to medium chaff, occasional fine lime temper. Rim dm 10 cm. B.1068.12.
20. Black burnished exterior, black interior and core; frequent medium grit temper. Rim dm 22 cm. B.1068.34.

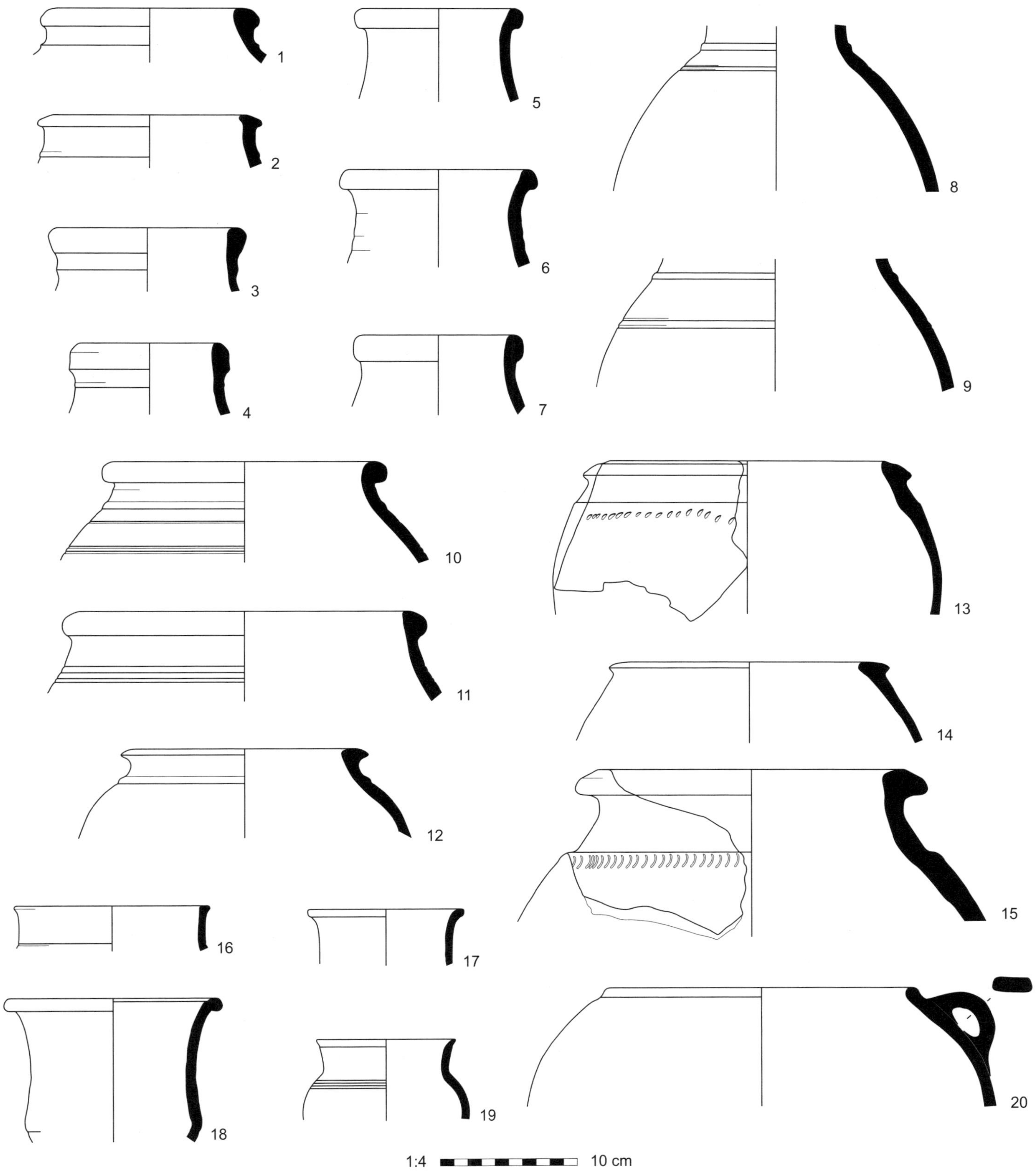

Figure C.23. Surface ceramics from THS 59: closed forms

Figure C.24. Surface ceramics from THS 59: open forms, bases, and potstand

1. Buff exterior, orange interior and core; frequent to abundant sand temper. Rim dm 27 cm. T11/2. B.1068.29.
2. Orange surfaces, thin black core; common to frequent medium chaff temper. Rim dm 26 cm. T11/2. B.1068.27
3. Orange surfaces, orange-brown core; common medium chaff temper. Rim dm 24 cm. B.1068.23.
4. Orange surfaces, orange-brown core; occasional fine chaff, occasional sand, occasional fine lime temper. Rim dm 16 cm. T11/2. B.1068.25.
5. Orange surfaces, thin gray core; frequent medium chaff temper. Rim dm 15 cm. B.1068.16
6. Buff surfaces, orange core; common fine chaff temper. Rim dm 23 cm. B.1068.15.
7. Yellow-buff surfaces and core; no visible temper. Rim dm 19 cm. B.1068.17.
8. Buff surfaces and core; frequent medium chaff temper. Rim dm 17 cm. B.1068.18.
9. Yellow exterior, buff interior, pink core; common to frequent fine to medium chaff, common medium lime temper. Rim dm 27 cm. T11/1. B.1068.19.
10. Buff surfaces and core; common fine grit temper. Rim dm 25 cm. T11/1. B.1068.3.
11. Orange-brown burnished surfaces, exterior vertically burnished, brown core; common medium chaff temper. Rim dm 24 cm. T11/1. B.1068.20.
12. Orange surfaces, thin brown core; frequent medium chaff, occasional fine lime temper. Rim dm 26 cm. T11/1. B.1068.21.
13. Orange surfaces, thin black core with buff margins; frequent medium to coarse chaff, occasional fine to medium lime temper. Rim dm 29 cm. B.1068.26.
14. Buff surfaces, brown core; common medium chaff, rare sand temper. Rim dm 30 cm. B.1068.24.
15. Buff surfaces and core; common medium chaff, occasional medium lime temper. Rim dm 27 cm. T11/12. B.1068.6.
16. Green surfaces and core; common fine chaff and sand temper. Rim dm 38 cm. B.1068.30.
17. Buff surfaces, orange core; common to frequent medium chaff, occasional fine dark grit temper. Rim dm 52 cm. T11/11. B.1068.5.
18. Buff to brown surfaces; common fine chaff and medium grit temper. Notched horizontal ridge. Rim dm 36 cm. T12/4. B.1069.13.
19. Buff surfaces and core; common fine to medium chaff temper. Upper rim dm 13.5 cm. B.1069.16.
20. Gray-green exterior, buff interior and core; abundant fine grit, occasional fine chaff temper. Base dm at carination 4 cm. T11/3. B.1069.2.
21. Buff surfaces; abundant sand temper. B.1069.3.
22. Buff surfaces, pink core; common fine chaff, occasional grit temper. Base dm 12.3 cm. T11/4. B.1069.10.
23. Buff exterior, brown interior, black core; abundant medium chaff temper. Base dm 7 cm. T11/4. B.1069.6.
24. Buff surfaces; abundant medium chaff, occasional fine grit temper. Base dm 7 cm. T11/4. B.1069.4.
25. Buff exterior, pink interior; abundant fine chaff and fine grit temper. Base dm 7 cm. T11/4. B.1069.5.
26. Buff surfaces and core; abundant medium chaff, occasional fine grit temper. Base dm 8 cm. T10/9. B.1069.9.

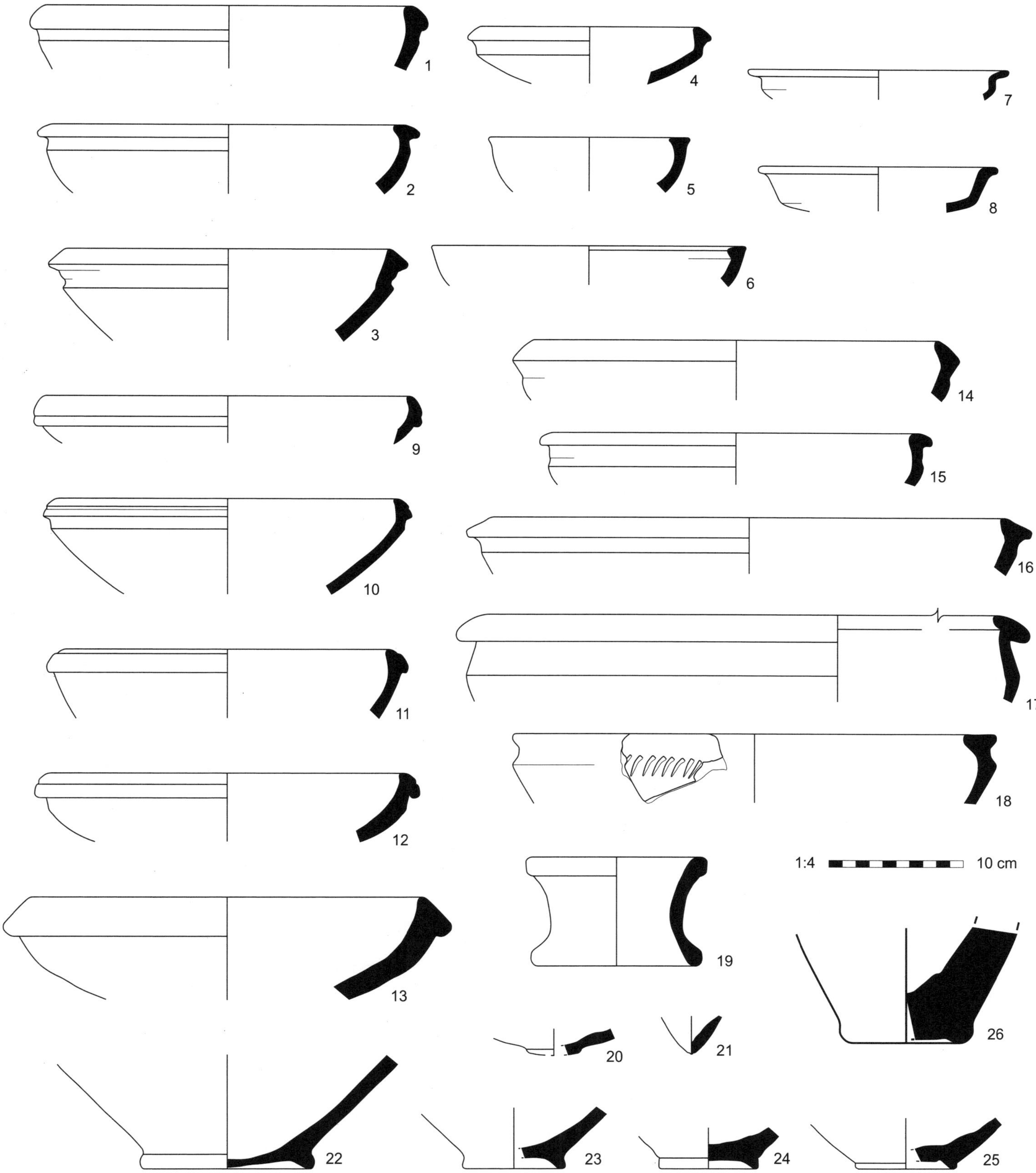

Figure C.24. Surface ceramics from THS 59: open forms, bases, and potstand

Table C.1. THS 1 (Hamoukar) typed sherds by period and collection unit

Collection Unit	Total Sherds	Period												
		5b	5a	6	7	11	12	13	14	15	16	19	20	21
1	168	—	1	1	6	—	—	—	—	—	—	—	—	—
2	153	—	—	—	4	—	1	—	—	—	—	—	—	—
3	211	—	—	—	11	—	—	—	—	—	—	—	—	—
4	251	—	1	5	16	—	—	—	—	—	—	—	—	—
5	59	1	—	—	—	—	—	1	—	—	—	—	—	—
6	105	—	—	—	4	—	—	—	—	—	—	—	—	—
7	116	—	—	—	7	—	—	—	—	—	—	—	—	—
8	68	—	—	—	1	—	—	—	—	—	—	—	—	—
9	55	—	—	—	3	—	—	—	—	—	—	—	—	—
10	189	—	1	3	6	—	—	—	—	—	—	—	—	—
11	122	—	—	1	2	—	—	—	—	—	—	—	—	—
12	293	—	—	1	25	—	—	—	—	—	—	—	—	—
13	295	—	—	—	17	—	—	—	—	—	—	—	—	—
14	129	—	—	—	5	—	—	—	—	—	1	—	—	—
15	97	—	—	—	3	—	—	—	—	—	—	—	—	—
16	258	1	—	—	4	—	—	—	—	—	—	—	—	—
17	287	—	2	—	7	—	—	—	—	—	—	—	—	—
18	247	—	—	—	7	10	—	—	—	—	—	—	—	—
19	242	—	—	1	2	8	—	—	1	—	—	—	—	—
20	270	—	—	1	3	10	—	—	—	—	—	—	—	—
21	288	2	1	—	—	3	—	—	1	—	—	—	—	1
22	185	—	—	—	4	1	—	—	—	—	—	—	—	—
23	248	—	—	2	12	1	—	—	—	—	—	—	—	—
24	154	2	—	—	4	—	—	—	—	—	—	—	—	—
25	251	1	—	1	5	—	—	—	—	—	—	—	—	—
26	130	5	—	4	4	1	—	—	—	—	1	—	—	—
27	110	—	—	—	13	—	1	—	—	—	—	—	—	—
28	156	2	—	—	9	—	—	—	—	—	—	—	—	—
29	188	12	12	—	4	—	—	—	—	—	—	—	—	—
30	248	5	2	2	2	—	—	—	1	—	—	—	—	—
31	202	19	18	2	4	—	—	—	—	—	—	—	—	—
32	197	25	13	—	8	—	—	—	—	—	—	—	—	—
33	108	—	—	—	7	—	—	—	—	—	—	—	—	—
34	83	—	—	—	1	—	—	1	—	—	—	—	—	—
35	136	—	—	—	4	—	—	—	—	—	—	—	—	—
36	138	1	1	—	13	—	—	—	—	—	—	—	—	—
37	227	—	—	—	19	—	—	—	—	—	—	—	—	—
38	190	—	—	—	6	—	—	—	—	—	—	—	—	—
39	119	1	—	—	15	—	—	—	—	—	—	—	—	—
40	125	—	—	—	7	—	—	1	—	—	—	—	—	—
41	98	2	—	—	3	—	—	—	—	—	—	—	—	—
42	120	2	—	—	6	1	—	—	—	—	—	—	—	—

Table C.1. THS 1 (Hamoukar) typed sherds by period and collection unit (*cont.*)

Collection Unit	*Total Sherds*	*Period*												
		5b	5a	6	7	11	12	13	14	15	16	19	20	21
43	158	5	1	—	3	—	—	—	—	—	—	—	—	—
44	256	58	1	—	—	—	—	—	—	—	—	—	—	—
45	246	1	—	—	6	—	—	1	—	—	—	—	—	—
46	252	—	1	—	4	—	—	1	—	—	—	—	—	—
47	293	—	—	—	11	—	—	6	—	—	—	1	1	—
48	201	1	1	—	1	—	—	—	—	—	—	—	—	—
49	396	1	1	—	3	—	—	—	—	—	—	—	—	—
50	21	—	—	—	21	—	—	—	—	—	—	—	—	—
51	56	—	—	—	5	—	—	—	—	—	—	—	—	—
52	92	—	—	—	10	—	—	—	—	—	—	—	—	—
53	69	—	—	1	8	—	—	—	—	—	—	—	—	—
54	44	—	—	—	3	—	—	—	—	—	—	—	—	—
55	130	—	—	—	4	—	—	—	—	—	—	—	—	—
56	137	—	—	—	11	—	—	—	—	—	—	—	—	—
57	279	—	1	—	22	—	—	—	—	—	—	—	—	—
58	195	—	—	2	5	—	—	—	—	—	—	—	—	—
59	213	—	—	2	12	—	—	—	—	—	—	—	—	—
60	8	—	—	—	8	—	—	—	—	—	—	—	—	—
61	125	—	—	—	8	—	—	—	—	—	—	—	—	—
62	181	—	—	—	9	—	—	—	—	—	—	—	—	—
63	89	—	—	—	4	—	—	—	—	—	—	—	—	—
64	125	—	—	—	33	—	—	—	—	—	—	—	—	—
65	114	—	—	—	6	—	—	—	—	—	—	—	—	—
66	134	—	—	5	3	—	—	—	—	—	—	—	—	—
67	23	—	—	—	—	—	—	—	—	—	—	—	—	—
68	68	—	—	30	—	—	—	—	—	—	—	—	—	—
69	57	—	—	—	4	—	—	—	—	—	—	—	—	—
70	125	—	—	1	10	—	—	—	—	—	—	—	—	—
71	122	—	—	—	14	1	—	—	—	—	—	—	—	—
72	119	—	—	—	2	—	—	—	—	—	—	—	—	—
73	89	—	—	—	7	—	—	—	—	—	—	—	—	—
74	65	—	—	—	3	—	—	—	—	—	—	—	—	—
75	87	—	—	—	16	—	—	—	—	—	—	—	—	—
77	60	—	—	—	5	—	—	—	—	—	—	—	—	—
78	62	—	—	1	2	—	—	—	—	—	—	—	—	—
79	77	—	—	1	2	—	—	—	2	—	—	—	—	—
80	139	—	—	—	13	—	—	1	—	—	—	—	—	—
82	143	—	—	1	4	—	—	—	—	—	—	—	—	—
83	53	—	—	—	17	—	—	—	—	—	—	—	—	—
86	59	—	—	—	2	—	—	—	1	—	—	—	—	—
87	50	—	—	—	10	—	—	—	—	—	—	—	—	—
88	107	—	—	—	6	—	—	—	—	—	—	—	—	—

Table C.1. THS 1 (Hamoukar) typed sherds by period and collection unit (*cont.*)

Collection Unit	*Total Sherds*	*Period*												
		5b	5a	6	7	11	12	13	14	15	16	19	20	21
89	76	—	—	—	7	—	—	—	—	—	—	—	—	—
90	65	—	—	1	13	—	—	—	—	—	—	—	—	—
91	91	—	—	2	14	—	—	—	—	—	—	—	—	—
92	95	—	—	—	16	—	—	—	—	—	—	—	—	—
93	102	—	—	—	6	—	—	—	—	—	—	—	—	—
94	211	1	—	1	12	—	—	—	—	—	—	—	—	—
95	145	5	2	—	4	1	—	—	—	—	—	—	—	—
96	86	1	—	—	1	—	—	—	—	—	1	—	—	—
97	19	1	—	—	3	—	—	—	—	—	—	—	—	—
98	63	—	—	—	4	—	—	—	—	—	—	—	—	—
99	54	—	—	—	2	—	—	—	—	—	—	—	—	—
100	125	1	1	—	6	—	—	—	—	—	—	—	—	—
101	102	—	—	—	3	—	—	—	—	1	—	—	—	—
102	82	—	—	—	7	—	—	—	—	—	—	—	—	—
103	60	1	—	—	3	—	—	—	—	—	—	—	—	—
104	61	—	—	—	10	—	—	—	—	—	—	—	—	—
105	64	—	—	—	8	—	—	—	—	—	1	—	—	—
106	158	1	1	2	4	—	—	—	—	—	—	—	—	—
107	224	4	3	—	1	—	—	—	—	—	—	—	—	—
108	271	28	2	—	1	—	—	—	—	—	—	—	—	—
109	157	—	—	5	8	—	—	—	—	—	—	—	—	—
110	136	—	—	2	7	—	—	—	—	—	—	—	—	—
111	67	—	—	—	28	—	—	—	—	—	—	—	—	—
*117	51	5	19	1	21	—	—	—	—	—	3	—	—	2
*126	31	2	1	2	21	—	—	1	—	—	—	—	—	—
*127	63	6	2	1	34	—	—	9	1	—	—	—	—	—
Totals	15,294	203	88	85	844	37	2	22	7	1	7	1	1	3

* Units marked with an asterisk are supplementary areal collections

Table C.2. THS 2 typed diagnostics

Period	*Type*	*Quantity*
4	T4/18	2
5b	T5b/2	1
	T5b/3	1
	T5b/4	1
	T5b/5	2
	T5b/11	4
5a	T5a/1	2
	T5a/2	1
	T5a/3	4
	T5a/4	2
	T5a/5	4
	T5a/6	4
7	T7/5	1
	T7/10	1
8	T8/6	1

Table C.3. THS 3 (al-ʻAsayla) typed diagnostics

Period	*Type*	*Area A*	*Area B*
4	T4/18	1	—
5a	T5a/1	—	3
	T5a/6	1	1
7	T7/5	1	—
11	T11/1	2	5
	T11/2	1	2
	T11/4	—	1
	T11/8	—	6
12	T12/1	2	—
	T12/3	—	2
	T12/5	—	1
13	T13/1	11	2
	T13/2	18	3
	T13/7	1	—
	T13/8	1	—
	T13/12	1	—
16	T16/3	—	1
	T16/4	1	—
17	T17/3	—	1

Table C.4. THS 4 typed diagnostics

Period	*Type*	*Quantity*
1	T1/6	2
2	T2/1	1
3	T3/2	1
7	T7/10	1
	T7/11	1
	T7/14	1
8	T8/1	1
10	T10/12	1
16	T16/3	1

Table C.5. THS 5 (Tell al-Duwaym) diagnostic types. Area A was not formally collected

Period	*Type*	*Area B*
4	T4/18	1
13	T13/2	2
	T13/8	1
16	T16/2	1
	T16/3	6
17	T17/4	3
19	T19/1	4
	T19/2	1

Table C.6. THS 6 typed diagnostics

Period	*Type*	*Quantity*
16	T16/2	3
	T16/3	8
18	T18/1	1
20	T20/2	2

Table C.7. THS 7 typed diagnostics

Period	*Type*	*Quantity*
16	T16/2	3
	T16/3	4
	T16/4	2
	T16/6	1
	T16/9	1
	T16/10	1
17	T17/3	1
	T17/4	3
	T17/5	1

Table C.8. THS 8 typed diagnostics

Period	*Type*	*Quantity*
2	T2/1	13

Table C.9. THS 9 typed diagnostics

Period	*Type*	*Quantity*
2	T2/1	21
17	T17/3	1

Table C.10. THS 10 (Khirbat al-Batta) typed diagnostics

Period	*Type*	*Area A*	*Area B*	*Area C*	*Area D*	*Area E*
1	T1/6	—	—	—	—	1
4	T4/5	—	—	1	—	1
	T4/18	—	—	—	—	5
5b	T5b/4	—	—	—	—	1
7	T7/14	—	—	1	—	—
8	T8/1	—	—	—	—	2
	T8/6	—	—	—	—	1
10	T10/6	—	1	—	—	—
11	T11/1	—	—	—	1	1
	T11/2	3	6	6	5	4
	T11/4	1	—	—	1	—
	T11/8	—	—	—	1	—
	T11/9	—	1	1	—	—
	T11/10	—	1	1	—	—
12	T12/2	—	—	1	—	—
	T12/5	—	—	2	—	—
13	T13/1	10	3	—	—	—
	T13/2	30	9	3	—	—
	T13/3	2	—	—	—	—
	T13/5	3	—	—	—	—
	T13/7	1	—	—	—	—
	T13/8	3	1	—	—	—
	T13/10	1	—	—	—	—
	T13/11	1	1	—	—	—
	T13/12	12	14	2	—	2
14	T14/9	1	—	—	—	—
16	T16/3	—	—	3	—	—

Table C.11. THS 11 typed diagnostics

Period	*Type*	*Quantity*
7	T7/11	1
10	T10/5	1
	T10/9	1
	T10/10	4
	T10/12	4
	T10/13	2
	T10/15	2
16	T16/3	1
21	T21/2	1

Table C.12. THS 12 (al-Asila) typed diagnostics

Period	*Type*	*Quantity*
1	T1/1	15
	T1/6	3
4	T4/2	1
7	T7/9	1
	T7/11	2
	T7/14	1
10	T10/3	1
	T10/10	2
	T10/11	1
	T10/12	10
	T10/13	3
16	T16/3	1

Table C.13. THS 13 typed diagnostics

Period	*Type*	*Quantity*
7	T7/14	1
10	T10/5	2
	T10/8	1
11	T11/1	4
	T11/2	3
	T11/4	3
	T11/8	2
12	T12/4	1

Table C.14. THS 14 typed diagnostics

Period	*Type*	*Quantity*
7	T7/11	1
10	T10/5	2
	T10/9	1
	T10/10	3
	T10/12	3
	T10/13	1
	T10/14	1
14	T14/0	1
	T14/4	1

Table C.15. THS 15 typed diagnostics

Period	*Type*	*Quantity*
2	T2/1	4
4	T4/4	1
	T4/5	1
5b	T5b/1	2
	T5b/3	1
	T5b/4	4
	T5b/5	2
	T5b/9	3
14	T14/4	1
15	T15/3	1
16	T16/3	1

Table C.16. THS 16 (Tell al-Sara) typed diagnostics

Period	*Type*	*Area A*	*Area B*
2	T2/1	1	—
4	T4/18	2	—
5b	T5b/3	1	—
	T5b/4	1	—
6	T6/8	4	—
7	T7/1	3	—
	T7/4	4	—
	T7/5	3	—
	T7/8	1	—
	T7/9	2	—
	T7/14	1	—
	T7/20	1	—
8	T8/1	21	—
	T8/2	2	—
	T8/6	1	—
10	T10/5	—	1
	T10/10	1	1
	T10/12	—	2
	T10/13	—	4
11	T11/1	1	—
	T11/2	5	2
	T11/3	2	1
	T11/4	2	1
	T11/8	2	3
	T11/14	1	—
12	T12/2	1	—
	T12/3	1	—
13	T13/1	5	—
	T13/2	2	—
	T13/11	1	—
15	T15/1	1	—
16	T16/2	2	—
	T16/3	4	—
17	T17/4	2	—
	T17/6	1	—
18	T18/1	1	—
21	T21/2	1	—

Table C.17. THS 17 (al-Masiha) typed diagnostics

Period	*Type*	*Quantity*
3	T3/2	1
4	T4/1	5
	T4/2	2
	T4/3	1
	T4/4	3
	T4/5	6
	T4/7	3
	T4/8	2
	T4/9	1
	T4/18	4
5b	T5b/3	2

Table C.18. THS 18 typed diagnostics

Period	*Type*	*Area A*	*Area B*	*Area C*	*Area D*	*Area E*
2	T2/1	—	—	—	4	—
4	T4/4	—	—	1	2	—
5b	T5b/4	—	—	—	1	—
	T5b/5	—	—	—	2	—
8	T8/1	5	1	2	5	—
	T8/6	1	1	—	—	—
10	T10/3	—	—	—	1	—
	T10/8	—	—	—	1	—
11	T11/1	—	—	1	1	—
	T11/2	—	—	—	1	—
	T11/4	1	—	—	2	—
	T11/8	—	—	2	—	—
	T11/10	—	—	—	1	—
14	T14/3	—	—	—	1	—
15	T15/1	1	—	—	—	—
16	T16/1	—	1	2	—	—
	T16/2	—	3	—	—	1
	T16/3	8	13	8	6	10
	T16/4	—	2	—	—	—
17	T17/4	4	1	3	—	6
	T17/5	5	2	—	—	1
	T17/6	2	—	—	1	1
18	T18/1	—	1	2	—	—
19	T19/1	1	10	11	1	3
	T19/2	1	3	—	—	2
	T19/3	—	—	3	—	—
	T19/4	—	3	—	—	—
	T19/5	—	—	1	—	—
20	T20/1	—	—	2	—	—
	T20/2	—	—	1	—	—
21	T21/1	—	—	1	—	—
	T21/2	—	1	1	—	2
	T21/6	3	5	3	—	—

Table C.19. THS 20 (Khirbat 'Ali) typed diagnostics

Period	*Type*	*Area A*	*Area B*	*Area C*	*Area D*	*Area E*	*Area F*
2	T2/1	10	3	14	1	—	—
4	T4/4	—	—	—	—	1	—
	T4/18	—	—	2	—	—	—
5b	T5b/1	1	—	2	—	1	—
	T5b/4	6	2	3	—	—	—
	T5b/5	—	—	1	—	—	—
7	T7/1	—	—	—	1	—	—
	T7/2	1	—	—	—	—	—
	T7/9	—	2	—	—	—	1
	T7/11	—	1	—	—	—	—
	T7/14	—	1	—	—	1	—
10	T10/12	—	—	—	2	—	—
11	T11/1	—	1	—	—	—	—
	T11/2	2	5	—	1	—	—
	T11/3	—	1	—	—	—	—
	T11/4	—	1	—	—	—	—
	T11/8	1	13	—	—	—	—
	T11/11	—	1	—	—	—	—
12	T12/1	—	1	—	—	—	—
	T12/4	—	—	—	—	1	—
	T12/5	1	—	—	—	—	—
14	T14/1	—	—	—	—	1	—
	T14/2	—	—	—	—	2	3
	T14/3	—	—	—	—	1	2
	T14/5	—	—	—	1	—	—
	T14/6	—	—	—	—	—	1
16	T16/3	—	—	1	—	—	1
	T16/4	—	—	—	—	—	1

Table C.20. THS 21 typed diagnostics

Period	*Type*	*Quantity*
4	T4/1	1
	T4/4	3
	T4/5	2
	T4/18	3

Table C.21. THS 22 typed diagnostics

Period	*Type*	*Qty*
5b	T5b/1	1
7	T7/1	1
	T7/2	1
	T7/4	1
	T7/9	2
	T7/15	1
	T7/20	1

Table C.22. THS 23 typed diagnostics.

Period	*Type*	*Area A*	*Area B*	*Area C*	*Area D*
7	T7/1	—	—	—	1
	T7/9	1	—	—	—
	T7/14	—	—	1	—
8	T8/1	—	—	1	—
	T8/2	—	—	1	—
	T8/6	1	—	—	—
10	T10/5	—	—	—	1
	T10/8	—	—	—	1
	T10/9	1	—	—	—
	T10/10	—	6	1	—
	T10/12	1	1	1	—
	T10/15	—	—	2	—
11	T11/0	—	—	1	—
	T11/1	1	1	2	—
	T11/2	1	2	4	—
	T11/4	2	2	1	—
	T11/8	1	1	—	—
	T11/9	—	1	—	—
12	T12/2	1	—	—	—
	T12/5	—	—	2	—
13	T13/1	—	—	1	—
	T13/2	1	—	3	2
14	T14/0	—	—	3	—
	T14/3	—	—	1	—
16	T16/3	—	—	—	1
20	T20/1	—	—	—	1
21	T21/6	1	—	—	—

Table C.23. THS 24 (Khirbat al-'Abd) typed diagnostics

Period	Type	Area																					
		A	B	C	D	E	F	G	H	I	J	K	L	M	N	O	P	Q	R	S	T	U	V
1	T1/1	—	—	—	—	—	—	—	—	—	1	—	—	—	—	—	—	—	—	—	—	—	—
2	T2/1	2	—	—	—	1	3	—	—	—	—	—	1	1	—	—	—	—	1	—	—	—	—
3	T3/5	—	—	—	—	—	—	—	—	—	1	—	—	—	—	—	—	1	—	—	—	—	—
4	T4/4	—	—	—	—	—	—	—	—	—	—	—	—	—	—	—	—	1	—	—	—	—	—
5b	T5b/4	—	—	—	—	—	—	—	—	—	1	—	—	—	—	—	—	—	—	—	—	—	—
	T5b/5	—	—	—	—	—	—	—	—	—	1	—	—	—	—	—	—	—	—	—	—	—	—
6	T6/1	1	—	—	—	—	—	—	—	—	—	—	—	—	—	—	—	—	—	—	—	—	—
7	T7/9	—	—	—	—	—	—	—	—	—	—	—	—	—	—	—	—	1	3	—	—	—	—
	T7/10	—	—	—	—	—	—	—	—	—	—	—	—	—	—	—	—	2	—	—	—	—	—
	T7/14	—	—	—	—	—	—	—	—	—	—	—	—	—	—	—	—	—	—	1	—	—	—
	T7/15	—	—	—	—	—	—	—	—	—	—	—	—	—	1	—	—	1	—	—	—	—	—
8	T8/1	5	12	12	7	9	7	—	4	10	5	1	—	7	—	—	—	—	2	—	4	—	—
	T8/2	—	1	1	1	1	—	3	1	6	6	—	—	—	—	1	—	2	—	2	—	1	—
	T8/5	—	—	—	—	1	—	2	2	1	3	—	—	—	—	—	—	—	—	—	—	—	—
	T8/6	—	3	—	2	—	1	2	2	4	4	—	—	2	1	2	2	—	—	—	—	—	—
10	T10/0	—	—	—	—	—	—	—	—	—	—	—	—	6	—	3	—	—	—	—	—	—	—
	T10/3	—	—	—	—	—	—	—	—	—	—	—	—	—	—	—	—	—	1	—	—	—	—
	T10/5	—	—	—	—	—	—	—	1	1	—	—	—	—	1	—	—	—	—	3	—	—	—
	T10/6	—	—	—	—	2	—	1	2	—	—	—	—	—	—	—	—	1	—	—	—	—	—
	T10/8	—	—	—	—	—	1	1	—	—	—	—	—	—	—	—	—	—	2	—	—	—	—
	T10/9	—	—	—	—	—	—	—	—	—	—	—	—	—	1	—	—	—	3	2	—	—	—
	T10/10	—	—	—	2	1	1	5	1	1	—	—	—	—	—	—	—	3	9	4	1	—	—
	T10/11	—	2	—	—	—	—	1	—	—	—	—	—	—	—	—	—	—	—	—	—	—	—
	T10/12	—	2	—	1	—	2	13	—	1	1	—	2	3	1	1	2	5	6	1	1	1	—
	T10/13	1	—	—	—	—	—	—	—	—	—	—	—	—	3	—	—	1	3	1	—	—	—
11	T11/1	—	1	—	—	1	—	—	—	—	—	—	—	—	1	—	—	—	—	—	—	—	—
	T11/2	—	1	—	—	1	3	—	—	—	—	—	—	—	3	—	—	—	—	—	—	—	—
	T11/4	—	1	—	—	—	1	—	—	—	—	—	—	—	—	1	—	—	—	—	—	—	—
	T11/8	—	2	1	—	—	2	—	—	—	—	—	—	—	1	—	—	—	—	—	—	—	—
	T11/14	—	—	—	—	1	—	—	—	—	—	—	—	—	—	—	—	—	—	—	—	—	—
12	T12/1	—	—	—	—	1	—	—	—	—	—	—	—	—	—	—	—	—	—	—	—	—	—
	T12/2	—	—	—	—	1	—	—	1	—	—	—	1	—	—	—	—	—	—	—	—	—	—
	T12/3	—	1	1	—	—	—	—	1	—	—	—	1	—	1	—	—	—	—	1	—	—	—
	T12/5	—	1	—	—	—	—	—	—	—	—	—	1	1	—	—	—	—	—	—	—	—	—
	T12/7	—	—	—	—	—	—	—	—	—	—	—	—	—	—	1	—	—	—	—	—	—	—
13	T13/0	—	—	—	—	—	—	—	—	—	—	—	—	3	—	6	—	—	—	—	—	—	—
	T13/1	—	—	—	—	—	—	—	—	—	—	—	—	—	—	—	—	5	—	—	—	—	—
	T13/2	—	—	—	—	—	—	—	—	—	—	1	—	—	—	1	1	24	1	—	—	—	—
	T13/3	—	—	—	—	—	—	—	—	—	—	—	—	—	—	—	—	1	—	—	—	—	—
	T13/7	—	—	—	—	—	—	—	—	—	—	—	—	—	—	—	—	6	—	2	—	—	—
	T13/9	—	—	—	—	—	—	—	—	—	—	—	—	—	—	—	—	1	—	—	—	—	—
	T13/11	—	—	—	—	—	—	—	—	—	—	—	1	—	—	—	—	—	—	—	—	—	—
	T13/12	—	—	—	—	—	—	—	—	—	—	—	—	1	—	—	—	1	—	—	—	—	—
	T13/13	—	—	—	—	—	—	—	—	—	1	—	—	—	—	—	—	—	—	—	—	—	—

Table C.23. THS 24 (Khirbat al-'Abd) typed diagnostics (*cont.*)

Period	*Type*	*Area*																					
		A	*B*	*C*	*D*	*E*	*F*	*G*	*H*	*I*	*J*	*K*	*L*	*M*	*N*	*O*	*P*	*Q*	*R*	*S*	*T*	*U*	*V*
14	T14/0	—	—	—	—	—	—	—	—	—	—	—	—	4	—	—	—	—	—	—	—	—	—
	T14/1	—	—	—	—	—	—	—	—	—	—	—	—	—	1	—	1	—	—	—	—	—	—
	T14/2	—	—	—	—	—	—	—	—	—	—	—	1	—	2	—	—	—	—	—	—	—	—
	T14/3	—	—	—	—	—	—	—	—	—	—	—	—	—	2	1	—	—	—	—	—	—	—
	T14/4	—	—	—	—	—	—	—	—	—	—	—	1	—	1	—	1	—	—	—	—	—	—
	T14/5	—	—	—	—	—	—	—	—	—	—	—	—	1	2	—	—	—	—	—	—	—	—
	T14/6	—	—	—	—	—	—	—	—	—	—	—	—	—	3	—	—	—	—	—	—	—	—
	T14/7	—	—	—	—	—	—	—	—	—	—	—	—	—	1	—	—	—	—	—	—	—	—
	T14/8	—	—	—	—	—	—	—	—	—	—	—	—	—	1	—	—	—	—	—	—	—	—
	T14/12	—	—	—	—	—	—	—	—	—	—	—	—	—	1	—	—	—	—	—	—	—	—
15	T15/1	—	—	—	—	—	—	—	—	—	—	—	—	—	—	—	—	—	3	1	—	7	2
	T15/2	—	—	—	—	—	—	—	—	—	—	—	—	—	—	—	—	—	—	—	—	—	4
	T15/3	—	—	—	—	—	—	—	—	—	—	—	—	—	—	—	—	—	—	1	—	—	3
16	T16/1	—	—	—	—	—	—	—	—	—	—	—	—	—	—	—	—	—	5	5	3	13	9
	T16/2	1	3	—	1	—	—	—	—	—	—	—	—	—	—	—	—	—	—	—	—	—	2
	T16/3	—	3	3	2	3	3	—	1	1	—	—	—	—	1	—	—	1	4	—	5	10	4
	T16/4	—	—	—	—	—	—	1	—	—	—	—	—	—	—	—	—	—	—	—	—	—	—
	T16/6	—	—	—	—	—	—	—	—	—	—	—	—	—	—	—	—	—	—	—	1	—	—
17	T17/1	—	—	1	—	—	—	—	—	—	—	—	—	—	—	—	—	—	—	—	—	—	—
	T17/4	1	5	3	6	—	—	—	—	—	1	—	—	—	—	1	—	—	2	—	—	—	—
19	T19/1	—	2	—	—	—	—	—	—	—	—	—	—	—	—	—	—	—	—	—	—	—	—
20	T20/4	—	—	2	—	—	—	—	—	—	—	—	—	—	—	—	1	—	—	—	—	—	—
21	T21/2	2	6	1	2	1	—	—	—	—	—	—	—	1	—	—	1	—	—	—	—	—	—
	T21/5	—	—	1	1	—	—	—	—	—	—	—	—	—	—	—	—	—	—	—	—	—	—

Table C.24. THS 25 (Hamoukar southern extension, Khirbat al-Fakhar) diagnostics from the central mounded area

Period	*Type*	*Area*																
		A	*B*	*C*	*D*	*E*	*F*	*G*	*H*	*I*	*J*	*K*	*L*	*M*	*N*	*O*	*P*	*Q*
4	T4/0	—	—	—	—	—	—	—	—	—	—	—	—	—	—	—	—	1
	T4/1	6	18	7	3	23	9	18	3	4	4	5	2	—	16	2	14	—
	T4/2	5	1	—	1	2	2	6	—	—	—	1	1	2	—	2	1	—
	T4/3	—	2	—	—	—	1	—	—	—	—	—	—	2	2	1	4	—
	T4/4	—	1	—	1	4	—	2	2	3	4	6	2	1	—	—	1	1
	T4/5	4	3	3	—	2	1	4	3	2	—	6	2	5	7	2	1	5
	T4/6	—	—	—	—	—	—	—	—	—	—	1	—	1	—	—	—	1
	T4/7	—	—	—	1	—	1	3	—	1	1	6	—	—	—	2	—	3
	T4/8	—	2	—	—	2	2	3	2	2	2	3	1	1	9	2	1	—
	T4/9	—	—	—	—	—	—	—	—	—	—	3	—	—	—	—	1	1
	T4/10	—	—	—	—	—	1	—	2	—	1	12	1	4	—	7	—	1
	T4/11	—	—	—	—	—	—	—	—	—	—	—	—	—	1	—	—	2
	T4/12	—	—	—	—	—	—	—	—	—	—	—	—	—	—	2	—	—
	T4/14	—	—	—	—	—	—	—	—	1	—	5	1	—	—	2	—	—
	T4/15	—	—	—	—	—	—	—	—	—	—	—	—	—	14	—	—	—
	T4/18	4	1	1	1	10	3	—	1	2	2	5	1	5	4	1	—	—
7	T7/2	—	—	1	—	—	—	—	—	—	—	—	—	—	—	—	—	—
	T7/4	—	—	1	—	—	—	—	—	—	—	—	—	—	—	—	1	—
	T7/5	—	—	—	—	—	—	—	—	—	—	—	—	—	—	—	1	1
	T7/9	—	—	—	—	—	—	1	—	1	—	—	—	—	—	—	—	—
	T7/11	—	—	1	—	—	—	—	—	—	—	—	—	—	—	—	—	—
	T7/12	—	—	—	—	—	—	—	—	—	—	—	—	—	—	1	—	—
	T7/14	—	—	—	—	—	—	1	—	—	—	—	—	—	—	—	—	—
	T7/15	—	—	—	—	1	—	—	—	1	—	—	—	—	—	—	—	—
11	T11/2	—	—	—	—	—	—	—	—	1	—	—	—	—	—	—	—	—
12	T12/1	—	—	—	—	—	—	—	1	—	—	—	—	—	—	—	—	—
	T12/2	—	—	—	—	—	—	1	—	—	—	—	—	—	—	—	—	—
13	T13/0	—	—	—	—	—	—	—	5	—	—	—	—	—	—	—	—	—
	T13/1	—	—	—	—	—	—	—	—	5	—	—	—	—	—	—	—	—
	T13/2	—	—	—	—	—	—	2	1	21	—	—	—	—	—	—	—	—
	T13/3	—	—	—	—	—	—	—	—	1	—	—	—	—	—	—	—	—
	T13/12	—	—	—	—	—	—	—	—	4	—	—	—	—	—	—	—	—
14	T14/0	—	—	—	—	—	—	—	—	—	5	—	—	—	—	—	—	—
	T14/1	—	—	—	—	—	—	—	—	—	—	—	—	—	—	—	2	—
	T14/2	—	—	—	—	—	—	3	—	1	6	—	1	—	—	3	4	—
	T14/3	—	—	—	—	—	—	—	—	1	4	—	—	1	—	1	—	—
	T14/4	—	—	—	—	—	—	—	—	—	1	—	—	—	—	—	2	—
	T14/5	—	—	—	—	—	—	2	—	—	2	—	1	—	—	1	1	—
	T14/6	—	—	—	—	—	—	—	—	—	3	—	—	—	—	1	—	—
	T14/7	—	—	—	—	—	—	—	—	—	8	—	—	—	—	—	—	—
	T14/8	—	—	—	—	—	—	3	—	—	—	—	—	—	—	—	3	—
	T14/9	—	—	—	—	—	—	1	—	—	—	—	—	—	—	—	—	—
	T14/11	—	—	—	—	—	—	—	—	1	—	—	—	—	—	—	—	—
	T14/12	—	—	—	—	—	—	2	—	—	2	—	—	—	—	—	—	—

Table C.24. THS 25 (Hamoukar southern extension, Khirbat al-Fakhar) diagnostics from the central mounded area (*cont.*)

Period	*Type*	*Area*																
		A	*B*	*C*	*D*	*E*	*F*	*G*	*H*	*I*	*J*	*K*	*L*	*M*	*N*	*O*	*P*	*Q*
16	T16/2	—	—	1	—	2	—	—	—	—	—	—	—	—	—	—	—	—
	T16/3	2	2	—	4	9	3	9	—	—	—	—	—	—	—	—	1	—
	T16/4	—	1	—	6	2	—	—	—	—	—	—	—	—	—	—	—	—
17	T17/2	—	—	—	—	1	—	—	—	—	—	—	—	—	—	—	—	—
	T17/3	—	—	1	1	7	—	—	—	—	—	—	—	—	—	—	—	—
	T17/4	—	—	1	—	10	2	2	—	—	—	—	—	—	—	—	—	—
	T17/5	—	—	—	1	1	1	—	—	—	—	—	—	—	—	—	—	—
	T17/6	—	—	—	1	1	—	—	—	—	—	—	—	—	—	—	—	—
19	T19/1	—	3	—	2	—	4	—	—	—	—	—	—	—	—	—	—	—
	T19/2	—	1	—	—	—	—	—	—	—	—	—	—	—	—	—	—	—
	T19/4	—	—	—	—	—	1	2	—	—	—	—	—	—	—	—	—	—
20	T20/0	—	—	—	—	—	—	—	—	—	1	—	—	—	—	—	—	—
	T20/1	—	—	1	—	—	—	—	—	—	—	—	—	—	—	—	—	—
	T20/2	—	—	1	—	—	—	—	—	—	—	—	—	—	—	—	—	—
21	T21/2	1	3	—	6	4	2	4	—	—	—	—	—	—	—	—	—	—
	T21/4	—	—	—	2	—	—	—	—	—	—	—	—	—	—	—	—	—
	T21/5	—	—	1	—	—	—	—	—	—	—	—	—	—	—	—	—	—
	T21/6	—	1	—	1	—	—	—	—	—	—	—	—	—	—	—	—	—

Table C.25. THS 26 (Khirbat Awa'id) typed diagnostics

Period	*Type*	*Quantity*
3	T3/1	4
	T3/4	1
	T3/5	4
4	T4/0	9
	T4/1	6
	T4/3	1
	T4/4	2
	T4/5	16
	T4/8	8
	T4/10	1
	T4/15	1
	T4/18	2
5b	T5b/7	1
7	T7/9	1
12	T12/3	3

Table C.26. THS 27 (Tell Fakhar) typed diagnostics

Period	*Type*	*Quantity*
4	T4/2	4
	T4/4	1
	T4/9	1
	T4/10	4
	T4/18	1
11	T11/1	5
	T11/2	2
	T11/4	2
	T11/5	2
	T11/6	1
	T11/8	8
	T11/10	2
	T11/11	2
	T11/14	1
12	T12/1	5
	T12/3	1
	T12/5	11
16	T16/3	1

Table C.27. THS 29 typed diagnostics

Period	*Type*	*Quantity*
3	T3/1	12
	T3/3	3
	T3/5	15
6	T6/6	1
7	T7/2	1
16	T16/3	1
21	T21/6	1

Table C.28. THS 30 typed diagnostics

Period	*Type*	*Quantity*
4	T4/2	3
	T4/3	1
	T4/4	4
	T4/5	6
	T4/8	1
	T4/18	15
7	T7/5	2
	T7/11	1
	T7/12	1
16	T16/3	1
17	T17/4	2

Table C.29. THS 31 typed diagnostics

Period	*Type*	*Quantity*
4	T4/1	3
	T4/2	7
	T4/4	5
	T4/5	8
	T4/9	12
	T4/18	9
5b	T5b/1	1
	T5b/4	4
5a	T5a/5	1
6	T6/6	1
7	T7/5	3
	T7/9	3
	T7/14	2

Table C.30. THS 32 (Khirbat 'Asaylan) typed diagnostics

Period	*Type*	*Area A*	*Area B*	*Area C*	*Area D*
2	T2/1	5	6	3	4
3	T3/4	—	1	—	—
4	T4/2	—	1	—	—
	T4/3	—	1	—	—
	T4/4	—	1	—	—
	T4/5	—	1	1	—
	T4/18	—	1	1	—
5b	T5b/2	1	1	—	—
	T5b/3	—	1	3	1
	T5b/4	—	—	1	2
	T5b/5	—	1	—	—
5a	T5a/1	1	—	—	—
7	T7/5	—	—	1	—
	T7/8	—	—	—	1
	T7/9	—	—	—	1
	T7/15	—	—	—	1
8	T8/1	4	11	5	1
	T8/2	1	2	—	1
	T8/6	—	2	2	—
	T8/9	—	1	1	—
10	T10/5	—	5	1	—
	T10/9	1	—	—	—
	T10/10	—	2	—	—
	T10/11	—	1	—	—
	T10/12	—	2	2	—
	T10/13	—	—	1	—
11	T11/1	1	1	—	1
	T11/2	8	6	2	4
	T11/3	—	1	—	—
	T11/4	3	9	1	4
	T11/6	1	—	—	—
	T11/8	8	5	6	5
	T11/9	2	3	—	1
	T11/11	2	2	3	—
	T11/12	—	4	—	—
	T11/14	—	—	—	3

Table C.30. THS 32 (Khirbat ‘Asaylan) typed diagnostics (*cont.*)

Period	*Type*	*Area A*	*Area B*	*Area C*	*Area D*
12	T12/1	1	—	1	—
	T12/3	—	3	—	—
	T12/5	1	1	1	1
	T12/6	1	—	—	—
13	T13/7	1	—	—	—
14	T14/3	—	2	—	—
	T14/6	—	1	—	—
15	T15/2	—	1	—	—
16	T16/1	3	—	—	—
	T16/3	1	—	—	—
17	T17/4	—	—	—	1
21	T21/5	1	—	—	2

Table C.31. THS 33 typed diagnostics

Period	*Type*	*Quantity*
4	T4/3	1
	T4/18	3
5b	T5b/2	4
	T5b/3	11
	T5b/7	2
10	T10/5	2
11	T11/11	1
16	T16/2	1

Table C.32. THS 34 (Tell al-Fakhar) typed diagnostics

Period	*Type*	*Area A*	*Area B*
10	T10/10	—	2
	T10/12	3	—
	T10/13	1	—
11	T11/1	—	3
	T11/2	—	1
	T11/3	—	2
	T11/4	—	1
	T11/8	—	4
	T11/10	—	2
12	T12/2	—	1
	T12/5	2	3

Table C.33. THS 35 typed diagnostics

Period	*Type*	*Quantity*
7	T7/1	1
	T7/12	1
10	T10/3	1
	T10/10	2
	T10/15	2
11	T11/4	2
	T11/8	3

Table C.34. THS 36 typed diagnostics

Period	*Type*	*Quantity*
5b	T5b/1	2
	T5b/4	11
	T5b/5	1

Table C.35. THS 37 (Umm Adham) typed diagnostics

Period	*Type*	*Area A*	*Area B*
5b	T5b/11	1	—
7	T7/2	1	—
	T7/4	7	—
	T7/9	1	—
	T7/12	1	—
	T7/20	1	—
8	T8/1	7	—
	T8/3	3	—
10	T10/4	—	2
	T10/6	2	—
	T10/10	4	5
	T10/12	3	—
	T10/13	—	2
11	T11/4	—	1
12	T12/5	—	4
16	T16/1	—	1
	T16/3	1	4

Table C.36. THS 39 typed diagnostics

Period	*Type*	*Quantity*
1	T1/1	23
	T1/6	4
	T1/7	3
4	T4/3	1
	T4/4	1
	T4/18	1
6	T6/1	3
7	T7/2	2
19	T19/1	2
21	T21/5	1

Table C.37. THS 40 (Khirbat Melhem) typed diagnostics

Period	Type	Area A	Area B	Area C	Area D	Area E	Area F	Area G	Area H	Area I
4	T4/3	—	—	1	—	—	—	—	—	—
5b	T5b/1	9	—	—	—	—	1	—	—	—
	T5b/2	2	—	—	—	—	—	—	—	2
	T5b/3	—	—	1	—	—	—	—	—	—
	T5b/4	3	—	—	—	—	1	—	1	8
	T5b/5	4	—	—	—	—	—	—	—	2
	T5b/9	1	—	—	—	—	—	—	—	—
	T5b/10	1	—	—	—	—	—	—	—	—
	T5b/11	8	2	6	4	1	2	8	9	3
5a	T5a/0	7	4	2	12	3	1	2	3	8
	T5a/1	3	7	9	10	6	11	17	11	7
	T5a/2	1	—	—	—	—	—	—	—	—
	T5a/3	1	—	—	—	—	—	—	1	5
	T5a/4	—	—	—	—	—	—	—	1	—
	T5a/5	5	2	3	2	1	—	3	4	5
	T5a/6	2	—	1	1	2	—	2	3	4
	T5a/7	7	1	4	1	2	2	4	2	4
	T5a/8	4	1	1	1	1	—	2	1	3
7	T7/1	—	—	—	—	—	—	—	1	—
	T7/2	1	—	—	—	—	—	—	—	—
11	T11/1	—	—	—	1	—	—	—	—	—
	T11/2	1	—	—	4	1	3	—	—	1
	T11/4	—	—	—	1	—	—	—	—	1
	T11/8	—	2	1	5	1	—	—	—	—
	T11/9	—	—	—	—	1	—	—	—	—
	T11/11	—	—	1	—	1	—	—	—	—
	T11/14	—	1	—	—	—	—	—	—	—
12	T12/3	—	—	1	1	1	—	—	—	—
	T12/5	—	—	1	1	—	1	—	—	—
16	T16/3	1	1	2	2	—	1	—	1	—
	T16/4	—	—	1	—	—	—	—	—	—
17	T17/4	—	1	—	—	—	—	—	—	—
20	T20/0	—	—	1	—	—	—	—	—	—
21	T21/0	—	—	—	3	—	—	—	—	—
	T21/6	1	—	—	—	—	—	—	—	—

Table C.38. THS 41 (Tell Na'ur) typed diagnostics

Period	*Type*	*Area A*	*Area B*	*Area C*	*Area D*	*Area E*	*Area F*	*Area G*	*Area H*	*Area I*	*Area J*
2	T2/1	16	29	25	7	1	10	—	—	—	—
5b	T5b/1	—	—	—	—	—	1	—	—	—	—
	T5b/3	—	—	—	—	—	2	—	—	—	—
	T5b/4	—	1	—	—	1	1	—	—	—	—
	T5b/5	—	—	1	—	—	—	—	—	—	—
	T5b/7	—	—	—	—	—	1	—	—	—	—
	T5b/10	—	2	1	—	—	—	—	—	—	—
6	T6/1	—	3	1	—	—	—	—	—	—	—
	T6/6	1	—	—	—	—	—	—	—	—	—
	T6/8	2	6	4	—	—	—	—	—	—	—
7	T7/1	—	1	4	—	1	—	—	—	—	—
	T7/2	3	—	2	—	—	—	—	—	—	—
	T7/4	1	3	7	1	2	—	—	—	—	—
	T7/5	3	1	3	2	—	—	—	—	—	—
	T7/9	—	2	—	1	—	—	—	—	—	—
	T7/15	1	—	—	—	—	—	—	—	—	—
	T7/20	2	2	1	—	—	—	—	—	—	—
8	T8/1	21	40	35	10	5	8	—	1	—	—
	T8/2	3	11	4	—	3	4	—	—	—	—
	T8/3	1	1	3	—	—	1	—	—	—	—
	T8/6	3	2	—	—	2	3	—	—	—	—
	T8/9	—	—	—	—	1	—	—	—	—	—
10	T10/10	1	—	—	—	1	2	—	—	—	—
	T10/12	—	1	—	—	—	3	1	—	—	—
11	T11/1	—	—	—	1	—	—	1	—	—	—
	T11/2	—	—	—	—	—	—	5	—	1	—
	T11/4	—	—	—	—	—	—	1	1	—	—
	T11/8	—	—	—	—	—	—	8	—	—	—
	T11/9	—	—	—	—	—	—	1	—	—	—
	T11/11	—	—	—	—	—	—	1	—	—	—
	T11/14	—	—	—	—	—	—	1	—	—	—
12	T12/1	—	—	—	—	—	—	1	—	—	—
	T12/2	—	—	—	—	—	—	1	—	—	—
	T12/4	—	—	—	—	—	—	1	—	—	—
	T12/5	—	—	—	—	—	—	—	—	1	—
13	T13/1	—	—	—	—	—	—	—	—	1	—
	T13/2	1	1	—	—	—	2	3	—	1	1
14	T14/1	—	—	—	—	—	—	—	1	—	—
	T14/3	—	—	—	—	—	—	—	—	—	1
15	T15/3	—	—	1	—	—	—	—	—	—	—
16	T16/1	—	—	—	—	—	—	1	—	1	—
	T16/3	—	—	—	—	—	2	1	2	2	—
	T16/4	2	—	—	—	—	—	—	—	—	—

Table C.39. THS 42 (Nasiriya Sharqiya) typed diagnostics

Period	*Type*	*Quantity*
10	T10/10	2
11	T11/1	1
	T11/2	1
12	T12/5	2
19	T19/1	3
	T19/4	1

Table C.40. THS 43 (Khirbat Barjis) typed diagnostics

Period	*Type*	*Area A*	*Area B*	*Area C*	*Area D*	*Area E*	*Area F*	*Area G*
2	T2/1	—	—	1	3	1	7	—
5b	T5b/1	—	—	—	2	—	1	1
	T5b/2	—	—	—	1	—	—	—
	T5b/4	—	—	—	2	—	1	—
	T5b/5	—	—	—	—	—	1	—
5a	T5a/3	—	—	—	—	—	2	—
	T5a/6	—	—	—	—	—	1	—
11	T11/1	—	2	1	1	1	3	—
	T11/2	1	5	5	6	—	4	—
	T11/3	1	—	—	1	—	—	—
	T11/4	—	—	3	1	3	—	—
	T11/6	—	—	1	—	2	—	—
	T11/8	—	—	4	10	12	8	—
	T11/9	—	—	—	1	—	—	—
	T11/14	1	—	2	5	3	—	—
12	T12/1	1	—	—	—	—	—	—
	T12/3	—	—	1	—	—	2	—
	T12/4	—	—	—	1	1	—	—
	T12/5	—	1	3	2	1	2	1
13	T13/2	1	2	2	4	—	—	1
	T13/11	—	—	1	—	—	—	—
	T13/12	—	—	—	3	—	—	1
14	T14/1	—	—	1	1	—	—	1
	T14/2	—	4	—	—	—	—	5
	T14/3	—	—	2	—	—	—	1
	T14/4	—	1	—	—	—	—	2
	T14/5	2	—	—	—	—	—	1
	T14/6	—	—	—	—	—	—	1
	T14/7	—	—	—	—	—	—	1
	T14/8	—	—	—	—	—	—	5
	T14/12	1	—	—	—	—	—	1
16	T16/3	—	—	—	—	1	—	—

Table C.41. THS 44 (Khirbat Taif) typed diagnostics

Period	*Type*	*Area A*	*Area B*
1	T1/0	1	6
	T1/1	8	4
	T1/2	1	—
	T1/6	—	1
	T1/7	1	6
3	T3/1	1	—
	T3/4	—	1
4	T4/1	1	—
	T4/2	1	—
	T4/5	4	—
5b	T5b/1	2	—
	T5b/2	—	1
	T5b/4	8	—
	T5b/5	3	—
7	T7/5	1	—
19	T19/1	1	—
20	T20/0	1	—

Table C.42. THS 45 (al-Saudiya) typed diagnostics

Period	*Type*	*Area A*	*Area B*	*Area C*	*Area D*
1	T1/1	—	1	—	—
7	T7/1	1	—	—	—
	T7/9	—	2	—	—
	T7/14	—	1	—	—
10	T10/3	1	—	—	—
	T10/5	—	1	—	—
	T10/10	4	1	—	1
	T10/12	1	—	—	—
	T10/13	2	—	—	—
11	T11/1	7	—	—	—
	T11/2	2	1	—	—
	T11/8	7	1	—	1
	T11/9	4	1	—	—
	T11/11	4	1	—	1
12	T12/5	2	—	—	—
13	T13/0	—	—	2	—
	T13/7	—	—	1	—
14	T14/2	—	—	1	—
	T14/3	—	—	—	3
	T14/6	—	—	—	1
	T14/8	—	—	—	1
15	T15/1	5	—	—	2
	T15/2	—	—	1	4
	T15/3	2	—	1	2
16	T16/1	7	1	—	4
	T16/2	—	1	—	3
	T16/3	—	3	6	—
19	T19/1	2	—	—	—
20	T20/1	—	—	—	1

Table C.43. THS 46 typed diagnostics

Period	*Type*	*Quantity*
3	T3/2	1
4	T4/0	11
	T4/5	3
5b	T5b/1	1
	T5b/4	1

Table C.44. THS 47 (Khirbat al-Sukar) typed diagnostics. Area B sherd counts are lost

Period	*Type*	*Area A*
7	T7/11	2
	T7/14	3
10	T10/12	1
	T10/13	1
13	T13/7	1
14	T14/1	1
	T14/2	5
	T14/3	2
	T14/12	2

Table C.45. THS 48 (Khirbat al-Shiha) typed diagnostics

Period	*Type*	*Area A*	*Area B*	*Area C*	*Area D*	*Area E*	*Area F*
6	T6/6	—	—	1	—	—	—
10	T10/10	2	1	—	—	—	—
11	T11/1	3	2	2	—	—	—
	T11/2	—	—	2	—	—	—
	T11/4	1	4	—	—	—	—
	T11/8	2	5	4	4	1	—
12	T12/1	—	—	—	—	1	—
	T12/2	—	—	—	3	—	—
	T12/3	2	1	2	1	—	—
	T12/5	1	3	1	—	—	—
13	T13/1	—	—	—	—	2	—
	T13/2	—	—	—	2	8	—
	T13/3	—	—	—	—	2	—
	T13/7	1	—	—	—	—	—
14	T14/3	—	—	—	—	—	2
	T14/6	—	—	—	—	—	1
15	T15/1	—	—	—	—	1	—
16	T16/2	1	—	2	—	—	—
	T16/3	2	3	4	—	—	—
17	T17/4	—	2	2	—	—	—
	T17/5	—	—	1	—	—	—
19	T19/1	—	2	—	—	—	—
	T19/2	—	1	—	—	—	—
20	T20/4	1	—	1	—	—	—

Table C.46. THS 50 (al-Botha) typed diagnostics. Area A was not formally collected

Period	*Type*	*Area B*
2	T2/1	1
16	T16/2	1
	T16/3	11
	T16/6	1
17	T17/3	1
	T17/5	3
	T17/6	4
21	T21/2	4

Table C.47. THS 51 typed diagnostics

Period	*Type*	*Quantity*
2	T2/1	9
6	T6/6	2
7	T7/1	1
	T7/9	4
	T7/10	1
	T7/11	1
	T7/14	5
	T7/15	1
10	T10/12	1
12	T12/2	2
	T12/7	1
13	T13/0	2
	T13/2	2
	T13/7	2
17	T17/4	1

Table C.48. THS 52 typed diagnostics

Period	*Type*	*Quantity*
2	T2/1	7

Table C.49. THS 53 typed diagnostics

Period	*Type*	*Quantity*
6	T6/7	1
10	T10/3	1
	T10/10	1
	T10/12	6
	T10/13	4
15	T15/1	1

Table C.50. THS 54 (Tell Tamr) typed diagnostics

Period	*Type*	*Area A*	*Area B*	*Area C*	*Area D*	*Area E*
4	T4/9	—	—	1	—	—
7	T7/4	—	—	—	1	2
	T7/5	—	—	—	1	4
	T7/11	—	—	—	—	1
	T7/14	—	—	1	—	—
8	T8/1	1	—	—	—	24
	T8/2	—	—	—	—	2
	T8/5	—	—	—	—	1
	T8/6	—	—	—	—	4
	T8/9	—	—	—	—	3
10	T10/5	3	—	—	—	1
	T10/9	1	1	—	—	—
	T10/10	2	—	—	—	—
	T10/12	1	—	—	1	5
	T10/13	1	—	—	—	—
11	T11/1	—	—	—	—	1
	T11/2	2	1	1	—	7
	T11/3	1	—	—	—	1
	T11/4	2	—	—	—	3
	T11/8	3	—	—	—	2
	T11/11	1	—	—	—	3
12	T12/1	1	—	—	—	1
	T12/5	—	—	1	—	1
13	T13/1	—	4	2	—	—
	T13/2	2	2	1	1	—
	T13/11	—	1	—	—	—
	T13/12	1	—	—	—	—
14	T14/2	—	2	—	1	—
	T14/9	—	2	—	—	—
15	T15/1	—	—	2	—	2
	T15/3	—	—	—	1	—
16	T16/1	—	1	—	6	—
	T16/2	1	1	2	6	—
	T16/3	2	3	4	12	6
	T16/4	—	—	—	2	1
	T16/6	—	—	—	3	—
17	T17/2	—	—	—	6	—
	T17/3	—	1	—	7	—
	T17/4	—	—	—	5	—
	T17/5	—	—	—	6	—
19	T19/1	1	—	—	2	—
21	T21/6	—	—	—	—	1

Table C.51. THS 55 typed diagnostics

Period	*Type*	*Quantity*
7	T7/11	1
	T7/5	1
11	T11/2	1
	T11/4	1
	T11/8	3
	T11/9	2
	T11/11	3
	T11/14	2
13	T13/12	1
14	T14/1	4
	T14/2	2
	T14/3	4
	T14/6	4
	T14/12	4
16	T16/2	2
	T16/3	2
17	T17/2	1
	T17/6	1
21	T21/2	1
	T21/3	1

Table C.52. THS 56 typed diagnostics

Period	*Type*	*Area A*	*Area B*	*Area C*	*Area D*
1	T1/1	—	2	—	—
2	T2/1	6	—	—	7
7	T7/1	2	—	—	—
16	T16/3	—	—	1	—
	T16/5	—	—	1	—
17	T17/3	—	—	3	—
21	T21/6	—	—	1	—

Table C.53. THS 57 typed diagnostics

Period	*Type*	*Quantity*
8	T8/6	2
10	T10/5	2
	T10/8	1
	T10/9	4
	T10/10	7
	T10/12	3

Table C.54. THS 58 typed diagnostics

Period	*Type*	*Quantity*
8	T8/1	1
	T8/6	4
10	T10/5	3
	T10/9	4
	T10/10	8
	T10/12	1
	T10/13	3

Table C.55. THS 59 typed diagnostics

Period	*Type*	*Quantity*
10	T10/9	2
11	T11/1	6
	T11/2	11
	T11/3	1
	T11/4	5
	T11/6	5
	T11/8	13
	T11/9	1
	T11/10	1
	T11/14	3

ملخص

الألفية الثالثة قبل الميلاد ، أصبحت حموكار مركزًا مدنيًا مزدهرًا تحيط به حقول مزروعة بكثافة. وكان مغطا وبقية الحوض بشبكة متطورة من الطرق والمسارات. يبدو أن توسع المستوطنة في العصر الحديدي يعود الى سياسة إعادة توطين بدو آراميين أو شعوب غزيت من أماكن أخرى سيطرت عليها الدولة. وجاءت المرحلة الأخيرة من التوسع الاستيطاني في الفترة الإسلامية المبكرة ، عندما كانت منطقة حموكار على الطريق بين نصيبين والموصل.

الملحق ألف (أ) هو فهرس المواقع الستين في منطقة حموكار ، مع معلومات حول أسماء المواقع وشكل المواقع ، وتاريخ الاستيطان. الملحق باء (ب) يصف ويوضح التسلسل الزمني للفخار، بما في ذلك من اجراء تقييم نقدي لجدوى الأنواع المختلفة. ويعرض الملحق جيم (ج) قوائم كمية للقطع الأثرية الهامة زمنيا التي وجدت في كل موقع ، ويوضح تجمعات كسر الفخار من المواقع المختارة.

شكر وتقدير. من دواعي سروري أن أشكر المديرية العامة للآثار والمتاحف في الجمهورية العربية السورية على منحي الاذن للعمل وعلى تشجيعها لي. على وجه الخصوص، أودّ أن أشكر المديرين العامين الحالي والسابق، عبد الرزاق معاذ و سلطان محيسن، ومدير الحفريات ، ميشيل المقدسي ، ومديرمحافظة الحسكة ، عبد المسيح بغدو. وقد كان كلّ من مدير حملة حموكار السورية الأمريكية ، ماجواير جيبسون من جامعة شيكاغو معهد الدراسات الشرقية وعمرو العظم من جامعة دمشق في غاية الكرك عندما أسندا إليّ مهمة القيام بالمسح الاثري للتل.

من الاستيطان المنخفض الكثافة ، ممّا يجعله موقع فريد في عصور ما قبل التاريخ في بلاد ما بين النهرين. في الألفية الرابعة، أمّنت منطقة حموكار للمستوطنات الأصلية و لمستوطنات توسع أوروك إمكانيات النمو. فتوسع تل حموكار إلى ١٥ هكتارًا في هذه الفترة. في منتصف الألفية الثالثة ، نما تل حموكار إلى ٩٨ هكتارًا ، مما جعله واحدًا من أكبر المدن في بلاد ما بين النهرين الشمالية. بعدها، في أوائل الألفية الثانية انحسر الاستيطان في المنطقة . ولكن في العصر البرونزي المتأخر والعصر الحديدي، ازداد عدد المواقع. بعد هذه المرحلة من النمو في الفترة الهلنستية والبارثية، شهدت المنطقة انخفاض في أعداد المواقع وانحسار في مساحة المستوطنات. ولكنها عادت الى الازدياد مرّة أخرى في الفترة الإسلامية المبكرة، قبل أن تنهار في الألف سنة الماضية ، قبل إعادة التوطين في القرن العشرين.

الفصل السابع يصف مشهد لا مثيل له من الحركة في حوض الخابور الأعلى. فقد تمّ تحديد وتعيين أكثر من ٦٠٠٠ كيلومترا من المسارات تعود الى عصور ما قبل العصر الحديث من خلال صور الأقمار الصناعية كورونا (CORONA). النمط الاكثر شيوعا بين تلك المسارات هو النوع الذي ينبثق من موقع مركزي. وكانت قد نشأت هذه المسارات من خلال تنقل المزارعين والرعاة من وإلى حقولهم ومراعيهم. وأما النمط الثاني من الطرق الجوفاء يربط عادة بين موقعين. وترتبط معظم الطرق الجوفاء بمواقع من منتصف إلى أواخر الألفية الثالثة قبل الميلاد ، وقت التمدّن الأقصى في الحوض. وترتبط مجموعة ثانية من المسارات بمواقع الفترة الإسلامية المبكرة. الدرجة العالية من الحفاظ على هذه المسارات تجعل من حوض الخابور من أفضل المشاهد حفاظًا على بقايا التنقل في العالم.

الفصل الثامن يلخص نتائج مسوح الاثرية للاستيطان والمشاهد الطبيعية و من ثمّ يضعها في سياق الشرق الأدنى القديم. وكان موقع تي إتش إس ٢٥ (THS 25) الواسع النطاق مركزًا للسكان وتصنيع الزجاج البركاني الأسود والتجارة في نهاية الألفية الخامسة قبل الميلاد ، ويبدو أن الموقع موقع فريد لفترة ما قبل التمدّن. حموكار ومواقع عدة في منطقتها كانت جزءًا من توسع أوروك في الألفية الرابعة قبل الميلاد. في

استمرّ من ١٩٥٩ حتى ١٩٧٢. هذه الصور مفيدة بشكل خاص لتحديد المواقع الصغيرة والمسارات القديمة. استخدم المسح أيضًا البيانات الرقمية الفوتوغرافية والخرائط التاريخية. على الأرض، تم تحديد المواقع عن طريق وجود التلال (الهضبات)، ووجود اللقى على السطح ، وعلى ضوء لون التربة. تم تقسيم المواقع الى مناطق فرعية وجمعت كل اللقى التي تساعد على التشخيص من كل واحدة منها. لم يتبع هذا المنهج في موقع واحد (تي إتش إس ٢٥ THS 25 ، خربة الفخار) بسبب كبر مساحته . في هذه الحالة، تمّ جمع اللقى باستخدام مزيج من جمع في منطقة التلال المركزية و في الوحدات على التلال الخارجية.

الفصل الخامس يستعرض عناصر المشهد الأثري. أبرز المواقع ما تبقى من المستوطنات القديمة التي يمكن تقسيمها الى ١) التلال منخفضة ، ٢) الأكوام العالية ، ٣) مستوطنات المدن السفلى ، ٤) المواقع ذوات التلال المركبة والتي لها خصائص من بعض أو كل ما ورد أعلاه ، و ٥) المواقع التي لا تشتمل على تلال. لقد تمّ التعرّف على معظم هذه المواقع من خلال صور الأقمار الصناعية (كورونا CORONA). كما تمّ دراسة ثلاثة أنواع من الميزات خارج الموقع أو المناظر الطبيعية. الانتشار الخفيف ولكن المستمر لقطع صغيرة من الفخار في الحقول بين المواقع ناتج عن عمليات التسميد القديمة فقد كان المزارعون يضعون النفايات من المستوطنة على الحقول من أجل زيادة إنتاجيتها. وقد تم قياس كثافة مجالات الانتشار هذه في مجموعات منتظمة. أدّى المسح أيضًا الى قياس الطرق الجوفاء ، والتي هي عبارة عن منخفضات ضحلة طولية لمواقع المسارات القديمة. هذه الميزات واضحة ولا سيما في صور الأقمار الصناعية كورونا (CORONA). وأخيرًا ، حدّد المسح آثار قنوات الري القديمة.

الفصل السادس يعرض نتائج أساليب هذا المسح. كشف المسح عن ستين موقعًا من ٨٠٠٠ سنة ماضية. كانت جميع مواقع من عصور ما قبل حسونة وحلف و عبيد قرى صغيرة الحجم. ظلّت معظم المواقع صغيرة في عصر النحاس المتأخر ١–٢ ، ولكن نما موقع تي إتش إس ٢٥ (THS 25) إلى ٣٠٠ هكتارا

كبيرة من سنة إلى أخرى. وقد سنحت هذه العوامل الجيولوجية والمناخية فرصًا للاستيطان البشري في الحوض. ولكنّها أيضًا شكلت عقبة أمام نمو المستوطنات خارج حدود معينة. وأخيرًا يصف هذا البحث تاريخ الاستيطان بعد القرن السادس عشر من خلال سجلات الدولة العثمانية ورحلات المستكشفين الغربيين. و قد كان حوض الخابور الأعلى في هذه الحقبة منطقة الرعي الشتوية للبدو العرب من رعاة الابل الذين أحبطوا الاستيطان الدائم من قبل المزارعين. ونتيجة لذلك ، فقد حوفظ على المشهد الاثري السابق للعصر الحديث بشكل جيد حتى زمن الانتداب الفرنسي ، عندما أجبرت القبائل البدوية على الاستيطان وتمت زراعة الحوض بأكمله. وقد أدّى هذا المزيج من الظروف البيئية المواتية للاستيطان وهجرة المزارعين من السهل حتى القرن العشرين الى الحفاظ الممتازعلى المشهد الأثري.

الفصل الثالث يعرض الأساليب المستخدمة في جمع اللقى من سطح تل حموكار. ويتألف الموقع من تل تبلغ مساحته ١٥ هكتارًا و من منطقة منخفضة إلى جنوب التل تقع على علو ٣–٤ أمتار فوق سطح السهل. تبلغ المساحة الكلية للموقع ١٠٥ هكتارًا ، ممّا يجعله واحدًا من أكبر مواقع العصر البرونزي في سوريا. ويحيط الموقع منخفضات خطية (طولية) وهي عبارة عن بقاية المسارات القديمة (الطرق المجوفة) التي تناقش في الفصل الخامس. حاليًا تغطي قرية تسمى الحرية ٤٠ هكتارًا من الموقع. تم جمع القطع الأثرية من السطح بصورة منتظمة في مجموعة وحدات مساحتها ١٠٠ متر مربع (١٠ x ١٠) وضعت على كل ١٠٠ متر عبر الموقع. وقد تم جمع ما يقرب من ١٦٠٠٠ قطعة أثرية وتحليلها. معظم أجزاء الموقع أفرزت ١٠٠ كسرة فخار في كل ١٠٠ متر مربع.

الفصل الرابع يصف الأساليب المستخدمة في المسح الأثري لـ ١٢٥ كيلومتر مربع المحيطة بحموكار. الأساليب المستخدمة وارتفاع معدل استرداد المواقع تجعل من مشروع مسح حموكار الأثري من أكثر الدراسات الاستقصائية كثافة في الشرق الأدنى. استخدم في المسح عدّة أنواع من البيانات الجغرافية. استخدم المسح صورًا التقطتها مخابرات الولايات المتحدة الأميركية عبر برنامج كورونا CORONA الذي

ملخص

ترجمة رنا ميقاتي

هذا العمل يعرض النتائج النهائية للمسح الاثري لموسم ١٩٩٩-٢٠٠٠ لمحيط تل حموكار، مدينة رئيسية من الألفية الرابعة والثالثة قبل الميلاد في محافظة الحسكة ، الجمهورية العربية السورية. يهدف هذا البحث الى فهم حجم التطور والترتيب المكاني لحموكار والمواقع المجاورة له من حوالي ٦٠٠٠ قبل الميلاد حتى الوقت الحاضر. كما يصف المشهد الأثري خارج حدود الموقع ، ولا سيما ما تبقى من الممارسات الزراعية القديمة ومشهد الاتصال. وتشمل الأساليب المستخدمة في هذا البحث جمع اللقى عن السطح بشكل منهجي ومكثف واستخدام مصادرالاستشعار عن بعد المختلفة (صور الأقمار الصناعية وخاصة كورونا CORONA) ، والتحليل المكاني المستند إلى نظم المعلومات الجغرافية (GIS).

الفصل الاول يعرض أهداف المشروع ، ويصف الطريقة التي استخدمت لتقسيم الزمن، كما يصف أيضًا تنظيم المجلد. يهدف المشروع إلى وصف تطور الاستيطان والمشهد الاثري حول مدينة رئيسية من المدن المبكرة . بالاضافة الى ذلك، للمشروع هدفان محددان : أولاً فهم سياق حموكار في فترة توسع أوروك في الألفية الرابعة قبل الميلاد ، والتحقيق في العلاقات المتبادلة بين المكان والبيئة خلال فترة توسعه القصوى في الألفية الثالثة قبل الميلاد.

الفصل الثاني يصف البيئة المادية والتاريخ الحديث للحوض. هذان هما أهم متغيران في فهم نشأة المشهد الأثري الحالي. شمال بلاد ما بين النهرين هي نتاج تشكّل جبال طوروس الثور وجبال زاغروس التي أسفرت عن تشكيل مجاري المياه الاساسية باتجاه شمالي- جنوبي والرواسب التي مازالت تحدد طبيعة البيئة اليوم. مناخ المنطقة موسمي جدًا: تهطل كل الأمطار تقريبًا خلال أشهر الشتاء وتتغيّرنسبها بدرجة

تل حموكار. المجلّد الأوّل

المدينية والمشاهد الثقافية في شمال شرق سوريا
مسح تل حموكار ١٩٩٩–٢٠٠٠

جايسون أ. أور

مع مشاركة

ماجوير جيبسن، محرر سلسلة تل حموكار

منشورات المعهد الشرقي. المجلد ١٣٧

المعهد الشرقي في جامعة شيكاجو